CW01184267

A Modern History of the Ismailis

The Institute of Ismaili Studies
Ismaili Heritage Series, 13
General Editor: Farhad Daftary

Previously published titles:
1. Paul E. Walker, *Abū Yaʿqūb al-Sijistānī: Intellectual Missionary* (1996)
2. Heinz Halm, *The Fatimids and their Traditions of Learning* (1997)
3. Paul E. Walker, *Ḥamīd al-Dīn al-Kirmānī: Ismaili Thought in the Age of al-Ḥākim* (1999)
4. Alice C. Hunsberger, *Nasir Khusraw, The Ruby of Badakhshan: A Portrait of the Persian Poet, Traveller and Philosopher* (2000)
5. Farouk Mitha, *Al-Ghazālī and the Ismailis: A Debate on Reason and Authority in Medieval Islam* (2001)
6. Ali S. Asani, *Ecstasy and Enlightenment: The Ismaili Devotional Literature of South Asia* (2002)
7. Paul E. Walker, *Exploring an Islamic Empire: Fatimid History and its Sources* (2002)
8. Nadia Eboo Jamal, *Surviving the Mongols: Nizārī Quhistānī and the Continuity of Ismaili Tradition in Persia* (2002)
9. Verena Klemm, *Memoirs of a Mission: The Ismaili Scholar, Statesman and Poet al-Muʾayyad fiʾl-Dīn al-Shīrāzī* (2003)
10. Peter Willey, *Eagle's Nest: Ismaili Castles in Iran and Syria* (2005)
11. Sumaiya A. Hamdani, *Between Revolution and State: The Path to Fatimid Statehood, Qadi al-Nuʿman and the Construction of Fatimid Legitimacy* (2006)
12. Farhad Daftary, *Ismailis in Medieval Muslim Societies* (2005)

A Modern History of the Ismailis

Continuity and Change in a Muslim Community

Edited by
Farhad Daftary

I.B.Tauris *Publishers*
LONDON • NEW YORK
in association with
The Institute of Ismaili Studies
London, 2011

Published in 2011 by I.B.Tauris & Co. Ltd
6 Salem Road, London W2 4BU
175 Fifth Avenue, New York, NY 10010
www.ibtauris.com

in association with The Institute of Ismaili Studies
210 Euston Road, London NW1 2DA
www.iis.ac.uk

Distributed in the United States and Canada Exclusively by Palgrave Macmillan,
175 Fifth Avenue, New York, NY 10010

Copyright © Islamic Publications Ltd, 2011

All rights reserved. Except for brief quotations in a review, this book, or any part thereof, may not be reproduced, stored in or introduced into a retrieval system, or transmitted, in any form or by any means, electronic, mechanical, photocopying, recording or otherwise, without the prior written permission of the publisher.

ISBN: 978 1 84511 717 7 (Hb)

A full CIP record for this book is available from the British Library
A full CIP record for this book is available from the Library of Congress

Library of Congress catalog card: available

Typeset in Minion Tra for The Institute of Ismaili Studies
Printed and bound in Great Britain by
CPI Antony Rowe, Chippenham, Wiltshire

The Institute of Ismaili Studies

The Institute of Ismaili Studies was established in 1977 with the object of promoting scholarship and learning on Islam, in the historical as well as contemporary contexts, and a better understanding of its relationship with other societies and faiths.

The Institute's programmes encourage a perspective which is not confined to the theological and religious heritage of Islam, but seeks to explore the relationship of religious ideas to broader dimensions of society and culture. The programmes thus encourage an interdisciplinary approach to the materials of Islamic history and thought. Particular attention is also given to issues of modernity that arise as Muslims seek to relate their heritage to the contemporary situation.

Within the Islamic tradition, the Institute's programmes seek to promote research on those areas which have, to date, received relatively little attention from scholars. These include the intellectual and literary expressions of Shi'ism in general, and Ismailism in particular.

In the context of Islamic societies, the Institute's programmes are informed by the full range and diversity of cultures in which Islam is practised today, from the Middle East, South and Central Asia, and Africa to the industrialized societies of the West, thus taking into consideration the variety of contexts which shape the ideals, beliefs and practices of the faith.

These objectives are realized through concrete programmes and activities organized and implemented by various departments of the Institute. The Institute also collaborates periodically, on a programme-specific basis, with other institutions of learning in the United Kingdom and abroad.

The Institute's academic publications fall into several distinct and interrelated categories:

1. Occasional papers or essays addressing broad themes of the relationship between religion and society in the historical as well as modern contexts, with special reference to Islam.
2. Monographs exploring specific aspects of Islamic faith and culture, or the contributions of individual Muslim figures or writers.
3. Editions or translations of significant primary or secondary texts.
4. Translations of poetic or literary texts which illustrate the rich heritage of spiritual, devotional and symbolic expressions in Muslim history.
5. Works on Ismaili history and thought, and the relationship of the Ismailis to other traditions, communities and schools of thought in Islam.
6. Proceedings of conferences and seminars sponsored by the Institute.
7. Bibliographical works and catalogues which document manuscripts, printed texts and other source materials.

This book falls into category five listed above.

In facilitating these and other publications, the Institute's sole aim is to encourage original research and analysis of relevant issues. While every effort is made to ensure that the publications are of a high academic standard, there is naturally bound to be a diversity of views, ideas and interpretations. As such, the opinions expressed in these publications must be understood as belonging to their authors alone.

Ismaili Heritage Series

A major Shi'i Muslim community, the Ismailis have had a long and eventful history. Scattered in many regions of the world, in Asia, Africa, and now also in Europe and North America, the Ismailis have elaborated diverse intellectual and literary traditions in different languages. On two occasions they had states of their own, the Fatimid caliphate and the Nizari state of Iran and Syria during the Alamut period. While pursuing particular religio-political aims, the leaders of these Ismaili states also variously encouraged intellectual, scientific, artistic and commercial activities.

Until recently, the Ismailis were studied and judged almost exclusively on the basis of the evidence collected or fabricated by their detractors, including the bulk of the medieval heresiographers and polemicists who were hostile towards the Shi'is in general and the Ismailis among them in particular. These authors in fact treated the Shi'i interpretations of Islam as expressions of heterodoxy or even heresy. As a result, a 'black legend' was gradually developed and put into circulation in the Muslim world to discredit the Ismailis and their interpretation of Islam. The Christian Crusaders and their occidental chroniclers, who remained almost completely ignorant of Islam and its internal divisions, disseminated their own myths of the Ismailis, which came to be accepted in Europe as true descriptions of Ismaili teachings and practices. Modern orientalists, too, studied the Ismailis on the basis of these hostile sources and fanciful accounts of medieval times. Thus, legends and misconceptions have continued to surround the Ismailis through the 20th century.

In more recent decades, however, the field of Ismaili studies has been revolutionized due to the recovery and study of genuine Ismaili sources on a large scale – manuscript materials which in different ways survived the destruction of the Fatimid and Nizari Ismaili libraries. These sources, representing diverse literary traditions produced in Arabic, Persian and Indic languages, had hitherto been secretly preserved in private collections in India, Central Asia, Iran, Afghanistan, Syria and the Yemen.

Modern progress in Ismaili studies has already necessitated a complete re-writing of the history of the Ismailis and their contributions to Islamic civilization. It has now become clear that the Ismailis founded important libraries and institutions of learning such as al-Azhar and the Dar al-'Ilm in Cairo, while some of their learned *da'i*s or missionaries developed unique intellectual traditions amalgamating their theological doctrine with a diversity of philosophical traditions in complex metaphysical systems. The Ismaili patronage of learning and extension of hospitality to non-Ismaili scholars was maintained even in such difficult times as the Alamut period, when the community was preoccupied with its survival in an extremely hostile milieu.

The Ismaili Heritage Series, published under the auspices of the Department of Academic Research and Publications of the Institute of Ismaili Studies, aims to make available to wide audiences the results of modern scholarship on the Ismailis and their rich intellectual and cultural heritage, as well as certain aspects of their more recent history and achievements.

Contents

	Preface	xiii
	Note on Transliteration and Abbreviations	xvi
	Notes on the Contributors	xvii
1.	Introduction	
	Farhad Daftary	1

Part I. Nizari Ismailis: Syria, Central Asia and China

2.	Modern History of the Nizari Ismailis of Syria	
	Dick Douwes	19
3.	The Nizari Ismailis of Central Asia in Modern Times	
	Hakim Elnazarov and *Sultonbek Aksakolov*	45
4.	The Nizari Ismailis of China in Modern Times	
	Amier Saidula	77

Part II. Nizari Ismailis: South Asia and East Africa

5.	From Satpanthi to Ismaili Muslim: The Articulation of Ismaili Khoja Identity in South Asia	
	Ali S. Asani	95

6. The Socio-Legal Formation of the Nizari Ismailis of East Africa, 1800–1950
   Zulfikar Hirji   129

7. Communities of Tradition and the Modernizing of Education in South Asia: The Contribution of Aga Khan III
   Shiraz Thobani   161

Part III. Nizari Ismailis: Contemporary Policies, Institutions and Perspectives

8. The Aga Khan Development Network and Institutions
   Malise Ruthven   189

9. Caring for the Built Environment
   Stefano Bianca   221

10. The Gender Policies of Aga Khan III and Aga Khan IV
    Zayn R. Kassam   247

11. At the Interstices of Tradition, Modernity and Postmodernity: Ismaili Engagements with Contemporary Canadian Society
    Karim H. Karim   265

Part IV. Tayyibi Musta'lian Ismailis

12. History of the Da'udi Bohra Tayyibis in Modern Times: The *Da'i*s, the *Da'wat* and the Community
    Saifiyah Qutbuddin   297

13. The Da'udi Bohra Tayyibis: Ideology, Literature, Learning and Social Practice
    Tahera Qutbuddin   331

14. A Brief Note on Other Tayyibi Communities: Sulaymanis
    and ʿAlavis
    Tahera Qutbuddin 355

    Glossary 359
    Select Bibliography 365
    Index 381

Preface

The second most important Shiʿi Muslim community after the Ithnaʿashari or Twelvers, the Ismailis have had a long and complex history dating back to the formative period of Islam. Subsequently, the Ismailis became subdivided into a number of major branches and minor groups. However, since the beginning of the 12th century, the Ismailis have existed in terms of two main branches, the Nizaris and the Tayyibi Mustaʿlians, who have been respectively designated as Khojas and Bohras in South Asia. The Tayyibis themselves were in due course split into the dominant Daʾudi and minority Sulaymani and ʿAlavi communities. Currently, the Ismailis of different communities are dispersed as religious minorities in more than 25 countries of Asia, the Middle East, Africa, Europe and North America.

Numbering several millions, the Ismailis represent a diversity of ethnicities and literary traditions, and speak a variety of languages and dialects. The majoritarian Nizari Ismaili community now recognize His Highness Prince Karim Aga Khan IV as their 49th hereditary Imam or spiritual leader. The Daʾudi, Sulaymani and ʿAlavi Tayyibi Ismailis are led by different lines of *daʿi*s with supreme authority while all the Tayyibi Imams have remained in concealment and inaccessible to their followers.

Until the middle of the 20th century, the Ismailis were by and large misrepresented with a variety of myths and legends circulating about their teachings and practices. This was due to the fact that they were almost exclusively studied and evaluated, in both Western and Muslim countries, on the basis of evidence collected or fabricated by their detractors. The perceptions of outsiders of the Ismailis have been drastically revised, however, by the results of modern scholarship in Ismaili studies, based on an increasing number of manuscript sources produced in different phases of Ismaili history.

The rich and varied Ismaili literature recovered and studied in modern times, especially since the 1940s, has particularly enhanced our knowledge of the medieval history and traditions of the Ismailis. But the modern period in Ismaili history, covering approximately the last two centuries, has not received its deserved share of benefit from the modern progress in Ismaili studies. A major reason for this stems from the fact that adequate textual sources on the modern history of the Ismailis in various regions have not always been available, while it remains extremely difficult for non-Ismaili scholars who do not have the relevant language skills to tap into the rich oral traditions existing in the regions where the Ismailis have lived throughout the centuries. In sum, it seems that a proper modern history of the Ismailis still awaits much preparatory work, which needs to be undertaken by the Ismailis of different regions themselves. Only then, may we begin to have a better understanding of the evolution of the Ismaili communities of various regions together with their heritage and literary traditions. The present publication represents a first attempt in that direction.

This volume contains chapters on the modern history of the Nizari Ismailis of several regions where these communities have traditionally lived. These chapters are mostly written by Ismaili scholars, both young and well established, who have the necessary language skills as well as familiarity with these communities' oral and literary traditions. One chapter takes up the issue of Nizari settlement in the West, an important phenomenon since the 1970s. Several chapters deal with the reforms and institutional initiatives of the last two Nizari Imams, Aga Khan III and Aga Khan IV, and their achievements. A separate part is devoted to the modern history of the Tayyibi Musta'lian Ismailis, now dominated by the Da'udi Bohras of South Asia. The authors of the Tayyibi chapters, too, are well placed as young scholars belonging to a prominent family within the leadership hierarchy of the Da'udi Bohra community and, as such, they have had access to the sources of information required for approaching their subjects.

The studies collected here should not be taken to represent the final word on their subject matters. Several chapters, in fact, may reflect work in progress, as the state of our knowledge on modern Ismaili history is still continuously undergoing revision and enhancement. One main aim here, as with all our research and publications at the Institute, has been to facilitate scholarship and contribute to further progress in the field of Ismaili studies.

It remains for me to express my deep gratitude to all the contributors who have shared with us in this volume the results of their regional or other studies of the modern and contemporary Ismailis, including their field research findings. I would also like to thank Kutub Kassam and Isabel Miller for their meticulous editorial work, and Nadia Holmes who prepared an earlier typescript of this volume. Needless to say, the studies presented here represent solely the views of their individual authors, and not necessarily those of the other contributors to this volume, nor should they be taken to imply in any sense their endorsement by The Institute of Ismaili Studies.

F. D.

Note on Transliteration and Abbreviations

The system of transliteration used in this book for the Arabic and Persian scripts is essentially the same as that adopted in the second edition of *The Encyclopaedia of Islam*, with a few modifications, namely *ch* for *č*, *j* for *dj* and *q* for *ḳ*. Diacritical marks are dispensed with, except those for *ʿayn* and *hamza*, for some of the dynastic and community names which occur frequently in the book.

Abbreviations used in chapter notes and Select Bibliography:

BSO(A)S	*Bulletin of the School of Oriental (and African) Studies*
EI2	*The Encyclopaedia of Islam*, 2nd edition
EIR	*Encyclopaedia Iranica*
JAOS	*Journal of the American Oriental Society*
JRAS	*Journal of the Royal Asiatic Society*

Notes on the Contributors

Sultonbek Aksakolov is a Research Assistant at The Institute of Ismaili Studies. He has an M.Phil. in Modern Society and Global Transformation from the University of Cambridge. He also worked as Researcher for the Silk Road Project at the University of Uppsala, Sweden. He has conducted research projects on the issues of identity among the emigrant Ismaili community in Southern Tajikistan and Russian Federation, and Russian and Soviet scholarship on Ismailism.

Ali S. Asani is Professor of the Practice of Indo-Muslim Languages and Culture at Harvard University where he offers courses on Islam, Islamic mysticism, Islam in South Asia and languages of South Asia. His books include *The Bujh Niranjan: An Ismaili Mystical Poem* (1991), *The Harvard Collection of Ismaili Literature in Indic Languages: A Descriptive Catalog and Finding Aid* (1992), *Ecstasy and Enlightenment: The Ismaili Devotional Literature of South Asia* (2002) and *Let's Study Urdu: An Introductory Course* (2007).

Stefano Bianca is a Swiss architect, architectural historian and urban designer who obtained his Ph.D. in 1972 and has since spent much of his professional life in the Muslim world. Between 1976 and 1991 he directed a number of major planning, urban design and conservation projects in cities such as Fez, Aleppo, Baghdad and Riyadh. From 1992 to 2006 he was the Director of the Aga Khan Historic Cities Programme at the Aga Khan Trust for Culture (AKTC) in Geneva, where he built up the programme's portfolio, with projects in Northern Pakistan, Zanzibar, Samarkand, Cairo, Mostar, Aleppo, Kabul and Herat. Dr Bianca has lectured and published widely on the subject of environmental planning, as well as Islamic culture, architecture, arts and gardens. His recent books include *Urban Form in the Arab World* (2000), *Hofhaus und Paradiesgarten* (2001), *Karakoram: Hidden Treasures in the Northern Areas of Pakistan* (2005) and *Syria: Medieval Citadels between East and West* (2007).

Farhad Daftary was educated in Iran, Europe and the United States, and received his Ph.D. from the University of California at Berkeley in 1971. He has held different academic positions, and since 1988 he has been affiliated to The Institute of Ismaili Studies, where he is Co-Director and Head of the Department of Academic Research and Publications. He is a consulting editor of *Encyclopaedia Iranica*, co-editor of the *Encyclopaedia Islamica* as well as the General Editor of the Ismaili Heritage Series, and the Ismaili Texts and Translations Series. An authority on Ismaili studies, Dr Daftary has written several acclaimed books in this field, including *The Isma'ilis: Their History and Doctrines* (1990; 2nd ed., 2007), *The Assassin Legends: Myths of the Isma'ilis* (1994), *A Short History of the Ismailis* (Edinburgh, 1998), and *Ismaili Literature* (2004). Most recently he co-authored (with Z. Hijri) *The Ismailis: An Illustrated History* (2008) on the occasion of the 50th anniversary of His Highness the Aga Khan's accession to the Imamate. Dr Daftary's books have been translated into Arabic, Persian, Turkish, Urdu, Gujarati and numerous European languages.

Dick Douwes studied Arabic Language and Culture at Nijmegen University, Netherlands. In 1993 he received his Ph.D. from Nijmegen University with a thesis on *Justice and Oppression: Ottoman Rule in the Province of Damascus and the District of Hama, 1785–1841*. From 1998 onwards he was academic coordinator and later executive director of the International Institute for the Study of Islam in the Modern World (ISIM), a joint research institute of the universities of Amsterdam (UvA), Nijmegen, Leyden and Utrecht. Since 2006 Dr Douwes has been a professor of the History of the Non-western Societies at the Faculty of History and Arts of the Erasmus University, Rotterdam. He has published on late Ottoman history in Syria and on religious plurality in the Middle East, as well as on Muslims in Western Europe. His publications include *The Ottomans in Syria: A History of Justice and Oppression* (2000).

Hakim Elnazarov is Coordinator of Central Asian Studies at The Institute of Ismaili Studies. He holds a university diploma in Islamic Studies and MEd from the Institute for Educational Development at the Aga Khan

University. He has worked in various capacities in the field of education in Tajikistan and East Africa, and his academic research includes religious education in Tajikistan, and the cultures and traditions of Central Asian mountainous societies. He has published a number of articles on education, languages and gender issues in Tajikistan.

Zulfikar Hirji is Associate Professor of Anthropology at York University (Toronto, Canada). He received his D.Phil. degree in Social Anthropology from the University of Oxford. His research focuses on the history and socio-cultural expressions of Muslim groups living along the Western Indian Ocean littoral from the 19th century up to the present day. He is co-author (with F. Daftary) of *The Ismailis: An Illustrated History* (2008). He has also edited *Diversity and Pluralism in Islam: Historical and Contemporary Discourses amongst Muslims* (2010).

Karim H. Karim is Co-Director of The Institute of Ismaili Studies. He previously was Director of Carleton University's School of Journalism and Communication in Ottawa, Canada. Professor Karim was a Visiting Scholar at Harvard University's Divinity School and Department of Near Eastern Languages and Civilizations in 2004. He has delivered distinguished lectures at several universities and has published internationally on social development in Muslim societies and the relationship of culture and communication to issues of diaspora, technology and globalization. Professor Karim received the inaugural Robinson Book Prize for excellence in Communication Studies for his *Islamic Peril: Media and Global Violence* (Montreal, 2003) and is the editor of *The Media of Diaspora* (Routledge, 2003). Professor Karim has also been honoured by the Governor-General of Canada for promoting interfaith collaboration. Prior to joining academia, he held positions as a Senior Researcher and Senior Policy Analyst in the Department of Canadian Heritage, was a reporter for Inter Press Service (Rome) and Compass News Features (Luxembourg) and worked as a Religious Education Coordinator in the Ismailia Association for Canada. Professor Karim holds degrees from Columbia and McGill universities in Islamic and Communication studies.

Zayn R. Kassam is Associate Professor and Chair of Religious Studies at Pomona College, Claremont, California, and is also on the faculty at Claremont Graduate University. She received her Ph.D. from McGill University and currently teaches courses on Islamic philosophy, mysticism, gender and literature, as well as courses on philosophical and mystical texts from a comparative perspective. Dr Kassam has been honoured with two Wig Awards for Distinguished Teaching at Pomona College, as well as an American Academy of Religion Excellence in Teaching Award. Author of numerous articles on gender and cultural issues, she recently published a book on Islam which is part of a series on the world's major religions.

Saifiyah Qutbuddin studied for her BA at the American University in Cairo, followed by an MA in Arabic Studies and Middle Eastern History. She received her Ph.D. from the University of Oxford with her thesis 'The Political History of the Ismaili-Tayyibi Daʿwa in Yemen'. Since then she has been researching and teaching Ismaili texts within the Bohra Ismaili community in India.

Tahera Qutbuddin is Associate Professor of Arabic Literature at the University of Chicago. Previously she taught at the University of Utah and Yale University. She obtained her Ph.D. in Arabic language and literature from Harvard University. She is the author of *Al-Muʾayyad al-Shirazi and Fatimid Daʿwa Poetry: A Case of Commitment in Classical Arabic Literature* (2005). Dr Qutbuddin has published several articles on classical Arabic literature, Fatimid/Ismaili studies, and Arabic in India.

Malise Ruthven is an independent scholar, and his publications include *Islam in the World* (1984), *The Divine Supermarket: Shopping for God in America* (1989), *A Satanic Affair: Salman Rushdie and the Wrath of Islam* (1990), and *A Fury for God: The Islamist Attack on America* (2002). His *Islam: A Very Short Introduction* (1997) has been published in several languages, including Chinese, Japanese, Korean, Romanian, Polish, Italian, Spanish and German. He is a regular contributor to the BBC and the *Times Literary Supplement*. His most recent books are *Fundamentalism: The Search for Meaning* (2004) and *A Historical Atlas of Islam* (with A. Nanji) (2004).

Amier Saidula is a Research Assistant at the Institute of Ismaili Studies. He has an LLM degree in Public International Law from the School of Oriental and African Studies, University of London, and is currently engaged in his doctoral studies in anthropology at Edinburgh University. He has translated several of the Institute's publications into Chinese and Uyghur languages.

Notes on the Contributors

Shiraz Thobani is a Research Associate at The Institute of Ismaili Studies. He holds a Ph.D. in Education from the University of Cambridge, where he undertook a sociological and policy study of Islam in the English education system. He lectures at the postgraduate level on education in Muslim societies, and is currently engaged in curriculum research and development in the Islamic context. He has also been involved in an advisory capacity with European and American institutions in curriculum-related ventures linked to intercultural and civilizational studies. He is the co-editor (with G. Jonker) of *Narrating Islam: Interpretations of the Muslim World in European Texts* (2010).

1

Introduction

Farhad Daftary

The origins of the Ismaili Muslims may be traced back to the formative period of Islam when different Shi'i and Sunni communities were elaborating their own distinctive interpretations of the Islamic message. The Imami Shi'is, who recognized a line of 'Alid Imams descending from 'Ali b. Abi Talib, the first Shi'i Imam, and his wife Fatima, the Prophet Muhammad's daughter, represented one such major community. The Imami Shi'is acquired their prominence under Imam Ja'far al-Sadiq. It was also in al-Sadiq's time that the central Imami doctrine of the Imamate was formulated. This doctrine, with minor modifications, has served as the central teaching of the later Ismaili and Twelver Shi'is.

On the death of Imam Ja'far al-Sadiq in 765, his Imami Shi'i following split into several groups, including two groups identifiable as the earliest Ismailis. By the middle of the 9th century, the Ismailis had organized a revolutionary movement against the Abbasids who, in the eyes of the Shi'a, had usurped (like the Umayyads before them) the rights of the 'Alids to the leadership of the Muslim community. The Ismaili movement was now led centrally by a hereditary line of 'Alids who guarded their true identity in order to escape Abbasid capture. By 899, the unified Ismaili movement, designated by the Ismailis themselves as *al-da'wa al-hadiya*, 'the rightly guiding mission', or simply as the *da'wa*, was rent by its first major schism over the question of the leadership or Imamate in the community. The Ismailis now became divided into two rival factions, the loyal Ismailis and the dissident Qarmatis. The loyal Ismailis upheld continuity in the Ismaili Imamate in the progeny of Isma'il b. Ja'far al-Sadiq, and also recognized the founder of the Fatimid dynasty and his successors as their Imams. The Qarmatis, who founded a powerful state in Bahrayn, acknowledged a line of seven Imams only, ending in Muhammad b. Ismaʿil b. Jaʿfar al-Sadiq. Thus they did not accept the Fatimid caliphs as their Imams.[1]

By the final decades of the 9th century Ismaili *daʿi*s, acting as religio-political agents of the *daʿwa*, were active in almost every major part of the Islamic world, from North Africa to Yemen, Syria, Persia and Central Asia. The early success of the Ismaili *daʿwa* culminated in 909 in the foundation of an Ismaili state or *dawla*, the Fatimid caliphate.[2] The revolutionary activities of the early Ismailis had finally resulted in the establishment of a state in which the Ismaili Imam was installed as Fatimid caliph, representing an effective Shiʿi challenge to the religious authority of the Abbasid caliph, who acted as the spokesman of Sunni Islam. The Fatimid period was in a sense the 'golden' age of Ismailism, when the Ismaili Imam ruled over a vast empire and Ismaili contributions to Islamic thought and literature attained their apogee. It was during the Fatimid period that the learned Ismaili *daʿi*s, who were at the same time the scholars and authors of their community, produced what were to become the classic texts of Ismaili literature dealing with a multitude of exoteric (*zahiri*) and esoteric (*batini*) subjects. Amongst such personalities, particular mention may be made of Abu Yaʿqub al-Sijistani (d. after 971), Hamid al-Din al-Kirmani (d. after 1020), al-Muʾayyad fiʾl-Din al-Shirazi (d. 1078) and Nasir-i Khusraw (d. after 1070).[3] Ismaili law, which had not existed during the pre-Fatimid secret phase of Ismailism when the Ismailis observed the law of the land wherever they lived, was also codified during the early Fatimid period.[4] It was indeed during the Fatimid period that the Ismailis made their important contributions to Islamic theology and philosophy in general and to Shiʿi thought in particular.[5] Modern recovery of Ismaili literature abundantly attests to the richness and diversity of the literary and intellectual traditions of the Ismailis of Fatimid times.[6]

In line with their universal aspirations, the Fatimids did not abandon their *daʿwa* activities on assuming power. Aiming to extend their authority and rule over the entire Muslim *umma*, and other states, they in fact retained a network of *daʿi*s, operating on their behalf as religio-political missionaries both within and outside Fatimid dominions. The Fatimids particularly concerned themselves with the affairs of their *daʿwa* after transferring in 973 the seat of their state to Egypt, which they had conquered in 969. Cairo, founded as a royal city by the Fatimids, became the headquarters of their complex hierarchical *daʿwa* organization. Supreme leadership of the Ismaili *daʿwa* and the Fatimid *dawla* were the prerogatives of the Fatimid Imam-Caliph. However, the Ismailis remained a minority community within the Fatimid state where the Sunni Muslims still predominated. The Ismaili *da'wa* had its greatest lasting successes outside the Fatimid dominions, especially in Yemen, Persia and Central Asia where different Shi'i traditions had long histories.[7] In Egypt, the Fatimids also patronized intellectual activities. They founded major libraries in Cairo, including one at the Dar al-'Ilm (House of Knowledge), founded in 1005, where a variety of religious and non-religious subjects were taught. Soon the Fatimid capital, Cairo, became a flourishing centre of Islamic scholarship, sciences, art and culture, in addition to playing a prominent role in contemporary international trade and commerce.

In 1094, on the death of al-Mustansir, the 8th Fatimid caliph and the 18th Ismaili Imam, the Ismailis became permanently divided into the Nizari and Musta'lian branches, named after al-Mustansir's sons who claimed his heritage. The succession to al-Mustansir was disputed between Nizar (1045–1095), his original heir-designate, and the latter's much younger brother Ahmad (1074–1101), who was actually installed as Fatimid caliph with the title of al-Musta'li bi'llah. Subsequently Nizar rose in revolt to assert his claims, taking the title al-Mustafa li-Din Allah, but he was eventually defeated and killed in 1095. Aiming to retain the reins of power in his own hands, the all-powerful Fatimid vizier al-Afdal had favoured al-Musta'li. Moving swiftly, on the day after al-Mustansir's death, he had placed al-Musta'li on the Fatimid throne. Supported by the Fatimid armies, the vizier quickly obtained for al-Musta'li the allegiance of the Fatimid court and the leaders of the Ismaili *da'wa* in Cairo. The Imamate of al-Musta'li, now firmly installed to the Fatimid throne, came to be recognized by the *da'wa* establishment in Cairo, as well as most Ismailis in Egypt, many in Syria, and by the entire Ismaili community in Yemen and that in Gujarat dependent on it. These Ismailis, who depended on the Fatimid regime and later traced the Imamate in al-Musta'li's progeny, maintained their relations with Cairo, now serving as the headquarters of the Musta'lian Ismaili *da'wa*. On the other hand, the Persian Ismailis, then under the leadership of Hasan-i Sabbah, defended al-Mustansir's original designation and upheld Nizar's right to the Imamate. Hasan, in fact, founded the independent Nizari Ismaili *da'wa*, severing his relations with the Fatimid regime and *da'wa* headquarters in Cairo. In Syria, now beyond Fatimid control, Nizar had followers who soon were organized by emissaries dispatched from Alamut, the headquarters of Hasan-i Sabbah. The Ismailis of Central Asia seem to have remained uninvolved in the Nizari-Musta'li schism for quite some time. It was much later that the Ismailis of Badakhshan and adjacent regions accorded their allegiance to the Nizari line of Imams. The two factions of the Ismaili *da'wa* henceforth became known as Nizari or Musta'lian, depending on whether they recognized Nizar or al-Musta'li as their rightful Imam after al-Mustansir.

The Musta'lian Ismailis themselves split into the Hafizi and Tayyibi factions soon after the death of al-Musta'li's son and successor on the Fatimid throne, al-Amir, in 1130. The Hafizi Musta'lians, who acknowledged al-Hafiz (d. 1149) and the later Fatimid caliphs as their Imams, disappeared soon after the collapse of the Fatimid dynasty in 1171. The Tayyibi Musta'lians recognized al-Amir's infant son al-Tayyib as their Imam after al-Amir, and then traced the Imamate in al-Tayyib's progeny. However, all Tayyibi Imams after al-Amir have remained in concealment, and in their absence the affairs of the Tayyibi community and *da'wa* have been handled by lines of *da'is* with supreme authority, known as *da'i mutlaq*.[8] Tayyibi Ismailism initially received the all-important support of the Queen Sayyida Arwa, the effective ruler of Sulayhid Yemen.[9] In fact, Yemen served for several centuries as the permanent stronghold of Tayyibi Ismailism.

By the end of the 16th century, the Tayyibis themselves had become further subdivided into the Da'udi (Dawoodi) and Sulaymani branches over the issue of the rightful succession to the position of their *da'i mutlaq*; and later a third branch appeared under the designation of 'Alavi Bohras. By that time, the Tayyibis of South Asia, known locally as Bohras and belonging mainly to the Da'udi branch, outnumbered their Sulaymani co-religionists centred in Yemen. The Tayyibis in general maintained the intellectual and literary traditions of the Ismailis of the Fatimid period, as well as preserving a good portion of that period's Ismaili Arabic literature.

The Nizari Ismailis, concentrated originally in Persia and Syria, have had a completely different historical evolution. The Nizaris acquired political prominence within the Saljuq dominions, under the initial leadership of Hasan-i Sabbah, who seized the mountain fortress of Alamut in northern Persia in 1090. This signalled the initiation of the Persian Ismailis' open revolt against the alien rule of the Saljuq Turks as well as the foundation of what was to become the Nizari Ismaili state of Persia with a subsidiary in Syria.[10] The Nizari state, centred at Alamut and with territories in different parts of Persia and Syria, lasted for some 166 years until its destruction by the Mongols in 1256. A capable organizer, Hasan-i Sabbah (d. 1124) designed a revolutionary strategy aimed at uprooting the Saljuq Turks, whose rule was detested throughout Persia. He did not achieve his goal, nor did the Saljuqs succeed in dislodging the Nizaris from their mountain strongholds despite their much superior military power. But Hasan did manage to found and consolidate the independent Nizari state and *da'wa*.

The Syrian Nizaris, too, eventually came to possess a network of castles, and pursued complex policies of war and diplomacy towards various Muslim powers as well as the Crusaders in a then politically fragmented Syria. The Syrian Nizaris reached the peak of their power and fame under Rashid al-Din Sinan, who led them as their chief *daʿi* for three decades until his death in 1193. It was also in his time that the Crusaders and other occidental observers began to fabricate and circulate, both in the Levant and Europe, a number of interconnected tales, the so-called Assassin legends, regarding the imagined secret practices of the Nizaris.[11] The Crusaders thus made the Nizaris famous in Europe as the Assassins, a misnomer rooted in a term of abuse.

After Hasan-i Sabbah and his next two successors at Alamut, who ruled as *daʿi*s and *hujja*s, the concealed Nizari Imam's chief representatives, the Imams themselves emerged at Alamut to lead their community, *daʿwa* and state.[12] The circumstances of the Nizaris of the Alamut period were drastically different from those faced by the Ismailis living in the Fatimid state, and the Tayyibi Mustaʿlians of Yemen. From early on, the Nizari Ismailis were preoccupied with a revolutionary campaign and the endeavour to survive in an extremely hostile environment. Accordingly, they produced military commanders and governors of fortress communities rather than many outstanding religious scholars. As a result, the Nizaris of the Alamut period did not produce a substantial body of religious literature. Nevertheless they did maintain a literary tradition and elaborated their teachings in response to the changed circumstances of the Alamut period. Hasan-i Sabbah himself was a learned theologian, and he is credited with establishing an impressive library at Alamut. Later, other major Nizari fortresses in Persia and Syria came to be equipped with significant collections of books, documents and scientific instruments. The Nizaris also extended their patronage of learning to outside scholars, including Sunnis, Twelver Shiʿis and even non-Muslims. Foremost among these mention may be made of Nasir al-Din al-Tusi (d. 1274), the renowned Muslim polymath who spent some three decades in the fortress communities of the Nizaris and voluntarily embraced Ismailism.

The Nizari Ismailis survived the Mongol destruction of their fortress communities and state, and this marked the initiation of a new phase in their history. In the unsettled conditions of the post-Alamut period, the Nizari communities of Syria, Persia, Central Asia and South Asia developed independently under their local leadership for some time, also elaborating a diverse range of religious and literary traditions in different languages. Many aspects of Ismaili activities in this long period have not been sufficiently studied due to a scarcity of reliable primary source materials. More complex research difficulties arise from the widespread practice of *taqiyya*, or precautionary dissimulation of true religious beliefs and identity, by the Nizari communities of different regions during the greater part of this period when they were obliged to dissimulate under a variety of disguises, such as Sufi, Sunni, Twelver Shi'i and Hindu, against rampant persecution.

In the aftermath of the destruction of their state, the Nizari Imams went into hiding and, for the most part, lost their direct contact with their followers. The scattered Nizari communities now developed independently under their local leaders designated as *pirs*, *mirs* and *shaykhs*. But by the middle of the 15th century, the Nizari Imams had emerged in Anjudan in central Persia, initiating what has been called the Anjudan revival in Nizari *da'wa* and literary activities.[13] During the Anjudan period, which lasted about two centuries, the Imams reasserted their central authority over the various Nizari communities. The Nizari *da'wa* activities now proved particularly successful in Badakhshan in Central Asia, and in the Indian subcontinent where large numbers of Hindus were converted and became locally known as Khojas. The Khojas developed a unique literary genre in the form of devotional hymns known as *ginans*, while the Nizari tradition elaborated there became designated as Satpanth or the 'true path' (to salvation).

The modern period in Nizari history may be dated to the middle of the 19th century when the residence of the Imams was transferred from Persia to India and subsequently to Europe. On the death of the 45th Nizari Imam, Shah Khalil Allah, in 1817, his eldest son Hasan 'Ali Shah (born in 1804) succeeded to the Imamate as the 46th Imam. Fath 'Ali Shah (1797–1834), the then reigning Qajar monarch of Persia, appointed the youthful Imam to the governorship of Qum and gave him one of his daughters, Sarv-i Jahan Khanum, in marriage. In addition, the Persian monarch bestowed upon the Nizari Imam the honorific title (*laqab*) of Agha Khan, meaning lord and master. Henceforth, Hasan 'Ali Shah became known in Persia as Agha Khan Mahallati, because of his royal title and the family's deep roots in the Mahallat area and its environs (Anjudan and Kahak); the title of Agha Khan, later simplified to Aga Khan, has been used on a hereditary basis by Hasan 'Ali Shah's successors to the Nizari Ismaili Imamate.

Aga Khan I lived a quiet life in Persia, honoured and highly respected at the Qajar court for the remainder of Fath 'Ali Shah's reign. The next Qajar monarch, Muhammad Shah (1834–1848), appointed the Imam to the governorship of the province of Kirman in 1835. This post had been held earlier for almost half a century by the Imam's grandfather who was the 44th Imam, Abu'l-Hasan 'Ali (d. 1792). Subsequently, the Imam faced a series of confrontations with the Qajar court and the enmity of the all-powerful grand vizier. Relations between the Imam himself and the Qajar establishment deteriorated, resulting in a number of military encounters in 1840. The Ismaili forces, led by the Imam and his brothers Sardar Abu'l-Hasan Khan (d. 1880) and Muhammad Baqir Khan (d. 1879), were eventually defeated by the superior Qajar armies.[14] As a result, in 1841 the Imam was obliged to flee to neighbouring Afghanistan, marking the end of the Persian period of the Nizari Ismaili Imamate which had lasted some seven centuries from the start of the Alamut era.

Accompanied by a large retinue as well as his cavalry, the Nizari Imam then advanced to Qandahar, which had been occupied in 1839 by an Anglo-Indian army. Henceforth, a close association developed between the Aga Khan and the British Raj. Subsequently, in 1842, the Imam proceeded to Sind and stayed at Jerruck (now in Pakistan), where his house is still preserved. From the time of his arrival in Sind, Aga Khan I established extensive contacts with his Khoja followers. In 1844 the Imam left Sind and after spending a year in Gujarat among his followers arrived in Bombay in 1846. British interventions for the Imam's return to his Persian ancestral homeland, as was the Imam's personal desire, failed, and, after an interim stay in Calcutta, the Aga Khan settled permanently in Bombay in 1848.

With Aga Khan I's settlement in Bombay there began the modern period in the history of the Nizari Ismailis. The Nizari Imamate was now established in India, with Bombay serving as the seat of the Nizari Imams. Hasan 'Ali Shah, Aga Khan I, was the first Nizari Imam to set foot in India and his presence there was greatly welcomed by the Ismaili Khojas who gathered enthusiastically to pay their homage to him and receive his blessings. The Imam soon established elaborate headquarters and residences in Bombay, Poona and Bangalore. He attended the chief *jama'atkhana* in Bombay on special religious occasions.

Aga Khan I spent the last three decades of his eventful and long Imamate in Bombay. As the spiritual head of a Muslim community, he received the protection of the British establishment in India, which strengthened his position. Nevertheless Aga Khan I encountered some difficulties in establishing his authority over the Khoja community. The South Asian Nizari tradition known as Satpanth had become influenced over time by elements of Hindu practice, while the Khojas had been obliged to dissimulate for long periods as Sunnis or Twelver Shi'is, also having close ties with certain Sufi orders. In the settlement of their legal affairs, too, the Khojas, like certain other Muslim groups in India, had often resorted to Hindu customs rather than the provisions of Islamic law, especially in matters relating to inheritance. These factors served as sources of ambiguity in terms of the Khojas' religious identity. In fact dissident Khoja groups appeared periodically in the course of the 19th century, claiming Sunni or Twelver Shi'i heritage for themselves. It was under such circumstances that Aga Khan I launched a widespread campaign for defining and delineating the distinctive religious identity of his Khoja following. The Imam also succeeded gradually in exerting control over the Ismaili Khojas through their traditional communal organization. He personally appointed the officers of the major Khoja congregations, including the *mukhi*s who acted as the religious and social heads of every local Khoja group (*jama'at*) and his assistant called *kamadia* (pronounced *kamriya*). Aga Khan I also encouraged a revival of literary activities among the Nizari Ismailis, pioneered by his eldest grandson Shihab al-Din Shah (d. 1884).[15] Aga Khan I died in 1881 and was buried in an impressive mausoleum situated in the Mazagaon area of Bombay.

Aga Khan I was succeeded as Imam by his eldest son Aqa 'Ali Shah, his sole son by his Qajar spouse. The 47th Imam was born in 1830 in Mahallat, where he spent his early years. He eventually arrived in Bombay in 1853 and, as the Imam's designated successor, regularly visited different Khoja communities, especially in Gujarat and Sind. He lived for some time in Karachi where his own Qajar wife, Shams al-Muluk, a granddaughter of Fath 'Ali Shah Qajar, bore him his future successor, Sultan Muhammad (Mahomed) Shah, in 1877. Aqa 'Ali Shah led the Nizari Ismailis for only a brief four-year period, during which time he concerned himself mainly with the educational standards and welfare of the Khojas. He also established contacts with the Nizari communities outside the Indian subcontinent, especially in Central Asia and East Africa. Aga Khan II died in 1885 and was buried in the family mausoleum at Najaf, Iraq, near the shrine of Imam 'Ali b. Abi Talib.

The Nizari Khojas, along with the Tayyibi Bohras, were among the earliest Asian communities to settle in East Africa.[16] The settlement of Asians in East Africa was greatly encouraged during the early decades of the 19th century by Sultan Sayyid Sa'id (1806–1856) of the Ibadi Al Bu Sa'id dynasty of 'Uman and Zanzibar. Aiming to develop the commercial basis of his African dominions, Sultan Sa'id encouraged the emigration of Indian traders to Zanzibar, where they enjoyed religious freedom under British protection. The Khojas, coming mainly from Gujarat, represented the largest group of Asian emigrants in Zanzibar. Asian emigration to East Africa increased significantly after Sultan Sa'id transferred his capital in 1840 from Muscat to Zanzibar. Subsequently, the Asian Ismailis moved from Zanzibar to the growing urban centres of the East African coastline, notably Mombasa, Nairobi, Dar es Salaam, Kampala and Tanga. Further penetration of the Asian Ismaili settlers into the interior of East Africa occurred after the establishment of British and German colonial rule in the region. By the early decades of the 20th century, the emigration of the Ismaili Khojas and Bohras to East Africa had practically ended.

Aqa 'Ali Shah was succeeded in the Imamate by his sole surviving son Sultan Muhammad Shah, Aga Khan III, who led the Nizari Ismailis as their 48th Imam for 72 years, longer than any of his predecessors. Aga Khan III's life and achievements are amply documented since he became well known as a Muslim reformer and statesman through his prominent role in Indo-Muslim as well as international affairs.[17] Aga Khan III spent his early years under the close tutelage of his Qajar mother, Shams al-Muluk (d. 1938), receiving a rigorous traditional education in Bombay, including studying Arabic and Persian literature. In 1898 the Ismaili Imam paid his first visit to Europe, where he later established permanent residences. He also maintained close relations with the British establishment throughout his life which brought immense benefits to his followers in South Asia and East Africa where they lived under British rule.

From early on, Aga Khan III made systematic efforts to establish the identity of his followers as distinct from the Twelver Shi'is and Sunnis. Thus his religious policy revolved for quite some time around defining and asserting the distinctive Nizari Ismaili identity of his followers, who were also urged to respect the traditions of other Muslim communities. This identity was articulated in the Ismaili constitutions that Aga Khan III promulgated for his followers in different regions and which served as the personal law of his community. While delineating their distinct Ismaili identity, Aga Khan III worked indefatigably to consolidate and reorganize the Nizaris into a modern Muslim community with high standards of education, health and general well-being. The participation of Ismaili women in communal affairs also received high priority in the Imam's reform programmes. The implementation of his reforms, however, required suitable institutions and administrative organization. The development of a new communal network, in the form of a hierarchy of councils, thus became one of the Imam's major tasks. Aga Khan III became increasingly concerned with reform policies that would benefit not only his own community but non-Ismailis as well. To that end he founded an extensive network of schools, vocational institutions, libraries, sports clubs, dispensaries and hospitals in East Africa, the Indo-Pakistan subcontinent and elsewhere. Aga Khan III remained in close contact with his followers, and guided them through his oral and written directives or *farman*s, which served as another communal mechanism for introducing reforms.[18]

Sir Sultan Muhammad Shah, Aga Khan III, the 48th Imam of the Nizari Ismailis, died in his villa near Geneva in 1957 and was later buried in a permanent mausoleum at Aswan, overlooking the Nile in Egypt. As a spiritual leader and Muslim reformer, Aga Khan III responded to the challenges of a rapidly changing world and made it possible for his followers, scattered in many different countries, to live in the 20th century as a progressive and educated community with a distinct Islamic identity. Aga Khan III was survived by two sons, Prince Aly Khan (1911–1960) and Prince Sadruddin (1933–2003). However, in accordance with his last will and testament, his grandson Prince Karim (Prince Aly Khan's son) succeeded to the Imamate as the 49th and the present Mawlana Hazar Imam of the Nizari Ismailis. He is internationally known as His Highness Prince Karim Aga Khan IV.

Born in 1936 in Geneva, Aga Khan IV attended Le Rosey, the renowned Swiss boarding school, before entering Harvard University, from where he graduated in 1959 with a degree in Islamic history. Aga Khan IV has continued and substantially extended the modernization and communal policies of his grandfather, also developing a multitude of new programmes, initiatives and institutions of his own for the benefit of his community and others. At the same time, he has concerned himself with a variety of social, developmental and cultural issues which are of wider interest to Muslims and the Third World countries. By 2007, when the Ismailis celebrated the 50th anniversary (Golden Jubilee) of his Imamate, Aga Khan IV had established an impressive record of achievement not only as the Ismaili Imam but also as a Muslim leader deeply aware of the challenges and dilemmas of modernity, as well as the conflicting and at times problematic interpretations of Islam. The present Imam of the Nizari Ismailis has indeed dedicated himself to promoting a better understanding of Islamic civilizations and the diversity of interpretations of the Islamic message.

Aga Khan IV closely supervises the spiritual and secular affairs of his community, regularly visiting his followers in different parts of Asia, the Middle East, Africa, Europe and North America. He guides the Nizaris through his own *farman*s. Aga Khan IV has maintained the elaborate council system of communal administration initiated by his grandfather, also extending it to new territories in recognition of the large-scale emigration of his followers from Asia and East Africa to the West since the 1970s. Aga Khan III had issued separate constitutions for his Khoja followers in East Africa, India and Pakistan. But in 1986 a new chapter was inaugurated in the constitutional history of the Nizari Ismailis, when their Imam promulgated a universal document entitled 'The Constitution of the Shia Imami Ismaili Muslims' for all his followers throughout the world. The preamble to the 1986 constitution affirms all the fundamental Islamic beliefs and then focuses on the Imam's *ta'lim* or teaching which is required for guiding the community along the path of spiritual enlightenment and improved material life. On the basis of this constitution, amended in 1998, a uniform system of councils with affiliated bodies is now in operation in some 20 regions of the world where the Nizari Ismailis are concentrated, including India, Pakistan, United Arab Emirates, Syria, Iran, Afghanistan, Kenya, Tanzania, Uganda, France, Portugal, the United Kingdom, Canada and the United States. Each of these territories also possesses an Ismaili Tariqah and Religious Education Board (ITREB) for the provision of religious education at all levels of the community and for publication of materials on different aspects of Islam and its Shi'i Ismaili interpretation.

The present Ismaili Imam has also initiated many new policies, programmes and projects for the educational and socio-economic benefits of his followers as well as the non-Ismaili inhabitants of certain regions in Asia, the Middle East and Africa. To that end, he has created a complex institutional network, generally referred to as the Aga Khan Development Network (AKDN). Implementing projects related to social, economic and cultural development, the AKDN disburses more than $300 million annually on its non-profitmaking activities. In the area of social development, for instance, the AKDN has been particularly active in East Africa, Central Asia, Pakistan and India in projects for health, education and housing services as well as rural development.

While Aga Khan III pioneered modern educational reforms in his community, the present Imam has extended that central interest of the Ismaili Imamate to higher educational institutions, founding The Institute of Ismaili Studies in London, the Aga Khan University in Karachi, with its Institute for the Study of Muslim Civilizations in London, the University of Central Asia in Tajikistan with branches in other Central Asia republics, and the Global Centre for Pluralism in Ottawa. Aga Khan IV has additionally launched a number of innovative programmes to promote a better understanding of Islam as a major world civilization with its plurality of social, intellectual and cultural traditions. The apex institution for the preservation and regeneration of the cultural heritages of Muslim societies is the Aga Khan Trust for Culture (AKTC), set up for promoting an awareness of the importance of the built environment in both historical and contemporary contexts, and for pursuing excellence in architecture.

The modern progress in Ismaili studies, initiated in the 1940s, has shed valuable light on many aspects of Ismaili history and traditions in the medieval era.[19] As a result, we now possess a much better understanding of the formative and early periods in Ismailism. Ismaili history during the Fatimid period, too, has become amply documented, as the bulk of the Ismaili texts and archival materials produced during that period have been recovered and studied in recent decades, and general and regional Islamic histories have been used more objectively by contemporary scholars. On the other hand, certain aspects of Nizari Ismaili history during the Alamut period remain shrouded in controversy and obscurity, as the bulk of the Persian Nizari texts of the period have not survived directly. Further research difficulties relate to Nizari Ismaili history and traditions in the post-Alamut period when adherents had to observe *taqiyya* in various forms, and the Nizari communities of Syria, Persia, Central Asia and South Asia elaborated different religious and literary traditions in Arabic, Persian and a number of Indian languages. These communities also developed largely independently of one another until modern times.

The studies collected in this volume represent a modest first attempt at piecing together a history of the Ismailis during approximately the last two centuries. In the Nizari Ismaili communities, this period coincided for the most part with the Imamates of three Imams, who during the individually long periods of their leadership, and building on the foundational work of their predecessors, delineated the distinctive Ismaili identity which had earlier been often interfaced or amalgamated with other religious traditions due to the widespread practices of *taqiyya*. In fact, as a result of such dissimulating tactics over extended periods, a number of Nizari groups completely lost their identity, especially in Persia and South Asia where they became duly 'assimilated' or 'acculturated' into the dominant Twelver Shi'i and Hindu communities of their surroundings.[20] It is within such a context that many of the policies of Aga Khan I and his grandson Aga Khan III can be fully understood. A second theme that emerges from the policies of Aga Khan III and his grandson and successor, the present and 49th Nizari Ismaili Imam H.H. Prince Karim Aga Khan IV, revolves around reform and modernization. The last two Imams responded to the challenges of their times and, as progressive Muslim leaders, introduced a coherent set of policies and institutional structures that ensured high standards of education, health and welfare for their followers. They have also been foremost amongst the modern Muslim leaders of the world in working for the emancipation of women and their participation in communal affairs. As a result of the concerted and progressive leadership of their last two Imams, the Nizari Ismailis have emerged in modern times as an exemplary Shi'i Muslim community with a distinct religious identity, while still enjoying a diversity of cultural and social traditions. The final part of this book has been devoted to the modern history of the Tayyibi Musta'lian Ismailis, dominated by the Da'udi Bohras of South Asian origins.

Notes

1. For further details, see F. Daftary, *The Isma'ilis: Their History and Doctrines* (2nd ed., Cambridge, 2007), pp. 87–126, and his 'A Major Schism in the Early Isma'ili Movement', *Studia Islamica*, 77 (1991), pp. 123–139, reprinted in his *Ismailis in Medieval Muslim Societies* (London, 2005), pp. 45–61.
2. On the Fatimid caliphate, see H. Halm, *The Empire of the Mahdi: The Rise of the Fatimids*, tr. M. Bonner (Leiden, 1996); his *Die Kalifen von Kairo. Die Fatimiden in Ägypten 973–1074* (Munich, 2003); M. Brett, *The Rise of the Fatimids: The World of the Mediterranean and the Middle East in the Fourth Century of the Hijra, Tenth Century CE* (Leiden, 2001); Ayman F. Sayyid, *al-Dawla al-Fatimiyya fi Misr* (2nd ed., Cairo, 2000), and Daftary, *The Isma'ilis*, pp. 137–237. The most significant contemporaneous Ismaili accounts of the rise of the Fatimids are contained in al-Qadi al-Nu'man b. Muhammad, *Iftitah al-da'wa*, ed. W. al-Qadi (Beirut, 1970); English trans., *Founding the Fatimid State*, tr. H. Haji (London, 2006), and Ibn al-Haytham, *Kitab al-munazarat*, ed. and tr. W. Madelung and P. E. Walker as *The Advent of the Fatimids: A Contemporary Shi'i Witness* (London, 2000). A thorough analysis of the sources on the Fatimids may be found in Paul E. Walker, *Exploring an Islamic Empire: Fatimid History and its Sources* (London, 2002).
3. On some recent studies of these *da'i*s and their contributions, see P. E. Walker, *Abu Ya'qub al-Sijistani: Intellectual Missionary* (London, 1996); his *Hamid al-Din al-Kirmani: Ismaili Thought in the Age of al-Hakim* (London, 1999); Verena Klemm, *Memoirs of a Mission: The Ismaili Scholar, Statesman and Poet al-Mu'ayyad fi'l-Din al-Shirazi* (London, 2003); Tahera Qutbuddin, *Al-Mu'ayyad al-Shirazi and Fatimid Da'wa Poetry* (Leiden, 2005), and Alice C. Hunsberger, *Nasir Khusraw, The Ruby of Badakhshan: A Portrait of the*

Persian Poet, Traveller and Philosopher (London, 2000).

4. Ismail K. Poonawala, 'Al-Qadi al-Nu'man and Isma'ili Jurisprudence', in F. Daftary, ed., *Mediaeval Isma'ili History and Thought* (Cambridge, 1996), pp. 117–143.

5. W. Madelung, 'Aspects of Isma'ili Theology: The Prophetic Chain and the God Beyond Being', in S. H. Nasr, ed., *Isma'ili Contributions to Islamic Culture* (Tehran, 1977), pp. 51–65, reprinted in W. Madelung, *Religious Schools and Sects in Medieval Islam* (London, 1985), article XVII; H. Halm, *The Fatimids and their Traditions of Learning* (London, 1997); and P. E. Walker, 'Fatimid Institutions of Learning', *Journal of the American Research Center in Egypt*, 34 (1997), pp. 179–200, reprinted in his *Fatimid History and Ismaili Doctrine* (Aldershot, 2008), article I.

6. See Ismail K. Poonawala, *Biobibliography of Isma'ili Literature* (Malibu, CA, 1977), especially pp. 44–132.

7. F. Daftary, 'The Ismaili *Da'wa* outside the Fatimid *Dawla*', in M. Barrucand, ed., *L'Égypte Fatimide, son art et son histoire* (Paris, 1999), pp. 29–43, reprinted in his *Ismailis in Medieval Muslim Societies*, pp. 62–88.

8. S. M. Stern, 'The Succession to the Fatimid Imam al-Amir, the Claims of the later Fatimids to the Imamate, and the Rise of Tayyibi Ismailism', *Oriens*, 4 (1951), pp. 193–255, reprinted in S. M. Stern, *History and Culture in the Medieval Muslim World* (London, 1984), article XI; and Daftary, *The Isma'ilis*, pp. 241–269.

9. F. Daftary, 'Sayyida Hurra: The Isma'ili Sulayhid Queen of Yemen', in Gavin R. G. Hambly, ed., *Women in the Medieval Islamic World* (New York, 1998), pp. 117–130, reprinted in his *Ismailis in Medieval Muslim Societies*, pp. 89–103; and Delia Cortese and S. Calderini, *Women and the Fatimids in the World of Islam* (Edinburgh, 2006), pp. 129–140.

10. F. Daftary, 'Hasan-i Sabbah and the Origins of the Nizari Isma'ili Movement', in F. Daftary, ed., *Mediaeval Isma'ili History and Thought* (Cambridge, 1996), pp. 181–204, reprinted in his *Ismailis in Medieval Muslim Societies*, pp. 124–148; and his 'Hasan Sabbah', *EIR*, vol. 12, pp. 34–37.

11. These tales are analysed in F. Daftary, *The Assassin Legends: Myths of the Isma'ilis* (London, 1994), pp. 88–127.

12. For an excellent brief overview of the Nizari state and *da'wa* during the Alamut period, see Marshall G. S. Hodgson, 'The Isma'ili State', in *The Cambridge History of Iran*: Volume 5, *The Saljuq and Mongol Periods*, ed. John A. Boyle (Cambridge, 1968), pp. 422–482, and F. Daftary, *A Short History of the Ismailis* (Edinburgh, 1998), pp. 120–158, while more detailed surveys are contained in B. Lewis, *The Assassins* (London, 1967), pp. 38–124, and Daftary, *The Isma'ilis*, especially pp. 310–402, 617–642.

13. See Daftary, *The Isma'ilis*, pp. 422–442.

14. Aga Khan I's own account of his early life and conflict with the Qajar ruling establishment in Persia, which culminated in his permanent settlement in British India, is contained in his autobiography entitled *'Ibrat-afza* (lith-

ograph, Bombay, 1278/1862); ed. H. Kuhi Kirmani (Tehran, 1325/1946). See also Naoroji M. Dumasia, *A Brief History of the Aga Khan* (Bombay, 1903), pp. 66–95; his *The Aga Khan and his Ancestors* (Bombay, 1939), pp. 25–59; H. Algar, 'The Revolt of Agha Khan Mahallati and the Transference of the Isma'ili Imamate to India', *Studia Islamica*, 29 (1969), pp. 61–81; his 'Mahallati, Agha Khan', *EI2*, vol. 5, pp. 1221–1222; James C. Masselos, 'The Khojas of Bombay: The Defining of Formal Membership Criteria during the Nineteenth Century', in I. Ahmad, ed., *Caste and Social Stratification among Muslims in India* (New Delhi, 1973), pp. 1–20; and Daftary, *The Isma'ilis*, pp. 463–476.
15. See W. Ivanow, *Ismaili Literature: A Bibliographical Survey* (Tehran, 1963), pp. 149–150; Poonawala, *Biobibliography of Isma'ili Literature*, pp. 283–284; and F. Daftary, 'Shihab al-Din al-Husayni', *EI2*, vol. 9, p. 435.
16. See Hatim M. Amiji, 'The Asian Communities', in J. Kritzeck and W. H. Lewis, ed., *Islam in Africa* (New York, 1969), pp. 141–181; Robert G. Gregory, *India and East Africa* (Oxford, 1971), pp. 17–45; and N. King, 'Toward a History of the Isma'ilis in East Africa', in I. R. al-Faruqi, ed., *Essays in Islamic and Comparative Studies* (Washington DC, 1982), pp. 67–83.
17. Aga Khan III left a valuable account of his life and career in his *The Memoirs of Aga Khan: World Enough and Time* (London, 1954).
18. See *Aga Khan III: Selected Speeches and Writings of Sir Sultan Muhammad Shah*, ed. K. K. Aziz (London, 1997–1998), 2 vols. The modernization policies of Aga Khan III are discussed fully in M. Boivin, 'The Reform of Islam in Ismaili Shi'ism from 1885 to 1957', in Françoise 'Nalini' Delvoye, ed., *Confluences of Cultures: French Contributions to Indo-Persian Studies* (New Delhi, 1994), pp. 197–216; his *La rénovation du Shi'isme Ismaélien en Inde et au Pakistan. D'après les écrits et les discours de Sultan Muhammad Shah Aga Khan (1902-1954)* (London, 2003); and M. Ruthven, 'Aga Khan III and the Isma'ili Renaissance', in Peter B. Clarke, ed., *New Trends and Developments in the World of Islam* (London, 1998), pp. 371–395.
19. For details, see F. Daftary, *Ismaili Literature: A Bibliography of Sources and Studies* (London, 2004), pp. 84–103, and his *The Ismailis*, pp. 1–33.
20. For some interesting anthropological case studies of these complex issues in the Muslim–Hindu context, see Dominique-Sila Khan, *Conversions and Shifting Identities: Ramdev Pir and the Ismailis in Rajasthan* (New Delhi, 1997), and her *Crossing the Threshold: Understanding Religious Identities in South Asia* (London, 2004), especially pp. 30–93.

PART I

NIZARI ISMAILIS: SYRIA, CENTRAL ASIA AND CHINA

2

Modern History of the Nizari Ismailis of Syria

Dick Douwes

The history of the Ismailis of Syria in the 19th and 20th centuries is characterized by two processes of reorientation: the first is spatial, resulting from migration from the Mediterranean mountains to the inland plains, and the second is spiritual and related to the recognition of Aga Khan III as Imam by what has become the majoritarian Nizari Ismaili community of Syria. In combination, these processes radically changed Ismaili lifestyles in Syria.

Currently about 1 per cent of the population of the Syrian Arab Republic is Ismaili. This small minority is divided into two Nizari Ismaili branches of the old Imamate tree: Qasim-Shahi and Mu'min-Shahi. The latter represent the 'traditional' Syrian Ismailis, but their numbers are very small. The Qasim-Shahis acquired their prominence on the Syrian stage towards the close of the 19th century, but today they constitute the large majority within the Syrian Ismaili population. Both communities are relatively close and there are no longer any 'sectarian' disputes amongst them. Moreover, today the Ismailis are among the most 'secularized' communities of the region.

In relation to the broader society, religious identity and association have always mattered in one way or another throughout the centuries. Modernity in its multiple guises – colonialism, nation-state, citizenship, secularism and, more recently, political Islam – does not seem to have made religious affiliations less important or problematic. Eventually, modernity brought about an increasing degree of participation in society and, subsequently, led to the greater visibility of the Ismailis. For the past half century, discussions of the dynamics within different religious communities and relations between these communities have been highly sensitive issues in Syria, because they are readily interpreted to reflect 'sectarianism'. In view of the fact that the modern history of the Ismailis has evolved in close interaction with other religious groups, particularly with Alawis and, later, with Sunni Muslims, they are generally reluctant to share their memories of certain events with 'outsiders'. As a result, many aspects of the modern history of the Ismailis require further investigation.

By the early 19th century, the Ismaili communities in Ottoman Syria were by and large located in the coastal hills and mountains between Tripoli and Latakiya. The Ismailis were heirs to the state of the 'fortresses of the mission' (*qila' al-da'wa*), and more precisely to the new Nizari Ismaili mission (*al-da'wa al-jadida*) in Syria. Once better known in Europe as the 'Assassins', the 'new mission' was comprised of a network of Ismaili fortresses and *da'i*s with their main centre at Alamut in northern Iran. In the 12th century, the Nizari Ismailis established strongholds in Syria, mainly in the coastal mountain range within the triangle of Tartus, Latakiya and Hama. Little is known of the religious milieu of this frontier area on the eastern Mediterranean at that time, except that it was home to various Muslim groups sometimes described as 'heterodox', as well as Christian communities.

Initially the Ismailis in Syria were concentrated in urban centres. With the demise of the Fatimid caliphate and the failure of the early Nizari *da'i*s to establish permanent footholds in Aleppo and Damascus, the *da'wa* aimed to acquire rural strongholds. After failed attempts in Afamiya and Shayzar to the northwest of the town of Hama, the *da'wa* turned to higher and more remote ground. The castles of Qadmus and Kahf, situated in a landscape of barren hills and deep valleys, were purchased. Together with Masyaf, these castles became the core of the Ismaili state that lasted for nearly a century and a half. Subsequent satellite strongholds were either conquered, purchased or constructed during the course of the 12th century. Under the leadership of Rashid al-Din Sinan (d. 1193), the greatest of the Nizari Ismaili *da'i*s in Syria, the Ismaili state was part of the broader political and military topography of the region.[1]

The submission of the last Ismaili castle, Kahf, in 1273 to the Mamluks ended the *da'wa* and political aspirations of the Ismailis in Syria. But the community survived in what was to become a politically marginal area under the Mamluks, who had not only subdued the Ismailis but also the remaining pockets of Crusaders. The Mamluks tolerated the Ismailis as a religious community, but kept them under close surveillance and ordered that their main centre, Masyaf, was to be administered in accordance with

Sunni Muslim prescriptions.² In official documents the Ismaili district continued to be designated as the *qilaʿ al-daʿwa* well into the Ottoman period.

Local Society in Coastal Syria

In the coastal mountains, the Ismailis were outnumbered by the Nusayris, who since the 1920s have been called Alawis. There is very little reliable information available on the historical demography of this area, but what is certain is that the Ismailis were gradually losing territory to their Alawi neighbours, notwithstanding indications that Ottoman authorities were generally favourably disposed towards the Ismailis when it came to local politics. Their long tradition of holding office, in particular as tax collectors, had made the leading Ismaili families relatively close associates of the provincial authorities. However, it was their interaction with the Alawi communities that shaped Ismaili history in late Ottoman times as well as to a large degree in the post-Ottoman French mandate period.

The Nusayriyya/Alawiyya is one of the lesser known branches of Shiʿi Islam. Unlike the Druzes, the Alawis are not an offshoot of the Ismailis but originated in earlier Shiʿi developments. The Alawis may have been dispersed over a much wider area in the past, but in Ottoman times they were by and large concentrated in the mountainous coastal strip to the north of Tripoli. They suffered severe persecution in the aftermath of the Ottoman–Safavid wars, apparently because of their association with the Qizilbash, the Shiʿi Turkomans who backed the Safavids. Alawi tradition is rich in its commemoration of those persecuted by Ottoman soldiery, and several of the Alawi clans in the coastal mountains traced their origin back to areas, such the Diyarbakir and Aleppo, which were cleansed by Ottoman forces of any potential opposition to the state.³

The relations between Ismaili and Alawi communities were complicated by the fact that leading Ismaili families, the so-called *umara* or amirs, often controlled official positions and economic resources in the areas where a growing majority of the population was in fact Alawi. The Ismaili amirs depended on Ottoman support in order to maintain their privileged status. Given the limited resources of the coastal mountains, life was difficult and competition for these resources fierce. Only its southern hills – the Safita and Wadi al-Nasara areas – and a small area in the hills near Latakiya were integrated in the regional market dominated by the production of silk and tobacco. Throughout the region, and particularly in the higher central and northern areas, banditry was common. In the

19th century, the coastal mountains were among the most deprived and poverty stricken areas of Greater Syria, a situation that continued well into the 20th century.[4]

According to both Alawi and Ismaili traditions, relations between the two communities were at times strained. Both significant and lesser incidents are prominently preserved in local collective memory and histories. Indeed a number of Ismaili and Alawi clans had a history of vendetta, including a few extremely violent encounters in the Qadmus and Masyaf areas. For instance, according to one popular Alawi tale, the Ismailis, after having captured Qadmus by treachery and with the support of the Turks, used the pretext of bringing a bride to gain entrance to the castle during the holy festival of al-Ghadir; and, subsequently, they killed 80 Alawi religious *shaykh*s and threw their bodies into a well. The Alawis also claim that on that occasion the Ismailis took away a number of sacred Alawi books as well as the blade of the sword of Imam al-Husayn, which, their tradition relates, was held in custody by a local Alawi clan for the awaited Mahdi. Not all stories have such a sensationalist angle, but the hostility of tone and language generally tended to be strong. *Shaykh*s were held in reverence and violent action against them was considered abhorrent and proof of having low standards of morality. Similar but less dramatic Ismaili tales exist about certain Alawi clans.[5]

It is difficult to attribute the recurrent clashes between the Ismailis and Alawis to a notion of religious rivalry between the two Shi'i communities. Society in the coastal mountains was organized along factional, clan lines and vendetta culture was part of the local code and was followed alike by Alawis, Ismailis and other communities. Factionalism was not only evident between the various religious communities but also within each of them. The deprived and harsh conditions in the area resulted in the fragmentation of political and religious authority. Internal conflicts and clashes were as common for the Alawi and Ismaili communities as inter-communal conflicts. However, the latter were sometimes larger in scope and therefore better remembered and documented, if only because Ottoman troops intervened with some regularity. Be that as it may, some of these recollections were committed to writing and published by Alawi and Ismaili authors, since the reconstruction of past events was not only shaped by a contemporary understanding of that past, but even more so by an urgent need to explain current conditions, namely the continuing problematic communal relations after the collapse of the Ottoman order in the wake of the First World War. For instance, the above tale of the theft of sacred books and the even more sacred blade of the sword of Imam al-Husayn by the Ismailis was published a few years after Alawi clans had attacked Qadmus in 1919. The author, an Alawi *shaykh*, maintains that the leading Alawi clan chief, Shaykh Salih al-'Ali, offered the Ismailis protection on the condition of the return of the sacred books and the blade. The Ismailis returned a false blade, thus leading to the Alawi attack on Qadmus.

Notwithstanding their historical feuds, the Ismailis and Alawis had much in common. On the devotional level, they shared the cult of the saints and their shrines. The hills and valleys are dotted with these shrines and other sacred sites. Many shrines were visited by local people irrespective of their particular religious affiliation, and some attracted visitors from Tripoli, Latakiya or even further afield.[6] The most popular shrines in the area were those of Mar Jurjus – Khidr in Muslim tradition – in the Wadi al-Nasara, and Shaykh Badr just to the north of the castle of Khawabi, a shrine that was held in high esteem by both Alawis and Ismailis. In cases of arbitration and reconciliation vows were taken at the shrine, a tradition that had survived since the Ottoman times. Khidr figured as the most prominent saint in the larger region from the Balkans to Central Asia, having numerous shrines dedicated to him. Various religious cults were very widespread in the coastal mountains, and the Khidr cult focused on the fertility of women and land.[7]

Another area of common ground between the two communities was based on the fact that some Nusayri clans were known to have Ismaili origins, reflecting the slow but prevalent trend towards the incorporation of smaller pockets of Ismailis into larger Alawi village clans, particularly in the northern and central parts of the coastal range. The declining Ismaili presence in these areas also led to a migration to the larger Ismaili towns and villages. Consequently, valleys and mountain ridges that had been populated by Ismailis for centuries became exclusively Alawi. The Ismailis evacuated most of the castles that had once belonged to their *da'wa*, as well as the valleys these castles controlled. By the mid-19th century the Ismailis were concentrated in three areas: Masyaf, Qadmus and Khawabi, areas linked to each other by a couple of days' journeying, and each was dominated by a fortress village. Small numbers of Ismailis continued to live in some adjacent valleys, such as Wadi al-'Uyun. From the early 19th century, Sunni Muslims replaced the original Ismaili inhabitants of the fortress village of Khawabi after the appointment of a Sunni tax collector by the Ottoman authorities in Tripoli. The last Ismaili family left Khawabi castle in the 1920s. A few pockets of Ismailis survived in villages and hamlets further north and in the hills near Tripoli (Akkar).

It is likely that in some of the towns in the wider area, such as Hama, there were one or two Ismaili families or even a small Ismaili community. However, it is doubtful whether these town dwellers adhered openly to the Ismaili faith.[8] All in all it is difficult to assess the total number of Ismailis living in this region in the late Ottoman period, but in all likelihood they did not exceed 10,000.[9]

Religious Traditions

Ismaili literary production in the Ottoman period consisted mainly of copying earlier Ismaili texts preserved by the Syrian community as well as the composing of religious poems (*anashid diniyya*). The texts that have survived were set down in small leather-bound books that the religious *shaykh*s carried with them.[10] The books that were copied or produced in the 19th and early 20th centuries – older books do not seem to have survived – are proof of a continuing literary and manuscript tradition. The Ismaili religious *shaykh*s handed down the sayings attributed to the first generations of Muslim leaders, in particular the Prophet's companion Salman al-Farisi and, of course, the first Shi'i Imam, 'Ali b. Abi Talib. Sayings and texts attributed to some of the other early Imams, in particular Ja'far al-Sadiq (d. 765), were also copied by the *shaykh*s, but clear references to later Imams seem to be absent. Most texts are attributed to Ismaili authors, including the famous Ikhwan al-Safa', or Brethren of Purity, and the Fatimid jurist al-Qadi al-Nu'man (d. 974), but some religious handbooks also included mystical texts that are not specifically Ismaili. The mystic Ibn Arabi (al-Shaykh al-Akbar) and his teachings on the *wahdat al-wujud* (oneness of being) also figured prominently in the Syrian Ismaili tradition with its strong mystical undercurrents. The activist mystic al-Hallaj (d. 922) was also revered by the Ismaili *shaykh*s of Syria in the late 19th and early 20th centuries.[11] The more specifically Syrian Ismaili sources in the religious repertoire of the *shaykh*s comprised roughly two types of texts: works attributed to Ismaili *da'i*-authors who shaped the local Syrian tradition such as Rashid al-Din Sinan, Shams al-Din al-Tayyibi and Hasan al-Mu'addil, and religious poetry composed by the Ismaili *shaykh*s of the Ottoman period.

Apart from the literary tradition, the shrine culture embodied links to the Ismaili past. The shrine dedicated to Rashid al-Din Sinan near Masyaf continued to attract devotees well into the 20th century, and the site has recently been renovated. Moreover the tombs of Ismaili *shaykh*s themselves served as places of remembrance and devotion, such as that of al-Hajj Khidr in the village of Aqar Zayti in the Khawabi area. The *shaykh* tradition represented the main source of the continuity of the Ismaili tradition, but it brought a degree of segmentation of the religious leadership when compared to the pre-Ottoman organization of the community led by a unified and unity organization of missionaries and chief missionaries. In the 19th century at least two *shaykh*-related orientations existed in the core area of Ismaili settlement, where villagers adhered to the local lineages of *shaykh*s. Similar *shaykh*-related spiritual affiliations existed among the Alawis. The main Ismaili *shaykh* lineages were those of the Suwaydanis and Hajjawis, the latter also being known as Khidrawis, a division that dated back to an earlier century. These lineages appear to have largely reflected the local balance of power between the families of the amirs, as the Ismaili clan leaders were called.

According to local folklore, these differences in spiritual leadership arose from the failure of one group to accept the intervention of the Imam in favour of another group or leader. For instance, in the Hajjawi recollection of events, Shaykh al-Hajj Khidr, who was a relative of a leading *shaykh*, Muhammad al-Suwaydani, became increasingly popular as a spiritual leader in the Qadmus area and in the end the amirs of Qadmus had him expelled. Al-Hajj Khidr and his followers took refuge in Khawabi and Kahf. Every five years, as it is remembered, a delegation of *shaykh*s set out from Syria to meet the Imam in India, to submit the tribute to him and receive his instructions. Al-Hajj Khidr was a representative in the mission from Khawabi led by Muhammad al-Suwaydani. When receiving the delegation, the Imam decided that the latter – who was in his 80s – was to be relieved of his duties. Instead he appointed al-Hajj Khidr as his chief missionary in Syria. On their return to Syria, the amirs of Qadmus, Masyaf and Wadi al-ʿUyun refused to recognize al-Hajj Khidr's authority. Some time later, as the story goes, the amirs of Qadmus tricked the followers of al-Hajj Khidr into a deadly trap: they invited them to a reconciliation banquet on a rock close to Qadmus and attacked them. Some managed to escape to the woods nearby, but the agents of the amirs searched the woods and in the process more were killed. The place is known as Sakhrat al-Ma'ida, or the Rock of the Banquet, at least among some of the descendants of the Hajjawis.[12]

This episode is part of the oral history of the area. As noted earlier, similar stories exist about conflicts between Ismailis and Alawis, and between various Alawi clans. Many of the stories may have been rooted in some historical reality, but they are perhaps more relevant for understanding the circumstances that existed at the time of their reconstruction. Although rich in detail, most such tales lack vital elements. In the account of the appointment of al-Hajj Khidr as the chief missionary, for instance, all the details relate to local matters. The story does not offer a single clue as to the identity of the Ismaili Imam in question,[13] nor his whereabouts (which as we now know must have been Awrangabad or some other locality in India where the Nizari Imams of the Mu'min-Shahi line then lived).

The Living Imam

Most Syrian Ismailis adhered to the Mu'min-Shahi line of the Nizari Imams.[14] It is not known whether communications with the Imams continued uninterruptedly in the first centuries of Ottoman rule.

The Ismaili historian 'Arif Tamir (1921–1998) quotes texts in which reference is made to later Mu'min-Shahi Imams living in India, including Amir Muhammad al-Baqir, who is believed to have been the last Imam of that lineage. In the main, Tamir bases his argument on verses composed by Sulayman b. Haydar (d. 1795), a revered *shaykh* from Masyaf, who referred to the contemporary Mu'min-Shahi Imam. Tamir argues that communication with the Imam was discontinued after widespread raiding by Alawi clans in the early 19th century when the Ismailis temporarily lost possession of Masyaf. Sulayman b. Haydar led the Ismaili refugees to the town of Homs where he died.[15] Ottoman troops from Damascus then came to the rescue of the Ismailis and restored order, handing back Masyaf to the Ismailis.[16] In spite of the uncertainties about the nature of relations between the Ismailis in Syria and their geographically remote Imams, the notion of the necessity of having a living Imam had clearly survived. Around 1880 the Suwaydani Shaykh Muhammad al-Haydar set out for Iran in search of the Mu'min-Shahi Imam. He failed to locate the Imam there, but collected some possible clues about his whereabouts – pointing to India – that were taken up by a small group of both Suwaydani and Hajjawi *shaykhs*. These *shaykhs* also failed to find their Imam but reported on their return to Syria that an Ismaili Imam appeared to be living in Bombay. Soon afterwards a new delegation of *shaykhs* left for Basra where they took a boat to Karachi and then journeyed overland to Bombay to meet the very young Imam of the Qasim-Shahi Nizari Ismailis, Sultan Muhammad Shah, Aga Khan III. Back in Syria, the news that contact had been established with the Imam spread rapidly, causing great excitement in the community. However, the *shaykhs* were hesitant to acknowledge Sultan Muhammad Shah as their Imam because of his Qasim-Shahi ancestry, a line of Imams which had adherents in various Nizari Ismaili communities in Iran and India, but perhaps not many in Syria. Curiosity about the young Imam caused yet another group of *shaykh*s to travel to Bombay, but on their return most of the *shaykh*s declared that they rejected Sultan Muhammad Shah's claim to the Imamate. However, some of the Hajjawi *shaykh*s did accept him as their rightful Imam and these *shaykh*s were also able to mobilize a growing number of followers within the Syrian Ismaili community.[17]

In his first letter to his Syrian followers, the Aga Khan appointed the Hajjawi Shaykh Sulayman al-Hajj as their *mukhi*, or religious leader, thus introducing the Khoja religious terminology into Syria. The religious instructions in the letter were 'orthodox' in content; they stressed the importance of performing the *salat* five times a day, fasting during the month of Ramadan and the *hajj* pilgrimage to Mecca.[18] In 1895 Shaykh Sulayman al-Hajj died of cholera when in Bombay. His companion, Shaykh Ahmad al-Muhammad al-Hajj, was then appointed as *mukhi*. Shaykh Ahmad is reported to have stayed for about a year in Bombay before returning to Syria, where he caused a sensation by introducing teachings and rituals that were perceived as a clear departure from local tradition.[19]

Shaykh Ahmad met with resistance when explaining the 'new order' and was even barred from Qadmus and Masyaf. However, he was supported by an influential family from Khawabi, the al-Jundis, who were related by marriage to the *shaykh*. When travelling to spread his mission to the Ismaili community of Salamiyya, Shaykh Ahmad feared he would be barred from Salamiyya, too, because some of the amirs of Salamiyya opposed his instructions. But there was also support for the *shaykh* because many of the inhabitants of Salamiyya and the surrounding villages had recently moved there from Khawabi. Reportedly, Shaykh Ahmad entered Salamiyya at noon on a Friday in the month of fasting, Ramadan. He went straight to the mosque where he participated in the Friday prayer. After the prayer, he was asked to explain the reforms. The *shaykh* stressed that those who wished to pray five times a day were free to do so, and those who wished to fast similarly had the right to do so. However, he is said to have argued that the Imam also sought to emphasize the inner spirituality of the rituals.

By the close of the 19th century, the distinction between the two main Ismaili traditions upheld by the *shaykh* families deepened and a rapidly growing number of Hajjawis now adhered to the Qasim-Shahi line of Imams, whereas the Suwaydanis remained devoted to the Mu'min-Shahis. It is difficult to reconstruct actual changes apart from the limited facts about alterations to certain rituals and the organization of the payment of tribute (*khums*) to the Imam.[20] Payment of the *khums* was to be a source of considerable trouble to the followers of the Aga Khan. In the first decade of the 20th century many *shaykh*s and other Ismailis from Khawabi and Salamiyya were arrested and tried by Ottoman authorities. Some died in prison, including Shaykh Ahmad al-Muhammad al-Hajj. Obviously the *shaykh*s had not anticipated this reaction from the Ottoman authorities, who interpreted recognition of a 'British Indian prince' as an act of treachery against the authority of the Ottoman sultan, and accused the followers of the Aga Khan of a variety of criminal offences.[21]

Ismaili Migrations

The Ottoman actions against the followers of the Aga Khan should be analysed in terms of the local political context of Salamiyya, a rapidly developing rural area on the fringes of the Syrian steppes. Most of the Aga Khan's followers were to be found in the Khawabi area, the traditional Hajjawi area, and in the recently settled area of Salamiyya southeast of the town of Hama. Migration to the fertile inland plain of Salamiyya began around the mid-19th century and gained momentum in the closing decades of that century. The fact that Salamiyya had been an Ismaili stronghold in the 9th century may also have been remembered, but by the 19th century Ismaili settlers in this previously nomadic area were largely motivated by hopes of a more prosperous life owing to exemptions from taxes and army conscription for the inhabitants. Among the very first settlers in Salamiyya were a number of Ismailis who benefited from a general Ottoman policy of the time which granted amnesty to fugitives from the law who were willing to settle in areas to the east of the Sultanic Road connecting Aleppo, through Hama and Homs, with Damascus. This had been rich farmland but the villages had been deserted for several generations.

Settling to the east of the inland towns of Hama and Homs was not without risk, because the pastureland and water resources of the Salamiyya area were controlled by nomadic Arab tribes who were reluctant to accept the appearance of a sedentary population in their midst. But apart from a few larger incidents in the first decade or so, the tribes came to tolerate the farmers under condition of payment of protection money. Until his death in 1868, Amir Isma'il, who was allowed to keep a militia of 40 armed horsemen, successfully managed to re-cultivate the ancient farmlands around Salamiyya. His son, Amir Muhammad, succeeded him as leader of the local Ismaili community.[22]

The first families to settle were the Hajjawis, including the Isma'il, al-Jundi and Mirza families of amirs who had recently lost many of their old privileges, in particular the collection of taxes in the Khawabi (al-Jundi), Kahf (Isma'il) and Marqab (Mirza) areas. A number of these families had been outlawed after violent entanglements in Qadmus, to which they had retreated.[23] From the beginning, the leading migrant amirs had actively sought to encourage Ismailis in the coastal mountains to settle in Salamiyya, not only from Khawabi but also the Qadmus and Masyaf areas. After a somewhat problematic start, they were successful, and the news of better prospects spread by word of mouth. Ismailis from small communities in the Akkar and Antioch areas migrated to Salamiyya. This would lead to the complete disappearance of Ismailis from those areas. Villages in the Qadmus and Khawabi areas, too, lost their centuries-old Ismaili presence, in particular in the Wadi al-'Uyun. Even close to the old Ismaili centre of Masyaf, the Ismailis in some villages were entirely replaced by Alawis and Greek Orthodox Christians. However, not all Ismailis went to Salamiyya. A number settled in the larger villages in the mountains, others in the nearby towns of Hama, Homs and Tartus, while some emigrated to the Americas.

The first satellite villages of Salamiyya, 'Izz al-Din and Sabbura, were founded in the 1860s, but both failed to prosper mainly owing to pressure from the local Arab tribesmen. In spite of these setbacks, new settlements were soon founded. Akkari families started farming around Kafat in about 1870, representing the first case of a satellite village to succeed. Other large villages settled by Ismailis in the closing decades of the 19th century included 'Aqarib, Talldarra and Sa'n al-Shajara. The latter, some 50 kilometres to the northeast of Salamiya, was the most remote Ismaili settlement in the Ottoman period and also contained an Ottoman army post.[24] Apart from the attractions of paying less tax and being exempt from military conscription, many villagers decided to migrate to the Salamiyya area because of deteriorating conditions elsewhere caused by the growth of large estates. For instance, the Ismaili settlers who founded the village of 'Aqarib had been expelled from their lands near the fortress village of Shayzar by a prominent family based in the town of Hama.

By the 1870s non-Ismaili settlers had also arrived in the region. Circassian refugees from the Caucasus settled in a number of villages to the north and south of Salamiyya. By their presence these new arrivals were of help to the Ismaili settlements. Alawi villagers were also attracted to the area. Finally an increasing number of nomadic tribesmen opted

Normalization and Conflict in Salamiyya

for a sedentary life, but this process only gained momentum in the first decade of the 20th century. By that time the apparatus of the Ottoman administration was more firmly established in the area.

Access to and control over land and labour resources constituted the main issues in the process of extending cultivation of land in the Salamiyya area. With an increase in the movement of both Ismailis and non-Ismailis to Salamiyya, competition for land also increased. On the one hand, the influx of migrants made the further spread of cultivation possible, but on the other hand the later migrants discovered that the more fertile lands and best water resources had, perhaps inevitably, already been taken by the earlier settlers. The first families to move to Salamiyya, including the amirs, controlled relatively large areas of land, not only in the immediate surroundings of the town but also in several of the nearby villages in which they had made investments in exchange for land. Their properties were not comparable to those held by the big landowners of Hama and Homs, but nonetheless they had established themselves firmly as a local elite. Apart from hiring Ismailis to work on their land, they recruited Alawis – often as seasonal labourers – and later on Arab tribesmen. Absentee landowners from the towns of Hama and Homs also developed a keen interest in farming on the steppes to the east of their towns and recruited Alawi villagers and Arab tribesmen to work their land.

The authority of the Ismaili amirs of Salamiyya did not remain unchallenged. Conflicts over land occurred regularly. For instance, newly arrived relatives of the amirs were given land that had been appropriated from earlier but less eminent migrants. The first migrants from Akkar lost their plots of land in Salamiyya in this way. Some of them returned to Akkar, but others founded the village of Kafat. The amirs also controlled a number of services for which the villagers had to pay dearly, such as grinding wheat and barley, for which they charged up to 50 per cent of the flour produced.[25]

The rapid expansion of settlements from the 1870s onwards and the arrival of a more mixed population of settlers, including Sunni traders from Hama, resulted in the administrative normalization of the area in the 1880s and 1890s. Salamiyya was made the administrative centre of a district that included large stretches of the plain and hills to the southeast of Hama, though part of this land had been turned into Ottoman Sultanic estates which were administrated separately. Local councils were introduced whose main responsibility was supporting Ottoman officials. At the municipal level, membership of these councils reflected the local prominence of individuals and, predictably, most members belonged to the families of the Ismaili amirs. The first mayor appointed in Salamiyya was Amir Isma'il al-Muhammad, the son of the then recently deceased Amir Muhammad. Then in the mid-1890s Amir Tamir Mirza took over the position.

Towards the end of the 19th century, local conditions in Salamiyya became rather unsettled following recurrent disputes over land. A settler from Qadmus, Himadi al-'Umar, had acquired a strong enough position to confront the leading amirs of Salamiyya. He had a popular following in and around Salamiyya, including some Alawis, and became a member of the district council in the late 1880s. His rise to prominence coincided with the abolition of the privileges of the settlers, such as the exemption from taxation, and, more importantly, from conscription. The most detailed information on Himadi al-'Umar is given by the Ismaili Shaykh 'Abd Allah al-Murtada (d. 1936), who was openly biased against the man. According to his reconstruction of the events, Himadi al-'Umar converted to Sunni Islam, volunteered to have his oldest son conscripted into the army and gathered around him a following by making various false promises. According to the *shaykh*, it was he who induced the Ottoman authorities to start recruiting Ismailis from Salamiyya into the army.[26] After a number of violent encounters between the followers of the Ismaili amirs and Himadi al-'Umar, Ottoman soldiers were dispatched to Salamiyya to restore order. Even today people are reluctant to share the local memories of this conflict with outsiders, partly because of the 'sectarian' aspects of the episode. What seems to be certain is that, as in many other localities, the normalization of local government and the introduction of conscription met with resistance. Also, as had happened in Qadmus, resistance against the authority of the amirs was growing.

The mounting tensions in Salamiyya rendered problematic the recognition of Aga Khan III as the Imam by a number of Ismailis. 'Abd Allah al-Murtada blamed Himadi al-'Umar for inciting the Ottoman authorities against the followers of the Aga Khan, claiming that in 1901 he had informed the authorities of the imminent transfer of the tribute payments, which were then immediately confiscated. Examining the documents presented at the trials that followed, it is evident that Himadi al-'Umar and his followers supported the move against the Ismaili *shaykhs* and amirs by giving evidence against them. Himadi al-'Umar claimed, among others, that they had tried to extort money from him as a contribution to the tribute collected for the Imam, and that they had attempted to kill him after he refused to give in to their demands. Indeed he was killed about five years later, possibly at the instructions of Amir Tamir Mirza who lived in hiding among Arab tribesmen after escaping arrest in 1901.

After the Constitutional Revolution of 1908 the remaining prisoners were released, among them Shaykh Nasr al-Muhammad, a brother of Shaykh Ahmad, who had died in prison. Shaykh Nasr became the new Ismaili *mukhi*. In 1910 the provincial authorities arrested him as he set out for India with the community's religious dues. The *shaykh* was exiled to the town of Bursa in Anatolia but was allowed to return after six months. The tribute was not returned to the community but invested in an agricultural school in Salamiyya that opened its doors in 1912.[27]

Troubles in the Mountains

Migration from the mountains to Salamiyya continued well into the post-Ottoman period. In the 1910s and early 1920s, conflicts in the mountains caused many to flee from the smaller villages, or even entire valleys, and hundreds of refugees arrived in Salamiyya. Among the Ismailis they included both Hajawis and Suwaydanis. A number of Suwaydanis settled in Salamiyya in the Qadamisa quarter named after Qadmus, the place of origin of most of these migrants.

Qadmus was a trouble spot in the late Ottoman period. The frequent conflicts over land and other resources caused a large portion of the Ismaili population of Qadmus to leave their homes for Salamiyya. Competition between the Ismaili amirs of Qadmus, too, placed strains on the local villagers and obliged many of them to migrate. The resulting shortage of agricultural labour led to further difficulties in the villages. The district was in the heart of the historic Ismaili lands in the coastal mountains, but by the late 19th century Alawis greatly outnumbered Ismailis. Many Alawis belonged to prominent clans, such as the Matawira, Rashawina and Khayyatin, which were also present in the adjacent districts and were able to mobilize armed bands in the event of a conflict. Furthermore within the Ismaili community in Qadmus a rather asymmetric situation arose as the families of the Ismaili amirs gradually began to outnumber those of the ordinary Ismailis.

With the collapse of Ottoman rule in the wake of the First World War, the ensuing highly unstable political conditions and contending political claims on Syria, public order broke down in Qadmus.[28] Given the clannish nature of the local politics, the conflicts that arose in the late 1910s cannot be readily attributed to class or sectarian factors. Moreover the sources required for reconstructing the events of the time are themselves highly problematic.[29] The main participants were the quarrelling Ismaili amirs of Qadmus, Alawi clan leaders from adjacent areas and ill-informed French officials who sought to intervene. Since these events developed in the broader context of the establishment of the French mandate authority and the initial strong local resistance against it, other parties intervened when the crisis in Qadmus deepened and spread to other areas, among them Sharifian officials from the entourage of King Faysal and nationalist activists from the main inland towns such as Damascus and Hama.

The situation in the Qadmus area was tense because a rival leadership had developed opposing the traditional authority of the Ismaili amirs. The new leadership was mixed, containing both Ismailis – including a few members of amir families – and Alawis. Conditions worsened when the young son of an Alawi clan leader was shot by an Ismaili. The Ismailis' failure to pay the customary blood money mobilized the Khayyatin clan against them. Mediation by Alawi clan leaders from Masyaf proved unsuccessful and in March 1919 the Ismailis were attacked, not only by the Khayyatin but also by some other clans. In May the conflict escalated and spread to Khawabi when, following a series of disputes over livestock and land, the Sunni community of Khawabi invited Alawi clans to retaliate against the Ismailis. During the attacks, over 100 villagers were killed and thousands fled to the coastal towns, with most Ismailis fleeing to Tartus. Apart from the Ismailis, Maronite and Greek Orthodox villages also came under Alawi attack.[30] By then the conflict had also acquired anti-colonial and nationalistic features as a consequence of French intervention. The first interventions were unsuccessful and led to a much broader conflict that became known as the 'revolt of Shaykh Salih al-'Ali', a local Alawi clan leader who, for at least a year or two, was part of the Syrian nationalist resistance against the establishment of the French mandate. French army units were deployed to curb numerous local revolts. Small armed groups of Ismailis assisted the French troops in extending their control over the southern part of the coastal mountains and hills.

Shaykh Salih al-'Ali was the son of a locally eminent Alawi *shaykh* in the Shaykh Badr area, near Khawabi. It appears that Shaykh Salih al-'Ali had a reputation as a rebel, having killed two Ottoman police officers who had harassed one of his father's wives. Some reports suggest that he was also a miracle worker at the shrine he had built for his father.[31] In the vacuum following the collapse of the Ottoman order, he and his band of armed followers had acquired a leading role in local politics and also, subsequently, in the resistance movement against the steady military and political advance of the French. The series of attacks in 1919 and the initial failure of the French to curb the local armed bands attracted nationalists from inland Syria, including officers of the Sharifian army. Early in 1920 rebels attacked the coastal areas of Tartus and Banyas. By that time the French were in the process of winning over the main Alawi clans of the southern part of the mountains. By the end of 1920 the pacification of the south was completed. Shaykh Salih al-'Ali escaped to the higher mountains, only to surrender himself in 1922 to the French authorities. He was pardoned and went on to become a respected dignitary who no longer resisted the French in their attempts to construct a separate Alawi polity, 'L'État des Alaouites', within the Syrian federation. After the revolt had subsided many Ismaili refugees returned to Khawabi.

Notwithstanding the severity of their confrontations, Ismailis and Alawis did not differ widely in their approach towards the mandate authorities. Their sentiments against renewed Sunni domination were also strong, in particular among the Alawis, and the French policies that threatened the autonomy of the Alawi 'state' met with opposition. In 1923 numerous petitions against the new French policies restricting their local autonomy were signed by Alawi, Christian and Ismaili notables alike. However, competition for office came to dominate local politics, resulting in drawn-out negotiations between various factions, with the Alawis persistently criticizing the prominence of Sunni Muslims and Christians in the public administration. Being a small community, the Ismailis were rarely represented in the new councils, except at the municipal level. As with the Maronites, there was only one Ismaili on the representative council of the Alawi state.

Within the evolving nationalist discourse, Shaykh Salih al-'Ali was to become a hero, whereas the Ismailis were to be remembered as being favourably inclined to the French authorities. This may not be an accurate understanding of events, but it reflects the popular memory of them.

After the establishment of French control, conditions improved and gradually relations between the Ismailis and Alawis in the Khawabi and Qadmus areas were normalized. There was only one significant incident, the Ba'amra dispute in the 1930s, in which the Ismailis and Alawis were contending parties. In 1933 Muhammad Ibrahim, an Ismaili notable from Masyaf, acquired the village of Ba'amra in a public sale following the bankruptcy of its original owner, the Alawi Shaykh Sulayman al-'Ali of the large Matawira clan. The sale caused great dissatisfaction among the local Alawis and in 1935 the villagers collectively abandoned Ba'amra;

Muhammad Ibrahim recruited about 30 families from Salamiyya to replace them. When these families arrived they were attacked and chased away by Alawis. One Ismaili was killed and four others seriously injured. Relations between Ismailis and Alawis in the Masyaf area remained tense for several years.[32]

Although Ismailis and Alawis have a long history of conflict, one should be careful not to give an overly 'sectarian' interpretation of these disputes. Nearly all such encounters started with disputes over local resources, in particular land, between clan leaders who, with some regularity, recruited armed bands from among their following. This does not necessarily imply that Alawis and Ismailis always supported their leading families, and indeed they often acted in unison. Internal conflicts occurred frequently, contributing greatly to the attrition of the Ismaili presence in the mountains they once controlled. In the broader context of political dynamics in the mandate period, the Alawi and Ismaili communities were closer, despite their earlier conflicts. The leadership of both communities was clearly apprehensive about possible marginalization in any larger, democratic polity where Sunni Muslims would constitute the majority. The history of independent Syria demonstrates that both communities were able to cope with the new challenges.

Social and Political Change

Since independence, the conditions in which the Ismailis lived have changed drastically, in particular during the 1960s. New forms of leadership have developed, partly at the expense of the old hierarchy of amirs and religious *shaykh*s. A number of Ismailis from the families of amirs or *shaykh*s have done well in the political, intellectual and cultural fields, but they increasingly had to do so without any traditional patronage, and in fact some clearly distanced themselves from the former privileged status of the amirs. The youth of the leading Ismaili families enjoyed a better start in life as compared to others; some were able, for instance, to study at the best university in the region, the American University of Beirut. But their social base was eroding. The mood in Syria had become secularist, nationalist and eventually socialist, and these trends met with a response from the Ismailis. After the socialist Ba'th regime came to power in 1963, the economic base of the traditional amirs was weakened considerably by land reforms. The establishment of a national universal education system offered an increasing number of ordinary Ismailis from rural areas the prospect of social mobility by acquiring qualifications and working in the government bureaucracy. Today the Ismailis of Syria form part of the country's best-educated strata and of the most secularized ones in the wider region.

From the mid-20th century onwards a few young intellectuals from notable Ismaili families, such as Mustafa Ghalib (1923–1981), a Qasim-Shahi, and 'Arif Tamir (1921–1998), a Mu'min-Shahi, acquired academic prominence in the community and started to write about the Ismaili faith. They showed little interest in writing about the beliefs and practices of their parents or grandparents. Instead they concentrated on providing texts from the Fatimid period, or writing on Qasim-Shahi history.[33] Ignoring the more recent, in particular Ottoman, history of Syria and its religious communities was a general trend because of the strong emphasis on the nationalist understanding that the Arabs had not been in control of their destiny since the domination of the Turks, Saljuqs, Mamluks or Ottomans, in the Middle East.

The short-lived union of Syria and Egypt as the United Arab Republic (1958–1961) met with growing resentment in Syria, in particular among Muslim minorities who were wary of the growing Sunni bias against them in provincial affairs. The Egyptian officials arriving in Syria were surprised by the diversity of Islamic communities there. The journal of al-Azhar University in Cairo, the famous institution founded by the Fatimids but for many centuries since a centre of Sunni Muslim learning, published a short report on the Ismailis under the title of 'The Fatimids are still among us!'[34] The dissolution of the United Arab Republic was generally greeted favourably in Syria.

The military coup of 1963 and the establishment of the Ba'th regime in Syria were received with mixed feelings, in particular in urban centres. However, in view of the prominence of both military and civilians from rural backgrounds in the new regime, including Sunnis, Alawis, Druzes and Ismailis, its main source of support was to be found in the rural areas, including rural towns such as Salamiyya. The reforms implemented by the Ba'th regime, in particular land reform, weakened the political power of the large, urban-based landowners. Consequently the villagers tended to grow favourably inclined towards the Ba'th regime, not only because of the land reforms but also the rural development programmes in the fields of education and health.

However, among the Ismailis, in particular in Salamiyya, reactions were mixed, basically because the fortunes of the more prominent families were negatively affected by land reform and other policies. Also the increasingly secular, if not anti-religious, policies of the Syrian regime in the late 1960s were not welcomed by all. Yet, quite a number of Ismailis were actively involved with the new regime, both on local and national levels. Although members of the notable Ismaili families also cooperated with the regime, the title of 'amir' was no longer a time-honoured epithet of prestige but instead was symbolic of the exploitation of the labouring rural classes, and in one or two cases it became simply a family name.

In Salamiyya, members of the large al-Jundi family had roles in government. Others from the Ismaili notable families became prominent in the 1960s, pursuing careers in the military and other fields.[35] The increasing participation of Ismailis in various levels of government in the early 1970s reflected the general trend towards emancipation of minority groups.

Religious Policy

It may be argued that the acknowledgement of Aga Khan III as Imam by the majority of the Syrian Ismailis created conditions favourable to a more rapid spread of secular ideals and lifestyles. Some of the policies of the Aga Khan, such as discouraging visitations to shrines and not invoking the blessings of saints, had a negative impact on the position of the religious *shaykh*s who were the custodians of the shrines. Cut off from the sacred world of saints and shrines, the local *shaykh*s were now faced with the difficult task of acting as a channel of communication between the Syrian Ismailis and the Khoja leadership in the entourage of the Aga Khan, further complicated due to language differences. In the Khawabi area, a number of shrines were dismantled, including the shrine of al-Hajj Khidr at 'Aqar Zayti, but most of the aged pine trees, traditionally considered sacred, survived. However, saints and shrines did not disappear from the religious life of the Ismailis overnight, and even now a small number of individuals remain faithful to the old traditions, occasionally visiting shrines, especially that dedicated to Imam Zayn al-'Abidin in an Alawi village to the north of Hama.

Communication between the Aga Khan and Khoja leadership, on the one hand, and the Syrian Ismailis, on the other hand, had been problematic from the outset, causing difficulties in conveying religious guidance for several decades. Restrictions imposed by the Ottomans following the arrest and trial of the Ismailis in the first decade of the 20th century had also hampered communication. Wars and revolts created further barriers. Some Indian Ismaili missionaries visited their co-religionists in Syria after the First World War, but the channels of communication with the Aga Khan and his entourage remained few and the position of the Syrian

Ismailis within the global Nizari Ismaili community was somewhat marginalized, if only because of their small numbers as compared to the Khoja community and its African diaspora.

Sultan Muhammad Shah sent his son Prince Aly Khan as an envoy to the Syrian community and his visits are still remembered locally. These periodic visits served to strengthen the bonds between the Syrian Ismaili community and the Aga Khan.[36] They commenced in 1931, when Prince Aly Khan visited both Salamiyya and Khawabi, where he opened the Muhammadiyya School. Prince Aly Khan became quite popular in the Ismaili community of Syria. In Beirut during a stop-over in August 1957 the newly installed Imam, Prince Karim Aga Khan IV, received a large delegation of the Syrian Ismailis who came to express their collective allegiance to him.[37]

After independence, events in Syria brought about a diminution of contact between the Aga Khan and his communal organization and the Syrian Ismailis. In the 1950s Sunni Muslim politicians and officials openly favoured their co-religionists, and they were biased against the Ismailis and other Muslim minorities in Syria. This trend continued during the union with Egypt. With the coming to power of the Ba'th party, the participation of minorities, including Ismailis, in politics increased markedly but the regime was secular and suspicious of any religious activity. Moreover the spread of Sunni Islam among the Ismailis of Salamiyya, following hostile encounters between the al-Jundi and the Ismaili amir families, curtailed any expansion of their activities, since their adversaries were close to the leadership of the Ba'th regime. However, in 1968 a new Ismaili centre opened its doors in Salamiyya, which included a library for general use by the inhabitants of Salamiyya. It was only after the coming to power of the more moderate Ba'th faction under the leadership of Hafiz al-Asad that the Nizari Ismailis were able to place the remains of Prince Aly Khan in a mausoleum next to the Ismaili centre in Salamiyya. Prince Aly Khan had been killed in a car accident in 1960, and earlier attempts to convey his remains from France to Salamiyya had proved futile owing to difficulties raised by the Ba'th regime.

It was in the course of the 1970s that newly formulated religious education policies for the Ismailis began to be implemented in Syria, also. The first professional teachers and preachers of the community were trained in Karachi. In the 1980s a number of others, including two young women, were enrolled at the special teacher-training programmes offered at The Institute of Ismaili Studies in London. The training of this new professional group coincided with the gradual disappearance of the traditional religious *shaykhs*. The last few remaining Ismaili *shaykhs* were elderly people, and the most famous of them, Shaykh 'Ali 'Idu, died in the 1990s. Until the mid-1960s the religious *shaykhs* had run a number of small schools in the Ismaili villages, providing religious as well as general education. Most of these schools were closed down after the reforms in education undertaken by the Ba'th regime. Others closed down at the passing of the *shaykhs* in charge of them. Only a few *shaykhs* continued their activities into the 1990s.[38]

Meanwhile the Syrian Ismailis were enjoying a rising standard of living. Their farmlands in the plains around Salamiyya were yielding better harvests. Under Aga Khan IV the organization of the Syrian community, like that of many other Nizari communities, was reshaped on the basis of the 1986 Constitution, with a National Council and an Ismaili Tariqah and Religious Education Board (ITREB) responsible for the provision of religious education at all levels in the community, and for the training of religious teachers. In the last two decades the Syrian Ismailis have been increasingly involved in programmes initiated by Aga Khan IV, in particular in the fields of education – including skills training such as computing – and culture.

With the passing of the last generation of Ismaili *shaykhs*, the art of composing religious poetry (*anashid*) also dwindled among the Syrian Ismailis, but a few individuals still continue to pursue this traditional literary genre. The writing and recitation of poetry is still very popular among the Ismailis of Salamiyya. Ahmad al-Jundi is by far the best-known modern poet, his poems also being popular outside Syria, but scores of others in the Salamiyya area have published – mostly locally – modern verse, reflecting the cultural vitality of the community.[39] Recent visits of Aga Khan IV to Syria contributed not only to community building, but also to the increased visibility of the Ismaili community in Syria.[40]

Notes

1. See Farhad Daftary, *Ismailis in Medieval Muslim Societies* (London, 2005), pp. 149–155; Peter Willey, *Eagle's Nest: Ismaili Castles in Iran and Syria* (London, 2005), pp. 40–44.
2. Maurice Gaudefroy-Demonbynes, *La Syrie à l'époque des Mamelouks, d'après les auteurs Arabes* (Paris, 1923), pp. 4, 114–115.
3. D. Douwes, 'Knowledge and Oppression: The Nusayriyya in the Late Ottoman Period', in *La Shi'a nell'impero ottomano* (Rome, 1993), pp. 149–169; for local Alawi history, see Muhammad al-Tawil, *Ta'rikh*

al-ʿAlawiyyin (Latakiya, 1924). For the Ottoman perspective on the community in the early modern period, see Stefan Winter, 'The Nusayris before the Tanzimat in the Eyes of Ottoman Provincial Administrators, 1804–1834', in T. Philipp and C. Schumann, ed., *From the Syrian Land to the States of Syria and Lebanon* (Beirut, 2004), pp. 97–112.

4. See Douwes, 'Knowledge and Oppression', and the source cited therein, and Jacque Weulersse, *Le pays des Alaouites* (Tours, 1940).
5. Al-Tawil, *Taʾrikh*, pp. 431–432; this book was published in 1924, a few years after widespread Alawi attacks on Ismaili property, including Qadmus which had been in Ismaili possession since the 12th century. See also D. Douwes, 'Tegenstellingen in noordwest Syrië in de periode 1840–1880' ('Controversies in Northwestern Syria, 1840–1880'), *Sharqiyyat*, 2 (1989), pp. 47–64.
6. The most famous visitor to shrines near Masyaf and Qadmus was the mystic Shaykh ʿAbd al-Ghani al-Nabulsi (d. 1731); see his *al-Haqiqa waʾl-majaz fiʾl-rihla ila bilad al-Sham wa-Misr waʾl-Hijaz*, ed. Ahmad A. Huraydi (Cairo, 1987), pp. 54–56. The *shaykh* defined the locals as *ahl al-bidʿa wa-dalal* (people of wrongful innovation and error) but noted that he was welcomed with great hospitality and escorted by the locals to several shrines.
7. On Khidr, see Patrick Franke, *Begegnung mit Khidr: Quellenstudien zum Imaginären im Traditionellen Islam* (Stuttgart, 2000).
8. The French author Maurice Barrès, *Une enquête aux pays du Levant* (Paris, 1923), p. 252, noted that after the Constitutional Revolution of 1908 some people living in the towns of Hama and Homs declared themselves Ismailis and demanded separate representation on the local councils. However, they were reminded that they had always stated that they were Sunni Muslims.
9. Muhammad Bahjat and Rafiq Tamimi, *Wilayat Bayrut* (Beirut, 1917), vol. 2, pp. 391–394, estimated that on the eve of the First World War, some 2,500 Ismailis lived in 12 villages in Qadmus and another 2,000 in 17 villages in Khawabi. Their survey did not include Masyaf and Salamiyya, nor Akkar.
10. A collection of these Ismaili books of Syrian provenance are now kept at The Institute of Ismaili Studies; see Delia Cortese, *Ismaili and Other Arabic Manuscripts: A Descriptive Catalogue of Manuscripts in the Library of The Institute of Ismaili Studies* (London, 2000).
11. Ibid.; see also Ahmad al-Jundi, *Lahw al-ayyam* (London, 1991), p. 48; ʿAbd Allah al-Murtada, *al-Falak al-dawwar fi samaʾ al-aʾimma al-athar* (Aleppo, 1352/1933), p. 33.
12. Mahmud Amin, *Taʾrikh al-Ismaʿiliyyin fi bilad al-Sham*, MS, ff. 137–139. The late author failed to get permission to publish this work. Large parts of it were, however, included in his *Taʾrikh Salamiyya fi khamsin qarn* (Damascus, 1983).
13. In a very brief late 20th-century reconstruction of the career of al-Hajj Khidr, who was the best-known *shaykh* among the followers of the Aga Khan, it is claimed that he was appointed as *daʿi* by the Qasim-Shahi Nizari

Imam Nizar II; see *Nafahat al-iman*, published by the Hay'at al-Tariqa wa'l-Thaqafa al-Diniyya al-Isma'iliyya (n.p., n.d.), p. 12.

14. It should be noted, however, that a number of contemporary Syrian (Qasim-Shahi) Nizaris, drawing mainly on the oral traditions of their community, question the validity of this view. They hold that the Qasim-Shahi Nizari branch always predominated in Syria and that, therefore, there was no substantial switch of allegiance by the Mu'min-Shahis to the Qasim-Shahi branch in the early decades of Aga Khan III's Imamate.
15. See 'Arif Tamir, 'Furu' al-shajara al-Isma'iliyya', *al-Mashriq*, 51 (1957), pp. 581–612. See also his entry 'al-Isma'iliyya', in *Da'irat al-Ma'arif*, vol. 13, pp. 315–335. His *Muraja'at Isma'iliyya* (Beirut, 1994), pp. 5–20, includes a *qasida* attributed to Shaykh Sulayman b. Haydar, in which Amir Muhammad al-Baqir is described as *al-hadir al-mawjud* and *al-imam sahib al-zaman*. To my knowledge other authors have not had access to these texts which were in the private library of 'Arif Tamir.
16. Dick Douwes, *The Ottomans in Syria: A History of Justice and Oppression* (London, 2000), p. 116.
17. This account is based on Mahmud Amin's *Ta'rikh al-Isma'iliyyin*, ff. 167–171, which is biased against those who rejected the Aga Khan as their Imam, and on Ahmad al-Jundi's somewhat more critical evaluation of the events, in his *Lawh al-ayyam*, pp. 46–53.
18. The letter, dated Dhu al-Qa'da 1307/1890, is kept in the archives of the Ismaili Council in Salamiyya.
19. Bahjat and Tamimi, *Wilayat Bayrut*, vol. 2, pp. 395–408.
20. The archives of the Ismaili Council in Salamiyya contain only a few letters from Aga Khan III to the Syrian community, and these deal mostly with collection and transfer of the religious dues.
21. For a detailed account of the trials, see Dick Douwes and Norman N. Lewis, 'The Trials of Syrian Isma'ilis in the First Decade of the 20th Century', *International Journal of Middle East Studies*, 21 (1989), pp. 215–232.
22. The migration to and the expansion of cultivation in the Salamiyya area has been reconstructed on the basis of numerous interviews by Mahmud Amin in his *Ta'rikh Salamiyya*. See also Norman N. Lewis, *Nomads and Settlers in Syria and Jordan, 1800–1980* (Cambridge, 1987), pp. 58–73.
23. Conflicts between the amirs' families about the collection of taxes in the Qadmus area had escalated to such a degree that an Ottoman provincial official of the influential Harun family of Latakiya was killed while mediating. In order to prevent any retaliation by Ottoman troops, two of the rebellious amirs were surrendered to Ottoman authorities. Reportedly, one of them was killed in the process, the other, Amir Isma'il, was imprisoned. When shipped to the provincial capital Beirut, he managed to escape and started a career as a rebel with a substantial following in the Qadmus area, pillaging villages and later retiring to Khawabi where he was protected by Shaykh Ahmad al-Muhammad al-Hajj. Amir Isma'il and his men were eventually

pardoned and they settled in Salamiyya. See Amin, *Ta'rikh Salamiyya*, pp. 144–157, and also Lewis, *Nomads and Settlers in Syria*, pp. 58–61.
24. For a detailed description of the migrations and the expanding cultivation, see Amin, *Ta'rikh Salamiyya*, pp. 158–231, and also Lewis, *Nomads and Settlers*, pp. 58–73.
25. Amin, *Ta'rikh Salamiyya*, p. 217.
26. Al-Murtada, *al-Falak al-dawwar*, pp. 249–251.
27. See also Zakariya Wasfi, 'Salamiyya', *al-Insaniyya*, 3 (1933), pp. 601–610, and 4 (1934), pp. 17–27, and his *Jawlat athariyya fi ba'd al-bilad al-Shamiyya* (Damascus, 1934), p. 283. This author was for many years director of the agricultural school in Salamiyya.
28. See Amin, *Ta'rikh Salamiyya*, pp. 221–225; Paul van Caldenborgh, *The Incorporation of the Alawi Community into the Syrian State during the French Mandate Period* (Ph.D. thesis, University of Nijmegen, 2005), pp. 59–64.
29. With one single exception, local Ismaili sources are silent on the post-Ottoman conflicts in which Alawis were involved, the exception being Shaykh 'Abd Allah al-Murtada of al-Khawabi, who published an angry account of the events in 1933 in his *al-Falak al-dawwar*.
30. On this conflict and its spread to adjacent areas, see Caldenborg, *Incorporation*, pp. 59–69.
31. Ibid., p. 60.
32. Ibid., pp. 146–148.
33. See, for instance, M. Ghalib, *Ta'rikh al-da'wa al-Isma'iliyya* (Beirut, 1953).
34. *Majallat al-Azhar*, no. 31 (1960).
35. Hana Batatu, *Syria's Peasantry, the Descendants of its Lesser Rural Notables and their Policies* (Princeton, 1999), pp. 153–154; Nicolaos van Dam, *The Struggle for Power in Syria* (London, 1996), pp. 66–67.
36. Ghalib, *Ta'rikh al-da'wa*, pp. 395–401.
37. Only a dozen families in Talldara and Salamiyya refused to recognize the Imamate of Prince Karim. They were known as Ismaili Sultani, but are said to have later adopted the name of 'Ali-Allahi.
38. For an overview of the last generation of religious *shaykh*s, see Amin, *Salamiyya*, pp. 311–314.
39. For a survey of modern poetry composed in Salamiyya, see Hisam Khadur, *Lamsat naqdiyya li-shu'ara' Salamiyya* (Salamiyya, 2000).
40. Over the last few years numerous smaller publications on the Aga Khan IV and on the Ismailis in general have been on sale in the larger bookstores in Syria, the most prolific author being Hisam Khudur from Salamiya. An occasional more religious Ismaili text has also been made available, such as *Salamiyya Raw'at al-A'ajib* by Shaykh Ahmad 'Ali Amin (Salamiyya, 2007). Apart from local production in Salamiyya a most remarkable publication is the small volume on the Ismailis (*al-Isma'iliyyun fi Suriya*) in his path-breaking series on religious minorities by Samir 'Abduh, published

in Damascus in 2008. On religious diversity in Syria, see Dick Douwes, 'Migration, Faith and Community: Extra-local Linkages in Coastal Syria', in *Syria and Bilad al-Sham under Ottoman Rule*, Leiden: Brill, 2010, pp. 483–495.

3

The Nizari Ismailis of Central Asia in Modern Times

Hakim Elnazarov and *Sultonbek Aksakolov*

The Nizari Ismailis of Central Asia are scattered across the vast terrain of the high mountain ranges of Pamir, Hindu Kush and Karakorum known as 'the roof of the world'. Six countries share borders in this mountainous area: Afghanistan, China, India, Kyrgyzstan, Tajikistan and Pakistan. The Ismailis mainly reside in the Badakhshan province divided between Tajikistan and Afghanistan, Chitral district and northern areas of Pakistan, and Tashkorghan county in the province of Xinjiang in China. The Hazara Ismailis who live in the central part of Afghanistan are also included among the Central Asian Ismailis.

The Ismailis of Central Asia represent a distinct set of religious, cultural and social practices, values, achievements and challenges. In recent years they have moved beyond their traditional homelands and settled across the globe, in a fashion similar to the rest of the transnational Ismaili community. They now reside in Russia, Canada, the USA and Europe.

In a broad historical and cultural sense, Central Asia has always exhibited intellectual dynamism and cultural pluralism, a place where major religions – Zoroastrianism, Nestorian Christianity, Buddhism, Manichaeism and Islam, as well as major ideologies (such as socialism, nationalism and liberalism) – have encountered each other as the region shifted its status (from central to marginal and back again) during its rich history.[1] The enrichment of the culture of Central Asian societies through these encounters can be observed in the diverse ethnic and linguistic features found among the Ismailis of the region: at present, covering some 15 ethnic and linguistic groups who inhabit the remote mountain valleys of Central Asia,[2] which are predominantly Ismaili. Most of these languages and cultures are ancient and epitomize valuable sources for understanding the linguistic, ethnic and cultural histories of the dominant ethnic groups in the region. With the spread of Islam in the region, the Persian language took over the local languages and became the *lingua franca* for communication, devotional literature and religious practices among the Ismaili communities, many of which, however, continue speaking their own particular dialects and languages.

The history of the Ismailis of Central Asia is one of the least recorded and explored areas of modern scholarship on Ismaili studies.[3] The reasons for this are manifold: (1) an underdeveloped historiographic tradition among the Central Asian Ismailis; (2) the scarcity of materials on the early history of Ismailism; (3) the annexation of the community by the former superpowers, namely Russia and Great Britain; (4) the persecution and marginalization of the community by the dynasties of neighbouring lands which pursued their own political agendas and ideologies; and (5) an absence of the necessary conditions for critical scholarship independently of ideological and political pressures.

Since the second half of the 19th century these communities have been variously investigated by Russian and Western orientalists. The subjects of their studies have been quite diverse. With the exception of a few studies on religious beliefs and practices, the bulk was of a philological, socio-political and economic nature. The history of Tajik Badakhshan during the Soviet period, for example, has been extensively recorded by Soviet historiographers while the Soviet linguists discovered Pamir to be a mosaic of ethnic and linguistic diversity to be studied for its own merit. However, the community's religious tradition features negligibly in the ethnographic studies of the Pamir region. For studies of Ismailism in central Afghanistan, northern areas of Pakistan and western China the situation is even worse.

The last decade, following the disintegration of the Soviet Union, has witnessed a resurgence of Central Asian studies, by both external and indigenous scholars, who have aimed not only to fill the void left by Soviet scholarship but also to re-examine the past and modern history of Central Asian societies. These studies have focused mainly on the socio-political and economic developments in the Central Asian countries. Thus the study of the religious life of the region's Ismailis remains marginal and wanting. The Institute of Ismaili Studies is one of the very few institutions that have managed to collect a considerable amount of archival and primary data on Central Asian Ismaili history and traditions in various languages. This chapter draws on these sources and presents the general trends and issues in the community's modern history from the end of the

19th until the beginning of the 21st century.

Earlier History

The Ismaili *da'wa* (mission) spread to Khurasan and Transoxania (*Ma wara al-nahr*) at the end of the 9th century. Between 903 and 954 a number of *da'i*s (missionaries), such as Abu 'Abd Allah al-Khadim, al-Husayn b. 'Ali al-Marwazi and Muhammad b. Ahmad al-Nasafi, propagated the *da'wa* in the region.[4] Under the Samanid amir Nasr II (914–943) the Ismailis achieved a degree of prominence and managed to convert influential dignitaries at the court, including the amir, his vizier and other dignitaries, and poets such as Rudaki. It was probably at this time that the Ismaili movement extended to Badakhshan proper at the frontiers of the Samanid state. The success of the Ismaili *da'wa* at the Samanid court soon brought forth a hostile reaction from the Sunni religious and military leaders who finally conspired against Nasr II and overthrew him. As a result the influential Ismaili *da'i* and philosopher al-Nasafi and his associates were executed in 943 in Bukhara while the Ismailis were harshly persecuted throughout Khurasan and Transoxania. Despite this tragedy the Ismaili mission was quickly revitalized by al-Nasafi's son Mas'ud, Abu Ya'qub al-Sijistani and others.[5]

The subsequent revival of the Ismaili *da'wa* in Central Asia is closely linked with the activities of the famous Ismaili *da'i*, poet, traveller and philosopher Nasir-i Khusraw (1004– after 1070), who was appointed as the *hujja* or chief *da'i* of Khurasan by the Fatimid Imam-Caliph al-Mustansir (1036–1094). Nasir-i Khusraw faced enormous challenges in spreading the mission and eventually ended up living in exile in the valley of Yumgan, a district in modern Afghan Badakhshan. There he found sanctuary in a land ruled by an Ismaili amir, 'Ali b. Asad. In Yumgan, he produced his main theological and philosophical works and a *Diwan* of poetry, while spreading the *da'wa* and the Ismaili interpretation of Islam among the inhabitants of Badakhshan and surrounding areas.

What forms Nasir-i Khusraw's activities took and how the Ismaili *da'wa* evolved in Central Asia after him remain rather obscure. From his *Diwan* one can only gather that he faced dangerous opposition and threats as he attempted to spread the *da'wa* in Balkh, and also Mazandaran in northern Persia. In Badakhshan, however, it appears that he achieved some measure of success: he is regarded as the founder of the Ismaili intellectual and spiritual tradition in Central Asia and is remembered as a *pir, shah, hazrat, sayyid* and *hujjat* by the modern community there. In time

Nasir-i Khusraw's image was transformed from historical to legendary; in Badakhshan centuries-old myths, stories, oral traditions and rituals performed by both Ismailis and non-Ismailis have become attached to his personality and life. Be that as it may, his theological and philosophical works have provided the doctrinal basis of Ismailism in the area. Owing to the remarkable presence of Nasir-i Khusraw in the oral, religious and intellectual traditions of the Central Asian Ismailis, their distinctive religious tradition is often referred to as the tradition of Nasir-i Khusraw.

Little is known about the subsequent medieval history of the Ismaili *da'wa* in Badakhshan. Though devoted to Nasir's mission, the Ismailis of Badakhshan remained outside the Nizari–Musta'li schism that split Ismailism into its two major branches in 1094. On the basis of oral tradition it is known that Nizari Ismailism was brought to Badakhshan during the later Alamut period by two *da'i*s sent by the Nizari Imams.[6] A certain Shah Malang was sent from Khurasan to Shugnan and took control of this area by ousting its ruler. Shah Malang was followed by another Nizari *da'i*, Sayyid Shah Khamush. According to tradition, these *da'i*s became the founders of some of the local dynasties of *mir*s and *pir*s. Badakhshan was ruled by various dynasties, including not only local Tajiks but also Turkic people. These dynasties were led by *shah*s, *mir*s or *bek*s – the wealthy landlords whose sovereignty depended very much on the internal and external political situation.[7] As a minority group, the Ismailis were often persecuted by the region's Sunni rulers.

Ismailis and the Great Game of the 19th Century

The advance of the Russian and British colonial powers into Central Asia at the end of the 19th century resulted in a series of contests for control of the region which are known in history as the Great Game. In the course of defining their borders, these two empires organized a series of diplomatic exchanges, military expeditions and scholarly investigations designed to gather information on the history, languages and religions of these uncharted lands.[8]

During this period the interest of the 'players' of the Great Game in understanding and exploring the social, cultural and religious traditions of Central Asian communities increased significantly. Many of the Russian military officers who controlled the northern territories of the Oxus river had a background in oriental studies and intensively recorded the social, political and cultural structure of the local communities. Their diaries and reports included information about the relations between the Ismailis and non-Ismaili Afghans and Bukharians who ruled over some parts of Badakhshan until the beginning of the 20th century. These reports were sent to their Turkestan headquarters and were used, in due course, to define the Russian policy for these mountain regions.

The situation was similar in Afghanistan and northern Pakistan, where the British military strove to strengthen their dominance over these regions' mountain communities. Major surveys were conducted by British officers in the northern parts of the Indian subcontinent. These reports were mostly of a political nature and were drawn up to enable the British in India to develop their expansionist policy in the north.[9] Among the most prominent military agents and travellers visiting Pamir was Captain John Wood, whose work is recognized as pioneering research in the systematic description of the Pamir and its people with a focus on the religious conditions, language and ethnicity of the inhabitants of the Ishkashim and Wakhan areas in Afghan Badakhshan.[10]

On the Russian side the earliest information on the religious beliefs of the Tajik Ismailis of the Pamir mountains and their relationship with the Sunni Muslims of the area was provided by Count Aleksey Bobrinskoy (1861–1938). In 1902 Bobrinskoy published a report on the Ismailis of Central Asia, which was based on his interviews with three Ismaili *pirs* as well as observations of the life of their *murid*s (followers) in the Russian territories of Wakhan, Ishkashim, Gharan, Shugnan and Rushan.[11] It appears that the research on the various aspects of the life of the Ismailis of Central Asia was accelerated because of the rivalry between the British and Russian empires over the areas of Pamir and Hindu Kush. Subsequently, after the annexation of Pamir by Russia, two main scientific expeditions were organized to explore the area in depth. The famous Russian scholars on Pamir and Ismailism, A. Bobrinskoy, Aleksandr A. Semenov (1873–1958) and Ivan I. Zarubin (1887–1964), participated in these expeditions (1898 and 1914) and collected data on the history of the Ismailis, their customs, folklore, languages and religious practices.[12]

Prior to these expeditions, an agreement was reached between Britain and Russia about the northern borders of Afghanistan along the Oxus river in January 1873, according to which Russia accepted the Afghan amirate's domination over southern Turkestan and Badakhshan. This agreement limited the further advance of the Russians in Central Asia. The Great Game ended with many compromises from the Russian side, giving more strategic advantages in the region to the British. According to the 1895 agreement, Russia agreed not to advance its troops further than the present Murghab district of Tajikistan while Britain limited itself to the Gilgit area (present-day northern Pakistan). In this treaty Russia lost the central junction point of Bazai Gumbed, from where trade routes crossed to China, Bukhara, Ferghana and India. The river Panj became the border between Afghanistan and Russia.[13]

This fragmentation of Central Asia in the colonial era had significant implications for the native population, including the Ismaili community in the region. On the positive side, the annexation of parts of Pamir by the Russians and British freed the Tajik Ismailis from the oppression of their Sunni Afghan and Bukharian rulers who regarded them as heretics and forced them to convert to Sunnism. Suspecting that the Ismaili *pir*s were in alliance with the Russian and British agents, the Sunni rulers regularly exposed the populations of Shugnan and Rushan to ruthless persecution, often genocidal in nature.[14]

As a result of the aforementioned delimitation, the already isolated but still religiously united settlements in the mountain ranges of Pamir, Hindu Kush and Karakorum lost their socio-cultural and economic ties. The artificial breaking of their spiritual ties was perceived as a good excuse by the colonial agents for penetrating each other's sphere of influence. It was, therefore, important to gain the loyalty and sympathy of the Ismaili *pir*s and their *murid*s. At the same time, the colonial powers, especially the Russians, remained suspicious of the services that the Ismaili *pir*s were offering. The Russian consulates in Kashghar and Bombay sent reports to their administrative centres in Tashkent and St Petersburg on the pro-British position of the then Ismaili Imam Sultan Muhammad Shah Aga Khan III and his *murid*s in Central Asia. The concern of the Russians was grounded in the tension and possible conflict between Russian and British forces, in which case the Ismaili population was expected to support the British.[15]

At the same time, centuries of isolation from the centres of the Ismaili *daʿwa* had left the Nizari Ismaili communities of Central Asia to develop their specific literary tradition, practices, independent leadership and organizational hierarchy, headed by *pir*s and *khalifa*s.[16] When, at the end of the 19th century and the beginning of the 20th century, the Ismailis of Badakhshan established formal links with their Imam of the time, Shah Aga Khan III, the *pir*s as the local hereditary religious authorities received the confirmation of their status directly from the Imam. The Russian rulers did not try to stop the Badakhshani Ismailis from sending their *zakat* payments to the residence of the Imam in Bombay. Despite their religious authority and leadership, the *pir*s were not regarded with favour by local and foreign rulers of Badakhshan, most of whom were not Ismaili.

In order to preserve their power and authority among the local rulers, the Ismaili *pir*s entered into a number of ambiguous alliances with the local and outside Sunni rulers of Badakhshan, Shugnan, Wakhan, Hindu Kush, Kashghar and the adjacent regions, including Afghan and Bukharan rulers, and even with the British and Russian colonial powers. Such alliances with local and neighbouring Sunni rulers included marriage between the families of Ismaili *pir*s and those of the rulers. In addition to paying taxes, the Ismaili *pir*s would also present the non-Ismaili rulers with various gifts. The available information suggests that there were a number of *pir*s at the end of the 19th and beginning of the 20th century who had their own subjects. Interestingly enough, however, their followers were scattered across Badakhshan. Thus one could find followers of the same *pir* in the territories of Zebak, Munjan, Darwaz, Shugnan, Ishkashim, Rushan, Wakhan, Kanjut, Chitral and Kashgar (Yarkand), reflecting the movement of individuals from the community within the region and their continued adherence to the *pir*s with whom they were historically associated.

The role of some of these *pir*s in the socio-political developments in the Pamir was remarkable. While the *pir*s were classified as either Russophile or Anglophile by some writers,[17] in reality many *pir*s led active, complex lives negotiating between the various internal and external forces in order to maintain the community, their own authority and fulfil their duty on behalf of their Imam. By the middle of the 19th century these positions had become hereditary, with *pir*s exercising significant influence upon their subjects. The *murid*s consulted their *pir*s on all aspects of their lives. This status prompted many *pir*s to actively engage in political events.

Chroniclers noted the brutal atrocities enacted by Afghan rulers on the Ismailis: the Afghans had no mercy even for women, the elderly or the young.[18] It is reported that the Shugnani Pir Sayyid Farrukhsho and his *murid*s planned a rebellion against the Afghans in 1883. After taking over the centre of Shugnan their rebellion was quickly defeated by an Afghan army sent from Kabul. After the failure of the revolt, a number of Rushanis led by Khudodod Mingboshi sent a letter to the representative of the amirate of Bukhara in Darwaz in November 1883 indicating the submission of Shugnan and Rushan to Bukhara. Pir Sayyid Farrukhsho and other prominent individuals of Shugnan, however, appealed to the stronger Russian Empire to take Pamir under its protection. However, the representatives of Tsarist Russia withheld any concrete support from the rebels at that time. As a result, Pir Sayyid Farrukhsho changed his tactics and decided to seek a compromise with the Afghan rulers, and he married his daughter to Abdullojon Sardor, the ruler of Khanabad. But this step neither helped the people nor saved Sayyid Farrukhsho's life. He was invited to Khanabad and then executed for his disloyalty to the Afghan amir. Following his father's death, Pir Sayyid Yusuf Alisho intensified his calls for the Russian annexation of the Pamir.[19]

Pamir was officially annexed to Russia in 1895, but it was in 1905 that Tsarist Russia actually established direct rule over the areas of present Gorno-Badakhshan Autonomous Oblast (GBAO). Although the Russian colonial authorities were primarily motivated by their own geopolitical interests, nonetheless they introduced a number of positive measures, including abolishing the enslavement of the Ismailis by their Sunni neighbours, banning their religious persecution and cancelling their tax payments. These steps led to the stabilization of political and economic conditions and the return of many refugees driven away by the Afghan and Bukharan repressions. Thereafter considerable changes took place in the region as a result of the Russian military presence in the western Pamir, with Khorog emerging as its centre. With the support of the *ishan*s (*pir*s), the Russian military personnel reorganized the region's system of irrigation canals, and planted new types of seeds and crops in place of opium cultivation. The service of Russian officer E. K. Kivikes (1866–1939), who openly confronted the Bukharan officials in order to protect the Shugnani people from them, is an example of commitment to the indigenous cause. His frequent appeals to the Governor-General of Turkestan played a substantial role in the dismantling of Bukharan and Afghan militias and ultimately the placing of western Pamir under a Russian protectorate.[20]

Ismailis in the 20th Century

The division of the Ismaili-populated region of Central Asia between Russia, Afghanistan, China and the British Empire in the late 19th and early 20th century initiated a new era in the political and social development of the now divided Ismaili communities. These developments were contingent upon the social and political orientations of the countries of which they became a part. The separation led to the severance of the historical ties between individuals, affecting the continuity of the unified Ismaili traditions within the community. One such major change was in the institution of the *pir*. The relationship between the *pir*s and the *murid*s, a backbone of the tradition, began to lose its prominence as many *pir*s were unable to maintain contacts with their former *murid*s, who as a result of the new political divisions now resided in new countries.

The political developments in Russia, British India, China and Afghanistan in the course of the 20th century have shaped the social and economic infrastructure of the region, making the disparity in the living conditions of Ismailis in different parts of the region strikingly vivid. A brief survey of the developments of the region, outlined in the subsequent sections, will illustrate the general trends in the social, economic and religious situation of the community in their respective nation-states.

Ismailis of Tajik Badakhshan

The toppling of the Russian tsar and the revolutionary upheavals of 1917 resonated throughout the mountains of Badakhshan as early as 1918. The Russian military garrison located in Khorog, which was loyal to the interim Russian government, was dispersed after receiving news of the Communist revolution, and the fragile security situation in Badakhshan was left in the hands of the locals. The Bukharian amirs took advantage of the situation and with the help of their local appointees captured Khorog fortress in March 1920 and declared Pamir part of the amirate of Bukhara. Their rule, however, did not last long; soon the Shugnanis revolted, disarming the Bukharian soldiers, and eventually the power was transferred to the Soviets. The first Soviet soldiers sent to guard the border arrived in Khorog in November 1920 and were welcomed by the locals who had already developed friendly relations with some of the Russian military. Later in 1921 the new Soviet-led military expedition headed by T. Dyakov, a special representative of the Soviet Turkestan Republic and in charge of the defence of its borders in the Pamirs, entered Khorog. This was the beginning of reinforcing their strategic position along the upper bank of the river Panj, thereby putting an end to the centuries of intervention by Afghan and Bukharian rulers.

Under the protection of the new regime with its political and economic promises the local people were encouraged to participate in the development of the country. The Soviet structures were established in each district; these structures, which entailed the presence of local activists in government administration, brought about radical transformation of the existing administrative and cultural systems, replacing the traditional ruling groups such as *kazi*s, *arbab*s, *aksakal*s and *mingbashi*s in the localities with elected organizations of peasants and farmers. The changes engendered a mixture of feelings in the local population: some were content with the Soviet presence and their intention to empower the peasants and oppressed classes, others were weary of the changes in the traditional structures of governance and administration, including the religious ones. In particular, the authority of the *pir*s and the wealthy landlords was undermined by the revolutionary reforms of the Soviets. The Soviets were persistent in their reforms and campaigned locally against the traditional norms and structures of power. They later gained the support of the majority of the population as more locals joined sides with the Soviets and as the Soviet Red Army successfully fought against the *Basmachi*s across the region.[21]

From 1921 to 1924 Tajik Badakhshan was part of the Soviet Turkestan Republic. In January 1925 it became part of the newly established Tajik Autonomous Republic. The establishment of the Badakhshan Autonomous Region was prompted by geographic, linguistic and ethnic considerations. Some historical sources and early ethnographic studies suggest that the people of Badakhshan or Pamir, regardless of their linguistic diversity and ethnic differences, referred to themselves as Tajiks of the mountains. This was seen as a major factor in the active participation of many Badakhshani or Pamiri Tajiks in the process of national delimitation in Central Asia, leading to the establishment of the Tajik Soviet Socialist Republic independent of the Soviet Uzbek Republic in 1929. A crucial role in founding the Tajik Republic was played by Shirinsho Shohtemur (1899–1937), who was originally an Ismaili from Badakhshan.

The Gorno-Badakhshan Autonomous Oblast (GBAO) was divided into several administrative units or districts including Shugnan, Rushan, Vanj, Ishkashim, Darwaz and Murghab, with some variations within these categories. Khorog became the administrative centre of the GBAO. With the exception of Murghab, Vanj and parts of Darwaz district, the rest of the region is predominantly Ismaili. In all of Badakhshan the Ismailis constitute around 80 per cent of the total population, with the remainder comprised of Sunni Muslims of Tajik and Kyrgyz origins.

During the Soviet period, the population of Tajik Badakhshan increased significantly. By the end of the 20th century the number of Tajik Ismailis exceeded 200,000, with approximately 100,000 living outside the province, mostly in Dushanbe, the capital of Tajikistan, and in the Khatlon region. The modernization projects launched by the Soviets proved advantageous for the economic and social development of the community. Within two decades, the Soviets had managed to create developmental infrastructures which covered a variety of institutions and establishments related to education, social, cultural and economic activities.

Developments in the spiritual and religious spheres were more complex and elusive. Initially the Soviets were less aggressive towards the religious beliefs of the mountain dwellers, cooperated with the local *pirs*, and even allowed them to send the tithes (*sarkor*) to the Ismaili Imam, Sultan Muhammad Shah, in India. The priority was to engage the local population in the political life of the country. At the end of the 1920s the authorities took a harsher stance against the religious activities of the community and its religious leaders. Propaganda by the Soviet authorities against the religious functionaries, accusing them of manipulating the local poor population, and disloyalty to the Soviet system, having instead allegiance to their Imam, the Aga Khan, was on the rise. In 1936 the border along the river Panj was completely closed in order to put an end to contacts with the Ismailis living across the border and to prevent delegations carrying the annual tithes to the Imam. Prominent religious authorities or *pirs* who still exercised some influence over the community were exiled or killed. Such was the tragic fate of the most influential *pir* of Shugnan, Sayyid Yusuf Alisho, who was killed in front of his *murids*. As the Soviet repressions increased, this sort of treatment was handed out also to other distinguished members of the community, many of whom were loyal Communists; under various pretexts they became the victims of Stalinist oppression, such as being petty-nationalists, agents of foreign powers and members of the local bourgeoisie.

Meanwhile the Soviet authorities had become aware of the difficulty of eradicating Ismaili religious traditions. Thus they began to accommodate these traditions in a way that would not only undermine the religious establishment but also serve the Soviet system, resulting in many campaigns against religion, superstitions and even traditional culture. With the abolishing of the institution of *pir*ship, the *khalifa*s undertook the role of the religious authority. In the past they had been appointed by the *pir*s as their representatives in specific localities and their duties included performing various religious ceremonies. Although they did not possess the same status and position as the *pir*s, they increasingly became the sole religious authorities versed in the religious knowledge which enabled them to fulfil the community's basic religious needs. The authority of the *khalifa*s was also reinforced by their lack of contact with the Ismaili Imam and the local Ismailis' lack of awareness of their history. Aiming to have full control over the *khalifa*s, the state streamlined the office and their appointment became subject to approval by the Soviet governing bodies. At the same time, the *khalifa*'s job was narrowed to merely carrying out the basic religious ceremonies, such as funerals, marriages and other rites of passage where the presence of the *khalifa* was deemed traditionally indispensable.

The practice of the religious ceremonies, especially the funeral ceremony with its coherent and complex set of rites and rituals infused with Ismaili content and teachings such as the *Charogh* (or *Chiragh*) *Rawshan*, ensured the continuity of the Ismaili traditions in the region during the Soviet era. At the same time, the Soviet authorities were hoping that with the passage of time, educational activities and secularization of society, the religious beliefs would increasingly give way to their atheistic world view. Local members of the Communist Party were expected to act as role models, and their attendance at religious ceremonies was discouraged by the party committees or governing bodies. However, the Soviet authorities fell short of offering alternatives to replace the established religious customs and to meet the spiritual needs of the Ismailis. The spiritual elevation experienced during the *Charogh Rawshan* ceremony, the recitation of *maddoh* (devotional poetry) with its philosophical, doctrinal and ethical messages, were significant elements of the people's Ismaili identity and served as indispensable elements of their existential reality. These religious practices were, moreover, devoid of overt political motivation and did not pose any challenge to the existing system. Indeed, at times, the Soviet system was praised during these ceremonies for the good it had brought to the Ismaili community.

During the Second World War, 1941–1945, the religious gatherings of the Ismailis turned into congregational prayers for the victory of the Soviet army against the German invaders, while many Ismailis fought against the Nazis on the battlefield. The *khalifa*s practised a form of traditional *daʿwa* (summons) to call the people to support the Soviet army against the German fascists.[22] In the post-war period, religion remained a separate domain in the life of the Ismaili community, not interfering with the social and political trends of the state.

By and large, this state of religious affairs remained unchanged until the end of 1980s when the new Communist leader Mikhail Gorbachev announced his *perestroika* (restructuring) and *glastnost* (openness) policies. His policies stimulated the restoration of religious influence within the wider social and political domains of society.

The Ismaili community of Tajikistan actively participated in the political developments of the years that led to Tajik independence and in the civil war between 1992 and 1997. They supported the nascent democratic and Islamic parties in Tajikistan, both of which recommended Davlat Khudonazarov, a prominent Ismaili figure, as a candidate for the presidency of an independent Tajikistan.[23] The defeat of the Islamo-democratic forces in the election and the deepening economic and political disparities between various regions of Tajikistan were used by the extremist groups to radicalize vulnerable elements amongst the country's youth and instigate a civil war in 1992.[24]

The civil war devastated the economy of Tajikistan and had a human cost of over 50,000 lives. It also led to the displacement of half a million Tajiks from their homes in the southern and central parts of Tajikistan. There was no significant military action in Badakhshan, but the effect of war on the region was overwhelming. In order to escape the conflict and killings, over 60,000 Ismailis living in the central parts of Tajikistan took refuge in Badakhshan, the land of their ancestors. Thousands of other Ismailis were forced to leave their homes and flee to Russia and other former Soviet republics. The influx of refugees from other parts of Tajikistan into Badakhshan put further strains on the tenuous economic state of the region which was cut off from central Tajikistan and its food supplies. A humanitarian crisis spread unchecked throughout Tajik Badakhshan until the Aga Khan Foundation mounted an intervention in 1993, bringing relief supplies and aid. Thereafter a new phase was ushered in with the development and transformation of Tajik society and the history of the Ismailis of Tajikistan, which is inextricably linked to the activities of the Aga Khan Development Network (AKDN).

Ismailis of Afghanistan

The Ismailis of Afghanistan can be categorized as two groups. The first includes those who inhabit the Badakhshan province in northeastern Afghanistan and are referred to as Badakhshani Ismailis. They reside predominantly in Shugnan, Wakhan, Zibak, Yumgan, Jurm, Rushan, Kiran-Munjan and Darwaz *wuluswali*s (districts). In other settlements of the province the Ismailis constitute a minority. In terms of ethnicity and languages they resemble their co-religionists in Tajikistan. Numbering around 200,000, the Ismailis constitute approximately one-third of the total population of the province. The second group of Ismailis, known as the Hazaras, are settled in an area called Hazaristan (formerly Hazarajat) in the central parts of Afghanistan. The Hazara Ismailis live predominantly in the provinces of Bamyan, Orozgan and Ghur and in Kabul city. The Hazara Ismailis are the second largest group of Hazaras in Afghanistan, after the Ithnaʿashari Shiʿis. The number of Hazara Ismailis is not known, but the total Hazara population is estimated at around 5 to 6 million.[25] There are several legends about the origins of the Hazaras. According to the most common one, they are said to be the descendants of

Mongols from Genghis Khan's army who settled in Afghanistan.

The present territory of Afghan Badakhshan was a quasi-independent part of the amirate of Bukhara before it fell under Afghan domination in the middle of the 19th century, when the Pashtun rulers of Afghanistan occupied the north with the military and political assistance of the British, then the colonial rulers of India. In reality, however, the area remained semi-independent but endured frequent incursions from outside powers. The occupation of Badakhshan by Afghans and Bukharans clearly demonstrated the ideological nature of their oppression since their rulers claimed to serve Islam by 'exterminating and subjugating the Ismailis living in this region'.[26]

During the reign of King 'Abd al-Rahman (1880–1901), Afghan Badakhshan lost its quasi-autonomous status. His government also kept the Ismailis in subjugation and they endured the coercive policies of the state. They were obliged to attend Sunni mosques and they practised *taqiyya* (precautionary dissimulation of faith). But the Afghan repression drove the Ismailis of Shugnan and Rushan to protest and they organized rebellions. The major Ismaili rebellion against the Afghan authorities occurred in 1925 when, due to increased taxation and conscription, the tribal chiefs protested against the policies of King Aman Allah (1919–1929). The rebels, led by Mahrambek from Rushan, detained the local administrator at the centre of Shugnan. But they were quickly defeated by government forces sent from Faizabad and fled across the Panj river to Soviet Badakhshan. In Khorog these refugees petitioned the Soviet government to provide them with support and grant them safety and citizenship. Having established friendly relations with the Soviets, the rulers of Afghanistan negotiated with them to resolve this crisis through diplomacy. The refugees were returned home and severe penalties were imposed on those who engaged in anti-state activities.[27] Subsequently the Badakhshani Ismailis in Afghanistan were further marginalized and they continued to be ruled by the Sunni majority who maintained their dominance over the Ismailis in the political, economic and legal domains. The situation of the Ismailis of Afghan Badakhshan remained largely unchanged until the establishment of the pro-Soviet government in the 1970s. The Ismailis supported the pro-Soviet government and acquired prominent positions in the bureaucratic apparatus of the province, and within a short period of time managed to improve their social and economic conditions. Their support of the socialist model of development and pro-Soviet government may have been influenced by the comparatively better quality of life enjoyed by the Ismailis living in Soviet and Chinese territories.[28]

With the collapse of the Soviet-backed government of Kabul, the Ismailis of Badakhshan were again caught up in the factional fighting between different groups led mainly by the Sunni warlords. From 1989 to 2001 the Mujahedin government of Afghanistan led by the former president Burhanuddin Rabani and Ahmad Shah Mas'ud[29] maintained its control over the Badakhshan region. There was, however, internal fighting among various groups who tried to control different parts of the province and in this the Ismailis were actively involved. During this turbulent period Ismaili leaders constantly changed their allegiance from one powerful commander to another.

The collapse of the Soviet Union in 1991 and the ensuing civil war in Tajikistan weakened border control between Tajikistan and Afghanistan, resulting in illegal crossings from both sides and illegal activities, such as drug trafficking into Tajikistan. In recent years a stronger control along the border on the Tajik side has led to a decrease in drug trafficking into Tajik Badakhshan. The current Afghan government with the help of the NGOs, such as the Aga Khan Development Network, has attempted to resolve the problem by encouraging the establishment of alternative sources of livelihood, improving the communication systems, and promoting the legal trade of goods and commodities between the two countries.

While the Ismailis living in the Soviet Union remained isolated from the central leadership of the Ismaili Imamate, different forms of organization developed in Afghan Badakhshan. The traditional Ismaili leadership through *pir*s retained its significance and the connection with the Ismaili Imamate remained more or less intact. However, owing to the political situation, the Ismailis frequently practised *taqiyya*. As a minority group, they tried to avoid any confrontation with the Sunni majority. But under the local leadership of their *pir*s and *khalifa*s, they continued to observe their religious ceremonies and ensured the passing on of their religious traditions.

The Hazara community experienced a different set of changes in the modern period. Their history is inextricably linked to that of their highly revered *pir*s. Apart from those on the genealogy of the Ismaili *pir*s or *sayyid*s of Kayan valley, there are no studies on the history, traditions and rituals of the Hazara Ismailis. The origin of the Kayani clan itself is traced back to the so-called 'Sayyids of Medina'.[30] Subsequently the *sayyid*s moved to Iran and in the second half of the 18th century one of the leaders of this clan, Sayyid Shah Sadeh, left Iran with his family and numerous followers to settle in Hazarajat in central Afghanistan. Sayyid Shah Sadeh became popular among the local populace for his piety, devotion and knowledge and was recognized as the leader of the Hazarajat Ismailis. The Ismaili *daʿwa* had already spread among the people of Hazarajat before the *sayyid*'s arrival. Around the 1830s one of the successors of Sayyid Sadeh travelled to Iran to see the then Ismaili Imam, Hasan ʿAli Shah, Aga Khan I, and was granted the status of *pir* of the Ismailis of Afghanistan. He subsequently settled in a place called Kayan in Baghlan province and the title of 'Kayani' was attached to the names of his heirs. The appointment of his son Shah Abdul Hadi as the *pir* further legitimized the leadership of the Kayanis over the Hazara Ismailis. In the course of time, the Kayani *sayyid*s succeeded each other as *pir*s and were involved in the national politics of Afghanistan, supporting and opposing different rulers. Some of these *pir*s were also talented poets, writers and scholars.

The nature of the relations between the *pir*s of the Hazara Ismailis and the Ismaili *pir*s in other parts of Central Asia in this period remain obscure. It can be assumed that the geographical and political isolation of the various groups of Ismailis in Central Asia did not permit the establishment of meaningful links between the Hazara Ismailis and the Badakhshani Ismailis. One of the Hazara *pir*s, Sayyid Temur Shah, is believed to have travelled to Badakhshan to meet the Ismaili *pir*s of Shugnan. He allegedly attempted to establish contact with some Ismaili *pir*s and *sayyid*s there in 1921 in order to mount a rebellion against the Soviets and to gain their allegiance for the Pashtun rulers of Afghanistan.[31] Pir Sayyid Temur Shah was succeeded by his brother Sayyid Nader Shah Kayani (1897–1961). In 1929 the coup of Bachayi Saqa ('son of the water deliverer') overthrew King Aman Allah. Bachayi Saqa, also known as Habib Allah Kalakani, took a strong line on what he regarded as dissident or non-conformist religious views and persecuted the Ismaili leaders, forcing some of them into exile in Tajikistan. But during the reign of the last Afghan king, Muhammad Zahir Shah (1933–1973), the Hazara Ismailis and their *pir*s were favoured for their loyalty and enjoyed a relatively peaceful existence. The situation of the Ismaili community in that period resembled that of a mini-state with its own legal, economic and administrative systems secured by armed forces. The city of Puli Khumri served as the capital of this Ismaili mini-state under the Kayani family.[32]

In contrast to the Ismailis of Badakhshan, who were generally supportive of the pro-Soviet government of Afghanistan, the leaders of the Hazara Ismailis were initially reluctant to accept the Communist regime in Kabul. As a result some of them were arrested, persecuted and executed. The history of the Hazara Ismaili *pir*s of Kayani origin indicates that they were not only religious leaders but also prominent politicians who actively participated in the conflicts and politics of Afghanistan to ensure they retained a relative degree of autonomy.

During the Soviet occupation of Afghanistan (1979–1989) and the Afghan civil war, the Ismailis tried to maintain their neutrality, but established close contacts with the Kabul government. As a result of successful negotiations with the Kabul authorities, the Soviet army was not stationed in the areas of Afghan Badakhshan populated by Ismailis and emigration from the province was almost negligible. The advance of the Taliban in the late 1990s resulted in a considerable number of Ismailis fleeing the country and taking refuge in Pakistan, while others migrated to North America and Europe.

The situation remained rather uncertain for the Badakhshani and Hazara Ismailis until the Taliban regime was ousted in 2001. The work of the Aga Khan Development Network in Afghanistan and the establishment of Ismaili institutions in the country laid the foundation for new developments, not only in the economic and social spheres but also in the religious domain. These Ismaili communities now have an opportunity to develop and revive their identity. New *jama'atkhanas* have been established across central and northern Afghanistan. In most places, former *khalifas* and *pirs* have assumed the roles of *mukhis* and *kamadias* in the established *jama'atkhanas*, and they continue to perform their religious rites and ceremonies.

Ismailis of China (Xinjiang Province)

Like the Ismailis of Badkhshan, the Ismailis in the Xinjiang Province of China are a minority within the broader Muslim population of the province. Furthermore they are ethnically defined as Tajik and speak mainly the Sariqoli and Wakhi languages which are spoken also by some of the Ismailis in Tajikistan. They are also linked to Badkhshan by close religious ties, since, according to tradition, the Ismaili *da'wa* spread in this part of Pamir through the disciples of Nasir-i Khusraw. Their history in the modern era is dealt with in detail by Amier Saidula in the next chapter of this book.

Ismailis of the northern areas of Pakistan and Chitral

The northern areas of Pakistan have historically been comprised of Gilgit, Baltistan and Chitral territories located in the northernmost part of British India. In 1895 for administrative convenience the British separated Chitral from the rest of the northern areas, and later it became a part of the North West Frontier Province (NWFP) of Pakistan. The settlements of the northern areas and Chitral are spread over the narrow valleys within the great mountain ranges of the Himalayas, Karakorum and Hindu Kush. The northern areas contain five districts, three of which (Gilgit, Ghezer and Diamer) are part of the Gilgit region, and two (Iskardu and Chache) constitute the Baltistan region. Chitral and Hunza, parts of Gilgit region, were historically the Ismaili populated areas. In Ghezer and the Hunza valley of Gilgit, the Ismailis represent the majority of the population, while in other areas they are minorities compared with other Muslims. All in all, about 22 per cent of the population of the northern areas of Pakistan are Ismailis, while in Chitral their number is less than 5 per cent of the total population.

Prior to the 20th century, each valley was independently governed by its own ruler or king. The kingdom of Hunza was considered one of the most powerful of the northern areas till the end of the 19th century. It was ruled by a dynasty of *mir*s for many centuries. They were referred to as *ayasho* – 'descendants from heaven'. Most of the members of this dynasty, including the last seven *mir*s, were Ismailis.[33] Unlike Hunza, in other valleys of the northern areas and Chitral political power remained in the hands of non-Ismaili rulers who were frequently caught up in internal fighting. By the end of the 19th century they had all been subjugated by the Sikh governor of Kashmir and eventually came under British control. With the demise of British colonial power in the Indian subcontinent, the northern areas and Chitral were incorporated into Pakistan.

After a series of unsuccessful negotiations with the *mir* of Hunza, the British deployed their army to the region and conquered it in 1892. Mir Safdarali Khan who had opposed the British fled to China with hundreds of his loyal subjects. To strengthen their influence over the local population, the British brought in the step-brother of the former *mir*, Muhammad Nazim Khan, and appointed him as the new ruler of Hunza. Henceforth Hunza functioned as a semi-independent entity where the external policy of the *mir* was determined by the British and later the central government of Pakistan. However, in internal matters, the *mir*s retained authority and exercised their power to settle domestic affairs. In 1976 Hunza's semi-independent status was terminated by the then Prime Minister of Pakistan Zulfiqar Ali Bhutto, who abolished all such autonomous principalities in all parts of Pakistan.

The spread of Ismailism to the northern areas is traditionally associated with *pir*s who originated from Badakhshan. According to local tradition, the Ismaili *daʿwa* was introduced into Hunza and surrounding areas in two phases.[34] The earliest conversions to Ismailism apparently took place in the 14th century when an Ismaili ruler from Badakhshan, Tag Moghul, conquered Hunza. The subsequent history of the *daʿwa* in the northern areas remains obscure until the conversion of the *mir* of Hunza to Ismailism at the beginning of the 19th century, marking the second phase of the *daʿwa* in the northern areas and particularly in the Hunza valley. According to tradition, one of the *mir*s of Hunza, Prince Salim (or Salum), was exiled to Badakhshan where he was influenced by a local *pir*. When he ascended the throne he established relations with a *daʿi* named Sayyid Shah Ardabil who subsequently converted the *mir* to Ismailism. When the *mir* died in 1823, the son of the *daʿi*, Pir Sayyid Husayn Shah, came to perform his funeral ceremony according to the Ismaili tradition. This was reportedly the first time in the history of Hunza when the *Charogh Rawshan* ceremony was held as part of the funeral ceremonies of a *mir*.[35]

The subsequent initiation of the population of Hunza into Ismailism is associated with Pir Sayyid Yaqut Shah and his successors, Pir Sayyid Shah Abdul Hamid, Pir Sayyid Ghulamali Shah, Khwaja Shah Talib and other *pir*s from Badakhshan and Chitral, who in the course of the 19th century frequently visited Hunza and increased the number of their followers in the area. But these *pir*s did not stay for long in Hunza and they maintained their authority through the *mir*s and their representative *khalifa*s who performed the practices of the faith for the community.

The Ismaili *daʿwa* in Chitral started much earlier, probably due to its closer proximity to Badakhshan and frequent visits of *daʿi*s or *pir*s to the area. Chitral was also the permanent residence of some *pir*s who had followers in Hunza and China. However, the hostility of the Mehtar, or king of Chitral, towards the *pir*s and their religious activities forced them to leave the locality and settle in China, in the Xinjiang province, and Hunza. In the course of the 20th century, due to the lack of political protection, many Ismailis fled from Chitral to other parts of the northern areas, and their number in Chitral decreased significantly. The influx of Pashtuns from the valleys to the mountainous areas of the NWFP presented additional challenges to the Ismaili community.

In the aftermath of the Great Game, the Ismailis of the northern areas have witnessed a significant modernization of the religious institutions and their increased amalgamation with the traditions of the Ismailis of the Indian subcontinent. This process was facilitated by the presence of the Ismaili Imam Sultan Muhammad Shah in Bombay and his active modernization of the community. In due course, a new institutional structure headed by *mukhi*s and *kamadia*s replaced the traditional system of *pir*ship. Most *khalifa*s assumed the roles of *mukhi*s in the local *jama'atkhana*s and continued to serve the community by performing traditional practices. The traditional rites and ceremonies are also performed sporadically by community members on their own initiative.

The strategic location of the northern areas of Pakistan favoured the construction of the Karakorum Highway, which runs through the region and links Pakistan with China. The improved internal communications network accelerated the development of the area and altered the community's centuries-old isolation. The Ismailis of the northern areas, who generally reside in the high mountain valleys, have been engaged in farming and animal husbandry. The growth in population in the last few decades and the lack of arable land prompted many Ismailis to move down to the major urban centres and in particular to Gilgit, the administrative and commercial centre of the northern areas, and further, to the south of the region. Many found alternative means of sustenance by engaging in small business, or joining the civil service and the Pakistani army.

In October 1960 Prince Karim al-Husayni, Aga Khan IV, visited the region for the first time in the history of the Ismaili Imams. The social and economic programmes of the AKDN and the Ismaili Imamate increased significantly in the northern areas in subsequent years resulting in a transformation in the quality of life for the people in the region. An emphasis on education in particular has enabled many Ismailis, especially women, to acquire skills and enter various professions.

Continuity and Change in the Traditions of the Central Asian Ismailis

The institution of *pir*ship was the backbone of the Ismaili tradition throughout the medieval and modern periods in most parts of Central Asia. The role of the *pir*s was not only to ensure the adherence of their followers to the Ismaili faith, but also to summon others to Ismailism when opportunities emerged. This was probably one of the reasons that their *murid*s were sporadically spread in various parts of Central Asia. Many *pir*s were not just exercising religious authority over their followers, but they were also political, scholarly and literary figures, contributing to the local and national heritage. The establishment of links with the Ismaili Imam in the second half of the 19th century further legitimized their position within the community. By the end of the 19th and the beginning of the 20th century, the relations of the community with their Imam, who by then had moved from Iran to India with new headquarters in Bombay, had also become better established. The *farman*s of the Imam, which were delivered via *hajjis*,[36] inspired the community to remain united. In addition to the written *farman*s, personal visits of the representatives of the Imam to Central Asia also commenced. They delivered the messages of the Imam and passed on new instructions regarding the religious affairs of the community. The most influential of these representatives was Pir Sabzali or Mashnari,[37] who visited most of the Ismaili populated areas of Badakhshan in Tajikistan and Afghanistan as well as northern Pakistan in the 1920s. He attempted to introduce religious practices similar to those observed by the Indian Nizari Ismailis, including the appointment of *mukhi*s and *kamadia*s and replacing the *Charogh Rawshan* ritual with *Tasbeh*, etc. Among other influential visitors to the region was Agha Samad Shah al-Husayni, who visited Hunza, Chezer and Kashgar at the beginning of the 1920s and initiated the construction of *jamaʿatkhana*s in these localities.

The modernization policies initiated by Pir Sabzali in the religious sphere did not yield significant results in Badakhshan. This was partly due to the presence of the Soviets in Tajik Badakhshan, and also to the reaction of the local religious hierarchy who found it difficult to abandon their centuries-old traditions. The fact that these changes were also likely to undermine the leadership and status of some of the *pir*s was another underlying factor. Be that as it may, some of the practices introduced by the missionaries eventually became ingrained in the local religious tradition and practices in parts of Badakhshan, and more firmly in northern Pakistan.

The institutional changes proceeded steadily in the Ismaili communities of the northern areas and Chitral in Pakistan, who unlike the Ismailis of Badakhshan and China, had retained their contacts with the Imam in the course of the 20th century. The positions of *pir*s and *khalifa*s were taken over by *mukhi*s and *kamadia*s who began to lead the religious ceremonies in the *jamaʿatkhana*s. Concurrent to this, the traditional structures and practices, such as the *Charogh Rawshan* ceremony, continued.

The isolation of the Central Asian Nizari Ismaili communities in mountain areas and in the narrow valleys and passes of the Hindu Kush, Pamir and Karakorum ranges resulted in the development of distinctive literary and oral traditions and religious practices centred on Nasir-i Khusraw's works.[38] The socio-political developments in the Central Asian context throughout the centuries have led to many changes in the oral tradition and practices of the region's Ismailis, who strove to preserve and negotiate their identity in a hostile environment where they were continuously persecuted by the different rulers. However, the theological, philosophical and didactic ideas of Nasir-i Khusraw, as reflected in his writings, have ensured the continuity of the evolving Ismaili tradition. It incorporates elements from the local practices and the prevalent Sufi teachings, with which the Nizari Ismailis established close connections in the post-Alamut period of their history. The bulk of the Ismaili literature that is preserved in Persian in the private libraries of the *khalifas* and other religious dignitaries in various parts of Badakhshan, Chitral, northern areas and among the Ismailis of China has been rather distinctive, enabling scholars to shed light on many facets of Ismaili teachings in medieval times.

A significant feature of the Central Asian Ismaili tradition is the very designation of Panjtani (literally, 'five bodies'), which the Central Asian Ismailis use to distinguish themselves from the Choryoris or Sunni Muslims. The label Choryori (literally, from Tajiki for 'four friends') is used by the Pamiri Ismailis to refer to the Sunni Muslims who acknowledge the first four caliphs (Abu Bakr, 'Umar, 'Uthman and 'Ali). The Panjtan or pentad refers to the Prophet Muhammad, his cousin and son in-law 'Ali, his daughter Fatima, and grandsons Hasan and Husayn. The Panjtan is symbolically represented by the five pillars inside every Pamiri house (*chid*) and is manifested also in certain local rituals and prayers. While the intellectual tradition was maintained through the compilation of treatises on Ismaili doctrine and history, based on the original works of Nasir-i Khusraw and other Ismaili thinkers, the practice of religion was transmitted through the oral tradition, observance of special rituals, holy days, rites of passage and visitations to sacred shrines or *mazars*.

The indigenous minstrel tradition of performing religious poetry is known as *maddohkhoni* and *qasidakhoni* (recitation of *maddoh* or *qasida*) among the Central Asian Ismailis. *Maddohs* are performed on various occasions, including funeral ceremonies and the *ayam* (holy events), in the home and sometimes in nearby *mazars*. Apart from its ceremonial function, *maddohkhoni* serves didactical, curative and preventive functions for health maintenance.[39] Classical Persian poetical genres, such as the *ghazal, rubayat, qasida, mathnawi* and *mukhammas*, are performed as *maddoh*. Musically the *maddoh* is comprised of three sections: *munajat, haydari* and *setayish*. The *maddoh* is essentially a vocal composition accompanied by one or two musical instruments, *rubabs* and/or *tanbur* with rhythmic support from the *daf*. The *maddoh* (literally, 'praise') is an important means of expressing Ismaili thoughts and sentiments. The main themes of *maddoh* are praise of God, the Prophet and his progeny, contemplation on the purpose and meaning of life and death, and submission to the will of God, praising his benevolence and goodwill, etc. The poetry of Nasir-i Khusraw and Sufi poets such as Jalal al-Din Rumi, Sana'i, 'Attar and others, forms a major part of the *maddoh* repertoire. The tradition of *maddohkhoni* survived the Soviet suppression of religious practices. The popularity of *maddohkhoni* increased as part of the religious revival in the latter years of Soviet rule and the post-Soviet period in Tajik Badakhshan.

Among the Ismailis of Afghanistan, northern Pakistan and China, the performance of religious poetry is known as *qasidakhoni*. The performance of *maddoh*s and *qasida*s was an essential part of the religious tradition of the community. They have a significance as vehicles for conveying the messages of Ismailism and ensuring the continuity of the Ismaili tradition in Central Asia. One of the major occasions when religious poetry is performed is the ceremony of *da'wat*. In the course of their history, the Ismailis used different strategies to propagate their *da'wa* which served both political and religious functions.[40]

At present, in the context of Central Asian Ismailism, the term *da'wat* refers mainly to specific religious rituals and ceremonies, such as *da'wati fana*, *da'wati baqa* and *da'wati qurbon*. These ceremonies are not observed on a daily basis but take place on designated occasions. *Da'wati fana* is also known as *Charogh Rawshan* ('luminous lamp') and *da'wati Nosir* ('Nasir's summons'). The ceremony is usually held at dawn on the third day after the death of an Ismaili in the presence of an assembly in the house of the deceased. *Charogh Rawshan* is the central element in the funeral ceremony and itself consists of a number of rituals accompanied by the recitation of *du'a*s, *salawat*s and a special text called *Charagh-nama* ('The Book of Light'), also known as *Qandil-nama* in parts of Badakhshan. Oral tradition attributes this ceremony to Nasir-i Khusraw and, hence, it is also called *da'wati Nosir*. Copies of these texts are held by each *khalifa* whose duty it is to conduct the ceremony. Some differences are observed in the performance of the *Charogh Rawshan* ceremony across the region, but the ceremony has identical meaning and function for the Ismaili community living in different parts of Central Asia. According to oral tradition, this ritual was revealed to the Prophet Muhammad by the angel Jibra'il to provide comfort for the Prophet at the death of his young son 'Abd Allah. The Prophet wished the same colourful light that he witnessed during his *mi'raj* (spiritual ascension) to be handed down through his progeny until the Day of Judgement.

Subsequently Nasir-i Khusraw allegedly introduced the tradition to Badakhshan as part of his *da'wa* activities in the area. Thus the ritual includes *salawat* and *durud* (praise) of the Prophet and his progeny. It is believed that the *charogh* symbolizes the divine light (*nur*) mentioned in the Qur'an (24:35), the Light of the Imamate illuminating the present world and the hereafter. The powerful metaphor of the *charogh* symbolizes the continuity of the Ismaili Imamate through the guidance of the successive living Imams.

In addition to *da'wati fana*, there are other ceremonies and rites which are also known by the name of *da'wat*. *Da'wati baqa* ('summons of eternity'), in contrast to *da'wati fana* ('summons of demise'), is held during the lifetime of an individual. Its purpose is to cleanse and purify the soul by *tawba* (taking a vow), not indulging in *gunah* (sin), refraining from the misdeeds of the *alami jismoni* (the physical world), and preparing oneself for the *alami baqa* (the eternal world). The participants are usually middle-aged people who are believed to be sufficiently mature to participate in this ritual. Performing the ritual is financially costly and it is not commonly held. It is therefore not incumbent, like *da'wati fana* which is held on the death of a person. *Da'wati baqa* is similar to the *hajj* pilgrimage, a journey that is not expected of the poor. Like the *da'wati fana* ceremony, *da'wati baqa* is a gathering or *majlis* which takes place at night, during which performances of *maddoh* or *qasida* also take place in the presence of a *khalifa* who leads the ceremony.

Like other Muslims in Central Asia, the Ismailis celebrate a number of festivals such 'Id al-Adha or Qurban, 'Id al-Fitr or Ramadan, and Nawruz. However, there are specific Ismaili ways of observing and interpreting these festivals. Among other festivals observed by Ismailis, mention may be made of *Jashni Shah Nasir-i Khusraw* and *Jashni Diwana Shah Wali*, believed to have been one of the great Ismaili *da'is*, which are popular in certain parts of Afghan Badakhshan.

As noted, centuries of isolation from the central leadership of the Ismaili community resulted in the development of a particular religious organization and hierarchy among the Nizari Ismailis of Central Asia. Traditionally the organizational hierarchy of the Ismailis of Central Asia had developed with the Imam as the supreme leader of community, followed by the ranks of *hujjat* or *pir*, *mu'allim* (teacher), *khalifa* (deputy of a *pir*) and finally *murid*. Apart from the position of the Imam, the terms and hierarchy of the structure were not always fixed, but remained fluid and underwent modifications over time. As a result of the institutional changes introduced by the previous and the present Ismaili Imams, the authority shifted away from *pir*s and *khalifa*s to the central or regional offices of the Ismaili Imamate. At the same time, the traditional forms of local leadership have maintained their symbolic presence among the Ismailis of Central Asia, in particular in Afghanistan and China.

Present Times: Challenges and Developments

The last decades have witnessed unprecedented developments in the social, economic, political and religious life of the Ismaili community in Central Asia. The dissolution of the Soviet Union and the transformation of the political and economic structure in independent Tajikistan were characterized by uncertainty, impoverishment and psychological dislocation. Following the civil war in Tajikistan, economic and political instability coupled with lack of opportunities for development impelled many Ismailis, in particular the younger generation, to leave their homeland for seasonal work in other parts of the former Soviet state, especially in Russia. The Russian Federation has become home to an increasing number of Tajik Ismaili migrants, now estimated at around 30,000. The bulk of these immigrants appear to have settled permanently in Russia.[41]

Migration patterns emerged much earlier in other Ismaili populated areas of Central Asia, including the northern areas of Pakistan and Afghanistan, due to a lack of arable land (in northern Pakistan) and prolonged war (in Afghanistan). The migration of Ismailis from northern Afghanistan to central Afghanistan and Kabul started as early as the 1970s, especially during the era of the Soviet presence in Afghanistan. The subsequent war in Afghanistan and the rise of the Taliban to power forced the majority of the Ismaili community in central Afghanistan, including the Hazaras and the Badakhshani Ismailis, to take refuge in Pakistan. By the end of the 1990s, a significant number of Afghan Ismaili refugees had emigrated to North America and Europe. Many Ismailis from the northern areas of Pakistan and Chitral migrated to the southern parts of Pakistan, especially Karachi, which is home to the largest South Asian Ismaili community at present. More recently, Ismailis from northern Pakistan have tended to settle in Islamabad. This is prompted by the presence of the AKDN headquarters in the capital, increasing number of international and national non-governmental organizations, and a generally better quality of life.

Residing in an isolated mountain area with unfavourable climatic conditions, the Ismailis of Central Asia have adapted to their environment, engaging in farming, animal husbandry and small-scale trading. The impassable mountainous terrain provides major obstacles to the economic development of the region. The governments of the region's countries and the international organizations working in the region are trying to address the geographic isolation of the region through the construction of new highways and bridges which it is hoped will promote the economic development of the region. The leading development agency in Central Asia is the Aga Khan Development Network which had already constructed several bridges over the river Panj at the outset of the new millennium, providing opportunities for the exchange of goods and services between the Tajik and Afghan populations of the region. There are also challenges specific to each country that are rooted in the internal social and political factors of that particular state and geographical locality.

The newly emergent conditions in the mountain regions of Central Asia put strains on the self-sustaining cultural processes which had hitherto survived and nourished the community in its geographic isolation. Some aspects of the culture, the traditions and local languages are being challenged by rapid changes in the social and economic spheres.

AKDN Activities in Central Asia

The main driving force behind economic development in the mountain societies of Central Asia in the last decade has been the Aga Khan Development Network (AKDN), a set of non-political, non-denominational independent organizations which implement 'the social conscience of Islam through institutional action'.[42] Building on the foundations laid by Sultan Muhammad Shah, Aga Khan III, these institutions have now gained international renown under the leadership of the present Imam, Aga Khan IV, for investing in developing human and material resources in the impoverished parts of the world.

AKDN institutions first began to operate in Central Asia in the northern areas of Pakistan. The earliest initiative here was the establishment of schools in 1946 during the Diamond Jubilee of Aga Khan III. Since then, over 100 Aga Khan Schools have been set up in the northern areas and Chitral operated by the Aga Khan Education Services (AKES). Other AKDN agencies such as the Aga Khan Health Services (AKHS) and the Aga Khan Rural Support Programme (ARSP) respectively operate an increasing number of health centres and promote agricultural productivity. Through its Historic Cities Support Programme (HCSP), the Aga Khan Trust for Culture (AKTC) has begun the restoration of historical sites in the northern areas, including the famous Baltit and Shidar forts. The latest endeavour in the northern areas is the establishment of the Professional Development Centres (PDC) in Gilgit and Chitral which operates under the stewardship of the Institute for Educational Development (IED) of the Aga Khan University (AKU) in Karachi. It provides training for various stakeholders involved in the management and improvement of schools.

The provision of humanitarian assistance to impoverished Tajik Badakhshan became the primary objective of the Aga Khan Foundation during the Tajik civil war, enabling the community to survive through difficult times of war and crisis. In recent years the activities of AKDN institutions have moved from relief work towards sustainable development of the region with a special emphasis on rural development, community empowerment and improving the quality of education. Among other AKDN initiatives is the Aga Khan Music Initiative (AKMI) which provides technical and financial support to local musical projects to preserve and promote the traditional music of Central Asia.

The present Ismaili Imam, Aga Khan IV, paid his historic first visit to Tajikistan in May 1995. Since then he has visited Tajikistan and other Central Asian countries on several occasions. On all these visits the Imam has constantly emphasized the importance of peaceful coexistence between peoples of various faiths, the development of civil society, of education and living within the ethical framework of the faith. In 2000 Aga Khan IV signed a protocol of agreement with the presidents of three Central Asian countries (Tajikistan, Kyrgyzstan and Kazakhstan) for the establishment of the University of Central Asia (UCA), a private secular university with campuses in the city of Khorog in Tajikistan, Naryn province of Kyrgyzstan and Tekeli in Kazakhstan. The primary objective of the UCA is to provide access to higher education for the isolated societies in the mountains of Central Asia and to develop knowledge, skills and abilities through a range of academic programmes at both undergraduate and graduate levels.[43]

Since 2001 the AKDN has been active in development projects in Afghanistan after the years of war and deprivation. AKDN institutions have reconstructed and built dozens of schools, hospitals and other social and economic facilities throughout the country. Special attention is paid to the restoration of the cultural heritage of Afghanistan. The AKTC works on the conservation and rehabilitation of traditional districts in Kabul and Herat. The conservation of the mausoleum of Timur Shah and restoration of the Kabul Gardens are among the more recent endeavours of the AKTC in Afghanistan.

Together with programmes in the economic and social spheres, the Ismaili Imamate has launched a religious education programme to enable the Ismaili communities of Central Asia to revive their religious heritage and identity. Religious education for the community is provided through the Ismaili Tariqah and Religious Education Committees (ITREC) and Boards (ITREB) which work with the local community. The ITREBs monitor the implementation of the *Ta'lim* or educational curriculum developed for primary schools by The Institute of Ismaili Studies in London, to educate the Ismaili children in their faith, in the history and cultures of Muslims in general and of Ismaili Muslims in particular.

Notes

1. See A. Nanji and S. Niyozov, 'Silk Road: Crossroads and Encounters of Faiths', in *The Silk Road: Connecting Cultures, Creating Trust* (Washington DC, 2002), pp. 37–43.
2. The Ismailis speak diverse languages which are believed to have been spoken by the Sogdians and Saks who inhabited Central Asia in ancient times. These minority languages, including Shugni, Rushani, Sarikoli, Wakhi, Ishakashimi, Brushaski, Chitrali, Sariquli, etc., are part of the Eastern Iranian group of Indo-European languages.
3. See Farhad Daftary, *The Isma'ilis: Their History and Doctrines* (Cambridge, 1990).
4. Ibid., pp. 121–122.
5. Ibid., p. 123.
6. Ibid., pp. 486–487.
7. See Bahadur I. Iskandarov, *Vostochnaya Bukhara i Pamir v period presoedineniya Sredney Azii k Rosii* (Stalinabad, 1960), pp. 36–37.
8. Most of this information comes from material held in archives in various countries and has been accessed in recent years by scholars. The critical analysis of this material will doubtless shed light on many aspects of the history, religious leadership, rituals and traditions of the Ismailis of Central Asia.
9. The first comprehensive document was prepared by a mission led by Colonel Lockhart which was authorized by the British Foreign Office of India to explore the then little-known territories at the northern borders of the British Empire in India. The exploration resulted in a report entitled 'Gilgit Mission' (1885) which dealt with the geographical, topographic, economic, social, political and cultural aspects of the Ismaili communities of the northern areas. Despite the valuable information on the economic

and political situation of the region and the geopolitical significance of the Ismaili populated areas that they collected, the expedition failed to provide reliable information on the religious belief system of the community, probably the result of their ignorance of Ismaili doctrine as well as their reliance on non-Ismaili informants who seem to have been hostile to their Ismaili neighbours. Prior to and even after the 1873 agreement, the British selected several experts-pundits from the local people in India and dispatched them from Chitral to Yarkand (Kashgar) via the Hindu Kush, Pamir and Sarikol. These experts were engaged in collecting material about the routes and settlements of the Pamir. For more details see Ghulam Abbas, *Critical Review of the Literature Evolved on the Ismaili Community of Northern Areas of Pakistan* (unpublished report, London, 2005).
10. For a brief summary of the research of British and Russian travellers, military agents and scholars, on Pamiris in the 19th century, see Frank Bliss, *Social and Economic Changes in the Pamirs* (London, 2006), pp. 67–75.
11. Aleksey A. Bobrinskoy, 'Secta Ismailiya v Ruskikh I Bukharskikh predelakh Sredniy Azii', *Etnograficheskoe Obozrenie*, 2 (1902), pp. 1–20.
12. D. Karamshoev, *Olimoni Soveti dar borayi Pomir* (Dushanbe, 1975).
13. Leonid N. Kharyukov, *Anglo-Russkoe sopernichestvo v Tsentral'noy Azii i ismailism* (Moscow, 1995), p. 63. See also *Istoriya Gorno-Badakhshanskoy Autonomnoy Oblasti* (Dushanbe, 2006), pp. 362–365.
14. Kharyukov, *Anglo-Russkoe Sopernichestvo*, p. 100.
15. The concern about the loyalty of the Ismailis of the Upper Oxus to their leader in India was well reflected in a message sent by the Russian representative in Pamir, Baron Cherkasov, to the Governor-General and the Russian Political Agent in Turkestan. See the appendix containing the text of a telegram to the tsar sent by a senior Russian consular officer from Bombay on 11 February 1904, in Bobrinskoy, 'Secta Ismailiya', and the appendix of the report by Baron Cherkasov in R. M. Masov et al., *Ohcerki po Istorii Sovetskogo Badakhshana* (Dushanbe, 1985), pp. 456–470.
16. Daftary, *The Isma'ilis*, p. 436.
17. See Kharyukov, *Anglo-Russkoe sopernichestvo*, pp. 110–111; T. Kalandarov, *Shugnantsi* (Moscow, 2005), p. 75; E. Hojibekov, *Ismailitskie Piri i yikh rol v obshestvenno-politicheskoi zhizni Shugnana (konets XIX i nachalo XX veki)*, (Ph.D. thesis, Dushanbe, 2002).
18. M, Nazarshoev, 'Dobrovolnoe vkhozhdenie Pamira v sostav Rosii yi ego progressivnoe znachenie', in R. M. Masov et al., *Ocherki po istorii Sovetskogo Badakhshana* (Dushanbe, 1985), pp. 36–65.
19. For more details, see Elbon Hojibekov, *Ismailitskie Piri* (unpublished thesis), p. 37.
20. See Davlat Khudonazarov, 'Russkiy pravitel Pamira, Pamyati Eduarda Karlovicha Kivikesa', *Journal Posev*, 3 (2006), pp. 29–34.
21. The term 'Basmach' refers to the anti-Soviet groups in Central Asia who considered the Soviets infidels and fought against the Communists until

the early 1930s. Currently there is an attempt to present them as a resistance movement against the Communist regime in Central Asia.

22. See Kh. Dodkhudoev, *Philosofiya krestyanskogo bunta* (Dushanbe, 1987), p. 38.
23. Davlat Khudonazarov, originally from Badakhshan, served as the chairman of the Union of Soviet Cinematography. He was also a member of the Supreme Council of the Soviet Union, and served in various committees of the Supreme Council of the USSR during the Gorbachev era.
24. Much has been written on the civil war in Tajikistan; for details see Oliver Roy, *The New Central Asia: The Creation of Nations* (New York, 2000).
25. Hafizullah Emadi, 'Breaking the Shackles: Political Participation of Hazara Women in Afghanistan', *Asian Journal of Women's Studies*, 6 (2000), pp. 143–161.
26. F. Bliss, *Social and Economic Changes in the Pamirs*, p. 63.
27. Vladimir Boyko, 'On the Margins of Amanullah era in Afghanistan: The Shugnan Rebellion of 1925', *International Journal of Central Asian Studies*, 7 (2002), pp. 67–78.
28. H. Emadi, 'Nahzat-e-Nawin: Modernization of the Badakhshan Ismaili Communities of Afghanistan', *Central Asian Survey*, 24 (2005), pp. 165–189.
29. Ahmad Shah Masʿud led the groups opposed to the Taliban in Afghanistan and was killed in September 2001 in a terrorist attack.
30. Sergey E. Grigoryev, 'K voprosu o rodoslovnoy ismailitskikh pirov Afghanistana', *Strani i narodi vostoka*, 30, Petersburkoe Vostokovedenie (1998), pp. 242–251.
31. See Kharyukov, *Anglo-Russkoe*, p. 121.
32. Ibid., p. 249.
33. Ghulam Abbas, *Mapping Religious Traditions of Ismaili Communities in the Northern Areas of Pakistan* (unpublished report, London, 2006), p. 15.
34. Faquir Muhammad Hunzai, 'A Living Branch of Islam: Ismailis of the Mountains of Hunza', *Oriente Moderno*, NS, 84 (2004), p. 6.
35. See Fida Ali, p. 21, quoted in Ghulam Abbas, *Mapping Religious Traditions*, p. 13.
36. The *hajji*s went to the Imam and delivered the tithe and brought back *farman*s. They were usually local people from a family of *pir*s who were designated to go to the Imam's headquarters in Iran and India.
37. 'Mashnari' was derived from the term 'missionary', which the local Ismailis used to refer to the Imam's representative.
38. F. Daftary, *A Short History of the Ismailis* (Edinburgh, 1998), p. 204.
39. Benjamin D. Koen, *Devotional Music and Healing in Badakhshan, Tajikistan: Preventive and Curative Practices* (Ph.D. thesis, Ohio State University, Columbus, Ohio, 2003), p. 104, and Gabrielle van den Berg, *Minstrel Poetry from the Pamir Mountains: A Study on the Songs and Poems of the Ismaʿilis of Tajik Badakhshan* (Wiesbaden, 2004).
40. Azim Nanji, *The Nizari Ismaʿili Tradition in the Indo-Pakistan Subcontinent*

(Delmar, NY, 1978).
41. According to a census conducted by the Ismaili cultural organization 'Nur' in 2002, the number of Ismaili migrants in Moscow and its vicinities amounted to 17,000 persons.
42. Aga Khan Development Network (AKDN): An Ethical Framework, available at www.iis.ac.uk
43. For more details visit http://www.ucentralasia.org and http://www.akdn.org.

4

The Nizari Ismailis of China in Modern Times

Amier Saidula

Islam has a long history in China dating back to the first Muslim pioneers who settled during the 7th century AD in cities on its southeast coasts. Arabic and Chinese chronicles of the period refer to Saʿad b. Abi Waqqas (d. 674), maternal uncle of the Prophet Muhammad, who led an official mission to the court of the Tang Emperor Gaozong (r. 650–683) in 651. The emperor endowed Islam with legitimacy by drawing parallels between Islamic thought and the teachings of Confucius, and allowed Muslims to practise their faith within the Chinese empire. This is reflected in the fact that important Muslim monuments such as the Great Mosque (*qin zhen dasi*) in the Tang capital Chang'an (present-day Xi'an), Huaishen ('Remembering the Sage') Mosque in Canton, as well as a Muslim tomb in Quanzhou (*madinat al-Zaytun*), all date from the same early period.

China has a variety of linguistic regions, generally corresponding to the geographic distribution of various minority communities. Today the state recognizes ten of the 56 official ethnic groups as Muslim, and these Muslim groups number over 20 million in aggregate. The urban Mandarin-speaking Hui (also known as Chinese Muslims) and the Turkic Muslims from Xinjiang (known officially as Xinjiang Uyghur Autonomous Region) constitute the majority of Muslims in China. Apart from the Indo-European-speaking Tajik Ismailis from the westernmost part of the country, the Muslims of China are predominantly Sunni.

Located in the northwest region of the People's Republic, Xinjiang is the largest provincial administrative region, making up one-sixth of Chinese territory. With its predominantly non-Chinese population, Xinjiang is ethno-linguistically diverse, politically sensitive and in geocultural terms the Central Asian part of China. Xinjiang was fully Islamicized by the

17th century. 'This process had begun earlier, its onset signalled by the 10th-century conversion of Satuq Bughra Khan and 200,000 tents of Turks.'[1]

The Chinese state defines a nationality as a group of people of common origin living in the same area and speaking the same language and having a sense of group identity in terms of their economic and social organization. Although the official criteria do not recognize religion as a valid sign of ethnicity, nevertheless an automatic religious identity is assigned to each ethnically defined group. Therefore official statistics calculate the number of believers by adding up the population census of all ethnic groups who profess the same faith. Hence Ismailis are known as Tajiks officially because all the Ismailis of China are Tajiks, although the corollary is not necessarily true, that all Tajiks are Ismailis.[2] The Tajiks account for one of the 13 'principal' ethnic groups (*zhuti minzu*) of Xinjiang.[3]

Strictly speaking, the Tajiks of Xinjiang, who speak the eastern Iranian dialects of Sariqoli and Wakhi,[4] have little in common with the Persian-speaking Tajiks of Central Asia. The Sariqoli dialect belongs to the Shughno-Rushani family of Pamiri languages, whilst the Wakhi of Xinjiang is identical with the Wakhi language spoken in the Ishkashim district of Badakhshan, the Wakhan valley of Afghanistan and the Gujal district of the northern areas of Pakistan. Persian, once the *lingua franca* and mode of religious expression in Central Asia, is virtually a foreign language to the Tajiks of Xinjiang. While most of the Persian-speaking Tajiks outside China adhere to Sunni Islam, the Tajiks of Xinjiang follow the Ismaili Shi'i tradition. Moreover the Soviet labelling of the ethnolinguistically similar Badakhshani Ismailis as Tajiks may have influenced the practice of the Chinese ethnographers in Xinjiang. In fact Soviet practice in Central Asia was the salient factor in awakening modern nationalism in Xinjiang. Many cross-national ethnic groups in Xinjiang conveniently assumed the ethnic appellation used by their co-religionists in Soviet Central Asia long before the establishment of the Communist regime.[5]

The modern territory of Xinjiang, consisting of the agricultural south and the steppe lands in the north bisected by the Tianshan range, was united in the 13th century under the Mongol Yuan dynasty. By then most of the eastern Iranian-speaking natives of the Tarim Basin had been absorbed into the Altaic-speaking community, who inherited the local culture which gave them their language.[6] The Tajiks in Xinjiang claim descent from the remaining Indo-European speakers located in the mountain heartland of the region. Various historical sources, as well as modern archaeological discoveries and works of classical Chinese literature, support this assumption.[7] Although centuries of coexistence with Turko-Mongol settlers have significantly altered the physical features of the native population, many Tajiks in Tashkorghan have retained distinctive Eurasian racial features. Usually citing the *Tang Dynasty Court History* (*Tangshu*), modern Chinese social scientists argue in support of the indigenous Tajik claim, on the basis of ethno-linguistic and racial similarities between modern Tajiks and their ancient forebears.[8] Similar records pertaining to the ethno-linguistic and racial attributes of the ancient inhabitants of the southern Tarim Basin and Sariqol (Tashkorghan) region appear in many ancient Chinese official and personal documents.[9]

Like the Tajiks of Tajikistan, the Tajiks of Xinjiang assert their Iranian heritage by associating with the rich culture of the ancient Iranian world. For instance, a recent publication on classical Tajik literature (*Tajik Adabiyat Tarihi*) published in Xinjiang includes the entire pageant of Persian literary giants in the local literary heritage.[10]

To date, the Tajiks in Xinjiang are one of the least studied ethnic groups in China. Apart from a few popular publications by native scholars addressing the subject, information about the community is almost wholly absent from anthropological literature on Chinese society written in any language. The obvious problem with the popular studies was their lack of objectivity and academic clarity; instead, their authors demonstrate a zest for seamlessly meshing political ideology with subjective opinions and a selective, piecemeal treatment of historical facts.

The following outline of the community's structure, beliefs and practices was pieced together from scanty textual and oral data accumulated in the past few years among the Tajik Ismailis in Xinjiang; the statistical figures were approximated from various publicly available official sources.

The Ismailis in China: A Profile

The Chinese state's practice of equating ethnic identity with religious identity and treating these categories as synonymous in reports and surveys is problematic. As a result, the official statistical data on the Tajiks in Xinjiang may fall short of reflecting a true picture of the Ismailis as a religious community.[11] Over the past 60 years the Ismaili community in China has faced some formidable challenges to its existence. The internal life of the community remains largely a *terra incognita* to outsiders. This chapter attempts to redress the balance by providing a summary sketch of the religious and cultural life of the Ismailis in Tashkorghan.

The Ismailis are mainly concentrated in Tashkorghan Tajik Autonomous County (*Ta Shi Ku Er gan Ta ji ke Zizhi Xian*). Tashkorghan is a mountainous locality at the westernmost part of the Xinjiang Uyghur Autonomous Region, and the only semi-urban area where three-quarters of the local population is Ismaili. The county is perched at the eastern end of the Pamir plateau with an average altitude of 2,800 metres above sea level. The 35,000 square kilometre land mass on the 'roof of the world' has 11 villages (*xiang*) and an international border (which is 888km long) under its jurisdiction. It is also famous as the only Chinese county bordering more than one country (Pakistan-held Kashmir, the northern areas of Pakistan, Afghanistan, Tajikistan and Kyrgyzstan). The nearest urban centre, Kashgar, is 294km to the northeast of the county, and the distance to the provincial capital Urumchi is 1800km. It lies roughly 5000km west of the national capital, Beijing.

According to the *Xinjiang Statistics Bureau Yearbook*, the total population of Tajiks in Xinjiang had reached 40,933 by the end of 2004, out of which around 28,000 were living in Tashkorghan. Besides that, a few oasis towns on the southern rim of the Tarim Basin also have small Tajik enclaves.[12] As part of the government poverty relief and relocation programme, 240 households from Tashkorghan were displaced in 2002 to a reclaimed salt desert village in Makit County in the Kashgar Region. There are small groups of members of the intellectual and political elites in Urumchi (Urumqi), the provincial capital, and Kashgar, the regional centre. In recent years, many retired cadres and successful business people have been moving away from Tashkorghan in search of a better material life in prosperous urban centres.

Historical Traditions

The history of the Ismaili religious tradition in Xinjiang is obscure and full of ambiguity. Nevertheless the patterns of religious rituals that are open to observation confirm unequivocally that their origin lies in the tradition initiated by Nasir-i Khusraw. Like their co-religionists in Central Asia, the Persian-language religious texts they most frequently consult are all attributed to Nasir-i Khusraw. As a tradition that has relied mainly on the oral transmission of culture from generation to generation, and given therefore the paucity of written texts, considerable difficulties are faced by researchers seeking to provide a clear account of this indigenous tradition. In addition, the remote geographical location has hindered communication with the surrounding civilizations and, as a result, the existence of the Ismailis of Xinjiang was barely acknowledged and documented by their neighbours. These factors, therefore, have necessitated a strategy of observing and listening to the present in order to make sense of the past. Yet, recent efforts in this direction have hardly scratched the surface owing to the ideological barriers put in place by the Communist regime in China, on top of other difficulties.

The following narrative of proselytization was taken from popular local accounts. The narrative purports to say that Pir Nasir-i Khusraw initiated the tradition of Ismailism himself, suggesting a history stretching over a millennium. According to this, Nasir-i Khusraw led a mission into the region with four of his close disciples, namely Sayyid Hassan Zarrabi, Sayyid Surab Wali, Sayyid Jalal Bukhari and Jahan Malikshah. He instructed some of the companions to settle down and continue the Ismaili *daʻwa* among the new converts. Many *pir*s in Xinjiang claim descent from those early Ismaili preachers.[13] A written version of this narrative, it is claimed, was also incorporated into the official version of Tajik history in China.

Apart from this story, we do not know much about the Imam–*murid* relationship before the 19th century. A popular story alleges that Imam Aqa ʻAli Shah, Aga Khan II (d. 1885), once visited Sariqol, and the legend was perpetuated through worship at sacred sites known as the 'footprints of the Imam' (*Aqa qadamgoh*). This tradition will be discussed further below. In fact, the few extant written communications from an Imam addressed to the Ismaili community in Xinjiang were the *farman*s of Imam Sultan Muhammad Shah, Aga Khan III. The last of such direct *farman*s, nominating five *mukhi*s in Xinjiang, was received in 1948 just before the closing of the border by the Chinese. As far as we know, the current Imam, Prince Karim al-Husayni, Aga Khan IV, is the only Ismaili Imam ever to have set foot in Xinjiang.[14]

Contemporary circumstances

For centuries, as members of the local literary ruling elite, hereditary religious leaders played an important role in keeping religious traditions alive. But in modern China, religion is no longer allowed to intervene in politics, and state endorsement is a prerequisite for fulfilling any religious duty or role of spiritual leadership. In theory, religious belief is an individual right protected by the Constitution of the People's Republic of China.[15] But the scope and scale of freedom enjoyed differs according to each individual's social status. While purely religious congregations are considered off limits for civil servants and school-age children, attending cultural events which incorporate aspects of religious ritual and practice are less restricted. Even adherence by high-ranking Communist officials to certain traditions regarded as superstition by the atheist regime is tolerated. The clergy is selected, licensed and remunerated by the state.

Before universal secular schooling was introduced in the 1930s, literacy and religious learning among the Ismailis was a privilege reserved for the hereditary *pir* families. Occasionally, *pir*s would train *khalifa*s from the local populace, and these individuals shared religious duties and a certain limited amount of social cachet with the *pir*s. This age-old practice continues on a much more restricted scale under the watchful eye of the Chinese state. Today education is secular and religious learning follows a strict state quota in Ismaili areas. As far as actual practices are concerned, no state legislation explicitly regulates religious education per se, but it is guided by many extra-judicial policy documents.[16] According to *Xinjiang Zongjiao Shiwu Guanli Tiaoli* (Xinjiang Religious Affairs Administration Regulation), only individuals over 18 years of age and remunerated by agencies other than the state may receive religious education and attend religious gatherings. Teaching religion to children of school age without state approval is a criminal offence. As a result, the younger generations know very little of their religious heritage. The religious tradition has been able to survive by virtue of being an integral part of ethnic culture and many aspects of this culture evolved around religious values.

The Ismailis call their places of worship *jama'atkhana*s. According to tradition, the first *jama'atkhana* in Tashkorghan was built by the end of the 19th century with the help of an official envoy from Imam Sultan Muhammad Shah, Aga Khan III.[17] The exterior design, with two small minarets set over the east gate, was a replica of Sunni mosques found in the area. The differences lie in the interior settings. As a public space, *jama'atkhana*s served the community not only as a place of religious congregation, but also as a centre of community service and an institution providing public welfare and charity. However, the government kept religious institutions in the country closed for over three decades, only allowing some limited practices to resume after the death of Chairman Mao.

By the early 1980s the regime had rectified its past intolerant attitude towards religion by removing the outright ban on all religious practices which had been imposed during the Cultural Revolution (1966–1976). During that short-lived period of leniency, many damaged and appropriated places of worship were repaired and restored to their original purpose. The state even initiated various restoration projects, and many abandoned *jamaʿatkhana*s benefited from this opportunity, with the result that the number of functioning *jamaʿatkhana*s increased to over 40, although the numbers of worshippers attending religious congregations barely increased in the same period. In fact, apart from the biannual Muslim *ʿid* congregations in local *jamaʿatkhana*s, very few believers pray together in Tashkorghan on a regular basis throughout the year.

Religious Hierarchy

The highest spiritual authority belongs to the living Ismaili Imam, and the local religious leaders who spread his teachings are called *pir*s. The religious hierarchy is organized as follows:

The Imam: the Ismailis believe that the living Imam is the *hujjat* (proof) of God. The Imam may appear in a different guise in each era (*dawr*) but his essence is eternal. The Imam is the guide and the gate to the eternal truth, because the Imam knows the true meaning of the divine message.

Mukhi: the term used for the community religious leader who has been nominated by the Imam through an official letter (*farman*). The title is not hereditary and the term of office ends with the demise of the title-bearer. As a recently introduced function, its relation to the traditional power structure is ambiguous since the office coexisted with, but did not alter, the traditional religious hierarchy. In fact it was interpreted as an additional structure set up to supervise the religious life of the community on the Imam's behalf and so responsible to the Imam only.[18] The previous *mukhi*s were appointed from amongst the prestigious local *pir*s in the areas of Tashkorghan and Yarkand.

Sayyid: a hereditary religious title that is passed down through the male line. *Sayyid*s claim their descent from the family of the Prophet Muhammad through his daughter Fatima, and ʿAli b. Abi Talib, the first Imam. The title allows them to preside over religious congregations, take students, accept gifts from their followers, communicate with the Imam directly and collect religious alms. They are called *pir* by ordinary people and each *sayyid* has a group of followers called *murid*s.

Khuja: this is also an important hereditary religious title whose origin has yet to be clarified. It has been suggested that *khuja*s earned their prestige through their service to the Imam, and it has even been assumed that *khuja*s were descended from those nobles who followed the Imam from

Persia to India. They also enjoy privilege in the community as religious leaders. Just like the *sayyids*, a *khuja* may preside over religious services, accept gifts, take apprentices, collect religious alms, receive direct *farmans* from the Imam and in the past they were also nominated as *mukhis*. The *khujas* have *murids* too and are addressed as '*pir*' as a matter of courtesy.

Khalifa: a religious scholar of humble descent who receives his religious training and mandate from an established *pir*. *Khalifas* are the most active lower-level religious functionaries, presiding individually over various religious congregations with the approval of a *pir*. However, they lack the prestige and hereditary trappings of aforementioned religious dignitaries.

Alam: an *alam* ('*alim*) is a scholar with basic religious training. Acting as independent agents, they take students and perform religious services in the absence of any of the aforementioned clergy. Today *sayyids*, *khujas* and *khalifas* serve the community after obtaining a state licence to practise their faith.

Religious Dues

Ismailis allocate one-tenth of their annual income to religious dues. Each *pir* collects two separate dues from his *murid* after the autumn harvest. The taxes are called *sarkuri* and *darwiza*. *Sarkuri* (Persian: *sar'i-kori*), roughly translated as 'official expenditure', was the principal religious tax offered by the Ismailis. Everyone, excepting the very poor and the destitute, is expected to pay the due. At the donor's discretion, the levy is collected either in cash or in kind. In early October the *pirs* collect the tax and offer blessings and prayers on the Imam's behalf. Once the collections have been completed, each *pir* prepares a detailed account of the donations, with the help of a literate elder (*muysafid*), which he distributes to his followers after the Friday congregation. After collective scrutiny, and correction if necessary, the account is sent with the donations to the Imam's treasury.

Darwiza is a non-obligatory local religious tax. It is a voluntary gift that the *pir* receives from a *murid*, and the *pir* is not obliged to disclose the details of the donation. The donors are free to decide on the amount of the gift and the time of donation according to their own priorities. Habitually many prefer to hand in their *darwiza* along with the *sarkuri* at the same time. The obligatory collection of dues was outlawed by the state in 1949, but sporadic voluntary donation is tolerated and treated as part of local cultural practice.

Religious Worship, Beliefs and Practices

Acts of worship at mazars (shrines)

Undertaking a devotional visit to a *mazar* (shrine) is a common practice among all Central Asian Muslims. In Xinjiang each locality has its own sacred places of worship. Some are, so to speak, general-purpose shrines which can be the focus of devotional acts for a variety of reasons, while others may have attributes related to specific needs. For instance, people generally visit shrines in order to ward off evil spirits (*jin-shaytan*), seek protection from the evil eye, bring peace and prosperity to the family, etc., but there are other special shrines from where it is believed that cures for certain ailments can be obtained, a curse reversed or infertility remedied. Worshippers bring food to the shrines to share with other pilgrims or to distribute among the poor and needy in order that their prayers may be granted.

There are many shrines in Tashkorghan which attract Ismaili and non-Ismaili pilgrims all the year around. Some are resting places of obscure saints or folk heroes, while others are simple locations associated with exotic legends such as *Rustam Buloq* ('the spring of Rustam') or *Mustagh Ata* ('father ice mountain'). Besides praying at the common Muslim shrines, the following few places are venerated by the Ismailis only.

Tombs

Two of the most famous Ismaili shrines in Xinjiang are the ancient mausoleums of *Bafamili Wal* ('the family of Wali'), and *Bafamili Mujarrad* ('the family of Mujarrad') in Datong village. These obscure tombs are built in the typical Central Asian style, being square, with a flat roof, lattice windows and a wooden door with geometric patterns carved on them.

Aqa Qadamgoh

*Aqa Qadamgoh*s ('footprints of the Aga Khan') are the sacred places where the Ismaili Imam allegedly received and blessed his followers.[19] These sites are marked with a pile of rocks and a coloured standard made of wood attached to the top of the pile, like a typical Sufi or shamanic shrine. All *qadamgoh*s are located far from residential areas, usually besides narrow goat trails. The passersby walk towards the pile of stones with both hands humbly crossed at the waist and touch the stones with their right hand. The ritual is called *daryub zoht*. The pilgrims leave some food or small sums of money at the site after the ritual.

Shingun Duldul

Shingun Duldul is a white horse-shaped fossil in Shingun valley to the west of the town of Tashkorghan. Legend has it that the stone was the favourite mount of Hazrat 'Ali, the first Imam. One day the horse ventured out of sight, was seduced by the devil (*shaytan*), then fell asleep when it was needed for a vital call of duty. For its disobedience the Imam turned the horse into stone. The place is considered sacred because it contains a cenotaph of Imam 'Ali, and only the pure and pious may see the stone.

Healing remedies

Dixtuv, or *tabibi*, *dini diwu* ('religious remedy/healing'), is sought for treating minor diseases. A *pir* or *khalifa* prescribes the remedy in exchange for a small gift. Usually they bless a pot of water by reciting verses from the Qur'an, before giving the blessed water to the sick person to drink. Alternatively they may copy out certain Qur'anic verses on a sheet of white paper with a wooden pen and black ink, and give it to the sick person to soak in a bowl of spring water until the ink fades and tinges the water, before drinking the water. The paper is then burnt and the smoke is waved around and above the invalid.

Pilgrimage

The customary annual Muslim pilgrimage to Mecca is known amongst the Ismailis as *hajj-i zahiri* (exoteric pilgrimage) and a personal *didar* of the living Imam as *hajj-i batini* (esoteric pilgrimage). It is believed that the *zahiri hajj* benefits the body whereas the *batini hajj* enlightens the soul. The Ismailis aspire to the *batini hajj*, although they also value the opportunity of a *zahiri hajj*.[20]

Festivals

The Ismailis also celebrate the two major Islamic festivals of 'Id al-Adha (*Qurban 'Id*) and 'Id al-Fitr or Ramadan (*Richo*). The *Qurban 'Id* prayer follows a large communal feast in front of the local *jama'atkhana*, each household contributing food for the occasion. The final day of the month of Ramadan is celebrated by a large congregation and collective prayer in the *jama'atkhana*.

Other beliefs and practices

Other religious practices, suggesting traces of much older belief systems, include the veneration of natural objects. For instance, the Chinese Ismailis offer prayers and make wishes when passing through three sacred pine trees called *Talmazur*, near Tashkorghan. In addition, they burn incense frequently in order to ward off the evil eye, reverse bad fortune or cure a chronic ailment.

Life-cycle Rituals

Marriage

The Ismailis of China are a patriarchal community. Like other Muslim communities, the senior male is head of the household and makes all the important decisions. In a traditional family, three or more generations live under the same roof, with a clear hierarchical order according to age and gender. Providing for the young and looking after the elderly is the duty of the male bread-winner, while the women bring up the children, serve the elderly and attend to household duties. It is a breach of custom for a young man to start an independent life without parental endorsement, and leaving the household without permission he automatically forfeits his right to inheritance. The senior male in the household manages and dispenses the family wealth through consulting with other male members of the family.

Other rituals and rites of passage, such as marriages and funerals, follow clearly articulated sets of rules and procedures. As a rule it is considered incumbent on the parents to arrange and pay for the weddings of their children. It is expected that all the formalities, starting from the initial *Qodadori* (asking a person for their daughter's hand) to the end of the matrimonial ceremony, will be arranged by the parents. Without involving the young couple, the families negotiate and decide on the exact amount of the dowry, fix the engagement and wedding dates, and agree on the numbers of guests each party may invite. The last piece of etiquette before the actual wedding is the pleading for approval for the impending marriage. Three days before the ceremony, the bride and groom's families hold a joint feast for those in the vicinity who have lost a relative in the last 12 months. After a hearty meal and exchanges of niceties, the mourners give their approval for the celebration by tapping on the hand drum (*dof* or *dorya*) with their finger.

Funerals

Funerals are another important form of life ritual with an elaborate set of rules. Apart from adhering to common Islamic religious rites of cleansing the body and praying for the soul of the deceased, the Ismailis also perform the ceremony of *Charogh Rawshan* on the night after the burial. This is a distinctive Ismaili practice which, it was believed, facilitated the journey of the departed soul to its final resting place. Besides this, there are a few noteworthy details of the funeral ceremonies unique to the Ismailis.

Before removing the body from the house for burial, the family burns incense and closes the skylight to cleanse the path for the departed. If the deceased is an unmarried girl, a *pir* or *khalifa* performs the *nikah* (wedding ceremony) and symbolically weds her to one of the five wooden columns in the traditional Ismaili house, thus helping the parents of the deceased to fulfil their obligation to marry their children in this world.[21]

Unless the news is announced after the funeral, everyone related to the deceased is expected to attend the memorial service. Those who hear about the death later on must make up for their absence at the funeral by a later visit.

For 40 days following the burial, the closest relatives of the deceased continue mourning and eschew personal comforts. The men grow their beards and the women leave their hair unattended. On the final day, a group of friends of the family gather at the household and help the bereaved to shave and bathe, and then persuade them to carry on with their life. This ritual is known as *tor zokht* ('removing the black').

Festivals

There are two major festivals celebrated by the Ismailis of Xinjiang, *Nawruz* or *Shawgun Bahor* (New Year) and *Pilik* (literally 'wick'; like All Souls this festival commemorates the departed). *Nawruz* is fixed on 21 March, and *Pilik* is celebrated on the 14th or 15th day of Barat, the eighth month of the Islamic calendar.

According to the Iranian lunar calendar, *Nawruz* (also known in Sariqoli as *ched chader* ('cleaning the house') marks the beginning of the new year. The Chinese state acknowledges the tradition by allowing the Tajiks in Tashkorghan to take a public holiday in order to celebrate the event. Before *Nawruz*, families clean their homes thoroughly and sprinkle the inner walls with wheat flour, called *putuk*, wishing for a prosperous year. After sunrise, people congregate in small groups and elect a group leader, called *Shawgun*, then follow the leader to visit friends and family in the vicinity with *Nawruz* greetings. Each household bakes a special cake for the occasion to share with visitors, and guests are welcomed on the doorstep by sprinkling *putuk* on their right shoulder. *Nawruz*, along with other local traditions, was banned under Mao but reinstated in the late 1980s. Today, with the exception of the Hui Muslims who follow the Chinese lunar calendar, all the Muslim communities in Xinjiang celebrate *Nawruz*.

Pilik is an exclusively Ismaili festival dedicated to the consecration of the dead by the living. Families commemorate their ancestors by lighting candles and praying for the souls of the departed while circling the light and pulling the fire towards their faces. The tradition suggests a possible Zoroastrian origin. The ritual lasts for two days. On the first day, members of the household remember the departed by lighting a family *pilik* inside the house, and on the second day they visit the cemetery in the evening where they light a *pilik* for each deceased relative and place it on their grave.

Originally *Zuwur zotht* ('irrigation') and *Teghm zuwost* ('seed sowing') were purely seasonal rituals, but nowadays the occasion starts with a *pir* or *khalifa* blessing the agricultural implements in the fields by reciting verses from the Qur'an.

Social etiquette

The Ismaili Tajiks in Tashkorghan follow a strict social etiquette in everyday life, and we may see part of it from the following description of greeting rituals. The community respect religious leaders and treat the elderly courteously, and it is through the formalities of greeting that such relationships are usually expressed. Greeting anyone senior to oneself by their first name without using the appropriate kinship terms, such as grandfather, mother, uncle, aunt, brother, sister etc., is considered disrespectful. The codes of conduct require the younger individual to kiss the hand of the elderly while addressing them appropriately, and their courtesy is reciprocated with a kiss on the forehead. On all occasions, the proper way of greeting a *pir* is by kissing his hand.

There are special occasions such as public functions or ceremonial gatherings when the patriarchal men of Tajik society lavish respect on their womenfolk. For example, during wedding banquets or funeral feasts, the best places in the house are reserved for women; they are ushered through the door first and food is served to them from the female quarter of the house.

Socio-Economic Conditions

Conditioned by the limits of highland topography and a harsh climate, Tashkorghan is suitable only for small-scale animal husbandry and growing hardy crops. The native population lives dispersed at high altitudes where natural resources are sparse and the land offers very little of economic value. For centuries the locals sustained themselves by cultivating small patches of arable land and rearing animals, and this continues unaltered to this day. Apart from a mineral-water plant and a hot spring sanatorium, there are no revenue-generating industries in Tashkorghan. The only major form of trade, which partly benefits the locals, is selling embroidered traditional dress and hats, but such operations are seasonal, small-scale private initiatives.

The Ismailis living in other parts of the province are farmers. Notwithstanding the seemingly advantageous location, favourable climate and more hospitable natural environment, the quality of material life on the fertile plain is conspicuously inferior to that in Tashkorghan. This is not surprising considering the increasing disparity in incomes between rural and urban areas of China in recent years. Tashkorghan might also have been poor if it had not been for the preferential high altitude subsidies provided by the state. The economy of Tashkorghan needs to develop entrepreneurial spirit and self-confidence, as only a fraction of local businesses are owned and operated by the Ismailis. Although government wages in the area are above the national average, salaried jobs are few and competition for them is intense.

Conclusion

In summing up, the Ismaili community in China is an ethnic, religious, linguistic and racial minority. As an autochthonous group, history connects them to the ancient eastern Iranian inhabitants of the region, and a shared ethno-linguistic and cultural heritage relates them to the present-day Pamiri Ismailis of Tajikistan. The local religious tradition, enriched with older indigenous spiritual practices, has evolved into a spontaneous mode of expression without any deviation from the core principles of Ismaili religious doctrine. This resilient mountain culture survived and developed over the millennia in socio-cultural autonomy and physical isolation. However, it is difficult to entertain a similar optimism about the future of the tradition.

In fact the religious policy of the Chinese regime is something of a mixed blessing. On the one hand, the omnipresence of the state may have protected the small and vulnerable communities against the negative effects of local nationalism or religious sectarianism. On the other hand, the state's attitude towards religion works against the continuity of the community's traditional practices in the long term.

Improving the local infrastructure may gradually bring the Ismailis closer to China proper in terms of physical distance and cultural homogeneity. But China's ever-growing global influence and expanding economy may also increase the state's confidence and determination to tame its subaltern Muslim subjects and to subsume the differences of minorities into the culture of the majority. In the long term, however, the continuity of Muslim cultures in Xinjiang would seem to depend upon the ability to negotiate a path between accommodating the changes initiated by the People's Republic of China and maintaining a separate cultural and religious identity.

Notes

1. James A. Millward, *Eurasian Crossroads: A History of Xinjiang* (London, 2007), p. 78.
2. In fact not all the Tajiks in Xinjiang are Ismailis. The Tajiks of Torlegh, a village in Aktu County, are Sunni Muslims although they share common cultural traditions with the Tajiks of Tashkorghan.
3. *Tashkorgan Tarih Materyalliri* (*Historical Sources on Tashkorghan*) (Kashgar, 2000).
4. The languages are named after the places where they are spoken.
5. For a detailed discussion refer to Dru C. Gladney, *Dislocating China: Reflections on Muslims, Minorities and Other Subaltern Subjects* (London, 2004).
6. Richard N. Frye, *The Heritage of Central Asia: From Antiquity to the Turkish Expansion* (Princeton, 1997).
7. Shrin Qorban Madalikhon Duanshiyun, *Zhong guo Tajike shi liao hui bian* (*Historical Sources Concerning Tajiks of China*) (Xinjiang, 2003), hitherto referred to as SMD.

8. The book describes the residents of Sariqol, Kashgar and the western part of Tarim Basin as *Sai ren* (Saka) with deep blue or brown eyes and a high and straight nose bridge, fair or brown hair and speaking a form of the *sute* (Soghdian) dialect (an ancient eastern Iranian language).
9. Shrin Qorban, *Zhong guo Tajike shi liao hui bian*.
10. Atikem Zamiri and Shrin Qorban, *Tajik Adibiyati Tarihi* (*History of Tajik Literature*) (Urumqi, 2005).
11. The Torlegh Tajiks are Sunni Muslims.
12. Small numbers of Ismailis live in Tajik ethnic villages in Yarkand (*Sha Che*), Hotan (*Hetian*), Poskam (*Zepu*), Qarghalik (*Ye Cheng*) and Aktu (*A Ketao*) counties respectively.
13. Duanshiyun, *Zhong guo Tajike*.
14. Imam Shah Karim al-Husayni Aga Khan IV visited Xinjiang in 1982.
15. Article 36 of 'The 1982 Constitution of the People's Republic of China', the first ever such legislation after the Cultural Revolution, guarantees religious rights in China. The 'Citizens of the People's Republic of China enjoy freedom of religious belief. No state organ, public organization or individual may compel citizens to believe in, or not to believe in, any religion; nor may they discriminate against citizens who believe in, or do not believe in, any religion. The state protects normal religious activities. No one may make use of religion to engage in activities that disrupt public order, impair the health of citizens or interfere with the educational system of the state. Religious bodies and religious affairs are not subject to any foreign domination.'
16. Ren jie, *Zhongguo Gongchandang de Zongjiao zhengce*. http://www.cnr.cn/xjfw/mzzj/200611/t20061121_504331906.html.
17. The name of the envoy is unclear. Some suggest it was Samad Shah, the British agent in Tashkorghan, while others think it was Pir Sabzali, the envoy sent to Xinjiang by Sultan Muhammad Shah, Aga Khan III, in the 1920s.
18. The exact number of the *mukhi*s nominated before the border was closed is yet to be clarified. The official publications identify five *mukhi*s altogether.
19. The Ismailis venerate *agha qadamgoh*s as sacred places where Aqa 'Ali Shah, Aga Khan II, dismounted from his stallion and rested, or received (*didar*) his *murid*s at that location. But the alleged visit does not appear in Imamate chronicles; therefore we may assume that those places might have been shrines both prior to and after the establishment of Islam, in common with similar traditions in the region.
20. Shrin Qorban, *Zhongguo Tajikliri* (*Tajiks in China*) (Urumqi, 1994).
21. Duanshiyun, *Zhong guo Tajike*.

PART II

NIZARI ISMAILIS: SOUTH ASIA AND EAST AFRICA

From Satpanthi to Ismaili Muslim: The Articulation of Ismaili Khoja Identity in South Asia[1]

Ali S. Asani

The historian Bernard Lewis writes that in the course of its evolution, Ismailism 'has meant different things at different times and places'.[2] A principal reason for the multivalent significance of the tradition has been its remarkable ability to adapt to different contexts and circumstances. Depending on the historical period and geographical/cultural location, Ismaili intellectuals, poets and preachers have expressed the central doctrines of their faith in terms of various theological and philosophical approaches. In the late 10th and early 11th centuries, for example, Fatimid Ismaili thinkers engaged in a philosophical synthesis of Neoplatonic and Gnostic elements to elaborate Islamic and, specifically, Ismaili ideas.[3] As a consequence of centuries-old processes of acculturation to varying milieus, Ismaili communities have come to display a significant degree of diversity in their beliefs and practices. Indeed the 48th Imam of the Nizari Ismailis, Sir Sultan Muhammad Shah, Aga Khan III, commenting on the pliable nature of Ismailism, observed that the tradition has survived 'because it has always been fluid. Rigidity is contrary to our whole way of life and outlook. There have really been no cut-and-dried rules.'[4]

Some scholars have attributed this Ismaili tendency to acculturate to different contexts to the doctrine of *taqiyya*, the strategy traditionally used by various Shi'i groups to hide or camouflage their religious beliefs in order to escape persecution. Historically the Ismailis rank among the most frequently persecuted minorities of the Muslim world, often forced into 'an underground existence'.[5] During certain historical periods, the intensity with which they were persecuted was such that entire communities were wiped out. One is reminded of the infamous edict of the Mongol ruler Genghis Khan against Ismailis, as reported by the Persian historian

Juwayni, in which he commanded that 'none of that people should be spared, not even the babe in its cradle'.[6] Yet it is also evident that the impulse to acculturate is innate to the ethos of Ismailism. A distinctive element contributing to this ethos is the strong emphasis on the *batin* (the spiritual and esoteric) over the *zahir* (the physical and exoteric). As a result, the Ismailis have been called the *batiniyya*, 'the followers of the esoteric, the inner'. This has meant that externals of culture, such as language or dress, have not been considered essential to Ismaili articulations of faith and identity.

Central to Ismaili traditions of esotericism has been the notion that a single spiritual reality underlies what may appear externally to be starkly different and disparate doctrines and creeds. As a result Ismailism has been able to respond to cultural diversity by tolerating, in the words of Paul E. Walker, 'a surprising intellectual flexibility and leeway'.[7] The motivation to integrate, reformulate and acculturate to different environments is hence part of the Ismaili legacy.[8] One of the consequences of this legacy is that during many periods of their history, the religious identity of many Ismaili communities was often ambiguous and difficult to define, since they drew upon and integrated many different kinds of ideology.[9] For instance, Ismaili authors in Persia and Central Asia from the 15th century onwards used the prevailing Sufi discourses to explain their doctrines, resulting in a style that Wladimir Ivanow, the prominent scholar of Ismaili history, described as 'Sufico-Ismaili' because it created ambiguities not only regarding the religious affiliation of authors of the treatises, but about doctrinal issues as well.[10]

Not surprisingly, ambiguity of identity has been a prominent characteristic of Nizari Ismaili communities in the western regions of the Indian subcontinent, namely Punjab, Sind, Gujarat and Rajasthan. According to community traditions, the emergence and development of the Nizari Ismaili tradition was associated with various *pirs* and *sayyids* who from the 11th century onwards were entrusted with the responsibility of propagating Ismaili doctrines in the area on behalf of the Ismaili Imams residing in Iran. Significantly these *pirs* and *sayyids* referred to their teachings as *satpanth*, 'the true path'. Hence their followers identified themselves as Satpanthis rather than Ismailis. The Satpanth tradition employed terms and ideas from a variety of Indic religious and philosophical currents, such as the Bhakti, Sant, Sufi, Vaishnavite and yogic traditions to articulate its core concepts.[11]

This chapter explores the processes by which the identity of a group of Satpanthis, called the Khojas, originally members of a small mercantile caste in western India, was gradually transformed over a period of some 150 years so that a significant number today regard themselves as Shi'i Muslims, specifically Nizari Ismailis, members of a transnational religious community led by the Aga Khans. In the pre-modern period, the Khojas were, to use Faisal Devji's apt description, simultaneously 'a Vaishnav *panth*, a Sufi order, a trader's guild and a caste'.[12] In the 19th and early 20th centuries, however, the presence of all these various strands became problematic for them as new socio-political frameworks, which were associated with the establishment of British imperial rule and the emergence of religiously based nationalisms, became increasingly dominant in South Asia. In a tense and polarized atmosphere in which notions of religious identity and the categories 'Hindu' and 'Muslim' were contested and also rigidly and narrowly demarcated, the Khojas, like many other Indian communities, were pressured to reshape their identity to better conform to externally defined norms. To complicate matters, internal dissent among the Khojas over issues of authority and governance led to intervention by the judicial system of British India. As a result, schisms developed among the Khojas and they splintered along religious (Hindu/Muslim) as well as sectarian (Sunni/Shi'i) lines. For those Khojas who in the aftermath of these divisions came to identify themselves as Ismailis, the Aga Khans employed the sanction of their office as hereditary Shi'i Imams (spiritual leaders) to affect the process of transforming Khoja identity from an Indic caste to Muslim denomination.[13] The story of the Khojas is narrated from two perspectives: first, by exploring their identity within the changing landscapes of pre-colonial, colonial and post-colonial South Asia and, second, by examining the impact of identity transformation on their devotional life and literatures, especially the *ginan*s, a genre of devotional poetry that has been quintessential to Satpanthi and Khoja identity.

Locating Khoja Identity within Changing Contexts

The pre-colonial experience

During the course of its historical development, the Satpanth tradition evolved into several branches. As a result, Satpanthis were divided into various sub-groups such as the Khojas, Shamsis, Nijyapanthis (Nizarpanthis), Momnas, Imamshahis, Mahamargis and Barmatis (Maheswaris). Each sub-group adopted a distinctive identity centred on the particular *pir* or *sayyid* it followed as well as the occupation or profession of its members. The Khojas, the subject of this chapter, are said to be disciples of the

15th-century Pir Sadr al-Din, the most prominent of the Satpanthi *pir*s. According to Azim Nanji, Pir Sadr al-Din appears to have played a key role in organizing and consolidating the Satpanth tradition. To him are attributed the greatest number of *ginan*s, the establishment of the first *jama'atkhana* (house of congregation) and the invention of the Khojki script (an alphabet for recording religious texts and keeping commercial accounts).[14] Khoja traditions assert that they belonged originally to trading castes of Sind and Gujarat, principally the Lohanas and Bhatias. Upon their joining Satpanth, Pir Sadr al-Din is said to have given his new disciples the title '*khwaja*' (a Persian term of which Khoja is a corruption) to replace the original Lohana '*thakkur*', both meaning 'lord' or 'master'.[15] The intent behind the new title was apparently to bestow a caste-like status on his followers, a concession to their social milieu in which caste was fundamental in defining status and societal relationships. Before the name of an individual the title '*khwaja*' served to indicate simultaneously occupational (merchant), social and religious identities.

Evidence from British gazetteers indicates that in early 19th-century Bombay the Khojas functioned socially as an endogamous caste. They had regular meetings to which adult males were summoned by a crier who went through the streets in Khoja neighbourhoods. At such gatherings, all kinds of disputes, including those related to marriages, were presented for arbitration. In case of violation of caste norms, members could vote on excommunication. There were also special caste dinners for which the group, as a corporate entity, owned its own cooking utensils.[16] In nomenclature and social customs they did not differ much from their Lohana and Bhatia brethren. *The Gazetteer of the Bombay Presidency* remarks that in northeast Kathiawar, Khojas were still addressed by the Lohana title *thakkur* and wore their waistcoats in the Lohana fashion.[17] Like other mercantile communities in the region, they had their own writing system, Khojki, which was a refined form of Lohanaki, the script used by the Lohanas.[18] In personal law the group was, according to Hamid 'Ali, 'caught within the meshes of Hindu customary law'.[19] The remarriage of widows, as in the case of many Indian castes, was a strict taboo, while inheritance of property was limited only to males.[20]

In terms of religious life, as in some other regions, a multiplicity of beliefs that were at once complementary and contradictory had been integrated by the Khojas. One of the mainstays of their devotional life was the singing of *ginan*s, hymn-like poems which the *pir*s and *sayyid*s are said to have composed in various local languages to propagate the teachings of Satpanth in the manner in which they could be best understood by the local population. The term *ginan* is derived from the Sanskrit word for 'knowledge', in the sense of esoteric truth or wisdom; hence the *ginan*s may perhaps be best understood as hymns of esoteric wisdom.[21] In the *ginan*s, the *pir*s and *sayyid*s translated the core concepts of Satpanth, in particular that of the Imam, into one or more of the four religious discourses then prevalent in western India. The choice of discourse and the terms and idioms employed varied, depending on various factors such as the period of composition, doctrinal and thematic content, and the historical context of the audience. As a result, the formulation of Satpanthi doctrine in the *ginan*s was multilayered and multivalent in character.

Some of the earliest *ginan*s, such as the *Dasa Avatara*, often hailed as a Satpanth classic, created an ostensible equivalence between the Vaishnava Hindu concept of *avatara* and the Ismaili concept of *imam*. In such *ginan*s, the *pir*s represented themselves as guides who knew the whereabouts of the long-awaited tenth *avatara* of Vishnu, meaning the Ismaili Imam who they proclaimed was living in the west (Iran). As a result, these *ginan*s portray Satpanth as the completion or culmination of the Vaishnavite Hindu tradition.

Other *ginan*s formulated their teachings within a Sufi framework, reiterating a relationship between Sufism and Ismaili thought found in Iran, especially after the 13th century.[22] Several Sufi orders, particularly the Suhrawardiyya and the Qadiriyya, had a significant presence in the areas in which the *pir*s and *sayyid*s were most active, namely in Punjab and Sind. The use of Sufi terminology in the Satpanthi tradition served, therefore, to emphasize its close links with traditions of Islamic mysticism. The Ismaili Imams and their representatives, the *pir*s, were portrayed as spiritually enlightened teachers who could guide the spiritual development of each disciple (*murid*). With the aid of spiritual practices such as *dhikr* (remembrance of the divine names), the guide (*murshid*) prepared the disciple for experiencing the ultimate goal of Islamic mysticism – the 'face to face encounter with God', or *didar*, 'vision of the divine'. As keeper of the mysteries of *batin*, the esoteric, the Imam became not only the guide but often also the object of the spiritual quest, in which one encounters spiritually the light (*nur*) of the Imam, who is frequently referred to as 'Ali. In this context, 'Ali refers not merely to the historical person, but is symbolic of all the Imams and, indeed, the 'Light of the Imamate', a pre-eternal and cosmic light believed to be inherited by all Shi'i Imams following 'Ali.[23] A fine illustration of a *ginan* that adopts such a Sufi framework is the *Bujh Niranjan*, a lengthy composition in medieval Hindi describing the stages and states of spiritual development using Sufi technical terms drawn from the Persian and Arabic tradition.[24]

A third discourse found in the *ginan*s is that of the Sants, a group of lower-caste 'poet-saints' who were part of a powerful anti-ritual and anti-caste movement that swept across India at the same time as the Satpanthi tradition appeared. Formal organizations or *panth*s, similar to Sufi orders or fraternities, crystallized around some of the Sants. Each *panth* consisted of disciples who had dedicated themselves to following the teachings of a particular Sant and his descendants. Guru Nanak, commonly regarded today as the 'founder' of the Sikh religion, was one such Sant and the path he preached was initially called *Nanakpanth*. Indeed there are strong parallels between the evolution of *Nanakpanth* into the formal 'religion' that is known as Sikhism today, and the Satpanth tradition and its later evolution into various modern manifestations in Islam and Hinduism. The very name Satpanth was meant to resonate with the larger Sant tradition, the Imams and *pir*s being perceived as *satguru*s, 'true guides'. Adopting much of the idiom of Sant poetry, the *ginan*s challenge the efficacy of ritualism and rote learning as paths to salvation. Instead they urged the faithful to follow the right path (*satpanth*) by adopting a righteous lifestyle, recognizing the transitory nature of the world (*maya*) and the evils of attachment to it. Knowledge of true reality is only possible through regular constant remembrance (*sumiran*) of the divine name (*nam/shabd*) given to those who follow the true path by the *satguru*, the true guide ambiguously identified in most *ginan*s as either the *pir* or the *shah* (the Imam), or both. The *pir*s and *sayyid*s who composed the *ginan*s are depicted as teachers (*guru*s) who guided them to the path of spiritual enlightenment (*darshan/didar*) and thereby to eternal bliss.

The Bhakti tradition, a movement of devotionalism prevalent in north India, provided a fourth framework of expression. Bhakti vocabulary was used by the *pir*s for expressing one of the core concepts of Satpanth: the relationship of devotion between disciples and the Imam. Not only was the Imam a guide, a repository of knowledge and divine light, but also the object of love and veneration. Indeed for many of his followers love and devotion to the Imam are absolutely essential for the attainment of the spiritual vision and union for which the believer yearns. The most powerful representative of devotion in Bhakti poetry is the *virahini*, the woman longing for her beloved, best exemplified by Radha and the *gopi*s (dairy maids) in their longing for Krishna. In the *ginan*s, the *virahini* becomes symbolic of the human soul which experiences *viraha* (painful longing) for the beloved, almost always identified as the Imam. As a result, many *ginan*s portray the believer as a *virahini*, waiting expectantly for the return of the beloved from whom she has been separated. An interesting consequence of the prevalence of the *virahini* symbolism is that many *ginan*s are written in a feminine voice, although their authors are predominantly male.[25]

The various understandings of the doctrine of the Imam among the Khojas were echoed in their eclectic religious practices as documented in the early 19th century. In addition to performing Islamic rituals of mixed sectarian origins, they recited during their religious ceremonies the Satpanthi *ginan Dasa Avatara*, referred to earlier. In terms of their prayers, they performed the traditional Arabic *namaz* on the two *'ids*; otherwise, they had their own ritual prayer in the Gujarati language with a liberal sprinkling of Arabic and Persian phrases which they recited daily.[26] Their funeral ceremonies, as well as their marriages, were performed by Sunni officiants.[27] Yet the Khojas were clearly Shi'i by virtue of their reverence for 'Ali, the first Shi'i Imam. They venerated their Imams in Iran as his descendants, regularly sending tribute to them and, if possible, undertaking the arduous pilgrimage to see them in person.[28] They also participated in all the traditional Shi'i rituals commemorating the martyrdom of Imam Husayn during the month of Muharram. Those Khojas who could afford the expense would have the bodies of their dead shipped to Karbala in Iraq for burial near the shrine of Imam Husayn.[29] The significance of Karbala for the Khojas was further underscored by the fact that in a purification ritual called *ghat paat*, they sipped holy water in which small pills of Karbala clay were dissolved.[30]

Christopher Shackle and Zawahir Moir remark that the world view of Satpanth, although drawn from seemingly disparate sources, is remarkably coherent, representing 'a creative achievement of the religious imagination perhaps more remarkable than that seemingly syncretic grafting of Hindu ideas on an Islamic base of a very individual type which has tended to attract disproportionate and sometimes dismissive comment in the analysis of outsiders'.[31] On the other hand, W. Ivanow characterized Satpanth as 'a transition between Ismailism, Sufism and Hinduism'.[32] On account of the uniquely constructed multivalent Satpanthi formulation, the Khojas could effectively participate in several social identities simultaneously and navigate between them with fluidity: they were members of a mercantile group who followed Satpanth, 'the true path', a tradition that could be simultaneously understood within both Islamic and Indic doctrinal frameworks. They owed allegiance to their *pir/imam/murshid*, a descendant of 'Ali residing in Iran. It was to him that they expressed devotion using the symbols and idioms taken from the love poetry associated with Krishna and the *gopis*.

In many ways, pre-colonial Khojas represented a creative model of engagement with diversity that may be partially understood through Tony Stewart's 'translation theory' as a basis for understanding encounters between traditions. Following this hermeneutic model, we may regard the use of multiple discourses in the Satpanthi tradition as an attempt on the part of those who composed *ginans* 'to be understood, to make themselves understood', in several different religious 'languages' depending on the context they were addressing.[33] Within the context of colonial India, as religious identities came to be essentialized and religious difference between Hindus and Muslims became a source of socio-cultural polarization, 'multilingual' doctrinal and social formulations such as those of Satpanth became difficult if not impossible to sustain.

The Khojas in colonial spaces

One of the features of modernity in South Asia is the ideological use of religion to categorize communities based on their adherence to a distinctive set of practices and doctrines. The British, who were to play a dominant role in South Asia from the mid-19th century onwards, 'understood organized religious life as constituted in the Church of England'.[34] As a result of their encounter with European conceptions of religions as distinct and, therefore, separate, many inhabitants of South Asia came to regard Islam and Hinduism as fixed monolithic entities, with their respective adherents separated from each other by well-defined boundaries. Traditions that seemed to combine elements of both, therefore, came to be seen as anomalous and even deviant. No doubt the widespread presence of 'Hindu-Muhammadan' groups of indeterminate religious identity was confusing to British officials who lamented the lack of 'pure Moslems' in India.[35] Naturally the Khojas, with the pluralistic character of their practices and 'multilingual' discourses through which they understood their faith, were difficult to categorize, creating many quandaries. For example, Hamid Ali comments that their legal position was such that it was 'as baffling to the [colonial] law courts as it (was) to the legislature'.[36] Were they Muslim or Hindu? If Muslim, then what kind of Islam did they practise? Not only was the exact nature of their religious identity questioned, but occasionally it also elicited rather caustic judgements. For example, a British colonial officer, Sir Bartle Frere, noted that the Khojas were considered heretical by many Muslims because they engaged in 'various remnants of idolatrous and mystical worship'.[37] Defining Khoja identity was, and continues to remain, problematic for academics as well. For instance, the late Aziz Ahmad, a scholar of South Asian Islam, grouped them along with other 'syncretic' sects of indeterminate identity, declaring that their chief interest was as 'curiosities of mushroom religious growth',[38] who added 'color to the bizarre pageantry of India'.[39] Ordinary Muslims and Hindus, he further remarked, considered such communities to be 'spiritual freaks'.[40] Clearly the unique blend of Khoja beliefs and customs was bewildering to outsiders. But by the mid-19th century, it was becoming perplexing internally as well. In 1847 Hubib Ebrahim, a Khoja witness in an inheritance case, declared to a British judge: 'Some say we are Soonees [Sunnis], some Sheas [Shi'a]. Our religion is a separate religion, Aga Khan is esteemed as a great man amongst us.'[41]

In the latter half of the 19th century and early 20th century, two sets of factors triggered a series of changes which led to the Khojas redefining themselves to better fit new and more narrowly defined categories of identity. The first set of factors was external to the community and related to the establishment of British colonial rule in India. The very 'idiom' of this rule, as Peter Hardy terms it, was communalist, systematically institutionalizing India into a nation of discrete communities defined along religious lines through various bureaucratic practices.[42] Census and ethnographic surveys highlighted religious rather than other markers of identity, forcing people to identify themselves primarily in religious terms. Through such colonial instruments, the peoples of the subcontinent began to perceive themselves as a series of distinct religious communities. Consequently many traditionally antagonistic sectarian groups and separately organized collectives were represented in the single category of either Hindu or Muslim.[43] Muslim elites, for example, started to view all the Muslims in India, notwithstanding their significant ethnic, linguistic, social and sectarian differences, as a single monolithic community united by their religion. Eventually, in an atmosphere infused with nationalist ideas and sentiment, some Muslim and Hindu leaders began to see religious communities as distinct nations. It is this conception that led to demands for the partition of the subcontinent on the basis of the two-nation theory.

British rule also brought with it Western culture and new institutions, particularly schools and colleges, many run by Christian missionaries dedicated to promoting Western models of education and European lifestyles. This development prompted a general concern among many Muslims because it was perceived as a potential threat to Muslim identity. In response, revivalist and reformist movements calling for fresh interpretations of Islam emerged, offering a spectrum of definitions concerning the maintenance of Islamic identity in the colonial context.[44] Many of these definitions, ranging from liberal to ultra-conservative, sought to differentiate sharply Muslim from non-Muslim using as guides the Qur'an, the *sunna* (practices) of the Prophet Muhammad and the traditions of the first generation of Muslims. None of them had space for the multivalent identity projected by communities like the Khojas. Such groups were perceived as 'syncretic', and they would have to align their concept of Islam in conformity with the majority community. The exercise of their faith would have to conform to externally defined notions of orthopraxy.[45] Practices and ideas, particularly those inherited from local Indian traditions, came to be regarded as innovations and, therefore, 'non-Islamic'. Consequently the late 19th and 20th centuries witnessed individuals, groups and entire villages being targeted for reform by grassroots Muslim reformers, such as the Faraizis, who sought to eliminate a whole range of practices, customs and ideas among Muslims that they considered 'Hindu' or 'un-Islamic'.[46] Conversely Hindu reformists, particularly groups such as the Arya Samaj, produced aggressive propaganda that was aimed at 're-Hinduizing' groups they considered to be Hindu in origin. Among the targets for 'Hinduization' were Satpanthi groups. In 1913–1914 the Arya Samaj embarked on a vigorous campaign to encourage the Guptis, a group who were outwardly Hindu but inwardly Satpanthi, to undergo the *shuddhi* 'purification' ceremony so that they could become proper Hindus.[47] As a result of such campaigns, some Satpanthi groups such as the Nijyapanthis and the Imamshahis, as Dominique-Sila Khan has shown, eventually came to identify themselves as Hindus.[48]

Suspicion of local indigenous cultures thought to be 'un-Islamic' or 'Hindu' and the privileged status accorded 'Arabo-Persian' elements as 'Islamic' radically changed perceptions of cultural elements such as language, literature, dress, music and dance. As these began to be viewed through the politicized lens of religious ideology, they were subject to either 'Islamization' or 'Sanskritization', which ultimately resulted in cultural polarization between Hindu and Muslim communities. As yet more elements of culture came to be perceived as 'Hindu' or 'Muslim', the area of common cultural ground between Muslims and Hindus in certain parts of India shrank.[49] In this way communities became demarcated on the basis of rigidly defined cultural boundaries. For instance, just as the Hindu nationalists felt it was no longer possible for Hindu poets to write in Urdu, which they perceived as an Islamic language, Muslim nationalists felt it inappropriate for Muslim poets to write in Hindi, regarded as a Hindu language. The sociologist Imtiaz Ahmed correctly observes that the ultimate result of such processes was a disjunction that had a profound significance in shaping interaction between Muslims and Hindus by sharpening cultural differences between them.[50]

In this tense milieu, groups such as the Khojas, who had articulated their identity using concepts and formulations that were uncommon by the standards of the Arabo-Persian perceptions of Islam, were forced to clarify their position vis-à-vis the general Muslim community. This, then, marks the beginning of a period of sustained dialogue and engagement of the Khojas with other Muslim groups in South Asia.

A second set of factors that was responsible for the reorientation of Khoja identity related to developments internal to the Khojas. Specifically these were consequences of the move in 1841 of Hasan 'Ali Shah Aga Khan I, the 46th Nizari Ismaili Imam, to India. Following political disturbances in Iran, the seat of the Nizari Imamate for several centuries, Aga Khan I came first to Sind where he allied himself with the British. After a short stay in Calcutta in 1848, he settled in Bombay, which at the time had the largest settlement of Khojas. The Khojas had a tradition of sending tributes to the Aga Khan's ancestors in Iran through specially designated emissaries. Some had even undertaken the arduous overland journey to Iran to pay their personal respects to their *pir/murshid*. Notwithstanding this spiritual allegiance, when it came to conducting their internal affairs, the Khojas, like contemporary Ismailis in other regions, had been rather autonomous. For instance, the managing of caste property in Bombay, including the *jama'atkhana*s, was the responsibility of a select group of Khoja commercial magnates who formed a kind of council of elders (*justi*). In addition to the *justi*, the *mukhi* (chief) and *kamadia* (treasurer), as well as a *sayyid/vakil*, were central figures of authority in the caste.[51] Their duties included the collection of religious dues from caste members for transmission to the Imams in Iran. Already in the early 19th century, some of the more progressive-minded magnates had been instrumental in instituting what were then perceived as modernizing reforms among the Khojas, such as the introduction of English in their schools.[52]

Soon after his arrival, Aga Khan I began asserting his own authority over all matters related to the Khojas. For instance, he began instituting changes to some of their practices and customs, insisting on stronger participation in Shi'i rituals. In 1847, in keeping with traditional Shi'a religious law, he championed a change supporting a daughter's right to inherit a share in her father's property rather than the traditional Khoja practice which did not allow daughters to inherit.[53] He also began to assert control over communally owned Khoja property, a move which upset the upper echelons of the Khoja hierarchy. Resenting his authority, some members of the Khoja elite challenged his control as well as his right to receive tribute from them.[54]

The British colonial courts became the arena where the disputes between the Aga Khan and his opponents were fought. When it was not possible for the community to settle matters internally, the aggrieved parties filed legal suits. A common strategy in these cases was for the plaintiffs to challenge the Aga Khan's authority over the Khojas by questioning their religious identity. Thus the dissenters claimed that the Khojas were originally Sunni and accused the Aga Khan of propagating 'heretical' ideas to bolster his authority. In response the Aga Khan asked those faithful to him to sign a document in which they pledged to desist from Sunni rites and to follow the customs of their Shi'i faith openly. He further instructed them that they no longer had to observe *taqiyya* (precautionary dissimulation of beliefs), as under British rule the exercise of all religions was free. The majority of the Khojas signed the document.[55]

Several years of further dispute between the followers of the Aga Khan and his opponents culminated in the Aga Khan Case of 1866 in which the Bombay High Court undertook the daunting task of defining Khoja identity. In a lengthy landmark judgement, the presiding judge, Justice Arnould, gave validation to the Aga Khan's authority over the Khojas: 'a sect of people whose ancestors were Hindu in origin, which was converted to and has throughout abided in the faith of the Shia Imami Ismailis, which has always been and still is bound by ties of spiritual allegiance to the hereditary Imam of the Ismailis.'[56] Unable to accept this judgement, the Aga Khan's opponents joined the Sunni fold, calling themselves Sunni Khojas.

In the late 19th century and early 20th centuries, a period when Sultan Muhammad Shah, Aga Khan III (d. 1957), was the Ismaili Imam, the community's sectarian boundaries were further narrowed as a result of another court case. This time the dissenters, who included Haji Bibi, a cousin of the Aga Khan, and other members of his extended family, claimed that the Aga Khan was, like themselves, Ithna'ashari (Twelver Shi'i) by faith. His authority over the Ismailis was that of a traditional Sufi *pir*, not a Shi'i Imam, and, as such, they too were entitled to a share of the revenue he received from the Ismailis. In 1908 a British judge presiding over the Haji Bibi case (as it came to be known) gave further legal validation to the Aga Khan's authority and reaffirmed the Ismaili identity of the Khojas.[57] Once again a group of dissenters seceded, this time forming the Khoja Ithna'ashari community. As a result of these schisms and legal decisions, the identity of those Khojas who remained loyal to the Aga Khan was being clearly differentiated from that of the Sunnis and the Ithna'asharis alike, the cornerstone of which was allegiance to a living Ismaili Imam.[58]

The British courts in India played a crucial role in legally defining and upholding the identity of the Khojas as a community of Muslims. Key to this articulation was the 1866 judgement of Justice Arnould. He carefully sifted through the evidence he had gathered from witnesses, looking for elements that he could fit within the framework of the categories 'Islam', 'Muslim', 'Hindu', 'Sunni', 'Shi'a' and 'Ismaili' deduced from the scholarship of Western historians of Islam. He regarded these experts as authorities who had objective knowledge of the subject and were, he felt, more reliable than the Khoja practitioners themselves.[59]

As a result of these legal categorizations and the pressure to conform from the courts, the Khojas like other Muslim groups found themselves being defined with reference to the sectarian categories of 'Shi'a' and 'Sunni' as understood generally in the wider context of the Indian subcontinent. In this way they began to see themselves increasingly in sectarian terms, that is, as Ismaili, Ithna'ashari or Sunni. Sectarian affiliation became a primary marker of identity, superseding other markers such as caste, ethnicity, etc., a trend echoed in many other communities in colonial India. During the course of the 20th century the Khojas who remained loyal to the Aga Khans began identifying themselves specifically as (Nizari) Ismailis. While the British courts may have contributed to defining the Ismaili identity of the Khojas legally, the issue had yet to be resolved in terms of their doctrines and practices. For this process, as we shall see below, the Khojas had to rely on the various reform initiatives instituted by the Aga Khans.

Wilfred Cantwell Smith has remarked that Muslim societies generally place a greater emphasis on orthopraxy (conformity to ritual practice) than orthodoxy (conformity to doctrine) as the yardstick to determine 'correct' Islamic practice.[60] In many Muslim societies, the degree of conformity to traditional ritual practice has become the index by which the 'Islamic' character of groups like the Khojas is now judged.[61] The multivalent nature of Khoja practices as well as the prevalence of 'Indian' or 'Hindu' elements in their literature figured prominently in the testimony presented during the various court cases brought against the Aga Khans. British judges made references to these practices and observances in endeavouring to understand the religious identity and origins of the Khojas. Those practices and beliefs which did not make sense within the

Western construction of categories such as 'Islam', 'Sunni' and 'Shi'a' were classified as irrelevant, ignorant, superstitious or simply false.[62]

Ismaili Khojas in post-colonial spaces

Such questions became particularly pressing in the aftermath of the partition of British India in 1947 and the creation of Pakistan. Muhammad Ali Jinnah, the popularly acclaimed founder of Pakistan, was by birth a Khoja and was educated as a lawyer in England. In pressing for a separate nation for the subcontinent's Muslims, he had in mind a polity that would provide Muslims with a safe haven in which to practise their religion and nurture their cultural traditions. More specifically he envisaged a Western-style liberal democracy in which the Muslim majority and non-Muslim minorities would be free to practise their religions without interference from the state. Soon after its founding, however, there were attempts to transform Pakistan into an 'Islamic' state rather than simply a Muslim homeland. The push towards a more 'Islamic' character came from Sunni religious scholars ('*ulama*') who had initially opposed Jinnah's vision of Pakistan and, indeed, had termed him the 'great infidel'. Along with Mawlana Mawdudi (d. 1947), the founder of the Jama'at-i Islami, they now felt that Islam, rather than any Western secular ideology, should underpin the newly founded state of Pakistan. In their view, this would ensure that Islamic ideals of economic and social justice would prevail in society. Eventually, to counter powerful forces of ethno-nationalism that threatened its integrity, the Pakistani state itself began to appeal to Islam as a binding ideological force which could hold together a nation composed of different ethnic groups.

Some regimes, notably that of Zia ul-Haqq (1978–1988), introduced 'Islamization' policies with a view to enforcing upon Pakistan's Muslim citizens religious and cultural practices that were deemed to be 'Islamically' correct. Such programmes proved to be inimical to the fabric of Pakistani society since they accentuated religious and sectarian differences. The identification of Islam as the state religion negatively influenced the status of non-Muslims, particularly Christians and Hindus, who were effectively rendered second-class citizens, at least as far as the right-wing religious political parties were concerned. Furthermore, by granting a privileged status to the Sunni interpretation of Islam (specifically to that of the Jama'at-i Islami) the state, in effect, marginalized alternative interpretations of the faith. Policies of Islamization thus resulted in heightened sectarian tension, not only between Shi'i and Sunni but even among

Sunni communities. This provoked heated debate on the determination of 'correct' Muslim identity. Groups such as the Ahmadiyya, who claim to be Muslim, were proclaimed non-Muslim by the state and subjected to religious persecution.[63] In this atmosphere of growing intolerance, the identity of the Ismailis also came under increased scrutiny and their position grew precarious. On the one hand, the significant involvement of the institutions of the Aga Khan Development Network in the following decades in improving the socio-economic, educational and health standards of both the Ismaili and non-Ismaili population in Pakistan has helped in fostering a great deal of goodwill towards the Ismailis in many different circles of Pakistani society. On the other hand, some right-wing Sunni groups such as the Jama'at-i Islami, Tablighi Jama'at and other Wahhabi-Salafi-influenced groups have launched vigorous campaigns to propagate their version of Islam among the Ismailis and other Muslim groups. In Karachi, a city with a large Ismaili population, such groups have built Sunni *masjid*s adjacent to Ismaili *jama'atkhana*s in an attempt to entice Ismailis to join the Sunni fold.

In post-colonial India, the Ismaili Khojas have not been questioned as intensely by other Muslims on the subject of their Islamic identity as in Pakistan. This is perhaps due to the general situation of Muslims in India as vulnerable minority groups who have collectively suffered considerable discrimination, notwithstanding the avowedly secular and pluralistic ideals on which the Indian nation was founded. Many Hindus have come to regard Ismaili Khojas as model Muslims since they appear to have better assimilated to Indian culture in contrast to those Muslims who articulate their identity using non-Indic, Arabo-Persian symbolism. Yet identification even as assimilated Muslims in contemporary India is not without its problems. Occasionally during communal riots the Ismailis, too, have suffered the fate of other Muslim communities, falling victim to attacks by right-wing Hindu mobs. For instance, during the riots in Bombay in the aftermath of the destruction of Babri Mosque in December 1992, the Muslim victims numbered many Ismailis. The genocide of Muslims in Gujarat in 2002, in which both the Hindu nationalist-dominated state government and police were deemed to be complicit, also had an impact on the state's Ismaili population, a small proportion of whom chose to emigrate from Gujarat.

The Re-articulation of Khoja Identity

The history of the Ismaili Khojas in the 20th century is best characterized as a series of responses to the ever changing political, social and cultural landscapes of colonial and post-colonial South Asia, which we have discussed above. Within this highly volatile milieu, Khoja understandings of themselves and their faith changed significantly. The plurality of frameworks which they had traditionally used to express their multivalent identity became increasingly difficult to sustain in the face of modernity and the polarizing forces of religious nationalism and communalism. Among those Khojas who defined themselves as Ismaili, the process of identity redefinition constituted part of a larger programme of social and religious reforms, initiated by Sultan Muhammad Shah, Aga Khan III, in the early 20th century. The impetus underpinning the Aga Khan's reforms stemmed from the need to respond to the growing impact of modernization, socio-economic transformation and nationalism on his followers, as well as the need to clearly define their identity as Shi'i Ismailis within the larger Muslim *umma* (community). To facilitate his policies, Aga Khan III established several new institutions that were better suited to governing and responding to the needs of his followers within the dynamic socio-political milieu of colonial India. In tandem with these efforts, there was a progressive re-articulation of the Ismaili Khoja interpretation and practice of their faith within a framework of Islamic and specifically Shi'i traditions. Following his death in 1957, Aga Khan III's programme of reforms was considerably intensified and accelerated by his grandson, Prince Karim, Aga Khan IV, and extended to other Ismaili communities across the world.

Reorienting understanding and practice of faith

To execute their ambitious programme of reforms, the Aga Khans used two important instruments: constitutions and *farman*s (directives). In 1905 Aga Khan III introduced the first of a series of constitutions in which the Ismailis were formally and legally defined in modern terms as a 'religious community' of which he was the head. This marked the initiation of a period during which he created new structures of national and provincial councils through which he implemented change in a variety of areas including governance, social welfare, health and education. As they evolved in the post-colonial era, these institutions became the primary agencies for implementing social and economic change among the Ismailis in India, Pakistan and the newly independent countries of East Africa. In the later decades of the 20th century, under the leadership of Aga Khan IV, they evolved into an international network that 'both expresses and expedites the modernization of the community while it also emphasizes and reinforces the singular role of the Imam'.[64] In addition to outlining the roles, responsibilities and regulations governing these institutions, the constitutions contained lengthy sections governing social customs, as well as personal and family law with detailed regulations on marriage and divorce. Over the course of the 20th century, these constitutions were revised several times to keep pace with the changes in contexts and circumstances (as discussed elsewhere in this volume).

The Aga Khans also issued *farmans* through which they conveyed to their followers counsel and direction on a wide range of issues, both religious and secular. In the eyes of their followers, the *farmans* embodied the ongoing and infallible guidance of the Imams; hence obedience to them was obligatory. Not surprisingly *farmans* became the most significant means through which the Aga Khans mandated reform in all aspects of the Ismaili community.[65] In the early 20th century, with the rapid spread of print culture in South Asia, *farmans* were compiled and published in books so that they could be widely accessible to Ismaili Khojas. In most of these early publications, the *farmans* were recorded in Indic vernaculars – Hindustani, Gujarati and Sindhi – while in later years English became more prominent, though translations into local languages were also made available. As the corpus of printed *farmans* grew, it developed into a bona fide genre of Ismaili religious literature, representing the word of the Imams. Readings of selected *farmans* became an important feature of Ismaili worship, indicative of their status as the principal source for contemporary normative understanding of the faith.

The programme of reforms instituted by the Aga Khans dramatically transformed Ismaili Khoja social, economic and religious life. In the area of religious life and practice, it appears to have had two intersecting objectives: first, to promote among the Khojas a better understanding of Ismaili concepts and practices using frameworks consistent with Shi'i and general Islamic traditions; and second, to articulate an interpretation of Islam that was relevant to the emerging contexts of colonial and post-colonial South Asia in a changing world.[66] The expression and application of these objectives among the Khojas was by their very nature a complex process involving changes in many dimensions of life. At the fundamental level it involved shifting the understanding of key doctrines away from local frameworks (increasingly viewed as Hinduistic) to ones that would be considered authentically Islamic. This meant that the Ismaili doctrine of the Imamate, instead of being understood within a frame of reference that was in parts ahistorical or mythological and intermingled with idioms from the Vaishnavite, Sant or Bhakti traditions, was now formulated within a broader framework of Islamic history, theology and mysticism, as well as Shi'i paradigms of religious authority.

A key component of religious reform under Aga Khan III was familiarizing the Ismaili Khojas with new ways of enabling the continuum of understanding of the faith, including the production of *farman*s, books, periodicals and pamphlets, in several vernacular languages, particularly Gujarati. It also involved the establishment of a network of schools to impart religious education to children with a curriculum that would reflect the new frameworks of understanding. Founded as early as 1903, these schools were initially called 'Sindhi' because the students were taught Khojki or Khwajah Sindhi, the special script of the Khojas in which religious material was recorded.[67] Interestingly the formulation of an explicitly Ismaili Muslim identity also resulted in changes in nomenclature. Traditionally Khoja names had been indistinguishable from those of their Lohana and Bhatia compatriots. Since these names were increasingly considered to be indicative of a 'Hindu' identity in the socio-political climate of 20th-century South Asia, they were gradually replaced by Arabic or Persian ones that resonated better with Muslim identity. As a result, while many Ismaili Khojas retained ancestral names now considered to be 'Hindu' (such as Nanji, Ramji, Dewji, etc.), Arabo-Persian names became increasingly common for generations born from the early 20th century onwards, as in the case of some other Muslim groups in India. In some instances, especially for families who experienced great societal pressure to conform to Islamic norms, even ancestral names were changed.[68]

After the partition of the subcontinent in 1947 and the rise of movements seeking to define Pakistan as an 'Islamic state', the trend towards 'Islamization' gained further momentum.[69] There was a rapid removal or reformulation of rituals, including those connected with birth, marriage and death, to render them more Islamic in character. The most important of the changes, however, was in regard to the daily prayer that the Ismaili Khojas recited three times daily. Khoja tradition attributed the composition of this prayer, simply called *du'a*, to their founding *pir*, Sadr al-Din. The prayer was by and large in the Indic vernaculars, Sindhi and Gujarati, with a number of phrases in Arabic. Among its contents were invocations for the intercession of the Imam who was depicted both as *pir* and *murshid*, the 'immaculate one'. In the 1950s this *du'a*, which had been modified several times during its history, was replaced by one entirely in Arabic.

The new *du'a* consists of six parts, each of which begins with one or more Qur'anic verses,[70] some of which are used as proof texts for the doctrine of the Imamate. Each part also contains intercessory prayers addressed to the Imams and concludes in a prostration (*sujud*) affirming obedience and submission to God (*Allah*). The introduction of the new prayer was significant for two reasons: first, the use of Arabic instead of an Indic vernacular aligned the prayer with a universal language of Islamic liturgical practice; secondly, it reflected a shift in the Khoja understanding of the doctrine of the Imamate from a Vaisnavite-coloured framework to one based on Qur'anic proof texts. The fact that the new prayer was to be universally recited by Nizari Ismailis the world over and was not unique to the Khojas indicates a psychological shift in orientation not only from 'Khoja' to 'Ismaili' but also from local to universal. It indicates that the contemporary Khoja practice was not merely in response to changing conditions in South Asia but, more importantly, an occasion to create a pan-Ismaili identity by developing a set of ritual practices that would be common to Ismailis wherever they lived and whatever their local cultural practices. This is a point we shall discuss in the conclusion.

Impact on devotional life and literature

How did this reorientation of various Khoja customs and practices bear upon their devotional life and literature? As noted earlier, the principal devotional literature of the Satpanth tradition were the *ginans* believed to have been composed by a series of *pirs* and *sayyids* who for centuries served as intermediaries between the Ismaili Imams in Iran and their Khoja followers in India.[71] Composed in several Indic languages and sung in various *ragas*, the *ginans* had been the focus of intense veneration as the embodiment of truth and wisdom. The recitation of *ginans*, alongside performance of ritual prayers, was part of the tradition of Satpanthi worship. Memorization of *ginan* texts formed an important element in the transmission of Satpanthi teachings from one generation to the next. Beyond their role in worship, the *ginans* permeated many aspects of communal and individual life.[72] Notwithstanding their special significance for the Khojas, the *ginans* were by no means the only genre of devotional literature in Khoja religious life. The 18th- and 19th-century manuscripts belonging to Khoja communities reveal that, in addition to the *ginans*, devotional literature from a variety of non-Satpanthi traditions also played a significant role in Khoja religious life. For example, we find in these manuscripts, juxtaposed to the *ginan*s, a diverse collection of texts: poems attributed to famous Sufi, Sant and Bhakti poets; *marsiya*, the traditional Shi'i elegies commemorating the martyrdom of the Shi'i Imam Husayn in Sindhi, Hindustani or Gujarati; religious narratives to be read during Muharram assemblies traditionally held by Shi'i communities; poems of devotion to the Prophet Muhammad and his family; *fal-nama*, or prognostication charts, attributed either to a Shi'i Imam or a *pir*, as well as various amulets, magical squares and formulae to be used for talismanic purposes.[73] The presence of such a broad spectrum of devotional literatures among pre-colonial Khoja communities is hardly surprising given the multivalent nature of their religious practice. Furthermore Michel Boivin suggests that by including such material in their manuscripts, the Khojas were adhering to the standard episteme for *pothi*s, prayer books, widely prevalent among different religious communities in Sind.[74]

With the reorientation of Khoja religious identity in the early part of the 20th century, much of such non-*ginan*ic literature found in the manuscript tradition fell into oblivion; it had effectively lost its significance and relevance in the then emerging formulations of faith. The *ginan*s, on the other hand, because they were quintessential to Khoja identity, continued to retain their importance, albeit in new ways. As a result, their character, content and function changed significantly so that they could be accommodated within the new orientations of the Ismaili Khoja community. Most noteworthy in this regard was the creation of an official canon of authorized texts of *ginan*s. The process of collecting and collating the texts was by no means an easy task since manuscripts were scattered far and wide, and there seems to have been no attempt to create a consolidated record. This is perhaps an indication that for pre-colonial Khojas, the *ginan*s may not have been initially conceived of as a scriptural corpus exclusively identified with one religious community, as they came to be regarded later with the emergence of the printed canon. In fact, as a result of the different orientation in which their identities developed in the 20th century, other Satpanthi groups such as the Imamshahis, with whom the Ismaili Khojas have historically shared the *ginan*s, have also come to consider them as part of their 'Hindu' heritage.[75] These contradictory characterizations of the *ginan*s are another indication that they represent a genre that is portable, surmounting modern constructions of religious boundaries. The explanation is also significant since it is underpinned by a perspective that is now almost universally associated with the *ginan*s, namely, that they were intended primarily as a literature of conversion, composed to call Hindus to the Ismaili interpretation of Islam. As Amrita Shodhan points out, this is a perspective that was first publicly articulated in the Aga Khan Case of 1866 and became definitive in the subsequent characterization of *ginan*ic literature.[76] Recent scholarship has raised a host of questions regarding the term 'conversion': its implication for our understanding of the processes involved in religious change; its use as a political tool by the colonial and post-colonial state; its inadequacy when explaining the spread of Islamic ideas across the subcontinent; as well as the role that literary genres such as the *ginan*s or Sufi folk poetry may have played in the process.[77]

Community traditions assert that Aga Khans II and III, in an attempt to produce a 'standardized' corpus of *ginan*s, entrusted the responsibility for collecting manuscripts to Lalji Devraj and his associates. On the basis of manuscripts they had collected, Lalji Devraj and his team recorded approximately 700 texts which they edited in varying degrees.[78] They eventually published them through the Khoja Press in Bombay. Founded in 1903 by Lalji Devraj, the press, later known as the Ismaili Printing Press (reflecting the shift in identity from Khoja to Ismaili) became the official publishing house for Ismaili Khoja literature. It used fonts specially manufactured in Germany for printing Khojki. In 1922 the publication of *ginan*s was transferred to the Recreation Club Institute, founded by Aga Khan III in 1919, to oversee publication of religious material as well as to engage in research on Ismailism. To prevent the circulation of non-official versions of *ginan* texts, private publication was discouraged; the Ghulam-i Husayn Chapkhanu, a private press which used to print lithographs of *ginan*s stopped doing so in the early 20th century. Since Lalji Devraj's publication activities were believed to have had the imprimatur of the Aga Khans, many Ismaili Khojas considered his editions to be bona fide and authoritative texts of *ginan*ic literature. His *Tapsil buk*, a catalogue of some 700 *ginan*s published in 1915, has been regarded as the official list of the early printed *ginan* texts.[79] In the 1970s, when further revisions in the texts of the *ginan*s were under consideration, the Lalji Devraj editions were used as the basis of the new revised versions.[80] The emergence of the Lalji Devraj editions as the authoritative canon was greatly facilitated by the fact that his team is said to have buried nearly 3,500 manuscripts which they had used as the bases for their editions.[81] This move limited the possibility for the emergence of competing versions of the *ginan* texts. More significant, however, is the fact that the Lalji Devraj editions excluded perhaps as many as 300 *ginan* texts from the 'official' corpus, since their contents were deemed to be inappropriate for the direction in which the Ismaili Khoja identity was evolving.

The creation of a 'standardized' corpus of *ginans* is significant because it also effectively amounted to a closing of a centuries-old tradition of *ginan* compositions, the last official exponent of this genre being a woman, Sayyida Imam Begum, who died in Karachi in 1866.[82] It also terminated the era of *pir*s and *sayyid*s, and by so doing contributed to further consolidate the spiritual authority of the Aga Khans among the Khojas. Although their Ismaili Khoja followers continued to recite the *ginan*s, their importance as sources of normative understanding of Khoja faith and practice gradually diminished. This all important function came to be increasingly performed by the *farman*s issued periodically by the Aga Khans. Since the *farman*s embodied the authoritative contemporary, ongoing guidance of the living Imams, they soon eclipsed the *ginan*s. As the tradition of *farman*s was consolidated and became readily available in print, its significance grew over the course of the 20th century. This development was to have significant impact on the contextual and relational functions of the *ginan*s, altering the ways in which the communities of believers interpreted and related to them. For example, *ginan*s came to be increasingly seen as commentaries on the inner meanings of the Qur'an. There was a notable shift in the type of *ginan*s that were recited. Those *ginan*s that were considered explicitly 'Hinduistic' in their mode of theological expression were abandoned or no longer recited. A noteworthy example of this is the *Das Avatara*, mentioned earlier. One of the classic *ginan*s of Satpanth literature, its recitation had completely ceased by the mid-1950s and in subsequent decades it disappeared from the general consciousness of the community. In the late 1970s, other compositions that explained Ismaili doctrine predominantly within an Indic framework were also dropped from active use. Similarly individual terms in *ginan*s that could also be interpreted as Hinduistic were changed and replaced by those seen to have a greater Islamic resonance. In effect this meant that words of Indic origin were replaced with Arabo-Persian ones. For example, 'Hari' was replaced by '"Ali', *'swami'* by *'maula'*, 'Gur Brahma' by 'Nabi Muhammad', and so on.[83] However, the definition of what constituted a Hindu element as opposed to an Islamic one became a major issue of contention with certain members of the community, who argued that terms from Indic languages with no specific theological connection to the Hindu tradition should be replaced by Arabo-Persian ones.[84] By the end of the 20th century, when the Ismaili Khojas came into greater contact with Ismaili communities in other parts of the world, many with distinctive cultural traditions of their own, the perspective in which they understood *ginan*s changed even further. The Ismaili Khojas, who had hitherto conflated the Ismaili tradition almost exclusively with the *ginan*s, came to realize that they were only one part of the global literary traditions of Ismaili devotional literatures that included genres in Arabic and Persian such as the *qasida*, *maddoh* and *manqabat*.

Towards a new historiography

The abandonment of traditional Satpanthi frameworks created the need for a new literature through which the Ismaili Khojas could develop broader and more universal understandings of Ismaili doctrine. To meet this need, the Recreation Club, which Aga Khan III established in 1919 to engage in research and publication on Ismaili history, commissioned the first comprehensive history of the Ismaili Imamate in Gujarati, the most widely spoken language among the Khojas. The task of writing this monumental history, documenting the reigns of 48 Ismaili Imams from the 7th to the 20th centuries, was assigned to 'Ali Muhammad Jan Muhammad Chunara (1881–1966), who had served for a short period of time as the social secretary to Aga Khan III. In addition to being a factory owner in Bombay, Chunara was a pioneering journalist and editor of *The Ismaili*, the Anglo-Gujarati weekly for the Ismaili Khoja community published in Bombay. Already in 1918, at the behest of the Ismaili Sahitya Utjek Mandal (the Ismaili Literary Society), he had written a brief history of the Fatimids in Gujarati. With the assistance of Husein Shariff Bharmal, Hasan Ali Rahim Nathani and others on the staff of the *The Ismaili* who were knowledgeable in various languages including Arabic, Persian, Urdu and English, Chunara spent eight years researching the sources.[85] Finally in 1936, the year commemorating Aga Khan III's Golden Jubilee, or 50 years as Imam, he published a 180-page work. Significantly his Gujarati history of the Ismaili Imamate had an Arabic title, *Nuram [Nuran] Mubin*, 'Manifest Light', a Qur'anic expression (4:174) that is interpreted by Ismailis as a reference to the 'Light of the Imamate' manifest in the world as a divinely ordained means of guidance for humanity. The work's Gujarati subtitle, *Allahni Pavitra Rasi*, 'God's Sacred Rope', echoes another Qur'anic phrase, *habli'llah*, 'God's Rope' (3:103), which is commonly interpreted in Shi'i sources as a reference to the institution of the Imamate. The use of these two phrases in the title thus underscores the increasingly Qur'anic bases for newly emerging Ismaili Khoja understandings of the Imamate.

In his preface ʿAli Muhammad Chunara commented that among his motivations for writing this book was the widespread ignorance among Khojas about their faith, as a result of which they fell prey to misinformation and propaganda spread by unscrupulous individuals who were intent on luring them away from the Ismaili community. He expressed the hope that, armed with the knowledge acquired from the *Nuram Mubin*, Ismaili Khojas would be able 'to stand on both feet'.[86] These remarks clarify a broader objective for the publication of his book; it was a means through which Ismaili Khojas could acquire sufficient knowledge with which to articulate and defend their faith. In this regard, the *Nuram Mubin* constituted a significant work within a larger corpus of literature written in Sindhi, Gujarati and Urdu, which was used as a response to a barrage of polemical attacks from groups opposed to the Aga Khan and the Ismailis. This anti-Ismaili polemic, particularly powerful in the first half of the 20th century, was intended to convert Ismaili Khojas to either Sunni or Ithnaʿashari Islam, or to Hinduism. In this battle for the hearts and minds of the Khojas, Chunara was a leading member of a group of articulate Ismaili loyalists with considerable literary skills. Through a range of Gujarati publications that included newspaper articles, pamphlets and small booklets responding to Ithnaʿashari Shiʿi and Arya Samaj attacks, textbooks on Ismaili history and religion, and even volumes of poetry, this group of Ismaili revivalists, as Zawahir Moir calls them, 'sought to create a renewed sense of Ismaili identity, strong enough to hearten and educate their supporters and refute their opponents'.[87] Many of these publications cited generously from the Qurʾan and the *hadith*s, sayings of and about the Prophet, reflecting the Islamically based nature of their arguments. Similar works defending the Aga Khan and Ismaili doctrines were also written by prominent Ismaili Khojas in Sindhi during the same period. Some of these treatises attempt to show Ismailism, in particular the *ginan*s, as expressions of the powerful currents of Sufism that form the bedrock of Sindhi culture.[88]

Since Aga Khan III recommended that his followers read the *Nuram Mubin* in order to learn the history of the Imams, the work was regarded as authoritative and sold briskly, necessitating several reprints. It was also translated into Urdu.[89] In the last decades of the 20th century, further publication of the *Nuram Mubin* ceased and the book was withdrawn from circulation. Although there were no official explanations for this development, we can speculate that there may have been two principal reasons. First, as discussed above, the book was initially written in the early decades of the 20th century in a context of virulent polemical attacks on the Ismaili faith and the legitimacy of the Aga Khans. As such the work, written in part to counter these attacks, adopted a perspective that was becoming rapidly outdated in the new circumstances in which Ismaili Khojas were living. Second, the book was highly hagiographical in nature, replete with miracles associated with the Imams and *pir*s. Some of these accounts were drawn directly from allegories in the *ginan*s which had been interpreted rather literally. As these accounts attracted criticism about their factuality, a more historical perspective was adopted, reflected in newer histories such as Sherali Alidina's *Ta'rikh imamat* (1952), a history of the Imamate in the Sindhi language, and the *Ta'rikh a'imma Isma'iliyya* (1978–1983), a four-volume work in Urdu. Both works avoid mythological and hagiographical discourses in their presentation of history and were published by the Ismaili Association for Pakistan, the official community institution authorized by the Imam to publish such material. In the 1990s these locally produced histories were superseded by works of modern historical scholarship published under the auspices of The Institute of Ismaili Studies in London – a reflection of the transnational direction in which Aga Khan IV was guiding Ismaili communities.

Conclusion: Transnationalizing Ismaili Khoja Identity[90]

This chapter has explored the experiences of the Ismaili Khojas as they rearticulated their identity in response to changes in the cultural and political milieus in pre-colonial, colonial and post-colonial South Asia. The Aga Khans, as we have seen, inspired and determined the direction the formation their identity took within this regional context. During the course of the late 19th and 20th centuries, as a result of economic and political pressures, some Khojas left South Asia to settle in other parts of the world, notably East Africa, the UK and North America. Though these diasporic Khoja communities faced a range of issues different from those in the South Asian context, they continued to rely on the guidance of the Aga Khans to help them adapt to these new environments. Through various institutions, the Aga Khans modernized the structure and ethos of the Ismaili Khoja communities, whether in South Asia or abroad, formulating doctrines, religious practices and forms of devotional literature so that they would be aligned with universally accepted idioms of the Islamic tradition, while at the same time reinforcing the core of the Shi'i Ismaili principles of the faith. Commenting on these efforts, Aly Kassam-Remtulla observes that, in addition to asserting the legitimacy of Ismailism within Islam, they were in fact important steps in forging a pan-Ismaili identity.[91]

We have already remarked on the pan-Ismaili dimension of some of these reforms. For instance, in the 1950s, an Arabic *du'a*, or daily prayer, presenting the doctrine of the Imamate within a framework based on Qur'anic verses, replaced a version which used Indic vernaculars (Gujarati and Sindhi) and drew heavily on the traditional Satpanthi formulations of doctrine. Since this Arabic prayer was introduced among non-Khoja Ismailis as well, it became a ritual commonly shared by Ismaili communities worldwide. We have also remarked how as a result of the reforms, the *farman*s, the directives by which the Aga Khans have guided their followers, eclipsed the *ginan*s as a source of normative doctrine and practice. As *farman*s have become readily accessible through the medium of print, they have become the primary source of religious guidance shared universally by Ismailis. Translations of *farman*s, which are on most occasions given in English, are also available in other important languages spoken by Nizari Ismailis today – Arabic, Persian, Tajik, Urdu, Gujarati, Sindhi and French. A *farman* which the Aga Khan makes in Dushanbe, Tajikistan, may be read in a *jama'atkhana* in Karachi, Mombasa, Toronto or Boston. In the last decades the Ismaili Khojas have come into closer contact with other Ismaili communities throughout the world. As a result they increasingly think of themselves in pan-Ismaili terms.

Historically the Aga Khans have played a key role in transnationalizing Ismaili Khoja identity in many different ways, such as encouraging immigration to different parts of the world when necessary,[92] the evocation of the notion of a worldwide Ismaili 'fraternity', a belief that Ismailis are all brothers and sisters with the Imam as their spiritual father, and the ethic of humanitarian service, that is, the obligation of Ismailis to help others, regardless of their race, nationality or religious persuasion, and that this kind of volunteerism amounts to service to the Imam.[93] More recent efforts in the direction of globalization have included the introduction of *Ta'lim*, a religious and cultural education curriculum designed by The Institute of Ismaili Studies in London for the education of all young Ismailis internationally. Available in several different languages, its curriculum is both pan-Ismaili and pan-Islamic in character.

In the last decade of the 20th century and the opening years of the 21st century, Prince Karim Aga Khan IV, through the institutions of the Aga Khan Development Network and a global constitution, has played a key role in facilitating all kinds of exchanges between Ismailis living in different regions of the world. Such exchanges became even more pronounced after the collapse of the Soviet Union with the establishment of contact with Ismaili communities residing in various Central Asian republics, especially Tajikistan, and Afghanistan, as well as Syria and Iran. As a result of these contacts, the Ismaili Khojas have not only become less 'Khoja-centric' in their understandings of Ismaili Islam but are also becoming more familiar with other Ismaili traditions and devotional literatures. As a result of institutional encouragement, it is now increasingly common to hear Ismaili Khojas reciting Persian or Arabic *qasidas* in their *jama'atkhanas*. On the other hand, non-Khoja Ismaili communities are also being reshaped by their contacts with certain Khoja customs and practices. Most notable in this regard is the globalization of the offices and the nomenclatures of the *mukhi* and *kamadia*, a quintessentially Khoja institution. These cross-cultural encounters have created a need for the articulation of an Ismaili identity that not only respects regional or local differences in culture and tradition but also recognizes certain universal commonalities in practice and doctrine. The role of Aga Khan IV in negotiating the delicate balance between tradition and modernity, diversity and uniformity, has thus become pivotal.

The increasingly international and cosmopolitan nature of the Ismaili community was given legal recognition in the form of a new constitution which Aga Khan IV ordained on 13 December 1986, his 50th birthday. This constitution was to be in effect for all Ismaili communities worldwide, superseding numerous local or regional ones. It expresses Ismaili identity in pan-Islamic and pan-Ismaili terms. Its preamble reiterates Ismaili doctrines within a universal Islamic framework: the Shia Imami Ismaili Muslims, as they are formally identified, who affirm the *shahada* (profession of faith), a universal marker of Muslim identity, as well as key Islamic concepts such as *tawhid* (monotheism) and prophecy, including the finality of the prophethood of Muhammad.[94] They acknowledge, like the earlier generations of the Ismailis, the pan-Shi'a doctrine of the Imamate, specifically Imam 'Ali's authority to interpret and expound on God's final message, the Qur'an, after the Prophet's death, and the continuation of the Imamate by heredity through his direct descendants. Underlining the longstanding connection of Ismaili thought with traditions of Islamic mysticism and esotericism, the Ismailis are characterized as *murids* belonging to a *tariqa*; they are linked to the Imam by a *bay'a*, or oath of allegiance; the essential function of the Imam being to illuminate 'the *murid*'s path to spiritual enlightenment and vision'.[95]

Additionally the new constitution emphasizes the transnational identity of the Ismailis through their allegiance to the Imam, as being united with each other and as part of a global brotherhood. It also identifies several international institutions, such as the Leaders International

Forum, a consultative body consisting of Ismaili leaders from various parts of the world who advise the Imam,[96] and others that form part of the Aga Khan Development Network, established to 'realize the social conscience of Islam' by promoting the social welfare of societies globally.[97] Thus the 1986 constitution marks a significant milestone in Ismaili history, symbolizing the transnationalization process, that is, the emergence of the Ismailis from their local and culturally specific formulations of faith into a global Muslim community sharing a distinctive identity and interpretation of the Islamic faith.

This chapter has attempted to show evolution in the identity and self-image of the Ismaili Khojas of South Asia over the last 150 years. A once tightly knit and closed caste-like community that drew comfortably on a multiplicity of heritages in the early 19th century found its multivalent acculturation a liability when it encountered modernity and the nation-state. The modern urge to categorize and divide based on difference, reflected in the ethos of the colonial and post-colonial nation-state, led to the splintering of the Khojas into various sectarian groups – Muslim and non-Muslim. For those who expressed their loyalty to the Aga Khans, this meant a shift from being merely members of a Satpanthi Khoja caste in western India to *murid*s (disciples) belonging to a *tariqa* of Shia Imami Ismaili Muslims living in over 25 countries around the world. While an institution of British colonial India played a facilitating role in defining in legal terms Khoja identity as being Ismaili, it was the hereditary Islamic institution, the Ismaili Imamate, that navigated the Ismaili Khojas through the whirlpools of cultural and political change in colonial and post-colonial South Asia. In the process, their fluid and multivalent pre-colonial identity was stripped of its traditional Indic plurality and transformed into a modern denominational one. Yet, through their Imams, the Ismaili Khojas entered a new world where they encountered a different kind of plurality – the geographical and cultural diversity of Ismaili communities worldwide. The charismatic authority of the Aga Khans and their vision were crucial to the implementation of monumental changes that impacted not only on religious teachings and practices but also socio-economic life.[98] It is the belief in a living Imam, who can give rulings with complete authority, the cornerstone of the Shi'i identity, that gives the Ismaili Khojas and their fellow Ismailis the world over a unique identity among Muslims today.

Notes

1. This essay incorporates and builds upon material from a previous article on this subject by the author, 'The Khojas of South Asia: Defining a Space of their Own', *Cultural Dynamics*, 13 (2001), pp. 155–168. The author wishes to thank Michael Currier and Shiraz Hajiani for their comments on earlier drafts of this essay.
2. Bernard Lewis, *The Assassins* (London, 1967), p. 138.
3. See Henry Corbin, *Cyclical Time and Ismaili Gnosis*, tr. R. Mannheim and J. W. Morris (London, 1983).
4. Aga Khan III, *The Memoirs of Aga Khan: World Enough and Time* (New York, 1954), p. 24.
5. Farhad Daftary, *The Isma'ilis: Their History and Doctrines* (Cambridge, 1990), pp. 2–3.
6. 'Ata-Malik Juwayni, *Ta'rikh-i jahan-gusha*, tr. J. A. Boyle as *The History of the World-Conqueror* (Cambridge, MA, 1958), vol. 2, p. 723.
7. Paul E. Walker, 'Abu Ya'qub al-Sijistani and the Development of Ismaili Neoplatonism' (Ph.D. thesis, University of Chicago, 1974), p. 8.
8. Azim Nanji, *The Nizari Isma'ili Tradition in the Indo-Pakistan Subcontinent* (Delmar, NY, 1978), p. 132.
9. For interfacing of some Ismaili and Jewish ideas in Fatimid Egypt, see J. Kraemer, *Maimonides. The Life and World of One of Civilization's Greatest Minds* (New York, 2008), p. 158.
10. W. Ivanow, *Ismaili Literature: A Bibliographical Survey* (Tehran, 1963), p. 11.
11. For a contextual approach to understanding Satpanth and the Nizari Ismaili tradition, see Ali Asani, *Ecstasy and Enlightenment: The Ismaili Devotional Literature of South Asia* (London, 2002), pp. 1–24.
12. Faisal Devji, 'Conversion to Islam: The Khojas' (unpublished paper, University of Chicago, 1987), p. 49.
13. According to Nizari Ismaili belief, the Aga Khans hold authority as Imams by virtue of being descendants of the Prophet Muhammad's daughter Fatima and son-in-law 'Ali ibn Abi Talib. Aga Khan III and Aga Khan IV are acknowledged as, respectively, the 48th and 49th Imams in direct descent from the Prophet.
14. Nanji, *Nizari Isma'ili Tradition*, pp. 72–77.
15. Wladimir Ivanow, 'Khodja', in *Shorter Encyclopaedia of Islam*, ed. H. A. R. Gibb and J. H. Kramers (Leiden, 1953), p. 256. Mumtaz Ali Tajddin Sadik Ali questions this commonly accepted derivation of the title Khoja but does not offer a reasonable alternative. He also claims that it was first used by Pir Satgur (*ca.* 11th century); see his 'Meaning of Khoja', in the *Encyclopaedia of Ismailism* (Karachi, 2006), p. 359.
16. J. C. Masselos, 'The Khojas of Bombay: The Defining of Formal Membership Criteria during the Nineteenth Century', in I. Ahmad, ed., *Caste and Social Stratification among Muslims in India* (New Delhi, 1973), pp. 1–20; and

Hatim M. Amiji, 'Some Notes on Religious Dissent in Nineteenth-Century East Africa', *African Historical Studies*, 4 (1971), pp. 603–616.
17. *Gazetteer of the Bombay Presidency* (Bombay, 1877–1914), vol. 9, part 2, p. 39.
18. Asani, *Ecstasy and Enlightenment*, p. 101.
19. Hamid Ali, 'The Customary and Statutory Law of the Muslims in India', *Islamic Culture*, 11 (1937), p. 355.
20. S. T. Lokhandwalla, 'Islamic Law and Ismaili Communities (Khojas and Bohras)', in S. T. Lokhandwalla, ed., *India and Contemporary Islam* (Simla, 1971), pp. 385–386.
21. On the tradition of *ginan*s generally, see Asani, *Ecstasy and Enlightenment*; Christopher Shackle and Zawahir Moir, *Ismaili Hymns from South Asia: An Introduction to the Ginans* (London, 1992); and Tazim Kassam, *Songs of Wisdom and Circles of Dance: Hymns of the Satpanth Isma'ili Muslim Saint, Pir Shams* (Albany, NY, 1995).
22. W. Ivanow, *Brief Survey of the Evolution of Ismailism* (Leiden, 1952), p. 29.
23. For a more detailed summary of doctrines in the *ginan*s, see Shackle and Moir, *Ismaili Hymns from South Asia*, pp. 20–24.
24. Ali Asani, *The Bujh Niranjan: An Ismaili Mystical Poem* (Cambridge, MA, 1991). Michel Boivin suggests that *ginan*s (such as the *Bujh Niranjan*) which employ a highly Persianized vocabulary may be more recent compositions, dating to the 18th and 19th centuries when there was a 'renaissance' in the *ginan* tradition associated with the 'Iranization' of Satpanth; see his 'New Problems Related to the History and to the Tradition of the Aghakhani Khojahs in Karachi and Sindh', *Journal of the Pakistan Historical Society*, 46 (1998), pp. 12–14.
25. Asani, *Ecstasy and Enlightenment*, pp. 54–70.
26. Mujtaba Ali, *The Origins of the Khojahs and their Religious Life Today* (Bonn, 1936), pp. 63–67.
27. Masselos, 'The Khojas of Bombay', p. 7.
28. J. Arnould, *Judgement of the Honourable Sir Joseph Arnould in the Khojah Case, otherwise known as the Aga Khan Case* (Bombay, 1867), p. 15; J. N. Hollister, *The Shi'a of India* (London, 1953), pp. 390–392.
29. Reginald E. Enthoven, 'Khojahs', in his *The Tribes and Castes of Bombay* (Bombay, 1920–1922), vol. 2, pp. 229–230.
30. Ali, *The Origins of the Khojah*s, p. 68; Hollister, *The Shi'a*, p. 389; *The Gazetteer of the Bombay Presidency*, 9 (1899), pp. 48–49.
31. Shackle and Moir, *Ismaili Hymns from South Asia*, p. 24.
32. Ivanow, *Brief Survey of the Evolution of Ismailism*, p. 20.
33. Tony K. Stewart, 'In Search of Equivalence: Conceiving of the Muslim-Hindu Encounter through Translation Theory', *History of Religions*, 40 (2001), pp. 260–287.
34. Amrita Shodhan, 'Legal Representation of the Khojas and the Pushtimarga Vaishnava Polities and Communities: The Aga Khan Case and the Maharaj

Libel Case in Mid-Nineteenth Century Bombay' (Ph.D. thesis, University of Chicago, 1995), p. 42.
35. Census Commissioner for India, *Census of India 1901* (Bombay, 1901), vol. 18: *Baroda*, part 1, p. 152, and *Census of India 1911* (Bombay, 1911), vol. 7: *Bombay*, part 1, p. 58.
36. Ali, 'The Customary and Statutory Law of the Muslims in India', p. 355.
37. As quoted in Amiji, 'Some Notes on Religious Dissent', p. 605.
38. Aziz Ahmad, *Studies in Islamic Culture in the Indian Environment* (Delhi, 1964), p. 156.
39. Ibid., p. 162.
40. Ibid., p. 163.
41. Reported in the *Bombay Telegraph and Courier*, 24 June 1947, as quoted in Amrita Shodhan, *A Question of Community: Religious Groups and Colonial Law* (Calcutta, 2001), p. 101.
42. Peter Hardy, *Muslims of British India* (Cambridge, 1972), p. 116.
43. Shodhan, *A Question of Community*, p. 38.
44. Barbara D. Metcalf, 'India', in *The Oxford Encylopedia of the Modern Islamic World*, ed. John L. Esposito (Oxford, 1995), vol. 2, pp. 190–191.
45. Asani, 'The Khojahs of South Asia', p. 159.
46. For a discussion of the reformist Faraizi movement in Bengal, see Rafiuddin Ahmed, *The Bengal Muslims, 1871–1906: A Quest for Identity* (Delhi, 1981), pp. 39–105.
47. Zawahir Moir, 'Historical and Religious Debates amongst Indian Ismailis 1840–1920', in M. Offredi, ed., *The Banyan Tree: Essays on Early Literature in New Indo-Aryan Languages* (New Delhi and Venice, 2000), vol. 1, p. 144.
48. Dominique-Sila Khan, *Conversions and Shifting Identities: Ramdev Pir and the Ismailis in Rajasthan* (New Delhi, 1997), and her *Crossing the Threshold: Understanding Religious Identities in South Asia* (London and New York, 2004).
49. Ali Asani, 'Muslims in South Asia: Defining Community and the "Other"', *Bulletin of the Royal Institute for Inter-faith Studies*, 2 (2000), p. 109.
50. Imtiaz Ahmed, 'Exclusion and Assimilation in Indian Islam', in Attar Singh, ed., *Socio-cultural Impact of Islam on India* (Chandigarh, 1976), p. 99.
51. Amrita Shodhan, 'The Entanglement of the Ginans in Khoja Governance', in T. R. Kassam and F. Mallison, ed., *Ginans: Texts and Contexts* (New Delhi, 2007), p. 171.
52. Shodhan, *A Question of Community*, p. 12.
53. Ibid., p. 86.
54. Hollister, *The Shi'a of India*, pp. 367–369.
55. Arnould, *Judgement of the Honourable Sir Joseph Arnould in the Khojah Case*, p. 17.
56. W. E. Hart, ed., *Report of Cases Decided in the High Court of Bombay* (Rajkot, 1907), p. 363.
57. *Bombay Law Reporter* (Bombay, 1908), pp. 409–495.

58. Aziz Esmail, 'Satpanth Ismailism and Modern Changes Within It with special reference to East Africa' (Ph.D. thesis, University of Edinburgh, 1971), pp. 197, 253.
59. Shodhan, *A Question of Community*, p. 101.
60. Wilfred Cantwell Smith, *Islam in Modern History* (Princeton, 1977), p. 20.
61. Hannah Papanek, 'Leadership and Social Change in the Khoja Ismaili Community' (Ph.D. thesis, Radcliffe College, Harvard University, 1962), p. 80.
62. Shodhan, *A Question of Community*, p. 111.
63. See Yohannan Friedmann, *Prophecy Continuous: Aspects of Ahmadi Religious Thought and its Medieval Background* (Berkeley, 1989).
64. Cynthia Salvadori, *Through Open Doors: A View of Asian Cultures in Kenya* (Nairobi, 1989), p. 232.
65. Diamond Rattansi, 'Islamization and the Khojah Isma'ili Community in Pakistan' (Ph.D. thesis, Institute of Islamic Studies, McGill University, 1987).
66. See Michel Boivin, 'The Reform of Islam in Ismaili Shi'ism from 1885 to 1957', in F. 'Nalini' Delvoye, ed., *Confluence of Cultures: French Contributions to Indo-Persian Studies* (New Delhi, 1994), pp. 197–216.
67. For Khojki script, see Asani, *Ecstasy and Enlightenment*, pp. 100–123.
68. Rafiuddin Ahmed notes a similar tendency among Muslims in Bengal in the late 19th and early 20th centuries: 'The craze for a Muslim, as distinct from Bengali identity, had its impact even on personal names. Poorer Muslims in Bengal traditionally had local first names indistinguishable from those of Hindus. These, to the ashraf and the mullahs, were unsuitable for Muslims ... the tendency was clearly in favour of Arabic and Persian names ... new-born Muslim babies were given appropriate Perso-Arabic names in the proper Islamic fashion ... and less-fortunate adults (were induced) to give up their Bengali names for "correct" Muslim ones.' See his *The Bengal Muslims 1871–1906*, pp. 112–113.
69. For this process in Pakistan, see Papanek, 'Leadership and Social Change in the Khoja Ismaili Community'.
70. The Qur'anic verses used include Sura 4:59, Sura 36:12, Sura 5:67, Sura 48:10, Sura 8:27.
71. On authorship and authority in the *ginan*s, see Asani, *Ecstasy and Enlightenment*, pp. 82–99.
72. For the role of the *ginan*s in Ismaili Khoja devotional life, see Ali S. Asani, 'The Ismaili *ginan*s as Devotional Literature', in R. S. McGregor, ed., *Devotional Literature in South Asia: Current Research, 1985–1988* (Cambridge, 1992), pp. 101–112.
73. Ali S. Asani, *The Harvard Collection of Ismaili Literature in Indic Languages: A Descriptive Catalog and Finding Aid* (Boston, MA, 1992), pp. 6–22.
74. Michel Boivin, 'Ginans and the Management of the Religious Heritage of the Ismaili Khojas in Sindh', in T. R. Kassam and F. Mallison, ed., *Ginans:*

Texts and Contexts (New Delhi, 2007), pp. 42–44.
75. See Khan, 'Rewriting the Ginans: Revolution and Resistance among the Imamshahis', in T. R. Kassam and F. Mallison, ed., *Ginans*, pp 103–116.
76. Shodhan, 'The Entanglement of the Ginans in Khoja Governance', p. 173.
77. Gauri Viswanathan, *Outside the Fold: Conversion, Modernity and Belief* (New York, 1998); see also Asani, *Ecstasy and Enlightenment*, pp. 13–20.
78. The methods that Lalji Devraj and his team used to edit texts need careful study. In the case of at least one *ginan*, the *Bujh Niranjan*, I have shown that in his edition of the text, some material was introduced that was not found in the original manuscripts. See Asani, *Ecstasy and Enlightenment*, pp. 91–92.
79. Shackle and Moir, *Ismaili Hymns from South Asia*, p. 16.
80. Ibid., p. 17.
81. Ibid., p. 16.
82. Amrita Shodhan suggests that Imam Begum was a controversial figure, especially for male members of the Khoja community who complained that their wives were so captivated by her that they neglected their household duties. See her 'The Entanglement of the Ginans in Khoja Governance', pp. 174–175.
83. For an attempt to 'Hinduize' the *ginans* among the Imamshahis, one of the subgroups of the Satpanthis, see Khan, 'Rewriting the Ginans', pp. 103–116.
84. Asani, 'The Ismaili Ginans as Devotional Literature', pp. 108–109.
85. Mumtaz Ali Tajddin Sadik Ali, *101 Ismaili Heroes* (Karachi, 2003), pp. 99–105.
86. 'Ali Muhammad Chunara, preface to first edition, *Nuram Mubin* (2nd ed., Bombay, 1950), p. 7.
87. Moir, 'Historical and Religious Debates amongst Indian Ismailis 1840–1920', p. 136.
88. Boivin, 'Ginans and the Management of the Religious Heritage of the Ismaili Khojas in Sindh', pp. 28–36.
89. In 1950 a second edition, revised extensively by Jaffer 'Ali Mohammed Sufi (d. 1961), was published by the Ismailia Association for India. Two further editions of the *Nuram Mubin* were published: the third edition appeared in 1951; the fourth, prepared by Sultan Nur Mohammed, was published in 1961.
90. The following discussion on transnationalization has benefited from Aly Kassam-Remtulla's thesis, '(Dis)placing Khojahs: Forging Identities, Revitalizing Islam and Crafting Global Ismailism' (AB Honors thesis, Department of Anthropology, Stanford University, 1998).
91. Ibid, p. 96.
92. For instance, in the late 19th and early 20th century, Aga Khan III encouraged the Ismaili Khojas to emigrate to East Africa to seek better economic opportunities after communities in Gujarat were hit by a severe drought and economic depression.

93. For the transnationalizing impact of the ethic of service among Nizari Ismailis, see Zahra Jamal, 'Transnationalizing Tradition: North American Ismailis Volunteering Abroad', unpublished paper presented at Middle East Studies Association Conference (November 2006), and her forthcoming dissertation on this topic to be submitted to the Department of Anthropology, Harvard University.
94. *The Constitution of the Shia Imami Ismaili Muslims* (1986), p. 6.
95. Ibid.
96. Ibid., pp. 12–13.
97. Ibid., p. 16.
98. Esmail, 'Satpanth Ismailism', p. 402.

6

The Socio-Legal Formation of the Nizari Ismailis of East Africa, 1800–1950

Zulfikar Hirji

At the dawn of the 19th century, few pundits could have predicted that within less than a generation large numbers of Ismailis from the Indian subcontinent would cross the western Indian Ocean to the shores of eastern Africa and go on to constitute one of the most vibrant and influential Muslim communities found in various parts of the African continent, including present-day Tanzania, Kenya, Uganda, Mozambique, Madagascar, South Africa, Congo, Rwanda, Burundi and the Ivory Coast. Certainly no one could have predicted that within 170-odd years a significant number of the children and grandchildren of these first waves of Ismaili migrants to Africa would once again be on the move to Western Europe and North America. While a comprehensive study of the Ismailis who settled in various parts of Africa remains to be written, this chapter examines the socio-legal formation of the Ismailis in East Africa from the advent of European colonization of Africa (*ca.* 1800) up to the emergence of nation-states (*ca.* 1960s). The settlement of the Ismailis in East Africa is but one chapter in a complex story of inter-continental movement and settlement continuing down through the generations. Arguably, however, this process demonstrates the manner in which the Ismailis and their leaders appropriated and adapted European forms of modernity in the colonial contexts of the western Indian Ocean.

Two initial observations should be made about the histories of Ismaili communities in Africa and elsewhere after the 1800s. First, these histories took place during a period when many world empires reached their apex and then gave way to independent nation-states. On the Indian subcontinent, from where the majority of the Ismailis who went to Africa originated, the British Raj gave way to the independent nations of India and Pakistan.

On the African continent, Britain initially 'scrambled' for African territories with other European powers including Germany, France, Portugal and Belgium. European imperial aspirations and the concomitant process of colonization eventually submitted to independent African nation-states including the East African nations of Tanzania, Kenya and Uganda – the areas where the Ismailis initially settled. Europe itself underwent profound socio-political changes during the 19th and 20th centuries. The Ismailis who migrated and settled on coastal and continental Africa were not immune to various geopolitical shifts and the resulting socio-cultural effects. In what follows, it is evident that the Ismailis and their Imams were responsive to these transformations and sought to put the community on a strong footing in this rapidly changing context.

The second observation that needs to be made about the history of the Ismailis who settled in Africa after the 1800s is that it occurred at a time when the Ismaili Imams had only recently emerged as public figures. It will be recalled that prior to the 1800s the Imams were based in Persia and for several centuries had limited contact with the various Ismaili communities in Central Asia, Afghanistan, the Middle East and South Asia. Many of these Ismaili communities had lived in varying degrees of isolation from their Imams and as a result had developed varied understandings and articulations of Ismailism in response to local and regional as well as social and cultural conditions. For example, many of the Ismaili communities on the Indian subcontinent, from where the vast majority of Ismailis who settled in Africa originated, adopted Ismailism sometime after the 13th century through the activities of a succession of Ismaili *pirs* (missionary-saints). Upon their conversion the appellation 'Khoja' was bestowed on some converts, the term being a Gujarati transposition of the Persian term *khwaja* meaning lord and master.[1] Until the 19th century these convert communities practised their faith in a dissimulated manner. Hence their Ismailism (religious beliefs and practices) displayed a complex interface with other traditions.

When the 46th Ismaili Imam, Hasan 'Ali Shah Aga Khan I (d. 1881), transferred his headquarters from Persia to India, the Khoja Ismailis came into full public view. For the next century and half, Aga Khan I and his successors, 'Ali Shah Aga Khan II (d. 1885) and Sultan Muhammad Shah Aga Khan III (d. 1957), proceeded to gather Ismaili communities on the subcontinent and elsewhere around them and over the better part of two centuries began to reform their social institutions and religious practices. These processes of reform have been continued by the present Ismaili Imam, Prince Karim al-Husayni Aga Khan IV (b. 1936), who succeeded to the Imamate in 1957. Part of the process of adaptation and change undertaken by the successive Imams in modern times involved establishing for the Ismailis in different parts of the world a framework of governance by which they could manage their communal affairs according to the tenets of Ismaili Islam and in tandem with the socio-political systems established in their regions of residence.

Because there are virtually no comprehensive contemporaneous accounts of the migration and settlement of the Ismailis in East Africa, various existing studies, including the present one, draw upon a limited range of primary sources including documents produced by officials of the state both in the colonial and nation-state periods, and a limited number of community documents including published compilations of the Imams' *farman*s (edicts/guidance) to members of the community, as well as the oral testimony of descendants of original settlers. In addition to these materials, the present study uses more fully the socio-legal documents produced by the colonial states in which the Ismailis featured, as well as the community's published constitutions. However, these sources need to be assessed judiciously, taking into account the context of their production and use. For example, European colonial records have to be read recognizing that colonial categorizations of individuals and groups according to race, religion or caste-group were what the socio-linguist Jan Blommaert has called 'artificial and imported socio-cultural entities, systems and structures', which might have limited or no relation to individual or communal self-understanding.[2] Thus, in the case of legal digests produced by the colonial courts in East Africa, a primary source for the present study, entries related to Ismailis are found under such headings as 'Khojas', 'Khoja Mahommedans', 'Khoja Ismailis', 'Ismailis', or 'Mahommedan Law'. Such categories reflect both the manner in which the colonial courts identified individuals and groups, but also the manner in which individuals chose to identify themselves in the setting of the colonial court. For example, when the term 'Khoja' is used on its own, it is unclear whether the individuals in question were Ismaili, Ithna'ashari or Sunni, as all three groups used the appellation 'Khoja' in the 19th and early part of the 20th centuries. In sum, any study of the social history of Ismaili communities in Africa after the 1800s is a complex endeavour requiring a judicious and critical use of a variety of materials from a limited number of diverse sources.

Background: The Ismailis in British India

The first substantial migrations of Ismailis from the Indian subcontinent to East Africa took place between the early 19th century and the first half of the 20th century.[3] These migrations coincided with the period when Britain was extending and adapting its own laws for use in its colonies and developing new legal processes to govern its overseas territories. First in India and then in various protectorates and colonies in Africa, Britain carried out a series of legislative experiments, the impact of which has continued to be felt in these regions to the present day.[4] The Ismaili migrations to East Africa also coincided with the time when the Nizari Ismaili Imams, starting with Hasan 'Ali Shah, Aga Khan I, relocated from Persia to India and began to consolidate a socially and culturally diverse body of followers on the Indian subcontinent and elsewhere.[5]

Amrita Shodhan has argued that during the 19th century, the interplay between the reformist activities of the Ismaili Imams and Britain's codification of India's peoples according to colonial understandings of caste, religion and sect transformed the Khoja *jama'at* (assembly or congregation) from a 'caste group' into a 'Muslim sect', the Khoja Ismailis. This transformation profoundly altered the Khoja identity and their forms of communal governance.[6]

Originally part of the Hindu Lohana merchant caste, the Khojas were a Gujarat-based urbanized or semi-urbanized trading caste that is thought to have adopted Ismaili Islam sometime between the 14th and 15th centuries owing to the missionary activities of Pir Sadr al-Din (d. *ca.* 1369–1416), who is also credited with giving the group the *khoja* appellation, which is generally held to be a transposition of the Farsi (Persian) term *khwaja*, meaning 'lord' or 'master'. Owing to their repeated persecution by Indo-Muslim rulers at different times in their history, by the 19th century the Khojas were conducting their religious and communal affairs in a secretive manner and (perhaps for some generations) were accustomed to living their lives observing varying degrees of *taqiyya* (precautionary dissimulation). Zawahir Moir has argued that in private, and particularly in the context of their *jama'atkhanas* (assembly or congregational halls), the Khojas recited the *ginans* (devotional poems primarily of a didactic and esoteric nature) composed by the *pirs* in various languages and local dialects of northern India including Sindhi, Gujarati, and Punjabi, and 'followed the Shi'a practice of offering prayer three times daily, professing faith in Allah, the Prophet Muhammad and Imam 'Ali'.[7] However, in public, 'many Khojas in Bombay and Gujarat bore Hindu names, dressed like Lohana Hindus and followed Hindu property law, but they also practised circumcision and mostly preferred to arrange their marriages and funerals through local Sunni *mullahs*'.[8] In this regard they were not unlike a number of other cognate groups on the subcontinent such as the Nizarpanthis, Imamshahis, Barmatis, Maulais and Shamsis, whose ancestors were also converted to Ismaili Islam by a succession of charismatic Ismaili *pirs*.[9] Their comparable ritual practices, mythologies and religious literature suggest that all these groups including the Khojas may be considered as adherents of the '*satpanth*' (true path), a tradition that interacted with and displayed a complex interface between Ismaili Muslim beliefs and practices and those of particular local forms of religion including Hinduism.[10]

Following Aziz Esmail,[11] Dominique-Sila Khan has suggested that the liminality displayed by the Khojas and other *satpanth* groups in terms of religious observances, as well as their strategic use of *taqiyya*, not only allowed such groups to escape persecution, but also enabled them to harness the intellectual resources of different traditions, manoeuvre between socio-cultural formations of caste and religion, and sometimes act as a bridge between them.[12] But in the 19th century the hitherto fluid religious expressions of Khoja identity became more problematic. At this time, Indian provinces came under British rule. British forms of governance in India were based on legal manuals that drew upon selected authoritative texts and customary practices of local groups. The processes undertaken to develop these juridical materials (or what collectively came to constitute 'Anglo-Indian law') betray the preoccupation that British officials such as Warren Hastings, the first Governor-General of British India (1773–1775), based at Bengal, had with determining the 'orthodox', 'pure' and 'pristine' forms of 'Islam' and 'Hinduism'.[13] These ideal forms were developed according to a Western European understanding of religion and the laws of religious groups. For example, with reference to Muslims, Carissa Hickling states that:

> British officials perceived in Islam a system of law which mirrored their own. Therefore, the *shari'a* was, for all intents and purposes, Muslim law to be directly equated with a set of legal prescriptions which could be used by British judges to rule on a complete range of personal issues. The 'sources' of Muslim law were identified as the Muslim Holy Book (*Koran*), the example of the Prophet (*sunna*), and the *shari'a*. Eighth and ninth-century scholars of the *shari'a* became the appropriate 'legal authorities' to consult. The opinions (*fatwas*) of these 'legal authorities' were treated as legal 'precedents', with their treatises being 'legal textbooks'.[14]

It was these types of processes that determined the direction that Britain's socio-legal project would take on the Indian subcontinent and elsewhere in the British Empire.[15]

When these laws began to be applied more widely throughout British India during the first half of the 19th century, some British officials began to recognize that there were many local groups whose practices and personal laws did not fall neatly into the prescriptive legal categories of 'Mohammadan' (Muslim) and 'Gentoo' (Hindu). Hence, in areas such as the Bombay Presidency, the legal system made allowances for liminal groups to continue operating as caste-based entities whose established traditions and customs prevailed, irrespective of the religious tradition (Hindu/Muslim) to which such customs could ideally be ascribed.[16] For the Khojas in particular the precedence of 'custom' or 'customary law' over 'religious law' was confirmed in the rulings of Justice Erskine Perry in two legal cases on female rights of inheritance that were filed in the Bombay High Court in 1847. In these cases Justice Perry ruled that the Khojas' 'Hindu derived custom' of denying females 'any share of their father's property at his decease' was to be upheld over what was conventionally outlined in the *shariʻa*. Perry's rulings were made even though the Khojas were classed as a Muslim caste-group and Aga Khan I had voiced his support for the application of the *shariʻa* in such matters through his representatives in the court.[17]

The 1847 law suit came at a time when Aga Khan I had begun to fully assert his right of leadership over the Khojas. He was publicly challenged by dissidents from within the Khoja collective, known initially as the *barbhai* (twelve brethren) and later as the Khoja Reform Party. These intra-communal challenges resulted in the *barbhai* backing a series of law suits against Aga Khan I which included the 'Great Khoja Case' of 1851 and the famous 'Aga Khan Case' of 1866.[18] The 1851 case, which was again tried by Erskine Perry, went against the Aga Khan, who had asserted his rights over communal property, religious dues and the appointment rather than election of *mukhi*s (treasurers or stewards) and *kamadia*s (assistant treasurers) in local Khoja *jamaʻatkhana*s. In this case, as in the case of 1847, Perry ruled in favour of customary practice. The 1847 and 1851 rulings would come to dog the Khoja Ismailis and their Imams in the years to come on both sides of the western Indian Ocean. In sum, during the first half of the 19th century, in matters of personal law and communal governance, some Khojas sought to uphold aspects of their liminal profile. If challenged they could rely on a sympathetic British judiciary to uphold a number of their customary practices, the opinions and assertions of the Aga Khan notwithstanding.

However, by the second half of the 19th century the situation changed. By this time India had fully become part of the British Empire, and the British were less tolerant of liminal groups and demanded more clarity about who was a Hindu and who was a Muslim. The changes in British policy clearly informed the rulings made in the Aga Khan Case of 1866 which was filed by the *barbhai* against the Aga Khan. On the face of it the case concerned a dispute between the *barbhai* and the Imam about property held by the Khoja *jama'at* in Bombay. However, the case was a more comprehensive challenge to the Aga Khan's authority over the Khojas on the part of the *barbhai*, whose members had been cast out of the larger Khoja collective of Bombay in 1862 as a result of refusing to sign a document circulated by the Aga Khan in Bombay that confirmed his authority as religious leader and outlined that the religious practices to be upheld by the community were to be those of the Shi'i Imami Ismailis. Thus during the hearings of the 1866 case, the *barbhai* claimed that the Khojas were Sunnis and not Shi'is so as to discredit the authority of Aga Khan I over them and his role in a range of their communal affairs including his right to collect religious dues from the members of the *jama'at* and have interest in their communal property. Despite the efforts of the *barbhai*, the court, presided over by Justice Sir Joseph Arnould, adjudicated in favour of the Aga Khan. Moreover it was in the text of Arnould's ruling that the Khojas came to be definitively classified as Ismaili Shi'is:

> A sect of people whose ancestors were Hindus in origin, which were converted to and has throughout abided in the faith of the Shia Imami Ismailis and which has always been and still is bound by ties of spiritual allegiance to the hereditary Imams of the Ismailis.[19]

This meant that Aga Khan I, who claimed direct descent from the Nizari Ismaili Imams of the Alamut period, was now legally recognized as the supreme religious leader of the Ismaili Shi'i Khojas and had the final authority in all their communal matters.

After the case, those who retained their opposition to the Aga Khan adopted Sunni Islam, and came to be known as Sunni Khojas. Others who had grievances chose to rejoin the Aga Khan's fold for a time, but they ultimately seceded from the Ismailis and turned to Ithna'ashari Shi'ism, forming the Khoja Ithna'ashari community. The Khojas who sided with the Aga Khan, the Khoja Ismailis, could now completely abandon all forms of *taqiyya* and their liminal mode of existence, and claim the histories and traditions of earlier generations of Shi'i Imami Ismailis as part of their religious heritage, particularly the tenet of having a living spiritual guide (*hazar imam*) in the person of the Aga Khan. Thus for Khoja Ismailis, the 1866 case marked the dawn of a new era in their development as a religious community in British India.[20]

For Shodhan, the dissolution of the Khoja collective and their socio-legal transformation from a caste-oriented collective with a somewhat fluid identity and multiple affiliations into a series of closely defined sects, each one of a particular religious tradition, meant that the Khojas, who hitherto had a strong tradition of self-governance, lost forever their ability to manage their affairs independently of the colonial state. The Khoja Ismailis were now defined and codified in the terms outlined by the British court and any disputes between their members could legally be dealt with by the British judiciary in terms accepted by the judiciary itself. Moreover, as a result of the 1866 case, the British court had provided the Imam of the Ismailis with the legal means to uphold formal membership criteria for the community and the terms by which his own authority over the Khoja Ismailis could be maintained without further challenge. In short, the Khoja Ismailis now became a socio-legal entity which the state could govern.

Juridical Connections: References to East Africa in Anglo-Indian Case Law

As mentioned above, the Khoja Ismailis of India were definitively recognized under British law in 1866 as a distinctive Shi'i Muslim sect under the leadership of Aga Khan I. During the court hearings, information was presented to the court about the contemporary demography of the Khoja Ismailis of India, which included some of the first detailed demographic information available on the Khoja Ismailis settled in Zanzibar on the East African coast. The court report states that:

> In Sind, as appears from the evidence in this case, they number 2,800 houses or families; in Kattywar about 5,000 families. In Cutch and Guzerat the numbers are not stated, but must be considerable; Bhuj, the capital of Cutch, having long been one of their principal seats. In Zanzibar (on the African Coast) there are 450 Khoja families – in Muscat 400 – and so on. In Bombay and its immediate neighbourhood they may probably number about 1,400 families, of whom about 400 side with the relators and plaintiffs, the rest with the Aga Khan.

> Beyond the limits of Bombay and its immediate neighbourhood no differ-

ence of religious opinion appears to prevail among the Khojas. All of the overwhelming majority of the Khoja community in all parts of India and the East, except Bombay, are the staunch adherents of Aga Khan: to take an illustration (which seems to be quite a fair one) from the evidence of witness no. 23, it appears that 445 out of the 450 families who compose the Khoja community of Zanzibar have recently [in 1861] signed a paper of adhesion to the Aga Khan and to the views he is understood to represent.[21]

While not explicitly stated in the judge's report, the court's admission of evidence from Zanzibar would have been legally permissible, as, by 1866 Zanzibar was effectively part of the British Empire, albeit with the Sultan of Zanzibar as its ruler.[22] The British had established a juridical presence in Zanzibar in 1839, and this 'jurisdiction was continued in the Treaty [between the Sultan of Zanzibar and Britain] of 1866'.[23] Although Indian settlers in Zanzibar were not regarded as British subjects until 1870, by 1866 the High Court of Judicature at Bombay acted as Zanzibar's court of appeal and 'had the power to "confirm and remit" the sentence and punishment imposed' in certain criminal and civil cases heard at the British Consul's Court at Zanzibar.[24] Certainly the court report suggests that evidence about the actions and opinions of members of the Zanzibar Khoja Ismaili *jama'at* was considered relevant on the basis that these families had migrated from India and formed part of what today might be called the 'Khoja Ismaili diaspora'.

What the court report also shows is that when Aga Khan I set out to secure his authority over the community in 1861 via petition, supporters and dissenters amongst the Khoja *jama'at* were to be found on both sides of the western Indian Ocean.[25] According to Hatim Amiji, there is a possibility that those families in Zanzibar who refused to sign their allegiance to the Aga Khan in 1861 may have been close business associates of the *barbhai* Khojas who raised the 1866 law suit.[26] For Amiji it is more certain that later secessionist movements and law suits filed in Zanzibar by members of the Khoja Ismaili community there were led by 'prominent Zanzibar merchants who had recently returned from India after being excommunicated and declared heretics by the Bombay Khoja [Ismaili] *jamat* in 1877'.[27] One of these suits will be discussed in due course below. Suffice it to say here that there were ongoing religious associations and economic ties between members of the Khoja communities in East Africa and India and that these may have underpinned some of the legal actions taken against the Ismaili leaders and community members on both sides of the Indian Ocean over the course of the 19th and 20th centuries.

Further evidence of the British courts' recognition of ties between the Ismaili communities in India and East Africa is made explicit in the case of 'Hirba'i vs Gorba'i', heard initially at the High Court of Bombay between 1873 and 1874 and then on appeal in 1875. This case, like the 1847 case mentioned above, involved female inheritance. On this occasion, it concerned the matter of intestate succession under Khoja Ismaili custom, specifically a mother's right to manage the estate of her deceased son over that of the widow in the event where there is no male issue.[28] Again, as in the Aga Khan Case of 1866, the judgement is informed by the practices and views of the Khoja Ismailis of Zanzibar, albeit with caveats.[29] For example, in the initial hearing in 1874, Judge Sir Charles Sargent stated:

> Now there is undoubtedly a considerable amount of evidence in this case to show that the great majority of the community consider that, according to the custom of their caste, the mother ought to have the management of the property in preference to a childless widow, and that that custom has (so far as there is any evidence before the Court) been invariably adopted by the *Jamats* of Bombay and Zanzibar, and also in all cases of private arbitration. The cases to which I have referred in discussing the evidence of the *Mukhi* and *Kamaria* establish this satisfactorily as to Bombay. With respect to Zanzibar, the evidence is, of course, not so satisfactory, because of the difficulty of testing the accuracy of the statements; but the witness who gave the information was a man of respectable position as a merchant, and he was confirmed by the *Mukhi* generally in this statement of custom, and in particular as to one of the instances cited by him. On the whole, looking at the close connection between the Khojas of Bombay and those at Zanzibar, I do not think I should be justified in disregarding that evidence.[30]

The assumption made by the judge was that the Khoja customs of Zanzibar were invariably the customs of those residing in India. The main issue here is that despite the case of 1866 in which the Aga Khan is recognized as the final authority of the community, in the case of certain customary practices of the Khoja Ismailis, such as inheritance, there remained the possibility of recourse to the British courts. The case not only shows the dialectical relationship between communal self-governance and colonial law, but also sheds light on the principles, i.e. customary law, which colonial law-making used to regulate communal practice. Hence in the appeal that followed in 1875, Chief Justice Westropp also upheld Khoja 'custom' over and above 'Hindu' or 'Muhammaden' law in matters of intestate succession. He stated:

> In considering a question of custom in a case among Muhammadans proper or Hindus we have always followed the doctrine laid down by the Privy Council, that the party seeking to establish a custom different from the ordinary law of his community, must provide that the custom is ancient and invariable, and considered to be legally binding.[31]
>
> Though the evidence at large is not such as in the case of Muhammadans proper or Hindus it would suffice to establish an ancient invariable custom, we think we must hold that it is sufficient to establish a custom in the community, such as this, placed midway between Muhammadans and Hindus. We think that, under such circumstances, the Court ought to act upon satisfactory proof that the custom has existed for a considerable time, and has been generally accepted by the great majority of the Khoja community.[32]

To add to this, the issue of which law governed succession among the Khoja Ismailis (and similar groups such as Memon Katchhis) in India had already been raised in 1847 in the case of 'Hirbae and Others *v.* Sonabae' heard by Perry.[33] According to Daftary, the position of Aga Khan I on this matter was that female inheritance among the Khoja Ismailis was to be governed according to Islamic law.[34] Notwithstanding this formal position by the Ismaili Imam, in 1847 Perry upheld Khoja custom which at the time followed the Hindu inheritance laws.[35] Indeed, with the arrival of Aga Khan I and his policies in India, the customary and legal affairs of the Khojas began to witness a transitional phase. Be that as it may, the role of custom seems to have been so important for Perry that in his final statement in the ruling, he reprimands 'the attempt of these young women [i.e. the plaintiffs] to disturb the course of succession which has prevailed among their [i.e. the Khojas'] ancestors for many hundred years' and asks them to pay costs 'as a price of an unsuccessful experiment'.[36] As we shall see, both the substantive aspects of the case and the principle of the judgement in favour of customary law, especially in matters of female inheritance, were to remain an issue for the Khoja Ismailis of East Africa in later decades.

Juridical Connections: References to India in East African Colonial Law

Zanzibar was where the British forged the first legal links between East Africa and India. As mentioned above, in 1866 Zanzibar became the site of the first British Consular Court. Subsequent developments reinforced Zanzibar's relationship to the High Court of Bombay. Between 1897 and

1914 the court at Zanzibar was a High Court which could hear appeals from other territories in East Africa. Despite its status, further appeals could be made to Bombay and finally to the Privy Council in England. However, after 1914, having gained further territory in East Africa (e.g. Kenya Colony and Protectorate, Uganda Protectorate and Tanganyika Territory), the British established a Court of Appeal for East Africa which held sessions in different parts of the region, and had direct and final appeal to the Privy Council in England. Although formal links to the High Court of Bombay were severed in the early decades of the 20th century, it was the introduction and continual use of Indian enactments (i.e. Anglo-Indian laws) related to both criminal and civil actions that had a lasting impact on British law in East Africa.

According to Morris, by 1902 'British East Africa had a body of Indian law covering the most important areas of litigation'.[37] The situation then began gradually to reverse itself when Indian acts were used to draw up local (i.e. 'African') ordinances and 'White settlers' demanded that English (and not Anglo-Indian) law be used to adjudicate their affairs. As a result, from the 1930s onwards, the East African courts relied less and less on laws made by the British in India, even though, in many parts of East Africa, certain Indian enactments remained in force well into the 1970s.

The impact of Indian enactments on the social formation of the Khoja Ismailis of East Africa becomes evident when examining cases reported in the various law reports of the higher courts of East Africa beginning in 1868, including the *East Africa Protectorate Law Reports* (E.A.L.R.), the *Law Reports of Kenya* (L.R.K), the *Law Reports of the High Court of Tanganyika* (T.T.L.R.), the *Law Reports of Uganda* (L.R.U.) and the *Zanzibar Protectorate Law Reports* (Z.P.L.R.).[38] These publications, like their counterparts in India (i.e. *Bombay Law Reports*), are law digests of judgements and relevant evidence presented in cases and appeals that came before a higher court; they do not provide a complete record of all the cases heard in a particular territory, nor do they contain all the evidence presented in any one case. These reports were meant to be used by British judges and magistrates and served to inform them about cases which had set precedents and orders in council that would assist law practitioners to understand their jurisdiction over matters of civil and criminal law, and matters of procedure.

With respect to cases concerning the Khoja Ismailis it is important to reiterate that such cases appear in the law reports' indexes under various categories including 'Khojas', 'Khoja Mahommedans', 'Khoja Ismailis', 'Ismailis', or 'Mahommedan Law'. These different ways of categorizing the Khoja Ismailis change over time and this may reflect the unsettled and evolving nature by which individuals and groups were identified by the court or the changing manner in which individuals and groups chose to identify themselves in the court settings. With these caveats in mind, there are, for example, 18 cases reported in the Z.P.L.R. and Z.L.R. between 1868 and 1950 that can be regarded as definitively relevant to the Khoja Ismailis (i.e. cases in which one of the litigants is identified as Khoja Ismaili or where the case report clearly suggests a Khoja Ismaili link).[39] In 13 of these cases the judgements make direct reference to cases heard at various Indian law courts including Bombay, Calcutta and Madras which shows the important role that Anglo-Indian case law played in adjudicating such cases.[40] However, it is curious that only one of these cases, 89/1894, makes direct reference to the precedent-setting cases mentioned above, i.e. the Aga Khan Case of 1866, the 1842 case of 'Hirbae v. Sonabae', and the (1874) 1875 cases of 'Hirba'i v. Gorba'i'. Two others, 674/1918 and 39/1939, make reference to the (1874) 1875 cases of 'Hirba'i v. Gorba'i'. It is instructive to study the first of these cases (89/1894) in greater detail in order to examine, among other things, how Indian enactments were used by British law-makers in East Africa.

The case 89/1894, 'Sakinabai, wife of Allarakhia Khaki v. Allarakhia Khaki', sought to determine if 'Khoja custom' or 'Mohammedan law' governed the amount of maintenance due (if any) to a wife who had left her husband, 'a Khoja merchant', because he had married a second wife who was the widow of his deceased brother. During the trial, the defendant, Alarakhia Khaki, pleads that under 'Khoja custom' the plaintiff, his first wife Sakinabai, is not entitled to maintenance or return of her valuables (i.e. ornaments) because she left his house with his consent and went to reside with her father. In his ruling, the judge invokes some of the Khoja Ismaili cases heard in India to show that they are not applicable to the case of 'Sakinabai Khaki v. Allarakhia Khaki'. He states that, 'Now all of these [Indian] cases are cases of property or inheritance, and the case before me is the status of wife, and the custom pleaded is repugnant to Mahommedan and Hindu law.'[41] Hence the judge rules against Khoja custom in favour of Mahommedan law and the defendant is asked to pay the plaintiff maintenance for the duration that she was away from the matrimonial home.

On the surface the judgement stands in clear opposition to the cases heard at Bombay in 1847, 1874 and 1875, all of which vigorously upheld Khoja customary law. However, as the judgement unfolds it becomes clear that the reason for the judge's ruling against custom is not related to a general disregard for custom. Rather, the judgement is made based on the fact that the judge regards the defendant's motives and actions to be underhand and the recourse to custom as opportunistic. In particular the report reveals that the defendant was no longer a member of the Ismaili Khoja *jamaʿat* of Zanzibar. Rather, at the time of the suit he was supported by members of the 'Soubaniahs', a Shiʿi Ithnaʿashari group of 400 adult males who had at some point in the past seceded from the original 1,200 adult males of the Ismaili Khoja *jamaʿat* of Zanzibar. The report also states that disputes between members of the two groups had lasted 'some 20 years' and the defendant and his supporters were using 'an ordinary case of maintenance by a wife to assume the dimensions of a test question in matrimonial questions of this kind as to the power of the [Soubaniah] Jamat [over that of the Ismailis]'.[42] Thus the judge suggests that even if the defendant had taken his grievance to the Khoja Ismaili *jamaʿat* for resolution rather than the court, having the status of an outcast would have limited the Khoja Ismailis from engaging with him and arbitrating on his behalf. For the same reason the judge states that 'even if custom had been established, it is doubtful whether it would have been binding on the defendant'.[43] In sum, the judge goes to great length to ensure that the proof required for customary law is retained and the custom is given its due respect; Khoja custom was not upheld in this case due to the religious status, motives and socio-religious affiliations of the defendant.

The specific judgement aside, the court report also reveals the positive regard the British judge had for resident Khoja Ismailis in Zanzibar. For example, the judge states that he considers members of the Zanzibar *jamaʿat* to include 'many of the most intelligent, active and influential members of the large Indian colony on the East Coast of Africa'.[44] Also, as indicated by the following two excerpts, the court report unwittingly provides information on how the Khoja Ismaili community in Zanzibar had governed itself up until 1894:

> There is, as is usual in all considerable Khoja communities, a Khoja Jamat established in Zanzibar. Of that Jamat there were original[ly] five heads, of whom the one only, viz. Remtulla Hemani, is living, but the mantles of the late heads have descended to their children and grandchildren, and some witnesses have spoken of these five heads as being authoritative as to Khoja custom. It has even been contended, or at least suggested, that Salehmahomed Jaffer has the most potent voice amongst this body of five because his grandfather, Sir Tharia Topan, was the most respected and influential member of the Jamat during his lifetime. The present five heads are, without the one exception I have referred to, new men, some

of whom have had very little experience of the ancient custom of Khojas and the rulings of the Jamat. I should prefer, in the matter of weight, the testimony of old and experienced men such as Lakha Kanji and Suliman Daood.[45]

...

In previous times this matter [i.e. the case] would have been left to the Jamat, and I take it that the evidence they have given shows not a custom which would have had force of the law, but the general and as far as I can see very reasonable rules which would have guided them. The Jamat had no written rules, but adjudication on the matters of this kind seems to have been left to them by members of the caste, and no doubt they would have come to act upon some more or less ascertained principle. This, moreover, would be in accordance with the principles of Mohammedian [sic] law, and the procedure which it pointed out under the Shiah law in the matrimonial disputes save that where two arbitrators would be appointed by the Judge (Mohammedan Law, by Mr. Justice Syed Ameer 'Ali, vol. II, p. 366) the matter would rather be referred to the Jamat, if the parties had not gone there of their own free will.

Based on this information, it would seem that up until 1894 the Khoja Ismailis in Zanzibar had a head-men system which (at least) served to adjudicate disputes within the *jama'at*.[46] This point is corroborated by an interview recorded by Sabrina Kassam in March 1982 with Rai Mohamedali Rashid (1915–after 1982), who after serving in various capacities in the Ismaili community in East Africa was appointed chairman of Mombasa Provincial Council in 1965. Rashid states that:

> *Punjebhai* is a *Cutchi* word and it denotes 'Brotherhood'. The term was used by Mowlana Sultan Muhammad Shah in 1899 during his visit to Africa when he appointed five *Punjebhais* (literally meaning five 'brothers') as leaders of the Jamat before 1905 when the first Supreme Council was established in Zanzibar. Later, a *Punjebhai* Committee of 30 to 40 enthusiastic members was formed under a Council whose motto was 'SERVICE'. After 1937 the Committee was given the name of 'Welfare Society' whose motto of 'Service-above-self' continues up to this day. Members were given the task of helping the Jamat in all possible ways, including finding employment. An analogy here would be the social welfare groups one finds in the Western world today, except that the professional psychological approaches were not employed in those days.[47]

The court evidence presented in Perry's report also indicates that up till 1894 there 'were no written rules' which governed the Ismaili *jama'at*.

There is, however, a clear suggestion that the judge felt it the role of the head-men and the *jamaʿat* to deal with disputes between their members in which 'established practice' and what the community understood as Shiʿi Ismaili law played their respective roles.

Hence the judge's detailed recollection of such forms and processes of communal self-governance among the Khoja Ismailis, and his positive portrait of the elders, whom he deemed to be the knowledge bearers of Khoja custom. But it also attests to how cautious colonial court judges were about intervening in communal matters and avoiding interfering with communal self-governance. However, it should be noted that the very nature of their presence and the use of the British legal systems by members of communal groups to deal with certain grey issues or to establish precedent put British law-makers in a powerful position to modify communal models. This would not go unnoticed by the communities themselves. Thus, willingly or not, ultimately the socio-legal apparatus of the colonial state and the cases presented before its courts were one means by which the British came to govern the Khoja Ismailis and similarly situated communities.

While cases concerning the Khoja Ismailis of Zanzibar provide some evidence of the role of Indian enactments in the governance of the East African community, the main evidence for the legal impact of specifically Indian Khoja Ismaili cases on East African law-making as a whole, and the Khoja Ismailis in particular, is to be found in the first volume of the Zanzibar Protectorate Law Reports (citing cases between 1868 and 1918), published in London in 1919. The appendix to the second volume contains the complete report of the Aga Khan Case of 1866 as it appeared in the Bombay Law Reports. In his introduction to the volume, Sir William Murison, the Chief Judge of Her Britannic Majesty's Court at Zanzibar, stated that:

> This remarkable judgement (which every Magistrate in Zanzibar should know by heart before he hears a Mahommedan case) details the history and division of the Mahommedan sects and the principal points in their rituals, and contains information which is invaluable to anybody concerned in the hearing of Mahommedan law suits in Zanzibar.[48]

This statement is prefaced by the judge's recognition of the 'polymorphous' nature of the law in Zanzibar wherein British common law as applied in England, Indian codes and acts, Mahommaden law, Hindu law and 'the multiplicity of customs prevailing among the various communities of Zanzibar' coexist.[49] In addition, whereas he regards Mahommedan law as the 'fundamental law of the Protectorate', Murison also argues about its limitations, particularly as it had been applied in India.[50] Finally, the judge notes Zanzibar's multilingual environment and particularly the prevalence of Gujarati speakers in the territory. As such, he regards Zanzibar as more of an 'Indian town' than 'the mainland towns, such as Mombasa and Dar-es-Salaam'.[51] It seems that Morrison's main point for those reading the volume is that governance in the Zanzibar Protectorate was a complex matter, and that locally placed British law-makers were charged to make proper use of the multiple juridical systems operating there. Moreover his remarks anticipate the role customary law was to play in the British government of their East African possessions from the 1920s onwards.

'Custom' was already a part of the law in India. In Africa it was Frederick Dealtry (Lord) Lugard (1858–1945), who was based in Northern Nigeria during the 1900s, who articulated custom as a principle of colonial governance and encapsulated it in the familiar term 'indirect rule'. Subsequently it was Sir Donald Charles Cameron (1872–1948) who put the principle into practice in East Africa for Tanganyika:[52]

> [Cameron] who had served in Nigeria under Lugard, defined the principle of indirect rule as that 'of adapting for the purposes of local government the institutions which the native peoples have evolved for themselves, so that they may develop in a constitutional manner from their own past, guided and restrained by the traditions and sanctions which they have inherited (moulded or modified as they may be on the advice of British Officers) and by the general advice and control of those officers'.[53]

According to Read, the actual application of indirect rule and customary law in the formation of colonial legal systems in East Africa and the management and application of cases was neither uniform nor simultaneously developed in all parts of East Africa; the juridical forms and processes varied, and they were implemented gradually and evolved according to the experiences of the British officials in the field.[54] What is of interest here is the extent to which such principles came to inform, by choice, coercion or default, the world views, social forms and practices of the communities to whom they were applied. While there are studies which examine this for 'indigenous' African communities, to the best of my knowledge there have been few, if any, detailed studies of how the development of colonial law in East Africa was received by and affected the peoples of Asia and the Middle East who had settled in the region.[55] Despite this gap in scholarship, it is not unreasonable to argue that groups who migrated to Africa from the Indian subcontinent, such as the Khoja Ismailis, took note of the manner in which the colonial power was governing and the principles they were using in order to develop their own modes of governance and laws.

Origins and Development of Ismaili Communal Governance in East Africa

Between 1905 and 1954 the Khoja Ismailis in East Africa published a series of documents called 'rules and regulations' for the community. The first of these was printed in 1905 by Hussein Chapkhano, Zanzibar, in Gujarati under the title *Khoja Shia Imami Ismailia Counsilna Kayadani Book: Prakaran Pelu tatha Biju* (The Rule Book of the Khoja Shia Imami Ismaili Council: Parts One and Two). It is this edition that was instated by Aga Khan III at Zanzibar along with the first Supreme Council for Africa during his second visit to the region in 1905.[56] A second edition of the rule book was published in Zanzibar in 1925 by Varas Mahomedbhai Remtulla Hemani, President of the Shia Imami Ismailia Supreme Council of Zanzibar, now under the English title *Rules of the Shia Imami Ismailia of the Continent of Africa*.[57] The third edition, *Rules of H.H. the Agakhan's Ismailia Councils of the Continent of Africa*, was published at Mombasa in 1937 by Count Abdulla Shariff Kanji, President of H.H. the Agakhan's Ismaili Supreme Council for Africa, and Count Gulamhussein Mahomed Nasser Jindani, Chairman of the H.H. the Agakhan's Ismailia Councils of the Continent of Africa. The fourth edition was published at Mombasa in 1946 under the title *The Constitution, Rules & Regulations of His Highness the Agakhan Ismailia Councils of Africa*, by His Highness the Agakhan Ismailia Supreme Council for Africa. Finally, the fifth edition was published at Mombasa in 1954 by the same Council under the title *The Constitution, Rules and Regulations of His Highness Aga Khan Shia Imami Ismailia Councils of Africa*. According to Daftary, this particular edition 'was promulgated after the Aga Khan had called a special conference of the East African councillors at Evian in 1952 to discuss the existing problems and the future prospects of the community'.[58]

A number of observations may be made about these rule books. First, it is important to note that much of the secondary literature inaccurately refers to *all* these publications anachronistically as 'constitutions'. Furthermore, Walji uses the term as if it were the book's title, i.e. 'the Constitution of 1905', as do others.[59] As is clear from the list above, the term 'constitution' first appears in the fourth of the series (1946) and in this instance it is used alongside the terms 'rules' and 'regulations'. Indeed it was only in 1962, under the aegis of the 49th Imam of the Ismailis, Prince Karim, Aga Khan IV, that His Highness the Aga Khan Shia Imami Ismailia Supreme Council for Africa at Nairobi published the book with the title *The Constitution of the Shia Imami Ismailis in Africa*. It is worth noting, however, that despite the books' changing titles (i.e. from 'rules and regulations' to 'constitution'), the community was asked by the Imam to regard these publications as 'constitutional' and 'authoritative'. For example, in a communication from Sultan Muhammad Shah Aga Khan III to the Ismailis of East Africa in 1924, the Imam requests 'all to obey Constitutional authority [of the] Supreme Council', the institutional body whose purpose and function was to govern the affairs of the community on behalf of the Imam in the local context.[60] In this regard it should, however, be noted that the Ismailis in Africa did not regard themselves as independent of the colonial state, but very much operating under a colonial system which allowed and encouraged communal self-governance. Thus it would be fair to say that the changing titles of the rule books from 1905 to 1954 (during the reign of the 48th Imam, Aga Khan III) is not merely a semantic issue but one of substance. The changes from 'rules and regulations' to 'constitutions' most likely reflect the manner in which the Ismaili community in Africa was itself developing and the changing context of the colonial state. On the one hand, the changes may reflect the attitude of a community that was going through the settlement process – still finding its feet in the context of a new land and the ever-expanding colonial state – as opposed to the term 'constitution' which implies a fully settled, coherent and self-confident group. On the other hand, it may have only been possible for the term 'constitution' to be used as British colonial rule began to give way to the independent nation-state.[61]

The second point to be made about the rule books is that the Gujarati-language rule book published in Zanzibar in September 1905 was unlikely to have been the 'first (Nizari) Ismaili Constitution' to be produced in the modern era.[62] According to Shodhan, a document in Gujarati entitled *Khoja Shia Imami Counsilni Kayadani Book* was published in Bombay by Eastern Press in 1901 and then republished in 1910 by the Bhandari Press, Bombay.[63] In terms of genre, the Ismaili rule books may not have been unique in the context of the Indian subcontinent as it came under British rule. Again, Shodhan has suggested that 'caste constitutions became a very regular feature of caste groups in India around the turn of the 19th century': they dealt with 'affairs that were seen as "private" or "internal" …. rituals of marriage were an important part of such discussions – how much should each side spend, what should be the give and take at such occasions'.[64] The Ismaili rule books, among a range of other statutes, also contain similar types of guidelines. However, Samira Sheikh has suggested that 'the Khoja Ismaili rule books appear to be far more developed and detailed than anything that is known to have been produced by other communities'.[65]

In terms of the origin and early development of the Ismaili rule books, it is also worth bearing in mind that in 1878 a Khoja Law Commission was established in Bombay to 'frame the Khoja Intestate Succession Act'.[66] This commission operated between 1879 and 1884 and its members included Aga Khan I and then Aga Khan II, a number of Sunni Khojas (i.e. those who had seceded from the Ismailis) and two European representatives.[67] Shodhan notes that controversies arose within the Khoja Ismaili *jama'at* in India because of the inclusion of seceders on the commission.[68] The commission 'failed to come to a decision about specific laws applicable to the community',[69] but the existence of such a commission suggests that there were already attempts to frame laws for the community in India, especially given the legal challenges faced by Aga Khan I from the dissident members of the Khoja collective. The presence of Europeans on the commission also indicates that some formalized interaction took place between the Aga Khans and British officials with respect to legal issues within the Khoja *jama'ats*.[70]

A third observation about the rule books relates to their distribution. As has been mentioned, the Ismailis of Africa were not the first Ismailis to have received such books nor were they the only ones. Within six months of instating the 1905 rule book in Zanzibar, the Ismaili community based in Gwadar (then part of the Sultanate of Oman and presently in southwest Pakistan) also received a Gujarati rule book under the title of *Khoja Shia Imami Ismailia Counsilna Kayadani Book: Bhag Pelo tatha Bijo*, printed in March 1906 by Induprakash Steampress, Bombay. Notably this document is almost identical with the one received in Zanzibar.[71] The Poona Ismailis also received a rule book entitled *Khoja Shia Imami Ismaili Council Poona Kayadao/Rules and Regulations of the Khoja Shia Imami Ismaili Council Poona*, published by Dahyabhai Velji Ahmadnagarvala, president of the Khoja Shia Imami Ismaili Council, Poona, and printed in English and Gujarati in Bombay for the Khoja Shia Imami Ismaili Council, Poona, on 25 July 1913, stating that it is the 'improved and enlarged third edition', suggesting at least two predecessors. A comparable document was published for the Ismailis in Rangoon entitled *Rules and Regulations of the Khoja Shia Imami Ismaili Council of Rangoon*, printed in English by Golam Rahman at the Standard Press, and *Khoja Shia Ismailia Councilna*

Kayada ane Kanuno, Rangun, in Gujarati for the Khoja Shia Imami Ismaili Council, printed by the Bombay Burma Press. Both English and Gujarati are bound into the same volume, a 'revised edition', published in 1914 at Rangoon. For the Ismailis of the Punjab and Frontier Provinces there was a volume entitled *Rules and Regulations of the Ismaili Jamats and Councils of the Punjab and Frontier*, printed in English only by Principal Gulam 'Ali Mukhi 'Ali Bhai Ismaili and Ismailia Supreme Council of the Punjab and Frontier, printed at the Mercantile Press, Lahore.[72] Thus within a very short period of time, many other Ismaili communities in the Indian subcontinent received rule books comparable to the one instated for African Ismaili communities at Zanzibar in 1905. It is worth considering that the speed and distribution of these books reflects a programmatic attempt on the part of the Ismaili Imam to develop structures and systems that would be recognizable to members of the community wherever they found themselves in the western Indian Ocean region and to the British colonial authorities that governed most of the region.

A fifth observation to be made about the rule books is that they were clearly meant for public consultation by all members of the community (not just for their appointed executives) and for the authorities at large. For example, Rule 244 (1925) states that 'These Rule-Books will be *publicly* sold at the various Council's [sic] Offices throughout Africa for Rs. 3/- per copy'.[73] Rules 30 and 31 (1946) make this point even more explicitly: '30. The Holy Laws shall be read publicly in the Jamathkhana at least once a year'; and '31. The book of these Holy Laws shall be obtainable at all Council offices throughout Africa on payment of Shs. 5/- per copy *to any one*.'[74] Moreover it is clear that the books could be shared with non-Khoja Ismailis. For example, Rule 26 (1946) states: 'These laws shall be produced without the slightest hesitation before the authorities whenever it is necessary to do so'.[75]

The requirement that the books be publicly accessible may also serve to explain why within a few years of their initial runs the books were published in both Gujarati and English. In East Africa, at least, the 1925 and 1946 versions were both published in English and Gujarati in the same volume.[76] The 1925 Gujarati version appears after the English with the title *Aphrika Khainda nee Sheeya Imami Ismailia Councilo na Kaydaao*, and the 1946 Gujarati version has the title *Aphrikanee Heejh Haines Dha Agakhan nee Ismailia Councilo na Bamdhashna, Niyamo, ane Kaydaao*. Both Gujarati titles are literal translations of the English titles. The 1946 version also makes clear that 'the laws published in English shall be recognized and accepted as legal and authoritative. The laws published in Gujarati shall be treated as a translation of the English laws.'[77] Moreover the 1946 version also makes clear that the 'laws' should 'be read literally and accordingly', and that 'in the event of any difference of opinion with regard to the interpretation of any rule of these laws, the interpretation decided upon by the Supreme Council shall be accepted, subject to appeal to Mowlana Hazar Imam His Highness the Agakhan'.[78]

On the one hand, the languages of publications are likely to have served the Khoja Ismaili immigrants from India who were predominantly Gujarati speakers, or were initially more familiar with Gujarati than they were with English. On the other hand, it may be suggested that books were produced in the English language in order to ensure that British officials could easily use these documents. However, on surveying all the law reports from the various East African territories, only one case, 23/1928 in the T.T.L.R., refers directly to the Khoja Ismaili rule books. It states that:

> the Ismailia Khojas in Dar es Salaam have established a distinctive political and social organisation for themselves. A publication called the Rules of the Shia Imami Ismailia Councils has been put in, which shows a Supreme Council at Zanzibar and also shows a sub-council at Dar es Salaam.[79]

That references to the rule books are not mentioned in other cases is somewhat curious. Nevertheless in the case above, the British judge does seem to have knowledge of the book and may have read it. In terms of this case, the existence of the rule book in 1928 confirms for the judge the community's organizational capacity and its ability to self-govern in a manner understood by the court, i.e. through a series of institutional structures.[80]

The sixth observation to be made about the rule books is that they show remarkable consistency over time (and between regions) in terms of their language, content and sequence of presentation. In terms of language, the books are full of juridical terms and processes. For example, in the 1925 book, rules 78 through 134 are all 'related to the procedure of cases'.[81] The excerpts below provide some flavour for the language employed in the books and the processes set out in them:

> 78. A person, desiring to bring a case before the Council shall do so by written petition …

> 87. In the course of the hearing of the case before the Council, all questions asked by the parties or by the members of the Council shall be relevant to the case. Should any irrelevant question be asked by parties or by a member the President shall have the power to refuse it. …

90. Judgements of all cases or decision in matters brought before the Council in Africa shall be written in as concise a manner as possible, that is, a summary of the facts and evidence, brought in the case, may be given in the judgement; but, the facts not pertaining to the case shall not be commented upon.

92. In cases or other matters that are being heard by the Council, first of all votes shall be taken to decide whether the case is proved or not proved or the party is guilty or not guilty. The votes of the majority shall be accepted. Should opinions regarding any punishment to be imposed or regarding any order to be made the decision of the side voting with the majority shall hold good.

99. Should it be necessary to summon a woman before the Council it should be done with due respect, questions be asked with all civility and she should be treated with proper consideration. ...

122. On presentation of the plaint by the plaintiff in a case before the Council summons shall be served on the defendant, a written statement may well be given by the latter. ...

With regard to the contents and sequence of presentation, each rule book begins with a preface which makes clear that the rules and Ismaili councils were created in order 'that the affairs of the Shia Imami Ismailia Jamats, residents of the different parts of the Continent of Africa, be managed and conducted systematically and regularly,'[82] stating that the Aga Khan was solely responsible for the appointment of office bearers in the hierarchy of community-based councils.[83] This is followed by rules of procedure for each council and the location of each. For example, Rule 33 (1925) states that:

Should a member absent himself from the [Supreme] Council consecutively for a period of six months without any reason, his absence shall only be excusable on the following grounds:-

1st. His having gone abroad.

2nd. Any serious illness which may have compelled him to keep indoors.

In the event of a member going to India his seat may be kept open for a period of one year, and in event of his going to other parts of Africa, for six months. No other reasons besides these will be considered excusable and he shall be suspended from the Council and the matter reported to

His Highness the Aga Khan by wire. Should the Council neglect to bring this clause into operation any Ismaili follower has the right to protest and lodge a complaint.[84]

These rules of procedure inform community members as to processes of appointment, reporting mechanisms, length of tenure for office-bearers, and rights and methods of appeal.[85] Then follow rules governing 'cases' and specific aspects of 'personal law' such as marriage, birth, divorce and social relations with members of the community. These rules provide information on many of the socio-cultural customs followed by the community of the day, especially with regard to marriage practices. For example, the rule book of 1925 states that:

> At Mombasa on 6th November 1905 His Highness the Aga Khan had declared that it was an act of virtue to curtail the expenditure after wedding etc., and therefore some of the office-bearers of the Jamat should set an example by taking the lead in this respect. In the same way all other office-bearers and every individual of our Community ought to assist, or in other words, co-operate with those gentlemen. By so doing they will be practising righteousness. All places ought to introduce such reforms for the good of their Community. (p. 47)

Such statements prompt our seventh observation: the rule books were meant for the social governance of the community. As is made clear in the rule mentioned above, appointed leaders of various councils were not only seen as adjudicators of the rules, but were enjoined to practise them in order to set an example. Hence, not unlike the principle of customary law, enacting custom appropriately was regarded as a measure of an individual's adherence to the laws of the community and allegiance to its leader. Hence Rule 91 (1925) states that:

> Should a Co-religionist in Africa commit a breach of the passed Rules and Regulations and act contrary to the customs etc. of the Community or ignore any resolution passed by the Council and should another of our Co-religionists report the matter, the Honorary Secretary, after securing evidence, shall send him a notice asking him to be present before the Council at a fixed time and give any explanations he may have to give in the matter. The Council, after due enquiries concerning the accused, shall give their decision.[86]

The eighth observation that can be made about the rule books is that they do not contain any references to other legal authorities, apart from the authority of the Imam of the time, Aga Khan III. As Shi'i Muslims, it is understandable that the rule books would not make reference to the law books produced by the Sunni schools of law (i.e. Hanafi, Shafi'i, Maliki, Hanbali). And given their attempts to distinguish themselves from the Ithna'ashari Shi'is, they would not make reference to the sources of their laws which include the works of learned *'ulama* such as 'Alama al-Hilli (d. 1325). Indeed in the rule books the final authority in all matters is the Ismaili Imam of the time.[87]

In sum, from 1905 to the 1950s, the Khoja Ismaili model of communal governance in East Africa developed in response to the changing socio-legal arrangements in the British Empire and in accordance with the Ismaili understanding of the Imam. Previously the Khoja Ismailis had had no such form of communal organization in their history, nor were there any set of rules comparable to those that were developed for them by the Aga Khans during the 19th and 20th centuries. The use of British colonial systems of governance that advanced through the reform programmes of the Ismaili Imams were not incongruent with Ismaili teachings about the role of the Imam who is constituted as a living spiritual guide. The concept of the Imamate as generally expounded in Ismaili thought makes clear the notion that the role of the *hazar imam* (present living Imam) or *imam-e zaman* (Imam of the time) is to offer the believers continual guidance on spiritual and temporal matters in accordance with the principles of Islam (as interpreted by the Imam), and in relation to the circumstances of the historical age and time. Hence it would be reasonable to assume that the era of initial Ismaili settlement in East Africa dictated a response by the Ismaili Imams that at the very least took into consideration the British colonial socio-legal systems which were in force on both sides of the western Indian Ocean – systems that were subsequently used by many modern nation-states as the basis of their own post-colonial formation.

Notes

1. See F. Daftary, *The Isma'ilis: Their History and Doctrines* (Cambridge, 1990), pp. 562–563; A. Asani, *Ecstasy and Enlightenment: The Ismaili Devotional Literature of South Asia* (London, 2002), p. 95.
2. J. Blommaert, 'Ujamaa and the Creation of the New Swahili', in D. Parkin, ed., *Continuity and Autonomy in Swahili Communities* (London and Vienna, 1994), p. 67.
3. General accounts of these migrations may be found in Shirin Walji, 'A History of the Ismaili Community in Tanzania' (Ph.D. thesis, University of Wisconsin, Madison, 1974); Aziz Esmail, 'Some Aspects of the History of the Ismailis in East Africa', unpublished paper presented to the

Historical Association of Kenya Annual Conference (1972), and Azim Nanji, 'Modernization and Change in the Nizari Ismaili Community in East Africa – A Perspective', *Journal of Religion in Africa*, 6 (1974), pp. 123–139. Additional information may be found in issues of *The Bombay Ismaili*, *Africa Ismaili* and other such community-based publications which were published in India and East Africa. For interesting oral testimony of Ismailis and members of other communities, see Cynthia Salvadori, *We Came in Dhows* (Nairobi, 1996). For classic surveys of Indians (also referred to as Asians), including Ismailis, in East Africa, see Robert G. Gregory, *India and East Africa: A History of Race Relations within the British Empire 1890–1939* (Oxford, 1971), and J. S. Mangat, *A History of the Asians in East Africa c.1886 to 1945* (Oxford, 1969).

4. H. F. Morris, 'The Reception and Rejection of Indian Law', in H. F. Morris and J. S. Read, ed., *Indirect Rule and the Search for Justice: Essays in East African Legal History* (Oxford, 1972), pp. 109ff; Richard Roberts and Kristin Mann, 'Law in Colonial Africa', in K. Mann and R. Roberts, ed., *Law in Colonial Africa* (London, 1991), p. 5.; A. Shodhan, 'Legal Formulation of the Question of Community: Defining the Khoja Collective', *Indian Social Science Review*, 1 (1999), pp. 147ff; A. Shodhan, *A Question of Community: Religious Groups and Colonial Law* (Calcutta, 2001), p. 6.

5. Daftary, *The Isma'ilis*, pp. 513ff. The period covered in the study coincides with the Imamates of Hasan 'Ali Shah, Aga Khan I, who first came to Bombay in 1848 and died there in 1881, Aqa 'Ali Shah, Aga Khan II (d. 1885) and Sultan Muhammad Shah, Aga Khan III (d. 1957). To get a sense of the diverse groups that existed under the Khoja Ismaili umbrella during this time, see for example, Zawahir Moir, 'Historical and Religious Debates amongst the Indian Ismailis, 1840–1920', in Mariola Offredi, ed., *The Banyan Tree: Essays on Early Literature in New Indo-Aryan Languages* (New Delhi and Venice, 2000), vol. 1, pp. 131–153.

6. Shodhan, 'Legal Formulation of the Question of Community', pp. 137–151; Shodhan, *A Question of Community*.

7. Moir, 'Historical and Religious Debates', p. 133.

8. Ibid., p. 133.

9. Dominique-Sila Khan, *Crossing the Threshold: Understanding Religious Identities in South Asia* (London, 2004), pp. 28–29, 46–50.

10. See Daftary, *The Isma'ilis*, pp. 484–485.

11. Aziz Esmail, *The Poetics of Religious Experience: The Islamic Context* (London, 1998), p. 40.

12. Khan, *Crossing the Threshold*, p. 50.

13. For a summary of these developments, see Carissa Hickling, 'Disinheriting Daughters: Applying Hindu Laws of Inheritance to the Khoja Muslim Community in Western India, 1847–1937' (MA thesis, University of Manitoba, 1998), pp. 61–65; Khan, *Crossing the Threshold*, p. 70.

14. Hickling, 'Disinheriting Daughters', p. 63.

Socio-Legal Formation of the Nizari Ismailis of East Africa 155

15. According to Samira Sheikh, a comparable situation may have occurred in the 17th century under the Mughals when other Satpanthi groups such as the Imamshahis had been forced to declare their religious affiliation, as were the Tayyibi Bohra Ismailis (personal communication, 13 June 2006).
16. Hickling, 'Disinheriting Daughters', pp. 65–66.
17. See Erskine Perry, *Cases Illustrative of Oriental Life: The Application of English Law in India* (2nd ed., New Delhi, 1988), p. 111; Hickling, 'Disinheriting Daughters', pp. 66ff, 72ff, 79ff.
18. W. E. Hart, ed., *Bombay High Court Reports Vol. XII, Part II* (1876), pp. 323–363. The same report also makes reference to a community in Zanzibar which paid allegiance to the Aga Khan via signature in 1861 (pp. 349–350). See Daftary, *The Isma'ilis*, pp. 515–516.
19. Arnould's judgement as reported in the Bombay High Court Reports (1876) reads that: [the Khojas were] 'originally Hindus of the trading class, inhabiting the villages and towns of Upper Sind ... [who] were converted [to Islam of the Shia Ismaili persuasion] by Pir Sadardin [a missionary from Khorasan sent by an ancestor of the Aga Khan] about 400 years ago', p. 343; see also Asaf A. A. Fyzee, *Cases in the Muhammadan Law of India and Pakistan* (Oxford, 1965), p. 545.
20. A previous court case heard in 1847 (see Perry, *Cases Illustrative of Oriental Life*, pp. 110–114), discussed below, concerning Khoja custom, paved the way for the 1866 case. Hart, ed., *Bombay High Court Reports*, pp. 323–363. Hatim M. Amiji, 'Some Notes on Religious Dissent in Nineteenth-Century East Africa', *African Historical Studies*, 4 (1971), pp. 605, 608, mentions a smaller community as early as 1820, based on evidence presented in the 1866 court case found in the Tanzania National Archives (G9/41) and a list of *mukhis* and *kamarias* for Zanzibar dating back to 1838, prepared by the Ismaili Association of Dar es Salaam. Shodhan, in *A Question of Community*, pp. 83–116, provides a detailed discussion of the court case based on the court records and other archival sources.
21. *Bombay High Court Reports* (1876), p. 344.
22. Comprehensive discussions of the history of Zanzibar's political evolution can be found in A. Sheriff, *Slaves, Spices and Ivory in Zanzibar* (2nd ed., London, 1990), and A. Sheriff and E. Ferguson, ed., *Zanzibar under Colonial Rule* (London, 1991).
23. William Murison, *Zanzibar Protectorate Law Reports, Volume 1 (1868–1919)* (London, 1919), p. viii.
24. Gregory, *India and East Africa*, pp. 21–22; Murison, *Zanzibar Protectorate Law Reports*, p. ix.; Amiji, 'Some Notes', p. 609, states that between '1840 and 1850, there was considerable controversy over whether the Khojas, Bhatias, were under the Sultan's jurisdiction or that of the British consulate'. If Gregory is correct then the situation was clarified by 1870. In any case, the admission of evidence from or about Zanzibar-based individuals would not have been permitted had there not been some legal reason to do so.

25. Amiji, 'Some Notes', p. 610. Amiji incorrectly states that this was the action of Aga Khan II.
26. Ibid., p. 610.
27. Ibid.
28. 'Appeal No. 255 [July 2, 1875]', in Hart, ed., *Bombay High Court Reports*, pp. 294–322.
29. Ibid., pp. 310, 313, 317.
30. Ibid., p. 317.
31. Ibid., pp. 319–320.
32. Ibid., p. 322.
33. Perry, *Cases Illustrative of Oriental Life*, pp. 115ff.
34. Daftary, *The Ismaʿilis*, pp. 514–515. According to Daftary, the Aga Khan's views on the matter were represented in court by his brother, Muhammad Baqir Khan (d. 1879).
35. Perry, *Cases Illustrative of Oriental Life*, p. 110.
36. Ibid., p. 129.
37. Morris, 'The Reception and Rejection of Indian Law', in Morris and Read, ed., *Indirect Rule and the Search for Justice*, p. 115.
38. *East Africa Protectorate Law Reports, Colony and Protectorate of Kenya Law Reports* and *Law Reports of Kenya London* (1897–1956); *Tanganyika Territory Law Reports, Dar es Salaam* (1930 and 1955–1959); *Uganda Protectorate Law Reports* and *Uganda Law Reports, Entebee* (1910–1974); *Zanzibar Protectorate Law Reports London* (1868–1918); *Zanzibar Law Reports, London* (1919–1961).
39. Z.P.L.R and Z.L.R [Case/Date]: 382/1878, 186/1880, 158/1880, [753/1891, 89/1894, 44/1902], 336/1903, [3/1907, 102/1907, 192/1907, 57/1908], 1,390/1908, [136/1911, 2,248/1913, 674/1918, 27/1935, 46/1936, 39/1939].
40. Cases listed above in square brackets are those in which the judgement makes reference to cases heard in India.
41. Z.P.L.R. (1919), Case 89/1894, p. 46. In the course of proceedings the judge refers to the Shiʿi Ithnaʿasharis as 'orthodox Shias' (Z.P.L.R. (1919), 89/1894, p. 46). However, it is unclear if the judge here is stating this as a matter of fact, or quoting a witness.
42. Z.P.L.R. (1919), 89/1894. p. 47. Additional information concerning the dispute turns up in *Mubarak Talika and Messages: Mowlana Hazar Imam's Guidance and Advice in Spiritual and Worldly Matters to Ismailis of Africa* (Shia Imami Ismailia Associations for Africa, 1955), Talika from Zurich, 26th June, 1943, p. 8, no. 29.
43. Z.P.L.R. (1919), 89/1894, p. 48.
44. Z.P.L.R. (1919), 89/1894, p. 45.
45. Z.P.L.R. (1919), 89/1894, p. 46. Note that Remtulla Hemani is the same as Varas Mahomedbhai Remtulla Hemani, President of the Shia Imami Ismaili Supreme Council of Zanzibar, who published the 1925 *Rules of the Shia Imami Ismailia of the Continent of Africa*.

46. There may be some significance in the number five here; it may have some relation to what the later rule books refer to as the 'Punjebhai' associations mentioned in the 1925 Rules, which literally means 'five brothers'.
47. *Africa Ismaili*, 11, 1 (March 1982), p. 44.
48. Murison, *Zanzibar Protectorate Law Reports*, p. xi.
49. Ibid., pp. ix–x.
50. Ibid., p. x.
51. Ibid., pp. x–xi.
52. See Lugard's *Dual Mandate in British Tropical Africa* (Edinburgh, 1922); see also T. O. Elias, 'The Evolution of Law and Government in Modern Africa', in H. Kuper and L. Kuper, ed., *African Law: Adaptation and Development* (Berkeley, 1965), pp. 187ff.
53. Morris, 'The Framework of Indirect Rule in East Africa', in Morris and Read, ed., *Indirect Rule and the Search for Justice*, p. 3.
54. James S. Read, 'Patterns of Indirect Rule in East Africa', in Morris and Read, ed., *Indirect Rule and the Search for Justice*, pp. 253–286 *et passim*.
55. Apart from Anderson's works on Islamic law in Africa (which tend to add yet another filter through which the law was developed), most studies have tended to focus on the political roles played by the 'Asian' communities. A good example is James Brennan, 'South Asian Nationalism in an East African Context: The Case of Tanganyika, 1914–1956', *Comparative Studies of South Asia, Africa and the Middle East*, 19 (1999), pp. 24–38.
56. Aga Khan III made nine visits to Africa during his lifetime: 1899, 1905, 1914, 1925, 1926, 1937, 1945, 1946 and 1948. I am grateful to Shahbuddin Gwadri for making a copy of this rule book available to me for review. The presence of this copy contradicts an article by Abdul E. Samji in the *Africa Ismaili*, 3, 10 (1970), pp. 73–76, which states that: 'Our first constitution was formed with the guidance of His late Highness Sir Sultan Mohamed Shah on 9th September, 1905 at Zanzibar although it was not printed till 1922 for general circulation', p. 73. Samji goes on to list new editions (under Aga Khan III) in 1925, 1937, 1946, 1947 and 1954, and then a complete revision in 1962 under Aga Khan IV (pp. 73ff).
57. Walji, 'A History of the Ismaili Community in Tanzania', pp. 86 ff., also refers to a set of by-laws of the Shia Imami Ismailia Councils of the Continent of Africa, published at Zanzibar in 1926 by Varas Mahomedbhai Remtulla Hemani. This was not available to me.
58. Daftary, *The Isma'ilis*, p. 525.
59. Walji, 'A History of the Ismaili Community in Tanzania', p. 76; Nanji, 'Modernization and Change', p. 128; Arif A. Jamal, 'Principles in the Development of Ismaili Law', *Yearbook of Islamic and Middle Eastern Law*, 7 (2002), p. 121. Daftary, *The Isma'ilis*, p. 524 is more accurate. The 1962 Constitution also is more accurate in so far as it revokes 'all other Constitutions and Rules ... governing the Community residing in Africa' (p. 2).

60. *Mubarak Talika* and *Messages*, p. 3.
61. It is possible that the change from 'rules and regulations' to 'constitution' may have had to do with the fact that the first language in which these documents were produced was Gujarati; the English terms 'rules' and 'regulations' are both direct translations of the Gujarati term '*kayada*'.
62. See Jamal, 'Principles in the Development of Ismaili Law', p. 121.
63. I am grateful to Dr Amrita Shodhan for identifying these documents for me (personal correspondence 12 January 2005). According to Shodhan, both publications were available in the Gujarat Vidyapeeth Copyright Library in Ahmedabad during the time of her research there in 1992.
64. A. Shodhan (personal correspondence, 6 July 2005).
65. Samira Sheikh (personal correspondence, August 2006).
66. Shodhan, *A Question of Community*, pp. 8, 15 n.12, 194, 201 n.9. Shodhan's evidence comes from documents housed in the Maharashtra State Archives and the *Nuram Mubin* of Chunara Vazirmohammad Janmohammad (1st ed., 1936; 4th ed. 1961); Daftary, *The Isma'ilis*, p. 517. Aga Khan II was also appointed to the Bombay Legislative Council in the 1880s, as was his successor Aga Khan III, who was appointed a member of the Legislative Council in November 1902 and served on it for two years. See Daftary, *The Isma'ilis*, pp. 519–520.
67. Shodhan, *A Question of Community*, p. 8.
68. Ibid., p. 15 n.12.
69. Ibid.
70. It is unclear whether similar 'rule' books were drawn up for Ismailis residing in Persia, Syria and elsewhere during this period, see Daftary, *The Isma'ilis*, pp. 533ff.
71. I am grateful to Shahbuddin Gwadri for making this document available to me.
72. I am grateful to Rizwan Mawani for alerting me to the presence of copies of the Poona and Rangoon rule books in the British Library. I should also like to thank Dr Perwaiz Hayat for providing me with a copy of the Punjab rule book. The front page of the copy is damaged and hence is missing the exact publication date, but the content and form are almost identical to those of Poona and Rangoon, suggesting a similar date of publication.
73. *Emphasis added*. 1925: 244, p. 70.
74. *Emphasis added*. 1946: 30, 31, p. 75. See also 1925: 73, p. 25.
75. 1925, p. 25; 1946: 27, p. 74.
76. I assume that the 1901 version was similarly published in both English and Gujarati; Walji does not mention this. The copy I have seen of the 1957 version is only in the English language.
77. 1946: 27, p. 74.
78. 1946: 29, p. 75.
79. T.T.L.R., vol. 1 (1930), p. 57.
80. T.T.L.R., vol. 1 (1930), p. 59. By extension, a person's authority in court was

judged according to their place and length of service in the Ismaili councillor hierarchy, and it would appear that members of the community knew this as well. Thus two of the witnesses summoned by the court are referred to in the report as 'leading members of the Khoja community', and when providing testimony these members claim authority by stating their long service as members of the Ismailia Council.

81. 1925, pp. 27–29; cf. 1946, pp. 30–38, and 1954, pp. 26–33.
82. 1925, p. 3. Virtually the same wording is used in 1946, p. 1, and in the Preface of the 1954 book.
83. Of the three books I have seen (1925, 1946, and 1954) none includes statements 'outlining the status of the Prophet Muhammad and the Ismaili Imams' as stated by Jamal, 'Principles in the Development of Ismaili Law'. For example, the 1946 rule book simply clarifies that the person being referred to as Mowlana Hazar Imam in the book is none other than H.H. the Aga Khan, 'who is known amongst his followers by the following names: "Hazarat Mowlana Dhani Salamat Datar, Pir Salamat, Sarkar Sahebi, Sarkar Saheb, Huzur, Huzur Pur Nur, Hazar Jomo, Dhani Salamat, Hazar Imam, Dhani Pir, Agakhan ..."' (pp. 1–2). By contrast, the 1962 Constitution does begin with a statement about the Prophet Muhammad as the last Prophet of Allah, that ʿAli is the first Imam of the Shia Imami Ismailis, and then goes on to describe the status of the Imam of the time (p. 1).
84. 1925, p. 15.
85. It is remarkable that such a complex and sophisticated system of rules and procedures was received, understood and digested by the majority of Ismailis in East Africa, who only a few decades earlier had probably been poor farmers and small-scale traders.
86. 1925, p. 30.
87. See Daftary, *The Ismaʿilis*, pp. 299ff, for the development of the Bohra community in India, and J. N. D. Anderson, *Islamic Law in Africa* (2nd ed., London, 1970), pp. 326–327, for Bohras in East Africa and their laws.

7

Communities of Tradition and the Modernizing of Education in South Asia: The Contribution of Aga Khan III

Shiraz Thobani

Between the late 19th and early 20th century, the idea of modern education, which had before then attained only limited practical realization, came to be given institutional form in an increasing number of national contexts, an endeavour in large measure impelled by the project of the modern state. As part of this process, difficult choices needed to be made, by politicians, policy-makers, as well as community leaders, on the alternative paths that had opened up for the reform of education. Out of necessity, these options required engaging with contentious issues, such as the respective responsibilities of the state, local bodies and religious organizations in the control of public and private education, the degrees of educational access and opportunity to be offered to different social classes, and the forms of knowledge which the school curriculum ought to contain. At a more general level, the choices expressed on these issues were directly inspired by, and ultimately bore consequence for, the overall ideal and character of schooling that was espoused by competing interests in society. The debates that raged on these and other related concerns in various contexts during this formative period call into question the claim that the concept of 'modern education' was a given, that it had been consensually and decisively framed as a social contract, and that the act of modernizing education simply called for the implementation of a preconceived blueprint.

An important corollary ensues from the above point. The unsettled venture of schooling, whose every major aspect was subject to question in this particular period, must lead us to view with reservation the commonly held and unquestioned assumption that modern education was a commodity crafted, in its entirety, in one specific locality of the world and duly exported to the rest of the globe. Given that this was a period of rapid and sweeping historical change, initially one of high imperialism and then of its escalating decline, when the political destinies of both industrial and emerging states were affected by domestic dissent and foreign threats, we find educational policies being vigorously contested in both these parts of the world. In more specific terms, decisions on institutional control, social opportunity and school knowledge had to be negotiated with major interests in countries seeking self-determination, just as they had to be in Europe.

What these contexts alert us to is that the history of education in the modern age, whether we are considering Europe or the colonized world, cannot be read simplistically as a confrontation between 'modern' and 'traditional' modes of education, but demands a nuanced grasp of the complex engagement between the diverse parties who were getting to grips with the need to strike a delicate balance between generational continuity and social change. Under these circumstances, such concerns prompted the recasting of conventional categories of education and a desire to make sense of nascent ones, including deliberating on their reciprocal relationship, which all necessarily called for the exercise of political and intellectual sensibilities.

In this chapter, I wish to probe into the process of the conceiving of education in the modern period from a situational perspective by examining the case of the Nizari Ismailis in British India, a community of tradition situated in this particular context amid several intersecting spheres of influence – Muslim, Indian and colonial – yet seeking also to reassert its own distinctive Shiʻi identity through its historical link with the wider Nizari Ismaili community. More specifically, I will consider the perspectives and positions articulated by the Ismaili Imamate on the modernization of education in South Asia, primarily in the early part of the 20th century, paying particular regard to the social and political contexts of the time.

Muslim Revivalism, Colonial Policy and Educational Pathways

Following the 1857 Indian Revolt, with the formal transfer of power from the East India Company to the British government, a new political space opened up in the Indian subcontinent in which questions that Muslims had previously sought to address became accentuated. What was to be their political status and role in a state which was no longer under Muslim rule, and which appeared unlikely to recover its former position in this

Communities of Tradition and the Modernizing of Education 163

new phase of history? What relations were they henceforth to establish with the British, on the one hand, and the Hindu majority on the other? And, most crucially, what role was Islam to have as a source for religious law, moral guidance and a social code in a colonized context? Confronted with these questions that would affect their future destiny, Muslim reformists took it as a matter of necessity to set out new paths for their communities that would best serve their interests in the changed political circumstances.[1]

Education, inevitably, became a central consideration in this programme of regeneration, conceived of as a potent agency for effecting the desired social renewal. We can identify here at least three distinct approaches to education that emerged in this period, representing what were ultimately fundamental, if contrasting, responses to the socio-political issues facing the Muslim communities of the subcontinent, and all of which became embodied in centres of higher learning set up by pioneering revivalists in the late 19th century: the traditionalist moral populism of the Deoband Dar al-'Ulum, the liberal modernist elitism of the Muhammadan Anglo-Oriental College at Aligarh, and the pan-Islamic clerical solidarity of the Nadwat al-'Ulama at Lucknow.[2]

The first of these approaches was adopted by the traditionalist 'ulama who, coming to terms with the reality of British rule in India, set their hope on the revival of Muslim communities in the subcontinent through a renewed commitment to and observance of Islam, to be realized largely through institutionalized education. In adopting this stance the 'ulama were in effect seeking to compensate for the displacement of the Mughal social order by substituting for it the ideal of a moral community, defined by pious commitment, ritual observance and codified behaviour.[3] A reconstituted *madrasa*, in the form of the Dar al-'Ulum established at Deoband in 1867, aimed to produce a new generation of 'ulama who, grounded in traditionalist Islam, would graduate as prayer leaders, preachers and teachers, disseminating their learning to the Muslim population at large.[4]

An alternative vision of the Muslim presence in India put forth by Sir Sayyid Ahmad Khan proposed, on the other hand, an active engagement of Muslims with colonial rule. If the question that stood before Muslims in the aftermath of 1857 was their status under a reconfigured system of rule, Sayyid Ahmad was convinced that their condition could not be ameliorated simply through a puritanical revival. If the quality of life of the Muslim masses was to be uplifted, it demanded an altogether new breed of modern leaders who could place themselves at the helm of social and political change in colonial India, and who, from this wider vantage point, could steer Muslims towards a better destiny.[5] With this aim in mind, Sayyid Ahmad set up the Muhammadan Anglo-Oriental College in Aligarh in 1875 at the heart of his educational project, offering a contrasting model of higher education for Muslims, the college's adopted name symbolic of and aspiring towards a confluence of multiple influences. The overall thrust was on liberal education within an Islamic context which would create not scholars immersed in the minutiae of tradition but public intellectuals engaged with the political and social realities materializing around them. Proposing what was, for its time, a bold paradigm, Sayyid Ahmad was intent on Aligarh College becoming a pioneering institution where Islam could be studied as a subject of intellectual enquiry, thus spurring the revitalization of Islamic thought. On this vital aspect, however, he was forced to concede to the *'ulama* when faced by their intransigence on the reform of religious education.[6]

In direct opposition to traditionalist revivalism and liberal modernism, and attempting to overcome the deficiencies of both, the Nadwat al-'Ulama saw the interests of Muslim communities best served by religious scholars steeped in the high classical texts of Islam, and who needed to be reconnected historically and geographically with the wider pan-Islamic legacy beyond the subcontinent. Seeking to bridge Deoband and Aligarh, Nadwa aimed at producing *'ulama* who could attain a fairly high level of mastery in classical scholarship, but who would also, by acting as spokesmen for the Muslims, be empowered to engage politically with their colonial overlords. Committed to the idea of producing a unified body of religious scholars in India to defend Muslim interests, Nadwa found itself contending with the intractable problem of procuring clerical solidarity and consensual understanding among diverse Muslim traditions.[7]

In all these three prominent paradigms of educational reform that emerged in the late 19th century, we can discern attempts at addressing major concerns pertaining to the welfare and progress of Muslims in colonial India. Critical issues, such as the link between government and community institutions, the profile and quality of leadership required by Muslims, the weight to be given to mass and elite education respectively, and, lastly, the relationship between 'modern' and 'traditional' disciplines in the curriculum, elicited contrasting measures from the three movements. We ought not to underestimate here the formidable nature of the challenge the early reformists took upon themselves in setting up new pathways for the educating of their Muslim constituencies, given the exigencies and complexities that confronted them. To say the least, it called for a spirited resolve to take on the responsibility of pioneering educational reform in uncertain times, but it also demanded, above all, a clear vision of an educated Muslim community and the place it needed to assume in the future of South Asia.

Despite these ground-breaking reformist moves, the prospects for the education of the Muslim population at the dawn of the 20th century remained bleak, weighed down as they were by near universal illiteracy on the one hand, and restricted by limited forms of higher education on the other. The plight of Muslims was compounded additionally by the passing of the first wave of reformers who had been at the vanguard of social and educational change, leaving a vacuum of leadership that needed filling with some degree of urgency. It was also in this period that swiftly changing socio-political conditions put the educational choices made by the earlier reformers to the test, when the implications of their particular approaches became more fully apparent. The Muslim leaders who emerged in the early decades of the new century were now faced with the difficult issue of whether to continue sustaining the founding initiatives of their predecessors, give fresh impetus to former ideals, or, more radically, set out new directions altogether for the education of Muslims.

A significant change in colonial policy on education in India at this juncture added, to what was already a complex issue, one more complicating factor of which the new leaders were forced to take heed. The year 1898, in which Sayyid Ahmad Khan died, marked the closing of one chapter in the history of Muslim education in colonial India. At the same time, it saw the inauguration of a new phase of educational policy with the appointment of Lord Curzon as the viceroy of India, who came resolved to reform Indian education as a matter of the highest importance. However, it was apparent that beneath a paternalistic desire to improve the general welfare of the colonized subjects lay an ulterior motive to assert greater control over the educational system, in both the public and private sectors, a desire prompted by allegations that the schools and colleges were inciting young Indians to sedition and rebellion against the British. It was argued with rising alarm that the spread of education, in collusion with other privileges and liberties, was undermining the very foundations of British rule and driving it into a 'shifting and unstable quagmire of sham Radicalism and anti-English feeling'.[8]

As a consequence, Curzon's efforts during his seven years as viceroy, from 1898 to 1905, involved introducing a raft of measures regulating all tiers of education. This marked a turning point in British educational policy in India which, until then, had observed the principle of *laissez-faire*, on the premise that it was not in the state's interest to intervene directly in education and that indigenous responsibility for schooling ought to be encouraged as far as possible.[9]

In the overall policy framework, the colonial government appears to have seen that it was to its advantage to support Muslim claims for greater education, allegedly in a bid to counter-balance the growing influence of the Hindu educated classes. As far back as 1871 the government had officially recognized concerns related to the education of Muslims, what it came to label as their 'educational backwardness', regretting that 'so large and important a class should stand aloof from co-operation with our educational system', and, in a bid to redress this situation, issued a resolution that sought to encourage English education among the Muslims. A commitment was made towards the promotion of secondary and higher education in Muslim constituencies, the inclusion of Arabic and Persian literature as part of this education and the appointment of qualified Muslim teachers in English schools.[10]

Despite the official enquiries and recommendations, the majority of the Muslim population continued to lag behind the Hindus and other communities, by no means in all parts of India but in areas which were predominantly rural and isolated. Disconcertingly, if government measures were proving to be ineffective in resolving this problem, so too were communal efforts. The educational strategies adopted by Muslim revivalists in the late 19th century had failed to alleviate, in any substantial measure, the mass illiteracy endemic to rural communities. The socio-economic status of Muslims, on the whole, remained largely stagnant in the early years of the 20th century, as did institutional development. The proposal to transform the college at Aligarh into a Muslim university had suffered a severe setback with the death of Sayyid Ahmad in 1898, throwing into question the commitment to create a modernized higher education institution for the Muslims of India that would also be a catalyst for the reform of primary and secondary education. The challenges that confronted the new Muslim leadership now appearing on the Indian national stage at this juncture were formidable, to say the least.

Prominent in this new leadership was the 48th Ismaili Imam, Sir Sultan Muhammad Shah, Aga Khan III, who came to assume a distinguished role not only in his inherited capacity as the spiritual head of his community and as a representative of Muslims in South Asia and other parts of the world but also as an international statesman. In 1896, at the age of 19, he visited the Aligarh College while travelling in northern India, where he had the occasion to meet Sir Sayyid Ahmad Khan who was then almost an octogenarian and in the final years of his life. Recalling this event decades later in his memoirs, the Aga Khan wrote: 'This was the origin of what was for many years one of the crucial concerns of my life – my interest in the extension and improvement of Muslim higher education, and specially the college and university at Aligarh.'[11] Six years later, in 1902, he found himself called upon to preside over the All-India Muhammadan Educational Conference, a central forum for the discussion of educational problems facing Muslims which Sayyid Ahmad had established in 1886. In his presidential address, cognisant of the far-reaching social implications that the endeavour of education held for the Muslims of India, the Aga Khan stated:

> We are, if I understand the purpose of this Conference aright, considering what in modern times are the ideals we must hold before our people and the paths by which they attain them; and upon the right answer to these questions depends no trifling matter, ... nothing less than the future of Indian Moslems.[12]

With this future destiny of Muslims very much in mind, the young Aga Khan redirected the attention of his audience to the pressing need of founding a Muslim university through the conversion of Aligarh College to university status, revitalizing an agenda that was to dominate the Conference for virtually two decades until this aim was finally realized in 1920. From these early beginnings, well into the first half of the century, the Ismaili Imam was to provide overall guidance on the issues concerning education not only for Muslims but for the Indian population as a whole.

The Aga Khan made use of a variety of platforms to voice his concerns on, as well as suggest possible solutions to, aspects of education requiring special attention. As a member on the Imperial Legislative Council between 1902 and 1904, during Curzon's viceroyalty, he found himself in a position in which he could discuss the needs of Muslims specifically, and those of Indians in general, while raising pertinent questions on the policies drafted by the colonial administration. He also contributed periodically to discussions on Muslim education in the All-India Muhammadan Educational Conferences, delivering keynote addresses to this forum in 1902, 1911 and 1936.[13] He dwelt on the subject of education on numerous other occasions, in his campaigns for raising funds for Aligarh University, in his addresses to Muslim leaders in India, East Africa and South Africa, as well as in the *farmans* or guidance he gave to his own Ismaili community. He also wrote at length on mass instruction and higher education in his early work, *India in Transition*,[14] and later reminisced about his role in the establishment of Aligarh University in his memoirs.[15] Viewed collectively, the speeches and writings of the Aga Khan, spanning a period of over half a century, are a valuable source for understanding the Ismaili Imam's position on education as a Muslim leader in the formative decades of the 20th century.

In engaging in the debate on education, the Aga Khan, like the other leaders of his time, had necessarily to contend with diverse forces influencing questions on Muslim education – colonial, nationalist and communal – forces that were intricately linked and assumed shifting relations with each other with the changing circumstances. In those turbulent times, it required all the tact and diplomacy the new Muslim leader could muster to rise above the factious and vested interests of conflicting parties and to draw attention to the broader goals which needed to be pursued. Finding himself strategically positioned amid these intersecting spheres of interest, the Aga Khan was ideally located to put forward a broad vision of Muslim education that took into account the different forces and influences actively at work on the subcontinent.

It is interesting to note that the issues which most concerned the Ismaili Imam were the very problems which underlay, in both European and colonial contexts, the defining of modern education – those centred on, but by no means restricted to, the management of education, social access and curricular emphasis. In the analysis below, I examine the nature of the problem that each of these concerns posed for Muslims in the context of colonial India, and the particular perspectives put forward by the Aga Khan, which collectively suggested to Muslim communities an alternative conception of education to the paradigms that had been elaborated in the late 19th century.

The Imperial State, Educational Governance and the Dual System

Perhaps the most contentious issue in the modernizing of education, faced by both established and emerging nation-states in the period under consideration, was the nature and extent of control that should be exercised over the educational system by the state, religious organizations and other voluntary bodies. It needs to be recognized that historically, in various regions of the world, religious communities had wielded considerable influence for centuries over mass education through communal instruction, divulging confessional teachings on their particular faiths to the young, with some inclusion of rudimentary literacy skills. In the modern period, with governments assuming greater control over public welfare, the question of the management of education turned into a source of conflict between marginalized religious groups and the state. In France the clash between state and church, culminating in the secularization of education in the late 19th century, and the sectarian grievances over state schools and religious instruction in England in this same period, provide clear examples of the struggle to demarcate areas of control between the public and private spheres of education.[16]

In British India we find a similar attempt by the colonial state, from 1898 onwards, to exert its control on education through a greater imposition of its will over the schooling of colonized subjects. The fundamental issue at stake in this case, linked to the question of the management of education, was nothing less than the very survival of British rule in India. In pursuing this goal the new administration under Curzon sought to bring both public and private schooling under greater colonial supervision, aiming to check the threat of the subversion of education by those keen to further the nationalist cause. The rationale put forward by the colonial administrators, advanced to some extent as a front for their underlying political objectives, was that there ought to be fewer grant-aided secondary schools and colleges so as to deliver a better quality of education. Similarly private schools, which were rapidly proliferating in this period, and which represented attempts by Indian communities to compensate for the lack of government provision, were perceived by the colonialists as needing to be assimilated into the state system or requiring better regulation. However, the demand for education proved to be too overwhelming to curb the increase of either public or private schools throughout India.[17] Moreover the secular, non-denominational system of state education enforced by the colonial administration made it necessary to permit religious communities to set up their own private educational institutions if communal tensions and grievances were to be avoided.

For the Muslims, perhaps more so than other communities in India, the question of the administration and control of education in the colonial context raised serious questions of how their young were to be raised. Between 1854 and 1898 the *laissez-faire* policy observed by the British had led to the emergence of a dual system of education for Muslims, with government schools on one side constituting the public domain, and, on the other, the *maktab*s and *madrasa*s, reduced essentially to Qur'anic schools, falling by default into the private sphere. The expansion of the *madrasa* system alongside government schools exposes an unsuccessful manoeuvre by Muslims to challenge the public–private dichotomy by promoting a system of education in which their children would be raised wholly within an Islamic framework of values. In selecting this path community leaders were of the opinion that Muslims ought to pursue a strategy of self-reliance, resulting in the *madrasas* failing to take advantage of the range of learning experiences, social exposure and vocational opportunities public schooling offered.[18] At the same time, however, there was not, generally speaking, the will to exploit the full potential of any private mode of schooling in which a more inclusive form of education could have been created in curricular and social terms.[19]

In effect traditionalist Muslims held that state education would compromise the integrity and identity of their young if non-Muslim pupils and teachers were present in their school environment, and if subjects not previously taught in the traditional curriculum were to be included. The public space pertaining to schooling could not be conceived of in pluralistic terms, for little commerce could be countenanced between the specifically denominational and the broadly heterogeneous environments in which Muslims lived. This stance may have derived from an exclusivist notion of faith which finds popular expression in the idea that Islam is 'a total way of life', and which at times is too readily carried over as a regulatory code into social institutions and communal relations. Since state education was under the control of the colonial administrators, the private sphere remained for the traditionalists the sole means of furthering their interests, realized through the separation of domains of knowledge as well as social groups, and the introverted proselytizing of Islam that became constrained, at the level of elementary education, to memorizing the Qur'an by rote.

How best to educate the young in a dual system of education was a dilemma that the Ismailis, like other communities in British India at the turn of the 20th century, could not ignore. From the outset the Aga Khan adopted a far-sighted but pragmatic view of this duality, seeking in it creative opportunities for social progress and advancement. Accepting the reality of India as a modern state, though a colony of the British Empire at this time, he resolutely affirmed the vital role that state education had to play in the emerging society of this region, recognizing that numerous communities were too impoverished to school their young with their own meagre resources, and that it was only the state which was in any position to make provision for universal education in India.[20] He therefore lobbied the colonial government to express a greater commitment to the educating of the masses of the people under its care, urging the Legislative Council to be more generous in its expenditure on education.[21] It was all too evident to the Ismaili Imam, from contemporary examples of countries in other regions, that the destiny of the state could no longer be considered in isolation from the education of its people.[22]

In adopting this position, the Aga Khan was affirming a principle that today is universally taken for granted and constitutes the very foundation of modern education, namely that the state is responsible, in the main, for the provision and maintenance of education. By definition, public education in non-authoritarian societies mandates that it be above the control of any specific group with its vested interests, enabling children to receive education without the fear of religious or political indoctrination. This, at least, is the ideal, and we have to acknowledge here that state education today leaves much to be desired. Yet, whatever its deficiencies, the public domain of education is a promising arena for encounter and dialogue among the young. Of equal importance is exposure to the general education it affords, which holds forth the prospect of broadening the outlook of young minds by opening them to the wider world. In calling upon the state to assume its proper responsibility in education at the turn of the 20th century, the Aga Khan was embracing these possibilities while recognizing the as yet untapped potential of public education as an indispensable agency for national development and social coexistence.

Public education by itself, however, was clearly not sufficient to serve the needs of all the diverse constituencies that made up colonial India – private schooling, too, could make a contribution to the emerging society. The concept of private education upheld by the Aga Khan was not the insular, communal *madrasa* system proposed by the traditionalists; in truth, he found much wanting in the 'old-fashioned Maktabs and Madrassahs which continue to give a parrot-like teaching of the Koran'.[23] He became committed, instead, to a concept of private schooling that was non-denominational in its overall policy, on the one hand, being open to children of all backgrounds, regardless of their faith, culture, gender or financial status, and, on the other, oriented towards providing education of a superior quality to the young. The first three Aga Khan schools were opened in Zanzibar in 1905, in Dar es Salaam in 1906, and in Mundra, India, in 1907, eventually leading to the founding of over 200 schools in Africa and Asia during the first half of the 20th century.[24] The setting up of these private schools was based on the view that whilst such institutions would be owned, financed and managed largely by different communities, this condition ought not to preclude them from respecting the principle of open access, making learning available to all who were in need of it. Being community-centred endeavours supported by the Imamate, the Aga Khan schools initially catered largely to Ismailis, but in opening up with passing years to an increasing number of children from other communities, whether Shi'i or Sunni, Hindu, Christian or Sikh, these schools became an invaluable public space within the private domain.

In essence then, the dual system of education, rather than being perceived as divisive by the Ismailis, was used to society's benefit and advantage by exploiting the strengths of both domains. Universal state-funded education as a social institution was accepted as essential to the development of the state, since it was designed to provide a common foundation of learning for the vast majority of the population. The private system, on the other hand, would be increasingly recognized for its versatility in offering innovative programmes and specialized services, thus acting as a catalyst for change in the public sector.

The dual system is not without its pitfalls, of course, and in the worst cases can engender divided societies in which privileged minorities or communitarian tendencies foster segregated school systems. However, private education can also become a potent means of breaking down social barriers if based on pluralistic principles, a stance that the Ismailis embraced at an early stage. Indeed the dual system came to be upheld as a close partnership between the public and private spheres, through which voluntary contributions complemented and enhanced the social welfare endeavours of the state. This was consonant with the emerging philosophy, in this period of political upheavals, that there was prudence in sharing the control of education between state and civil society. This was the best safeguard a society had against the abuse of education arising from the concentration of power in a single absolute authority, an approach the ramifications of which would become starkly clear with the rise of fascism and totalitarianism. In this framework of partnership, communities of tradition had an important role to assume as civil bodies in contributing to the good of the whole, a position embraced unreservedly by the Aga Khan and one which was far removed from the sectarian insularism and power politics of education that emerged among traditionalist and fundamentalist religious groups of the 19th century.

Social Access, Universal Education and the Elite

If the control of schooling was one of the major issues in the defining of modern education, the question of social access in this period was no less prone to controversy and dispute. In the industrializing nations, the policy of access had been translated, at the level of principle, in terms of the ideal of universal education, but in policy and practice had become heavily determined by class interests. While primary education was generally made available to the working classes by the end of the 19th century, the provision of secondary and higher education remained largely confined to the upper and middle classes, a situation which continued well into the 20th century. The division of education along class lines in Europe arose from a complex group of factors – historical, political and economic – whose interplay could be discerned in the ruling class's attempts to address growing anxiety about the increasing threat posed by the labouring masses to the political and economic *status quo*. There was a grudging recognition that if socialist uprisings were to be prevented from turning into bloody revolutions, political power in democratic states would have to be conceded to the proletariat, sooner or later, if only because of their numerical superiority. However, while the *idea* of universal education became acceptable as a means of purchasing social stability and political enlightenment, it was applied with more than a little reservation to the privileged sphere of secondary and higher education which, to a large degree, remained the preserve of the elite, since it provided an entree to the worlds of power and wealth.

In British India a parallel dichotomous policy arose on social access to education, based in this instance more along racial rather than class lines: one form of education for the colonial overlords and another for the colonized subalterns. Curzon's policies at the turn of the 20th century acknowledged, to some extent, the need for expanding primary schooling in India, but secondary and higher education, as we have noted, were viewed as clear threats to imperial rule, producing lawyers, intellectuals and activists who were increasingly demanding national independence.[25] While the colonial administrators themselves were in most cases the product of the public-school system and Oxbridge colleges, having received a form of education geared towards creating politicians, statesmen and career diplomats, this same form of education was looked at askance and generally frowned upon, if not altogether discouraged, in the Indian context. The creation of an elite class in India, in this age of high imperialism, was viewed with suspicion, and when it did arise, the Indian graduates failed to attract the same level of acceptance in colonial society as the British, finding themselves to be no more than, in fulfilment of Macaulay's expectations, 'a class of interpreters' between the colonialists and the colonized masses.

Despite these constraints, the Muslim leadership of the late 19th century succeeded in establishing a limited number of colleges of higher education, in centres such as Aligarh, Deoband and Lucknow. We have noted the difficulties faced by these colleges in producing the educated elite that the Muslim communities required, unable to reconcile in their aims, policies and programmes the political and religious conceptions of leadership. At the same time, the question of primary school education remained inadequately addressed, pre-empted by the setting up of Qur'anic schools that failed to reduce the high level of illiteracy among Muslims. This sharp disjunction between the two poles of elementary and higher schooling was, needless to say, caused by the lack of an overall integrated policy of education for the Muslim communities. The outcome at the turn of the century, in the absence of firm state support for universal education, was that millions of Muslims, alongside Hindus and other communities, were deprived of a basic education, whilst the privileged few being trained in the handful of Muslim centres of higher education were either detached from the masses, or, if in contact with them, ill prepared to initiate programmes of social regeneration.

The reluctance on the part of the leadership, both colonial and Muslim, to approach education as a continuous and progressive development from early nurturing to higher tutelage bore serious implications not only for individual growth but for social progress as a whole, an issue that was of deep concern to the Aga Khan. Alerting the policy-makers to the implications of this lack of continuity, he advised them against tackling the problem of education in India in a piecemeal fashion and placing undue emphasis on one tier of schooling at the expense of another. Rather, the most effective means of resolving the dilemma, in his view, was to address both lower and higher education simultaneously, in a way in which a natural balance could emerge between the two. 'A system of education working up from the bottom and down from the top concurrently,' he suggested, 'must surely find the centre of its gravity and enormously promote the interests of India.'[26] The two ends of schooling were integrally linked to each other, and, recognizing that without a sound foundation of primary education a system of higher education would become difficult to sustain, he warned that '[n]o solid superstructure can stand safely on softer soil'.[27] To link the two tiers of education, he advocated applying the principle of meritocracy, whereby the most promising of primary level pupils would be able to advance to secondary schools and then on to university.[28]

Drawing attention to the need for elementary schooling, the Aga Khan stated repeatedly that the way to lift not only Muslims but millions of other Indians all over the subcontinent out of their severe poverty was through the institution of universal primary education, a case he vigorously argued at various political levels. As early as 1903 we find him making the following plea to the Imperial Legislative Council, reflecting his conviction that mass education was the first charge on a modern state:

> My Lord, has not the time come for the commencement of some system of universal primary education, such as has been adopted by almost every responsible Government? The extreme poverty of this country has recently been much discussed both here and in England, and all sorts of causes have been found and given to explain the undoubted fact. But, my Lord, in my humble opinion the fundamental cause of this extreme poverty is the ignorance of the great majority of the people.[29]

Both the material progress and spiritual fulfilment of the masses depended on their access to basic education:

> Most of the ills of India can be ascribed to the general want of knowledge. ... The small proportion of literacy to the whole uninstructed mass ... is appalling. ... The poverty and disease so general in India is largely attributable to mass ignorance. ... From higher standpoints this weight of mental destitution is a grievous handicap. It renders the mass of the people incapable of real spiritual culture ... and tends to degrade religion in all its varied forms to the level of an unreasoning superstition.[30]

The general education of the common people was also essential if they were to be prepared for political participation. Until the Indian educational system became more universally accessible, the Aga Khan argued, the average Indian would be ill equipped to form opinions about public questions, making the illiterate susceptible to political manipulation and agitation.[31] The colonial administration, in his view, ignored the education of the masses at its own peril, neglecting a boundless source of human capital that could be put to constructive purpose if possessed of requisite skills and knowledge. Nation-building was an impossible project to realize if the vast majority of the population did not have the means to rise above the debilitating conditions in which they found themselves. 'If less drastic measures are taken,' the Aga Khan warned presciently in 1918, 'India will remain handicapped by general ignorance when the economic world position, after the war, provides her with extraordinary opportunities for development.'[32]

The concept of mass education upheld by the Ismaili Imam was an inclusive one. He was all too aware of the inequalities suffered by disadvantaged social groups seeking to gain access to schools. As long as these discrepancies existed, he argued, it would be difficult to attain the level of social cohesion required for a nation to exist, a concern he voiced in his address to the All-India Muhammadan Educational Conference in Delhi in 1911:

> The colossal ignorance of the Indian masses militates against uniting them as a nation. ... I firmly believe that primary education should be free and compulsory, and it should be so devised that its benefit may extend equally to the minorities, as to the majorities of the Indian communities. ... [I]f it is to be efficacious and serve the noble purpose which it is intended to do, then it must be free from all and any taint of an invidious distinction between one category of poverty and another.[33]

While the necessity for universal primary education was beginning to gain greater acceptance from governments across the globe, it had yet to be implemented fully, not only so as to embrace minority groups but also by taking full stock of the neglected problem of female education. The question of the education of girls, which is implicit in the term 'universal education', received scant attention in this period. The Aga Khan was one of the few Muslim leaders in India drawing attention to the vital need for the education of women, and, where resources were limited, perceiving it as deserving precedence over male education. He pointed to the immense benefits that could accrue from educated mothers who were better placed to pass on knowledge and skills to their families. He also foresaw the impending changes in society when women would be called upon to make an equal contribution alongside men to social progress and national development. With these considerations in mind, he made a strong plea for the application of compulsory and free education for both boys and girls, including its fair apportioning between them, impressing upon policy-makers the requirement that 'progress towards general education should everywhere be based on the equitable principle of not permitting the enormous disparity between the literacy of the two sexes to continue.'[34]

Universal primary education, for both boys and girls, was only one pole of public provision, however, through which social advancement could be procured. The other was that of higher education, which needed to deliver a yield of leaders, thinkers, scientists and professionals of the highest calibre if a society was to realize its true potential. Mass education, by itself, was not adequate for bringing about social reform if it lacked political direction and professional support. In upholding the necessity for higher education as a complement to mass instruction, the Aga Khan avoided the elitist inclinations reflected in the purposes some of the earlier Muslim reformists ascribed to institutions of advanced learning. The elite were not perceived as a class unto themselves, removed from and oblivious to the plight of the masses, but located within the very heart of society, from where they could make an enduring material, intellectual and moral contribution to social progress.

In the context of traditional communities, if graduates were to be of use to their people, centres of higher learning had to draw their inspiration and ideals from their historical roots:

> It must be our aim in founding our University, not to produce at a great cost merely an institution where the wisdom of the East and the science of the West may be acquired and degrees conferred upon the meritorious, but to found an institution that will play the same part in the life of the [Muslims] of India, as do the great Universities in Europe in the life of the Europeans. But one must remember that to copy any model must mean an ultimate failure; for an institution must be in keeping with the traditions and historic circumstances of the people it desires to serve.[35]

It was with this aim in mind that the Aga Khan devoted himself, with great zeal and by mobilizing the support of other Muslim leaders, to converting Aligarh College into a fully fledged Muslim university, an aim that was finally fulfilled in 1920. In being raised to the status of a modern university, Aligarh College avoided to some extent the course adopted by the traditionalist *madrasa*s which, in essence, and despite the reforms undertaken, ended up as little more than theological seminaries, being preoccupied with the propagation of religious sciences to the neglect of pioneering scholarship in a wider array of fields.

In his campaign for a Muslim university, the Aga Khan strenuously countered the criticism that Aligarh would be narrowly sectarian, reassuring his critics that its graduates would go forth 'through the length and breadth of the land to preach the gospel of free enquiry, of large-hearted toleration and of pure morality'.[36] He urged from the outset that Sanskrit be taught at Aligarh, together with the history and evolution of Hindu civilization, religion and philosophy, so that Muslims could better understand their Hindu neighbours.[37] In this spirit he gave his wholehearted support to the proposal of a Hindu university at Benares as a parallel venture to the Muslim university of Aligarh. Events, however, were to force the political landscape in India to change dramatically in the interwar years, and then especially after the end of the Second World War, culminating in the partition of the subcontinent into India and Pakistan. Reflecting in his memoirs on the role that Aligarh played in the creation of Pakistan, the Aga Khan wrote:

> Often in civilized history a university has supplied the springboard for a nation's intellectual and spiritual renascence ... we may claim with pride that Aligarh was the product of our own efforts and of no outside benevolence; and surely it may also be claimed that the independent, sovereign nation of Pakistan was born in the Muslim University of Aligarh.[38]

Looking back on this achievement, the Aga Khan gave due recognition to the political consequences of the establishment of Aligarh University, but he also drew attention to its real calling as a centre aspiring to rekindle the ideals and values of the Islamic faith.[39] This vision of higher education for Muslims, together with his adherence to the principle of universal primary education, informed the heart of his project for the modernizing of Muslim education in colonial India. The Aga Khan's stand on a broad access to education, based on egalitarian principles, sought to bridge the divide that had appeared in this period between the masses and the ruling classes in Europe and other regions. This hope of opening up access to learning, at both elementary and higher levels, may appear to be idealistic in the context of the time, given the reluctance of the colonial government to invest seriously in Indian education, and the demographic reality of the subcontinent which required the provision of very large numbers of schools and teachers in order for the goal of universal education to be achieved. Despite these obstacles, the Aga Khan stood by his belief that the denial of education, as much to the few as to the many, led ultimately to social deficiency and degeneration, as did those forms of education divided by race, class or gender.

Forms of Knowledge and Curricular Divides

Issues on the control of and access to education were crucial to the defining of modern education. No less was the question of the curriculum, posing the problem of what forms of knowledge were to be considered relevant for emerging societies in the new age. In Europe a prolonged debate raged in the 19th and early 20th centuries on the weight to be accorded to classical studies, on the one side, and on the other to 'upstart' disciplines such as the sciences and modern languages, not recognized previously as legitimate subjects in the school curriculum. The conflict between classical humanism and modern subjects crystallized in the 19th century along class lines, with the former, by virtue of its association with aristocratic breeding in the past, being considered the preserve of the elite, whereas the latter, supposed as dealing essentially with technical knowledge and skills, became initially assigned to vocational schools catering largely to students from the lower classes. In the main it was not until the second half of the 20th century that the ideal of a balanced curriculum, underpinning a broader concept of liberal education and striving to override class divisions, would gain firm acceptance among policy-makers.

In British India, school knowledge was looked upon with increasing suspicion by Curzon's colonial administration, as noted earlier, and attempts were made to regulate what was taught in schools and universities through greater control over the official syllabuses and prescribed textbooks. Radicalizing literature, whether from the European classical canon or modern thought, was deemed unsuitable for the 'Asiatic mentality'. Curzon's apprehension about this matter provoked him to adopt a censorious attitude towards books on university reading lists, pronouncing, for instance, Burke's *Reflections on the Revolution in France*, an undergraduate text prescribed for the BA course at Calcutta University, as 'dangerous food for Indian students'. Other works by European writers, such as Carlyle, Byron, Macaulay and William Butler, were also considered inappropriate, it being assumed they would further incite an already prevalent hatred of alien rule.[40] If the issues of curricular privileges and restrictions were stoking the flames of class struggle in Europe, in British India they were increasingly arousing the desire for independence.

Educating for self-determination was a goal no less aspired to by Muslims than other communities in India, and, consequently, what was taught to their young mattered significantly. For Muslims, the issue of school knowledge was compounded by the divide between 'traditional' Islamic subjects and 'modern' disciplines that became institutionalized through the dual system of *madrasas* and government schools, a policy whose consequences are still unfolding before us in the early 21st century. It was the entrenchment of this dichotomy in higher education, in particular, that posed a serious concern to Muslim leaders seeking to modernize communal education. If neither the Dar al-'Ulum nor the Nadwat al-'Ulama had succeeded in realizing a curriculum that engaged with both religious and non-religious forms of knowledge, the programme at Aligarh College, too, was wanting to the extent that it failed to present Islam as a subject of modern academic enquiry in its curriculum. Given the circumstances of the time, it is perhaps expecting too much for the historical religious sciences to have been brought into intellectual engagement with contemporary disciplines in these fledgling colleges, but had such ventures been initiated, it is possible that opportunities would have opened up for the revitalizing of Islamic thought, not to mention the flourishing of a more creative interface between Islam and non-religious subjects in the primary and secondary tiers of schooling.

To the Aga Khan, the adoption of a policy of epistemic separation by the Muslim communities was gravely misplaced:

> If the present method by which the Ulema being brought up on one line of studies and the scientific youth on a different one continues, ... there will be a fundamental misunderstanding in the outlook of intellect and faith in the soul of the nation.[41]

The Ismaili Imam was of the view that, with the passing of time, the impulse towards scientific enquiry in the Muslim past, inspired by the Qur'anic portrayal of nature as part of divine creation, had become subdued in contemporary understandings of Islam. To remedy this situation, the Aga Khan urged, referring to the newly established state of Pakistan, that the universities should have a faculty of Islamic religious and philosophical studies attached to the ordinary, postgraduate curriculum. The atmosphere of science needed to permeate religious studies, and *vice versa*, as was the case with divinity studies in European universities.[42] These views reflected a marked departure from earlier positions adopted by traditionalist Muslim leaders, steering away firmly from a policy of bifurcation of institutional forms and curricular content.

The Aga Khan did not hesitate to embrace the inclusion of 'modern' subjects in the education of young Muslims, not accepting that these new areas of enquiry were antithetical to Islam, but, on the contrary, seeing them answering the Islamic call for each believer to pursue knowledge, as a matter of obligation, wherever and in whatever form it was to be found. Religion, in his consideration, was not in conflict with science as these were two complementary streams of understanding with a common wellspring in man's innate desire to fathom the mysteries of the universe.[43] He viewed Islam, in fact, as the faith of the philosophers, which could not contradict 'the best thought of the present' but held the potential of relating harmoniously to disciplines with which it was in apparent tension.[44] These sentiments point to the deep anxieties of the period, provoked by ascendant scientism and positivist philosophies which were making reductionist judgements on the value of the sacred in human life. Like other Muslim thinkers of his time, the Ismaili Imam held that the profundity within Islam could intellectually challenge these claims.

Wishing for Muslim policy-makers to overcome their partialities and suspicions of emerging forms of knowledge, the Aga Khan strongly advised the setting up of colleges of science and technology in India, and after the partition, in Pakistan, to rival the best of such institutions in the West. He also cautioned that the teaching of Urdu, Hindi and other vernaculars be considered if the young were to appreciate their heritage.[45] Art, literature and music were subjects for which the Aga Khan had deep and abiding passion, and he was very much for young minds being exposed to these varieties of humanistic expression. The ideal of the school curriculum which he espoused was underpinned by a rounded notion of knowledge to prepare the young for modern life, but which also cultivated their appreciation of human genius, excellence and achievement.

This was a liberal conception of education but by no means a libertine one, for as the spiritual head of a Muslim community, the Aga Khan was deeply sensitive to the role of tradition in human society. He saw it as essential that the education of young Muslims should acquaint them, above all, with their religious and historical traditions, in a manner which engendered reflective thought rather than mechanical commitment. Indeed this exposure needed to arouse in the young the same spirit of intellectual endeavour and inspiration that was reflected in the work of the great Muslim thinkers, poets and scientists of the past. Muslims could not afford to approach their faith in a passive manner if it was to speak to the changing conditions faced by them – they had to reconnect with the spiritual and ethical ideals of Islam in order to become revitalized themselves. Referring to the subject of religious education at the All-India Muhammadan Educational Conference in Rampur in 1936, the Aga Khan remarked:

> Other religions have taken in formalities, but Muslims have outformalized the formal. Both Christians and Hindus have made progress in scientific education but Muslims have lagged far behind. ... This does not mean that the faith of Islam is not true. Nay Islam is the most rational, most social, of all faiths.
>
> It only means that our substitution and interpretation of Islam totally fails us. To this work, gentlemen, however unpleasant and offensive it may be to the conservatives, thought is necessary if we are to keep alive the name of Muslim University and Muslim Educational Conference, ... Howsoever unpleasant it may be, this task of reinterpreting Islam will have to be done.[46]

The Aga Khan urged that the subject of Islam become incorporated as an area of intellectual enquiry in higher education, expecting the highest level of scholarship to develop in the field of Islamic studies. This aspiration can be understood in the context of the growing need among

Muslim leaders of the time for intellectual responses, derived from within Islam itself, which would address the fundamental questions posed by the contemporary ideologies of capitalism, communism and nationalism, all of which were beginning to exercise considerable sway over events in the 20th century. Having witnessed the devastation wrought by the two world wars, the Ismaili Imam believed it ever more necessary to draw upon the impulse for peace that lies at the core of the great spiritual and ethical traditions of humanity. His understanding of Islamic education, embodying the principles of social plurality and coexistence, is aptly captured in the intellectual role he desired for a Muslim university which he envisaged as being,

> a true centre of Islamic faith and culture, in which can be expounded and practised the principles of our religion, its universality and its real modernity, its essential reasonableness, its profound spirit of tolerance and charity and respect for other faiths.[47]

This 'real modernity' and 'essential reasonableness' of Islam also compelled Muslims to engage with the dichotomy between 'religious' and 'secular' knowledge which had become the norm in both European and Muslim societies. The Aga Khan's philosophy as a whole inclined him towards an ideal of liberal education, understood in the broadest sense of that term, anchored within the Islamic vision of the limitless pursuit of knowledge and respectful of the spirit of the personal quest and intellectual endeavour.

Conclusion

The contribution of Aga Khan III to the debate on education in colonial India in the opening decades of the 20th century needs to be appreciated in the context of the complexity of forces and circumstances that conspired to shape the modernization of education in this region of the world. What the Ismaili Imam and other Muslim leaders in India found at the turn of the century was that their communities had to make a number of strategic choices for the schooling of the young, and these would determine not only what conception of education would be embraced but how the destinies of their people would be shaped. While some communities of tradition in European and colonized societies leaned towards one or another extremes in education, whether these were political, social or epistemological in nature, the Aga Khan attempted to steer the Muslims in general, and the Ismailis more specifically, as far as the prevailing circumstances allowed, towards approaches that would bridge these dichotomies so as to provide an integrating system of education best suited to preparing the young for the emerging challenges. Thus we find him seeking to connect, in conceptual and programmatic terms, public and private domains of education, elementary and higher schooling, as well as religious and scientific forms of knowledge.

The direction adopted by the Aga Khan on education also sheds light on the concept of social progress he envisaged for Muslim communities. The Indian Muslim leadership of the late 19th century had left as its legacy three seemingly irreconcilable paradigms of reform: what we have designated as traditionalist moral populism, pan-Islamic clerical solidarity and liberal modernist elitism. The Ismaili Imam sought to rescue the best of the ideas contained within these positions while rejecting outright their deficiencies. His views on education demonstrate a questioning but constructive political engagement with the colonial authorities rather than a resort to communal insularism or an amorphous transnational solidarity. He also distanced himself from the extremes of populism and elitism, seeing the vital necessity of reaching out to both the masses and the intellectuals at the same time. Most of all, he avoided tendencies towards reducing the whole of education to a narrow presentation of tradition, or, conversely, rendering tradition into an insignificant category within a liberal notion of education. Modern education for Muslims, he was convinced, need not imply the rejection of their faith, but that the spirit of Islam should inspire continuous intellectual growth, not closure, as the basis of learning.

What was put forward by the Aga Khan, then, was not a theory of education in the narrow, pedagogical sense of that term but a broad outlook based on considered views and evolving positions, informed of the multiple contexts in which modern thinking on education was being shaped. The principles underlying the positions he adopted drew inspiration from the spiritual, ethical and intellectual ideals within the Ismaili tradition, principles such as the unfettered pursuit of knowledge in all its forms, the progressive nurturing of the mind, and the responsibility of the community to reach out to those in need of assistance. In the succeeding Imamate, these principles would be recontextualized by His Highness Aga Khan IV into international humanitarian endeavours encompassing a range of educational interventions in developing regions of the world.

Notes

1. C. L. Thorpe, *Education and the Development of Muslim Nationalism in Pre-partition India* (Karachi, 1965).
2. B. D. Metcalf, *Islamic Revival in British India: Deoband, 1860–1900* (Princeton, 1982); D. Lelyveld, *Aligarh's First Generation: Muslim Solidarity in British India* (Princeton, 1978).
3. Metcalf, *Islamic Revival in British India*, pp. 348–354.
4. Ibid., pp. 87–103.
5. Lelyveld, *Aligarh's First Generation*, pp. 102–146; Metcalf, *Islamic Revival in British India*, pp. 317–335.
6. Ibid., pp. 328–330; Lelyveld, *Aligarh's First Generation*, pp. 130–134.
7. Metcalf, *Islamic Revival in British India*, pp. 335–347.
8. A. Basu, *The Growth of Education and Political Development in India, 1898–1920* (Delhi, 1974), p. 10.
9. Curzon sought to exert direct state control over the education system through greater centralization, tighter fiscal discipline over grants and expenditures, the reconstitution of university senates, the regulation of secondary schools, the vetting of prescribed textbooks, and curbing of the growth of private schools that had expanded significantly between 1880 and 1900. See Basu, *The Growth of Education and Political Development in India*, pp. 6–59.
10. This policy was to be further reinforced by the Indian Education Commission of 1882–1883 which made 17 recommendations directed at 'special encouragement' for Muslim education. See H. Malik, *Sir Sayyid Ahmad Khan and Muslim Modernization in India and Pakistan* (New York, 1980), p. 142; A. R. Khan, *The All-India Muslim Educational Conference: Its Contribution to the Cultural Development of Indian Muslims 1886–1947* (Oxford, 2001), pp. 8–10.
11. Aga Khan III, *The Memoirs of Aga Khan: World Enough and Time* (London, 1954), p. 60.
12. Aga Khan III, Sultan Muhammad Shah, *Aga Khan III: Selected Speeches and Writings of Sir Sultan Muhammad Shah*, ed. K. K. Aziz (London, 1997–1998), vol. 1, p. 205.
13. Ibid., pp. 92–106.
14. Aga Khan III, *India in Transition: A Study in Political Evolution* (Bombay and Calcutta, 1918), pp. 215–232.
15. Aga Khan III, *Memoirs*, pp. 60–61, 107, 145–147.
16. J. N. Moody, *French Education since Napoleon* (Syracuse, NY, 1978); P. Chadwick, *Shifting Alliances: Church and State in English Education* (London, 1997).
17. Basu, *The Growth of Education and Political Development in India*, pp. 6–12, 229–231.
18. Malik, *Sir Sayyid Ahmad Khan and Muslim Modernization in India and Pakistan*, pp. 125–136, 182–186.

Communities of Tradition and the Modernizing of Education

19. Khan, *The All-India Muslim Educational Conference*, pp. 3–4.
20. *Aga Khan III: Selected Speeches*, vol. 1, p. 380; vol. 2, p. 1117.
21. Aga Khan III, *Memoirs*, p. 104; and his *India in Transition*, p. 218.
22. Aga Khan III, *India in Transition*, pp. 215–228; *Aga Khan III: Selected Speeches*, vol. 1, pp. 364–376.
23. *Aga Khan III: Selected Speeches*, vol. 1, p. 206.
24. http://www.akdn.org/agency/akes.html#intro.
25. Basu, *The Growth of Education and Political Development in India*, pp. 13–59.
26. *Aga Khan III: Selected Speeches*, vol. 1, p. 374.
27. Ibid., p. 380.
28. Ibid., p. 371.
29. Aga Khan III, *India in Transition*, p. 218.
30. Ibid., pp. 215–217.
31. *Aga Khan III: Selected Speeches*, vol. 1, pp. 368.
32. Aga Khan III, *India in Transition*, p. 221.
33. *Aga Khan III: Selected Speeches*, vol. 1, p. 380.
34. Aga Khan III, *India in Transition*, pp. 217, 221–222.
35. *Aga Khan III: Selected Speeches*, vol. 1, p. 378.
36. Aga Khan III, *Memoirs*, p. 145.
37. Ibid., p. 146.
38. Ibid., p. 61.
39. Ibid., p. 147.
40. Basu, *The Growth of Education and Political Development in India*, pp. 28–29, 38–39.
41. *Aga Khan III: Selected Speeches*, vol. 2, p. 1291.
42. Ibid., pp. 1291–1292.
43. Ibid., pp. 1359–1360.
44. Ibid., pp. 1116–1117.
45. Aga Khan III, *India in Transition*, p. 229.
46. *Aga Khan III: Selected Speeches*, vol. 2, pp. 1116–1117.
47. Aga Khan III, *Memoirs*, p. 147.

PART III

NIZARI ISMAILIS: CONTEMPORARY POLICIES, INSTITUTIONS AND PERSPECTIVES

8

The Aga Khan Development Network and Institutions

Malise Ruthven

The Aga Khan Development Network (AKDN) is a cluster of institutions – including for-profit and not-for-profit entities – which have grown up or proliferated over more than a century. They now constitute one of the world's largest private development agencies, which now operates in more than 30 countries. Building on institutions created by Aga Khan III (1885–1957) to serve the needs of the Ismaili community in India and East Africa, the Network has been established and vastly extended under his successor, Aga Khan IV, to provide health, educational and cultural services for people of all faiths and backgrounds in the countries where it operates, and to stimulate development by investing in socially productive for-profit and not-for-profit institutions and companies. There are now more than 140 separate entities belonging to the Network with some 58,000 full-time and part-time employees – not including thousands of others engaged in the numerous national and international partnerships through which AKDN operates, and an estimated 20,000 full-time equivalent volunteers.

The range of activities is broad: as well as hospitals, clinics, schools and two universities (each of which has campuses in several countries) and comprehensive rural development programmes in Africa and South and Central Asia, the Network (through its investment arm AKFED – the Aga Khan Fund for Economic Development) operates or participates in numerous business enterprises, including power generation and telecommunications, hotel management and tourism, aviation, food processing and packaging. Its cultural sphere embraces the Aga Khan Award for Architecture, the most prestigious award of its kind for the developing world, the Historic Cities Support Programme, the Central Asian Music

Initiative and ArchNet, one of the world's largest online architectural resources, and the Aga Khan Museum, all functioning under the umbrella of the Aga Khan Trust for Culture (AKTC).

Given the complexity of its organization and the range of its activities, the AKDN eludes familiar definitions based on normal organizational categories. It is neither a non-government organization (NGO) concerned with international development nor a faith-based charity (although it has some characteristics of both). In several countries its representatives enjoy diplomatic status and have close relationships with governments, allowing them to engage in policy discussions at the highest levels. However, they are not state actors and operate within a tradition of strict political neutrality. While the Network includes profit-making enterprises and owns extensive holdings in real estate and other investments, it does not fit the model of the business conglomerate that claims to be committed to 'good corporate citizenship': the ratio of profit and non-profit sectors in the Network, both in terms of employment and expenditure, is much more evenly balanced than one finds in the corporate realm. Though relatively well endowed, its financial resource base is limited, falling well below the endowments measured in billions of organizations such as the Ford Foundation. Unlike grant-giving foundations it implements many of its projects directly. The innovations it has pioneered in the fields of rural development and urban conservation are widely admired and emulated by other organizations and governments, both separately and in partnership with the AKDN.

The various agencies belonging to the AKDN are incorporated as legal entities in the countries where they operate. As the Living Imam of the Nizari Ismaili community, the Aga Khan's responsibilities are to interpret the Ismaili faith in the context of the times, to provide security and a good quality of life for his community in accordance with their present-day needs and to benefit other peoples, Muslim and non-Muslim, amongst whom Ismailis reside. A cluster of institutions combining for-profit and not-for-profit enterprises, the AKDN is a vehicle for realizing the social conscience of Islam through institutional action.

In addition to its not-for-profit structures, the Network's profit-making enterprises clustered under AKFED are integral to the Aga Khan's development strategy. They are not conventional capitalist entities aimed at maximizing profits but rather companies whose primary aim is to foster economic development. Here, as with his other activities, he takes a long-term view, aiming to ensure that the businesses become self-sustaining by achieving 'operational break-even', within a 'logical time frame'.[1]

The Network's institutions can be grouped under the broad categories of health and education, rural, economic and financial development, civil society development, architecture and urban conservation, culture and media and, finally, humanitarian activities concerned with disaster prevention and emergency relief. These are not, however, discrete or separate spheres. While there remain some challenges in coordinating the management strategies of the various bodies that make up AKDN, an integrated whole, in which each programme or commercial area benefits from its interactions with the others, remains vital to the Network's outlook.

As Imam of the Ismailis, the Aga Khan firmly believes that in Islam *din* and *dunya* – 'religion and world' – are not to be treated as separate realms but constantly intersect and interact, with the pursuit of material gain framed within the calculus of ethical concern. All believing Muslims hold that humans are enjoined by God to act in accordance with the ethical guidelines of Islam. Since the Prophet was a man of action as well as a preacher, Muslims are required to translate ethical principles into action. For Ismailis the Imam of the Time facilitates the imperative of social action by providing the appropriate institutions – a duty the present Imam takes very seriously. He seeks out the best advice for his projects, regardless of the religious orientation of his advisors, and finds ways of including that advice in his programmes. As the sole authoritative interpreter of the tradition, he sees to it that those programmes are underpinned by the ethics of Islam. Service to God, in his view, is not just to be made through religious worship but through service to humanity.

All the AKDN institutions are aimed in different ways at helping economically disadvantaged people to improve their condition, to turn their backs on the kinds of dependency that thwart human aspirations and undermine human dignity. These institutions also provide outlets for the culture of volunteerism that is a vital part of the Ismaili tradition. Broadly speaking the Network's institutions can be grouped under the following categories.

Social Development: Health and Education

A modern approach to healthcare and education has deep roots in Ismaili philanthropy as well as in the progressive approach of the last two Imams who have successively presided over the community for more than 120 years. In the 19th century the wealthy Ismaili merchant Sewa Hajji Paroo (1851–1897) founded a hospital in Bagamayo, on the coast of what is now

Tanzania. At a time when education was largely controlled by Christian missionary organizations, his younger contemporary Alidina Visram (1863–1916) founded the first non-denominational school for Indian children in Mombasa. The present Imam's grandfather, Sir Sultan Muhammad Shah, Aga Khan III (1885–1957), established schools, clinics and hospitals in India and East Africa. A passionate advocate for the modernization of Muslim education in India, it was largely due to his efforts that the Muhammadan Anglo-Oriental College of Aligarh, founded by Sir Sayyid Ahmad Khan in 1875, acquired university status in 1920.[2] In his *farmans* (directives), Aga Khan III urged his followers to eliminate illiteracy by building primary schools for their children. In 1934, for example, he instructed the Iranian Ismailis to use 80 per cent of the tithes they normally remitted to the Imam on building schools. Ismaili schools were asked to collect fees from the better-off in order to subsidize their poorer brethren. The need for free and compulsory education for all the Ismailis was stressed with the stronger emphasis on girls' education and a preference for primary and secondary education for all rather than university for the minority. Aga Khan III was passionately committed to women's education. Contributions from his Indian followers to his Diamond Jubilee in 1946, when he symbolically 'received' his weight in precious stones, were used to fund schools for girls in Ismaili villages in the Hunza and Gilgit areas of what is now northern Pakistan. Altogether, Aga Khan III was responsible for establishing some 200 schools in East Africa and South Asia during the first half of the 20th century, beginning with the first – in Zanzibar – in 1905, followed by Dar es Salaam in what was then Tanganyika in 1906 and Mundra in Gujarat in 1907.

In German East Africa, Ismailis were the first Asian group to start small private schools under the supervision of local committees.[3] Up to the 1930s Ismaili schools were financed entirely from community resources and annual grants from the Aga Khan.[4] Later, because they admitted a substantial number of Africans to their schools, they received grant-in-aid from the colonial government. From 1952 English became the medium of instruction in both primary and secondary schools, setting in motion the process by which the Khoja Ismailis who originated in Gujarat have become a predominantly Anglophone community, with significant numbers of Portuguese and French speakers now residing in Portugal, France and Canada.

Education is fundamental to healthcare, especially in the case of women in traditional societies, where even basic literacy can produce a dramatic reduction of child mortality. Aga Khan III was committed to improving the health of his people as well as their minds. In East Africa he established clinics and bore the cost of the first free dispensaries to be established in Dar es Salaam in 1929. This and other dispensaries were the nucleus of what eventually became four hospitals run by the Aga Khan Health Services in Mombasa, Nairobi, Kisumu and Dar es Salaam. In 1946 his son Prince Aly Khan (1911–1960) founded the new Prince Aly Khan Hospital in Bombay on land he donated for the purpose. Funds raised at the time of Aga Khan III's Platinum Jubilee in 1956 – celebrating the 70th year of his Imamate – contributed to the building of the Aga Khan Hospital in Nairobi which opened shortly after his death and is now part of the Aga Khan University.

Building on a legacy

When Prince Karim Aga Khan succeeded to the Imamate in 1957 at the age of 20, he took on the responsibility for a number of institutions in health and education that had already been established in South Asia and East Africa. There are now more than 300 Aga Khan schools serving just under 60,000 pupils in three East African countries (Kenya, Uganda and Tanzania), three South Asian countries (India, Pakistan and Bangladesh) and two Central Asian countries (Tajikistan and Kyrgyzstan) where the Aga Khan Educational Services (AKES) operate. Although historically based in areas of Ismaili settlement, the schools are non-denominational and the great majority of pupils are non-Ismailis. In addition to the schools for which the AKES have direct responsibility, the Aga Khan University (AKU) – through its Institute of Educational Development (IED), established in 1993 (Karachi) and 2000 (East Africa), supports the AKES and different government education systems as well as other non-state or private schools.

The School Improvement Programmes (SIPs)

The IED offers Ph.Ds, Masters and a variety of diplomas in education and research, its main focus being on improving classroom performance by linking actual practice with research. In addition to AKU-IED, the Aga Khan Foundation (AKF) and AKES have an even longer history of supporting SIPs across South and Central Asia as well as eastern Africa, with many of these operating at increasingly larger scale in partnership with local government systems and affecting hundreds of schools and many thousands of students.

The outcome of most research over the last few decades – influenced to a considerable degree by the pioneering work of Jean Piaget, the Swiss philosopher and researcher, into early childhood development – has been a shift from teacher-centred to pupil-centred learning. The fundamental insight animating this shift is that in the final analysis, all education is self-education. The aim of education is not so much to impart knowledge to children as to teach them how to learn and to support them in their learning so that they succeed as it becomes increasingly difficult and complex. The shift towards a more child-centred and child-friendly approach has been a gradual one and has met with some resistance from teachers who fear that such methods might prevent them from meeting targets set by government. While child-centred learning is becoming a new orthodoxy, there remains considerable debate among educationists as to how effective its methods are in delivering improvements in measurable subjects such as reading and arithmetic. This in turn is fuelling new discussion and experimentation among educationalists, leading to emerging approaches that combine child-centred principles with the need to improve strategies and knowledge related to the teaching of core subjects. Methods commonly used by the SIPs include:

> active learning in small groups; encouraging pupils to interact, help each other and discuss; conveying high expectations; providing children with learning aids; encouraging pupils to pose their own questions and seek answers to those questions; encouraging pupils to think; attending to individual student's needs; pupils intellectually engaging with tasks, creating, shaping, and integrating what they are learning with what they already know.[5]

The classrooms where SIPs have taken hold are bright, with colourful posters, charts, maps, diagrams and pictures that include examples of children's work, which contrast with the dingy, sometimes grimy walls of the old-fashioned 'chalk and talk' schools. Shells and seeds, teacher-made board games, flash cards and storybooks are amongst some of the materials used as teaching and learning aids for maths, languages, science and other subjects. Obviously the physical resources available to teachers in developing countries are limited. However, SIPs assisted by specially trained staff from AKF, AKES and IED are showing teachers how to make teaching aids from inexpensive, locally available materials.

The School Improvement Programmes run by the AKF and AKES are now having a direct impact on several hundred schools in its programme areas. These include more than 600 schools in Pakistan, almost 300 in India

– mainly in the arc of northwest India linking Mumbai–Ahmedabad–Jaipur and New Delhi, plus several schools in Hyderabad, capital of Andhra Pradesh; more than 260 schools in Afghanistan, more than 800 in Kenya, more than 200 in Uganda, 20 in Tanzania, 345 in Gorno-Badakhshan, 29 in Kyrgyzstan, more than 100 in Mozambique and 12 in the urban area of Lisbon, Portugal. Though some of these programme areas have been, and still are in some cases, places with substantial Ismaili populations, the vast majority of beneficiaries are non-Ismailis, including substantial numbers of non-Muslims in Africa, including Central Kenya and Uganda, and India.

Introducing school improvements at primary and secondary level remains a challenging proposition. SIPs, whether applied at primary or secondary level, involve challenging the innate conservatism – and vested interests – surrounding current teaching practices. A unique characteristic of AKDN school improvement programmes is the emphasis on reaching out to the private sector (including community and NGO-run schools as well as not-for-profit schools such as those run by AKES). In recent years AKDN has fostered a number of interesting private–public partnerships in Pakistan, India and Africa. While education ministers may formally welcome efforts from the voluntary sector to improve their schools, the realities are a great deal more complex. AKDN's experience shows that SIPs are most effective where they are able to mobilize and leverage community support for education. In addition relevant professional development for teachers, and importantly for head teachers and other education managers, has repeatedly been shown to be essential for the improvement of teaching in schools.

The Madrasa Early Childhood Programme

Perhaps the most innovative of the SIPs and pre-school programmes that are a now a major part of the Aga Khan's work in education is the Madrasa Early Childhood Programme in East Africa. It began as a pilot project in the coastal region of Mombasa in Kenya in the mid-1980s where local Muslim community leaders asked the Aga Khan if he could help set their children on the path to university. They felt that Muslim children were losing out to children from other communities in the competition for higher education and jobs.

After studies by the AKF in conjunction with local Ismailis and other Muslim community leaders a new curriculum was devised. A crucial step involved persuading the local Sunni Imams that these methods were fully compatible with the traditional values of Swahili society. The 'integrated' pre-school curriculum developed in consultation with them brought together language, songs and stories from Swahili culture, key values and teachings from Islam and the child-centred High Scope methodology adapted for local use. The approach promoted early literacy and numeracy skills, and social development (working and playing with peers) for children between three and six years of age. The programme's cultural sensitivity was enhanced by locating the pre-schools in existing traditional *madrasas*.

The most significant element of the programme has been the synergy between the local community's engagement and commitment and the professional expertise (along with a rich array of suitable teaching and learning aids) arising in large part from the training and follow-up support provided by the Madrasa Resource Centres (MRCs). In some cases MRC staff spend up to a year discussing the programme and potential partnership with local communities before they are ready to establish their own *madrasa* community pre-schools.

Special emphasis is placed on ensuring that girls and women participate in the programme and take on leadership roles both in the pre-schools and in the Centres. Although fees are charged and set by the communities themselves, pressures to increase the number of children in the classes for financial reasons are resisted since it would affect the quality of teacher–child interaction. Local women who have completed Grade 8 or higher are trained as teachers and head teachers. Each local management committee is required to have at least three women. The directors and staff of the three Centres in Mombasa, Zanzibar and Kampala are a mixture of women and men.

In the late 1990s the Aga Khan Foundation worked with the Madrasa Programme to pilot an innovative local 'mini-endowment' scheme for 148 Madrasa Pre-schools. Each endowment combined funds from local sources with donor agency funds. The endowments were eventually pooled in each country and managed by National Endowment Steering Committees (NESCs), and community and Madrasa Programme representatives. A regional endowment advisory committee provides periodic guidance and support to the NESCs. All investments are within the East Africa region. Each national association of graduated Madrasa Pre-schools decides what portion of the dividend will be reinvested, and how much should be distributed to participating schools. The funds distributed to schools are generally used to pay teachers' salaries, to improve learning facilities, to supply teaching and learning materials and provide a contingency fund for emergencies.

Although the goal of reaching financial sustainability has yet to be achieved, the programme is highly regarded throughout East Africa and beyond. As of 2008, with funding from a range of international agencies, more than 200 communities in Kenya, Tanzania and Uganda are being supported. So far, more than 54,000 children have enjoyed the benefits of the system.

Over the past 15 years the Aga Khan Foundation has expanded its work in the field of early childhood education beyond East Africa, with significant programmes in South and Central Asia, as well as Egypt, Syria and Portugal. In all, some 370 early childhood settings are being supported, benefiting many thousands of children up to the age of eight, along with their parents.[6]

The Aga Khan Academies

An initiative that will make a significant contribution to raising the quality of education is the network of Aga Khan Academies planned for major cities and regions in the developing world including Portugal. The new academies are purpose-built schools designed to be 'centres of excellence' that demonstrate a standard of quality in education not typically seen in these regions. The first Aga Khan Academy opened in Mombasa, Kenya, in 2003 and the second is undergoing construction in Hyderabad, India. Four more are under development in Maputo, Antanarivo, Dhaka and Damascus. The academies have a dual purpose: to provide an outstanding education for exceptional students of all backgrounds who have the potential to become leaders of civil society; and to enhance the quality of teaching in the surrounding region by means of an ambitious outreach programme of professional development.

The philosophy behind the establishment of the academies is similar to that in the field of health: creating nodal points of excellence that will extend beyond a particular institution into society at large.

The curriculum is built around the International Baccalaureate (IB) – a programme that is gaining ground internationally since its beginnings in Geneva in 1968. Since 2000 the number of IB students worldwide has been growing by about 15 per cent per year. At the latest count IB programmes are being followed by more than half a million students at some 2,000 schools or more in 125 countries, divided more or less equally between the state-funded and private sectors.

The primary aims of the founders of the IB system, who included Kurt

Hahn, a refugee from Nazism in Germany, and Alec Peterson, a professor of education at Oxford, was to create a system whose overall purpose was 'not the acquisition of general knowledge, but the development of the general powers of the mind to operate in a variety of ways of thinking' that would help to 'break down the barriers of national prejudice'.[7]

The IB programme avoids the narrow focus on testing procedures epitomized by the British A-levels (still widely used in East Africa and South Asia), an exam taken at 16–18 that encourages students to cram a good deal of specialized knowledge into their senior years. The emphasis in the International Baccalaureate is on continuous assessment and project work. Before receiving their IB diplomas students are required to undertake a course in the theory of knowledge, to complete a 4,000-word essay based on their own research on a subject of their choosing, and to involve themselves in at least one creative or sporting activity, as well as in community service. One of the foremost of these schools now following the IB programme is Le Rosey in Switzerland, where the present Aga Khan was himself educated before going to Harvard University.

The Aga Khan University (AKU)

The apex of the health–education nexus is the Aga Khan University, established in 1980 as a college for nursing. A teaching hospital opened in 1985 in Karachi; its fine pink stucco buildings are set in parkland with a man-made lake and trees skilfully landscaped to maximize the use of limited space.

Chartered as an international university in 1983, AKU's objective is to promote human welfare by disseminating knowledge and providing instruction, training, research and services in health sciences, education and other disciplines. AKU is a non-denominational institution open to all on the basis of merit. Although admission to its academic programmes are 'needs blind', special emphasis is placed on the development of women. By maintaining high academic standards and programmes relevant to the needs of developing societies, by working with government on issues of health and education policy, and by delivering critical social services, AKU has had a nation-wide impact in Pakistan. With the launch of academic programmes in Kenya, Tanzania, Uganda, Syria, Afghanistan and Egypt – as well as in London – AKU is now established as an international institution with 11 sites in seven countries worldwide.

For its first two decades the university's primary focus was on health sciences. Its alumni now occupy important teaching posts internationally, mainly in Kenya and the United States. Student enrolment is entirely based on merit, without regard to ethnicity, gender or national origin. More than 40 per cent of the students receive some form of financial aid. Students come from all over Pakistan and several other regions, including North America and the Middle East. The rigorous admission process includes a competitive entrance exam and interviews. AKU prides itself on the diversity of its student body. Students can choose to live on the medical campus which has separate hostels for men and women. Forty-eight per cent of the academic staff are women – a proportion that compares favourably with many Western universities.

The Aga Khan University has achieved a commanding position in research in a remarkably short time. It now accounts for between 30 and 40 per cent of all biomedical research in Pakistan. Recent landmarks include a system for monitoring the taking of medicine by patients, discoveries in the genetics of high blood pressure and the development of new systems for injection safety. Community health is a primary focus of the university's research.

Now in its third decade the university is planning an ambitious programme of expansion. Two new campuses for Faculties of Arts along with Professional Graduate Schools are planned in Karachi, Pakistan and Arusha, Tanzania. Both of these new campuses are on greenfield sites consisting of more than 1,000 acres each, at an estimated cost of more than $400 million each.

According to its prospectus each Faculty of Arts and Sciences is expected to have between 1,500 and 1,600 students and 'will offer a liberal arts education with the aims of developing skills in critical thinking and analysis, raising proficiency in verbal and written communication, enhancing human resource development in the region and advancing understanding' in a range of disciplines. This is a radical programme in societies where religious traditionalism has often held sway.

The Institute of Ismaili Studies

Founded by Aga Khan IV in 1977, The Institute of Ismaili Studies is not, strictly speaking, part of the AKDN but as it operates under the Imamate in tandem with other educational endeavours such as the Aga Khan University and the University of Central Asia, it bears mentioning here briefly. The Institute has developed a number of activities including a Graduate Programme in Islamic Studies and Humanities and has established links with some leading institutes of higher education in the West and in the Muslim world. Distinguished scholars from other academic institutions are invited to teach the students who come from diverse backgrounds and many of whom have gone on to pursue doctoral studies at the School of Oriental and African Studies, Oxford and Cambridge Universities and Edinburgh.

The Institute's Department of Academic Research and Publications pursues intensive scholarly research and translation programmes, including the Ismaili Text and Translation Series which produces editions and English translations of Arabic and Persian works from the Ismaili literary tradition, particularly the medieval period, and the *Encyclopaedia Islamica* which is an abridged translation from the Persian original. Amongst current projects mention may be made of a complete edition and annotated translation of the *Rasa'il Ikhwan al-Safa*. Monographs on the traditions of the Ismailis and their history are published in the Ismaili Heritage Series, as are proceedings from the conferences and symposia that the Institute hosts. Scholars from the department regularly attend conferences elsewhere presenting papers on their research. The department includes a Central Asian Studies Unit and a Qur'anic Studies Unit. The former concentrates on the study of the culture and traditions of the Ismailis of Central Asia, notably of Tajikistan but also of Afghanistan, China and northern areas of Pakistan. The Qur'anic Studies Unit undertakes a series of publications on Qur'anic traditions of exegesis as well as other aspects of Qur'anic studies. Recently a programme of publication and seminars on the study of Shi'i Islam generally was initiated in the department, with a series of publications and conferences underway. The English publications are translated into Arabic, Persian and other languages spoken in the Nizari Ismaili community.

The library of the Institute, with its significant holdings of manuscripts and other materials, is a major resource for scholars of Ismaili studies. Several catalogues of the Institute's Arabic manuscripts have already been published.

Other departments of the Institute produce materials on Islam and its Ismaili traditions for primary and secondary school levels in the languages used by the Nizari Ismaili community, employing modern pedagogical approaches to the development of curriculum materials. The Institute's departments also produce materials and organize events for the benefit of the Nizari community at large.

Rural Development

The Aga Khan Rural Support Programme (AKRSP) in northern Pakistan is regarded by many development agencies, including the World Bank, as one of the world's most effective aid programmes. Originally based in the Northern Areas and Chitral (NAC) – regions of significant Ismaili settlement – the programme encourages villagers to set up their own village organizations (VOs) and women's organizations (WOs) with a view to choosing and carrying out their own projects, such as the digging of irrigation canals (kuhls), the construction of roads and small hydro-electrical plants (hydels). Hundreds of kilometres of kuhls have been excavated, bringing several thousand hectares of new land under cultivation. The link roads constructed by villagers, along with dozens of bridges, have enabled subsistence farmers living in distant valleys to benefit from commercial and other opportunities occasioned by the construction of the Karakorum Highway (KH) connecting Pakistan with western China.

The irrigation schemes are part of the broader programme of natural resource management aimed at improving agricultural productivity in a region where around 60 per cent of all household incomes derive from farming, and are likely to remain on that path. AKRSP strategies have included improving yields of wheat and maize by introducing new varieties, the promotion of potato cultivation in an area whose altitude makes potatoes less vulnerable to viral infections, the increased production of animal fodder (alfalfa, oats and maize) and the introduction of exotic varieties of cherries, apples, pears and apricots for the lowland market. The local cattle have been improved by cross-breeding. AKRSP's forestry programme – co-funded by the Norwegian government – has planted some 40 million trees. Some 1,500 private nurseries have been established.

In the Chitral district where the slopes of the Hindu Kush are conducive to microhydel schemes, about 170 were constructed between 1991 and 2001 providing the region with the highest concentration of such schemes in the world. The average grant from AKRSP has been around $10,000. The turbines in the hut-sized power stations are driven by water piped from the fast-flowing glacial streams or torrents. The technology is not complicated and ordinary maintenance is entrusted to village specialists after basic training by AKRSP engineers. To date more than 16,000 households have benefited from the electricity, which is mostly used for lighting, reducing pollution from kerosene lamps, but there are provisions for low-wattage water heaters and power tools for small enterprises such as stone-polishing. Families now have access to TV and radio, and children have more time to study. Appliances such as washing machines and butter churns have been introduced, reducing the time women have to spend on household chores.[8]

Building social capital

Improved technologies and the better management of natural resources, however, are only a part of the story. In the AKRSP philosophy they are the outcome of social action, and not just of technology or management expertise. Change, including technological change, will happen, especially in a globalizing world where even the remotest human communities are exposed to macro-economic forces. But change can be managed so as to protect the most vulnerable, and to preserve what is most valuable in a more traditional way of life: the sense of social cohesion and group solidarity, the sense of neighbourliness one finds in societies where people have to cooperate in order to survive.

Social capital is the reservoir of knowledge, expertise and motivation that, taken together, makes it possible for people to transform the material conditions governing their lives. A vital part of AKRSP's strategy in nurturing it has been to learn from local people and to build that knowledge into their programmes wherever possible, while training them in new techniques and methodologies.

Microfinance

One of the most enduring results of AKRSP has been the development of microfinance institutions, which have a particular bearing on the status of women. Since women do not own land in this region and have few other assets, the savings programme has provided them with an opportunity to have something of their own. It empowered them by providing them with their own accounts. It also motivated them to obtain employment in order to increase their savings. By the end of 2002 the women of NAC had accumulated savings of Rs 121 million (more than $2 million) out of the 430 million rupees ($7.2 million) jointly amassed by the VOs and WOs, proving that very poor people can save if encouraged to do so.

The savings, used as collateral against loans, have also given women the opportunity to borrow money on credit. Women from very poor households have especially been the beneficiaries of loans for consumption purposes – meaning, of course, that children have also benefited. Microloans for consumption, advanced against the 'social collateral' provided by the WOs where group pressure is applied to guarantee repayment, helps ease the seasonal fluctuations to which women and children were particularly vulnerable. A loan for pulses or rice taken out in winter can help see the children through to summer. In the past the most vulnerable members of the family often died.

Village Organization banking, pioneered by AKRSP in northern Pakistan, has been remarkably successful in giving villagers, both men and women, a new sense of control over their lives. By the year 2000, however, the system had reached a crossroads, where it faced a number of choices. One alternative was to maintain the degree of village autonomy that had built up over the preceding decades. However, the path that was eventually chosen was to bring the whole VO banking system within the purview of the First Microfinance Bank, established in 2002. AKRSP and AKFED are its two main stakeholders and its headquarters is in the capital, Islamabad. Any loss of village autonomy has been compensated for by the financial sustainability enjoyed by a larger operation including in the lowlands of Punjab and Karachi, as well as by the professionalization of the banking system and the flexibility given to managers in assessing projects and individuals for loans.

Since its establishment in 2005 the Aga Khan Agency for Microfinance has brought together over 25 years of microfinance activities, programmes and banks that were administered by sister agencies within the Aga Khan Development Network. AKAM is now active in 13 countries and has over 3,000 staff in Central Asia, the Middle East and Africa.

The underlying objectives of the agency are to reduce poverty, diminish the vulnerability of poor populations and to alleviate economic and social exclusion. It aims to help people become self-reliant and eventually gain the skills needed to move into the mainstream financial markets. This endeavour is governed by principles of long-term sustainability, efficiency and financial discipline.

Operating in both rural and urban settings, AKAM's institutions have helped poor people from a variety of cultures and backgrounds to expand their incomes and improve their quality of life. AKAM is a not-for-profit, non-denominational, international development agency created under Swiss law. Its headquarters are in Geneva, Switzerland. It is governed by an independent Board of Directors under the Aga Khan's chairmanship.

As of 2007 AKAM served over 230,000 clients and had a loan portfolio worth more than US$110 million. AKAM is committed to the development of innovative products designed specifically with the poor in mind, and its philosophy is to ensure that poor households have access to a seamless provision of financial services. While a large percentage of AKAM lending is for economically productive purposes such as farming, livestock rearing, trading and small-scale production, loans are also available for housing, health and education. Where permitted by local legislation, AKAM also provides savings and deposit services and has over 110,000 savings clients.

AKAM has also recently begun to provide micro-insurance coverage in some countries, designed to protect families from the high costs associated with illnesses or accidents, or from the loss of crucial household assets such as farm animals. Clients in some institutions also have access to business development services and facilities for domestic and international money transfers.

The AKRSP template

'Learning by doing' is an AKRSP mantra. The programme's ideas were strongly influenced by a programme in Bangladesh – the Comilla experiment – and various cooperative movements in 19th-century Europe and 20th-century South Asia. But it is a template, not a blueprint. The VOs do not exist just to implement projects. They are vehicles for articulating and giving expression to the needs and hopes of ordinary people. The aspiration to improve people's lot has universal resonance. The ability to translate this idea into action is much more difficult, not least because human beings are complex creatures with competing needs, aspirations and outlooks. The AKRSP template factors these complexities into its operations from the beginning. The key is organization. Development programmes in many parts of the world fail because the absence of good organization means that people from the community where projects are being carried out do not participate. The AKRSP's point of departure is organization. The AKRSP template is not a model but a framework for learning by experience within an organized range of priorities. It builds upwards from the bottom without predetermining the project's ultimate shape, adapting itself to the prevailing conditions.

The programme's success can be measured in part by the level of external donor support. Between 1982 and 2000 the main donors were Western governments and their agencies: 34 per cent of the funding came from Britain, 20 per cent from Canada, 16 per cent from the Netherlands, 8 per cent from Norway. This support has grown enormously over more than two decades. External contributions (mainly from Canada and the Ford Foundation) in 1982–1983 accounted for around 21 per cent of AKRSP's budget. In 2000 they amounted to almost 90 per cent.[9] In the course of an 18-year period assessed by the World Bank, the Ismaili contribution through the Aga Khan Foundation, including its branches in Pakistan, Canada, the United States and the United Kingdom, amounted to less than 14 per cent. However, this percentage excludes the personal contribution the Aga Khan makes by providing two helicopters, complete with experienced and expensive crews, out of his own resources.

The success of AKRSP in attracting international donor support is not just a testimony to its achievements in raising the living standards of Pakistani mountain villagers. It is also a recognition of the flexible way that the template can be adjusted to apply to programmes almost anywhere where rural people are mired in poverty. The first test of replicability – an important criterion with donor agencies – came with the application of the programme outside the core Ismaili areas where the Aga Khan name was guaranteed to generate support. The programme did encounter some resistance in the mainly Twelver Shi'i areas of Nagar and Baltistan, and some opposition in Chitral where there are mixed communities of Sunnis and Shi'is (Ithna'asharis and Ismailis). However, thanks to the Aga Khan's leadership and the tactical skills of the staff, this resistance was largely overcome. In Chitral special efforts were made to overcome resistance after the AKRSP board passed a ruling that two-thirds of infrastructure investments must go to non-Ismaili communities.

The replicability of the AKRSP template, however, extends far beyond its original matrix in northern Pakistan. The programme has spawned at least eight rural support projects outside the Aga Khan Development Network, in Pakistan, including the National Rural Support Programme, the Punjab Rural Support Programme, the Kushali Bank, the Chitral Agricultural Development Project, the Sarhad Rural Support Corporation and Ghazi Barotha Taragiati Idara, and several other organizations that had established some 20,000 community organizations by the year 2000, five times the number established by AKRSP. These programmes were directly influenced by the AKRSP approach and in many cases were being run with help from former ARKSP staff members. More significant, perhaps, in the development culture as a whole has been the 'export' of AKRSP outside Pakistan, to India, East Africa and Tajikistan.

AKRSP in India

Applying the AKRSP template in India presented an entirely different set of challenges. At the outset the physical environment where AKRSP (I) began its work could not have been more different from that of northern Pakistan. Compared to the soaring buttresses of the Karakorums and the rugged valleys of the Hindu Kush, the plains, forests and hills of Gujarat seem to belong on a different planet. The decision to establish a programme in Gujarat was influenced by the Ismaili presence there, although in operational terms this was a smaller factor than it was in northern Pakistan. Of the three districts chosen for pilot projects, only Junagadh has Ismailis, though they are by no means the poorest of the farmers in this area. The two other programme areas selected were in the Bharuch district and in Surendranagar. All three areas posed serious environmental challenges. The coastal district of Junagadh is known as India's groundnut belt, where exploitation of groundwater for irrigating groundnuts, wheat and other crops has led to such a degree of sea intrusion that drinking water has to be brought in by truck. The Bharuch area, though enjoying an annual rainfall of 1,200mm with potential for rain-fed farming, supplemented by irrigation in the dry season, is nonetheless very poor, with a large tribal population and a high degree of seasonal migration. Surendranagar, with 450mm annual rainfall, is the most drought-prone area in the state. Its rocky soil has been depleted by deforestation and severe over-grazing, while the highly permeable soil makes water storage a problem. As well as farming and horticulture, improving water supplies and access to the forest and its products for tribal peoples were among the principal objectives in all three programme areas.

AKRSP's input is mostly intellectual; it is 'soft power' rather than 'hardware': how to organize a society and a savings regime, where to place check-dams for irrigation purposes, how to construct them, which crops will find a market. The challenge of 'soft power' is the challenge of people – of helping to fashion what Immanuel Kant famously called 'the crooked timber of humanity' into productive modes of behaviour where the burdens of scarcity, drudgery, insecurity and dread are replaced by opportunity and hope. AKRSP does not neglect the hardware. In India its low-tech check-dams are functional: using drystone and wire-mesh construction techniques is just as effective as concrete, and halves the cost of construction. Other 'low-tech' programmes include providing simple biogas systems where methane from cattle manure is converted into gas for cooking. But soft-power considerations are paramount.

A scheme for building outside toilets in Gujarat not only yields benefits to family health and hygiene but to education, since girls are no longer deterred from attending school because of the absence of toilets. In India AKRSP holds regular workshops on gender awareness for its staff.

Another technology now being used in India consists of drip irrigation, where individual plants are watered by tiny holes from miniature plastic tubes. The system is much more economical with water and more efficient and less wasteful in hot climates than systems that rely on sprays or channels, as there is little loss from evaporation and plants are served individually. Drip irrigation is an appropriate emblem for all that is best in rural development schemes. It is literally and metaphorically about fine-tuning the distribution of water, the most essential of all natural resources, maximizing use, minimizing waste, making sure that every drop goes exactly where it is needed. The AKRSP model has been employed elsewhere in countries where AKF operates: in Tajikistan, Kenya in the 1990s and more recently in Mozambique, Syria and the Kyrgyz Republic, and on a very large scale in Afghanistan where it includes measures to provide viable alternatives to livelihoods based on the cultivation of illicit drugs. In Pakistan the government extended the AKRSP model to regions of the country outside NAC with technical assistance from AKRSP.

In the long term the AKRSPs may not be able to reverse the tide of urbanization that has generated the slums of cities such as Karachi, Mumbai and Nairobi, due to macro-economic forces. But they can succeed in limiting the impact of these forces, at least for some of the poorest rural people. By opening the channels for capital to reach rural hinterlands that might otherwise be neglected, the programme is allowing some people to remain in the countryside and to benefit from the access they gain from entering a larger market and, ultimately, a larger universe of human expectations.

Economic Development: AKFED

As with the Network's health and education services, the for-profit entities of AKDN originate in measures taken by Aga Khan III to improve the welfare of his community by diversifying its economic base. The Jubilee Insurance Company (JIC) was established in East Africa in 1936. Despite its name the company actually functioned more like a bank – anticipating by several decades the microfinance banks that now form part of AKDN. Though aimed at lower- and middle-income families seeking to start new businesses or expand existing ones, anyone could borrow from it providing they could provide two guarantors. Following a similar pattern the Diamond Jubilee Investment Trust Company (DJIT) was founded in 1946. Its initial focus was to provide loans for the construction of commercial buildings and housing but it rapidly spread out into other business ventures, including stationery and printing, import–export and textiles, as well as cotton farming. The most successful enterprises were the building societies or housing associations formed to help lower-income Ismailis who could not afford to construct their own homes.

After succeeding to the Imamate in 1957 Prince Karim Aga Khan commissioned a survey to estimate the cost effectiveness of JIC, DJIT and other companies, and to evaluate the extent to which they could be harnessed for wider projects of social and economic development. IPS – Industrial Promotion Services – is a venture capital company with a remit to invest in local companies, while also guiding Ismaili entrepreneurs into industrial ventures they were unwilling or unable to undertake by themselves. The IPS companies are now part of AKFED – the Aga Khan Fund for Economic Development – an entity which acts as the Ismaili Imamate's economic development arm.

With the advent of independence, the Aga Khan was keen to encourage Ismailis to move into manufacturing.[10] Then, under the Aga Khan's direction, the institutions were repositioned to make them more attractive to non-Ismaili investors including Africans. In time IPS's role was expanded to engage in partnerships with individuals and the public sector in order to promote development by creating capacity and employment in the emerging markets. Early industrial activities involved import substitution, with local companies producing goods such as soap, suitcases, barbed wire and hosiery.

At the same time, IPS investments in Africa served the Aga Khan's broad agenda of indigenizing industrial development, with local IPS companies acting as national institutions rather than African branches of international conglomerates. The aim was to encourage local entrepreneurship and stimulate local economies to create opportunities for employment and sustainable development. The financial entities were similarly diversified. Their destinies in East Africa were inevitably tied to the different paths that those countries adopted after independence. In market-oriented Kenya the Diamond Jubilee Investment Trust (DJIT) grew from strength to strength. In 1972 it opened its doors to the public and was listed on the Nairobi stock exchange.

In Uganda DJIT went into abeyance under the regime of Idi Amin. After the expulsion of people of South Asian origin in 1972 the Aga Khan decided not to fold it up but to leave it to quietly slumber. A similar policy was adopted in Tanzania under the socialist regime of Julius Nyerere. In recent times, the Trusts have become banks in Uganda and Tanzania, but have not, as yet, gone public.

Diamond Trust Bank – or DTB as it has come to be known – operates in Kenya, Tanzania and Uganda. It serves the wider needs of the retail as well as the consumer segments of the market. Through an efficient and growing network, the bank is poised to serve a wide cross-section of the populations of all three countries. In line with the ethos of the AKDN the bank places a high emphasis on best practices. The AKDN reputation for probity is its greatest asset. DTB's reputation rests on its board and on its staff who have been able to maintain the bank's image of a professional institution with high levels of service and governance.[11]

The financial sector in Indo-Pakistan

In the Indian subcontinent, where the Ismailis tended to be more closely tied to their rural roots, financial evolution was slower, partly because of the disruption caused by the partition in 1947. The Ismaili savings cooperatives established under Aga Khan III were reformed in order to widen the circle of lenders and borrowers. This eventually resulted in larger accumulations of capital opening the way to fully fledged banking operations at the beginning of the 21st century when the banks moved to broaden their base beyond community funding and expanded to include internationally reputed financial institutions. By 2003 AKDN was managing over 40 microfinance banks and microcredit programmes across Africa, the Middle East and South and Central Asia.

Tourism promotion

The tourist enterprises, including the Serena hotel chain, form part of AKFED. Since its launch in 1984, when it absorbed Industrial Promotions Services (IPS) and Tourism Promotion Services (TPS), AKFED has made impressive contributions to the developing economies of Africa, Central Asia and South Asia. By promoting tourism at the high end of the market, with game lodges in Kenya and Tanzania and first-class hotels in Nairobi, Maputo, Kampala, Kigali, Zanzibar, Islamabad and Kabul, AKFED brings foreign currency into the host economies and contributes to their exchequers through taxation while limiting the cultural impact of tourism. Tourism at the high end of the market does less environmental damage than mass tourism, because the numbers of visitors are relatively small. For the same reasons it may have a less problematic cultural impact.

With AKFED's strong equity position, which means in effect that it is not beholden to banks or shareholders, it is free to take on the burden of risk by investing in 'underserved' regions remote from the tourist track. The Serena chain of hotels, lodges and resorts in Afghanistan, Kenya, Mozambique, Pakistan, Tajikistan, Tanzania, Zanzibar, Uganda and most recently Rwanda contribute to the local economies by training staff and by encouraging or reviving the local crafts that are reflected in the hotel interiors.

Tourism and conservation

The promotion of high-end tourism is integral to the Network's conservation programmes. The Serena Inn in Zanzibar's Stone Town is a case in point. Zanzibar is a destination popular with Americans, Australians and Europeans, who arrive in considerable numbers during the tourist season. This five-star hotel, however, is part of a complex development project linking tourism with urban conservation and the revival of Zanzibar's craft industries. The project is part of the regeneration strategy for Stone Town devised by the Aga Khan Trust for Culture (AKTC) in collaboration with the European Commission and the Zanzibar government's Stone Town Development and Conservation Authority. Stone Town is one of the oldest Islamic cities in the southern hemisphere, the outcome of centuries of Indian Ocean trade. A spectacular example of its architecture is the Old Dispensary with its elaborate wrought-iron staircases, classical pilasters and ornate fretwork balconies in Anglo-Indian style created by Gujarati craftsmen. Originally built by the Ismaili entrepreneur Tharia Topan as a hospital to commemorate Queen Victoria's 1887 Golden Jubilee, it is now a cultural and arts centre following a meticulous programme of restoration by the Aga Khan Trust for Culture. In order to bring the building back to its original Victorian splendour, the AKTC architects had to train craftsmen such as plasterers, carvers and metalworkers, increasing the skills and knowledge of Zanzibar's artisan community. Zanzibari craft products – including hardwood furniture with contemporary designs – are now being exported to Europe, America and Australasia.

The restoration of the Old Dispensary is part of a wider scheme for regenerating the whole of the waterfront, which became littered with ramshackle sheds and disfiguring concrete barriers in the decades following the Zanzibar revolution, when Soviet influence was in the ascendant, resources were lacking and government had priorities other than the preservation of buildings associated with colonial or Arab-Omani rule. The Serena Inn not only contributes towards further conservation measures by recycling its profits into the Aga Khan Network; it has the more subtle role of raising awareness among Zanzibaris, generating pride in their city after generations of neglect when older buildings regularly collapsed, inappropriate new buildings were added and the decorated ceilings of Arab palaces were wrecked by smoke from the open fires on which homeless migrants (originally squatters) from the countryside cooked their food.

AKFED's strategies

AKFED is no ordinary enterprise. It invests in high-risk ventures with the specific aim of reversing the downward spiral in which instability generates poverty and vice versa. By encouraging other investors to follow its lead, it acts as a magnet for capital while reinvesting its profits in further business development. In Afghanistan, for example, the concentration of equity has the built-in strategic purpose of reversing the spiral of negativity such as afflicts the country, as it does many other war-torn states. One of the remits of AKFED is specific to such situations. As its mission statement explains, it is to make 'bold but calculated investments in situations that are fragile and complex, often assisting in rehabilitation and confidence building in economies that have suffered from civil conflict or war'. AKFED is not in business just to make money; its priority is to build the confidence that alone can generate wealth and social opportunities for the people among whom it operates.

The Serena Hotel in Kabul, an island of luxury in Afghanistan's war-torn capital which has suffered at least one serious terrorist attack, is one example of AKFED's commitment to the country's future. Another is Roshan, the Telecom Development Company of Afghanistan, the mobile phone company created from a partnership that AKFED formed in 2003 with Monaco Telcom International (MTI) and MCT, an American venture-capital fund since acquired by Teliasonera. With 51 per cent of the equity, AKFED is the leading sponsor. Roshan's growth has been phenomenal. It now has 2 million subscribers in some 180 towns and cities, with about 55 per cent of a rapidly growing market. With more than $300 million invested to date, it is the country's largest private investor as well as its largest corporate tax payer.

Staff at its main call centre in Kabul, where the women work alongside men (a rare occurrence in this traditionally segregated society), are required to be fluent in Dari and Pashto, and must be able to read their computer screens in English. The call centre presents a model of international corporate culture adapted to local conditions. The company, like its competitors, offers discounted rates to women. In Afghanistan – especially in the Pashto-speaking areas – conservative readings of Islamic tradition blend with but also conflict with the traditional tribal code known as the Pushtunwali. Both codes limit a woman's social mobility. The mobile phone enables women to enjoy a measure of 'virtual mobility' outside the circle of their immediate family members to which many remain confined. In 2007 Roshan joined with the government in providing resources for a programme in support of some 130 rural schools in Badakhshan, Baghlan and Bamyan provinces. More than 60,000 students and 2,000 teachers have benefited from the programme which includes in-service training for teachers, special-learning kits and other packages of new instructional materials. In addition some 40 war-damaged schools have been reconstructed or rehabilitated with the company's help from Roshan.[12] The most innovative of Roshan's initiatives involves the use of cutting-edge medical technology in conjunction with the Aga Khan University Hospital and the French Medical Institute for Children, a hospital now being run by Aga Khan Health Services. This pioneering project will link Afghan hospitals via broadband to medical specialists in Karachi and Western countries, avoiding the need for many Afghans to travel overseas for specialist treatment – or for hard-pressed surgeons, specialists and their volunteer support teams to visit Afghanistan under charitable auspices, as happens at present. The services will include video consultations with specialists and the instantaneous electronic transfer of digital images, X-rays, ultrasound and CAT scans.

AKFED has stakes in some 90 companies in 17 countries worldwide. Its investments include those that are still grouped under IPS established in the 1960s; the tourism ventures grouped under TPS; agricultural companies such as Kenya's Frigoken which supplies canned and frozen beans for the international market, and Ivoire Coton, a company that furnishes seed, working capital, ginning and transport services to 45,000 small farmers in the Ivory Coast, as well as sugar plantations in Burkina Faso, where AKFED has a major stake in the national airline. IPS companies are involved in packaging products such as cocoa, flour, coffee and cement, using jute and polypropylene bags and drawing on expertise originally obtained in Bangladesh where several Ismaili families owned jute mills.

The range of products in which AKFED has invested include the corrugated packaging used for Kenyan flower exports (currently the country's largest export after tea), plastic bottles and jerrycans for Ivory Coast, Burkino Faso and Senegal, and garments made for the US market in Kenya. The larger enterprises in which AKFED has invested include several power plants: a 450-megawatt generator fuelled by natural gas at Azito on the Ivory Coast, the oil-fired Tsavo plant near Mombasa which puts an additional 74 megawatts onto the Kenyan grid, and Pamir One hydro-power station above Khorog in Tajikistan, a regenerated Soviet plant that is now able to supply electricity to this region all year round. In addition the company is in the process of initiating pilot sales to Afghanistan. In Uganda AKFED has joined with Sithe LLC, the global power company owned by Blackstone, the giant private equity group which manages assets worth some $31 billion, to finance the construction of the $870 million Bujugali Dam near the point where the White Nile leaves Lake Victoria. The project will provide vital energy for Uganda and western Kenya. Given the risks, companies such as Blackstone would be much less likely to bring in foreign capital without AKFED's involvement.

Capital and human capacity

Development means building human capacity and expertise, as well as much needed capital. The Aga Khan believes that the drudgery, toil, sickness and ignorance that afflict people in the regions where AKFED works are best addressed by harnessing the power of global capital. But every investment must be balanced by respect for the environment and considerations of social utility. His strategies favour long-term investments and strong equity positions so that he and his staff, together with their partners, can take a 'hands-on' approach to management. As a long-term investor AKFED is committed to creating sustainable enterprises and business in emerging economies and is well placed to work in collaboration with other AKDN agencies to promote the Network's social and humanitarian agenda.

The Nation Group[13]

The Aga Khan's inaugural tour of East Africa in 1958 convinced him that the rising generation of educated Africans needed a decent newspaper. From his talks with African politicians and Ismaili community leaders he knew that independence was not only inevitable but would come much sooner than the 10–15 years envisaged by the Colonial Office in London. He established the Nairobi-based *Nation* newspaper and media group, now the leading media empire in East Africa. In 1973 the Aga Khan made 40 per cent of his holding available. A further public issue in 1988 reduced his holding to 45 per cent. The Aga Khan had always intended that shares should be made available to Africans: not only should his newspapers be written and read by Africans, they should also be owned by them. By 2005 the *Nation* Group maintained substantial media interests in Kenya, Uganda and Tanzania. It was employing in excess of a thousand people.

The quality of the *Nation*'s journalism reflected the Aga Khan's commitment to raising standards throughout the company by attracting talented journalists and providing training, both in-house and overseas. This was particularly the case in respect of the editorial staff where he saw early on the importance of developing journalism as a worthy occupation that should be remunerated like other professions. In 2003 he transferred his 45 per cent holding to AKFED.

Culture: Architecture and Development

The genesis of the Aga Khan Award for Architecture (AKAA) was in the early 1970s when the Aga Khan began to promote the idea of architecture as an engine for development. An important milestone was the construction of the Aga Khan University Hospital, Medical College and School of Nursing in Karachi. The Pakistani government granted the Aga Khan Foundation an impressive greenfield site on the edge of the city. At the Aga Khan's request the architect and his team visited historic sites in Spain, Morocco, Tunisia, Egypt and Persia to evaluate different styles of Islamic architecture and discover how qualities of living as well as architecture could be incorporated into the university hospital's design. The result is series of buildings that could be described as Islamic in feeling, without harking back to the past or adhering to any particular dynastic or regional school.

In contrast to the Pritzker Prize and other awards that tend to celebrate 'hero-architects', the AKAA pays as much attention to restoration projects and sanitation schemes that improve the built environment as to the design of buildings and their architectural qualities. The network of professionals commissioned to nominate projects includes planners and social scientists as well as architects. The Master Juries who grant the Awards include many distinguished intellectuals as well as practising architects. The process has been as important as the results: the preliminary evaluations are made by a team of architects based in Geneva. The short-listed items are then passed to a Master Jury nominated by the Steering Committee. The Award's team of trained architects in Geneva reconfigure dossiers and re-draw plans to make the process as fair as possible. A crucial role is played by the technical experts sent to investigate each nominated project. The Master Jury of distinguished architects, philosophers and social scientists do not see the projects on site, but must take full account of the technical experts' reports and the guidance implicit in the Award's various mandates.

An important outcome of this process has been the volume and quality of the documentation. Many of the projects have been recorded in monographs and illustrated books, containing photographs, drawings and diagrams with essays by experts and transcripts of seminars. By addressing issues such as cultural symbolism, conservation strategies, housing improvement and rural and urban development, and preserving the debates they engender, these publications have helped to establish 'a corpus of conceptual tools' for 'tackling all sorts of problems related to modern development as well as preservation of cultural heritage'.[14] The Award's activities have also been recorded in *Mimar*, a high-quality periodical that ran from 1981 to 1992. *Mimar*'s valuable data has been preserved in ArchNet, based in Cambridge Massachusetts, an electronic database that is now one of the world's largest online architectural resources.

A conclusion that might be drawn from the Award process is that there is an emerging possibility for an architecture that is 'Muslim' primarily because it serves Muslim communities and inhabits their built environment. This architecture may draw its inspiration from local vernaculars. However, it is not 'Islamic' in the obviously identifiable way that resonates only with the classical traditions that many people associate with Islam. The Award process has been seminal in bringing low-cost developments such as sewage disposal or informal housing improvement into the mainstream of architectural concern.

The Aga Khan Trust for Culture (AKTC)

From its beginning the Award for Architecture included the conservation, upgrading and restoration of historic buildings as part of its brief. However, once it appeared that this approach was insufficient to arrest the decline of landmark monuments in Islamic cities, the Aga Khan established the Trust for Culture (AKTC) with its broader agenda for preservation, conservation and the rehabilitation of historic Islamic cities in danger of collapse or of being overwhelmed by the exponential urban growth afflicting many cities in the developing world. The Historic Cities Programme (HCP) is the implementing agency of the Trust. With its own team of architects and conservation experts on hand to draw up plans and carry them through, HCP has been able to attract several important funding partners such as the Getty Grant Programme, the World Monuments Fund, the Ford Foundation, the Swiss, Swedish, German and Norwegian bilateral aid organizations, as well as the World Bank. In enlisting support from local governments and municipalities, the HCP goes beyond mere physical conservation of historic buildings. It injects new life into them by providing them with new functions as cultural or social centres for local communities as well as magnets for tourism.

AKTC's most outstanding project to date has been al-Azhar Park in Cairo, a large public park with lawns, flowering shrubs, artificial ponds and pavilions situated on what was formerly a rubbish dump next to the old Ayyubid wall of the city. The Park, which opened in 2004, was 20 years in the making – four of them in construction, 16 devoted to preparation and meeting planning, technical and administrative challenges.

When early excavations needed for site re-grading exposed part of the old Ayyubid city wall, the project was expanded to include the rehabilitation of the adjacent al-Darb al-Ahmar district and the restoration of key monuments in the area. From being 'just a park' – a formidable enough ambition in itself – the project now became an exercise in sustainable development, based on the proposition that economic, cultural and environmental initiatives must be elements of an integrated strategy for improving the life of communities.

The al-Darb al-Ahmar project established by AKTC, with funding from the Egyptian-Swiss Fund for Development, the Ford Foundation, the World Monuments Fund and the Social Fund for Development, has developed a long-term strategy to protect the community and improve its living standards in the face of the inevitable changes engendered by the Park. As Cairo's 'lung' or foremost green space, the Park is quietly transforming the whole area of the old city by generating both private and public investment. The numerous restoration projects in the area allow young people to learn traditional crafts such as carpentry and stone dressing. However, AKTC does not believe that it is always necessary to create jobs locally. One of the project's most successful initiatives has been to establish an employment bureau and counselling service to enable local people to find jobs outside the area. A microfinance initiative has been established to help local enterprises, especially those run by women. The project has been active in creating civil society institutions such as al-Darb al-Ahmar Business Association and the Family Health Development Centre.[15]

In addition to al-Azhar Park and al-Darb al-Ahmar projects in Cairo, recent or current projects overseen by the AKTC and HCP include the rehabilitation of Stonetown, Zanzibar; the Baltit, Altit and Shirgar forts and surrounding villages in the northern areas of Pakistan; Mostar in Bosnia-Herzegovina; the citadel of Aleppo and the ancient Ismaili castle of Masyaf and Qal'at Salah al-Din in Syria; the 'paradise garden' of Babur and the restoration of several historic buildings and houses in Kabul, Afghanistan, including the mausoleum of Timur Shah; the restoration of the gardens surrounding Humayun's Tomb in Delhi. There are plans afoot for the regeneration of the densely populated slum surrounding the shrine of Shaykh Nizam al-Din in Delhi and for a new park in Aleppo. The list, already formidable, lengthens by the day.

Nearly all of these schemes move beyond mere conservation by regenerating the social lives of the communities in which they are located, injecting a sense of ownership and pride. For example, the restoration of the Baltit Fort at Karimabad in northern Pakistan has gone hand in hand with a community-driven plan to upgrade the homes that lie below its walls, by providing them with new sanitation and generally demonstrating how ruined old houses can be restored and improved.

The restoration projects undertaken by the Aga Khan, through the AKTC and HCP, are contributing to a seismic shift in cultural attitudes. The once despised traditional quarters of Islamic cities are beginning to 'look smart'. The outlook of the governing elites in most Muslim countries has shifted since the 1970s, when planners and bureaucrats associated the souks and casbahs with backwardness. The AKTC is showing how a new kind of adjustment is becoming necessary: to survive successfully historic cities must be able to function economically without relying solely on tourism.

Architectural education

Outstanding buildings and conservation areas, however important, are not in themselves sufficient to transform the outlook of the cohorts of architects, bureaucrats, politicians, entrepreneurs and planners responsible for maintaining and extending the built environment. Soon after launching the Award, the Aga Khan established an endowment for a joint programme for Islamic architecture at Harvard and MIT (the Massachusetts Institute of Technology in Cambridge). His aim, he explained at the time, was to encourage a general recognition of the strength and diversity of Muslim architectural traditions, so that when these were combined with the latest construction technologies they would result in a more appropriate built environment. The aim is to teach practitioners and teachers by offering post-professional Masters programmes for students who had already acquired basic qualifications – typically students in their middle to late 20s who had already acquired two or three years' practical knowledge of their trade. The programmes – including Ph.D. programmes in landscape architecture and Muslim architectural history – are in the process of defining the field of Islamic art and architecture globally. As well as influencing the built environment of Muslim countries where architects are returning to practise, the programmes are popular with students pursuing careers in museums and art galleries in the West.

Conclusion: The Pursuit of Excellence

The pursuit of excellence – measured by international standards – is a discernable feature, almost a defining characteristic, of the Aga Khan 'brand'. In the context of the developing world, where standards are often lax, the institutions that carry his name are models to be emulated.

The Aga Khan often regards his role as that of a facilitator or catalyst – a word that recurs in his speeches – rather than an originator. Many of the programmes that are adapted and adopted for his institutions – in health, education and development – may have been pioneered elsewhere, in the case of the Comilla project, or the programmes for early childhood development. What is distinctive about his approach, however, is his attention to detail and the meticulousness with which he interrogates the experts, whom he constantly challenges with persistent and detailed probing to come up with new insights and perspectives, to ensure that programmes are suited to the social milieus where the AKDN operates.

In recent years the range of activities and extent of the AKDN commitments have grown exponentially. The list is indeed a formidable one: the University of Central Asia with its three mountain campuses planned in Tajikistan, Kyrgyzstan and Kazakhstan; two new institutes, for the study of Muslim Civilizations affiliated to AKU in London and for the Study of Pluralism in Ottawa; a brand new museum in Toronto to house various collections of Islamic art including that acquired from the estate of the Aga Khan's uncle, Prince Sadruddin; the Music Initiative for Central Asia in collaboration with the Silk Road Project inspired by the Chinese-American cellist Yo-Yo Ma; the Aga Khan Academies; a new university city north of Karachi; refurbishing the existing AKU hospitals in Karachi and Nairobi, since medical equipment must be replaced every decade; a new park for Aleppo; extending the Historic Cities programme into the Nizam al-Din area of Delhi.

When the present Aga Khan succeeded to the Ismaili Imamate in 1957, the Ismailis consisted of a disparate group of communities in widely different parts of the world, united by their common allegiance to their Imam. With the establishment of the Aga Khan Development Network and the elaboration of Jamati institutions, continuity is now assured. There is an organized framework through which the various agencies concerned with the welfare and progress of both the Ismaili and the wider communities in which they reside or used to reside are coordinated. The great majority of the beneficiaries of these agencies are now non-Ismailis. The AKDN is a dynamic organization whose outreach is constantly expanding as co-funders come into the system. At the same time, the body at its core, the Ismaili Imamate, has itself become more institutionalized.

The content of the present Imam's legacy is not less valuable for being impossible to quantify. Health, education and development are only keywords: they barely hint at complex human realities – the joy of a parent whose baby recovers from dysentery, the satisfaction that comes from exercising knowledge and skill, the opening of new horizons, mental and physical, made possible by the construction of a bridge or road, the access to knowledge powered by electricity.

The Nizari Ismailis have been fortunate in having two outstanding leaders, grandfather and grandson, who between them have guided the community for 125 years, from 1885 to the 21st century. Both, in different ways, have proved remarkably successful in adapting an ancient tradition to modern conditions. Neither of them, however, would claim exclusive credit for his achievements. As descendants of the Prophet Muhammad and human vessels for the Light or spirit of 'Ali, the first Shi'i Imam, they would see themselves as exemplars of a model of leadership which stretches back 14 centuries. The esoteric theology that legitimizes that tradition is not accessible to everyone, but its value may be judged by its practical results, and the promise it holds for the future.[16]

Notes

1. *International Herald Tribune*, 7 July 2007.
2. Aga Khan III, *The Memoirs of Aga Khan: World Enough and Time* (London, 1954), pp. 114–116.
3. Shirin Remtulla Walji, 'A History of the Ismaili Community in Tanzania' (Ph.D. thesis, University of Wisconsin, Madison, 1974), p. 139.
4. Ibid., p. 187.
5. Joanne Capper, Shelomith Nderitu and Paul Ogola, 'School Improvement Programme of the AKES Kenya at Kisumu, Western Kenya: An Evaluation', Aga Khan Foundation (Geneva, 1997), p. 44.

6. Geoff Brown, Janet Brown and Suleman Sumra, 'The East African Madrasa Programme: Evaluation Report', AKF (Geneva, 1999); Kathy Bartlett, 'The Madrasa Early Childhood Programme in East Africa', AKF (Geneva, 2003). My thanks to Kathy Bartlett for updating these figures in May 2008.
7. Alexander D. C. Peterson, *Schools Across Frontiers: The Story of the International Baccalaureate and the United World Colleges* (London, 1987), p. 1.
8. World Bank, *The Next Ascent* (Washington DC, 2002), pp. 108–109.
9. Ibid., p. 96.
10. Peter Hengel, *Weite Wege* (unpublished memoir, Gstaad, n.d.).
11. Martin Browbridge, 'The Causes of Financial Distress in Local Banks in Africa and Implications for Prudential Policy', UNCTAD Discussion Paper no. 132 (March 1998), p. 13.
12. *Kabul Times*, 27 May 2007.
13. Details on the Nation Media Group that follows are taken mainly from an unpublished history of the newspaper by Gerald Loughran with notes by Gerald M. Wilkinson.
14. See the article by Stefano Bianca in this volume.
15. See F. Daftary, E. Fernea and A. Nanji, ed., *Living in Historic Cairo: Past and Present in an Islamic City* (London, 2010), especially pp. 172–293.
16. For a more detailed account of the AKDN and the progress of the Nizari Ismaili community under the last two Aga Khans, see M. Ruthven (with Gerard M. Wilkinson), *Children of Time: The Aga Khan and the Ismailis* (London, forthcoming).

9

Caring for the Built Environment

Stefano Bianca

This chapter addresses the importance of the built environment as a focal point for the comprehensive human development efforts pursued by the Aga Khan Development Network (AKDN) and, more particularly, by the Aga Khan Trust for Culture (AKTC). Moreover it attempts to shed light on the function of certain identity-building processes associated with the built environment, i.e. how buildings can become charged with deeper meaning and how, in turn, they can dispense cultural identity to the individuals and communities actively involved in shaping them. Understanding the interdependence between mentally perceived images and symbols, on the one hand, and their various physical expressions, on the other, is crucial for assessing and protecting the essential qualities of a living cultural heritage. Moreover it can result in more appropriate development procedures, capable of reviving the values inherent to the built environment.

Such understanding seems particularly urgent with respect to the current complex situation in the Islamic world, where perennial cultural traditions are often threatened by modes of development incompatible with these traditions, with sometimes explosive consequences. Unfortunately the prevailing inter-cultural discourse, rather than disentangling and resolving such conflicts, often aggravates them by reverting to simplistic theories (such as the much talked about 'clash of civilizations') that are driven by polarizing political agendas and seem to ignore the existence of deeper human dimensions and concerns. To be sure, the alleged clash does not apply to opposed ethnic and cultural entities but to conflicting ideologies which are too narrow-minded to be equated with the inner driving forces of cultures and civilizations.

Ideological conflicts of this type are by no means a new phenomenon, for the rise of Islamic fundamentalism came as a response to equally aggressive materialistic ideologies that have been imposed on non-Western societies since the time they became subject to colonial regimes. New philosophies rooted in the secular creed of 'progress' – regardless of their Marxist or capitalist guise – have profoundly disrupted the so-called developing societies and generated a latent or overt dualism within their cultural systems. The very term 'developing' already implies a certain arrogance by assuming the undoubted superiority of one particular and rather limited type of modern civilization. Based as it is on prejudice and lack of tolerance, this blinkered outlook does not favour a fruitful dialogue. It needs to be replaced by more balanced and more pluralistic approaches, acknowledging that the real victims of such ideological clashes are the non-Western communities rich in local cultural traditions, as they are suddenly forced to react to alien parameters enforced via political and economic pressures.

For this very reason, the concept and the implicit agenda of 'development' requires critical scrutiny from each recipient's perspective. Understanding other values, mentalities and needs, harnessing local cultural assets and contextualizing technological achievements through adapted modes of intervention are major challenges for any organization dealing with heritage conservation and urban rehabilitation in Islamic countries – or, for that matter, in the developing world at large. For promoting a single – and highly unsustainable – way of life all around the globe under the banner of 'civilization' can no longer be the goal of international cooperation.

The Aga Khan Trust for Culture and the Built Environment

The history, the function and the future face of the built environment in Muslim societies have become major thematic concerns of various institutions of the Aga Khan Development Network over the past three decades. The corresponding research and evaluation processes were initiated by His Highness the Aga Khan in 1978 through the establishment of the Aga Khan Award for Architecture – the world's most important architectural prize – and one year later through the endowment of the Aga Khan Programme for Islamic Architecture at Harvard and MIT with its various outreach programmes covering the Muslim world, the latest addition (ArchNet) being based on advanced tools of electronic interaction. In both cases the objective was to promote and disseminate adequate approaches to planning and design in Islamic countries, taking into account the historic roots and specific local traditions, as well as the needs arising from current evolution and transformation processes.

In 1988 these efforts were greatly strengthened with the formal establishment of the Aga Khan Trust for Culture as the overarching institution dealing with cultural development in the Islamic world. Step by step, new programmes were established by the Trust, such as the Historic Cities Programme, the Music Initiative, the Humanities Programme and the Museum Division, thus reaching out into other cultural domains. Architecture, however, has remained at the core of the Trust's mandate – the built environment being understood as the most tangible and complete expression of culture and its many social ramifications.

Since the early years of the Award for Architecture, and particularly with the establishment of the Trust, it became clear that architecture was not to be considered in its functional and aesthetic dimensions only, but as a matrix, as it were, of wider human development – including cultural aspirations, social networks and economic needs and opportunities. The built environment was understood in its multi-dimensional aspects, covering historic buildings as well as modern architecture, private houses as well as public facilities, urban sites as well as rural and informal settlements, landscapes as well as public open spaces. For its procedures, the Award adopted a three-year cycle for search, evaluation and celebration, attaching particular importance to a project's impact on respective local communities. User satisfaction and a project's operational sustainability became other important considerations in prize-giving.

This comprehensive way of looking at planning, design and implementation was investigated and confirmed through a series of seminars organized by the Award's Steering Committee in the late 1970s and 1980s, with the intention of exploring, through field visits, the various aspects of the built environment in the Islamic world and its correlation to pressing socio-economic development issues. His Highness the Aga Khan took a keen personal interest in these debates which brought together an international range of leading thinkers, practitioners and academics in various locations both Western and Eastern.

The seminars revolved around such themes as cultural symbolism, conservation strategies, housing improvement, public facilities, rural and urban development, etc. The resulting publications helped establish an important corpus of conceptual tools tackling all sorts of problems related to modern development as well as preservation of cultural heritage. Over the years, the Award has created a network of engaged thinkers, some of them serving as Steering Committee or Master Jury members, and fostered a debate (a 'space for freedom') such as had never existed before in the Islamic world. The award-giving ceremonies, organized every three years in prominent historic sites of the Islamic world with the participation of local political leaders, became instrumental in broadcasting the message to professionals, architectural schools, governmental institutions and the specialized media. A series of substantial books has also been published by the Award to disseminate the recommendations of the Steering Committee and Master Jury members, and to share the debates and conclusions of various educational seminars with a wider public.[1]

A decisive boost was given to the Aga Khan Trust for Culture in the early 1990s, when the Aga Khan decided to go beyond mere identification, evaluation and celebration of third parties' projects and to become engaged, through the Trust, in active implementation of a range of urban conservation and rehabilitation projects. This move was undertaken with the intention of building up a portfolio of significant demonstration projects in various regions of the Islamic world and in different thematic domains, such as landmark conservation, adaptive re-use, urban renewal, community development and local capacity building. The institutional vehicle to achieve this purpose was the Historic Cities Programme (HCP), capitalizing on the body of knowledge and connections accumulated during earlier decades of Award activities. First established in 1991, the HCP has since grown rapidly to become the Trust's major programme in terms of resource allocation and direct impact on the built environment.

The Activities of the Historic Cities Programme

The Historic Cities Programme (HCP) follows the Trust's humanitarian, not-for-profit orientation and is non-parochial in the choice of its projects, since it does not limit itself to regions and sites where Ismailis have a presence or represent a majority of the population. HCP thus has the mandate to become involved in various countries of the Islamic world; yet it has to be selective with the allocation of its limited resources in order to avoid excessive dispersion and to reach the necessary depth and critical mass in dealing with the chosen sites and communities.

Obviously, speaking of the 'Islamic world' as a whole is a simplification which calls for some caveats. The built environment of the Islamic world has never been as homogeneous as this general term may imply, and is even less so today. To be sure, there has always been a strong affinity between the individual architectural traditions within Islam, where certain ritual or social practices have related three-dimensional expressions. Within this overarching unity of spirit, there exists a rich variety of regional cultures, which reflects different climates, different pre-Islamic heritage components and particular vernacular building traditions. Other, more recent factors which created differences between the newly emerged Islamic nations are the political divisions imposed during and after the colonial period, as well as the economic disparities between rich (oil-producing) countries and their poorer cousins. Ironically it is the richer countries that, within decades, have lost most of their architectural heritage as a result of excessive and uncontrolled development. Meanwhile most poorer countries have retained a wealth of sites and historic cities which, however, are threatened by physical decay resulting from poverty, and forms of social and economic upheaval that have brought with them problems in the care and maintenance of the built environment. The common problem remains how to revive a cultural identity based on living and evolving local traditions – whether by rehabilitating historic cities or by establishing meaningful models of contemporary architecture.

Regardless of regional differences, the need for conservation and urban rehabilitation programmes all over the Islamic world is daunting, and selecting sites for HCP interventions poses a problem which can probably never be resolved in perfectly equitable terms. Acknowledging this dilemma, the Programme has had to adopt a pragmatic approach, basing its choices on a number of criteria which are designed to ensure the lasting success of individual initiatives and enable them to have a lasting effect and to demonstrate the viability and the benefits of the approach selected. Apart from enlisting the support of local government and the local communities directly concerned, one of the major concerns was to go beyond physical conservation or restoration and to introduce new functions for historic buildings, i.e. compatible activities which can inject new life into their architectural shell, provide the means for proper operation and maintenance, and increase the pride and sense of ownership of local inhabitants. Socio-economic, institutional and educational agendas were thus implicit in the projects from the very beginning.

HCP's initial project portfolio in 1992 was defined by three projects which His Highness had already envisaged in earlier years, before the Programme was formally established, and for which HCP now became the appropriate institutional instrument. These were, first, the restoration of Baltit Fort in Hunza (completed in 1996); second, the restoration of the Old Dispensary in Zanzibar (completed in 1997); and third, the construction of the Azhar Park in Cairo – a large project which was delayed by the prior construction of three large water-reservoirs on site and which later acquired a new level of complexity due to the Programme's gradual change in scope and approach, with the result that it was eventually completed in 2004.

During the initial phase of HCP, activities were largely confined to classical conservation or rehabilitation projects. However, it was soon recognized that individual projects needed to be embedded in wider planning and development initiatives and rooted in local community aspirations. Pursuing a more comprehensive approach was deemed essential in order to guide new building activities in historic areas, to consolidate the context of individual restoration projects, to introduce suitable adaptive re-use functions and to foster residents' involvement and commitment. Community motivation, in particular, was seen as a necessary pre-condition for the implanting of proper planning and rehabilitation principles and in order to spark the internal processes which enable projects to become alive, productive and self-perpetuating.

The logical consequence of the new approach was to place the restoration of historic buildings in a coherent physical and social urban context, with a view to building up a critical mass for positive change in sensitive locations. Accordingly, an innovative type of Area Development Projects was conceived, drawing on a variety of disciplines and addressing physical rehabilitation in close interaction with socio-economic development potential. Eventually this led the Programme to pursue an integrated preservation and development approach, where restoration of historic buildings could interact productively with urban renewal, housing and infrastructure improvement, socio-economic development initiatives, local institution building, small enterprise development, microcredit schemes, etc., thus making HCP's endeavours coincide with the wider scope of AKDN objectives.

Integrated Cultural Development (a concept which distinguishes HCP projects from classical conservation initiatives pursued by other agencies) was first carried out in Zanzibar and in the Hunza valley, in the north of Pakistan. In Zanzibar the restoration of the Old Dispensary building and its conversion into a Cultural Centre was set within the framework of a strategic action plan for the Old Stone Town – the most cosmopolitan historic city of East Africa which saw its cultural heyday in the 19th century under 'Umani rule. Various action areas were singled out for coordinated conservation and development initiatives. For the Stone Town waterfront – the most important of them – major landscaping and redevelopment activities were envisaged in Forodhani Park and in the harbour zone, in conjunction with the restoration of a number of other landmark buildings, such as the Old Customs House, and the conversion of the former telecom building into a hotel (now the Zanzibar Serena Inn). Enhancing the representative waterfront was combined with upgrading of traditional houses inside the Old Stone Town, demonstrating how the principles of the action plan were to be implemented plot by plot, with categories of intervention ranging from conservation to typological reconstruction or adapted new infill.

The Hunza valley, located in the high Karakorum range between China, Central Asia and the Indian subcontinent, features an important legacy of vernacular forts, palaces, religious buildings and cultural landscapes that have only recently become accessible by modern transportation means – although they had been part of the old Silk Road network and later played a role in the Great Game of the colonial period. The restoration of the 700-year-old Baltit Fort at Karimabad, one of the landmarks of the area, went hand in hand with the community-driven upgrading of the decaying historic settlement beneath it, which saw the introduction of modern sanitation facilities. Demonstrating to residents how ruined old houses could be restored and improved went a long way to reversing existing trends to abandon the historic village and to build dispersed new houses on precious agricultural land. The upgrading of the historic settlement, therefore, was not merely a conservation exercise, but an essential breakthrough in implementing a wider environmental planning strategy which would preserve the resources and assets of the region, and enable a rational and economical development instead of an uncontrolled urban sprawl.

The results achieved through active cooperation with the local community in Karimabad were convincing enough to lure communities in other historic villages, such as Ganesh and Altit, into similar partnerships. The continued planning and rehabilitation work in these villages was underpinned by nurturing the growth of local 'town management societies' – an attempt to encourage more active models of self-governance and to make targeted local groups responsible for the management of their territory. The demonstrative effect of these projects in Hunza in turn spurred other communities in the Baltistan valleys to engage in similar projects and has produced a new awareness of the heritage assets in the northern areas of Pakistan.[2] The HCP staff, in turn, benefited from these experiences, since they enabled the Programme to conceptualize integrated, community-based conservation and development projects in other areas. The lessons learned were first applied to similar initiatives in Samarkand and Mostar, carried out during 1995–1998 and 1999–2004 respectively.

The most extensive of HCP's initiatives has been its Cairo project, located in one of the most prestigious cities of Islam. Al-Qahira ('the City Victorious') was founded in AD 969 by the Fatimid dynasty and thus occupies a special place in Ismaili history, although it no longer houses an Ismaili community. Project activities began in the mid-1990s with the construction of the Azhar Park, adjacent to al-Darb al-Ahmar district on the eastern edge of the Historic City. One could say that this initiative represented *mutatis mutandis* the first 'grand project' in an Arab country that uses a large-scale redevelopment project (i.e. the conversion of a derelict site of 30 hectares into a new urban park) as the engine for an incremental, in-depth rehabilitation of the adjacent historic district. It is this comprehensive scope, as well as the care for the fine grain of the historic fabric, that distinguishes it from other, perhaps more spectacular, redevelopment projects in the Persian Gulf countries, where the focus is on the work of 'signature' architects and where historic urban structures are either non-existent or doomed to disappear.

Al-Darb al-Ahmar, known as one of the poorest districts of historic Cairo, has been marginalized owing to its peripheral location along the 12th-century Ayyubid city wall, at some distance from the central bazaars. It is bordered by a 30-hectare-wide strip of land which for centuries was used as a dump for rubble and solid waste, thus accumulating a number of artificial hills over time. The district's housing stock, mostly of 19th- and early 20th-century origin, is quite dilapidated because of lack of maintenance. In spite of the rural immigration and the demographic changes that occurred in the early 20th century, al-Darb al-Ahmar retains a relatively stable and coherent social fabric, with many people living and working in the same place and with the existing public open spaces providing focal points for a vibrant community life. Furthermore the area features a large number of interesting historic buildings, including the old city wall, many mosques, mausoleums, fountains and Qur'anic schools from the Ayyubid and Mamluk periods, as well as ruins of interesting palaces and residences dating variously from the Fatimid period to the 19th century. One of its attractions is the interaction of historic buildings with a lively residential community that is still engaged in many crafts – a sound mix which, in addition, offers an unexploited tourism potential.

The interventions conducted by HCP have consisted of a progressive sequence of projects, starting with the 'Herculean' transformation of the huge barren land along the borders of al-Darb al-Ahmar into an attractive urban park. From its highest points, the site now offers a wonderful 360-degree panorama of the historic landmarks of Cairo, from the Pyramids to the chain of minarets of the Historic City, to Saladin's citadel and to the domes of the many historic mausoleums in the 'city of the dead'. Its rugged topography was deliberately used to provide a rich variety of landscape experiences. A central avenue is focused on a view of the citadel, bordered by palm trees and pavilions and punctuated by many fountains. There is also a meandering system of pathways adapted to the hilly structure of the site. Further points of attraction are a café on the lower southern plain (the pavilions and terraces of which border an artificial lake and an orchard), as well as the more luxurious hill-top restaurant. Both facilities are generating income for continued maintenance and upgrading of the Park.

The implementation of the new Azhar Park has completely transformed the image of this part of Cairo. Once considered a backyard of the old city, the place has been turned into a popular destination for visitors from all over Cairo, as well as foreigners. Al-Darb al-Ahmar is no longer located on the edge of a rubbish dump but instead overlooks a paradise-like public garden easily accessible to its residents. Moreover the city has reclaimed its original historic appearance, as 1.4 kilometres of the 12th-century Ayyubid wall, which had gradually disappeared under accumulating debris, were revealed again in their full splendour. The discovery and progressive restoration of the Ayyubid city wall with its interior galleries and the reinstated old city gates (now serving as new entrances from al-Darb al-Ahmar to the Azhar Park) is a story of its own.

The houses that have been built during the last one or two centuries from the city side against the Ayyubid wall (and even on top of it) and which are an integral aspect of Cairo's urban history raised particular conservation issues. Negotiation with the Egyptian Supreme Council of Antiquities was needed before embarking on their restoration, because they had been earmarked for eventual demolition. In fact an old antiquities law still calls for a 30-metre-wide strip to be cleared on the inner side of the city wall – a major intervention which would have had adverse social consequences. Moreover such action would not have enhanced the monument but rather jeopardized its survival by isolating it from the adjacent urban fabric.

The various physical rehabilitation initiatives in al-Darb al-Ahmar were started in 1999 and considered as part of an ongoing *process* rather than a finite project, such as the Park or the wall. The basis for this series of interventions was a concept of micro-scale research and implementation that covered the whole urban fabric plot by plot, starting with the row of buildings along the wall. Data on the physical state of buildings was collected, as well as information on the living conditions and aspirations of the inhabitants. Tailored to each case, a wide range of interventions has been applied, from scientific restoration of major monuments to emergency repairs on housing and typological infill projects, as well as infrastructure repairs and the improvement of public open spaces. A widespread housing improvement scheme (including microcredit) was initiated in 2004–2005 with the participation of residents. A grand, late 19th-century residential building along the wall, which was about to collapse, has been fully restored and now serves as combined project office and community centre, where residents of al-Darb al-Ahmar can organize social events, find advice or receive training.

To reclaim the architectural heritage of al-Darb al-Ahmar, two landmark complexes, the Khayrbek Mosque and the Umm al-Sultan Sha'aban Mosque, have also been restored. The historic houses, schoolrooms and other annexes attached to them are now being used for community-related purposes in the domains of health, education, skills enhancement and microcredit management, and to accommodate newly created NGOs. They are focal points for a wide range of socio-economic development initiatives which were conceived of as an integral part of the long-term rehabilitation process and provide residents with many new opportunities to improve their livelihoods. The latest addition to HCP's Cairo activities is the so-called urban plaza complex, now under construction along the northern edge of the site. The future urban plaza will be a multi-functional complex combining cultural, commercial and leisure functions, with internal courtyards and terraces. It will provide an additional grand entrance to the Park and will feature a museum and an exhibition centre to introduce visitors to the history of Islamic Cairo and to the archaeological discoveries made along the historic wall.[3]

While it is still too early to make a final evaluation of the benefits of HCP's interventions in Cairo, it can be said that the Azhar Park, including its high-end facilities, has been adopted whole-heartedly by the various strata of Cairo's population – a material expression of which is higher than expected income from sales of entry tickets and from the restaurants. According to an agreement with the Cairo Governorate, the financial proceeds from the Park operation and the urban plaza will be used for further enhancement of the Park and the neighbouring areas of al-Darb al-Ahmar, thus providing cross-subsidies for less profitable improvement schemes. The environmental upgrading of al-Darb al-Ahmar, initiated by the Park and the wall projects, is unleashing an internal dynamic which should soon attract private-sector investment to the area, thus providing greater momentum to the ongoing urban rehabilitation process and making it more self-sustainable. To facilitate this process, the AKTC team is contributing overall planning guidelines, technical assistance in individual project development and liaison with the local authorities.

HCP's Cairo initiatives have been described at greater length here, because they provide the best example of how a wide range of combined, incremental development activities – all of them reflecting the realities on the ground rather than being derived from abstract, pre-conceived planning schemes – can generate a powerful momentum for positive change. By taking on a life of their own, these initiatives are able to spread into wider urban areas. It is this humble, yet ambitious 'nuclear' approach which has been used by the Programme to produce urban revitalization schemes in various historic cities in the Islamic world. The most recent initiatives have been implemented in the old cities of Aleppo (since 2001), Kabul and Herat (since 2003) and Lahore, with others going on in Delhi, as well as various historic sites in Mali.

In Aleppo the enhancement of the public open spaces around the famous citadel – arguably the most accomplished historic defence structure in the Arab world still standing – adds an urban dimension to the conservation projects on the three Syrian castles (Aleppo, Masyaf and Qal'at Salah al-Din) that had been completed earlier by HCP. The improvement of this important civic space constitutes another major 'area development project' that will help revitalize the historic centre of Aleppo and make it more attractive to residents and visitors alike.[4] In Kabul a whole district of the surviving but badly damaged historic city has been rehabilitated in close cooperation with its residents, simultaneously with the restoration of the Garden of Babur – the first Mughal emperor – as a public and civic space. Moreover the restoration of the Timur Shah mausoleum has been completed in the context of a wider planning and landscaping scheme for the embankment of the Kabul river and the central markets. Together with corresponding urban rehabilitation initiatives in the centre of Herat, these projects demonstrate how cultural heritage can be preserved in difficult post-conflict situations in Central Asia. The restoration of the Gardens of Humayun's tomb in Delhi further demonstrates the Programme's commitment to Mughal architecture, and new area conservation and development initiatives are now being pursued in the adjacent district of Nizam al-Din. Subsequently the Programme has extended its portfolio by engaging in conservation and urban rehabilitation projects in Mopti and Djenneh, as a long-term commitment to the preservation of the distinctive earthen architecture of Mali, an important region of Islamic culture in sub-Saharan Africa.

The Relevance of the Built Environment and its Meaning in the Islamic Context

Instead of providing further details on the Historic Cities Programme (covered by other publications), the following pages intend to cast some light on the deeper rationale underlying the Programme's activities. No attempt at implementing urban rehabilitation strategies can avoid the question of why people should be concerned with the survival of their cultural and architectural heritage. In other terms: are conservation and revitalization merely nostalgic (or, worse, elitist) concepts imposed on a local population which is much more concerned with better living conditions and modern 'development', whatever the interpretation of this term may be? Does cultural heritage have a role to play in the future, or is conservation merely an attempt to freeze the past? Is there no hope of reconciling the apparent dichotomy between conservation and modern development?

To answer such questions, one has to refer to considerations of a more philosophical or psychological nature which deal with the mode of interaction between human beings and their built environment. This implies going beyond the purely material or functional attributes of physical structures, particularly since people do not conceive of their surroundings simply in utilitarian terms, but also and more intensely in imaginary ways, i.e. via visual symbols and archetypes. Projecting through architectural means a meaningful image of reality and a corresponding 'sense of place' is thus essential for ensuring the individual and collective well-being of the users of man-made spaces. In turn, what defines a user's attitude towards his built environment is the mental perception (and interpretation) of the given site qualities which elicit an emotional and spiritual resonance in him, and thereby make him attach values and judgements to seemingly 'neutral' physical shapes and structures.

In traditional societies, whether in the European Middle Ages or in pre-modern Eastern cultures, what used to motivate people in their environmental actions was the urge to live up to ideal images which embodied their beliefs and their collective identity. Without such visions neither Christian cathedrals nor Hindu and Buddhist temple mounds, nor some of the carefully planned palatial complexes of the past, would ever have been built. Man's means for achieving a holistic cultural universe have been his artistic capacities and his ability to conceive and materialize images of a higher spiritual order. While animals are restricted to a sort of 'automatic', i.e. cybernetically determined interaction with their natural habitat, human beings, through the tools of culture, have the possibility of conceptualizing different worlds. For human beings are equipped with creative imagination – the gift which, throughout the centuries, has enabled them to integrate physical and metaphysical realities and to shape inspiring places, buildings and works of art that go beyond mere material commodities.

Underlying man's urge to give form to his loftier visions is the eternal human quest for 'meaning', i.e. the need to enhance temporal earthly life by relating it to the timeless sources from which it emanates. In more concrete terms, this involves both the perception of spiritual values through matching intuitive and intellectual capacities, as well as the translation of such values into tangible forms and practices of daily life. To infuse man-made creations with meaning can be seen as the primary incentive of any human intervention in the environment, be it by architects, craftsmen or anonymous builders. It is the embodiment of meaning in a given place or structure that conditions man's response to it, providing him with a confirmation of his identity and enabling him to reproduce it and give it variety through many other expressions of human culture.

It is this positive exchange of give and take through the generations that has built up the substance, the inner unity and the outward coherence of past civilizations, rooting man in meaningful cultural patterns. In terms of urban structures, it has produced the unique balance between freedom and order so characteristic of historic cities in many regions. The term *genius loci* as the matrix of a pluralistic, yet consistent cultural production best sums up the qualities resulting from such interactive processes.

The blindness of modernity to those realities that transcend material and economic facts has severely limited its access to meaning, and eroded the capacity to produce built environments that can express qualities more substantial than sheer economic power, eccentric originality or a short-lived fashion. Moreover it has also led most professionals, whether historians, architects or administrators, to discard or misinterpret the inheritance of far more complete traditional cultures surviving in the present age. Intuitively many may still feel the subliminal presence of lost dimensions of our own being in the artefacts of the past. Yet the prevailing consensus is that traditional cultural expressions no longer represent a living reality and no longer embody essential human values capable of being revived from within. Instead they tend to be perceived as dead foliage, as it were, as meaningless formal relics of a distant past, worthy of scientific interest at best.

Emptying the built environment of its deeper values and its communicative qualities eventually introduced a gap between tradition and modernity, and went a long way to disrupt the self-regulating and self-reproducing systems of traditional cultures, thus preventing an inner continuity. It might be argued that the organic integrity of living cultural traditions was torn apart and its demise gave rise to two equally unviable visions: that of a fossilized heritage and that of an utopian Brave New World. As a result the divide between concepts of nostalgic 'conservation' and futuristic 'development' emerged, isolating them as diametrically opposed approaches. While apparently in contradiction to each other, they both suffer from the same kind of sterility because of their lack of response to vital human needs. In fact the most advanced rational planning constructs and the most painstaking archaeological preservation attempts simply represent two sides of the same coin – their common feature being the inability to incarnate a vibrant and fulfilling presence, which would be a fluid link between the past and the future.[5]

In this context it needs to be pointed out that the attribute 'historic' – conventionally used to justify conservation – corresponds to a paradigm invented in Europe in the 19th century and should not be seen as representing a quality in itself. The very concept of history in the modern sense is a secularized form of the linear concept of time found in various religious traditions including Christian eschatology. During the 19th and 20th centuries, with science and technology seeming to take to some degree the place of religion, the notion of a positivist utopia emerged which replaced the Christian salvation myth with a vision of endless man-made progress.[6] Authentic cultural values – and this holds true for all pre-modern cultures around the globe – do not depend on today's historic categories. They are constituted (and constantly renewed) by the performance of Tradition as a living system that is capable of self-sustained cultural production, incremental innovation and a creative integration of external influences.

The internal function of cultural traditions can be compared to that of cellular organic systems, the life of which is predicated on permanent processes of *auto-poïesis* (self-creation), to reflect a key-term used in recent biological research.[7] The basis of *auto-poïesis* is a structure where each part (or each individual cell) mirrors the larger whole and therefore has the inbuilt faculty of autonomous growth and self-renewal. Living cultural systems operate in similar ways, relying on a continuous and consistent metamorphosis without changing their fundamental principles. In order to be able to renew itself and still retain its essential qualities, a cultural tradition must constantly refer to timeless, immutable spiritual principles and archetypes, while adapting its various expressions to accidental material constraints, such as changing needs and circumstances. In accordance with the limits of the *conditio humana*, crystallized physical forms can never fully exhaust the intrinsic meaning of the images they incorporate, since the metaphysical values contained in symbols and archetypes are ultimately beyond formal expression. Yet, paradoxically, they depend on visualization through the arts, for they can only be experienced and shared through the medium of specific forms that appeal to the human senses – and above all to man's innate sense of beauty as an indicator of spiritual truth.[8]

For a Tradition to remain alive, creative and productive, two conditions apply. Firstly, its inner principles must be valued and experienced as a meaningful reality; secondly, they must be absorbed, internalized and enacted by individuals of a distinct and coherent social group managing their own territory – a process which will almost automatically create both a strong inner unity and a rich variety of material cultural outcomes. The built environment will then emerge as a lively expression of shared identity, providing a template for consistent individual and collective action. Indeed the manifestations of Tradition transmit a specific sense of 'wholeness' which cannot be generated artificially, for it must grow organically from within, i.e. out of the spiritual seeds nurtured in the cultural terrain.[9] Thus Tradition relies on the daily, almost ritual implementation of archetypical attitudes at grass-roots level; it will perish (or degenerate into a sterile theoretical construct) once the shared emotional connections with the spiritual sources of truth and identity are weakened, and once the chain of continuous reproduction and transmission is interrupted.

The inherited, pre-industrial built environment of Islamic societies, as it has survived up to this day in numerous historic cities and countless rural settlements, is a particularly strong testimony to the general principles of Tradition outlined above, and there are several reasons for this. First, Islam is a religion which, from the beginning, encouraged a coherent social and civic order.[10] For its realization it has relied on the strong social bonds inherent to ancient tribal societies, enhancing and superseding them by religious affiliation. Through its doctrine of divine unicity (*tawhid*), it has succeeded in bringing spiritual and worldly concerns together and in fostering strong patterns of daily life and modes of behaviour anchored in religious practice. The coherent translation of such deep-rooted collective attitudes into the physical structure of the built environment was greatly facilitated by the fact that the craftsmen and builders were part of the chain of Tradition. They had a knowledge, conscious or intuitive, of the meaning of architectural and ornamental forms and established a visual language that seems to have been understood by society as a whole. Traditional Islamic architects and craftsmen were fully integrated into society and rarely emerged as 'individuals'. In turn, most people knew how to build and adorn their own houses in their vernacular tradition.

Another Islamic concept that has shaped attitudes towards the built environment is the idea of man being the vicegerent and the steward of God's creation, as put forward in the Qur'an. The idea of responsibility and custodianship for nature – the fundamental resource of the built environment – is thus inherent to the faith. And, as is emphasized again and again in the Qur'anic messages, nature is not a 'dead' object or simple commodity but is invested with the Divine presence, as revealed through visible signs and symbols (*ayat*). Embedded in this concept of man as God's vicegerent on earth is the idea that he should neither assume the omnipotence of the one and only God nor attempt to become his own master. This is coupled with the acknowledgement that earthly existence is relative and transient, while the timeless and the absolute are found with God only – an attitude which went a long way to prevent utopian thinking and arrogant presumptions in man-made endeavours, establishments and institutions. As the theologian-philosopher al-Ghazali once put it, the world is merely a caravanserai where travellers meet during their terrestrial journey.

Some of the basic cosmological concepts of Islam are expressed in a powerful archetypical imagery that has inspired the shaping of the traditional built environment and the way it has been perceived and lived in. Perhaps the most fertile of such visions, capable of being mirrored in the man-made habitat, is the image of the paradise garden. Vividly evoked in many sections of the Qur'an, it establishes a close connection between spiritual and sensual experience. Moreover the paradise garden transfigures, enhances and formalizes an existing natural resource – the oasis – which is the only means of survival in a desert environment. Apart from being an element of pleasure and relief, water plays a particular role as the symbol of immaculate eternal life. Through the ritual ablutions, it assumes a religious function, renewing man's primordial state of purity which, during prayer, enables him to communicate with God. Thus water channels and fountains are ubiquitous features in the Islamic townscape, whether inside mosques, palaces and private houses or in common open spaces. Often they are integrated in enclosed garden courtyards that provide a man-made micro-cosmos, reflecting the wider universe within their restricted boundaries.

One could say that the use of water in the built environment emphasizes the virtual omnipresence of the Divine in the material world – a principle which is also present in the idea that the presence of the sacred is not limited to formal places of worship, with the exception of the central sanctuary of the Ka'ba in Mecca, where prayers from all parts of the world converge by virtue of the *qibla* orientation. The simple act of addressing God after performing ablutions can turn any given site into a place of prayer. Thus, due to the immanent presence of the Divine, the whole world is a potentially sacred site.

This understanding of the immanence and the omnipresence of the Divine had interesting consequences for the way the built environment was structured, its functions and how it is experienced by those who make use of it. Mosques, for instance, are generally not singled out of the urban tissue as isolated sacred spaces, as is the case with many churches or temples. They are also seen as congregational places which allow for many other functions beside prayer, and thus they tend to be embedded and physically integrated in larger complexes of markets, schools (*madrasas*), bathhouses (*hammams*) and caravanserais, making up a multi-functional cluster of public facilities controlled by the legal provisions of a charitable endowment (*waqf*). The courtyards of large public facilities also provide a coherent system of integrated common open spaces in the heart of the city.

Private houses, in contrast, are endowed with a greater sacred character than is usually the case in other cultures. They are considered sanctuaries (*haram*) of intimate family life, with special emphasis on the screening of the female domain. This has favoured the ubiquitous use of enclosed precincts catering for protected and largely self-contained interior spaces, as featured in most typologies of Islamic architecture. The preference for introverted buildings is also dictated by climatic conditions. The result is the use of central courtyards catering for light and air, which increases the autonomy of each residential unit and enables individual houses to coalesce wall-to-wall into clusters forming coherent sub-components of the urban fabric. This structural principle allowed the urban morphology of traditional Islamic cities to become homogeneous and extremely compact. Within the dense urban fabric, protection of the private sphere is obtained by careful control of accesses and entrances, and clearly marked thresholds between public and private spaces.[11]

The coherence of the traditional Islamic built environment was further enhanced by the use of a common artistic language in the architectural decoration of both religious and secular buildings. Through its focus on calligraphy, geometrical ornamentation and the arabesque, Islamic art gained a wide range of applicability, enabling it to merge easily with solid architectural structures. Ornamental patterns cover large wall surfaces, adorn significant door and window frames and often fill the cavities under domes, squinches and corbellings, thus managing the transition from square to spherical architectural components. The *muqarnas*, a unique form of Islamic architectural decoration, represents a striking three-dimensional transposition of geometric systems – and, beyond that, a meditative illustration of the complementary principles of differentiation and integration that are at work in the complex patterns of Creation. In many cases, architectural decoration envelops the structural parts of a building like a beautiful fabric, veiling its material character and transforming it into a lofty enigma of transcendent reality. Such intentions correspond to the traditional Islamic philosophy of life, the objective of which is to render the material world translucent with the radiance of the supreme reality.

Reconciling Tradition and Modernity

The preceding paragraphs contain indications of the type of conflicts that can exist between modern development procedures and the traditional built environment of local communities. While this is not the place to dwell in great detail on the historic impact of modern Western civilization on the traditional societies in the Islamic world, it must be borne in mind that the pressure began to be felt during the colonial period and has intensified in the second half of the 20th century, when new Islamic states emerged from the political divisions created by the colonial powers. In fact political independence was often followed by increasing economic and cultural dependence, as these countries were faced with a double and sometimes contradictory challenge: on the one hand, to strive for the benefits and opportunities of material advancement offered by Western innovations in science and technology during the 19th and 20th centuries; on the other hand, to protect and strengthen their traditional cultural identity against the influence of the secular ideologies underlying many of the achievements of technological progress.

No serious development endeavour in the Islamic world of today can ignore this basic dilemma, which is inherent to the current geopolitical context. The challenge is particularly arduous because of the conceptual implications of the Western notion of 'progress'. Since the Renaissance, European civilization has been obsessed with measurable, rational and material aspects of life to the exclusion of other dimensions. This movement culminated in Positivism, which in turn unleashed the autonomous and unfettered development of modern science and technology, thus doing away with the traditional view of an integrated, 'animated' cosmos. Modern civilization boasts of its unilateral dependence on reason but, paradoxically, the more it does so the more it becomes prey to irrational forces that can manipulate the course of history. In this process of rationalization, lasting cultural references were progressively annihilated, and, eventually, the loss of spiritual energy capable of holding together all material expressions of life led to a gradual disintegration of values and to a corresponding deficit in meaning.[12] The expansion of such a type of progress could only be achieved at the expense of cultural depth, identity and coherence.

Nowadays local cultural traditions, as far as they have survived, are exposed to the spread of globalization driven by modern technology. They are condemned, it seems, either to find their own path to renewal or else to be extinguished. Freezing past cultural expressions with a view to protecting and preserving them is not a solution to this dilemma. Many traditional structures may no longer be reproduced literally, i.e. in the external shape in which they had crystallized in the past, nor is archaeological conservation of the historic built environment a viable solution, except in the case of a limited number of single monuments.

However, this should by no means imply that the only alternative is to replace local cultural expressions with foreign imports based on alien cultural models and attitudes. The fallacy of standard modern development ideologies is to believe that modernization must always proceed through the abrupt and comprehensive replacement of supposedly obsolete traditional cultures and social patterns, despite their inherent faculties of adaptation and resilience, which have proved themselves throughout centuries of successful earlier evolution. Opinionated modernists are unable to conceive of more subtle modes of cultural exchange or of an evolutionary transformation based on indigenous values and principles – simply because their philosophical prejudices trap them in a self-defeating cycle from which they cannot extricate themselves. Accordingly, many modern development paradigms automatically go for radical interventions that involve the destruction of traditional systems and the mechanical substitution of existing elements, instead of strengthening the roots of existing indigenous cultures which could in fact be helped to flourish independently once again.

To remain true to themselves, traditional cultures have to follow their own entelechy, i.e. their own inbuilt order and finality. Yet they should not be regarded as rigid and inflexible – a judgement hinging on a modern bias for permanent and abrupt revolutions too readily identified with 'progress'. Cultural exchange, transformation and innovation have always been a natural and essential part of evolving traditions. But in order to achieve a genuine metamorphosis, change needs to re-interpret the guiding spiritual values and principles of a given culture and to be anchored in stable and meaningful cultural and social patterns. Only then can any newly introduced structures respond to the material, emotional and spiritual aspirations of the people; only then will change become sustainable through the collective commitment of the individuals involved; only then will it be possible to creatively absorb and internalize any external influences. The key issue, therefore, is to control and modify the forces of change, i.e. to enable a society to pursue a type of development which it can control itself and in a fashion which draws on its inner resources. This clearly means utilizing all forms of cultural potential in concert, rather than stressing isolated material aspects to the exclusion of other human faculties and needs.

The previous section has made it clear how culture in its many forms – perpetuated through time – acts as both the matrix and the repository of meaning, and that this can be seen as the strongest incentive for human beings to become productive and achieve social cohesion. Therefore, one may conclude, no development project which wants to realize human potential to the fullest extent can dispense with culture. Or, in other words, culture and development should never be allowed to become divergent or antagonistic forces. For just as development cannot be socially and intellectually absorbed or become truly effective without being part of culture, no more can culture remain creative and innovative if treated as a superficial addition to individual development pursuits.

The main question, then, is how a viable integration of both forces in terms of genuine 'cultural development' can be achieved – or, rather, consciously restored, since it was a natural trait of past civilizations. Establishing a viable synthesis is not just a matter of mediating between traditional cultural resources and modern technological tools, but of making them truly interactive and mutually reinforcing. This raises the issue of how modern tools and procedures can be made subservient to wider human needs rather than subjecting people to technology and exposing them to associated ideological and economic pressures. The problem here is one of compatibility, and it can only be resolved once modern development tools are modified and adapted so as to soften potential clashes and to avoid the repression of indigenous cultures.[13]

The first step towards fostering compatibility is to reveal the limitations and the hidden ideological bias of allegedly neutral modern development concepts – such as the unquestioned identification of new forms of industrial development with social progress and the belief that science and technology as such can succeed in creating 'paradise on earth'. Since the 19th century the Positivist ideologies underpinning Western civilization have established their own fundamentalist myth. They have been quick to dismiss or attack the spiritual foundation of religious traditions but curiously seem to have remained unaware of their own pseudo-religious dogmatism and indeed of their missionary zeal, which is often propelled by commercial agendas rather than by genuine humanitarian concern. Therefore, in order to avoid potentially harmful wholesale transfers, unravelling the ideological assumptions of composite modern development 'packages', singling out contradictory elements and adapting or re-inventing its applicable components is a matter that requires considerable diligence.

In parallel with the careful defusing of foreign development models or the extraction from them of those elements which are compatible with indigenous traditions, the major agents and the various potentials of the respective culture must be identified, strengthened and developed in order to enable it to respond to changing external conditions. Restoring the internal strengths and the cultural resilience of a society means it will be able to absorb the impact of external cultures creatively – rather than being paralysed by them. The simultaneous process of deconstructing and recomposing may eventually lead to some sort of 'organic' grafting in which the chances of rejection are minimized and new forms of hybrid traditions are allowed to emerge.

Instead of stifling existing resources, innovation must unlock and increase dormant potential and nurture organic growth from within. Thus the most important issue is to enable local cultural systems to reclaim their own vitality and creativity by encouraging internal life processes (*auto-poïesis*) which will be sources of self-renewal and self-sustainability. Indeed traditional societies have enormous potential at their disposal waiting to be recognized and harnessed in proper ways. This includes firm spiritual convictions, strong group solidarity and social networking, entrepreneurial initiative, talents for improvisation and for hands-on action with regard to their physical needs, as well as the capacity to negotiate and resolve internal conflicts. These resources should rather be strengthened by offering commensurate fields of action than frustrated by the imposition of rigid bureaucratic procedures. In this context, proper institutional capacity-building with targeted and responsive local communities is essential, in order to ensure that, by assuming a sense of territorial ownership and responsibility, they can reap the fruits of the evolutionary processes in which they are engaged.

The type of 'social engineering' suggested here may sound more abstract and more complicated than it actually is. What it requires, however, is an open and sincere dialogue between sensitive development professionals and active local communities as partners in a joint and open-ended process of discovery. The task of external professionals is to seek to understand the values, aspirations and social ramifications of a given traditional culture, to suggest productive ways of using a range of adapted development tools, and to offer advice on strategies designed to produce better internal resource development. The task of local groups and their representatives is to look with fresh eyes at their own traditions and to assess the implications of introducing new techniques and procedures. They also need to mobilize community support for innovative projects, to anticipate and resolve possible internal conflicts and to negotiate forms of internal compensation for any inequities triggered by social and economic change.

This brief description of a desirable form of interaction makes it clear that 'cultural development', in order to take root, cannot be imposed from the top; nor can it rely on centralized procedures and remote systems of control. At the same time as responding to global factors of change, new solutions have to be developed, implemented, sustained and monitored in the local context and with the direct participation of the constituencies concerned. The experimental character of this endeavour has to be recognized, and proper feedback systems need to be built into the development process. This means allowing for a flexible and differentiated incremental approach, rather than imposing preconceived, large-scale blueprints which are not adapted to the social and physical realities on the ground. As the projects of the Historic Cities Programme previously mentioned have demonstrated, such localized in-depth cooperation can unlock unexpected resources in communities, enabling them to face the challenge of development with a greater degree of autonomy.

The ongoing work of the Aga Khan Trust for Culture, modest as it may be, represents an exemplary contribution to the attempt to revitalize existing cultural heritage, ensuring that coming generations retain valid options and can make informed choices about their future built environment. Moreover in today's explosive political context where religious concepts (whether of Christian or Islamic origin) have been distorted and usurped to justify aggressive political ideologies, it provides a pragmatic demonstration of the essential role of culture in human society. For it shows how an integrated type of human development can be nurtured on the narrow stretch of common ground left to the human beings caught between two opposing radical ideologies, i.e. a totalitarian secular fundamentalism and a militant religious dogmatism. Broadening this common ground and overcoming the sterile dichotomy between two reductionist movements (both claiming exclusive validity and both equally unviable because of their approach) will increase the chances for tolerance, pluralism and rich cultural diversity which are preconditions of a fulfilling human existence.

Restoring meaning to the built environment is part of this essential endeavour, since providing people with a deep sense of place and belonging helps to anchor them in their earthly existence while opening a window onto the metaphysical realm. Caring for the built environment is about turning man's fragmentary world into the symbol of a more comprehensive, timeless order and helping him discover that his interior and his exterior universes are one.

Notes

1. See, for instance, some of the Award's publications: *Modernity and Community: Architecture in the Islamic World* (London, 2001); *Architecture and Polyphony: Building in the Islamic World Today* (London, 2004), and *Intervention Architecture* (London, 2007), as well as Philip Jodidio, *Under the Eaves of Architecture* (Munich, 2007).
2. For further details, see Stefano Bianca, ed., *Karakoram: Hidden Treasures in the Northern Areas of Pakistan* (Geneva and Turin, 2005).
3. For further details see Stefano Bianca and Philip Jodidio, ed., *Cairo: Revitalising a Historic Metropolis* (Geneva and Turin, 2004), as well as the internal HCP publication on al-Darb al-Ahmar. See also F. Daftary, E. Fernea and A. Nanji, ed., *Living in Historic Cairo: Past and Present in an Islamic City* (London, 2010), pp. 171–293.
4. For further details, see S. Bianca, ed., *Syria: Medieval Citadels between East and West* (Geneva and Turin, 2007).
5. George Steiner in his *Real Presences* (Chicago, 1989) gives an excellent account of the difference between 'first-hand' and 'second-hand' realities,

describing how modern civilization is being inundated by 'second-hand' derivatives and is thus losing its awareness of more primordial realities and experiences.

6. Octavio Paz in his *Convergences* (New York, 1987), pp. 121–122, writes: 'Modern time is the offspring of Christian time. The offspring and the negation: it is an irreversible time that follows a straight line, but it lacks a beginning and will have no end; it has not been created and it will not be destroyed. Its protagonist is not the fallen soul but the evolution of the human species, and its real name is history. Modernity is grounded in a twofold paradox. On the one hand, meaning resides neither in the past nor in eternity but in the future, so that history is also called progress. On the other hand, time does not have a foundation in any divine revelation or immutable principles; we conceive of it as a process that continually negates itself and thus transforms itself. ... Or rather, our time lacks substance; what's more, its action is the criticism of any and every substantialism. Thus Revolution takes the place of Redemption. ... Technology begins as a negation of the image of the world and ends as an image of the destruction of the world.'

7. See Fritjof Capra, *The Web of Life* (London, 1996), and, more recently his *The Hidden Connections* (London, 2003) – books which provide a fascinating introduction to the 'post-modern' approaches of science, demonstrating how emerging scientific concepts corroborate perennial, pre-modern philosophies and world views. Of particular interest is the parallelism between self-generating and self-renewing cellular systems of organic nature and corresponding social systems.

8. A profound elucidation of Tradition and its perennial values, pertaining to the Islamic context, can be found in the extensive works of René Guénon, Frithjof Schuon, Titus Burckhardt and Sayyed Hossein Nasr. See, for instance, T. Burckhardt, *Mirror of the Intellect: Essays on Traditional Science and Sacred Art* (Cambridge, 1987).

9. Christopher Alexander in his *The Timeless Way of Building* (New York, 1979) speaks compellingly about the sense of 'wholeness' reached through traditional forms of architectural production.

10. See, for instance, Louis Gardet, *La cité Musulmane* (Paris, 1954).

11. For a more detailed structural analysis, see Stefano Bianca, *Urban Form in the Arab World: Past and Present* (London and New York, 2000).

12. This process has been analysed by several European writers as the main disease of the nascent modern world in the late 19th and early 20th centuries. See, among others, René Guénon in his *Le Règne de la quantité et les signes des temps* (Paris, 1945), or Hermann Broch in his novel *The Sleepwalkers* (New York, 1947). Both went a long way in demystifying the illusions and obsessions of the 19th and 20th centuries.

13. It is hardly necessary to mention here the violent reactions which can occur when repressed traditional societies (or their defenders) take revenge on

an aggressively enforced Westernization by turning back the very tools of modernity against those institutions, individuals or symbols which represent the 'aggressor'. John Gray, in *False Dawn: The Delusions of Global Capitalism* (London, 2002), makes the point that 'the growth of scientific knowledge and expertise has not produced a convergence of values, or a universal civilization. Instead, it interacts with the diverse cultures humans have always had and gives them new weapons with which to propagate their different values'. See also the same author's *Al Qaeda and What it Means to be Modern* (London, 2003).

10

The Gender Policies of Aga Khan III and Aga Khan IV

Zayn R. Kassam

This chapter examines developments pertaining in part to Nizari Ismaili Muslim women in the last century through an analysis of the views of their 48th and 49th Imams, Sir Sultan Muhammad Shah, Aga Khan III (r. 1885–1957), and His Highness Prince Karim al-Husayni, Aga Khan IV (r. 1957–present). While much research still needs to be carried out regarding the status of Ismaili Muslim women both in the period prior to and during that under discussion, at the present time the situation of Ismaili women differs according to their geographical and cultural location, and depends upon a variety of factors including but not limited to the legal regime under which they fall, economic status, the degree to which healthcare and education is available to them, and global, regional and national political conditions – all of which are factors that must be taken into account for women globally, regardless of their faith tradition.

According to the Constitution of the Shia Imami Nizari Ismailis, Ismailis follow the legal regime of the countries in which they reside. Thus, for instance, Ismaili women living within the boundaries of the Europe–America–Australia orbit are afforded protections as found for women generally within those contexts. Similarly, Ismaili women living in Pakistan or Afghanistan are subject to Pakistani or Afghan law, respectively, and as such, are protected only to the extent that the legal regimes in those countries allow, and, furthermore, can be subject to the often legally sanctioned cultural practices obtaining in those areas. For instance, under the Taliban, Ismaili women in Afghanistan were subject to veiling while in public, as are Ismaili women in Iran and Saudi Arabia where head-covering is mandatory by law, despite the fact that head-coverings are no longer a religious requirement for Ismaili women.

In terms of economic status, the Aga Khan health and educational institutions have done much in the areas where they operate to make access to healthcare and education available to all regardless of race, religion, gender or class. Where they do not operate, healthcare and education become matters either of state provision or of whether individual Ismaili women belong to a class that can afford to pay for such services. Canadian Ismaili women, therefore, have access to healthcare and education as provided by the Canadian provincial governments, and Kenyan Ismaili women have the choice of attending either the state institutions or the Aga Khan institutions at minimal cost; Chinese Ismaili women, on the other hand, may only have access to state-funded education and healthcare where it is available. In all cases, a privileged background allows a woman access to superior educational institutions, if desired, along with better medical care than that offered by the state. Finally, the larger cultural expectations of gendered social roles play a part in determining the extent to which women are able to participate in the decision-making processes pertaining to the larger political and social life of the community in which they live. Thus, for instance, Mobina Jaffer is the first Muslim and Ismaili woman to be appointed to the Canadian Senate; Nurjehan Mawani was the first Muslim woman to chair the Immigration and Refugee Board of Canada, where she introduced historic legislation to make the threat of female genital surgery plausible grounds for granting refugee status, a move that has since been followed by other countries such as the United States; Tazim Kassam was the first Muslim woman to chair the Study of Islam Section at the prestigious American Academy of Religion in the United States, and is also the first Muslim woman to chair the Department of Religious Studies at Syracuse University; while Zain Verjee is the first Ismaili Muslim woman to be appointed to a high-profile position at CNN, the global news agency (Christiane Amanpour was probably the first Iranian woman).

The achievements of Ismaili Muslim women such as these are as much due to their own efforts as they are to the Ismaili community ethos set into motion by Aga Khan III and continued under Aga Khan IV, both of whom took steps to advance women's status so as to enable the full realization of their potential. In addition the educational and cultural systems of the societies in which Ismaili women live are important factors in determining the ways and means by which they define and achieve their goals, and, concomitantly, Ismaili women, like their civic and cultural counterparts, are constrained by the larger impediments operating in a society which may affect the degree to which women can participate in the lives of their civic and national communities and institutions. Their expectations may be determined by whether or not they are allowed to vote in the larger society (for instance, this is not so in Kuwait and Saudi Arabia), whether or not they may run for political office, pursue certain careers, work or travel outside the home without male permission, whether or not they require family permission to choose a spouse, or if they can make decisions regarding their health and bodies. In other words, it is clear that amelioration of the status of Ismaili women cannot be attained without similar advances in the status and role of women generally in those societies in which Ismaili women live, and that social advancement of this one group cannot occur without the advancement of the society as a whole.

Sir Sultan Muhammad Shah, as the supreme spiritual head of the community, fulfilled his mandate as *Imam-i Zaman* (Imam, or spiritual leader of the time, to be distinguished from the Sunni appellation of *imam* that denotes the leader of the prayer or *salat*) to provide guidance for his community that was in keeping with the times. His desire to modernize the Ismaili community for which he was responsible was not divorced from his concern for the Muslim *umma* generally. Indeed he included the 'woman question' in his interest in the relations between Muslim-majority societies and the world as a whole.

His writings on the need for women's suffrage in India illustrate the point. An active member of the Muslim League in the events leading up to the partition of India when the British left the subcontinent, Aga Khan III was well aware of the debates surrounding Indian self-rule. The British conceptualized India as a place that was culturally and spiritually backward, and saw themselves as carrying 'the white man's burden' (as per the title of the poem by Rudyard Kipling), that is, the responsibility of colonizing and ruling other peoples in an effort to bring them civilization, defined as the wholesale adoption of a European way of life. The Indian independence movement was met with arguments against the Indian capacity for self-rule. Arguments against Indian self-rule were buttressed by the 'woman question', as it was widely held by the British that the treatment of women in colonized cultures such as Egypt and India could provide evidence of the 'backwardness' of Islamic and Indian societies and hence justified 'enlightened' British rule. In the Indian case, works such as James Mill's *The History of British India* (1818) treated 'practices found among particular groups and in particular regions of India, such as the self immolation of widows (*sati*), female infanticide, the veiling of women (*purdah*), child marriage, and enforced widowhood, ... as emblematic of all India and of Indian culture as a whole. As such, therefore, these practices afforded a basis not only for the ideological justification of the "civilizing mission" of British imperialism in India, but also for arguments about the "barbarity" of Indian culture.'[1] It was in this context that Katherine Mayo wrote her infamous work, *Mother India*, first published in 1927, in which she argued that the many ills that beset Indian society, such as those related to childbirth, child marriage, veiling and the treatment of women generally, made Indians incapable of self-rule and justified continued British rule in India. As Mrinalini Sinha persuasively argues, by identifying these practices as 'timeless' cultural practices and conveniently ignoring the colonial government's 'repeated opposition to a number of reform measures, including bills sponsored by Indian legislators for raising the age of consent and abolishing child-marriage, nor the many reform initiatives for women undertaken by Indian men and women themselves',[2] the American author made it seem that Indian political backwardness stemmed from the condition and treatment of Indian women, a trope found in colonial and imperialist discourses on Muslim lands as well.

It is against this background that Aga Khan III's views on the 'woman question' must be viewed. While acknowledging that Indian women were chained by prejudice and folly from taking their rightful place in society, and that India could not take a place among the free nations of the world until the principle of equality between the sexes was accepted by Indians, he argued that Indian women were no less capable than their emancipated sisters elsewhere. In this respect he argued that women were as capable of earning their own livelihood as were men; Indian women played a crucial role in the advancement of society and were perfectly capable of taking up roles of responsibility in society:

> Biologically the female is more important to the race than the male. While average women are capable of earning their own livelihood like men, they are the guardians of the life of the race, and only through their natural constitution are they able to bear the double burden. Experience shows the strong probability that the active influence of women on society, under free and equal conditions, is calculated not only to bring about practical improvement to the domestic realm, but also a higher and noble idealism into the life of the State. ... No progressive thinker of today will challenge the claim that the social advancement and general well-being of communities are greatest where women are least debarred, by artificial barriers and narrow prejudice, from taking their full position as citizens. Hence it is with deep sorrow that the admission must be made that the position of Indian women is unsatisfactory, that artificial obstacles to their full service of the commonwealth are everywhere found, and that,

from the point of view of health and happiness alike, women suffer needlessly through chains forged by prejudice and folly. .... These and other social evils have so handicapped India that it is impossible to conceive of her taking a proper place in the midst of free nations until the broad principle of equality between the sexes has been generally accepted by her people. The present abrogation of this principle is the more to be deplored since the natural intelligence and ability of Indian womanhood are by no means inferior to those of their emancipated sisters.[3]

Comments such as these argue against the essentialist notion that women are inferior to men in matters of public affairs by reason of their biology. Indeed, in arguing subtly against the notion that the woman's place was limited to the home by suggesting that a woman was quite capable of earning a living, Aga Khan III also indicated that women's contribution to the political realm was equally necessary and should not be hampered by the obscurantist notion that they should not enter politics. In 1919 the Southborough Committee on Franchise, headed by Lord Southborough and supported by Sir James Meston, rejected a proposal to give the vote to women in India. Sir Sultan Muhammad Shah publicly criticized this rejection and its official explanation that women in *purdah* would find it difficult to cast their votes in a letter to *The Times*. This letter ended with a call to action to women in India as well as a reprimand to the outdated patriarchal and colonizing attitudes of the British officials in India: 'I feel it my duty to the hundreds of venerable and sensible *purdah* ladies of position I know in India to register this protest against the obsolete views of men who have attained to place and power in India, but who have never taken the trouble to know the people among whom they do office work.'[4]

Aga Khan III's views on Indian women's right to vote had been articulated earlier in his *India in Transition*, where he had laid out his views that India was capable of self-rule. There he wrote:

We must not build up the fabric of the autonomous State on weak and one-sided foundations. I am confident that an assembly to the election of which Indian women had contributed would keep nearer to the facts and needs of life, to the real and actual in the country, than one selected by men alone. ... Is it to be maintained that the women of India are less capable than the men of realizing the need for sacrifice [demanded by public life]? Or are we to impose on them the acceptation of responsibility to society at large without participation in the political shaping of the State? The progressive modernization which depends on co-operation and understanding between the rulers and the ruled will be impossible in

India unless women are permitted to play their legitimate part in the great work of national regeneration on a basis of political equality.[5]

These remarks derive from the vision of a democratic state and point out that it cannot properly be so unless the voices and experiences of women are included in the determination of the political direction of the country. They tacitly assume the full humanity of women and their agency and ability to determine what is in the best interests of the state by including their lived experience and understanding of the condition of the people. They also dismiss the notion that women, by dint of their biology and their concern with child-bearing, child-rearing and home-making (a construction of womanhood that bears little relation to the reality of the lives of women), cannot be full citizens of their countries or have a voice in political matters except to the detriment of the state. One might speculate that such an opinion was a veiled counterargument to the (in)famous and oft-quoted *hadith* recorded by Bukhari, 'Those who entrust their affairs to a woman will never know prosperity', which has been cited by Muslims whenever they wish to withhold the right to participate in politics from women. Fatima Mernissi has challenged the veracity of this *hadith*, arguing that the source for it was a man named Abu Bakra, who had previously been convicted of giving false testimony, which rendered the source of the *hadith* inadmissible according to the criteria established by the principal *hadith* collectors of the day (for whom soundness or otherwise of an individual's character was an important consideration when categorizing a *hadith*).[6]

It was not just in the political realm that Sultan Muhammad Shah felt that women needed to be heeded and given a voice. He also felt deeply, when looking into the Muslim past, that a grave error had been committed in the medieval era by the Abbasid dynasty (750–1258) in restricting the intellectual development of women. In his presidential address to the All-India Muhammadan Educational Conference held in Delhi in 1902, he invited the attendees to consider the cause of the general apathy he perceived in Indian Muslim society. He put this question to them:

> Throughout the whole length and breadth of India how many national schools are there in existence which educate Moslem boys and girls in their faith and at the same time in modern secular science? ... There are, indeed, a certain number of old-fashioned Maktabs and Madrassahs which continue to give a parrot-like teaching of the Koran, but even in these places no attempt is made either to improve the morals of the boys or to bring before them the eternal truths of the faith. As a rule, prayers

are but rarely repeated, and when said, not one per cent of the boys understand what they say or why.[7]

These remarks suggest that education for girls was not widespread, nor did religious education go beyond learning the requisite prayers and verses of the Qur'an to include comprehension, discussion and an enlarged understanding of what the faith teaches.

Calling for an engaged encounter with the world, having identified aloofness from the world as the first cause of the apathy he perceived among Indian Muslims, Aga Khan III proceeded to name the second cause as the terrible position of Muslim women. The passage is reproduced here:

> A second cause of our present apathy is the terrible position of Moslem women. ... There is absolutely nothing in Islam, or the Koran, or the example of the first two centuries, to justify this terrible and cancerous growth that has for nearly a thousand years eaten into the very vitals of Islamic society. The heathen Arabs in the days of ignorance, especially the wealthy young aristocrats of Mecca, led an extremely dissolute life, and before the conquest of Mecca the fashionable young Koraishites spent most of their leisure in the company of unfortunate women, and often married these same women and, altogether, the scandals of Mecca before the conquest were vile and degrading. The Prophet not only by the strictness of his laws put an end to this open and shameless glorification of vice, but by a few wise restrictions, such as must be practiced by any society that hopes to exist, made the former constant and unceremonious companionship of men and strange women impossible.
>
> From these necessary and wholesome rules the jealousy of the Abbassides, borrowing from the practice of the later Persian Sassanian kings, developed the present system ... which means the permanent imprisonment and enslavement of half the nation. How can we expect progress from the children of mothers who have never shared, or even seen, the free social intercourse of modern mankind? This terrible cancer that has grown since the 3rd and 4th centuries of the Hijra must either be cut out, or the body of Moslem society will be poisoned to death by the permanent waste of all the women of the nation. But Pardah, as now known, itself did not exist till long after the Prophet's death and is no part of Islam. The part played by Moslem women at Kardesiah and Yarmuk, the two most momentous battles of Islam next to Badr and Honein, and their splendid nursing of the wounded after those battles, is of itself a proof to any reasonable person that Pardah, as now understood, has never been conceived by the companions of the Prophet. That we Moslems should

saddle ourselves with this excrescent of Persian custom, borrowed by the Abbassides, is due to that ignorance of early Islam which is one of the most extraordinary of modern conditions.[8]

In his presidential address Sir Sultan Muhammad Shah was addressing two issues of key concern to him: women's seclusion from men, and the custom of keeping *purdah*, or veiling, which in its extended form is also understood as separating the spheres of female activity from that of men's. As Stowasser points out in her study of the Qur'an, there is nothing therein to justify veiling in the form that we now know it. Rather, the verses pertaining to *hijab*, which denote a physical curtain of separation and were mandatory only for the Prophet's wives, were seamlessly turned into a portable veil for Muslim women in emulation of the veiling practices observed by women of the elites found in Mediterranean and Persian societies under the control of the Arabs during the Abbasid era.[9] The issue of practices that were put into place by the Prophet Muhammad during his time that would curtail illicit relations between men and women are amply evinced in the Qur'an. For instance, the Qur'an (2:221) forbids marriage to idolatresses, as well as marriage to one's father's wives, one's mother, daughters, sisters, father's sisters, mother's sisters, brother's daughters, sister's daughters, foster mothers, foster sisters, mothers-in-law, step-daughters of women with whom one has had conjugal relations, wives of blood sons, and to two sisters from the same family, and all married women (4:22). Such restrictions, when read against the grain, suggest that such practices were probably being observed, hence the need for the restrictions.

The historian Leila Ahmed identifies the Abbasid period as one during which the tradition of Islamic discourse was set in place. Such discourses include the legal regimes governing the lives of women, the Qur'anic commentaries that were drawn upon for crafting these legal regimes, and the collection, collation and fixing of the various *hadith* collections. Each of these were inscribed with the gender presuppositions of the age, that is, the patriarchal society in which the Abbasids found themselves. While patriarchy itself was not invented by Islam, and was already present in 7th-century Arab culture, the societies that formed the Islamic empire were also organized according to patriarchal norms and mores which were easily absorbed into the commentarial, legal and social institutions established under the Abbasids.[10] Thus Leila Ahmed argues that the egalitarian voice of the Qur'an was subsumed under the law-maker's instrumental use of the Qur'an, which cited verses that originally spoke about social and legal arrangements prevalent in the society to which the Qur'an was revealed but which were now read and inscribed in law without consideration of the original social context. Thus, for instance, the verse on polygamy was restricted to the matter of caring for orphans, and further restricted to treating all four wives equally, and it is immediately followed by a verse in which it is declared that the Divine being was well aware that treating four wives equally is an impossibility, thereby implicitly making the case for monogamy. However, the legal regimes saw fit to focus their energies on sanctioning polygamy for Muslim men and determining how each wife might be treated equally rather than focusing on the impossibility of the task or limiting the admissibility of polygamy to situations concerning orphans.

Leila Ahmed, Amina Wadud and Asma Barlas have each argued that the Qur'an offers women full ontological and moral equality with men, as evinced in verses that state that men and women are created from a single soul (4:1), and both are equally accountable to God for their actions and for their religious beliefs and responsibilities (33:35), and that each shall receive the reward of their labour, suggesting that women's labour is valued (and not restricted to the private sphere).[11] Thus it was the essentialist notion of women as less than men, and as having a lower stature than men that was clearly the target of Aga Khan III's criticism of the Abbasid era as one in which social customs and laws were laid down, leading to the virtual 'imprisonment and enslavement of half the nation'. Clearly this is not how he understood the status and roles of women from a reading of the Qur'an itself or his understanding of the foundational norms of the community. Indeed he furnishes evidence for the fact that Muslim men and women in the early community mingled openly, although he upheld the need for sexual behaviour to be regulated, as was done in the Qur'an. However, in his view, regulation in the form given to it in later ages was excessive, viz. segregating women from social intercourse with men and placing them in *purdah*, or between four walls (Persian, *chahar diwari*). Speaking as a Muslim public figure, whose Islamic credentials included tracing his genealogy back to the Prophet, the Ismaili Imam saw no contradiction with Islamic principles of gender justice in his campaign for Indian women, both Muslim and Hindu, to be granted the right to vote, to have access to an education both in and about the faith, and in secular subjects, to participate fully in public life alongside men, to enter the labour force, and to be seen as intelligent individuals capable of independently charting the course of their private family lives as well as the public life of the nation.

Turning now to his role as the Imam or supreme spiritual leader of his community, the Shia Imami Nizari Ismailis, Diamond Rattansi has argued that Aga Khan III implemented many measures that would enable Ismaili women to assume their rightful place as partners with men in all matters pertaining to life and in developing their human potential to the fullest extent. For instance, prevalent practices among some members of the South Asian (Khoja) Ismailis included infant marriages, barring widows and divorcees from remarriage, and payment of large dowries. Each of these practices were abolished by Aga Khan III, with the added comment, largely unheeded, that if the rich spent less on marriage celebrations then the poor would follow. He also condemned polygamy and encouraged marriage between the different ethnic groups that constituted South Asian Ismailis.[12] In this manner, the Ismaili Imam was able to demonstrate to the community that young girls and women were not to be viewed as items of exchange between men, nor were widows or divorcees to be stigmatized for the loss of a husband (thereby subtly shifting emphasis to the woman herself rather than her virginity), nor were they to suffer the indignity of polygyny except in rare cases such as barrenness, thereby striking at the idea that women existed for the sole pleasure of men.

The Ismaili Imam's public views on women were no different from his exhortations to his own community of followers. In the Foreword to Syed Zaidi's *The Position of Women Under Islam* he asserted:

> I have not the least doubt that the whole spirit and teaching of the Holy Prophet—whatever their temporary aspects may have been—encouraged the evolution of all legitimate freedom and legitimate equality between men and women. The responsibility before God for prayers, for action, and for moral decisions is the same for men and women, according to the Prophet's Holy Message. Women already 1350 years ago were made economically independent of men, while in England as late as 1880 a woman's property belonged to her husband. The Prophet also broke with that system and made women financially independent and gave them their proper due in succession to their various relatives' estates.
>
> Pious and believing Muslims who really wish to understand the Holy Message of the Prophet and not just its passing aspects would immediately set to work with the object of bringing about the full and legitimate evolution of Muslim women in Islamic society until such time as they can honestly hold their own with the men.
>
> ...
>
> I firmly believe that in encouraging education amongst my religious followers, and in trying as far as possible to give them equality—women

with men—I have carried out the spirit of the Holy Message of my Ancestor.[13]

Here we see the Imam's understanding of the message of the Qur'an as it pertained to women as not one that limited their full responsibility in prayer, action and moral matters or as suggesting that women were to be financially dependent on men. In reading the Qur'an as vouchsafing women 'all legitimate freedom and legitimate equality', Aga Khan III upheld the full human dignity of women and subverted patriarchal assumptions of women as the weaker sex whose morality must be guarded by men or whose sole function was to attend to child-rearing rather than being economic agents in their own right. To effect such a change of consciousness within his own community, he chose education as the means by which women could take charge of their own destinies and work together with men to build a just and equitable society. In his *farmans* or guidance to the community,[14] especially to women, he addressed the issue of how men and women should relate to one another. For instance, in 1899, at Bagamoyo in Uganda, he said to the community that men and women were exactly equal in the Ismaili faith, and that unrelated men and women should treat each other as siblings or as parents, thereby ensuring a modicum of respect and familial bonding that would prevent one from harming the other and keep matters of sexuality in their proper place. In Karachi in 1920 he advised Ismailis not to be so foolish as to keep women in a cage and behind a veil, for one who kept a woman in such bondage was not an Ismaili. In Mombasa in 1937 he made the comment that today was not the time, unlike the old days, when the male was in front and the woman behind. Rather, men and women should be in step with each other.

Aga Khan III thus reinterpreted the idea of *mahram* found in the Qur'an (24:31) to extend it to all men within a woman's sphere of activity. The commonly held Muslim idea that men and women must be segregated from each other is extrapolated from the Qur'an (24:31) to indicate that a woman must not enter into social intercourse with men unless she is accompanied by a member from her *mahram* (the list of relatives provided in the verse 24:31). The verse simply exhorts women not to display their *zina* (commonly translated as adornment and interpreted to mean women's sexual attributes) to men other than their *mahram*. Clearly Sultan Muhammad Shah was mindful of the need to control illicit sexual interaction between the sexes, and thus he reminded his followers that all men and all women were to be as siblings or parents to each other, except naturally when there was a marital contract. In internalizing the respectful manner in which the sexes were to treat each other, he simultaneously retained, on the one hand, the non-sexual interaction necessary to preserve the moral comportment of the sexes to each other, and on the other hand, the dignity of each and the possibility for social and professional interaction between the sexes.

Such a move, opening the possibility of men and women entering into social and professional interaction, was accompanied by Sultan Muhammad Shah's publicly stated views on the necessity for education for women. In a rather radical statement, given the time of its writing, he asserts that such necessity is not for instrumental purposes so that women might fulfil their role as nurturers and in order to give men more effective support, but, rather, for women's own happiness and welfare:

> Yet the change in the feminine standpoint has been coming very gradually, largely owing to a very serious mistake made by mere man at the starting-point of reform. The constant argument has been that of the necessity for providing educated and intelligent wives and daughters, sisters and mothers, for the men. This well-meaning but insolent assumption that it is for some relation, however advanced from present standards, to the other sex that women need intellectual cultivation, has inevitably tended to direct the movement into narrow and deforming channels. The time has come for a full recognition that the happiness and welfare of the women themselves, must be the end and purpose of all efforts toward improvement.[15]

Such views were paralleled in the exhortations he made to the Ismaili community. For instance, in 1915 in Bombay he advised girls to study thoroughly at school, and if told by their elders not to go to school, to say to them, 'No! We will go to school and study thoroughly.' In Karachi in 1920 he argued, in a statement made to the community, that educating girls was necessary, for if by chance a girl were to end up married to a husband of bad character or one unable to earn an income, then how would she be able to support him or be happy herself? In Zanzibar in 1925 he commented that fathers lacked the motive to educate girls but that they must do so, since all the knowledge that was available in the world should remain open for girls to acquire and learn. Indeed he went so far as to say that girls should be provided with an education so that they could run their own lives, telling the girls present that if their fathers denied them an education they should insist that they wanted one. In Nairobi in 1926 he argued that boys and girls were identical, just as one eye is like the other, thereby undercutting the idea that there are essential differences of intellectual capacity and ability between men and women based on their different biological capacities. In Mombasa in 1937 he told the all-male Education Board, the community institution responsible for providing education, to prepare women to enter the professions in order to enable them to earn their own livelihoods. Again in Mombasa in 1945 he advised parents with limited financial resources to educate the female child first.

The coupling of education with the ability to support oneself financially cannot be underestimated. In paving the way for Ismaili women to go to school, to receive both the quality and length of education that would make it possible for them to enter the professions and to strive for financial self-sufficiency, Aga Khan III laid the groundwork for moving the community away from its inherited cultural patriarchal mores and attitudes towards a partnership model where women worked alongside men to meet the challenges the community would face in the 20th century, including the Ugandan crisis of 1971–1972 and emigration to Western countries. Ismaili male and female children were socialized to accord education the highest degree of importance, to view service to one's community, nation and the world as an Ismaili/Islamic mode of being in the world, to stress the importance of family and faith in one's daily life, and to struggle for individual and collective spiritual advancement. Addressing his community in Mombasa in 1945, Sultan Muhammad Shah emphasized not only that girls should be provided with the best education but that they should also acquire spiritual power through trust and faith. He went so far as to say that he had made girls free and independent, for the truly moral person was not one, as he was to say in Cannes in 1952, who is caged and locked up but one who, having seen the attraction of the bad, has elected to choose the good.

In locating morality within the realm of responsibility of both males and females, and in instilling the idea that they could interact freely without fear of sexual predatoriness by treating each other as siblings and relatives, Sultan Muhammad Shah opened the way for Ismaili men and women to work together on projects for the community or for the wider world. In giving women access to education, he furthered the possibility of partnership through mutual respect for each other's sphere of knowledge, for it is difficult for male children to look down upon the intellectual capacities and abilities of female children when they are in school together, and it is not sex that is the determinant of intelligence but rather hard work and natural intelligence.

In decoupling women's relationships with men from financial dependence upon men, he also gave men the added awareness that women could not be coerced into unhappy domestic situations with the threat of withdrawing financial support, while giving women the awareness that with a good education, a woman could support herself and her children if need be and did not have to take charity should her husband be unable to work, or had died or if she were divorced. These were the possibilities opened up for Ismaili men and women by Sultan Muhammad Shah. He set up institutions that would give both sexes access to education, but further research needs to be conducted into how many Ismaili women were in fact appointed to positions of responsibility within community institutions during his lifetime (as they routinely are now). In 1944 Shirin Gulamali Jivraj was the first Ismaili woman in East Africa to be appointed to the Aga Khan Provincial Council for Kenya.[16] As yet, no studies have been conducted to assess the levels of education and professional qualification that Ismaili Muslim women had attained by the time of Aga Khan III's death in 1957. For, despite his efforts, the community could not give up patriarchal modes of behaviour overnight. The role of the male as the head of the household and as the primary decision-maker for all the major decisions, financial or otherwise, has persisted to this day, although women defer to this for the sake of family harmony while continuing, in each generation, to enter the professions, own and run businesses and be appointed to leadership roles within the community and in the public sphere.

If Sir Sultan Muhammad Shah, Aga Khan III, could be considered a visionary Muslim leader who revolutionized the manner in which women were to be viewed and treated, and who exhorted women to get an education, hold on to their faith, assume financial independence and assume their full roles in society, his successor, His Highness Prince Karim al-Husayni, Aga Khan IV, may be considered an institution builder whose programmes have simply made equity of gender access a given. Aga Khan IV will no doubt be remembered in the historical record as having taken the institution building begun by his illustrious grandfather to new heights and extending the reach of his organization to serve all peoples wherever it operates. The four cornerstones that constitute his vision are an emphasis on the daily practice of one's faith, both in the community and individually; the importance of the intellect, considered a divine gift, in meeting the challenges of the existential condition; the centrality of service, including volunteering as the fundamental attitude through which to construct one's place in the world; and drawing on the principles of Islam to organize one's actions in the humanitarian and ecological fields, including valuing meritocracy and pluralism in the formation and sustainability of civil societies. In all these, there is no privileging of one gender over the other.

In the vast institutional network created by Aga Khan IV, overseen by the apex institution known as the Aga Khan Development Network (AKDN), a threefold structure comprised of economic development, social development and culture hosts approximately 16 institutions whose mandates, broadly speaking, are to identify challenges and to construct and implement strategies to meet them. Such institutions include the Aga Khan Fund for Economic Development (overseeing the work of institutions such as Tourism Promotion Services, and Industrial Promotion Services); the Aga Khan Foundation (AKF), overseeing the work of the Aga Khan Educational Services, the Aga Khan Health Services, and the Aga Khan Planning and Building Services; and the Aga Khan Trust for Culture (overseeing the work of the Aga Khan Award for Architecture, the Education and Culture Programme, and the Historic Cities Support Programme).[17] Three additional institutions that fall within the social development category are the Aga Khan University, the University of Central Asia, and the Aga Khan Agency for Microfinance.

More work is needed to determine the percentage of women who participate in the governing bodies of all these institutions. The 2005 report of the Aga Khan Foundation, for instance, does not name the board members. However, according to its report, the priorities of the AKF programmes are listed as: education, rural development, health, civil society, with particular emphasis on community participation, gender, the environment, pluralism and human resources. There is no question that women are involved at every stage of programme development, building and implementation, both as deliverers and as recipients of services and work alongside men. Sultan Muhammad Shah's goal was to enable women to take their place in society alongside men by removing patriarchal attitudes towards women and replacing the tripartite patriarchal roof under which women passed from being managed by their fathers to being managed by their husbands and subsequently by their sons, with an education which would ensure that women were financially independent. The present Aga Khan has sought to address the structural intersections within which gender inequities are imbricated. For instance, without paying attention to the myriad structures of the societies in which women live – economic, environmental, medical, educational, cultural – any attempts to ameliorate women's lives would only be short-term. Thus AKF's objectives are outlined in larger terms:

> Make it possible for poor people to act in ways that will lead to long-term improvements in their income and health, in the environment and in the

education of their children; b) Provide communities with a greater range of choices and the understanding necessary to take informed action; c) Enable beneficiaries to gain the confidence and competence to participate in the design, implementation and continuing operation of activities that affect the quality of their lives; and d) Put institutional, management and financial structures in place ensuring that programme activities are sustainable without Foundation assistance within a reasonable timeframe.[18]

In focusing institutional energies so as to address larger structural issues such that they ameliorate the lives of all those affected by the programmes, the potential of women can be developed alongside that of men and children to enable them to participate as fully as possible in creating sustainable communities that can live in a globalized world. In other words, attention to gender is built into the very structures of the programmes created by AKF, as can be gathered from reading the available AKF reports. The goals outlined by AKF do not explicitly mention gender, but as is clear from the list of priorities that provide the guiding principles for programmes, gender continues to be an essential and salient point both for development and implementation. An example of the gender-inclusive and integrated approach to development can be found in the following example of development initiatives in India, drawn from the AKF Annual Report for 2005:

> The Foundation is improving the quality of education available to marginalized and excluded communities in over 1,000 schools. AKF and its partners are working alongside state governments through the Sarva Shiksha Abiyan programme—a national programme to improve education quality—introducing new methods and approaches that take into account social and cultural practices and involve local government bodies.
>
> To address rural poverty and improve livelihoods, the Foundation is supporting activities for 400,000 people across four states in the semi-arid and rain-fed regions of western and central India. Over 1,400 community organizations have been formed, of which 50 percent of the 33,000 members are women. Knowledge and resource centers have also been established in collaboration with state governments to provide training and make available essential information on rural livelihoods to enable communities to equip themselves with the latest techniques and practices.
>
> Integrated community health interventions reach out to a population of over 240,000. The promotion of community-led approaches ensures access to quality, affordable child survival programmes, maternal health,

and other essential community health services in collaboration with public and private health systems. AKF's environmental health, water supply and sanitation activities reflect the needs of women and take into account their dignity and safety. Recently, Karan village in Siddhpur Taluka of Gujarat—an area covered by the Aga Khan Planning and Building Services—received the Nirmal Gram award for complete sanitation coverage.[19]

The importance of such cross-sectional approaches to gender development cannot be underestimated. In conclusion, while Aga Khan III's challenge was to address the cultural barriers facing Muslim women, including Ismaili women, with respect to developing human capital, the present Aga Khan IV is seeking to make a difference to global inequities through the mobilization of efforts that include entire communities regardless of race, gender, class, religious affiliation and disability in building a better future for all.

Notes

1. Katherine Mayo, *Selections from Mother India*, ed. M. Sinha (New Delhi, 1998), pp. 28–29.
2. Ibid., p. 32.
3. Aga Khan III, Sultan Muhammad Shah, *Aga Khan III: Selected Speeches and Writings of Sir Sultan Muhammad Shah*, ed. K. K. Aziz (London, 1997–1998), vol. 1, p. 111.
4. Letter to *The Times* (8 August 1919), quoted in *Aga Khan III: Selected Speeches*, vol. 1, p. 114.
5. *India in Transition*, cited in *Aga Khan III: Selected Speeches*, vol. 1, pp. 112–113.
6. Fatima Mernissi, *Women and Islam: An Historical and Theological Enquiry* (Oxford, 1991), pp. 49, 60.
7. *Aga Khan III: Selected Speeches*, vol. 1, p. 206.
8. Ibid., vol. 1, pp. 210–211.
9. Barbara Freyer Stowasser, *Women in the Qur'an: Traditions and Interpretation* (New York, 1994), pp. 92ff.
10. Leila Ahmed, *Women and Gender in Islam* (New Haven and London, 1992), pp. 65–67.
11. Amina Wadud, *Qur'an and Woman* (Kuala Lumpur, 1994), pp. 15–26, and Asma Barlas, *'Believing Women' in Islam: Unreading Patriarchal Interpretations of the Qur'an* (Austin, TX, 2002), p. 172.
12. Diamond Rattansi, *Islamization and the Khojah Isma'ili Community in Pakistan* (Ph.D. thesis, McGill University, 1987), pp. 38–39.
13. Syed Zaidi, *The Position of Women under Islam* (Karachi, 1935).

14. All the exhortations cited below are to be found in the Gujarati collection of Aga Khan III's *farmans* to the Ismaili community in a work entitled *Kalam-e Imam-e Mubin (The Sayings of the Manifest Imam)*, now out of print.
15. Aga Khan III, *India in Transition: A Study in Political Evolution* (Bombay and Calcutta, 1918), p. 258.
16. Personal communication from my father, Rahim Kassam Jivraj, 26 February 2007. Shirin Gulamali Jivraj was his aunt.
17. http://www.akdn.org/agency/akf.html.
18. AKF Annual Report for 2005, p. 50.
19. Ibid., pp. 22–23.

11

At the Interstices of Tradition, Modernity and Postmodernity: Ismaili Engagements with Contemporary Canadian Society

Karim H. Karim

There are between 70,000 and 80,000 Shia Imami Ismaili Muslims (also known as Nizari Ismaili Muslims, or simply, Ismailis) in Canada. The largest settlements are in Toronto and Vancouver, with substantial communities (*jamat*s; *jamaʿat*s) located in Calgary, Edmonton, Montreal and Ottawa. Ismaili migration to Canada occurred in the 1950s, with significant increases taking place between the 1970s and 1990s.[1] The expulsion of Ugandan Asians in 1972 was the cause of a notable growth in the community. Another large group of refugees arrived from Afghanistan in the 1990s. Most Canadian Ismailis have origins in South Asia. Other *jamati* members include those with European, Iranian, Arab, African and Central Asian ethnic backgrounds. The bulk of the community migrated to Canada from the East African countries of Uganda, Kenya and Tanzania; they are mostly of Indian (Gujarati) origin. There has also been immigration to Canada from Congo, Madagascar, Mozambique, South Africa, Iran, Tajikistan and Bangladesh. Others have arrived via Europe, notably the UK, France and Portugal, South America and Australia, where they had settled for varying periods of time. An increasing number of Ismaili immigrants now come from India and Pakistan. Many *jamat*s in Canada include recent converts of Euro-Canadian origins – mostly through marriage. In addition to those individuals who arrived as immigrants or joined the community through conversion, two generations of Ismailis have now been born in Canada.

The Canadian *jamat*, which is now the largest in a Western country, has been formed in part by the events abroad such as the Ugandan exodus, the Iranian Revolution, the wars in Afghanistan and the collapse of the Soviet Union, as well as Canada's willingness to accept the people displaced by such events. The community has a strong sense of Canadian citizenship alongside their transnational understanding of a global *jamat*. Ties are maintained with the lands of emigration as well as with other places with an Ismaili presence. Exhortations to Canadian Ismailis by the global leader of the community, His Highness Prince Karim Aga Khan IV, to make Canada their home as well as to support the transnational activities of the Aga Khan Development Network, have produced a sense of belonging to both the Canadian nation and the Ismaili transnation. In this, the community is beginning to engage with two major characteristics of our modern world: globalization and broad-based cosmopolitanism.[2]

But can Muslims be 'modern'? In the popular Western imagination Islam and modernity appear to be polar opposites. In dominant media discourses Muslims are presented as inescapably mired in a traditionalism that is the antithesis of modernity.[3] Critics of their migration to North America, Europe and Australasia tend to view them as incapable of integrating into these societies. Some public commentators have even proposed restrictions on immigration from countries where Islam is the major religion. This situation has worsened in the last few years following terrorist acts in which Muslims have been implicated.

Yet, parallel to this, in Canada the Nizari Ismailis have also been depicted positively as welcome contributors to the country. This way of portraying adherents of Islam is not entirely unique. Individuals of various Muslim backgrounds have been shown to be adapting well to modernity. Much has been written about the efforts of the 19th-century intellectuals, Jamal al-Din Asadabadi (Afghani), Muhammad Abdu and others who attempted to engage with Western philosophy of the 19th and 20th centuries.[4] However, such perceptions of Muslim modernists usually tend to focus on the work of individual thinkers and their disciples. Examples may appear in the daily media of individuals in majority-Muslim states who have embraced Western ideas but they are seen as exceptions in populations that are hostile to modernity. Even Western views about Turkey as the most secular of Muslim-majority countries are not bereft of suspicion about the population's dominant tendencies towards traditionalism. Despite the numerous individuals and families of Sunni, Ithna'ashari Shi'i or other Muslim backgrounds who have culturally adapted in Western societies, their group identities are often seen as unable to integrate even into multicultural milieus. However, communal portrayals of Ismailis, especially in Canada, generally show them at ease with Western norms.

But this is not an uncomplicated, one-dimensional image – either on the part of the dominant society or members of the community themselves. It operates, as such perceptions usually do, at various levels. The context of the particular situation as well as the medium through which it is viewed contributes to the shaping of its perception. Images of Ismaili Canadians are refracted through the particular prisms of tradition, modernity and postmodernity, both singly and simultaneously. Even as it shapes a future in a land that is at the forefront of modernity, this community continues to draw on centuries of history that unfolded in the cradle of civilization. Although commitment to tradition or modernity varies from person to person, no one is completely unaffected by either. Even the most secularly oriented Ismaili Canadian is not entirely unaware of the community's diverse corpus of tradition and, on the other hand, the most tradition-minded adherent has not remained untouched by its modernist aspirations.

Writing about the unfolding of Ismaili settlement in North America, Fariyal Ross-Sheriff and Azim Nanji state that members of the community draw upon 'their religious tradition as well as modernity to shape new forms of organization and provide an equilibrium upon which to build their lives'.[5] This dialectic between tradition and modernity is not a clash of opposites: it can instead be understood as a sincere dialogue between two individuals who have differing inclinations but who commonly seek the path of living in accordance with Islam (*al-sirat al-mustaqim*, Qur'an 1:6; literally, 'the straight path'). The search for balance between tradition and modernity extends into interaction with the postmodern. The struggle to find *al-sirat al-mustaqim* and to remain on it does not end at any point, but is destined to continue as the conditions of life inevitably change. No conclusion can be contemplated in physical life because the passage of time constantly brings new challenges. As in the postulations of Jacques Derrida,[6] solutions remain contingent on changing circumstances. Meaning would be lost if one settled entirely for only tradition or modernity or postmodernity. The ongoing search that maintains the balance between these three axes sustains the dynamism of continually discovering (contingent) answers to the changing contexts of life. This experience unfolds unendingly in the intervening spaces – the interstices – between tradition, modernity and postmodernity. Meaning is to be found in the interstices and in the struggle of the search itself. In the words of Aga Khan III, Sultan Muhammad Shah: 'Struggle is the meaning of life. Defeat or Victory is in the hands of God but struggle itself is man's duty and should be his joy.'[7]

Before proceeding to examine the struggles that occurred at the interstices, it is necessary to explore certain aspects of contemporary views on tradition, modernity and postmodernity. This will be an aid in providing the larger Western and Muslim contexts for the engagement of Canadian Ismailis with their current environment.

Tradition

We accept the word 'tradition' as a normal part of our everyday vocabulary. However, as with most words that have significance in public debate, it is often manipulated ideologically to promote specific interests.[8] Generally speaking, tradition evokes a view of the past as proffering values that are distinct from but, nevertheless, inform the ethos of the present. It denotes ideas and customs handed down from a previous era. These are then passed on from one generation to another, having their origins in myth, honoured ancestors, a golden age of high culture or divine revelation. Tradition usually contains the idea of something of value, but can also be used in negative senses. Someone who is a 'traditionalist' is held to be too rigid and inflexible to keep up with the times.

Tradition as a concept does not seem to have existed before the advent of 'modernization'. The idea of tradition had to be invented to provide an antithesis for modernization.[9] Aziz Esmail notes:

> traditional societies are the one kind of society which are singularly free from the idea of tradition. In the Islamic world, for instance, there is considerable talk, which has been going on now for an odd fifty years or so, about the Muslim 'tradition', the Muslim 'heritage', and so on. These are peculiarly modern preoccupations, however.[10]

One of the ways in which modernity has been defined is through juxtaposition with the Islamic tradition. The discourses of development in the 1950s, 1960s and 1970s presented modernity and Islam as binary opposites. According to one influential book, *The Passing of Traditional Society: Modernizing the Middle East*, published by Daniel Lerner in 1958, adherence to tradition was an obstacle to attaining modernity. He insisted that the norms of Muslim cultures had to be abandoned in order to acquire the 'rationalist and positivist spirit' of modernization. Lerner viewed Islam as conflicting with development, against which it was 'absolutely defenceless'.[11] Even Hisham Sharabi, a prominent Arab social scientist, asserted in 1966 that 'in the contemporary Arab world Islam has simply been bypassed'.[12]

Such a linear and teleological view of a progression from tradition to modernity posits elements of religion as outmoded in the contemporary world. It takes on an ideological posture by systematically excluding tradition from having any relevance in the present. The ideology of modernism conflates modernization with Westernization. It insists that all peoples of the world should necessarily mimic the path to development set out by Western societies. There are enormous economic and political benefits for the West if the rest of humanity always followed its lead. Traditionalism emerged as a counter-ideology, seeking to oppose modernism. Just as the latter politically supports and benefits specific institutions and structures, traditionalism upholds the status of those who promote its own world view.

However, there is more than one way of looking at traditionalism. The post-colonial scholar Ashis Nandy speaks of a 'critical traditionalism' which is 'reflective as well as self-critical, which does not reject or bypass the experience of modernity but encapsulates or digests it'.[13] Drawing from the examples of Mahatma Gandhi and Rabindranath Tagore,[14] Nandy presents this traditionalism as one that does not view contemporary science as alien, even though it may criticize its alienating tendencies. Traditionalism also questions the concept of objectivity while not denying its creative possibilities. Ultimately, critical traditionalism posits wisdom over knowledge and the intellect over intelligence.

Those who belong to the school of 'perennial philosophy' (*philosophia perennis*) have written about tradition as a representation of the essential expressions of the human spirit.[15] They write about the eternal truths that history or time does not negate – tradition remains as relevant today as it was in ancient times. The modern condition does not invalidate tradition since the fundamental spiritual needs of human beings remain constant.

A recent collection of essays expounds that 'traditional Islam' implies 'both horizontal continuity with the Origin and a vertical nexus which relates each movement of the life of the tradition in question to the metahistorical Transcendental Reality'.[16] It expresses a form of contemporary Islamic thought that is critical of 'modernist Islam'. Fuad S. Naeem's chapter in the book carries out an exposition of the critique by the early 20th-century traditional scholar Maulana Ashraf Ali Thanvi of 'modernists [who] mistake the power of the modern West with the truth of its ideas and thereby seek to modernize Islam in order to make it more powerful'.[17] Taking a *shariʿa*-centric approach, Thanvi held there was no need to reform Islamic tradition since it already contained in itself the requisite principles for its renewal.

Basheer M. Nafi identifies tradition in Muslim contexts with *taqlid*, which refers to the conformity to legal and doctrinal precedent. He describes *taqlid* as that which is 'dominant, conventional and established'[18] in Muslim discourses. However, he does not see this as implying a monolithic consensus on all issues. Nafi views the wide variations in the opinions of Muslim judges and muftis as evidence of the traditional society's profound 'belief in the limitations of man and the uncertain nature of his pursuits'.[19] He contrasts this with the strong sense of certainty that modernity propounds.

Farid Esack also points to the plurality of sources that make up Islamic tradition, including those that conflict with each other. He indicates how a tradition can be diverse and internally at variance; but this is what gives it its dynamism.[20] The dialectics between different strands within Islamic tradition have continued to nourish it for 14 centuries. There is a process of gradual recovery of the pluralism of the Islamic heritage among contemporary Muslims. In the particular context of the Ismailis in Canada, we see the interaction between the varying strands of their traditions as they converge from different sources of emigration.

Before closing this discussion on tradition, mention must be made of the common translation of the Prophetic *hadith* as 'tradition'. More precisely, the word denotes 'saying, tale'.[21] *Sunna* ('custom') refers to his practices and actions. The Prophet's life remains central not only to the thought of those who follow *taqlid* but also the modernists among Muslims.

Modernity

This section seeks to address 'modernity', which, like 'tradition', is a word that is a receptacle for many meanings. It is dominantly used to refer to a constellation of ideas that include individual freedom, change as a positive value, progress, reason as the path to true knowledge, science as a truth-seeking discourse, (instrumental) rationality, democracy, the nation-state, industrialization, industrial division of labour, expansion of markets, rapid capitalist growth, urbanization, mass society, mass education, mass culture, distinctions of high and low culture, bureaucratization of society,[22] and the separation of church and state. The origins of the concept are unclear. According to various accounts, its beginnings are to be found as early as the invention of printing technology by Gutenberg (1436) or as late as 1945, when the Second World War ended. The first use of the Latin term *modernus* occurred in the 6th century CE, but it was not until 1622 and 1849, respectively, that the English word 'modernity' and the French

At the Interstices of Tradition, Modernity and Postmodernity 271

'modernité' appeared.[23] Whether one chooses to place the inception of modernity in the Renaissance, the Reformation, the Enlightenment or the Romantic Era, the consensus seems to be that it was well established in the West by the 19th century. It was then spread to the rest of the world through colonialism.

However, there was a fundamental difference in the historical and cultural context of the ways in which the narrative of modernity has unfolded in the West and elsewhere. Tabish Khair notes that:

> Western modernity is seen as a response to *Western* tradition. But in the non-West, modernity is seen as disjunct from tradition. Modernity is something that is traced to another space and time – either Europe or the effects of European colonization.[24]

The template for modernization is usually Western. It tends to be forcibly placed upon the history and culture of other places, where it often does not fit. In dominant discourses of development, the failure to 'modernize' is not seen as a problem with modernization theory but a failing of those upon whom it is thrust.

Basheer Nafi's essay 'The Rise of Islamic Reformist Thought' outlines the ways in which Muslim societies responded to Western modernity. In accordance with dominant models, tight control was established over society and land through the intense bureaucratization of the state apparatus, the extension of communications and transportation networks, the homogenization of educational systems, the imposition of European legal frameworks and the expropriation by the state of religious endowments (*awqaf*). All this had the objective of unifying the nation-state and strengthening the power of central government. The 19th and early 20th centuries were also marked by intense intellectual activity: 'While some Muslim elements were calling for a rapid and wholesale embrace of Western ideas and institutional models, and others were holding to the past, rejecting any form of change, reformist *'ulama*, intellectuals and statesmen sought to chart a way between accommodating the new condition and preserving the Islamic identity of society.'[25]

The broad range of reformers had a common purpose in safeguarding Islamic distinctiveness in the face of the forceful challenge of modernization and at the same time overcoming what they saw as the debilitating layers of questionable traditional practices. Their twofold mission sought to contain 'the Western challenge by creating a synthesis between modern values and systems and what they perceived as eternal Islamic values and systems and questioning the credibility, even the Islamicity, of the dominant traditional modes of religion'.[26] Espousing the notion of progress, the reformers challenged what they saw as the blind adherence of Muslim society to juristic opinions developed over previous centuries and asserted the mutability of the *shari'a*. They urged the revival of the independent reasoning (*ijtihad*) as an integral aspect of Islamic methodology.

Despite their noteworthy efforts, these 19th- and early 20th-century Muslim reformers, such as Afghani, Abduh, Rida and Iqbal, were not able to determine the directions which Muslim-majority states eventually took. While occasionally paying lip service to reformist thought, governments mainly pursued policies of Westernization. By the late 1970s the alienation that this approach had engendered in Muslim societies gave rise to a more radical response usually termed as 'fundamentalism' or 'Islamism'. Nafi suggests that the work of reformists in breaking the dominance of the traditional *'ulama* opened the way for Islamists, most of whom do not have theological training, to pursue their forceful challenge against the state. Their political activism would not have been made possible if the reformists had not 'prepared the ground for the laymen, the modern Muslim intellectual and the Muslim professional to speak on behalf of Islam'.[27]

A number of commentators see Islamists as part of the broad stream of modernity. Bjorn Utvik states that they have been 'insistent advocates of technological and economic development'[28] and that they promote a meritocratic participation in politics and business. Roxanne L. Euben points to the strong tendency among Islamists towards a binarism that is characteristic of certain aspects of modernity – the polarization of the Cold War is mirrored in the way that the influential Islamist ideologue Sayyid Qutb viewed relations between the West and Muslims.[29] John Gray asserts that like other radical products of modernity such as Marxism, Nazism and neo-liberalism, Islamism adheres to what he thinks of as the 'modern myth' of remaking the human condition.[30]

Other contemporary heirs of the 19th- and early 20th-century reformists include Muslim scholars trained in the contemporary humanities and social sciences. Some of them also have traditional Islamic training. Many of them live and work in Western countries, often because of the greater opportunities these settings afford for free expression. They use the tools of contemporary scholarship to examine Muslim theology, history and sociology. Enlightenment and post-Enlightenment concepts are regularly employed when academic audiences and also when the Muslim faithful are addressed.

Ebrahim Moosa states that whereas the reformists viewed modernity as an ally, 'twenty-first-century critical Muslim scholars are much more apprehensive of its allure and offer a critique of modernity'.[31] While the former supported women's rights and the study of the contemporary sciences, most of them did not proceed to apply the intellectual tools of the day to scrutinizing traditional Islamic sciences. Moosa says that Muslims need to move beyond apologetics that distort those aspects of history and theology which do not appear to conform to contemporary standards. He criticizes the tendency to look for corroboration of past practices:

> this desire to find justification in the past, in a text or the practice of a founder, suggests that Muslims can act confidently in the present only if the matter in question was already prefigured in the past. ... Does this mean that Muslims can engage in discourses of justice, egalitarianism, freedom, and equality only if there is some semblance that the scripture of the Prophet or some of the learned savants (imams) of the past endorsed, hinted, or fantasized about the possibility of such discourses?[32]

Moosa states that these tendencies invalidate the actual experiences of Muslims in their efforts to construct the path to innovation, change and adaptation. There is an increasing insistence among contemporary Muslim intellectuals, according to Tariq Ramadan, to take account of 'the concrete realities of our societies' and 'produce a *fiqh*, a legislation appropriate to our times'.[33]

Ramadan, a prominent voice among Muslims in the West, has promoted the development of a 'Western Islam'.[34] Muslim intellectuals living in North America, Europe and Australasia are engaged seriously with modernity in the West. There has been an attempt to give impetus to a movement of 'progressive Muslims' in the USA and Canada. Included in the 'essential concerns of progressive Muslims' articulated by Omid Safi are: a critical review of the broad range of Islamic tradition; looking anew at Islamic scriptural teachings on social justice in the context of the contemporary world; striving for an 'Islamic feminism'; and a pluralistic openness towards human sources of compassion and wisdom that goes beyond Islamic ones.[35]

Aziz Esmail refers to a 'pluralistic, universal point of view' that safeguards the particularity of the Muslim community and moves 'from the inside to the outside' to gain an awareness of humanity's ethical and spiritual aspirations.[36] He proposes a common project among communities, particularly of the Abrahamic faiths, which would also critically assess cultural assumptions among Muslims. Esmail promotes a search that goes past these historical accretions in order to understand the core of the vision that gave expression to the principles of Islam. He suggests that Muslims in the West have an opportunity, through achieving harmony with their surroundings, to place the scientific and humanistic resources of modernity 'in the service of the spiritual and ethical vision of their faith'.[37]

Whereas the orientations of these contemporary Muslim scholars vary, they all urge for a critical intellectual approach when examining Muslim traditions, a non-adversarial engagement with the West, and respect for both pluralist and universal values. They reject the notion of modernization that grants a privileged status to Western understandings of intellectual and material development. Instead they uphold the necessity of truly universal values and the importance of inter-faith and inter-cultural explorations of the common heritage of humanity, while continuing to realize the particular significance and contribution of the Islamic vision.

Postmodernity

The idea of postmodernity developed in reaction to certain features of modernity. Postmodernity is characterized by tendencies such as the decentralization of authority in contrast to modernity's vision of consolidated power structures, hybridity instead of bipolarity, contingency in place of certainty, and continual change as opposed to stasis. True to its inclinations towards ambiguity and shifting terrain, the meanings attached to postmodernity are even more varied than those contained in the concepts of tradition and modernity. Azim Nanji notes that 'we live in a world where modernism has become post-modernism and ... post-modernism itself is being revised so that it is not entirely clear in which realm one finds oneself at any given point'.[38]

'"Postmodernism" originally referred to an antimodernist movement in architecture.'[39] Jean François Lyotard was among the first to try and make sense of it. He suggested that the postmodern artist or writer works without pre-established rules and categories, and that her work is actually a search for the rules and categories to guide it. '*Post modern* would have to be understood according to the paradox of the future (*post*) anterior (*modo*).'[40] This unsettling of linear time, that is key to modernity's central idea of progress, characterizes postmodernism's non-teleological approach to the unfolding of life.

Several major socio-cultural and economic features of the contemporary world can be seen, at least partially, as having been influenced by postmodernist perspectives. These include multiculturalism, globalization, transnationalism, diasporic cosmopolitanism, and post-colonialism. There is no clear disjuncture between them and modernity, but various vital aspects of each one of them departs from it. Multiculturalism seeks to validate the non-hegemonic diversity of cultural groups within a nation-state; globalization and transnationalism dissipate the modern focus on the nation; the cosmopolitanism of diaspora cuts across standard notions of national identity; and post-colonialism poses a strong challenge to the ideas that support the structures of Western dominance in the world. Post-colonial theorists have popularized the concept of 'alternative modernities', to describe the displacing of Westernization from its status as the only modernizing path.[41]

The eclectic consumption of the products of many cultures in a way that negates the distinctiveness of each and all is also viewed as a feature of postmodernism. Muslims participate along with other people in a global consumerism that has served to rearrange relationships that were constructed by both tradition and modernity. Ziauddin Sardar holds the central feature of postmodernism to be the exposition of meaninglessness, as conveyed through contemporary novels, film and television and supported by the global economy.[42] However, he states that it is not completely in opposition to modernity: 'Postmodernism does not represent a discontinuity with history, a sharp break from modernity, but an extension of the grand Western narrative of secularism and its associated ideology of capitalism and bourgeois liberalism.'[43]

According to Akbar Ahmed's assessment, postmodernism has emerged in the social environments made possible by modernism – democracy, urbanism, the growth of the middle class and mass media. But it is also characterized by 'a questioning of, a loss of faith in, the project of modernity; a spirit of pluralism; a heightened scepticism of traditional orthodoxies; and finally a rejection of a view of the world as a universal totality, of the expectation of final solutions and complete answers'.[44] Ahmed draws a link between postmodernism and 'ethno-religious revivalism'.[45] In Muslim contexts, the 'post' of modernism addresses the failures of Western models of politics, development and secularism in non-Western societies. The broad-based response among different sets of Muslims has included attempts to carry out a re-engagement with tradition, to 'Islamize knowledge', and, at the militant edge, physically attack Western interests.

Alternative modernities in Muslim societies includes what Alev Çinar describes as Islamist ideology's use of modernizing strategies and techniques to develop nationalist institutions that also draw from the Turkish past.⁴⁶ Similarly, religious courts in Malaysia are involved in defining Islam's role with respect to modernity and national sovereignty as well as the development of civil society.⁴⁷ There is also an attempt among Muslim thinkers to refine concepts included in modernity, such as secularism, in order to allow for an engagement with the truly universal and symbolic aspects of the human experience.

The conditions of postmodernity have produced situations in which the proliferation of different forms of media, notably the Internet, have permitted the rapid dispensation of '*fatwas*' by lay persons. This has served further to erode traditional forms of authority, intensifying what had been put in motion by the modernist reform movement. There has been some engagement with respect to pluralism in the context of Islam. However, Aziz Al-Azmeh's contention that 'there are as many Islams as there are situations that sustain it'[48] seems to point towards an unrestrained relativism that would result in the utter fragmentation of authority and community. It appears to invoke the kind of meaninglessness that is a major source of the criticism of postmodernism. Muqtedar Khan laments that 'postmodern incursions have subverted not only the foundations of truth, but also the possibility of ever establishing any truth claims'.[49]

Whereas modernism suppressed non-Western voices, Sardar states that postmodernism 'seeks to represent Other cultures and give their voices an opportunity to be heard'.[50] But he does not view the latter as promising a genuinely multicultural world where one can assert one's identity by liberating oneself from parochial concerns and take everyone else seriously. He sees both modernism and postmodernism as representing opposing 'extremities'[51] between which society will swing in the coming decades.

This commentator suggests that we are destined to live out the contest between the ideas of modernism and postmodernism. Muslims the world over are experiencing the swing of the pendulum, along with the rest of humanity. In the West, tradition, modernity and postmodernity are all in contestation in the lives of Muslims who reside there. They live in the interstices of what Homi Bhabha (borrowing from Frederic Jameson) refers to as the 'third space' that lies between national and immigrant identities. This place is 'the cutting edge of translation and negotiation, the *in-between* space'[52] where cultures meet, giving new meaning to one's identity and relations with others. The Ismaili Muslims living in Western countries like Canada find themselves inhabiting these spaces that are junctures between tradition, modernity and postmodernity.

The Canadian Context

Whereas the Canadian socio-cultural and political environment in which Ismailis live is similar to that in other Western countries, it does have some significant differences. Canada has a place in the world that is different from that of countries like the USA, the UK, France and Portugal – the other major Western locations where the members of the community have settled. While these countries, including Canada, are all in the broader Western alliances like NATO and OECD, the latter is not seen as a nation with overt imperialist ambitions, either past or present. As a former colony (dominion) of Great Britain, Canada has a special relationship with the mother country, but it is also respected by other former colonies in Africa and Asia, including fellow members of the Commonwealth and La Francophonie. However, Canada has a close relationship with the USA, due to its geographical proximity to this superpower, and is a member of the G7/G8, which has a significant influence on global economic affairs.

The evolution of Canada's policies on the immigration of 'non-white' peoples has been in step with those of other Western nations. It had race-based barriers to immigration until the 1960s. The change in policy was partially the result of a general international recognition of the basic concepts of human rights, a process in which Canadians played an important role. Canada was the first country to initiate a multiculturalism policy in 1971, and is presently the only one to have a fully fledged multiculturalism law (passed by act in 1988). While the policy remains contentious, in Canada its origins reflect the history of the relationships between its various indigenous and immigrant peoples.

The interpretation of multiculturalism in Canada varies from that in the USA (where public discourse has often been framed in single issues such as education and is not dealt with directly by the federal government) and the UK (where race relations tend to dominate discussions about it). Multiculturalism has validated the public presence of cultural diversity in Canada, particularly in the country's institutions. Whereas the languages and cultures derived from the British and French heritage remain dominant, room has been made for others in certain expressions of public life. It is at the individual level that the policy has had the most inclusive impact. People of various origins have been given opportunities to hold some of the highest offices in the country. The position of Governor-General of Canada, the official representative of the British monarch (who is the head of the Canadian state), has reflected the increasing variety of identities found in the Canadian population. In the past this appointment was exclusively the reserve of members of the British aristocracy. It was made more broadly inclusive in recent decades, with individuals of French, German, Ukrainian, Chinese and Haitian origins occupying the office. The government has also broadened the official Table of Precedence, which determines the placement of representatives of various religions during state ceremonies, beyond the Anglican and Roman Catholic churches.

However, attempts to include people from various backgrounds in the working of public institutions can meet with resistance. For example, in the early 1990s proposals to change the headgear of the Royal Canadian Mounted Police in order to incorporate the Sikh turban and traditional aboriginal hair braids were seen as extremely contentious, but were eventually introduced. The issue of tradition was invoked by some members of society who felt that modernist and postmodernist arguments were disregarding the heritage of the fabled police force, which is viewed by many as integral to the country's identity.

Multiculturalism is modernist in so far as it seeks to frame cultural diversity within the nation-state – a central political feature of modernism. The policy is conceptualized as a means of containing cultural conflicts and enhancing national cohesion (although its critics view it as a means of division). Instead of a situation where rival groups resort to competing with each other for access to public resources, the Canadian government has presented multiculturalism as a social framework within which these groups can learn to work together. But the policy is also postmodernist in that it challenges the modernist ideals of a state composed of a single people, speaking the same language and preferably having the same culture if not the same ethnicity. Certain European states, such as France, have historically been able to impose such monolithic characteristics on to their populations. The USA has long favoured the assimilationist model of 'the melting pot'. Robert Fulford, a prominent Canadian cultural commentator and critic of multiculturalism, nevertheless describes Canada as a country that is not dominated by a sole master narrative and is therefore 'a postmodern dominion'.[53] Following years of agonizing over the lack of a strong national identity, especially with respect to its powerful neighbour, the USA, most Canadians appear to have settled into describing their country as multicultural.

However, this is by no means a final stage in Canadian cultural history. Tradition, as embedded in the heritage of the dominant national groups (i.e. those descended from the British and French) as well as in that of the aboriginal peoples, and of all other groups, comes periodically into play in national debates. At the same time, modernism, as it appears in numerous expressions ranging from the structure of state institutions to school curricula to cutting-edge technological innovations, is also part of the daily public narrative. Postmodernism manifests itself most compellingly in art forms, providing for the exploration of novel ideas and hybrid fusions that stretch the mind, challenge conventional forms of morality and chart out ways of living in a pluralist future. But a constant discursive competition between tradition, modernity and postmodernity does not put to rest the debate on how to be Canadian. Canada's lack of a monolithic and fixed national identity opens up areas in which minority groups can contribute to the common conversation. Like others, Ismailis find their own explorations between tradition, modernity and postmodernity overlapping with the country's larger discussions.

Ismaili Engagements in Canadian Spaces

The Ismaili presence in Canada can be traced back to 1952 when Safar Ali Ismaily arrived from Pakistan as a student and eventually decided to stay. His brother Mustansir Billah soon followed and became the father of the first Ismaili child born in Canada. The Ismailis were active with the other (primarily Sunni) Muslims in Ottawa, where they settled. They played a key role in founding the Ottawa Muslim Association and in building the national capital's first permanent mosque.[54] 'We wanted it to have a traditional design with a dome and a minaret,' said Safar Ali Ismaily.[55] It was important for the recently arrived Muslims to reproduce what they viewed as the traditional architecture of their homelands in this northern country. Later, in the 1990s, Ismailis in Edmonton and elsewhere worked with other Muslims to have the Al Rashid Mosque, the first in Canada, officially designated as a heritage site.[56]

Tradition is central to the religious practice of Ismailis in Canada. Islamic scripture, philosophy and history are invoked on a regular basis. The past remains ever present, even in the engagements with modernity and postmodernity. Parin Dossa's ethnographic study of Ismaili immigrant women in Calgary and Vancouver demonstrates how they negotiate the demands of their work places in these cities while striving to maintain the traditional rhythms of family and communal life.[57] Attending *jamatkhana* (the Ismaili place of congregation) is central to the lives of a significant section of the community, gathering for prayers before dawn and at sunset. Tradition is deeply imbedded in ritual practices, which are traced to various points in history going back to the time of the Prophet.

The vast majority of Canadian Ismailis are from East Africa and are of South Asian origin. Their traditional practices draw from the particular Khoja Ismaili heritage of western India. This culture developed for some seven centuries in relative isolation from other Ismaili communities in Syria, Iran, Afghanistan and Central Asia. It produced a vibrant lyrical corpus of *ginan*s which continue to play an important part in the lives of many Khojas in Canada. These hymns, which incorporate religious, ethical and philosophical elements, had been integral to the conversion process in Gujarat, Kutch, Punjab and Sindh. *Ginan*s resonate far beyond the confines of the *jamatkhana* where they are sung regularly. Ali Asani notes that:

> Individual verses can be quoted as proverbs; verses can be recited in homes to bring *baraka*, spiritual and material blessing; housewives, in a usage that stresses the links between the *ginan*s and folk tradition, often recite them while working or as lullabies; audio cassettes with *ginan*s sung by 'star' singers or recordings of *ginan mehfil*s can be found in many an Ismaili home and even their cars![58]

It is around the subject of *ginan*s that several discussions on issues such as identity, belief and propriety are taking place. These debates have often brought to the fore varying Ismaili experiences and interpretations of tradition, modernity and postmodernity.

One of these discussions has centred round matters of propriety with respect to *ginan*s. These hymns are sung in *jamatkhana*s without musical accompaniment. Instruments such as the harmonium, tabla, tanpura and the electronic synthesizer are used in *ginan mehfils/mushairos* ('concerts'). The official Ismaili institutional structure has discouraged the recording and dissemination of such performances, citing in part the disdain for the use of instrumental music in dominant Muslim discourses. But the availability of freelance recordings that are sold in ethnic grocery stores catering to Ismaili customers and on Internet sites has made this approach untenable.[59] The response of the Ismaili Tariqah and Religious Education Board (ITREB) of Canada, the body designated by the Ismaili Imam to provide direction on religious matters to the community, has been to offer guidance on the standard of performance and the propriety of certain limited kinds of musical accompaniment in the recording of certain frequently sung *ginan*s.[60] Acting in what Max Weber describes as the rationalist manner of a modern organization,[61] ITREB's approach, of developing standards, is a modernist solution to a postmodernist situation in which contemporary technology and the market have led to the proliferation of freelance *ginan* audiotapes and CDs.

The guardianship of the *ginan* tradition has provided occasions for other discussions that touch on the contemporary study of this corpus. Until the recent past, authoritative discourse on the hymns was widely viewed as being the preserve of the traditionally trained preachers (*waezeen*). However, the rise of the academic study of *ginan*s by Ismaili scholars attached to Western universities has brought to the fore another set of commentators. The latter bring to bear the analytical methods of the contemporary humanities and social sciences on the corpus. This is not always viewed with favour by the traditionally trained *waezeen*. Tazim Kassam, author of *Songs of Wisdom and Circles of Dance*,[62] states that she came under pressure not to publish her book. She gives a personal account of the contingencies of tradition and modernity which were implicated in the question of the right to engage in public discourse about *ginan*s. Starting from a modernist position derived from her training in religious studies, Kassam was compelled through this challenge to move to a postmodernist assessment of the relationship between power and knowledge. This intellectual exploration also included an examination of her own multiple identities, particularly the position of the scholar as an 'insider-outsider' engaged in the study of their own tradition.[63] Increasingly, Ismaili intellectuals are having to draw on forms of methodology that go beyond merely analysing their heritage and to think reflexively about the numerous socio-cultural factors that impinge on their interstitial placement as believers and academics.

It is ironic that despite the avid discussions on a Khoja Ismaili lyrical tradition, the community has not until recent times placed a high value on cultural creativity. The activities of the Aga Khan Trust for Culture and the Arts and Culture Portfolio in the community's organizational structure have encouraged artistic production, but support for cultural engagement was sporadic until the last decade or so. One Khoja cultural form that has had longstanding populist appeal is that of *geets* (songs) in praise of the Imam. A number of 'non-professional' composers, singers and musicians have written and performed *geets* for the community. They have usually worked in isolation, sometimes passing down musical knowledge from generation to generation and interacting with other musicians of South Asian origin. The Imam's infrequent visits to the community usually provide the occasion for *geet* performances for the *jamat*. They have also provided opportunities for the production of new compositions, as happened in anticipation of the Aga Khan's first visit to the community (1978) and the silver (1982) and golden jubilees (2007) of his Imamate.

'Mara Mowla Canada Padharshe' (1978)[64] is one of the most memorable and popular *geet*s. Its literal English translation, 'My lord shall visit Canada',[65] does not capture the depth of the sentiments it expressed for a migrant community longing for the Imam's auspicious visitation following years of personal and collective struggle in an unfamiliar environment. The *geet* was composed by the Vancouver-based musician and vocalist Shamshu Jamal, whose profession was in the accounting field. He drew on the Canadian *jamat*'s emotional anticipation as well as his own religious sensibilities and profound understanding of Indian music and Gujarati lyrical traditions.[66] It became an international hit among Khoja Ismaili communities, with the names of particular locations where the Imam visited subsequently being substituted for 'Canada' in different renditions of the song. It is noteworthy that an Ismaili artist who contended regularly with the modern condition through his profession had turned to tradition to play a role in facilitating a re-integration of the newly established Canadian *jamat* with the transnational Ismaili community.

Similar creativity has been exhibited by the Ismaili Muslim Youth Choir, which was founded in Toronto in 1984, and was the first Muslim choir in North America. The choir has performed at several community and outreach activities, including for Aga Khan IV, the Canadian Prime Minister and Jordanian royalty. Its youthful members' repertoire includes Urdu *naat*s (in praise of the Prophet), *hamd* (in praise of Allah), *ghazal*s, and songs in various languages. Some of the choir's key accomplishments included bringing innovative and hybrid musical accompaniment to previously *a capella* performances for Eid al-Milad An-Nabi, composing English choral music for a Muslim audience in a Gospel style, and adding complex textural layers of harmony to a wide range of music from traditional and contemporary South Asian songs to Christian hymns, Jewish compositions and Zulu spirituals.[67]

Drama has been another popular art form among the Canadian *jamat*. The performances take place on an occasional basis and are usually the efforts of groups of individuals rather than permanent dramatic societies. Some Ismailis in Canada are also involved as amateur and professional participants in ethnic and mainstream productions. Plays supported by the Ismaili institutional structures usually have a moral or religious theme. The recent productions of *Hayy ibn Yaqzan* (2002) and *JOINDA* (2005) presented an historical sensibility and varied dance styles that became the means for highlighting the theme of diversity as the community engages with its own pluralism. Both shows, which had a kaleidoscopic presentation of traditional and contemporary performance modes, resonated well with audiences who seemed to appreciate this juxtaposition in Ismaili contexts.

The achievements of one Canadian Ismaili writer have been of an international nature. Moyez Vassanji, whose novels frequently feature a fictional Indian Muslim group called 'Shamsis' (who are loosely based on the Khojas), has garnered major literary prizes and other honours. Several of his books narrate the travails of Shamsis in East Africa and North America. They tell stories about the lives of these Indian Muslims as they engage with modernity in the two settings while holding on to their traditions. A recurring theme in Vassanji's work is the interstitial positioning of Indians in African and North American locations. *The In-Between World of Vikram Lall*, narrated from Canada by the main (Hindu) character, is about his life in Kenya where he felt caught between the colonial British and the indigenous Africans.[68] Vassanji's postmodernist narrative not only weaves back and forth across racial, religious and national boundaries but also excavates the moral ambiguities of the past and present that are usually smoothed over in standard accounts. His stories do not provide a picture of an idealized world of Indian settlement either in East Africa or in North America.

Ian Iqbal Rashid is another award-winning Ismaili Canadian artist who is also raising uncomfortable questions through his work. He has written about the intersections of identity with racial and sexual politics, but is most well known as a film-maker. His most widely distributed movie has been *A Touch of Pink* (2004), whose plot summary reads:

> Alim is an Ismaili Canadian who lives in London, thousands of miles from his family, for one very good reason – he has a boyfriend. His ideal gay life begins to unravel when his mother shows up to find him a proper Muslim girlfriend and convince him to return to Canada for his cousin's extravagant wedding.[69]

The tradition of marrying within the community and to someone of the opposite gender is brought into the public eye even as Canadian society at large is contending with inter-racial and same-sex marriage. We have here immigrant Ismailis in the West engaging in the larger socio-political debates through their artistic productions, which draw on the culture with which they are most familiar. The personal, familial and communal experiences of Ismailis are in this way entering into broader societal discourses. Whether other members of the *jamat* are happy with this or not, the relatively free expression of opinion permitted in liberal Western societies allows individuals to make such statements in public.

One of the recurring features of the history of Ismailism has been the management of the public and private expressions of identity. This endeavour has had implications for the very survival of the community at certain critical junctures. Ismailism is characterized by its greater inclination towards the esoteric (*batini*) aspects of Islam as compared to most other branches of the religion. The esoteric, by its very nature, is difficult to explain to those who have not been initiated into the faith. The community has come under attack in its history because of the *batini* nature of its religious outlook. Ismailis, like other Shi'i communities who also suffered rigorous bouts of persecution, adopted *taqiyya* – a means of veiling their identity and beliefs.[70] The hereditary Imams themselves went into concealment at various times, sometimes for centuries. Given this history as well as the current reality of a community that is spread around the world, including some places where its members are still susceptible to persecution, the Ismaili institutional structure remains mindful of the potentially wide-reaching repercussions of statements made in any one location. We have here a dilemma for a transnational community that is engaging at the cutting edge of global modernity while it remains vulnerable to contingencies that are dependent on its geographical placements.

The Ismaili Imamate has pursued a vigorous programme of modernization since the early 20th century. Aga Khan III's contributions were integral to the Muslim reformists' promotion of education, particularly in South Asia and East Africa. He built an institutional structure for his own community to ensure that Ismailis would be prepared for the contemporary world.[71] A set of councils and trusts founded according to modernist forms of institutional organization were guided by a nascent communal constitution. These structures have been significantly enhanced by his successor, Aga Khan IV, who has also established the much broader non-denominational and transnational Aga Khan Development Network (AKDN). The Aga Khan Foundation is a key organization in this network, carrying out socio-economic projects in developing countries while mobilizing funds and expertise in industrialized ones.

Upon moving to the West, the Ismailis have continued to play a vital role in supporting the Imam's initiatives and programmes. Apart from locating the headquarters of the AKDN in Europe, the Aga Khan has also established major institutions such as The Institute of Ismaili Studies and the Institute for the Study of Muslim Civilisations in the UK. In Canada, the network has established the Global Centre for Pluralism and the Delegation of the Ismaili Imamat; they are located on the most prestigious avenue in the Canadian capital whose other structures include the official residences of the Prime Minister and the Governor-General of Canada.

Also under development are the Aga Khan Museum and Ismaili Centre in Toronto and a park in Burnaby, British Columbia.

Media coverage of the community and its individual members in Canada over the last few years shows that the term 'Ismaili' is now readily recognized and is used without background explanation in news stories. The annual World Partnership Walk organized by the Aga Khan Foundation Canada results in significant press reports of Ismailis raising funds for development. Feature articles such as those commemorating anniversaries of the Ugandan exodus or stories about individuals with notable achievements have come to refer to Ismailis in a matter-of-fact way. The election of several members of the community to the federal and provincial parliaments, the appointment of a senator and the awarding of national honours like the Order of Canada to several Ismailis have also led to significant public attention. Additionally the visits of the Aga Khan to Canada receive substantial amounts of coverage in the media. As with other portfolios in the Canadian Ismaili institutional structure, relations with the media also operate along modern lines, and Haroon Siddiqui, a *Toronto Star* editor, noted that the Ismailis 'are miles ahead of other Muslim groups in their sophisticated media skills'.[72] However, all this attention has led to occasional questioning of the community's reluctance to talk about aspects of *jamati* life.

Whereas most of the Canadian news media appear to be respectful of the community's privacy, Douglas Todd, a prominent journalist writing for *The Vancouver Sun*, has made demands for greater 'self-disclosure'. He seems to be operating within an interpretation of open society that expects organizations to be prepared to tell representatives of the press everything they want to know. He argues that since Ismailis are taking on the role of 'public champion of the advancement of mutual understanding between different races, religions, ideologies and nations', they will need to reveal everything about themselves if they are to proceed with 'real engagement'.[73]

Contemporary ideas about the role of the press in society are based on the interaction of the media, government and civil society in the public sphere. However, all discourses in a society do not exclusively take place in a common, monolithic arena: there coexist with the dominant public sphere numerous smaller spheres or 'sphericules' making up the activities of diverse social groups.[74] These 'sphericules' intersect with the public sphere but do not coalesce with it. They legitimately maintain their own distinctness and exist autonomously, separate from the dominant arena of social interactions, particularly in Western liberal societies.

Along with the freedom of the press, privacy remains an important right in contemporary society. Ismailis seek to engage in some of the most pressing issues of the day. The laws of Canada enable them, like all other citizens, to participate in public debate. This right does not require persons to make disclosures about the nature of their community organizations or the nuances of their beliefs. Canadian Ismailis seem determined to participate in the public sphere, including the media, while at the same time they seek to safeguard the privacy of their community life. They remain committed to tradition even as they position themselves at the frontiers of modernity.

At a separate level of social organization, multiculturalism enables various cultural groups to coexist within the country. The Canadian concept of immigrant integration does not demand assimilation into a melting pot. Newcomers are encouraged to acquire personal skills to participate in the larger society's economic, social and political spheres. Sociological research has shown that young Ismailis in British Columbia generally approach Canadian and Ismaili values without dissonance.[75] Canadian multiculturalism 'has played a critical role in the establishment of the Isma'ili community in Calgary'.[76] This appears to be quite representative of the *jamat* in the rest of the country.

The *jamat*'s own cultural diversity is benefiting from adopting a pluralistic approach. A deliberate policy has been developed to incorporate non-Khoja Ismailis, a large number of whom are from Afghanistan, into the community. They are being appointed to the various boards and committees that form the *jamat*'s governing structure. Dari, which is widely used by Afghan members of the community, is also increasingly used in religious services. An indicator of the success of the community's internal policy of pluralism is that Khoja Ismailis are beginning to sing Farsi *qasida*s (poetic hymns) from the Central Asian Ismaili traditions while the Afghan members of the *jamat* recite *ginan*s. Nevertheless the process of integration remains a work in progress.

The AKDN's initiative to establish the Global Centre for Pluralism stems from the favourable experience Ismailis have had of Canada's multiculturalism policy and practices.[77] The joint project between the AKDN and the Canadian government will explore the possibility of sharing insights into pluralism with the rest of the world. The 'Centre will function as a global repository and source for knowledge and know-how about fostering pluralistic values, policies, and practices in a variety of settings'.[78]

Transnationalism, a feature of postmodernity that has become integral to the Ismaili world view, is the means by which this community takes national policies to a global level. The AKDN has become adept at working with a variety of governmental partners to enhance the quality of life through its educational, health and social development programmes both inside and outside Ismaili communities. A number of Canadian Ismailis and Canadians of other backgrounds are serving in various countries under the aegis of the AKDN; several are at the head of institutions.

Multiculturalism emerged as a Canadian solution to a particular historical and political problem. The policy was primarily aimed at resolving conflicts between competing interests in the nation-state, which is a product of the modern age. Ismailis, finding themselves part of this modernist project, are also applying this approach to their own community's diverse traditions. They are now working with the Canadian state to harness their own transnational postmodernity, using pluralism as a human resource in the quest to enhance the quality of life in other regions. But Aga Khan IV emphasizes the point that this is very much part of the Islamic tradition in which pluralism has 'profound roots'.[79] Tradition remains deeply implicated in Ismaili encounters with modernity and postmodernity.

Conclusion

Ismailis in Canada find themselves engaged in a tripartite 'dialectic' of tradition, modernity and postmodernity. A substantial proportion of Canadian Ismailis remain steadfast in their adherence to their religio-cultural heritage. They strive to uphold Islamic values and carry out religious practices with regularity. Members of the community view their tradition as the source of guidance for the ethical conduct of their lives in Western contexts. Their adherence to the present Ismaili Imam is central to this tradition.

The community has also embraced modernity. Their leader has encouraged them to engage with the conditions of the contemporary world. He informs them that there is no contradiction between the pursuit of education in secular institutions and the requirements of their faith. Indeed they are exhorted to excel in the contemporary world. The global *jamat* has reorganized itself over the last century on modernist lines. Beginning with Aga Khan III, the Ismaili Imamate has established a network of communal institutions that seek to promote *jamati* members' quality of life. These institutions are structured and operate according to modernist principles.

Canadian Ismailis also find themselves in a world where aspects of postmodernity intersect with their lives. Multiculturalism and transnationalism are integral to the outlook of the community. Most Ismailis have embraced them and seek to play a key role in encouraging the larger world to use them to resolve conflicts and promote the broader interests of humanity. Artists and intellectuals in the community are engaging with postmodernity and participating in contemporary debates in the public sphere. Their experiences with their heritage and community frequently provide them with a context for their contribution. The Canadian Ismaili *jamat*'s traditions, modernist tendencies and postmodernist forays are being brought to bear on each other in diverse ways so as to make sense of its members' contemporary circumstances.

The seeming paradox between the strong Ismaili leanings towards the esoteric aspects of Islam and a very public effort to implement Qur'anic values through socio-economic development is explained by the continual striving to maintain a balance between the spiritual and material dimensions of human existence. Engagement with tradition, modernity and postmodernity is conducted in search of equilibrium. This struggle is viewed as being a continual and never-ending search for meaning. It occurs at the junctures between tradition, modernity and postmodernity. Whereas all these three axes are pertinent, becoming fixed in any one would put an end to the dynamic of continual striving that is the basis of Ismaili responses to the ever-changing circumstances of life. Interstitial spaces are liminal sites that foster creativity.

The many freedoms that Canadian society offers to Ismailis operate in dialectical interaction with the community's systems of religious belief and social propriety. Members of the *jamat* come into contact with a range of ideas that contend with their heritage. In some ways this situation is reminiscent of the community's historical encounters with external influences which sometimes led to a re-examination of Ismaili traditions, as in the period preceding the establishment of the Ismaili state in North Africa in the 10th century.[80] Ismaili tendencies towards maintaining the privacy of certain aspects of their faith have been coeval with their determination to engage with the world. The current response of the literati and of the generally well-educated *jamat* to tradition, modernity and postmodernity is taking place as the community asserts itself in the global public sphere. Historical tradition provides a precedent in which Ismailis once governed an empire while concurrently maintaining a separate, enclosed sphere of activities for the far-flung community. Ismaili Imam-Caliphs ruled over the pluralistic Fatimid Empire, attending to the common needs of their subjects through public institutions and those of their own adherents through organizations centred around the Ismaili *da'wa* (mission).[81]

As Ismailis interact with contemporary Canadian society in the 21st century, they are simultaneously re-living certain aspects of their long history and charting out courses in contexts that are very different from those encountered previously. Their traditional acknowledgement of the need to respond to changing conditions has been manifested in the value they place upon the importance of continued religious guidance from the Imam of the time as well as the believer's use of the intellect.[82] This approach has been instrumental in enabling the community to survive the travails of history; it has continually adapted itself to contemporary conditions while holding fast to its Islamic heritage. However, the arrival of large numbers of Ismailis in the West has thrown up unique challenges. Not only does the religious community have to contend with the sometimes forceful secularism of post-Enlightenment society, but is also dealing with qualitatively new circumstances which all of humanity is facing for the first time.

The Canadian Ismaili community's engagements with its past and its current surroundings have begun to have a noticeable impact on the larger society. Continuing Ismaili endeavours in the interstices between tradition, modernity and postmodernity hold the prospect of an intensification of such developments in the coming decades.

Notes

1. For an overview of the early settlement of Ismailis in Canada, see Azim Nanji, 'The Nizari Ismaili Muslim Community in North America: Background and Development', in Earle H. Waugh, Baha Abu-Laban and Regula B. Qureshi, ed., *The Muslim Community in North America* (Edmonton, AB, 1983), pp. 149–164.
2. See Arjun Appadurai, *Modernity at Large: Cultural Dimensions of Globalization* (Minneapolis, MN, 1996); Karim H. Karim, 'Nation and Diaspora: Rethinking Multiculturalism in a Transnational Context', *International Journal of Media and Cultural Politics*, 2:3 (2006), pp. 267–282.
3. See Karim H. Karim, *Islamic Peril: Media and Global Violence* (Montreal, 2003).
4. See Albert Hourani, *Arabic Thought in the Liberal Age 1798–1939* (London, 1962); Majid Fakhry, *A History of Islamic Philosophy* (2nd ed., New York, 1983).
5. Fariyal Ross-Sherriff and Azim Nanji, 'Islamic Identity, Family and Community: The Case of the Nizari Ismaili Muslims', in E. H. Waugh et al., ed., *Muslim Families in North America* (Edmonton, AB, 1991), p. 102. A

constant theme in the Aga Khan's advice to his followers is the need to strive for balance between the spiritual and material aspects of life. See Aga Khan IV, *Precious Gems* (Karachi, 1960).
6. Jacques Derrida, *Writing and Difference*, tr. Alan Bass (London, 2004).
7. Aga Khan III, *Precious Pearls* (3rd ed., Karachi, 1961), p. 109.
8. See Abidin Kusno, *Behind the Postcolonial: Architecture, Urban Space and Political Cultures in Indonesia* (London, 2000), pp. 71–94; Karim H. Karim, 'Relocating the Nexus of Citizenship, Heritage and Technology', *The Public: Journal of the European Institute for Communication and Culture*, 4 (1997), pp. 75–86.
9. See Eric Hobsbawm and Terence Ranger, ed., *The Invention of Tradition* (Cambridge, 1983).
10. Aziz Esmail, 'Introduction', in Farhad Daftary, ed., *Intellectual Traditions in Islam* (London, 2000), p. 8.
11. Daniel Lerner, *The Passing of Traditional Society: Modernizing the Middle East* (Glencoe, IL, 1958), p. 58.
12. Hisham Sharabi, 'Islam and Modernization in the Arab World', in J. H. Thompson and R. D. Reischauer, ed., *Modernization of the Arab World* (Princeton, 1966), p. 26.
13. Quoted in Dipesh Chakrabarty, *Habitations of Modernity* (Chicago, 2002), p. 40.
14. Tagore was also an early commentator on the difference between Westernization and modernization, and embraced the latter as 'independence of thought and action'; quoted in Alastair Bonnett, *The Idea of the West: Culture, Politics and History* (New York, 2004), p. 88. Tagore's double orientation towards both tradition and modernity emphasizes the grey area between the two.
15. See Jacob Needleman, ed., *The Sword of Gnosis: Metaphysics, Cosmology, Tradition, Symbolism* (Baltimore, MD, 1974).
16. Joseph E. B. Lumbard, 'Introduction', in Joseph E. B. Lumbard, ed., *Islam, Fundamentalism, and the Betrayal of Tradition: Essays by Western Muslim Scholars* (Bloomington, IN, 2004), p. xiii. The quote is from Seyyed Hossein Nasr's *Traditional Islam in the Modern World* (London, 1987), p. 13.
17. Fuad S. Naeem, 'A Traditional Islamic Response to the Rise of Modernism', in Lumbard, ed., *Islam, Fundamentalism, and the Betrayal of Tradition*, p. 111.
18. Basheer M. Nafi, 'The Rise of Islamic Reformist Thought and its Challenge to Traditional Islam', in Suha Taji-Farouki and Basheer M. Nafi, ed., *Islamic Thought in the Twentieth Century* (London, 2004), p. 29.
19. Ibid., p. 38.
20. Farid Esack, *On Being a Muslim: Finding a Religious Path in the World Today* (Oxford, 1999), p. 195.
21. Annemarie Schimmel, *Islam: An Introduction* (Albany, NY, 1992), p. 52.
22. Mary Louise Pratt, 'Modernity and Periphery: Toward a Global and

At the Interstices of Tradition, Modernity and Postmodernity   291

Relational Analysis', in Elisabeth Mudimbe-Boyi, ed., *Beyond Dichotomies: Histories, Identities, Cultures, and the Challenge of Globalization* (Albany, NY, 2002), p. 23.
23. Ibid., p. 24.
24. Tabish Khair, 'Modernism and Modernity: The Patented Fragments', *Third Text*, 55 (2001), p. 13.
25. Nafi, p. 39.
26. Ibid., p. 40.
27. Ibid., p. 53.
28. Bjorn O. Utvik, 'The Modernising Force of Islam', in John L. Esposito and F. Burgat, ed., *Modernising Islam: Religion in the Public Sphere in the Middle East and Europe* (London, 2003), p. 64.
29. Roxanne L. Euben, *Enemy in the Mirror: Islamic Fundamentalism and the Limits of Modern Rationalism* (Princeton, 1999), p. 165.
30. J. Gray, *Al Qaeda and What it Means to be Modern* (London, 2003), p. 3. For a discussion that explores the primordial origins of this myth, see Karim H. Karim, 'Cyber-Utopia and the Myth of Paradise: Using Jacques Ellul's Work on Propaganda to Analyze Information Society Rhetoric', *Information, Communication and Society*, 4 (2001), pp. 1–22.
31. Ebrahim Moosa, 'The Debts and Burdens of Critical Islam', in Omid Safi, ed., *Progressive Muslims: On Justice, Gender, and Pluralism* (Oxford, 2003), p. 118.
32. Ibid., p. 122.
33. Tariq Ramadan, *Islam, the West and the Challenges of Modernity*, tr. Saïd Amghar (Leicester, 2001), p. 324.
34. Tariq Ramadan, *Western Muslims and the Future of Islam* (Oxford, 2004).
35. Omid Safi, 'Introduction: The Times They are A-changin' – A Muslim Quest for Justice, Gender Equality, and Pluralism', in Omid Safi, ed., *Progressive Muslims: On Justice, Gender, and Pluralism* (Oxford, 2003), pp. 7–15.
36. Aziz Esmail, 'Islam and Modernity: Intellectual Horizons', in Azim Nanji, ed., *The Muslim Almanac* (Detroit, MI, 1996), p. 487.
37. Ibid., p. 486.
38. Azim Nanji, 'Contemporary Expression of Islam in Buildings: What Have We Learned?', in Hayat Salam, ed., *Expressions of Islam in Buildings* (Geneva, 1991), p. 220.
39. Sohail Inayatullah and Gail Boxwell, ed., *Islam, Postmodernism and Other Futures: A Ziauddin Sardar Reader* (London, 2003), p. 190.
40. Jean François Lyotard, *The Postmodern Condition: A Report on Knowledge*, tr. Geoff Bennington and Brian Massumi (Minneapolis, MN, 1984), p. 81.
41. See, for example, Paul Gilroy, *The Black Atlantic: Modernity and Double Consciousness* (Cambridge, 1992).
42. Inayatullah and Boxwell, ed., *Islam*, p. 192.
43. Ibid., p. 209.
44. Akbar Ahmed, *Postmodernism and Islam: Predicament and Promise*

(London, 1992), p. 10.
45. Ibid., p. 13. However, not everyone is agreed that Islamism is an expression of or influenced by postmodernism; see Euben, *Enemy in the Mirror*, pp. 164 ff.
46. Alev Çinar, *Modernity, Islam, and Secularism in Turkey: Bodies, Places, and Time* (Minneapolis, MN, 2005).
47. Michael G. Peletz, *Islamic Modern: Religious Courts and Cultural Politics in Malaysia* (Princeton, 2002).
48. Aziz Al-Azmeh, *Islams and Modernities* (London, 1993), p. 1.
49. M. A. Muqtedar Khan, *American Muslims: Bridging Faith and Freedom* (Beltsville, MD, 2002), p. 62.
50. Inayatullah and Boxwell, ed., *Islam*, p. 123.
51. Ibid., p. 124.
52. Homi Bhabha, *The Location of Culture* (London, 1994), p. 38.
53. Robert Fulford, 'A Postmodern Dominion: The Changing Nature of Canadian Citizenship', in W. Kaplan, ed., *Belonging: The Meaning and Future of Canadian Citizenship* (Montreal, 1993), pp. 104–119.
54. Karim Kurji, 'Profile: Safar Ali Ismaily', *Canadian Ismaili* (July 1988), p. 47. Information was also collected through several personal interviews with Safar Ali Ismaily and Mustansir Billah Ismaily in September and October 2006.
55. Safar Ali Ismaily, personal interview (7 October 2006), Ottawa.
56. Yasmin Chagani, 'Century of Muslims', *The Ismaili Canada* (July 1999), p. 8. See also Karim H. Karim, 'Crescent Dawn in the Great White North: Muslim Participation in the Canadian Public Sphere', in Yvonne Haddad, ed., *Muslims in the West: From Sojourners to Citizens* (New York, 2002), p. 267.
57. Parin A. Dossa, 'Women's Space and Time: An Anthropological Perspective on Ismaili Immigrant Women in Calgary and Vancouver', *Canadian Ethnic Studies*, 20 (1988), pp. 45–65.
58. Ali S. Asani, *Ecstasy and Enlightenment: The Ismaili Devotional Literature of South Asia* (London, 2002), p. 29.
59. Rizwan Mawani, 'The Nizari Ismaili Community and the Internet', *ISIM Newsletter* (June 2003), pp. 44–45.
60. Shamshu Jamal, Mohamed Virjee, Nimet Jaffer, Saajia Amiri and Gyan Kumar, *Melodious Recitation of Ginans*, vol. 1 (Vancouver, 2005).
61. Max Weber, *The Theory of Social and Economic Organization*, tr. A. M. Henderson and Talcott Parsons (New York, 1947).
62. Tazim R. Kassam, *Songs of Wisdom and Circles of Dance: Hymns of the Satpanth Isma'ili Muslim Saint, Pir Shams* (Albany, NY, 1995).
63. Tazim R. Kassam, 'Balancing Acts: Negotiating the Ethics of Scholarship and Identity', in José Ignacio Cabezón and Sheila Greeve Daveney, ed., *Identity and the Politics of Scholarship in the Study of Religion* (New York, 2004), pp. 133–161.

At the Interstices of Tradition, Modernity and Postmodernity 293

64. Shamshu Jamal and Khurshid Noorali, *Paheli Mulakaat: Ismaili Religious Geets – To Commemorate Shah Karim Hazar Imam's First Visit to Vancouver B.C. Nov. 14/1978* Compact Disc (Vancouver, BC, 2005).
65. A more culturally accurate rendering would be: 'My lord will grace Canada with his holy presence.'
66. Shamshu Jamal, personal interview (1 July 2005), Ottawa.
67. Fayyaz Vellani, a former conductor of the choir, provided information on the choir.
68. M. G. Vassanji, *The In-Between World of Vikram Lall* (Scarborough, ON, 2003).
69. Sujit R. Verma, 'Plot Summary for A Touch of Pink (2004)', *Internet Movie Database* http://www.imdb.com/title/tt0374277/plotsummary. Accessed 29 October 2006.
70. Farhad Daftary, *Ismailis in Medieval Muslim Societies* (London, 2005).
71. Esmail Thawerbhoy, 'The Imam of the Socio-Economic Revolution', *Ilm*, 3 (1977), pp. 18–22.
72. Haroon Siddiqui, 'Perceptions and Misrepresentations of Islam and Muslims by the Media', *Islam in America*, 3 (1996), p. 41.
73. Douglas Todd, 'Openness will pose a continuing challenge for Ismailis', *The Vancouver Sun* (11 June 2005), p. C5.
74. See Todd Gitlin, 'Public Sphere or Public Sphericules?', in Tamar Liebes and James Curran, ed., *Media, Ritual, Identity* (London, 1998), pp. 168–175; Karim H. Karim, 'Public Sphere and Public Sphericules: Civic Discourse in Ethnic Media', in S. Ferguson and L. R. Shade, ed., *Civic Discourse and Cultural Politics in Canada* (Westport, CT, 2002), pp. 230–242.
75. Jennifer Hyndman, Arif Jamal and Marianne Meadahl, 'Young Ismailis Embrace Canadian Values', Simon Fraser University News Release (Vancouver, 19 September 2006); Robert Dalton and Naznin Virji-Babul, 'Expressions of Cultural Identity in the Drawings of Two Ismaili Muslim Children', in T. Pelton, G. Reis and S. Stewart, ed., *Connections* (Victoria, BC, 2006), pp. 11–23.
76. Rani Murji and Yvonne Hébert, 'Collectivized Identity among Shi'a Imami Isma'ili Muslims of Calgary', paper presented at 'Youth in the Plural City: Individualized and Collectivized Identities', Rome (25–28 May 1999).
77. Aga Khan Development Network, 'Aga Khan Welcomes Government of Canada's Partnership in New Global Centre for Pluralism', Ottawa, 18 April 2005, Press Release http://www.akdn.org/news/2005April18.htm. Accessed 29 October 2006.
78. The Global Centre for Pluralism, 'Why Establish a Global Centre for Pluralism?' http://www.pluralism.ca/backgrounder.shtml. Accessed 29 October 2006.
79. 'Remarks by His Highness the Aga Khan on the Occasion of the Signing of the Funding Agreement for the Global Centre for Pluralism', Ottawa, 25 October 2006. http://www.pluralism.ca/speeches/speech_oct25-2006.

shtml. Accessed 29 October 2006.
80. Daftary, *Ismailis in Medieval Muslim Societies*, pp. 207–230.
81. Ibid., pp. 62–88.
82. Aga Khan Development Network, 'Ismaili Imamat', http://www.akdn.org/imamat/imamat.html. Accessed 29 October 2006.

PART IV

TAYYIBI MUSTAʿLIAN ISMAILIS

12

History of the Da'udi Bohra Tayyibis in Modern Times: The *Daʿi*s, the *Daʿwat* and the Community

Saifiyah Qutbuddin

The Tayyibi *daʿwat* – so-called after the 21st Fatimid Mustaʿlian Ismaili Imam al-Tayyib b. al-Amir who went into seclusion or *satr* in 524/1130 – has been led by an uninterrupted series of *daʿi al-mutlaq*s, initially based in Yemen and then shifting to India in 946/1539, where the community's roots go back to the 5th/11th century. Despite a fairly turbulent history, the Indian community has survived and flourished, and gradually expanded to comprise a worldwide diaspora. My aim here is a historical rather than an anthropological or ethnological analysis of the main body of Tayyibi Mustaʿlian Ismailis, the Da'udi Bohras. The Bohras have a profile unique among Muslim denominations. This historical analysis will highlight the way the Bohras have managed to retain their cohesion and vibrancy as a community characterized by a distinctive traditional orthopractic culture and a compatible positive modernization; it will also illustrate how their leaders, the *daʿi*s, have been the driving force in guiding the destiny of the community and shaping its evolution in changing times.

The 19th century marked the beginning of a new chapter in Bohra history. It ushered in a period of relative peace for the *daʿwat*, mainly due to the establishment of British supremacy in India, after long years of persecution by Sunni rulers. After some unsettled years, a new centre, Surat, had just been established as the headquarters of the *daʿwat*. Surat, a trading post in Gujarat directly controlled by the British East India Company, offered not only protection from religious persecution but increased financial opportunity. Also extremely significant in terms of *daʿwat* history, the reins of *daʿi*-ship had been taken up by Sayyidna ʿAbd ʿAli Sayf al-Din, whose dynamism and long-lasting reforms earned him the epithet of 'rejuvenator' (*mujaddid*), who laid down a refurbished and enduring infrastructure for the *daʿwat*, and revitalized it in all spheres, whether religious, administrative, cultural or literary. His legacy was perpetuated by his successors. A hundred years and seven *daʿi*s later, another Sayf al-Din, a new 'rejuvenator', assumed the reins of the *daʿwat* early in the 20th century.[1] Sayyidna Tahir Sayf al-Din transferred the *daʿwat* headquarters to the developing metropolis of Bombay (now Mumbai). His astute response to the new realities of the 20th century included the best of what the new ideas and advances had to offer while reaffirming the community's traditional roots, thereby providing security from the bewildered confusion that beset certain other religious denominations. His farsighted and proactive leadership set the course of the *daʿwat* for the new century.

While several major political and cultural factors informed the fortunes of the Bohra community during the modern period, the *daʿi*s' far-reaching authority over the direction of the *daʿwat* and in shaping the community's history is also unmistakably noticeable. The *daʿwat* is conceived in Bohra doctrine as a spiritual kingdom; in the Imam's absence the *daʿi al-mutlaq* – vicegerent and sole representative of the concealed Imam – is the *de facto* head, empowered with the absolute authority vested in the Imam. He is aided in his mission by two other dignitaries of high rank (*rutba*), the *ma'dhun* and the *mukasir*. Belief in the unbreakable chain of *daʿi*s and in the veracity and authority of the appointed *daʿi* is the basic criterion for membership in the Tayyibi Daʿwat and the Bohra community. The Bohras refer to themselves as 'children of the *daʿwat*'. The *daʿi*'s unique role as father figure and supreme leader commanding absolute loyalty is inspired by a deep and personal adoration; the personal charisma and centrality of the *daʿi* in the formulation of the solidarity and very identity of the Bohra community has been remarked upon by other, non-Bohra, scholars.[2] In the context of Islam as a 'way of life', the *daʿi*'s concern and influence regarding the spiritual well-being of his followers extends to all facets of life. Hence he not only firmly regulates those aspects dealing with purely religious matters but takes an active and effective interest in the social and educational welfare of the community, and is intimately involved in the personal lives of his followers. While the Bohras naturally experience historical developments as part of the society and time in which they live, the manner and extent of their engagement with such developments is intrinsically influenced by the *daʿi*'s guidance.

In the modern period, Bohras as citizens of India have been affected by changing political situations and new ideological trends, including the British presence in India, Indian independence, the partition of India, governments led by different political parties, the revolutionizing technological advances of modernization, ideological movements like the women's liberation movement, wider educational opportunities and new arenas and techniques of business. The community's response, the impact of and interaction with these external influences, was governed by the *daʿi*s. In general a self-confident openness to positive external developments and a policy of tolerance and diplomacy can be seen in the *daʿwat*'s relations with others and its adjustment to new and possibly antagonistic ideological, political and social forces, which paved the way for dealing with new challenges thrown up by the modern world with a considerable degree of success.

An in-depth study of the Bohras reveals that their unique interpretation of Islamic law as essentially applicable to all ages, their reason-based philosophy and ethic of broad-mindedness, their tradition of business, and finally their *daʿi*-centred organizational structure and cohesion, have all facilitated a unique adaptation of modernity. A business-oriented livelihood and outlook have encouraged interaction with other cultures and the adoption of the dictates of progress. Implicit belief in Fatimid-Ismaili doctrine – which holds that reason and religion are fundamentally compatible and interdependent, and which preaches that 'wisdom' should be grasped wherever it is found – has enabled them to embrace all the practical accomplishments of modern science and technology which do not explicitly contradict Islamic ideals. The role of the *daʿi* in monitoring the community's response to modernity without deviation from religious ideals – inevitable variation of the degree of conformity in different sectors within the community apart – is crucial in the reinforcement of traditional orthopraxy, in directing and endorsing the incorporation of modern innovations, in setting the authoritative standard for change and continuity, and, not least, in providing a potent focus for spiritual loyalty and cultural cohesion.

Brief Survey of the *Daʿi*s

Sayyidna[3] ʿAbd ʿAli Sayf al-Din, 43rd *daʿi* (1213–1232/1798–1817)

Sayyidna ʿAbd ʿAli Sayf al-Din's forceful personality and total self-confidence, invaluable traits in his captaincy of the Bohra community, are a byword in *daʿwat* tradition. With passion and skill he breathed fresh life into the spirit of the community. He was a learned scholar and prolific writer; the Jamiʿa Sayfiyya, formerly the Dars-i Sayfi (the primary educational institution of the *daʿwat*) bears his name, as does the *daʿwat*'s central administration, the Wazarat al-Sayfiyya. He remains one of the wisest, most dynamic leaders of the *daʿwat*, overcoming chronic ill health, personal tragedies and crippling disasters to invigorate every aspect of the Bohra community.

Sayyidna Muhammad ʿIzz al-Din, 44th *daʿi* (1232–1236/1817–1821)
A new family was introduced to lead the *daʿwat*: Sayyidna Muhammad ʿIzz al-Din, the relatively inconspicuous and untried son of Shaykh Jeevan-ji of Aurangabad, was groomed meticulously in utmost secrecy by the 43rd *daʿi* and presented as his successor. His brief time as *daʿi* saw the smooth continuation of his predecessor's legacy.

Sayyidna Tayyib Zayn al-Din, 45th *daʿi* (1236–1252/1821–1837)
Also selected and trained for the rank by Sayyidna ʿAbd ʿAli Sayf al-Din, the long eventful reign of Sayyidna Tayyib Zayn al-Din – the elder brother of his predecessor – is alluded to as containing intimations of *'zuhur'*, a time when an Imam exercised sovereignty among the people, due to the pomp and recognition surrounding the *daʿi*'s official visits and activities, and the rare freedom enjoyed by the Bohras in practising their religion. Among his contributions to the field of education is the classification of key *daʿwat* texts into a graded sequence of study still pertinent today.[4]

Sayyidna Muhammad Badr al-Din, 46th *daʿi* (1252–1256/1837–1840)
Sayyidna Muhammad Badr al-Din's biographer writes his story with 'sorrowful heart and tear-filled eyes'.[5] Except for a long felicitous sojourn in Pune, tragedy overshadowed his life: his father Sayyidna ʿAbd ʿAli Sayf al-Din died when he was seven; early in his *daʿi*-ship, a devastating fire swept Surat, destroying thousands of homes and livelihoods, including almost all the *daʿwat* buildings and a large number of irreplaceable *daʿwat* manuscripts. He died at the young age of 30, the ninth and last *daʿi* of the Badri dynasty that had begun with the 34th *daʿi* Ismaʿil Badr al-Din (1065–1085/1655–1674).

Sayyidna ʿAbd al-Qadir Najm al-Din, 47th *daʿi* (1256–1302/1840–1885)
The issue of legitimate *daʿi*-ship and the *nass* controversy has tended to obscure the positive realities of Sayyidna ʿAbd al-Qadir's unprecedented 47-year term in office. He was the first Indian *daʿi* to carry out his decision to undertake the *hajj* pilgrimage. People from different faiths came, as they do now, to seek the *daʿi*'s blessings. The *daʿwat* weathered serious blows to its constitutional foundation, but he left the Bohra community a

legacy of extraordinary generosity and filial benevolence.

Sayyidna ʿAbd al-Husayn Husam al-Din, 48th *daʿi* (1302–1308/1885–1891)
The seasoned and tried Sayyidna ʿAbd al-Husayn Husam al-Din, with a long record of dedicated service, succeeded his brother after a virtual campaign of vilification against him by his enemies had failed to have him disinherited. He was acclaimed for his oratory. Among his lasting contributions is the Fayd-i Husayni, an agency to facilitate pilgrimage travel which became the major resource for Bohra pilgrims, and the establishment of *musafirkhana*s (guest-houses) for travellers; there are now lodges for visitors in most pilgrimage sites in India and abroad.

Sayyidna Muhammad Burhan al-Din (I), 49th *daʿi* (1308–1323/1891–1906)
Sayyidna Muhammad Burhan al-Din's 15-year term was divided by his son Sayyidna Tahir Sayf al-Din into three periods – the first fraught with internal and financial difficulty, the second spent in intensive consolidation of administrative and other matters, and the latter years a time of stability, prosperity and productivity. The clearing of the prolonged debt that had burdened the *daʿwat* is counted among the 49th *daʿi*'s greatest achievements.

Sayyidna ʿAbd Allah Badr al-Din, 50th *daʿi* (1323–1333/1906–1915)
The appointment of the mild-mannered, low profile Sayyidna ʿAbd Allah Badr al-Din as *daʿi* was generally unexpected. His term was comparatively peaceful and stable, a reflection of the calm apparent in the world at large before the First World War.

Sayyidna Tahir Sayf al-Din, 51st *daʿi* (1333–1385/1915–1965)
Sayyidna Tahir Sayf al-Din delivered the oration at the inauguration of his term like, it was said, a second ʿAbd ʿAli Sayf al-Din. He too came to be called 'Muʾayyad-i Asghar' or the 'Second Muʾayyad', a reference to the great Fatimid *daʿi* and intellectual al-Muʾayyad fiʾl-Din al-Shirazi, for his intellectual scope and mastery of the pen and for his contribution to the perpetuation and augmentation of a rich literary heritage; his erudition elicited respect and recognition from scholars outside the community as well. He, too, firmly established the paramount authority of the *daʿi*, kept the reins of *daʿi*-ship firmly in his hands, and brought the same vigour and resolution as his predecessors to his task. He, too, at the commencement

of another century, breathed fresh spirit into the *da'wat*: painstakingly, through coaxing, exhortation and sheer personal dynamism, he brought cohesion and renewed vitality to a community depleted by confusion and lassitude. It was a rapidly changing world, and the 51st *da'i* ushered in a dynamic new era in the *da'wat*. Under his direction, the *da'wat*, its members and its policies progressed towards successful participation in the modern age while reaffirming and renewing allegiance to the source of their identity.

The 28-year-old Tahir Sayf al-Din was immediately plunged into a battle with opponents. The dissidents, headed by the sons of the wealthy industrialist Adamji Pirbhoy, decided to take their challenge of the *da'i* to the civil authority of the country's courts; several cases were fought over a period of years within the national legal system, first under the British government and later the Indian, most prominent among them the Chandabhai Gulla Case and the Burhanpur Dargah Case. The new *da'i* had practically no seasoned counsellors; while benefiting from existing legal talent within the community, tough decisions regarding the conduction of the lawsuits were taken solely by the *da'i*. Lawyers involved in *da'wat* cases today find guidance in the sagacious arguments presented by the 51st *da'i* in court. He finally won every legal suit.

Tahir Sayf al-Din's concerted efforts during the early years focused on clearing the doubts regarding the *da'i*'s legitimacy. The exponents of the *inqita' al-nass* theory had been functioning clandestinely within the community since the time of Sayyidna 'Abd al-Qadir Najm al-Din, whose successors had adopted a policy of forbearance and conciliation for various reasons, including the dread of causing a fatal rift in the community and the consideration that several prominent *da'wat* figures were involved. Sayyidna Tahir Sayf al-Din confronted these challengers head on, in writing and in speech. He presented arguments for the doctrinal essentiality of a *da'i al-mutlaq*, with particulars about the *nass* of the 47th *da'i* in his first Ramadan *risalat* (treatise) titled *Daw' nur al-haqq al-mubin* (1335/1916–1917). The verdicts in British court cases concerning this issue further added to the success of his efforts. As a result the *da'i*'s position and authority within the community were greatly strengthened.

Sayyidna Tahir Sayf al-Din transferred the headquarters of the *da'wat* to Bombay (now Mumbai, capital of the state of Maharashtra); the *da'i*'s residence, Sayfi Mahal, and the Sayfi Masjid – the largest *masjid* ever built by a *da'i* and the city's principal Bohra *masjid* – are focal points of the Bohra landscape in Bombay. Bohras tended to gravitate towards and settle in centres of commerce and trade. Bombay, which by now had a Bohra population of about 5,000, had replaced Surat with its 2,000–3,000 strong community as the most populous Bohra centre. While Surat had been one of the major port cities of British India, it was becoming less important as a mercantile centre, and it was Bombay that was destined to become the commercial capital of modern India. Gujaratis had dominated the political and economic scene in Bombay during the colonial period, and it was mainly Gujarati entrepreneurs who helped to create the metropolis of Bombay; among them, Bohra businessmen also quickly filled the niches in the mercantile industry created by the expanding trade with Europe, and even established virtual monopolies in areas such as hardware and glass. While most Bohras owned shops or small businesses, a fair number went into banking and larger industrial ventures.

Sayyidna Taher Sayf al-Din's term covered more than 50 years, spanning an extremely eventful half-century in world history. The atmosphere in the Bohra community was one of animated activity, of seizing opportunity, of advancement and progress in all aspects of life. Many of the world's revolutionary events found echoes in the *da'wat*. It was a time of two world wars; in the *da'wat* there was turbulent activity and conflict with dissidents. The industrial/technological revolution encouraged a move towards technical and professional training among the Bohras; as the world became a smaller place with advanced communication and speedier travel, the *da'wat* administration was tightened and firmer central control established, while Bohras around the world had experienced a greater cultural unity and closer contact with the *da'i*. Expanding cosmopolitanism, the nationalism following Indian independence from British colonialism, and the globalization of the world economy, all had a considerable impact on the Bohras and the *da'wat*'s political and financial policies, initiating a degree of participation in national affairs and a recognition of their place in the forum of Indian Muslims especially, and then within the international Muslim forum.

These changes and trends were, by all accounts, directed by the vision and the firm hand of the 51st *da'i* in accordance with fundamental religious principles. On the one hand, he was fully alive to the need for dealing realistically with the complex problems of modern life; he had a hands-on manner of operation which ensured his awareness of and involvement in the details and decisions regarding developments in the *da'wat*. On the other, since the close-knit network of the community was opening up to a greater cosmopolitanism, to outside influences and ideological currents, a corresponding emphasis on the reinforcement of essential traditional values and practices, of the community's ideological roots, became a critical priority.

Having put into place the process for religious reaffirmation – fully restoring the authority of the *da'i*'s position, bringing about a resurgence of faith and participation in religious tradition focusing particularly on the youth – Tahir Sayf al-Din opened the community to accepting the beneficial aspects of modernity on a large scale. Secure in their ideology and tradition, Bohras had not undergone the crisis of identity of Islam versus modernity experienced by certain other Indian Muslims after the dissolution of the Mughal Empire and its replacement by British rule; no psychological or ideological obstacles had prevented the learning of new languages and the adopting of new ways of communication and trade. Instead all manifestations of progress that did not contradict fundamental religious principles were welcomed without qualms.

Sayyidna Tahir Sayf al-Din now launched comprehensive reform programmes in several areas of the community, especially administration, finance, education and societal norms. The administrative apparatus was better regulated, systematized and reinforced. Housing and cooperative schemes were encouraged. Along with the regulation and greater facilitation of religious education, *da'wat*-sponsored institutions for secular education were introduced and technical and career-oriented training was encouraged. Tahir Sayf al-Din, a prolific writer of works in both prose and poetry which are a central part of the *da'wat* literary corpus, held regular *sabaq*s for Bohras of various categories – the number reaching an incredible 30 or more classes a day during one period. He emphasized the need to educate the Bohras, the youth especially, in religious tradition to strengthen and reinforce their commitment to the *da'wat*, at the same time advocating secular education, particularly through the medium of the English language, and vocational and technical training. One measure of the success of the drive towards wider education is that the community, including women, achieved virtually 100 per cent literacy at a time when the average literacy in India was around 10 per cent and that of women and Muslims in particular far less. Bohra women were encouraged to seek education, to attend communal prayer and ceremonial/religio-social gatherings and to take an active part in community affairs. Voluntary associations for women as well as men – such as the Sayfi Women's Organization – were formed and drew a large membership involved in extensive social work. Modernity was reflected in the dress code as well. Bohra dress had been, save for a few minor adaptations, the dress of the society in which they lived. As the community opened up, the style of dress also changed. Men began to adopt the Western dress code that was gaining ground in professional and business circles. The *da'i* allowed women as well to wear other forms of dress within the required canon of religious propriety, while their traditional dress (*rida*) was also modified to allow for a more mobile lifestyle. The Bohras and their *daʿi* began to acquire a known public identity on the national scale. The partition of India in 1947 was a time of heightened communal emotion and danger for all in the region, and many Indian Muslims left for Pakistan either freely or as a result of coercion. Despite threats of dire consequences from a senior Hindu leader if he did not leave, the *daʿi* decided to remain in his homeland and directed his followers to do the same; other Muslims testified that his resolute stance also motivated them to remain. Particularly after independence, the Bohras assimilated to a degree with other Indian Muslims, supporting, for instance, the Congress Party against more right-wing Hindu parties and participating in the Muslim Personal Law Board. The *daʿi* was hailed as a pious, open-minded and wise leader, his public identity highlighted by his meetings and correspondence with government officials of British and independent India, as well as other public figures. The Bohras also began to publicly identify with the international Muslim *umma*.

For the first time, a *daʿi al-mutlaq* now visited Bohra communities established in countries outside India. It was the first time many of these Bohras had seen their *daʿi*. He visited Ceylon several times. He made a historic journey in 1953–1954 to the Far East, where he visited Rangoon (Burma), Bangkok (Thailand), Jakarta (Indonesia), Sarbaya and Penang (Malaysia), Singapore and Hong Kong, and in 1963 he went to East Africa. The *daʿi* was welcomed and honoured by political leaders in all these places. He also made long annual visits to Karachi, which has the second largest Bohra population after Mumbai, even after partition. His wide-ranging travels included several landmark pilgrimage journeys. He was the first *daʿi* to visit the Fatimid capital Cairo since the end of the dynasty's rule some 800 years earlier; he was also the first Bohra *daʿi* to visit places of historical significance for the Bohras in Palestine and Syria.

Sayyidna Tahir Sayf al-Din completed 50 years as *daʿi* in 1963. His Golden Jubilee was celebrated with great pomp by the Bohra community worldwide. Eminent public leaders and scholars also participated in the commemorations and expressed their appreciation for the *daʿi*'s work; others sent messages of felicitation and tribute for his guidance of his community, his promotion of the cause of Islam and his personal contributions to humanity. Sayyidna Tahir Sayf al-Din died on 19 Rajab 1385/12 November 1965; his mausoleum, Raudat Tahira, remains a focal point of Bohra devotional sentiment.

Sayyidna Muhammad Burhan al-Din (II), 52nd *daʿi* (1385/1965 – present)
Sayyidna Tahir Sayf al-Din was succeeded by his eldest son Sayyidna Muhammad Burhan al-Din – nominated by him when only 19, a point referred to at almost every public oration since – which ensured the renewal of faith and promised security in the endurance of tradition. Sayyidna Muhammad Burhan al-Din's term has reaped the fruits of the 51st *daʿi*'s labours. When the 52nd *daʿi* took up the reins of the *daʿwat*, he continued on the path set by his father. He appointed as *maʾdhun* his young brother Sayyidi Khuzayma Qutb al-Din. He confirmed the late *daʿi*'s brothers, Sayyidi Salih Safi al-Din as *mukasir* and Sayyidi Ibrahim Zayn al-Din as *raʾs al-hudud*. Many of the guidelines and activities of the *daʿwat* regarding political policies, social welfare, etc. continued for a time along the course established, and several trends begun by the 51st *daʿi* were further developed. Inevitably, as the passage of time has brought changes and developments, and new people with new ideas and attitudes have gained prominence in the establishment, some modifications, alterations and new directions have become apparent.

The Bohra community in Sayyidna Muhammad Burhan al-Din's time has kept in step with the developing times in all practical aspects of life. The trend towards more widespread and higher education has continued; while business is still the form of livelihood most encouraged, modern times have seen the emergence of more and more professionals, doctors, lawyers, scientists, engineers, architects, etc.; the participation of women in community affairs, their education and even careers are now taken for granted, and Bohra women enjoy a degree of involvement in and contribution to the community far above that of the average Indian Muslim woman. The *daʿwat* machinery, too, has continued to evolve: finances have improved dramatically, and education and welfare facilities among the community continue to improve and reach further. While the administrative format remains basically the same, more departments have been added, the infrastructure has been revolutionized with the coming of the computer age and new centres are being established at a rapid rate to accommodate the dispersal and expansion of the community.

Simultaneously, a more rigorous Islamic-centred approach in all aspects of life – including dress code, finance, etc. – is being propagated by the establishment. This emphasis is motivated in part by the desire to counteract anti-traditionalist, anti-authority aspects of Westernized modernization. Bohras who have settled in Western countries are perhaps particularly prone to such influence, but these trends are rapidly pervading Indian society, especially the youth, and have penetrated the Bohras as well. Inter-communal marriages are increasing, and permission is given with reluctance to such unions, as it is believed that they have negative consequences in the long term for the community inasmuch as they usually generate a dilution of tradition and a weakening of the bonds of loyalty to the *da'wat* in subsequent generations. The convening of religious functions has increased, and attendance is huge particularly when the *da'i* himself is present. Construction of devotional and pilgrimage-related structures also takes place on a much wider scale, and several ambitious renovation projects have been completed.

Much of this construction is now inspired by the Fatimid affiliation of the Bohras – one of the major features of Sayyidna Muhammad Burhan al-Din's time is the physical reinforcement of the Bohra's Fatimid identity, their involvement with the one-time Fatimid capital, Cairo, and their leader's persona as 'Fatimid *da'i*' in Egypt and other Arab countries. The Bohras see themselves as the inheritors of the Fatimid legacy. Their socio-religious norms reflect aspects of Fatimid culture (to give but one example, the choice of the colour white, the official Fatimid colour, for traditional male clothing), while *da'wat* literature and education is the inheritance and perpetuation of Fatimid religious learning. Sayyidna Muhammad Burhan al-Din travelled to Cairo shortly after becoming *da'i*, by invitation of the Egyptian government to inaugurate the *Ra's al-Husayn* cenotaph in 1966.[6] He has come to be known in the Arab world as 'Sultan al-Bohra', and is referred to as 'Azamat al-Sultan'. His renovation of the 4th/10th-century Fatimid *masjid* of Imam al-Hakim in Cairo, al-Jami' al-Anwar (one of the largest *masjids* in the world), which had lain for many centuries in virtual ruin, was a landmark undertaking in the Tayyibi *da'wat*'s history and proved to be of particular significance to the Bohra community.[7] It was responsible for the settlement of a fairly large Bohra community there; students from the Jami'a are given the opportunity to study in al-Azhar University. Since the restoration of al-Anwar (inaugurated in 1980), a 'neo-Fatimid' style has come to dominate the style of *da'wat* monuments, in which architectural forms and design motifs found in Egyptian Fatimid architecture are utilized, with copious use of marble and gold leaf, particularly in *mihrabs*. In renovated Indian monuments, stone structures have generally been replaced with marble; the Indian element that blended with the Islamic/Mughal has been retained in some renovated structures, but in all new edifices the 'neo-Fatimid' style prevails. The 1997 rebuilding of al-Masjid al-Mu'azzam in Surat is an example of this style.

Currently the 96-year-old *da'i* continues to lead an active community life and governs the *da'wat* in all its various aspects. As a direct result of their love and staunch allegiance to the person of the *da'i*, the Bohra community scattered all over the world has preserved an impressive degree of vigour and cohesion.

Historical Trends in Political Policies and Internal Dynamics

The modern period has been by and large one of prosperity and relative calm for the Tayyibi *da'wat*, particularly when compared with the preceding epoch. In India the *da'i* was respected historically as an illustrious spiritual personage by the Hindus and Sikhs, as well as Muslims. The Bohras have been noted for their attitude of harmony, non-confrontation and goodwill in their interaction with people of other creeds. However, as a minority Shi'i community, they have frequently suffered hostility and persecution. Their distinctive public observance of religious practices, such as the celebration of 'Id on an astronomically fixed day (rather than by the sighting of the moon), separate Friday prayer, the practice of *matam*, etc., has antagonized Sunni Muslim denominations; the slaughter of animals for meat has sometimes additionally angered vegetarian Hindus (factors also important in the broader context of Hindu–Muslim unrest in the country). The noticeable cohesion and effectual social welfare among the Bohra community, celebrations, and latterly their better lifestyle and advanced level of education have aroused the jealousy of some of the poorer and less well-organized among their co-religionists. A primary factor in inter-communal tension has been the Bohras' material affluence, which, say historic accounts, excited the avarice of Hindu and Sunni rulers and governors in pre-independence days, and has since led to the targeting of commercial property in communal violence.

The political authorities have both protected and persecuted Bohras through the ages. The political policies of the Indian *da'i*s have been informed by their traditional perception of themselves as a *gharib qawm*, literally 'poor people', or a defenceless and politically weak people, in Misra's words 'a persecuted and harried community',[8] a small minority beleaguered by a potentially hostile majority. Hence the *da'is*' policy has been to keep a low profile and to solicit where possible the goodwill of the ruling powers of the land. To this end, the *da'i*s of pre-independence India cultivated cordial relations with local *nawab*s and *raja*s, such as the Maratha Peshwas, and the rulers of the princely states such as the Sindhias of Gwalior, the Holkars of Indore and the Gaekwads of Baroda.

The *da'i* 'Abd 'Ali Sayf al-Din and the Bohras had cordial relations with the foreign mercantile powers making political inroads in India, particularly the British, who began to gain ascendancy and consolidated their dominance in almost the whole of India by the early 19th century. After suffering years of sectarian persecution, the Bohras welcomed the sympathy and protection of the British. The Bohras' positive experience with and historical perception of the British Raj is a fact that postcolonial scholars would perhaps be uncomfortable with – the negative sides of British colonialism continue to be the subject of academic and political discussion – but for the Bohras, British rule meant a friendly authority comparatively free from religious prejudice, which not only established a large degree of political stability but also initiated positive reforms in the infrastructure of the country and offered expanded business opportunities, a cosmopolitanism and cultural benefits. While Surat had been among the most populous and important of the Bohra settlements, control of it by the British East India Company was probably a key factor in the *daʿi* Yusuf Najm al-Din and his successors choosing it for the *daʿwat* headquarters.[9] The Bohra merchants were an active and influential sector of the city's trade, and the goodwill was mutual. ʿAbd ʿAli Sayf al-Din mentions in a *risalat* (official letter/treatise) that a Frenchman, having received impressive reports about the *daʿi*, immediately agreed to a request to vacate the seaside villa he had hired so that the *daʿi* could convalesce there. In Surat at least, after suffering the aggression of Shivaji and the Hindu Marathas, many of the leading Muslim families supported the British, and even during the upheavals of 1857 the area remained tranquil. In contrast to the peace and security in Surat, continued harassment of the Bohras by local rulers in various other areas is reported. The author of *Mawsim-i bahar* describes graphically how the persecuted Bohras – possibly referring to the area around Morbi, where the *daʿi* was resident at the time – lived in a constant state of uncertainty, while their financial situation deteriorated;[10] community leaders in Ratangarh-kheri and Jaatha (in present Madhya Pradesh) were interned by the Maratha Peshwa Baji Rao II.

During the 46th *daʿi*'s sojourn in Pune, British officers were so cordial it was said that no previous Indian *daʿi* had received such accolades from a political power. A letter written by the 47th *daʿi* in reply to a British agent contains an overview of the *daʿis*' long friendly association with the British in India, outlining instances of mutual help and support.[11] In his time, British sovereignty passed from the East India Company to the Crown following the uprising of 1857. The *daʿi* was conferred the title 'First Class Sardar of the Deccan'; this title, along with its benefits, was also conferred on his successors. Earlier *daʿi*s had been offered *jagirs* (land grants), which were refused because of the political obligations they entailed. British governors and residents enjoyed the *daʿis*' hospitality and sought their advice; local British officials participated in ceremonial occasions such as weddings; the British military provided escorts and protection for *daʿis*; British authorities facilitated Bohra trade ventures abroad. It is not, therefore, surprising that *daʿwat* history recalls British rule as an era that brought security, stability and progress.

Although the Bohras had, in the interests of their own survival, chosen to take the path of least resistance with the powers that be, they were not isolated from the aspirations of the people among whom they lived. They sympathized with the independence movement of India – many Bohras were active participants, with the *daʿi*'s blessings – and had good relations with the freedom fighters; Mahatma Gandhi was offered the *daʿi*'s bungalow for his stay in Dandi during the Salt March, which was later donated to the nation as a historic site. After independence, cordial relations continued particularly with the Congress Party and its leaders, and the *daʿi*, while still abstaining from directly participating in politics, continues to meet and act as host to national and international political leaders.

Ironically Bohras in India have suffered historically from the prejudice of Muslim rulers while enjoying comparative freedom from religious restrictions and persecution under Hindu rulers; this experience continued in post-independence India. Particularly since the 20th century, the Bohras began to assimilate themselves, albeit to a limited degree, into the Indian and then the international Muslim community. The 51st *daʿi* was successful in establishing a greater rapport with members of other Muslim denominations. By word and action, he emphasized the basic unifying factors of Islam rather than the differences among various Muslim communities. In the national elections held in 1935, the Bohras in Bombay – where the voting franchise was dominated by Muslims – supported Muhammad ʿAli Jinnah of the Muslim League. The *daʿi* as an influential community leader gained a highly respected voice in national Muslim affairs. Receptions hosted by the *daʿi* for visiting international Muslim leaders, the Aqsa restoration appeal and the Palestine Conference were an assertion of the Bohra community's pan-Islamic association and sympathies. Sayyidna Tahir Sayf al-Din presented the *kiswa*, red draperies that were hung in the interior of the Kaʿba, in 1931 and 1937, and donated the intricately crafted silver and gold cenotaphs (*zarihs*) for the tombs of Imam ʿAli (1942), Imam Husayn (1937), and Raʾs al-Husayn in Cairo (inaugurated in 1966). The *daʻi* has participated in international conferences related to religion.

Sayyidna Tahir Sayf al-Din placed the Bohra community on the national map of India. Under his direction, the Bohras began to achieve national recognition as a positive constituent of the country's society, and their strong religious roots, code of conduct, business acumen, discipline and tolerant outlook have been frequently praised by eminent public figures. Bohras have risen to occupy prominent civil posts such as Sheriff of Bombay and Chief Justice of the Indian High Court and even the Supreme Court. Since the mid-20th century large numbers of Bohras have begun to settle in the Middle East and the West. The *daʻwat* has acquired an international public identity, particularly with the *daʻi*'s visits to the new community centres; he is officially recognized abroad as the head of a known religious community, welcomed as a guest of governments and has even been awarded civic honours in several countries.

While the role and activities of the Public Relations Office instituted in the time of the 52nd *daʻi* are still limited, eschewing presenting statements or explanations in the press, good relations are built outside the community through the general conduct and actions of Bohras. In ʻAbd al-Qadir Najm al-Din's time, the Governor of Ratlam wrote of the *daʻi* and his followers with admiration in his book *Tarikh-i Malwa*.[12] Apart from their live-and-let-live attitude where ideology is concerned, in the 19th and 20th centuries the *daʻi*s contributed generously towards relief and charity for Hindus as well as other Muslims. Private meetings between *daʻwat* dignitaries and religious and international political leaders, including leaders from all denominations and all political parties, are a means of promoting goodwill.

The Bohras have, for the most part, enjoyed a peaceful and productive coexistence with Hindus, Muslims and other communities. However, inter-communal conflicts have erupted, and continue to do so, from time to time, disturbing the customary smooth relations.

Internal dissent

Historically, episodes of dissent within the community have usually been based on a rival claim to the leadership. Dissenters – termed *munafiqin* in the *daʻwat* – have tended to develop and utilize further this doctrine in order to support their claims. As far as is evident from accounts of such movements, social disaffection of any sort has not usually been an issue, at least not a declared motive. The *daʻi*s' policy has usually been one of prompt refutation, accompanied by attempts at reconciliation and re-absorbing, as far as possible. Some dissenters have seceded from the *da'wat* to form separate sects which are still in existence today, such as the Mahdibaghwalas; some have returned to the *da'wat*, either individually or the entire group (members of the Hujumiyya sect who had seceded in the time of the 33rd *da'i* returned during the time of the 43rd *da'i* 'Abd 'Ali Sayf al-Din; the 75 remaining followers of Majdu', a prominent dissident during the time of the 40th *da'i*, returned during Tayyib Zayn al-Din's time). From about the middle of the 20th century, 'social reform' became the main slogan of dissenters, who demanded the restoration of what they regarded as the 'original' Bohra tenets which they held had been distorted by the *da'i* and the establishment. While they claim to accept the *da'i* as their leader, albeit limited to what they define as the spiritual sphere, the dissenters continue to dispute the perimeters of his authority[13] and to seek outside intervention for perceived injustices. The period under study saw a few occasions of internal dissent, which had varying degrees of impact.

The inqita' al-nass theory

A very serious sedition or *fitnat*, in every way, occurred in the time of the 47th *da'i*, Sayyidna 'Abd al-Qadir Najm al-Din, a controversy about his authority as legitimate *da'i al-mutlaq* that pervaded the fabric of the community even in the highest circles, causing an internal upheaval that threatened the very dogmatic bedrock of the *da'wat*. The *nass*-validity issue has tended to dominate the historical accounts of the reign of the 47th *da'i*, with almost all non-Bohra sources uncritically replicating – for various reasons – the dissident view; the argument for the 47th *da'i* is hardly even mentioned. Historical records supply evidence that the 46th *da'i* had always spoken of, written about, alluded to and treated 'Abd al-Qadir Najm al-Din in a manner which left no doubt that he regarded him as his successor, clearly stating his choice publicly on several occasions. Hence the Ma'dhun Sayyidi Hibat Allah Jamal al-Din (d. 1274/1858) addressed him in a letter as *al-mansus alay-hi miraran* ('the heir oft-designated-by-*nass*').[14] His succession was decreed by authoritative scholars to be by a valid witnessed *nass*, no objection is reported to have been raised at the time, nor was any other candidate put forward. The *da'i*-ship began smoothly, with all the usual traditions of transition: the oath of allegiance, the letters and poems of congratulations, the routine financial entries under the name of the new *da'i* in the ledgers (*daftar*). Many years later, however, doubts were raised about the legitimacy of his *da'i*-ship by disaffected elements of the Bohra elite aiming to undermine the *daʿi*'s supreme authority. They actively propagated the claim that he had not received the mandatory formal designation of *nass* from his predecessor; coining the *inqitaʿ al-nass* theory, viz., that the tradition of *nass* necessary for a legitimate *daʿi al-mutlaq* had been severed, they proclaimed that ʿAbd al-Qadir Najm al-Din was simply a *nazim daʿi*, a 'manager *daʿi*' who had no spiritual authority. The *daʿi*'s supporters cited specific instances of *nass*; the *daʿi* himself was constrained to draft a response to his accusers.[15] Fifty years later, in court session, a British judge heard both sides of the argument and ruled categorically in the pro-*nass* party's favour.[16]

It is significant that the challenge was raised openly so long after ʿAbd al-Qadir Najm al-Din's assumption of *daʿi*-ship, when most of the eminent scholars of the time of the 46th *daʿi* and earlier were no longer alive to answer the accusations, including the witnesses to the appointment and scions of the ʿIzzi and Zayni families with direct knowledge of the affair. Sayyidna Tahir Sayf al-Din placed the controversy 15 years into ʿAbd al-Qadir Najm al-Din's term, based on the death in 1271/1854 of the pre-eminent *daʿwat* notable Sayyidi ʿAbd ʿAli ʿImad al-Din, perhaps the most influential of the *daʿi*'s supporters. It culminated in the launching of a direct challenge to the *daʿi*'s authority some 40 years into his term by a group calling itself *Hilf al-Fadaʾil*, comprised of people occupying prominent positions in the *daʿwat* establishment, sons of the late *hudud* who had endorsed the *nass*, plus a few members of the *daʿi*'s family. Their demand for the management of the *daʿwat* by consultative assembly (*shura*) was in effect a claim for the devolution of supreme authority within the *daʿwat* upon themselves. Their purpose, says Professor Robert Serjeant, was to usurp the *daʿi*'s power and acquire control over the *daʿwat* revenues;[17] several founders of the *Hilf* also had personal grudges against the *daʿi*.

The *daʿi* did re-establish his authority, the principal dissidents rendered him public obeisance and desisted from further open sedition, but a certain amount of damage had been done, and the consequences and costs of the conflict and the measures taken to protect the *daʿwat* would be felt for many years. The stature of the *daʿi* in the community had been undermined by years of rumour. To dilute the opposing *shaykh* faction, the *daʿi* began conferring the title of *shaykh* more commonly, with the result that it became less esteemed; to lessen their hostility, he allocated the income from prominent administrative areas to powerful potential trouble-makers in the *daʿwat*, reducing the *daʿwat*'s overall income; *dars* instructors had participated in the affair and hence the institution suffered. Most importantly for the *daʿwat*, the dissenters had used their status to create doubts in the minds of a significant portion of the Bohra community; the new doctrines of the invalidation of the *da'i*'s spiritual authority continued to survive in prominent circles and had repercussions for succeeding *da'i*s, becoming a much used weapon in the hands of would-be challengers. It would take the strenuous efforts of the 51st *da'i* to finally set the issue at rest.

The Mahdibaghwalas

The early years of the 49th *da'i*'s term were fraught by the turmoil of religious dissent and internal challenges to the *da'i*'s authority. The wealthy Bohra contractor Adamji Pirbhoy, who served as Sheriff of Bombay in 1897–1898, earlier a spirited supporter of the *da'i*s and an ardent admirer of the *da'i*'s father 'Abd al-Qadir Najm al-Din, began to solicit for more power in the *da'wat* administration. Influential *da'wat* personages still espousing the *inqita'* theory were able to exert tremendous pressure on the *da'i*.

Early in his term, a certain 'Abd al-Husayn b. Jeeva-ji began actively advocating this theory. Following in the footsteps of Majdu', he claimed that he had established direct contact with the concealed Tayyibi Imam and been appointed to the highest ranks in the *da'wat*. 'Abd al-Husayn, called by his followers 'Malik Sahib', publicly challenged the *da'i* in 1314–1315/1897, and succeeded in attracting many followers in the areas of Nagpur and Burhanpur, central India. They were known as Nagpuriyas or Mahdibaghwalas, from the city and locality of their congregation. Several refutational treatises were written by *da'wat* scholars, and efforts by the establishment to bring back the separatists were fairly successful, particularly following disillusionment with the claimant and his promises.[18] A small number still survive in Nagpur.[19]

After 'Abd al-Husayn's death, a faction of the Mahdibaghwalas formed a separate group, the Pidribaghwalas, on the question of leadership. In the time of the 51st *da'i*, 48 Bohras left the community to join this group, who had begun to proclaim that 'the Period of *kashf* [disclosure] had started' and the *shari'a* had been abrogated. They came to be called Artalisiyas (literally, 'forty-eighters').

Legal battles with the dissidents

Sayyidna Tahir Sayf al-Din had to face internal challenges very soon after he assumed the *da'i*-ship. Foremost among his opponents were the sons of the above-mentioned business tycoon Adamji Pirbhoy, who was now old and reportedly had been influenced against the *daʿi* by his sons. Shibani Roy suggests that having acquired enormous wealth, these businessmen aspired to the *daʿi*'s powers and expected deferential treatment from him. Disappointed, they resolved to ruin his good name; they saw the British courts as a suitable arena for their battle which they fought to the end, even ruining themselves in the process.[20] The Pirbhoys had joined forces with the main dissident faction, exponents of the theory of the invalidation of the spiritual *daʿi*-ship, and were active in causing discord within the community and with the government.

Among the most famous cases were the Chandabhai Gulla Case[21] (in which, for the first and only time, the *daʿi* himself gave a protracted personal testimony) and the Burhanpur Dargah Case. The legitimacy and extent of the *daʿi*'s authority within his community became an issue in both cases, and though victory is claimed by both sides, the final verdicts, in each case, seem to have been outstandingly in the *daʿi*'s favour. The first, instigated by the Pirbhoys in 1917, originally concerned the *daʿi*'s sole trusteeship of the *gulla* (offertory box) in the shrine of Chandabhai Seth and connected properties. While the court did not accept as legal the notion of an unaccountable trustee[22] – a ruling which enabled the plaintiffs to claim victory in the case – they cleared him of the allegation of mismanagement of funds and denied the request for a change of trusteeship. A wider issue brought up deliberately by the *daʿi* during the case and resolved in court was the position and rights of the *daʿi al-mutlaq* and the *inqitaʿ al-nass* theory to which the plaintiffs subscribed. The Bombay High Court in 1921 delivered a verdict in favour of Sayyidna Tahir Sayf al-Din's legitimate *daʿi*-ship.[23] This ruling, further reinforced by the Privy Council judgement of December 1947,[24] helped to clear the uncertainties that had plagued a substantial portion of the Bohra community for half a century, and, though the dissidents made an attempt at recovery by calling Sayyidna Tahir Sayf al-Din 'a court *daʿi*', it crushed the backbone of the dissident protest movement.

The Burhanpur Dargah Case filed in 1925[25] focused on the *daʿi*'s right to excommunicate. The plaintiffs were a group of trustees and students of the Burhanpur Hakimiyya School, who had been excommunicated by the *daʿi*'s *ʿamil* on a charge of disobedience and anti-*daʿi* activities. The creation of this school – the first *daʿwat*-sponsored school for secular education – was driven by influential *daʿwat* personages subscribing to the *inqitaʿ* theory and malcontents for whom secularism was also a means of undermining the *daʿi*'s supreme authority, and Sayyidna ʿAbd Allah

Badr al-Din had granted his permission reluctantly. The school became a hub for the anti-*da'i* faction, who cited the *da'i*'s reluctance as indicative of opposition to secular education. Tahir Sayf al-Din's vigorous encouragement of secular education effectively disposed of that contention. The excommunication was declared invalid by the court owing to certain necessary procedural prerequisites not having being fulfilled.[26] This 1931 judgement incidentally is quoted frequently by dissidents, as in it the validity of Sayyidna 'Abd al-Qadir Najm al-Din's *da'i*-ship is deemed doubtful; they usually do not mention the Chandabhai Gulla Case ruling, or the later Privy Council Appeal and other cases which decisively overturned this particular point. Control of the Hakimiyya School finally reverted to the *da'i* after 30 years, following a Supreme Court judgement that ruled for the dismissal of the litigious trustees. The hostile 1931 judgement had inherently recognized the *da'i*'s right to excommunicate. In 1949 in independent India the Prevention of Excommunication Act was passed which targeted, amongst other castes and Muslim Biradaris ('Brotherhoods'), the Bohras.[27] A series of appeals against the Act as unconstitutional were made by the *da'wat*. The Act was initially upheld by the Bombay High Court in 1953, but the final Supreme Court Judgement of 9 January 1962 ruled in the *da'i*'s favour, accepting the right of religious denominations to excommunicate non-conforming members.[28] These court verdicts did help to reinforce the *da'i*'s authority within the community, while Sayyidna Tahir Sayf al-Din had succeeded in forcing the dissidents into the open and exposing their motives. The issue of excommunication, particularly sensitive in the present socio-political climate, was raised again after the 51st *da'i*'s demise and continues to be controversial; excommunication has virtually ceased to be exercised by the *da'i*.

'Youth' and 'Reformist/Progressive Bohras'

Since the latter half of the 20th century, two distinct currents of internal opposition have emerged: a small but vocal group calling themselves 'Reformist' or 'Progressive' Bohras, considered outside the community by the establishment,[29] and the localized 'Youth' movement in Udaipur (Rajasthan).[30] While radically different in ideology, they have sometimes joined forces to achieve a common political aim: the curtailing of the *da'i*'s authority. While in a way there has been a sea-change in the format of internal dissent, the leaders of these movements are the successors of the group that sought the invalidation of spiritual *da'i*-ship: the ideological guru of the Udaipur 'Youth', a former professor of the Jami'a Sayfiyya named Ahmad Udaipuri, is an upholder of the *inqitaʿ al-nass* theory, while the 'Reformists', by demanding the limitation of the *daʿi*'s authority, quite simply seem to be looking for a '*nazim dai*' instead of a *daʿi al-mutlaq*. Both groups recruit supporters for their cause under the banner of social reform.

Youth: A large-scale upheaval has been disrupting the sizeable Bohra community of Udaipur since the 1970s. Initially, conflicting political rivalries aligned into pro- and anti-establishment lines divided the Bohras into two camps, the loyalist Shabab and the self-styled Youth (a translation of the Arabic '*shabab*'). This rivalry took on a more religious tone when Ahmad Udaipuri returned to his hometown and assumed control of the movement, infusing its ideology with his religious views. Violent disagreements between the groups provoked civil unrest in Udaipur. The Youth took control of the four Bohra *masjid*s; it was only after a lengthy legal struggle that one mosque was returned for interim use to the loyalist Bohras. The Rajasthan High Court judgement of May 1984 established a vital legal precedent by upholding the religious principle of *raza*, the legal requirement of the *daʿi*'s permission for communal worship in *daʿwat* mosques.[31] It was only in the late 1990s that a significant section of the Youth returned to the *daʿwat*; there are reports that the movement is alive today, though perhaps more discreetly.

Reformists: The immediate father of the Reformist Bohras was Noman Contractor, a self-made industrialist. Contractor emerged as a leader of the anti-*daʿi* movement – which he named the Pragati Mandal ('Progress Committee' – hence 'Progressive Bohras') – in the 1960s, and this generated renewed dissident activity. His influence contributed to defiance of the *daʿi* in the immigrant Bohra community in East Africa, but Sayyidna Tahir Sayf al-Din's visit to that country broke the dominance of the dissident movement there. Dissidents in Tanzania were able to cause official trouble during the 52nd *daʿi*'s visit. Contractor also exploited the internal conflict in Udaipur, though the Youth are basically antagonistic to the Reformist ideology and leadership. The Reformists again sprang to action in Bombay following the political victory of the Janata Party led by Morarji Desai, a long-time opponent of the Bohras, in 1977. At their instigation the Nathwani Commission report on alleged human rights infringements in the *daʿwat* was submitted in 1979; as the members and informants alike were dissident sympathizers, the report lacked objectivity and no action was taken by the government on its recommendations. The Reformist dissident movement is spearheaded today by the scholar and journalist Asghar Ali Engineer, a former disciple of Contractor.

Engineer has for the past two decades been indefatigable in promoting the Reformist cause to Indian society and the world and is the source most quoted in the press in matters relating to the Bohras, one of the reasons why Blank judges the dissidents to be 'winning the public relations war' outside the community, though they have little apparent support inside it.[32] The Reformists project themselves as modern secular-minded individuals fighting against a traditionalist and repressive religious authority; this image is also promulgated by members of their elite regarded as part of today's intelligentsia, largely for having made closely guarded *da'wat* texts available to Western scholarship. The *da'wat* views such unauthorized use of its texts, either obtained illegally or lent to them with strict oaths of confidentiality, as stealing. While emotions remain intense and mutual mistrust is as strong as ever, actual confrontations between the dissidents and the loyal Bohras are now few.

Internal Dynamics: Socio-Administrative Structure and Developments

Finance and welfare

Historically the livelihood of the overwhelming majority of the Bohra community has depended, as the most commonly accepted etymology for their name suggests, on some form of commerce. Traditionally and doctrinally, trade and business are actively encouraged in preference to other forms of employment. There have been prosperous Bohra businessmen operating in India since the time the community was first established. At the end of the 19th century the Bombay Gazetteer described them as the 'trading Bohoras' – large-scale merchants trading with Arabia, China, Siam and Zanzibar, mostly local traders or petty shopkeepers – and referred to them as 'the richest and most prosperous class of Musulmans in Gujarat'.[33]

The period from the 19th to the 21st century saw a greater extension of Bohra commercial ventures in countries outside India, with prosperous immigrant communities forming in the Eastern and Western hemispheres. In the 19th century, taking advantage of the resources of the British East India Company, Bohras began to venture abroad to other areas in the British Empire, like the Maldives, Ceylon (now Sri Lanka) and East Africa, encouraged and frequently helped financially by their *da'is*. The severe famine of 1228/1813 also gave an impetus to the Bohras affected to seek their fortunes elsewhere. The transfer of power to the British Crown in 1857 produced a boost in relations with the British and further emigration and financial advancement for the Bohras. The Bohras' business ventures expanded; Bohra traders along with other enterprising Indians launched successful businesses in the Far East, in Burma, Singapore, Hong Kong, China and Japan. Bohras established import–export businesses, operated rubber and tea plantations and played an important role in the spice trade; the Hong Kong–Kowloon ferry was founded by a Bohra, Abdul-Ali Ebrahim, whose descendants are still leading businessmen in Hong Kong. During the latter decades of the century, Bohras were migrating in ever greater numbers to Bombay and participating in and contributing to the growth of this booming financial metropolis, though within its cosmopolitan milieu they still retained their conservative socio-religious mores. Numerous *masjid*s and *jama'at-khana*s ('communal halls') were built by leading businessmen, many in places where there had been none before; by the 49th *da'i*'s time there was a *masjid* in almost every Bohra community. The British presence in Surat had also facilitated for the first time close contact with Western culture, and increased affluence reportedly inspired a taste for European material comforts and made itself manifest in more luxurious homes and lifestyles in cities like Surat and Bombay.[34]

Da'wat funds[35] are traditionally spent, besides on religious, administrative and political purposes of the *da'wat*, on welfare and constant financial, material and medical aid to needy individuals, and in times of calamity. Natural disasters and the subsequent relief efforts, and other inescapable expenditures created a huge burden of debt, but finally, towards the end of the 19th century, the 49th *da'i* succeeded – particularly through the untiring labours of Sayyidna 'Abd Allah Badr al-Din – in paying off every creditor, achieving the full clearance of the debt that had plagued the *da'wat* for about 150 years.

The 20th century witnessed growing material prosperity for the Bohras, who were among the foremost Indian entrepreneurs to take advantage of the expanding markets and growing trade opportunities of the era. Financial opportunities were also one of the main motives – besides education – in the demographic expansion of the Bohras in the West, particularly the United Kingdom, Canada and the United States; the economic motive is paramount in the migration to the Persian Gulf emirates of Bohra men, whose families back in India reflect their increased prosperity.[36]

While previously the juridical 'tools' for legalizing ostensibly *riba* ('interest' or 'usury') transactions prescribed by Fatimid jurisprudence were allowed and used, the present *daʿwat* establishment, with its more rigorous approach, counsels against any such transactions. In India itself, community members are encouraged to explore forms of Islamic financing. Local *Bachat Yojna* or cooperative saving schemes are operating successfully in Bohra communities almost everywhere and have helped petty traders tremendously. The *daʿwat* runs several 'Qarzan Hasana', or interest-free loan schemes, which are the first recourse for most Bohras seeking financial credit particularly on a larger scale. Several new institutions promoting social welfare, charity and finance have been activated, which provide financial and material aid and interest-free loans to a large number of Bohras. Bohras and others benefit from the *daʿwat* healthcare facilities, including the recently renovated Sayfi Hospital in Mumbai. The *daʿi* continues to provide aid in times of calamity like earthquakes or riots. The *daʿwat* provided substantial financial aid and launched rehabilitation efforts when required after the Hindu–Muslim riots in Bombay in 1992 and Gujarat in 2002.

Education

Religious learning is an indispensable prerequisite and thus a major preoccupation of the *daʿi*s; religious education has been historically a priority, as a means to foster spiritual merit, to perpetuate the rich literary heritage of the *daʿwat* and to reinforce the bonds of faith. Various facilities have been set up by the *daʿwat* for religious education, including *madrasa*s, and the time-honoured traditions of *waʿz* (sermons) and *sabaq* (informal classes on religious texts) have continued uninterrupted through the ages. *Daʿwat* literature and learning are discussed in the next chapter; here we shall give a brief historical overview of the period under study.

Sayyidna ʿAbd ʿAli Sayf al-Din initiated a literary efflorescence, the crux of which was the theological seminary 'Dars-i Sayfi'. He initiated a programme of intensified and strictly regulated education. The study of the Arabic language reached a new height; juridical issues were interpreted and discussed. Books and treatises on various subjects were written, as were poems in Arabic as well as Indian languages. The *daʿi*'s exacting standards for religious merit ensured that the honour of *haddiyat*[37] (the status of *hadd*, which carries with it the title of *shaykh*) was bestowed rarely; among the eminent *hudud* – scholars, writers, poets and bureaucrats – of his time, the most prominent was Sayyidi[38] ʿAbd ʿAli ʿImad al-Din b. Shaykh Jiva-bhai Shahjahanpuri (d. 1271/1854), one of the most celebrated scholars in *daʿwat* history. Under Sayyidna Tayyib Zayn al-Din's direction, the standard of the instructional excellence and living facilities of the Dars rose further, while the number of students multiplied. In the aftermath of the *inqita' al-nass* controversy in 'Abd al-Qadir Najm al-Din's time, the Dars was marginalized, but significant advances were made in the sphere of *da'wat* education and learning; the introduction of the *Lisan al-Da'wat*[39] texts made *da'wat* learning more accessible to lay Bohras. *Madrasa*s had continued to flourish and increase steadily in the 19th century.

In the 20th century, along with increasing facilities for religious education, the *da'wat* officially began to encourage and sponsor secular education. When Tahir Sayf al-Din became *da'i*, the number of existing *madrasa*s rose from 30 to 300 within a few years. The Dars-i Sayfi, renamed the 'Jami'a Sayfiyya', was overhauled and expanded along the lines of a modern seminary, its syllabus being revised to include secular subjects such as science and English. A *da'irat al-ta'lim* (department of education) was instituted to regulate *da'wat madrasa*s and schools. Modern primary and secondary schools for boys and girls offering secular education with *diniyyat* (religious studies) as an extra class were established, as were colleges for higher education. Sayyidna Muhammad Burhan al-Din further modernized the Jami'a; with its methods of teaching reformed, the library better equipped and reorganized, the capacity greatly increased, the Jami'a has developed into a religious seminary accorded official recognition as an institution for higher learning in various countries. It has its own autonomous department in Badri Mahal and receives the personal interest of the *da'i* himself. New *madrasa*s continue to be built, and the *da'wat* sponsors hundreds of schools.

Administrative developments: centralization

Participation in the *da'wat*'s socio-religious administration is ideally regarded as '*khidmat*', service for the religion, not just a means of livelihood but a way of earning spiritual merit. While the bureaucrats receive a salary (*wazifa*), there are also many volunteer groups, committees, etc., who render social services for the *da'wat* for no financial recompense.

The 19th and 20th centuries saw substantial development in the administrative machinery of the *da'wat*. Soon after his assumption of *da'i*-ship, 'Abd 'Ali Sayf al-Din initiated a process of reorganization and reinvigoration designed to restore the practices underpinning the *da'wat*'s moral values, tighten the religio-cultural norms and lay down the foundation for a more efficiently run community – a process whose effects are perceptibly manifest in the workings of the *da'wat* today. Policies were clearly laid out and carried through; the fiscal system was better regulated; normative customs of displaying reverence for the *da'i* were strictly required; official clothing was firmly regulated; practical guidelines were issued and long-lasting reforms instituted aimed at systematizing the administration with an emphasis on qualifications and the *da'i*'s paramount authority. Sayyidna 'Abd 'Ali Sayf al-Din had been brought up and prepared for the *da'i*-ship by his brother and predecessor Sayyidna Yusuf Najm al-Din, whose influence as the ideal of ascetic piety permeated his entire life. Leaning towards austerity and asceticism in his personal habits, he had an almost puritanical outlook in matters of the *da'wat*, reflected in his insistence on the principles of justice and integrity and in his edicts regarding, for instance, vigorous enforcement of *shari'a* prohibitions and discouragement of outside influences on religio-cultural practices. A ten-chapter manifesto (*taqlid*) sent by the *da'i* as a guiding maxim to all *'amils* offers counsel on social, financial and religious matters, and displays considerable political acumen in the way it finely combines diplomatic skill and integrity, practical considerations of administration and high moral standards.[40] A key facet of Sayyidna 'Abd 'Ali Sayf al-Din's reforms was tighter control by the *da'i*. All *da'wat* matters were conducted with his personal authorization. He instilled reverence for the status of the *da'i* and respect for his supreme authority. He was closely involved in the affairs of his followers; his influence penetrated all aspects of their lives, not least their ethics and behaviour. He was the arbiter of social norms, particularly in religious ceremonial, and resolute in ensuring observance of correct protocol. Many of the rules and regulations of the 43rd *da'i* persisted after him, though management of *da'wat* affairs varied in different *da'i*-ships according to circumstances, personnel and the personality of the *da'i* himself.

The attempt to dilute, if not negate, the *da'i*'s authority by constituting a consultative assembly (*shura*) responsible for *da'wat* administration in the time of Sayyidna 'Abd al-Qadir Najm al-Din was short lived. The increased independence of *'amils* and administrators was curtailed by the 49th and 50th *da'is*. Sayyidna Muhammad Burhan al-Din's rectification of administrative slackness included changes in key staff members and consolidation of the authority of the *da'i*'s office. A manifesto (*dastur al-'amal*) for *'amils* issued in Shawwal 1316/March 1899 provided guidelines for the regulation of finances, the responsibilities of various personnel and the ordering and pruning of social customs, marriage rituals, etc., in order to curtail un-Islamic Indian/Hindu practices.[41] Sayyidna 'Abd

Allah Badr al-Din also took steps to amend deficiencies in local *jama'at* administrative practices.

The 51st *da'i*, having shifted the headquarters of the *da'wat* to Bombay, housed the central administrative offices, named *al-Wazarat al-Sayfiyya*, in Badri Mahal,[42] and organized *da'wat* administration into well-defined departments with clear-cut responsibilities. Better records were kept and official forms for various *da'wat*-endorsed transactions and activities were standardized. More than 350 *da'wat* community centres were established in various towns, and they formed the basis for local cooperation, administered to social and educational needs, and provided community services. In the 52nd *da'i*'s time, the administration continues to keep pace with rapid demographic expansion. Local centres for religious worship presided over by *wazarat* representatives are increasingly established among new communities, while the central office itself, fully computerized, can obtain detailed statistics, maintain a regular awareness of developments and respond speedily to local needs of Bohra communities any where in the world.

Yemen

Yemen was the seat of the *da'wat* for more than 400 years, and continues to have a large Bohra population, though the numbers are greatly depleted. This was particularly due to persecution by the Imams who ruled the Zaydi kingdom of northern Yemen before it became a republic in 1962. The Zaydi Imams of San'a' had traditionally sought the detraction of the *da'wat* and the *da'i al-mutlaq*s throughout a turbulent history. One such instance was reported in 1935: following the signing of a treaty with the Hijaz in 1934, Imam Yahya attempted to enforce mass conversions of the Bohras, who were already being compelled to propagate Zaydi doctrine in their *madrasa*s.[43] In 1329/1911, in the Haraz region – which has the largest concentration of Bohras in Yemen, living in almost constant hostility with their Zaydi neighbours – Zaydis surrounded Bohra villages; the Bohras gathered near the tomb of the 3rd *da'i*, Hatim b. Ibrahim (d. 596/1199), in Hutayb, and in the ensuing battle managed to repel the Zaydis.

After the transfer of the *da'wat* headquarters to India in the middle of the 10th/16th century, Yemen was treated as a special province; the administration was placed under the overall control of an indigenous Yemeni *na'ib* (deputy, of the *da'i*), who supervised all the *'amil*s, also Yemeni, of various Bohra centres in the country. The *da'i*s continued to maintain regular correspondence with the Yemeni community. After

Sayyidna 'Abd al-Qadir Najm al-Din's brief stopover at the port of Mocha on return from the *hajj* – when Bohras from all over Yemen came to pay their respects – he gave particular care to the revitalization of the Yemeni community. He appointed a new deputy, and after returning to India sent noted scholars and *hudud* to revive *da'wat* practices.

In 1961 Sayyidna Tahir Sayf al-Din sent his son Muhammad Burhan al-Din, then the *ma'dhun*, on a ground-breaking trip to Yemen to assess the condition of the Bohra community there and reinforce its links with the *da'wat*. He received an official welcome from the British in Aden. Yemen has since become a frequent pilgrimage destination. Early in Sayyidna Muhammad Burhan al-Din's time, Yemen was brought under the direct control of the central administration. Problems with the *na'ib* precipitated his removal and the termination of the post itself in 1971. Now Yemen has two main *'amil*s, one based in San'a' and the other in Haraz. They continue to supervise *'amil*s in smaller towns but their powers are limited. Yemen continues to rate a certain degree of special attention from the *wazarat* and the *da'i* himself. *Da'wat* policy encourages Yemeni Bohras to visit India (particularly to enrol in the Jami'a) and attend communal gatherings. Yemeni Bohras have in general become more integrated with the Indian Bohras but continue to preserve certain elements of their distinctive dress and culture.

Religio-cultural identity

A greater self-awareness has been engendered among the Bohra community, fostering a self-conscious articulation of communal cultural identity. Several factors have contributed to this: expanding demographics, a general 'opening outwards' in all ways and constant contact with outsiders, combined with increased internal interaction among Bohras and greater central control, perhaps also a need to guard against the onslaught of Westernization, and, not least, a recognizable public profile. One form this articulation takes is the preservation of a distinctive individuality by, for instance, wearing the prescribed traditional dress – part of a wider trend of reasserting the community's Islamic identity manifested in a punctilious enforcement of *shari'a* law in areas such as finance and lifestyle. Routine communal gatherings in the local *masjid* or *markaz* are vital to recharging loyalty to the faith and keeping the blood of the community flowing, so to speak, but an illustration of increased solidarity is the huge congregation of thousands of Bohras travelling from all over the world every year to be present at the 'Ashura sermons commemorating

Imam Husayn's martyrdom held by the present *daʿi*. These occasions also serve as an international forum for Bohras to keep in touch with traditional Bohra culture and forge closer ties. The Internet has greatly facilitated the exchange of information and ideas amongst Bohras. Previously two monthly community magazines which started circulation in the 20th century had been the major sources of community news for Bohras; they still draw a wide readership. Forms of constant contact such as these have helped to sustain a close-knit social network and a distinct cultural identity.

The *daʿi*'s role in the community's solidarity and the formulation of its distinctive identity is crucial. The *daʿi*s, in their role as spiritual fathers, always kept their doors open for the community and listened to their problems. The 51st *daʿi* formalized this practice by instituting the custom of regular audiences (called *bethak*), where Bohras came to seek the *daʿi*'s advice and help in religious, financial and personal matters, or just to receive his blessings. His charismatic and welcoming presence drew Bohras, including the young generation and, for the first time, women, in increasing and unprecedented numbers; this trend has continued in the time of his successor. Every day the *daʿi*'s office answers a multitude of letters and Internet *arzi*s (petitions) soliciting guidance on spiritual and temporal matters; an *arzi* department has now been added to the administration.

Whilst love for the *daʿi* as leader and spiritual father has always been a basis for fealty, the *daʿi*'s actual presence amongst far-flung Bohra communities and his personal attention to their welfare does a great deal to strengthen loyalty to the *daʿwat* and reinforce confidence in their identity. In the past, when each journey was a long and arduous affair, the *daʿi*s travelled in India to places with *daʿwat* communities. Fatimid historical sites have always had an evocative appeal for the Bohras, and Cairo and Syria have become among the most visited pilgrimage locations since the pioneer visit by Sayyidna Tahir Sayf al-Din. The *daʿi*s' pilgrimages are not just occasions of personal spiritual fulfilment, but opportunities for a vast portion of the community to participate in a holy undertaking with their spiritual leader and to reinforce their faith and their bond with their fellow believers.

While striving to adhere to Islamic fundamentals of belief and practice, at the same time the modern period has seen the Bohra community become ever more technologically advanced and very much a part of the modern world. Their rationalist philosophy and dynamic leadership ethic enables them to welcome and participate in progress and development and to take advantage of all technological and practical advances of today's world. They do not shun modernization as incompatible with traditional forms of religion; instead they attempt to incorporate its benefits, indeed use them as vehicles to promote solidarity and vitality among their community. They claim to practise a religious philosophy that is 1,400 years old, yet is still progressive, outward-looking and germane; the love, loyalty and belief invested in the person of the *daʿi* is the basis of their firmly rooted solidarity.

Bibliographical Note

The limits and character of this study have to a certain extent been delineated by the historical information available in the sources. I have used both *daʿwat* historical works, most of which are in manuscript or lithograph form,[44] and published studies on the Bohras by other scholars for this article. Historical works by Indian *daʿwat* scholars are generally centred on the lives and activities of the *daʿi*s, different works comprising varying amounts of personal detail; information about the community has to be more often than not derived indirectly, while actual numbers and statistics are rare. The most comprehensive primary sources for *daʿwat* history in the 19th and 20th centuries are works by three *daʿwat* historians: Shaykh Qutb al-Din b. Sulaymanji Burhanpuri (d. 1241/1826), *Muntazaʿ al-akhbar fi akhbar al-duʿat al-akhyar*, vol. 2 (MS); Muhammad ʿAli b. Mulla Jivabhai, *Mawsim-i bahar*, vol. 3 (lithograph, Bombay, Rabiʾ I 1301/1884); and ʿAbd al-Tayyib b. Haydar ʿAli Diwan, (i) *Izhar al-qawl al-Tayyib fi akhbar al-duʿat al-hudat* (MS, 1335 AH), (ii) *al-Sira al-radiyya: Kitab akhbar al-duʿat al-hudat jamiʿ al-khayrat* (lithograph, Jabalpur 1356/1937), (iii) *Hadiqat al-tarikh: Risala mutadammina akhbar al-sadat Al Bharmal-ji* (lithograph, Bombay, 1369/1949). Several treatises of the 51st *daʿi* Sayyidna Tahir Sayf al-Din (d. 1385/1965), the *Rasaʾil Ramadaniyya*, contain a great deal of historical information, sometimes extracted from earlier works; oral reports originating from this *daʿi* in particular are invaluable especially for the period following Sayyidna ʿAbd al-Qadir Najm al-Din (d. 1302/1885), which is when the *Mawsim-i bahar* was written. Treatises written in the time of the preceding *daʿi*s yield some historical information when searched diligently. *Daʿwat* publications on the careers of the 51st and 52nd *daʿi*s are numerous, the most historically useful among them being *A Golden Panorama: Life and Works of His Holiness Dr. Syedna Taher Saifuddin* (Bombay, 1385/1965), and Mustafa Abdulhussein, *al-Dai al-Fatimi Syedna Mohammed Burhanuddin* (London, 2001), pictorial biographies of the 51st and 52nd *daʿi*s respectively. Published material on modern Bohra history by outside scholars is rather limited. Jonah Blank's anthropological study of modern Daʾudi Bohras, *Mullahs on the Mainframe: Islam and Modernity among the Daudi Bohras* (Chicago, 2001), the most in-depth and positive treatment to date, provides a historical overview. The Mustaʿlians/Tayyibis have received a degree of coverage in Farhad Daftary's work *The Ismaʿilis: Their History and Doctrines* (Cambridge, 1990; 2nd ed., Cambridge, 2007). Satish C. Misra's section on the Bohras (particularly chapter 2, 'The Bohra Community and their *Daʿi*s in Gujarat') in his *Muslim Communities of Gujarat* (Baroda, 1964) is among the most detailed of the earlier sources. Sayyid Abu Zafar Nadwi's Urdu history, *ʿIqd al-jawahir fi ahwal al-Bawahir* (Karachi, 1936), is the most comprehensive history written by a non-Bohra. Works by dissident sources presenting their version of *daʿwat* history include Ali Asghar Engineer's *The Bohras* (Delhi, 1980); earlier works by authors who later turned dissident include Ismailji Hasanali Badripresswala's *Akhbar al-duʿat al-akramin* (Rajkot, 1356/1937), and the much-used *Gulzar-e Dawoodi* by Mian Bhai Abdul-Husain (Ahmedabad, 1920).

Notes

1. Incidentally this passage of time also saw a change of 'dynasty' in the incumbency of *daʿi*-ship – though the office is not, unlike the Imamate, hereditary – from the Badri family to the Al-e Jeevan-ji family, of which line the present *daʿi* is the eighth.
2. See, for instance, Jonah Blank, *Mullahs on the Mainframe: Islam and Modernity among the Daudi Bohras* (Chicago, 2001), particularly chapter 6, 'Maintenance of Political and Spiritual Hegemony', pp. 159–161, where the author also provides comparative analyses of leadership in other Islamic sects, and pp. 172–174.
3. 'Sayyidna', mostly spelt 'Syedna' (possibly in accordance with English pronunciation), literally means 'our leader'. Bohras and non-Bohras call the *daʿi* by this title, by which he is also known in official circles. Bohras also address him as 'Mawlana' (our lord) or simply 'Mawla' (lord), or 'Aqa-mawla', and less frequently as 'Huzurala' (exalted presence). He is sometimes referred to as 'His Holiness'. In pre-independence times he was also known as 'Mullaji Sahib' or 'Bada Mullaji Sahib'.
4. This list has been translated by Asaf A. A. Fyzee, 'The Study of the Literature of the Fatimid *Daʿwa*', in George Makdisi, ed., *Arabic and Islamic Studies in Honor of H.A.R. Gibb* (Leiden, 1965), pp. 232–249.
5. Muhammad ʿAli b. Mulla Jivabhai, *Mawsim-i bahar* (Bombay, 1301/1884), vol. 3, p. 693.

6. The cenotaph marking the spot where the head of the martyred Imam Husayn, which was brought to Cairo in the 6th/12th century, is interred. It was donated by Sayyidna Tahir Sayf al-Din towards the end of his life, and the invitation was originally extended to him.
7. Other Fatimid *masjids* in Cairo that had fallen into disrepair were also renovated in 1996: al-Aqmar, al-Juyushi and al-Lu'lu'a. See Paula Sanders, 'Bohra Architecture and the Restoration of Fatimid Culture', in M. Barrucand, ed., *L'Égypte Fatimide, son art et son histoire* (Paris, 1999), pp. 159–165.
8. Satish C. Misra, *Muslim Communities of Gujarat* (Baroda, 1964), p. 16.
9. The British took Surat from the Marathas in 1759, and assumed the undivided government of the city in 1800.
10. Muhammad 'Ali, *Mawsim-i bahar*, vol. 3, p. 608.
11. Translated from the original Persian in Sayyid Abu Zafar Nadwi, *'Iqd al-jawahir fi ahwal al-Bawahir* (Karachi, 1936), pp. 260–264. Some occasions of official recognition by the British are given in Robert B. Serjeant, 'The Fatimi-Tayyibi (Ismaili) Da'wah', in Dominique Chevallier, ed., *Les Arabes et l'histoire créatrice* (Paris, 1995), pp. 59–77.
12. The *da'wat* library has a manuscript of this work.
13. The dissidents have created websites using the Da'udi Bohra name, which are a forum for the airing and discussion of grievances and criticisms of the *da'i* and establishment.
14. The letter in question is in the present *da'i*'s possession.
15. This document can be found in Muhammad 'Ali, *Mawsim-i bahar*, vol. 3, pp. 749–750.
16. Chandabhai Gulla Case, discussed below.
17. Serjeant, 'The Fatimi-Tayyibi (Ismaili) Da'wah', p. 71.
18. In John Hollister's view, *The Shi'a of India* (2nd ed., London, 1979), p. 295; 'The *hujjat*-pretender proved to lack the necessary knowledge and the whole affair looked like an effort to make worldly gain.'
19. Accounts of this movement are provided in 'Abd al-Tayyib b. Haydar 'Ali Diwan, *Izhar al-qawl al-Tayyib fi akhbar al-du'at al-hudat* (1335 AH, MS); Sayyidna Tahir Sayf al-Din, *Daw' nur al-haqq al-mubin* (Bombay, 1335/1916), p. 167, and Misra, *Muslim Communities*, pp. 51–52.
20. Shibani Roy, *The Dawoodi Bohras: An Anthropological Perspective* (Delhi, 1984).
21. High Court of Judicature at Bombay Suits No. 918 and 941 of 1917, judgement of Justice Marten delivered 19 March 1921.
22. On this point, too, however, a later ruling (Bombay High Court Appeal Judgement, 22 December 1922) allowed two separate offertory boxes to be placed in the shrine, the collection in one accountable, the other labelled the *da'i*'s personal property; it was the latter which always filled rapidly.
23. A document purportedly signed by the 49th *da'i* and stating that the *da'is* from the 47th were merely *nazim da'is* was examined by the court in the Chandabhai Gulla Case and judged by the presiding Justice Marten to be

invalid: the signature did not match that of the *daʿi*, and the witness who presented the document was unreliable.
24. Privy Council Appeal (No. 79 of 1945) from a judgement (25 October 1934) of the Nagpur High Court reversing the judgement of the Subordinate Judge of Burhanpur (2 January 1931).
25. Civil Suit No. 32 of 1925.
26. Judgement delivered by Subordinate Judge of Burhanpur, 2 January 1931.
27. Bombay Act XLII of 1949, Bombay Code III, 1949–1954, p. 3045.
28. Sardar Syedna Taher Saifuddin Saheb v. State of Bombay, AIR 1962, S.C. 853.
29. For an account of the 'Reformist' movement by one of its leading figures, see Asghar Ali Engineer, *The Bohras* (New Delhi, 1980), chapter 6. For more critical views, see Roy, *The Dawoodi Bohras*; Serjeant, 'The Fatimi-Tayyibi (Ismaili) Daʿwah', pp. 70–72; Blank, *Mullahs*, chapter 9.
30. Shibani Roy's *The Dawoodi Bohras* is an anthropological study of the Udaipur Bohras.
31. S.B.C. Appeal No. 5 of 1984, interim judgement delivered on 22 May 1984 by Justice M.C. Jain in the Rajkot (Rajasthan) High Court.
32. Blank, *Mullahs*, p. 234.
33. *The Gazetteer of the Bombay Presidency*, ed. James A. Campbell (Bombay, 1899), vol. 9, p. 24.
34. See, for instance, the description by Sir John Malcolm, writing in 1823, of 'modern' Bohra houses in Surat with 'European improvements' in *The Gazetteer of the Bombay Presidency*, ed. Campbell, vol. 9, pt. 2: Musulmans and Parsis, p. 29 n.1. This taste for luxury is reported in *daʿwat* sources to have adversely affected the zeal for learning and devout practice.
35. For *daʿwat* sources of income, see Blank, *Mullahs*, pp. 198–201.
36. In a recent survey of Indian Bohra households, Jonah Blank, *Mullahs*, p. 203, ascertained that three-quarters of the respondents were occupied in business, a fairly small percentage were involved in white-collar professions, an even smaller number cited teaching or manual trades, while 4.2 per cent listed their occupation as industry.
37. *Haddiyyat*: abstract noun of Arabic word *hadd*, pl. *hudud*, a grade which implied *daʿwat* learning and service; senior *shaykh*s were sometimes called *miyansaheb*.
38. Sayyidi: literally 'my lord', a lesser title than 'Sayyidna' accorded to men of religious/scholarly eminence or rank in the *daʿwat*.
39. *Lisan al-Daʿwat*: literally language of the *daʿwat*, a Gujarati dialect written in Arabic script, with a substantial incorporation of Arabic words especially.
40. This *taqlid* is included in its entirety in Muhammad 'Ali, *Mawsam-i Bahar*, vol. 3, pp. 615–625.
41. See Misra, *Muslim Communities*, p. 51.
42. In 1331/1912–1913, Sayyidna ʿAbd Allah Badr al-Din inaugurated the 'Mahall al-Azhar al-Badri', commonly known as Badri Mahal, which served

as the *daʿi*'s Bombay residence and later became the official *daʿwat* administrative headquarters.

43. Hollister, *Shiʿa of India*, p. 294. A Yemeni *shaykh* related that the Zaydi Imams had hundreds of Bohras of the Hamdan tribe killed, and their bodies piled one on top of the other in huge mounds (personal communication).

44. The MSS I have used here are all from the *daʿwat* library. A section of the *Muntazaʿ al-akhbar* has been edited and published by Samer F. Traboulsi (Beirut, 1999).

13

The Da'udi Bohra Tayyibis: Ideology, Literature, Learning and Social Practice

Tahera Qutbuddin

The Da'udi Bohra Tayyibis are a community of Shi'i Muslims who belong to the Musta'lian branch of the Ismailis and trace their religious and literary heritage to the Fatimid Imam-Caliphs of North Africa and Egypt. They are mostly indigenous Indians who converted to Islam in the 5th/11th century at the hands of missionaries initially sent by the Fatimid Imam-Caliph al-Mustansir. At some point they came to be known as 'Bohra' (and sometimes 'Bohri', used both in the collective and singular forms); in the Gujarati language this word means 'honest or trustworthy man in dealings and social intercourse', or simply, 'trader'.[1] The 'Da'udi' in their name refers to Da'ud b. Qutb Shah, one of their spiritual leaders.[2]

The Tayyibi Bohra have an intricate spiritual lineage. When al-Mustansir died in 487/1094, the Indian Bohra, together with the Egyptian and Yemeni Ismailis, supported his son al-Musta'li, who became the next Fatimid Imam-Caliph; the Persian and Syrian Ismailis supported his brother Nizar. Upon the death of al-Musta'li's son al-Amir in 524/1130, the Indian Bohra, along with the Yemeni Musta'lian Ismailis, broke away from the overlordship of the succeeding Hafizi Musta'lian regime in Fatimid Egypt. They professed allegiance to al-Amir's infant son al-Tayyib (hence the name 'Tayyibis'). Al-Tayyib, they believe, went into physical 'concealment' and in his line the Imamate continues, father to son, the Imams being represented during their absence by *da'i*s. Over the centuries, schisms occurred within the Bohra community over the question of legitimate leadership. Today there are a number of branches of the Tayyibi Bohra, based on the line of *da'i*s they accept as legitimate, of which the largest is the Da'udi Bohra one (henceforth, 'Bohra' in this chapter refers to the Da'udi Bohra).

The earliest Tayyibi *daʿi*s were Yemenis and the number of Indian Tayyibi Bohra grew during their time. It increased further after the transfer of their headquarters to India in 946/1539. Currently they number approximately 1 million adherents. They are concentrated in South Asia (mostly India and Pakistan), with a 13,000-strong indigenous Yemeni community and immigrant communities worldwide.

Despite their rich heritage and complex history, very little academic study of the Bohra has been forthcoming. This deficiency is largely due to the fact that most of their texts remain in manuscript form and are relatively inaccessible, and also because few academics master the languages necessary for such a study. The few earlier publications on the subject in English have mostly been polemical treatises written by members of dissident groups.[3] Fortunately the scholarly void has recently begun to be filled. Robert Serjeant's article titled 'The Fatimi-Taiyebi (Ismaili) Daʿwah. Ideologies and Community'[4] touches upon some important aspects of Bohra belief and history, and Jonah Blank's book-length anthropological work discusses in detail their utilization of modernity as a tool to facilitate religious practice.[5]

My own work here engages two fields of Tayyibi studies that have not been the subject of prior academic scrutiny: the strong tradition of text-focused Tayyibi learning, and the rich body of Tayyibi literature, in Arabic and in the Bohra Gujarati dialect called Lisan al-Daʿwat[6] (more on this dialect later). Furthermore this article presents new aspects of two other domains of study (engaged partially earlier, with a different approach, by Serjeant and Blank): the distinctive Tayyibi ideology and Indo-Islamic social practice (with some remarks on *daʿwat* administration). This study synthesizes data obtained from the following three sources: (1) perusal of a large number of previously unutilized primary texts in five languages – mainly Arabic and Lisan al-Daʿwat, also some Urdu, Persian, and Hindi – through a first-hand examination of Tayyibi Daʿwat manuscript libraries in Mumbai and Surat; (2) direct observation of religious assemblies and teaching sessions; and (3) personal interviews conducted with Bohra in India and Yemen concerning their beliefs and practices. Focusing on the 19th and 20th centuries, the following pages present a systematic description and analysis of these four key aspects of the Daʾudi Bohra Tayyibi world: ideology, literature, learning and social practice.

Ideology

The Bohra call their religious organization the *da'wat hadiya* (the 'rightly guiding mission'), and themselves *muminin*, believers (singular, *mumin*). The following beliefs constitute the fundamental tenets of their ideology. Their first precept is the profession (also held by all Muslims) of the unity (*tawhid*) of God. The Bohra believe Him to be the Creator who is beyond imagination or thought. Another primary doctrine is the belief (held by all Shi'a) in the existence of a spiritual leader (Imam) in every age, who is divinely guided, sinless and perfect, and who is the link between God and humankind, receiving His light and disseminating it to the people. This spiritual leadership (Imamate) commenced from the time the first human being walked the earth, and continues without interruption till the time the heavens and earth are annihilated. Further, it is in a single line of descent, passing from father to son, each Imam appointing his successor before his death. In this line came the Prophet Muhammad and his legatee (*wasi*) 'Ali b. Abi Talib, followed by a line of Imams who were descendants of Muhammad and 'Ali (the link being their mother Fatima, daughter of Muhammad and wife of 'Ali). References to these doctrines regarding the Imamate are present in almost all Fatimid texts.[7]

In addition to the spiritual authority of the Imam, he is the supreme temporal leader, whether or not his terrestrial leadership is manifest at any given time.[8] The first ten Imams of the Muhammadan era did not wield worldly power. The next ten Imams held political dominion, its materialization coming in 296/909 with the founding of the Fatimid caliphate in North Africa by the 11th Imam-Caliph 'Abd Allah al-Mahdi (d. 322/934). In 358/969 Fatimid rule extended to Egypt and the seat of the caliphate moved to Cairo. In 524/1130, upon the death of the 20th Fatimid Imam-Caliph al-Amir, his six-month-old son al-Tayyib succeeded him as the 21st Imam.[9] As mentioned earlier, al-Tayyib went into physical concealment (*satr*) and in his line the Imamate continues. The present Imam is the *imam al-zaman* (the Imam of the Time), and, since his identity is veiled, the Bohra know him by the name of his forefather, al-Tayyib.

Al-Tayyib's role of divine leadership is fulfilled during the period of his concealment by the *da'i al-mutlaq*, an Arabic phrase meaning 'one who calls' (to God and the Imam), and is given 'absolute (authority)'. He is also identified as the *da'i al-satr* (*da'i* during the Imam's concealment). The *da'i* is the Imam's representative and vicegerent (*na'ib*). Belief in his spiritual and temporal authority is a cardinal doctrine, and deemed essentially equivalent to belief in the spiritual and temporal authority of the Imam. The *da'i*-ship, like the Imamate say the Bohra, continues in an unbroken line – albeit without the condition of biological affiliation – each *daʿi*, like the Imam, appointing his successor before his death.[10] It will endure until such time as the Imam makes himself manifest (*zuhur*), or until the last Imam appears, proclaiming the Last Day. The Fatimid *hujjat* and Sulayhid queen, al-Malika al-Hurra (d. 532/1138), upon the instructions of the 20th Imam, appointed the first *daʿi*, Dhuʾayb b. Musa (r. 524–546/1130–1151). The *daʿi*-ship has continued uninterruptedly since then for nine centuries, and the present *daʿi* (*daʿi al-zaman*) is Sayyidna Muhammad Burhan al-Din (b. 1333/1915), the 52nd in the line.[11]

In Fatimid religious hierarchy, the rank of *daʿi al-mutlaq* is one of the nine ranks (*hudud* or *maratib*, singular, *rutba*) under the Imam. During the period of the Imam's concealment, the *daʿi al-mutlaq* has a special status because he represents the concealed Imam absolutely. The *maratib* ranked higher than the *daʿi al-mutlaq* are with the Imam in concealment. The two ranked below him are manifest, and aid the *daʿi* in his work of guidance. Thus the Bohra pledge allegiance to three *maratib* who conduct the *daʿwat* in the absence of the Imam: first and foremost, the *daʿi al-mutlaq*, and, subordinate to him and appointed by him, the *maʾdhun al-mutlaq* (the one granted absolute permission), followed by the *mukasir* (the breaker of 'false arguments'). The present *maʾdhun* is Sayyidi Khuzayma Qutb al-Din (b. 1359/1940), and the present *mukasir* is Sayyidi Husayn Husam al-Din (b. 1338/1920). All three are sons of the 51st *daʿi*.

The institution of *daʿwat* is embodied in the person of the Imam and, during his concealment, in the person of the *daʿi*. This doctrine stems from the belief that if the Imam and the *daʿi* were not present to carry out the mission of the *daʿwat*, there would be no *daʿwat*. Allegiance (*walayat*) to them is believed to be incumbent upon each follower, as is obedience to them in all matters. The authority of the *daʿi*, stemming from the authority of the Imam, is thus in principle absolute, encompassing both the spiritual and temporal realms. The permission (*raza*)[12] of the *daʿi* is, in theory, required in every matter. In matters pertaining directly to the *daʿwat*, this mandate is strictly enforced: religious matters such as leading the congregation in prayer, collecting the *zakat*, performing marriages, disseminating *daʿwat* learning and perusing *daʿwat* books are all believed to be subject to authorization by the *daʿi*.[13] With regard to civic issues, and in the absence of political jurisdiction, the *daʿi*, like the Imam historically, yields to the law of the land.

Allegiance to the Imam and *daʿi*, together with love (*mahabbat*) for them forms the primary criterion for salvation. Another important principle is that of service (*khidmat*): serving the *daʿwat* in every capacity, physical, intellectual and financial, is incumbent upon the Bohra and a significant way of earning religious merit. The obverse side of the coin of allegiance is *bara'at* (disassociation), and every Bohra is required to disengage categorically from anyone who harbours malicious designs towards the *da'wat* or *da'i*. Expositions on these doctrines of the *da'i* and the *da'wat al-satr* are found in writings about the cycles of time from the early Fatimid period, and in theological and poetic texts from the initial Yemeni period of the Tayyibi *da'wat*.[14]

The Islamic *shari'at* is an intrinsic part of Bohra religion, and the dual aspects of knowledge (*'ilm*) and practice (*'amal*) are complementary, each reinforcing and necessitating the other. Adhering to Islamic canon law, the Bohra uphold seven 'pillars' (*da'a'im*) of Islam (compared to five prescribed in other legal schools). These are (1) allegiance to the Imam and *da'i* (*walayat*); (2) ritual purification (*taharat*); (3) ritual prayer (*salat*); (4) almsgiving (*zakat*, to be collected and distributed by the *da'i*);[15] (5) fasting (*sawm*); (6) pilgrimage to Mecca (*hajj*); and (7) struggle against evil (*jihad*).[16] Bohra doctrine also espouses the social injunctions of the *shari'at*, including both personal and civic laws. It expects women to veil in public, encourages men to grow beards and preserves *shari'at* codes pertaining to marriage, divorce, custody, death rites and inheritance. It urges compliance with the Islamic financial canon, including a proscription of interest (*riba*). It enjoins adherence to humane values such as kindness and compassion, and sound moral and ethical behaviour such as truthfulness, integrity and loyalty to one's country.

The Bohra canonical legal text is the *Da'a'im al-Islam*, written by the 10th-century Fatimid jurist al-Qadi al-Nu'man, and authorized by the Fatimid Imam-Caliph al-Mu'izz.[17] This work is in two volumes. The first volume explicates the seven pillars or worship rites, and the second expounds upon other *shari'at*-related issues, including family law and regulations about mundane things such as food, dress, personal hygiene, gifts and oaths. The Bohra creed asserts that all aspects of existence fall under the aegis of religion, and in this sense the *shari'at* governs all segments of a believer's life.

Bohra doctrine requires an oath to be sworn, promising fealty and obedience to the Imam and *da'i*, and an undertaking to conform to the belief and practice outlined in it, by anyone who would be a *mumin* – each Bohra child upon attaining puberty, any non-Bohra adult wishing to convert and any dissident wishing to be received back into the fold. This is the *mithaq* (covenant), also known by its synonyms *bay'at* (pledge of allegiance), and *'ahd'* or *'ahd al-awliya'* (compact of (God's) elect). The Bohra believe this practice dates back through the ages to the first Imam who took the *mithaq* of those who accepted his daʿwat, and that the *mithaq* was administered by all the earlier prophets, by Muhammad, ʿAli, the Imams and the *daʿi*s to their adherents.[18] The text of the *mithaq* forms the blueprint for Bohra belief, delineating the key elements of Bohra ideology and practice.[19] All the articles of faith discussed earlier in this section are outlined in it. The introductory section of the text emphasizes that the oath can only be administered if the initiate accepts the covenant willingly and without coercion; if doubts exist, commitment should be postponed until such time as certainty is achieved. In the *mithaq* ceremony, the *daʿi* or his representative reads the text, outlining the conditions for becoming a Bohra, and the initiate responds by saying *naʿam* (Arabic, 'yes', I swear an oath to the effect that I accept these conditions). Engagement in the *mithaq* constitutes formal acceptance of the doctrines of the *daʿwat* and the authority of the Imam and *daʿi*.

In addition to these fundamental concepts and practices, Bohra piety has some unique features, such as distinctive supererogatory rites of worship. On nights of special sanctity, they perform the *washshiq* and *wasila*. The *washshiq* is a ritual prayer after the mandatory *ʿisha'* prayer, usually consisting of 24 *rakʿat*s (prayer cycles). The *wasila* follows the *washshiq*. It is a ritualized but spontaneous entreaty to God in Lisan al-Daʿwat by the prayer-leader, appended to a liturgical recitation in Arabic.

Bohra religious assemblies for everything other than ritual prayer are called *majalis* (singular, *majlis*, literally 'sitting'). The individual presiding over a *majlis* is termed the *sadr*. He sits in a central space surrounded by male members of the congregation; women usually sit in concealed enclaves or in the main space with a divider between them and the men, from where they can view the proceedings without being seen themselves. In women-only *majalis*, a female *sadr* presides. In every *majlis*, the congregation chants religious poems and the *sadr* frequently delivers a sermon of varying length (ranging from half an hour to two hours called *bayan*, literally 'clear exposition'). On occasions of celebration, the *sadr* and community elders ceremonially taste a sweet drink called *sherbet* (Arabic, 'drink'). This is followed by *vadhavanu*,[20] in which a member of the congregation circumlocutes over the *sadr* a small tray holding some sweets and two coconuts, these fruits being considered auspicious in the Indian tradition. In certain *majalis*, such as the *majlis* for the first of the month, the assembly comes forward one by one to kiss the hand of the *sadr*, a custom reinforced by Fatimid tradition as well as Indian princely etiquette. This practice is called *salam*, probably taking the name from its original Arabic sense of greeting.

Majalis devoted exclusively to a long sermon, usually lasting two to four hours, are called *majalis al-waʿz* (Arabic 'advice, counsel') or simply, *waʿz*. These are held during the first ten days of Muharram (in this case, also called *majalis al-ʿaza*'), and at other times of commemoration or celebration during the year. The origins of both the concept and format of the *majalis al-waʿz* can be traced to the Fatimid *majalis al-hikma* ('sessions of wisdom'), particularly to the *majalis* delivered by al-Muʾayyad fiʾl-Din al-Shirazi.[21] The Bohra *waʿz* addresses topics that range from theology, ethics and philosophy to literature, history and moral counsel. Its climax comes with the recounting of the story of the martyrdom of Husayn, and this narrative is interspersed with the recitation of elegies (*marthiya*).

The *daʿi* personally presides on a regular basis at religious gatherings, leading worship, delivering *waʿz* and officiating at *majalis*. In Ramadan he leads the Bohra in ritual prayer. Annually during Muharram his *waʿz* is held every year in different cities throughout the world. Up to 100,000 to 200,000 Bohra men, women and children gather to hear him speak. Some of his *waʿz* are relayed in audio and video format via the Internet or satellite, often live, to Bohra congregations worldwide.

The anniversaries of the births and deaths of figures prominent in the *daʿwat* spiritual hierarchy are days of *barakat* (divine grace), which the Bohra celebrate or commemorate with a *majlis*. Birth anniversaries are called *milad* or *salgirah*, and celebrated with a '*khushi ni majlis*' (*majlis* of celebration). Death anniversaries are called *ʿurs*, or, in the case of a martyr, *shahadat*, commemorated with a *majlis* of Qurʾan recitation, where all attendees simultaneously and inaudibly recite separate chapters of the Qurʾan for the benefit of the soul of the deceased. The Qurʾan recitation is followed by the '*sadaqallah*' ('God spoke Truth'), a prayer in Arabic beginning with those words for the deceased, recited aloud by the *sadr*. Next comes a recitation of elegies for the deceased, followed by elegies for Imam Husayn.

Visiting the shrines of deceased saints, called *ziyarat*, is a meritorious act.[22] The shrine visitor kisses the tomb of the saint, places rose petals or sweet basil leaves on the grave and recites the Qurʾan *surat*s of *al-Fatiha* and *Yasin* for the benefit of the soul of the deceased. On the eve of *ʿurs* – a particularly propitious time for *ziyarat* – visitors ceremonially spread upon the tomb a fragrant paste of sandalwood and rosewater called *sandal*.

In keeping with Fatimid tradition, the Bohra follow the fixed astronomical version of the Islamic Hijri lunar calendar; at times their feast days occur before or after those of other Muslim denominations. For example, they always fast the full 30 days during Ramadan each year, rather than varying it according to the sighting of the moon.[23] Many Bohra religious events are identical to those followed by Sunnis and the Twelver Shi'a. A celebration shared with other Shi'is is 'Id-i Ghadir, which according to all Shi'is marks the day the Prophet Muhammad publicly appointed 'Ali as his successor at the spring of Ghadir Khumm; this celebration is an affirmation of the fundamental Bohra doctrine of *walayat*.

Literature

The Tayyibis believe the entire corpus of their scholarly canon possesses a sacred nature as well as authoritative force. They assert that it derives directly from the Qur'an, the source of all knowledge. In this vein, they strictly discourage speculative writing. Any religious opinion must be backed by a *sanad*, a report from a person in a position of spiritual authority, one who has the right to practise *istinbat*, the derivation of interpretations and rulings. By virtue of the *da'i*'s reception of the Imam's direct spiritual guidance (*ta'id*), he is automatically recognized as the highest spiritual and scholarly authority in the community. Because of this supreme authority, and in view of the fact that the most learned person in the community is to be appointed *da'i*, the principal works of Tayyibi literature have mostly been produced by the *da'i*s and to a lesser extent by their *ma'dhun*s, *mukasir*s and other *hudud*.

Most Tayyibi scholarship is in Arabic, the sacred language of the Qur'an, even today in India. However, there are some works that have been composed in Lisan al-Da'wat, like *nasihat*s (poems of history and moral counsel), the historical work *Mawsim-i bahar*, and translations of key Arabic texts.[24] The use of Urdu is visible in elegies for Imam Husayn and in some panegyric poetry. Persian has also influenced Tayyibi literature to a certain extent through the incorporation of vocabulary into the vernacular and, more rarely, through the composition of Persian panegyrics.

In Tayyibi literature there are ascending levels of texts corresponding to ascending levels of learning. The beginning level is that of *zahir* (exoteric knowledge), which includes jurisprudence, history, belles-lettres, instruction in proper behaviour and texts of exhortation and edification. The next level is that of *tawil*, the deeper, allegorical meaning of the Qur'an, the Prophetic *hadith* and the *shari'at*. Much of the material in *tawil* works is explained as a symbolization of, or metaphor for, the stations of the spiritual hierarchy. The third and highest level of knowledge is that of *haqiqat* (literally, reality or actuality, often denoted by its plural *haqa'iq*). This term indicates metaphysical works expounding a philosophy of life that focuses on the nature of God's oneness (*tawhid*), the origin (*mabda'*) of creation and the return (*ma'ad*) to eternal life. The second and third levels, *tawil* and *haqiqat*, are collectively termed *batin* (literally, 'hidden', 'interior').

All Tayyibi writings are based on mother texts produced in the Fatimid period (10th to early 12th centuries) in the esoteric fields of *haqiqat* and *tawil*, and the exoteric domains of jurisprudence, history, literature and theology, by such celebrated scholars as Ja'far b. Mansur al-Yaman, al-Qadi al-Nu'man, Hamid al-Din al-Kirmani, and al-Mu'ayyad fi'l-Din al-Shirazi.[25] Upon the concealment of the Imam, the attention of the Yemeni Da'wat scholars focused largely on the field of *haqiqat*.[26] Da'wat scholars began to record, in written treatises, doctrines that had been expounded earlier in great secrecy and exclusively by oral means. In large part this mode of writing served the need of the hour, which was to prove to the community, in the physical absence of the Imam, the theological and metaphysical necessity for his existence. This task accomplished, the literature of the Tayyibi Da'wat saw a shift in orientation to history and heresiography; after the move of its headquarters to India four centuries later, a large number of the works produced were historical studies or refutations of seceding groups.[27] There are no *haqiqat* works from this period. Throughout its different periods, a consistently important component of Tayyibi literature was Arabic poetry. Major *diwan*s of poetry were composed in the tradition of al-Mu'ayyad's devotional poetry,[28] which used Tayyibi theological motifs to praise the Imam or *da'i*. The following are some of the most important *diwan*s in the Tayyibi Da'wat up to the 19th century: the *Diwan*s of the Tayyibi Da'is 'Ali b. Muhammad,[29] and Idris 'Imad al-Din in Yemen, and the *Diwan* of Sayyidi 'Abd al-Qadir Hakim al-Din in India (all mss).

The 19th and 20th centuries – our period of focus for this study – witnessed a veritable renaissance of Tayyibi literature. Two literary giants, both titled Sayf al-Din, succeeded to the leadership of the Tayyibi Da'wat as the 43rd and 51st incumbents. They made significant personal contributions to the *da'wat* library and fostered an atmosphere of learning in which a large number of intellectuals flourished and substantial scholarly works were produced. The reign of the first Sayf al-Din, named 'Abd-i 'Ali, was one of renewal in many ways. Since the overwhelming majority of *da'wat* texts were in Arabic, an important aspect of this revitalization was his emphasis on the mastery of its grammar and rhetoric as prerequisites to *da'wat* learning. He himself produced a *Diwan* of poetry that scholars of his age acknowledged as a masterpiece of Arabic literature.[30] In deference to his immense learning and erudition, they titled him 'Mu'ayyad-i Asghar' (the Younger Mu'ayyad) and 'Nu'man-i Thani (the Second Nu'man). This *da'i* also composed a poem of counsel (*nasihat*) in Lisan al-Da'wat for his six-year-old son, the future 46th *da'i* Muhammad Badr al-Din, beginning with the affectionate charge 'Encrust pearls of knowledge in your heart' (*'Ilm na moti jaro*).

Additionally Sayf al-Din directed the production of short prose treatises (*risalat*, plural *rasa'il*), which various scholars wrote in his name.[31] The *risalat*s of the *da'i*s were originally composed either as annual epistles giving news of *da'wat* activities to the community in Yemen and exhorting them to worship God, thus often composed in the month of Ramadan or Rajab, or elegiac epistles giving news of the demise (*na'y*) of the former *da'i*. The earlier ones were usually quite brief (characteristic of epistles), later ones were longer and contained academic material (characteristic of treatises). These *risalat*s, too, have the formal characteristics of epistles.

Several of the scholars of Sayyidna 'Abd-i 'Ali Sayf al-Din's reign wrote works encompassing the fields of *haqiqat*, history, jurisprudence, administration and poetry. The most important was another 'Abd-i 'Ali, titled 'Imad al-Din (popularly known as 'Imad al-Din Sahib), who rose to prominence in the reign of this *da'i* and lived into the reign of the 47th *da'i*. 'Imad al-Din Sahib came from a lay Bohra family, but by dint of his remarkable scholastic efforts rose to great heights in the *da'wat*. He studied under the *da'i* 'Abd-i 'Ali Sayf al-Din and achieved such mastery over *da'wat* learning that the *da'i* entrusted him with the training of three scions from the ruling family who all later became *da'i*s themselves.[32] The second of these – the 47th *da'i* Najm al-Din – bestowed the *rutba* of *mukasir* upon him and appointed him his heir-designate. Before 'Imad al-Din Sahib could assume the helm of the *da'wat*, however, he died in 1271/1854. He left an indelible mark on the literary constitution of the *da'wat*, having composed one of the highest-level *haqiqat* texts of the *da'wat*, the *Lubb al-lubab* (The Quintessence of the Essence), and a large number of lyrical poems in Arabic, Lisan al-Da'wat, and Urdu, mostly in praise of Sayyidna 'Abd-i 'Ali Sayf al-Din, along with some *nasihat*s. These have been collected in a *Diwan* and are immensely popular. Another well-known work from 'Abd-i 'Ali Sayf al-Din's period is the *Muntaza' al-akhbar fi akhbar al-du'at al-akhyar*, a two-volume work on the history of the Tayyibi Da'wat since the concealment of the Imam in 524/1130, up to the author's time in 1240/1824, by Shaykh Qutb al-Din b. Sulaymanji Burhanpuri (d.

1241/1826).³³ Yet another scholar, named Sayfi Sahib (d. 1236/1820), wrote a detailed commentary on the chapter on marriage from the *Daʿaʾim al-Islam* titled *Kitab al-najah fi ahkam al-nikah*, and four other *fiqh* works (mss). The most prolific Tayyibi Lisan al-Daʿwat poet, Sayyidi Sadiq ʿAli Sahib (1233/1818), composed a large number of historical, theological and ethical *nasihat* poems during Sayyidna Sayf al-Din's reign that are recited in *daʿwat majalis* to this day.³⁴

The literary renaissance sparked by Sayyidna ʿAbd-i ʿAli Sayf al-Din continued after him. In the reign of his successor, Muhammad ʿIzz al-Din, an anonymous author began the first work dedicated to Qurʾan *tawil* to be composed since Fatimid times, with a verse-by-verse explanation based on the Fatimid *tawil* works, the two-volume *Tafsir ʿIzzi*. Unfortunately the author does not appear to have completed the work, leaving sporadic gaps in the text and going only up to part of the second *sura*, *al-Baqara*. Other *daʿwat* scholars wrote texts on history, jurisprudence and esoteric Qurʾanic interpretation. They composed refutations of the doctrines of seceding groups including the Sulaymaniyya and the Mahdibaghwalla.

Two *daʿis* and two decades later there began another notably productive literary period, coinciding with the reign of the 47th *daʿi*, ʿAbd al-Qadir Najm al-Din. He himself composed numerous Arabic poems of high literary style that were collected in his *Diwan*, including an Arabic poem in an Indian metre (with the opening line: *Hal mazharu Dhiʾl-ʿArshi siwa sinwi al-Rasuli – fi kulli zuhuri*). A distinctive feature of his reign was the emphasis on Lisan al-Daʿwat, manifested in original works and translations. Al-Qadi al-Nuʿman's *Kitab al-taharat* was translated from Arabic to Lisan al-Daʿwat.³⁵ One of the most valuable historical works of the later Tayyibi Daʿwat, the *Mawsim-i bahar* of Muhammad ʿAli Rampuri b. Mulla Jiwabhai (d. 1315 or 1316/1897–1899), was composed in Lisan al-Daʿwat. This was a three-volume history of the *daʿwat* in India from its inception to the date of publication of the work.³⁶ Because it was written in Lisan al-Daʿwat, it made Bohra history directly accessible – for the first time – to the full Bohra community, rather than just to the scholars within it. It also provided the first systematic historical record of the period between the reigns of Sayyidna Sayf al-Din and Sayyidna Najm al-Din, from the publication date of the *Muntazaʿ* in 1240/1824 to that of the *Mawsim* in 1299/1882.

A little later, in the reigns of the 49th and 50th *daʿis*, another important scholar flourished. This was a third ʿAbd-i ʿAli, Sayyidi ʿAbd-i ʿAli Muhyi al-Din (d. 1326/1908), son of Sayyidna Husam al-Din, who composed poems of praise for the Imams and *daʿis* and some moving elegies for

Imam Husayn. He is remembered as a wise and learned man, and the teacher and mentor of the *daʿi* who was to become the most prolific scholar of the Tayyibi Daʿwat, Sayyidna Tahir Sayf al-Din.

Sayyidna Tahir Sayf al-Din became *daʿi* in 1333/1915 at the age of 27. Two years later he composed his first treatise (*risalat*), *Dawʾ nur al-haqq al-mubin* (The Glow of the Light of Clear Truth). The focus of this work was the establishment of the validity of the *daʿi*-ship of the 47th *daʿi* – about which a group of dissenters had raised doubts – and consequently all the *daʿi*s following him. This *risalat* played a large part in the regeneration of the prestige of the *daʿi*'s office. Simultaneously it laid out the doctrinal basis for a clear demarcation of what had earlier been a somewhat fuzzy line between the two opposing factions, of believers in the validity of the *daʿi*-ship and doubters therein, prescribing the ideological backing for Tahir Sayf al-Din's policy of dealing with dissidents. Those who disbelieved or doubted could either choose to regain belief in the spiritual authority of the *daʿi* or they could leave his fold; they would not be permitted to stay within it and hold that the *daʿi* was not legitimate.

In 1337/1919 Tahir Sayf al-Din wrote a second treatise, and for the next 47 years of his *daʿi*-ship until his death in 1385/1965, he went on to write one almost every year. Forty-four *risalat*s have been published, all written in Ramadan – following the tradition of the earlier *daʿi*s – and characterized as *Rasaʾil Ramadaniyya*.[37] About a third of their material – mostly in lengthy *tahmid* form – is from the pen of Tahir Sayf al-Din himself, and the rest consists of eclectic selections from a vast number of *daʿwat* works, with prefaces written by the *daʿi*. Their contents include history, philosophy, jurisprudence, ethics, literature and allusions to *haqiqat*. Although expounding on assorted topics, each *risalat* usually has one primary theme, referred to in its title. For example, the second *risalat*, titled *Thamarat ʿulum al-huda* (Fruits of Rightly Guiding Knowledge, 1337), treats the subject of knowledge. The 18th *risalat*, titled *Masarrat al-fath al-mubin* (Felicities of the Clear Victory, 1353), chronicles victories of the *daʿwat*. This *daʿi* also composed an abridgement of the *haqiqat* work *Lubb al-lubab*, titled *Thamarat al-lubb al-latifa*, along with a lengthy introduction.

In addition to his prose-writing skills, Tahir Sayf al-Din was a distinguished poet. He composed a large number of Arabic poems (over 10,000 verses) mostly in praise of the Imams and *daʿi*s which have been collected in a two-volume *Diwan*.[38] These poems are a summa for the beliefs (called *tasawwurat*) of the Tayyibis, expressed in beautiful Arabic verse. Among his poems is a moving elegy on Imam Husayn that is recited by the Bohra regularly, beginning *Ya sayyida al-shuhada'i* (O prince of martyrs!), and a poem on the Tayyibi philosophy of the intellect (*al-'aqlu fi'l-insani a'la'l-jawhari*). He also composed in Lisan al-Da'wat two *nasihat* and two *marthiya*s. Moreover many of his *wa'z* have also been recorded in writing and on audio tape, as have a large number of his Urdu and Arabic speeches.[39] In recognition of Sayyidna Tahir Sayf al-Din's vast scholarship, Aligarh Muslim University bestowed an honorary doctorate upon him, and later its nominating committee unanimously appointed him chancellor for three consecutive terms till he died in 1965. Tahir Sayf al-Din's scholarly works have become comprehensive repositories of *da'wat* learning.

Sayyidna Tahir Sayf al-Din personally trained his son and successor, the present *da'i* Sayyidna Muhammad Burhan al-Din (b. 1333/1915). The year after becoming *da'i*, Sayyidna Burhan al-Din composed a *risalat* in the tradition of his father, titled *Istiftah zubad al-ma'arif* (1385/1966). Since his early youth, he has continued to deliver *wa'z* expositions several times annually, and to compose panegyrics in praise of the 51st *da'i* and of the Imams, recently collected in a *Diwan*.[40] In recognition of Burhan al-Din's scholarship, al-Azhar University in Cairo bestowed an honorary doctorate upon him in 1966.

Miscellaneous Bohra works published in the last 200 years include several prayer manuals.[41] These are named '*hafti*', perhaps from the Gujarati word '*hafta*' (week) and the Persian word '*haft*' (seven), because of the weekly *du'a*'s contained therein. Some popular historical works and educational textbooks have also been published.

The Bohra libraries in Mumbai and Surat contain the largest collection of Fatimid and Tayyibi manuscripts in the world (approximately 524 titles, 10,000 manuscripts, in Mumbai and several thousand more in Surat). The Mumbai library is under the direct control of the *da'i* and is considered his personal archive; it is not accessible to the public. It houses the most valuable manuscripts of Tayyibi Ismaili literature, including manuscripts that are up to 600 years old. Quite a few autograph copies are housed in this library. The Surat library is affiliated to the Bohra seminary Jami'a Sayfiyya (discussed in the next section) and has been modernized in the last decade, with an online database. There is also a department for manuscript conservation, and many of the valuable works housed at the two libraries are being digitally preserved.

The Bohra literary culture is focused on manuscripts. Rather than printed books, students chiefly read and study from manuscripts, which continue to be copied regularly by hand. Each Jami'a student, for example, is required to copy a manuscript and present it to the Jami'a library before graduation. Private manuscript collections also exist in the Bohra community. Members of the *da'i*'s family and other scholars own a fair number of manuscripts, although these are usually not more that a couple of hundred years old. Individuals belonging to the Tayyibi community in Yemen are said to own secret caches of early manuscripts, even including some titles that are considered lost, but these, as yet, remain undisclosed.

Learning

Religious learning (*'ilm*) and religious practice (*'amal*) are the two principal criteria for advancement in the Tayyibi Da'wat. This being so, religious education is most rigorous in the *da'i*'s household, where secular education is considered valuable but secondary. The *da'i* himself often teaches his children and other relatives. He also imparts knowledge to the community at large through *wa'z*, *bayan* and periodic less formal expositions called *sabaq*. All *da'wat* knowledge, but most especially *haqiqat*, is believed to pass 'from mouth to ear' (*min famin ila udhun*) – the text is but a notation, while actual knowledge is inscribed in the student's heart by the teacher. The *da'i*'s permission is required for the study of all *da'wat* texts, especially the *batin* texts, and, within the *batin*, most especially the *haqiqat* texts.

Religious learning is available to the general Bohra community in several formats. One of these is the Jami'a Sayfiyya, an important academy of Bohra religious studies. In the 17th century, the 34th *da'i*, Isma'il Badr al-Din, founded it as an institution that provided free board and lodging to students who came to study with the *da'i* in Jamnagar. It remained a peripatetic kind of *madrasa*, moving with the *da'i* until, in the early 19th century, the 43rd *da'i* Sayyidna 'Abd-i 'Ali Sayf al-Din expanded it along more formal lines in Surat. In the early 20th century the 51st *da'i* Sayyidna Tahir Sayf al-Din further developed it along the lines of a modern seminary. The present *da'i* added a branch in Karachi, Pakistan, in 1983. In 1998 he founded under the Surat Jami'a aegis a new institute named Ma'had al-Zahra' for the memorization and study of the Qur'an. The *da'wat* funds the Jami'a and provides free tuition and board to students. The number of applicants has increased steadily over the years, and many more applications are received than there are spaces. In 2006 the Surat Jami'a had 149 professors and 717 students (440 male, 277 female). The Karachi Jami'a had 60 professors and 452 students (231 male, 221 female).

In most towns with a Bohra population, there are religious schools (called *madrasa*s) for children. To allow children to attend secular school on weekdays, *madrasa*s hold classes either in the evenings or on weekends. Outside India and Pakistan, the Dubai *madrasa* is one of the best-attended, with two hours of classes on religion every afternoon, five days a week. Religion classes are also held in Bohra-administered secular schools. A large number of religious teachers are Jami'a-trained professionals. Others are volunteers, some of whom are trained at the Zaynabiyya institute in Sidhpur. This institute has been operational since 1979, and by 2006 had 760 trainees (599 male, 161 female).

Many adults attend regular religious classes (*sabaq*). The local *'amil* or *madrasa* head teacher (*mu'allim*) teaches these, usually on a weekly basis. In Mumbai, members of the *da'i*'s family, the *Qasr-i 'Ali*, teach many of these classes. The Jami'a conducts an optional annual examination for *sabaq* attendees. The first texts taught in these classes are from the *zahir* category, often the *fiqh* works, particularly the *Da'a'im al-Islam*, along with a *risalat* by Sayyidna Tahir Sayf al-Din. After some years of training, a *tawil* text is taught, and after several more years and only to a select few, permission is granted to study *haqiqat*.

The *da'wat* administering body for schools, *madrasa*s and all religious education structures is the Da'irat al-Tarbiyyat wa al-Ta'lim (popularly called Attalim) which supervises religious study curricula used in Bohra *madrasa*s worldwide and publishes and distributes elementary religious study manuals and prayer books. According to recent studies, the Bohra have significantly higher educational levels than the Indian norm, for the *da'wat* leadership encourages women as well as men to pursue both religious and secular education.[42] In addition to institutions of religious learning, the *da'wat* also owns and runs several secular educational institutions. Bohra schools and colleges exist today in most cities with a Bohra population, and are most numerous in India; in Greater Mumbai itself there are 30 Bohra secular schools. Worldwide, there are 470 Bohra schools. These are open to non-Bohra as well, but require the Bohra children to take religious classes in addition to the regular secular curriculum.

Social Practice and Administration

Although influenced in a limited fashion by Arab and Persian social norms, Bohra social practice is above all a blend of Islamic 'orthopraxy' and Mughal–Rajput Indian culture. An example of this amalgamation is the Bohra language mentioned earlier, named Lisan al-Da'wat or '*Da'wat ni zaban*' (literally, 'the language of the *da'wat*'). Its substructure is the

Indo-Aryan language Gujarati, a derivative of Sanskrit, spoken mostly in the Indian province of Gujarat. The grammar and sentence structure of Lisan al-Da'wat appear to have remained in accord with Gujarati without any perceptible change. (A close parallel to the evolution of Lisan al-Da'wat might be that of Urdu, currently the national language of Pakistan, which is a blend of the Sanskrit-based Hindustani with Arabic and Persian.)

The vocabulary and script of Lisan al-Da'wat have become progressively more Islamized. Arabic and Persian vocabulary is gradually displacing the Gujarati Sanskrit-based lexicon; this is especially true of vocabulary related to religious matters, such as the use of the Arabic *din* (religion) rather than the Gujarati *dharam*, and the use of the Persian *ruza* (fast) rather than the Gujarati *vrat*. The Bohra *nasihat*s provide a clear illustration of this gradual absorption: *nasihat*s composed by Sayyidi Luqman-ji b. Shaykh Da'ud in the 12th/18th century have a much smaller Arabic Persian lexical content and a much larger Sanskrit-derived Gujarati one than *nasihat*s composed by Sayyidi Sadiq 'Ali Sahib in the 19th century; these latter, in turn, are less Arabicized than *nasihat*s composed by Sayyidna Tahir Sayf al-Din in the 20th century. The script in which Lisan al-Da'wat is currently written is Arabic-Persian *naskh* rather than Gujarati Devanagari. But some Bohra publications even today are written in the Devanagari script (e.g. the weekly magazine *Nasim-i sahar*), and significant numbers of lay Bohra use the Devanagari rather than the Arabic script. The shift in script, too, has been gradual and remains an ongoing one.

The Bohra mode of attire is similarly a mélange of the Islamic and the Indian. Women wear the Islamically mandated veil (which they call *rida'*) outside the home, comprised of a full-length skirt (*lenga* or *ghaghra*) and a triangular garment (*parr* or *pardi*) covering the head and bosom down to the hips; the *parr* has a flap that is sometimes used to cover the face. The *rida'* has evolved into its present form in the last 30 years or so; earlier, Bohra women wore different versions of the veil. Bohra men wear plain white calf-length robes (*kurta-saya*), with loose cotton trousers (also called *idhar*), and a white crocheted thread cap (*topi*) with some gold and black. Business attire is often Western-style trousers and shirt, with many choosing to include the *topi* as head covering. On ceremonial occasions the clergy wear a more elaborate costume, a full-length white muslin robe with a gathered waist (*jama*), folds of white muslin arranged over the shoulder (*dupatta*), and a white turban (*paghri*). Many of these garments – the *jama*, for example – are similar to those worn earlier in the Mughal court. Others, such as the *kurta*, are commonly worn in a shorter version by a large number of Indians today.

The wearing of traditional community dress (called *qawmi libas* or *libas-i anwar*) is *de rigueur* at Bohra religious and social gatherings and is encouraged at all times. This emphasis is of a dual nature: observation of Islamic law and preservation of Bohra cultural identity. According to the legal or cultural nature of the directive, there are gradations in the required dress code. The veil, as mentioned earlier, is required for women since it is considered mandated by Islamic law. The wearing of the Bohra cap by men, on the other hand, is encouraged rather than required, since it is a religio-cultural stipulation rather than a legal prescription.

Most Bohra social gatherings have a meal component, inspired by the promise of divine reward for those who feed the hungry. Very often the invitees are many in number, 500 guests being quite common for a wedding feast. In the event of a large religious gathering, all attendees are invited to a meal called *niyaz* (Persian, literally 'supplication'), which is offered by individuals or organizations. Since Muharram 1423/2002, Sayyidna Burhan al-Din has hosted a *niyaz* meal for all those attending his *waʿz* worldwide on the same day, virtually all the 1 million members of the Bohra community. Large communal *iftar* meals are also common during the fast of Ramadan. Like the *niyaz*, banquets for specific celebrations are given specific names. A meal to which all the Bohra living in a particular city are invited is called a *jamaʿat*. A banquet to which the *daʿi* or a high-ranking *daʿwat* personage is invited is termed a *ziyafat*.

A central administration headed by the *daʿi* oversees the administration of all Bohra affairs. All personnel are answerable to the *daʿi*, who lays out the broad parameters for their performance and inspects specific matters from time to time. The central offices of all the administrative departments are in the Badri Mahal complex in Mumbai, which also contains the offices of the senior administrators, including the brothers and sons of the *daʿi*. One of the important departments is al-Wazarat al-Sayfiyya, which appoints and supervises local representatives (called ʿamil, plural ʿummal) in cities, towns and villages. In 2006 there were 340 ʿamils worldwide. Each ʿamil is the head of the Bohra council in his city (called the *jamaʿat* committee), which is made up of people from the local community. Most ʿamils are graduates of Jamiʿa Sayfiyya, and combine religious knowledge with administrative skills. Under the ʿamil is a local man – called the *wali mulla* – who is appointed to lead the ritual prayer in the former's absence. Additionally, each *jamaʿat* is divided into sectors named *muhalla*, and each of these is locally administered by a governing body (called a *tanzim* committee). *Jamaʿat*s from the same district are grouped together for administrative purposes and are collectively called a *jamʻiyyat*. In towns where the number of Bohra is small, an *ʻamil* is generally not appointed, and instead a *wali mulla* leads the ritual prayer.

There are numerous Bohra social organizations that undertake a range of activities including the maintenance of *masjid*s and communal areas, charity schemes and the organization of trips to pilgrimage sites, social gatherings and athletic events. Bohra charity organizations are numerous and include giving free medical facilities, scholarships, interest-free loan schemes, orphanages, free food and clothing, and subsidized or free housing. The larger charities are funded and overseen by the *daʻwat*, under whose auspices many are administered by local Bohra communities. Community members often contribute funds to these charities, especially at the initial set-up stage. Branches of many of these organizations exist in most cities of the world which have a substantial Bohra population.

All in all, and despite their relatively small numbers, the Tayyibi Da'udi Bohras are a remarkable Indian Muslim community. Their unique and stable interpretation of the Islamic belief system, their rich and ongoing tradition of written Arabic exposition, their valuable manuscript collections, their focused attention on, and singular mechanisms for, providing religious and secular education to the entire community, and their amalgam of the Islamic-religious and the Indian-cultural in social practice, makes them occupants of a special niche among the Muslims of the world.

Notes

1. From the Gujarati word *vehvar* meaning 'dealings' or 'honest dealings'. See the Gujarati lexicon by L. R. Gala and P. L. Soda, *Gala Vishal Shabdkosh* (Mumbai, 2000), p. 637, *vahevaru*. This etymology seems the most plausible one, as the majority of the early Bohra were, in fact, traders, and as the Bohra are also called 'Vohra' ('b' and 'v' being interchangeable at the beginning of words in Gujarati). Another etymology of 'many sects or paths' derived from the Hindi phrase *bahu rah* is proposed by S. T. Lokhandwalla, 'The Bohras, A Muslim Community of Gujarat', *Studia Islamica*, 3 (1955), p. 120 n. 1. This etymology seems less convincing since converts to all religions are usually from different sects and paths that is not a feature novel enough to affect nomenclature.
2. The 'Da'udi' (popularly transcribed 'Dawoodi') in 'Da'udi Bohra' refers to their recognition of the *daʻi*-ship of Sayyidna Da'ud b. Qutb Shah who reigned from 999/1591 to 1021/1612 and was opposed by Sulayman b. Hasan, the first *daʻi* of the Sulaymani Bohra. A third group is the 'Alavi Bohra. Doctrinal differences among all groups appear to be minimal. Historical

details for the Sulaymanis and 'Alavis are provided in the following chapter.
3. See 'Bibliographic Discussion' in Jonah Blank, *Mullahs on the Mainframe: Islam and Modernity among the Daudi Bohras* (Chicago, 2001), pp. 301–307.
4. In Dominique Chevallier, ed., *Les Arabes et l'histoire créatrice* (Paris, 1995), pp. 59–77.
5. Blank's *Mullahs on the Mainframe* also contains a glossary, the most up-to-date bibliography on the Bohra, and a useful bibliographical discussion. An earlier, informative study on the Bohra of Udaipur is by Shibani Roy, *The Dawoodi Bohras: An Anthropological Perspective* (Delhi, 1984).
6. I have followed in this chapter the Bohra pronunciation of words, including the word '*daʿwat*' (with a final *t*, rather than *daʿwa*). Like many other words borrowed from Arabic with the feminine ending *–a(t)*, *daʿwa* in Bohra Gujarati usage takes the Persianized form with final *–t*, thus *daʿwat* (cf. in this paper *khidmat, baraʾat, walayat, taʿat, mahabbat, hujjat, taharat, rakʿat, shahadat, barakat, ziyarat, surat, haqiqat, nasihat, risalat, jamaʿat, jamʿiyyat, diyafat*). Those with masculine gender are pronounced with a final *–a* (cf. *rutba, madrasa, mahalla*). For a classification and analysis of the *–at* ending in Bohra Gujarati's sister languages of Urdu and Hindi, see John Perry, *Form and Meaning in Persian Vocabulary: The Arabic Feminine Ending* (Costa Mesa, CA, 1991), pp. 158–163.
7. See Fatimid Imamate doctrines in al-Qadi al-Nuʿman's chapter on *walayat* in his *Daʿaʾim al-Islam*, ed. Asaf A. A. Fyzee (Cairo, 1951), vol. 1, pp. 3–120; trans. A. A. A. Fyzee, revised by Ismail K. Poonawala as *The Pillars of Islam* (New Delhi, 2002–2004), vol. 1, pp. 17–122; and Hamid al-Din al-Kirmani's *al-Masabih*, ed. and English trans. Paul E. Walker as *Master of the Age: An Islamic Treatise on the Necessity of the Imamate* (London, 2007), pp. 71–127.
8. A concise explanation of the historical blending of these spiritual and temporal authoritative roles is an article by Paul E. Walker, 'The Ismaʿili Daʿwa and the Fatimid Caliphate', in M. W. Daly, ed., *The Cambridge History of Egypt*: Volume I, *Islamic Egypt, 640–1517*, ed. Carl F. Petry (Cambridge, 1998), pp. 120–150. See also Paula Sanders, 'The Fatimid State, 969–1171', in Petry, ed., *The Cambridge History of Egypt*, vol. 1, pp. 151–174.
9. References to the birth of al-Tayyib, his appointment (*nass*) to the Imamate by his father al-Amir and his subsequent disappearance are found in a 6th/12th-century Syrian chronicle titled *al-Bustan al-jamiʿ liʾjamiʿ tawarikh ahl al-zaman* by ʿImad al-Din Abu Hamid al-Isfahani (ed. Cl. Cahen, in his 'Une chronique Syrienne du VIe/XIIe siècle', *Bulletin d'Études Orientales*, 7–8 (1937–1938), pp. 121–122), and in Ibn Muyassar's *Akhbar Misr*, ed. A. F. Sayyid (Cairo, 1981), pp. 109–110, probably from the lost chronicle of Ibn Muhannak (d. 549/1154). Two sources for this data from Yemen are Muhammad b. Tahir (d. 584/1188), *Majmuʿ al-tarbiyya* (ms), and Idris ʿImad al-Din (d. 872/1468), *ʿUyun al-akhbar wa-funun al-athar*, vol. 7, ed. Ayman Fuʾad Sayyid as *The Fatimids and their Successors in Yaman* (London, 2002), pp. 254–257.

10. During the *daʻi*-ship of the 47th *daʻi* ʻAbd al-Qadir Najm al-Din, a group of dissenters claimed that his appointment (*nass*) was invalid, and that he was merely an administrator they termed '*nazim daʻi*' (caretaker *daʻi*), without spiritual authority, accountable to the community. In 1921, after Ibrahim and Karim, sons of Adamji Pirbhoy, filed a suit against the 51st *daʻi* Tahir Sayf al-Din, the British High Court in Bombay ruled for the validity of the *nass* conferred on Sayyidna Najm al-Din (*Record of Proceedings in the High Court of Judicature at Bombay*, Suit no. 941 of 1917, 'Conclusion re Dai-ul Mutlac', pp. 984–985). In 1947, the Privy Council in London upheld the judgement in favour of the *nass* (*Privy Council Appeal No. 79 of 1945*, pp. 12–13). For details of the *nass* and the establishment position on this matter, see the treatise *Dawʼ nur al-haqq al-mubin* by Sayyidna Tahir Sayf al-Din. For the anti-establishment position refuting the *nass*, see Ismail K. Poonawala, *Biobibliography of Ismaʻili Literature* (Malibu, CA, 1977), pp. 14, 224, 237–238; Asghar Ali Engineer, *The Bohras* (New Delhi, 1980), p. 135.

11. A brief overview of Sayyidna Burhan al-Din's life and work is contained in Mustafa Abdulhussein, 'Burhanuddin, Sayyidna Muhammad', in *The Oxford Encyclopedia of the Modern Islamic World*, ed. J. L. Esposito (Oxford, 1995), vol. 1, pp. 237–238. A Daʻwat publication about him by the same author is *al-Dai al-Fatimi, Syedna Mohammed Burhanuddin: An Illustrated Biography* (Oxford, 2001).

12. *Raza* is the Bohra pronunciation. The Arabic is *rida*, the more common meaning of which is 'being well-pleased', but which also means 'permission' or 'consent'.

13. All Tayyibi *haqiqat* texts contain a pledge at the beginning which mandates that without the permission of the *daʻi*, the reader may not read the text, nor transcribe a word of it, nor impart any part of the knowledge contained therein.

14. A Fatimid reference to these doctrines regarding the *daʻi*-ship (from the beginning of the Fatimid caliphate, two centuries before the concealment of the 21st Imam) is Jaʻfar b. Mansur al-Yaman (contemporary of al-Qadi al-Nuʻman who died in 363/974), *Sirat Mansur al-Yaman* (lost), excerpts cited by *daʻwat* scholars through the centuries, and most recently by the 51st *daʻi* Tahir Sayf al-Din in his treatise *Dawʼ nur al-haqq al-mubin* (Mumbai, 1333/1915, pp. 80–81). References to these doctrines are found in almost all Tayyibi sources. See, for example, the poems of the 5th *daʻi*, ʻAli b. Muhammad (*Diwan*, ms, see in this context the Ph.D. thesis by Rabab Hamiduddin titled *The Qasidah of the Tayyibi Daʻwah and the Diwan of Syedna ʻAli b. Muhammad al-Walid, d. 612/1215*, University of London, School of Oriental and African Studies, 2000). Works refuting the positions of seceding groups also contain expositions of these doctrines, an important source being a treatise by Sayyidi Luqmanji b. Habib Allah (d. 1173/1760), ms, quoted by Sayyidna Tahir Sayf al-Din in his treatise, *Salsabil hikam ghadaq* (Mumbai, 1364/1945), p. 124.

15. See al-Qadi al-Nuʿman, *Daʿaʾim*, vol. 1, ch. '*zakat: dhikr dafʿ al-sadaqat*', pp. 257–258.
16. The struggle against evildoers may be by the sword, the tongue and the heart (see al-Nuʿman, *Daʿaʾim*, vol. 1, ch. '*jihad: dhikr al-raghaʾib fi al-jihad*', pp. 343–344). The greatest *jihad*, however, is the struggle against one's own base soul; cf. exposition by al-Kirmani cited by Tahir Sayf al-Din in his *Amthal sidrat al-muntaha* (1377/1958), pp. 176–177.
17. Some other Bohra sources of law are al-Nuʿman's *Kitab al-iqtisar*, ed. Muhammad Wahid Mirza (Damascus, 1957); *Kitab al-Hawashi* and *masaʾil* works such as the *Masaʾil Aminji b. Jalal*, ms. A useful work in this context is A. A. A. Fyzee's *Compendium of Fatimid Law* (Simla, 1969).
18. A partial text of the Fatimid *mithaq* is preserved in the works of the Mamluk historians al-Nuwayri, *Nihayat al-arab*, vol. 25, ed. M. J. ʿA. al-Hini and ʿA. al-Ahwani (Cairo, 1984), pp. 217–20, and al-Maqrizi, *al-Khitat* (Bulaq, 1270/1853–1854), vol. 1, pp. 396–397. Heinz Halm, in his article, 'The Ismaʿili Oath of Allegiance (*ʿahd*) and the "Sessions of Wisdom" (*majalis al-hikma*) in Fatimid Times', in Farhad Daftary, ed., *Mediaeval Ismaʿili History and Thought* (Cambridge, 1996), pp. 91–115, argues that 'the close correspondence between the *ʿahd* of the Fatimid period and the one used today by the Bohra serves as further evidence for the assumption that the form of the oath has remained essentially the same throughout the centuries, and that there existed only *one* form, which the *daʿis* used all over the world. The Bohra as the heirs of the Fatimid tradition and literature have preserved this form' (p. 98).
19. See al-Qadi al-Nuʿman's statement in his *Asas al-taʾwil*, ed. ʿArif Tamir (Beirut, 1960), chapter on the Prophet Solomon, pp. 278–279, stating that the key elements of Fatimid belief are embodied in the *mithaq*.
20. Probably from the Gujarati *vadhave* (to increase), and/or *badhaʾi* or *vadhaʿi* (felicitations or welcome, also implying *barakat* or increase through grace, and from the same root; 'b' and 'v', as mentioned earlier, being interchangeably used); perhaps indicating a prayer for an increase in the life, happiness, well-being, wealth, and so on for the person who is the object of the *vadha-vanu*.
21. Al-Muʾayyad fi'l-Din al-Shirazi (d. 470/1078) was the *bab al-abwab* ('Gate of Gates', highest rank after the Imam in the spiritual hierarchy) and *daʿi al-duʿat* (chief missionary) under Imam al-Mustansir. His magnum opus is the *Majalis al-Muʾayyadiyya* in 8 vols.: vols. 1–3, ed. Hatim Hamid al-Din (Oxford, 1986; Bombay, 1987 and 2005); vols. 1 and 3, ed. Mustafa Ghalib (Beirut, 1974 and 1984). The *Majalis* were originally delivered as weekly sermons to the Ismailis in Cairo and later collected in book form.
22. For details of Bohra shrines with brief historical notes on the saints buried there, see *Tuhfat laʾali akhbar al-hudat*, ed. Hudhayfa Muhyi al-Din (Mumbai, 1414/1993). See also www.mazaraat.com.
23. See Daniel de Smet, 'Comment déterminer le début et la fin du jeûne de

Ramadan? Un point de discorde entre Sunnites et Ismaéliens en Égypte Fatimide', in U. Vermeulen and D. de Smet, ed., *Egypt and Syria in the Fatimid, Ayyubid and Mamluk Eras* (Leuven, 1995), pp. 71–84.

24. For details of Arabic composition in India see Tahera Qutbuddin, 'Arabic in India: A Survey and Classification of its Uses, Compared with Persian', *JAOS*, 127, 3 (2007), pp. 315–338.

25. Relevant bibliographical works are: Ismail K. Poonawala, *Biobibliography of Isma'ili Literature*, Wladimir Ivanow, *Ismaili Literature* (Tehran, 1963), first published as *A Guide to Ismaili Literature* (London, 1933), a pioneering work based on an incomplete manuscript of al-Majdu' (d. 1183 or 1184/1769 or 1771), *Fahrasat al-kutub wa al-rasa'il*, popularly known as *Fihrist al-Majdu'*, ed. 'Ali N. Munzavi (Tehran, 1966), an older work, but still useful for its summaries of contents (not provided by the later bibliographies).

26. Significant works in other genres were also produced, albeit less copiously, including: the historical writings of Idris 'Imad al-Din, ethical works and a hagiography of 'Ali by Hatim Muhyi al-Din, several *Diwans* of poetry, *ta'wil* books, treatises on contemporary *hudud*, and refutations of the Zaydiyya (all manuscripts, except 'Imad al-Din's *'Uyun al-akhbar*).

27. Works produced in India from the mid-16th to 18th century include jurisdic *masa'il* such as the writings of Aminji b. Jalal, *ta'wil* treatises, history works such as the *Sitt rasa'il* of Khawj b. Malak (see entry on him by Abdeali Qutbuddin in the *Encyclopaedia Iranica*) and the *Tadhkirat* by Sayyidi Hasanji Badshah (second half of 11th/17th century) on the martyrdom of Sayyidna Qutb al-Din, biographies of *da'wat* luminaries, refutation of seceding denominations (especially the Sulaymanis and the Hujumiyya) by Luqmanji b. Habib Allah and other scholars, correspondence, ethical works and poetic *diwans* (all manuscripts).

28. See my book *Al-Mu'ayyad al-Shirazi and Fatimid Da'wa Poetry: A Case of Commitment in Classical Arabic Literature* (Leiden, 2005).

29. Cf. Rabab Hamiduddin, *The Qasidah of the Tayyibi Da'wah and the Diwan of Syedna 'Ali b. Muhammad al-Walid*.

30. See Abdeali Qutbuddin, *The Meaning of Love in the Poetry of Syedna Abdeali Sayfuddin* (MA thesis, University of London, School of Oriental and African Studies, 1995).

31. Among the short *risalats* published in Sayyidna Sayf al-Din's name are the following brief treatises: (a) four composed in the month of Ramadan and characterized as *Rasa'il Ramadaniyya*, (b) two elegiac (*na'y*) treatises, one for his brother and predecessor in office, Sayyidna Yusuf Najm al-Din, the other for another brother and *mukasir* Sayyidi 'Abd al-Qadir Hakim al-Din, (c) two on administrative matters, one titled *Risala fi taqlid al-'ummal*, a code of conduct and guidance for local Da'wat administrators or *'amils*, and the second titled *al-Risala al-Sayfiyya fi tartib al-hudud*, about changes in the hierarchy of his *hudud*. Other prose works include three epistles (*sijill*, two to his representative in Yemen), an abridgement of the biography of

Sayyidi Luqman-ji Sahib, and a *fiqh masa'il* work titled *al-Masa'il al-Sayfiyya* (all mss).

32. These students were Sayyidna Sayf al-Din's son Muhammad Badr al-Din (46th *da'i*), Badr al-Din's successor 'Abd al-Qadir Najm al-Din (47th *da'i*), and the latter's brother and successor 'Abd al-Husayn Husam al-Din (48th *da'i*).
33. Partial ed., covering 1st to 27th *da'i*, by Samer F. Traboulsi (Beirut, 1999); full text in ms. Shaykh Qutb was 9th in ranking of Sayyidna Sayf al-Din's *hudud*, and is buried in Pune in the cemetery named after him. The history he transcribes up to the time of the 19th *da'i* Idris 'Imad al-Din is obtained almost entirely from the latter's *Nuzhat al-afkar* (ms); later history is culled from various unnamed sources.
34. Shaykh Sadiq 'Ali b. Mulla Sultan 'Ali Surti was 12th in the ranking of Sayyidna Sayf al-Din's *hudud* and is buried in the cemetery known by his name in Surat. His *nasihat*s have been published in a lithographed collection titled *Zahr rawd al-nasa'ih* (Mumbai, 1399/1979). For a thematic analysis, see Balvant Jani, 'The Devotional Element in the Nasihats of the Bohra Writings in Gujarat', in A. W. Entwistle and F. Mallison, ed., *Studies in South Asian Devotional Literature* (Paris and New Delhi, 1988–1991), pp. 224–238.
35. The translation is entitled *Miftah al-taharat*, translator not named (lithograph, Madras, 1290/1873).
36. Volume 3 was completed first and lithographed in 1299/1882, vols. 1 and 2 appeared in 1301/1884.
37. An index volume with the tables of contents for volumes 1 to 30 has been published under the title *Miftah khaza'in al-'ulum* ed. 'Imran b. Shaykh Hasan bhai (Surat, 1365/1946); the last five *risalat*s have not yet been published.
38. *Jawahir al-balagha al-ladunniyya* ([Dubai], 1414/1993).
39. Fifty-seven Urdu speeches by Sayyidna Tahir Sayf al-Din have been collected in *Kalim al-fasaha wa al-balagha*, ed. Shaykh Ibrahim al-Yamani ([Bombay], 1380/1960), and nine Arabic ones in *Kunuz al-fasaha wa al-balagha*, ed. Shaykh Ibrahim al-Yamani ([Bombay], 1372/1953).
40. Sayyidna Muhammad Burhan al-Din, *Abha zuhur riyad al-'ilm*, ed. Hudhayfa Muhyi al-Din (Mumbai, 1418/1997 and 1421/2000).
41. The most important *hafti*s are the following: (1) *Sahifat al-salat* (most comprehensive manual, contains instructions for all the important prayer rituals and *du'a*s for the year, and other important information related to prayer rituals associated with the life of each Bohra, such as birth and death rituals), (2) *Bihori ni hafti* (special Ramadan prayers and *du'a*'s, and prayers for Laylat al-Qadr, printed as *Khaza'in barakat al-du'a*), (3) *Roz parwani hafti* (commonly known as just '*hafti*,' *du'a*s to be prayed every morning, printed with the title *Ghamam al-rahma*), (4) *Shehrullah ni hafti* (*du'a*s for after *fajr* and *zuhr* prayer during Ramadan, printed as *Sahifat ad'iya*

ramadaniyya), (5) *Mansak al-hajj* (Hajj rites), (6) *Al-Barakat wa al-qurubat* (*ziyarat hafti*, Qur'an verses, *salams*, *du'as* and verses of poetry to be recited at shrines of Imam Husayn and *da'wat* luminaries), (7) *Azhar kanz al-maghani* (poems to be recited at various occasions during the year, such as *'urs* and *milad*).

42. Blank, *Mullahs on the Mainframe*, pp. 207–228, which also provides statistics.

A Brief Note on Other Tayyibi Communities: Sulaymanis and 'Alavis

Tahera Qutbuddin

Sulaymani Bohras or Makarima[1]

The Sulaymani Bohras follow a different line of succession to that of the Da'udi Bohras from the 27th *da'i* onwards, i.e. three *da'i*s after the shift of the Tayyibi *da'wat* headquarters to India in 946/1539. They believe that the rightful 27th *da'i* was not the Da'udi Bohra incumbent, Da'ud b. Qutb Shah, but rather a nephew of the 21st *da'i* named Sulayman b. Hasan (d. 1005/1597), after whom they are named Sulaymani. Sulayman was Indian, but had been the local representative (*'amil*) in Yemen for the 26th *da'i* (who lived in India), upon whose death he claimed the *da'i*-ship with the support of the majority of the Yemeni Tayyibis. He travelled to India to challenge Da'ud b. Qutb Shah, but died there without garnering much support from the Indian Tayyibis. He was succeeded by his son, Ja'far (d. 1050/1640), who returned to Yemen. From then on, the seat of the Sulymani *da'wat* has remained in Najran, the mountainous northeast district of Yemen, and all but the first three Sulaymani *da'i*s after the schism (Sulayman, his son and grandson), and the 46th (Ghulam Husayn, d. 1357/1938) have been Yemenis from the Makrami family of the Yam tribe. Najran was annexed to Saudi Arabia in 1936, and currently the seat of the Sulaymani *da'wat* is in Najran city in southern Saudi Arabia. The present incumbent is the 51st *da'i* Shaykh 'Abd Allah b. Muhammad al-Makrami (r. since 2005). The Arab Sulaymanis call themselves 'Makarima', from the family name of their *da'i*s, while the Indian Sulaymanis continue to use the name 'Sulaymani Bohra'. The demographics of the Sulaymanis are difficult to ascertain with any degree of certainty, but their numbers seem to have decreased rather than increased in the past few decades. In Yemen and Saudi Arabia they number between 50,000 and 200,000 persons. In India they number about 8,000.

The Arab Sulaymani-Makarima population is currently concentrated in the regions of Najran in Saudi Arabia and Haraz in Yemen. In the Haraz district of Yemen, they live in the northeast, in the villages of Shariqa, Lihab, Salul, Sa'fan, Bani Za'id and Lihab, also in Kahil and Akamat al-Sawda'. There are also Sulaymani-Makarima living in the Hamdan district north of San'a' in the villages of Tayba, Dila', Ghayl Bani Mu'nis and 'Aras, and in the district of Ibb. Almost the entire Yam tribe is Sulaymani, and there are Sulaymanis also among the tribes of Hamdan and Wa'ila.[2] In Saudi Arabia the community faces serious conflict. In April 2000 their main Mansura *masjid* was raided by the authorities, three leaders were arrested and religious manuscripts confiscated. Saudi officials have made comments to the effect that they consider the Sulaymani-Makarima infidels. Perhaps because of the intense pressure from the Saudi government, the Arab Sulaymanis have begun emulating the Saudi Wahhabi creed and practice in the past two decades. According to the Yemeni Da'udis, the Sulaymanis in Yemen and Najran have stopped holding religious *majalis*, even ceasing to commemorate 'Ashura.[3] They still visit the shrines of the *da'i*s for *ziyarat*, but they have stopped making obeisance or kissing the grave. Moreover they have begun entertaining the idea of popular election of the *da'i*, versus the traditional creed of appointment (*nass*) by the predecessor.

In India the affairs of the Sulaymani Bohra are conducted by the *da'i*'s *mansub* residing in Vadodara (formerly Baroda, in the state of Gujarat); the position is currently occupied by an individual named Muhammad Shakir. There are Sulaymani Bohras living in Hyderabad (Deccan), Ahmedabad and Mumbai. They have a centre in Mumbai named Badri Bagh. There is also a small community in Pakistan. The community outside the Najran-Haraz area seems to have little contact with the *da'i*, and there appear to be few dealings between the Yemeni and Indian Sulaymanis. The former differ considerably in lifestyle and culture from the latter. The Indian Sulaymani community has also gradually distanced itself culturally from its Gujarati roots, and its members now speak Urdu like the majority of the Indian Muslims. A prominent Sulaymani Bohra family of the 19th and early 20th century was the Tyabjis, to which belonged the first Indian Muslim barrister Badruddin Tyabji and the prominent Ismaili scholar Asaf A. A. Fyzee (1899–1981). The Tyabji family advocated two 'progressive' aims: modern education (especially the English language) for both men and women, and the discarding of the veil.[4] Technologically, however, they do not seem to be very advanced today.[5]

'Alavi Bohras[6]

The 'Alavi Bohras,[7] popularly known as Alya Bohra, also follow a different line of succession to the Da'udi Bohras from the 29th *da'i* onwards, two *da'is* after the split from the Sulaymanis. They believe the rightful *da'i* was not the majority Da'udi Bohra incumbent 'Abd al-Tayyib Zaki al-Din (d. 1041/1631) but rather a grandson of the 28th *da'i* named 'Ali Shams al-Din b. Ibrahim (d. 1046/1637). They are named after this 'Ali, calling themselves 'Alavis, and their mission the *da'wat hadiya 'Alaviyya*. Three *da'is* later, in 1090/1679 the seat of the 'Alavi *da'wat* was moved from Ahmedabad to Vadodara, which (except for a brief interlude in Surat in the 12th/18th century) remains the headquarters of the 'Alavis to this day. The present incumbent 'Alavi *da'i* is Sayyidna Tayyib Diya' al-Din (r. since 1974), the 44th *da'i* of the line. The 'Alavi Bohras have a library of 450 Ismaili manuscripts, some up to 500 years old, at their centre in Vadodara.[8]

Currently 'Alavi Bohras are a close-knit community numbering approximately 8,000, with the majority in Vadodara, and smaller groups scattered in Mumbai, Surat, Ahmedabad and other towns in India, where they have *masjids* and *musafirkhanas*. Some have migrated to the United States and Europe, as well as the Middle East. 'Alavi Bohras are mostly traders and dominate the optical market in Vadodara. They are now increasingly venturing into professions such as law, medicine and computer sciences. Their customs, beliefs and hierarchical set-up are similar to those of the Da'udi Bohras, including the *mithaq*, language (Lisan al-Da'wat) and mode of dress.

Notes

1. Studies on the Sulaymani Bohras include: Farhad Daftary, *The Isma'ilis: Their History and Doctrines* (2nd ed., Cambridge, 2007), pp. 295–300 (a brief chronological history); Satish C. Misra, *Muslim Communities in Gujarat* (Baroda, 1985), pp. 27–31 (an account of the schism); Asaf A. A. Fyzee, 'A Chronological List of the Imams and Da'is of the Musta'lian Ismailis', *Journal of the Bombay Branch of the Royal Asiatic Society*, New Series, 10 (1934), pp. 8–16, and his 'Three Sulaymani *Da'is*: 1936–1939', *Journal of the Bombay Branch of the Royal Asiatic Society*, New Series, 16 (1940), pp. 101–104. I was able to obtain additional information from interviews and communications with Da'udi Bohras who live alongside the Sulaymanis

in Yemen, and from news reports about recent conflicts in Saudi Arabia. A polemical monograph on the beliefs and practices of the Makarima is Ahmad b. Musfir al-'Utaybi, *Dahaqinat al-Yaman: Tahqiqat wa mutala'at fi milaff al-Isma'iliyya* (Amman, 2002).

2. See Human Rights Watch 2008 report, 'The Ismailis of Najran', at http://hrw.org/reports/2008/saudiarabia0908.

3. In April 2002 (Muharram 1423) the Makarima held 'Ashura commemorations after many years of non-observance, using in their *wa'z*, according to the Da'udis, the Da'udi work *Agharr al-majalis* and the elegy for Imam Husayn (*Ya sayyida al-shuhada'i*) composed by the 51st Da'udi *da'i*. The Makrami *shaykh* was subsequently arrested, and, according to an ABC news report, at least 40 people were killed in the violence that ensued.

4. See Theodore P. Wright, 'Muslim Kinship and Modernization: The Tyabji Clan of Bombay', in Imtiaz Ahmad, ed., *Family, Kinship, and Marriage among Muslims in India* (New Delhi, 1976), pp. 217–238.

5. I was not able to find any Sulaymani Bohra websites, for example, compared to over a thousand Da'udi sites.

6. Studies on the 'Alavi Bohras are almost nonexistent. Daftary, who has met the community's leadership in Vadodara, has a brief entry on them in *The Isma'ilis*, pp. 280–282. In the present short note, I have used additional materials provided by the son of the 'Alavi *da'i*, Bhaisaheb M. Nur al-Din. Their recently opened website also contains much information about their history, beliefs and particularly current events (with photographs and audio visual material) at http://www.alavibohra.org/index.htm.

7. Popularly and incorrectly known as ''Alya Bohra', they refer to themselves officially as ''Alavi Bohra'.

8. For scans of some of their manuscripts, see their website at http://www.alavibohra.org/library.htm ('library' section).

Glossary

adhan: Muslim call to prayer. There are slight differences between the Sunni and Shiʿi calls to prayer made five times a day.

ahl al-bayt: literally, the people of the house; members of the household of the Prophet, including especially, besides Muhammad, ʿAli, Fatima, al-Hasan, al-Husayn and their progeny.

ʿAlids: descendants of ʿAli b. Abi Talib, cousin and son-in-law of the Prophet and also the first Shiʿi Imam. Descendants of ʿAli and Fatima, the Prophet's daughter, through their sons al-Hasan and al-Husayn are also called Hasanids and Husaynids, comprising the Fatimid ʿAlids.

ʿ*alim* (plural ʿ*ulama*'): a scholar in Islamic religious sciences.

ʿ*amil* (plural ʿ*ummal*): local representative of the Tayyibi *daʿi mutlaq* (q.v.) in cities, towns and villages.

amir (plural *umara*'): commander, prince; also the title used by many independent rulers.

amr: the divine command or volition.

ʿ*awamm* (or ʿ*amma*): the common people, in distinction from the *khawass* (q.v.).

bab: literally, gate; the Ismaili religious term for the administrative head of the *daʿwa* (q.v.) in the Fatimid *daʿwa* hierarchy, the highest rank after Imam; the equivalent of the term *daʿi al-duʿat* (q.v.), mentioned mainly in non-Ismaili sources.

batin: the inward, hidden or esoteric meaning behind the literal wording of sacred texts and religious prescriptions, notably the Qur'an and the *shariʿa* (q.v.), in distinction from the *zahir* (q.v.).

daʿi (plural *duʿat*): literally, summoner; a religious missionary or propagandist, especially amongst the Ismailis; a high rank in the *daʿwa* (q.v.) hierarchy of the Ismailis.

daʿi al-duʿat: chief *daʿi*; the administrative head of the *daʿwa* (q.v.); see *bab*.

daʿi mutlaq: *daʿi* with absolute authority; highest rank in the Tayyibi-Mustaʿli *da'wa* organization; also the chief *da'i* (q.v.) acting as the administrative head of the (Da'udi, Sulaymani and 'Alavi) Tayyibi *da'wa* organization.

da'wa: mission; in the religio-political sense, *da'wa* is the invitation or call to adopt the cause of an individual or family claiming the right to the Imamate; it also refers to the hierarchy of ranks, sometimes called *hudud* (q.v.), within the particular religious organization developed for this purpose, especially amongst the Ismailis.

dawr (plural *adwar*): era, cycle of history; the Ismailis held that the religious history of mankind proceeded through seven *dawrs*, each one initiated by a speaker or *natiq* (q.v.).

faqih (plural *fuqaha'*): an exponent of *fiqh* or Islamic jurisprudence; a Muslim jurist in general.

farman: royal decree, written edict. For the Nizari Ismailis it refers to any pronouncement, order or ruling by their Imams.

Fatimids: descendants of 'Ali b. Abi Talib and Fatima, the Prophet's daughter, corresponding to Hasanid and Husaynid 'Alids (q.v.); also the name of the Ismaili dynasty of Imam-Caliphs from 297/909 to 567/1171.

fuquha': see *faqih*

ghulat (plural of *ghali*): exaggerator, extremists; a term of disapproval for individuals accused of exaggeration (*ghuluww*) in religion and in respect to the Imams. Criteria for defining 'exaggeration' changed over time.

ginan (*gnan*): a general term, derived from a Sanskrit word meaning contemplative or sacred knowledge; used in reference to the indigenous religious literature of the Nizari Khojas and some other communities of South Asia. Composed in a number of Indic languages, the hymn-like *ginans* are recorded mainly in the Khojki script.

hadith: a report, sometimes translated as Tradition, relating an action or saying of the Prophet. For the Shi'i communities, it also refers to the actions and sayings of their Imams. Muslims regard *hadith* as a source of Islamic law, second in importance only to the Qur'an.

haqa'iq (plural of *haqiqa, haqiqat*): truths; as a technical term it denotes the gnostic system of thought of the Ismailis. In this sense, the *haqa'iq* are the unchangeable truths contained in the *batin* (q.v.); while the law changes with every law-announcing prophet or *natiq* (q.v.), the *haqa'iq* remain eternal.

hudud (plural *hadd*): ranks; a technical term denoting the various ranks in the *da'wa* (q.v.) hierarchy of the Ismailis, also called *hudud al-din*.

hujja: proof or the presentation of proof. Amongst the Shi'is, the term has been used in different senses. Initially it meant the proof of God's presence or will and as such it referred to that person who at any given time served as evidence among mankind of God's will. In this sense, the application of the term was systematized by the Imami Shi'is to designate the category of prophets and Imams and, after the Prophet Muhammad, more particularly of the Imams. The original Shi'i application of the term *hujja* was retained by the pre-Fatimid Ismailis who also used *hujja* in reference to a dignitary in their religious hierarchy, notably one through whom the inaccessible Mahdi (q.v.) could become accessible to his adherents. The *hujja* was also a high rank in the *da'wa* (q.v.) hierarchy of the Fatimid Ismailis. In Nizari Ismaili *da'wa*, the term generally denoted the chief representative of the Imam, sometimes also called *pir* (q.v.)

ilhad: deviation from the right religious path; heresy in religion. The Ismailis and other Shi'i groups were often accused of *ilhad* by Sunni Muslims. A person accused of *ilhad* is called *mulhid* (plural *malahida*).

'ilm: knowledge, more specifically religious knowledge. Amongst the Shi'is, it was held that every Imam possessed a special secret knowledge, *'ilm*, which was divinely inspired and transmitted through the *nass* (q.v.) of the preceding Imam.

jama'atkhana: assembly house; congregation place, with a special prayer hall, used by the Nizari Ismailis for their religious and communal activities.

kalima: word; specifically the divine word, logos; a synonym of *kalimat Allah*.

kamadia: see *mukhi*.

kashf: manifestation, unveiling; in Ismaili doctrine, it is used specifically in reference to a period, called *dawr al-kashf*, when the Imams were manifest, or when the *haqa'iq* (q.v.) would be no longer concealed in the *batin* (q.v.), in distinction from *satr* (q.v.).

khawass (or *khassa*): the elite, the privileged people, in distinction from the *'awamm* (q.v.).

khutba: an address or sermon delivered (by a *khatib*) at the Friday midday public prayers in the mosque; since it includes a prayer for the ruler, mention in the *khutba* is a mark of sovereignty in Islam.

madhhab (plural *madhahib*): a system or school of religious law in Islam; in particular it is applied to the four main systems of *fiqh* that arose among the Sunni Muslims, namely, Hanafi, Maliki, Shafi'i and Hanbali, named after the jurists who founded them. Different Shi'i communities have had their own *madhahib*. In Persian the word *madhhab* is also used to mean religion, a synonym of *din*.

ma'dhun: literally, licentiate; a rank in the *da'wa* (q.v.) hierarchy of the Ismailis following that of the *da'i*. In the post-Fatimid period in particular, *ma'dhun* came to be used generically by the Ismailis in reference to the assistant of the *da'i*.

Mahdi: the rightly guided one; a name applied to the restorer of true religion and justice who, according to a widely held Muslim belief, will appear and rule before the end of the world. This name with its various messianic connotations has been applied to different individuals by Shi'is and Sunnis in the course of the centuries. Belief in the coming of the Mahdi of the family of the Prophet, *ahl al-bayt* (q.v.), became a central aspect of the faith in Shi'ism in contrast to Sunnism. In Shi'i terminology, at least from the 2nd/8th century, the Mahdi was commonly given the epithet *al-qa'im* (q.v.), 'riser', also called *qa'im al Muhammad*, denoting a member of the Prophet's family who would rise and restore justice on earth.

mukhi: a name originally used by the Indian Nizari Ismailis in reference to the head of the local Nizari community, *jama'at*, who officiated on various occasions in the local *jama'atkhana* (q.v.). The *mukhi*'s assistant was called *kamadia* (pronounced *kamriya*). The terms *mukhi* and *kamadia*, with various pronunciations, were in time adopted by the Nizari communities outside South Asia.

murid: disciple; specifically, disciple of a Sufi (q.v.) master; member of a Sufi order in general; also frequently used in reference to an ordinary Nizari Ismaili in Persia and elsewhere in the post-Alamut period.

mustajib: literally, respondent; a term denoting an ordinary Ismaili initiate or neophyte.

nass: explicit designation of a successor by his predecessor, particularly relating to the Shi'i view of succession to the Imamate, whereby each Imam, under divine guidance, designates his successor. The Tayyibi-Musta'li *da'i*s are also designated by the rule of the *nass*. One who has received the *nass* is called *mansus*.

natiq (plural *nutaqa'*): literally, speaker, one gifted with speech; in Ismaili thought, a speaking or law-announcing prophet who brings a new religious law (*shari'a*), abrogating the previous law and, hence, initiating a new *dawr* (q.v.) in the religious history of mankind.

pir: the Persian equivalent of the Arabic word *shaykh* (q.v.) in the sense of a spiritual guide, Sufi (q.v.) master or *murshid*, qualified to lead disciples, *murid*s (q.v.), on the mystical path, *tariqa* (q.v.), to truth (*haqiqa*); also used loosely in reference to the Imam and the holders of the highest ranks in the *da'wa* (q.v.) hierarchy of the post-Alamut Nizari Ismailis; also a chief Nizari *da'i* in a certain territory, in this sense it was particularly used by the Nizari Khojas in reference to the administrative heads of the *da'wa* in the Indian subcontinent.

qadi (plural *qudat*): a religious judge administering Islamic law, the *shari'a* (q.v.).

qadi al-qudat: chief *qadi*.

qa'im: 'riser'; the eschatological Mahdi (q.v.). In pre-Fatimid Ismailism, the terms Mahdi and *qa'im* were both used, as in Imami Shi'ism, for the expected messianic Imam. After the rise of the Fatimids, the name al-Mahdi was reserved for the first Fatimid Imam-Caliph, while the eschatological Imam and seventh *natiq* (q.v.) still expected for the future was called the *qa'im* by the Ismailis.

qasida: a poetic genre of a certain length, normally concerned with the eulogy of a personality; in Persian it is a lyric poem, most frequently panegyric.

qiyama: resurrection and the Last Day, when mankind would be judged and committed forever to either Paradise or Hell; in Ismaili thought, it also came to be used in reference to the end of any partial cycle in the history of mankind, with the implication that the entire hierohistory of mankind consisted of many such partial cycles and partial *qiyama*s, leading to the final *qiyama*, sometimes called *qiyamat al-qiyamat*. The Nizaris of the Alamut period interpreted the *qiyama* spiritually as the manifestation of the unveiled truth (*haqiqa*) in the spiritual reality of the current Imam, who was also called the *qa'im al-qiyama*.

risala (plural *rasa'il*): treatise, letter, epistle.

satr: concealment, veiling; in Ismaili thought, it is used specifically in reference to a period, called *dawr al-satr*, when the Imams were hidden from the eyes of their followers, or when the *haqa'iq* (q.v.) were concealed in the *batin* (q.v.), in distinction from *kashf* (q.v.).

shari'a (or *shar'*): the divinely revealed sacred law of Islam; the whole body of rules guiding the life of a Muslim. The provisions of the *shari'a* are worked out through the discipline of *fiqh*.

shaykh: old man, elder; any religious dignitary; in particular an independent Sufi (q.v.) master; in this sense called *pir* (q.v.) in Persian; *shaykh* (plural *mashayikh*) is also a high rank in the *da'wa* organization of the Da'udi Tayyibis.

Sufi: an exponent of Sufism (*tasawwuf*), the commonest term for that aspect of Islam which is based on the mystical life; hence, it denotes a Muslim mystic; more specifically, a member of an organized Sufi order, *tariqa* (q.v.).

tafsir: literally, explanation, commentary; particularly the commentaries on the Qur'an; the external, philological exegesis of the Qur'an, in distinction from *ta'wil* (q.v.).

ta'lim: teaching, instruction; in Shi'ism, authoritative teaching in religion which could be carried out only by an Imam in every age after the Prophet.

taqiyya: precautionary dissimulation of one's true religious beliefs, especially in time of danger; used widely by the Twelver (Ithna'ashari) and Ismaili Shi'is.

tariqa: way, path; the mystical spiritual path followed by Sufis (q.v.); also any one of the organized Sufi orders. It is also used by the Nizari Ismailis in reference to their interpretation of Islam.

ta'wil: the educing of the inner meaning from the literal wording or apparent meaning of a text or a ritual, religious prescription; as a technical term among the Shi'is, particularly the Ismailis, it denotes the method of educing the *batin* (q.v.) from the *zahir* (q.v.); as such it was extensively used by the Ismailis for the allegorical, symbolic or esoteric interpretation of the Qur'an, the *shari'a*, historical events and the world of nature. Translated also as spiritual or hermeneutic exegesis, *ta'wil* may be distinguished from *tafsir* (q.v.).

'ulama': see *'alim*.

umma: community, any people as followers of a particular religion or prophet; in particular, the Muslims as forming a religious community.

wasi (plural *awsiya'*): legatee, executor of a will; also the immediate successor to a prophet; in this sense, it was the function of *awsiya'* to interpret and explain the messages brought by prophets, *anbiya'*.

zahir: the outward, literal, or exoteric meaning of sacred texts and religious prescriptions, notably the Qur'an and the *shari'a* (q.v.), in distinction from the *batin* (q.v.).

Select Bibliography

Abdul Husain, Mian Bhai. *Gulzare Daudi for the Bohras of India*. Ahmedabad, 1920.
Abdulhussein, Mustafa. 'Burhanuddin, Sayyidna Muhammad', in *The Oxford Encyclopedia of the Modern Islamic World*, ed. John L. Esposito. Oxford, 1995, vol. 1, pp. 237–238.
___ *al-Dai al-Fatimi, Syedna Mohammed Burhanuddin: An Illustrated Biography*. London, 2001.
Adamji, Ebrahimjee Noorbhai. 'My Journeys to the Interior', in Cynthia Salvadori and Julia Aldrick, ed., *Two Indian Travellers: East Africa 1902–1905*. Mombasa, 1997, pp. 1–97.
Aga Khan III, Sultan Muhammad Shah. *India in Transition: A Study in Political Evolution*. Bombay and Calcutta, 1918.
___ *The Memoirs of Aga Khan: World Enough and Time*. London, 1954.
___ *Precious Pearls. Farman Mubarak Hazrat Imam Mowlana Sultan Mohammad Shah*. Karachi, n.d.
___ *Aga Khan III: Selected Speeches and Writings of Sir Sultan Muhammad Shah*, ed. K. K. Aziz. London, 1997–1998.
Aga Khan Award for Architecture. *Modernity and Community: Architecture in the Islamic World*. London, 2001.
___ *Architecture and Polyphony: Building in the Islamic World Today*. London, 2004.
Aga Khan Trust for Culture. *Historic Cities Programme: Karimabad and Baltit Project Development*. Geneva, 1996.
Ahmad, Aziz. *Studies in Islamic Culture in the Indian Environment*. Delhi, 1964.
___ *An Intellectual History of Islam in India*. Edinburgh, 1969.
___ *Islams and Modernities*. London, 1993.
Ahmed, Akbar. *Postmodernism and Islam: Predicament and Promise*. London, 1992.

Ahmed, Imtiaz. 'Exclusion and Assimilation in Indian Islam', in Attar Singh, ed., *Socio-cultural Impact of Islam on India*. Chandigarh, 1976, pp. 85–105.

Ahmed, Leila. *Women and Gender in Islam*. New Haven and London, 1992.

Ahmed, Rafiuddin. *The Bengal Muslims, 1871–1906: A Quest for Identity*. Delhi, 1981.

Aitken, E. H. *Gazetteer of the Province of Sindh*. Karachi, 1907; 2nd ed., Karachi, 1986.

Alexander, Christopher. *The Timeless Way of Building*. New York, 1979.

Algar, Hamid. 'The Revolt of Agha Khan Mahallati and the Transference of the Isma'ili Imamate to India', *Studia Islamica*, 29 (1969), pp. 61–81.

___ 'Mahallati, Agha Khan', *EI2*, vol. 5, pp. 1221–1222.

___ 'Aqa Khan', *EIR*, vol. 2, pp. 170–175.

Ali, Ameer. 'A Cry from the Indian Mahommedans', *The Nineteenth Century* (1882), pp. 193–215.

Ali, Hamid. 'The Customary and Statutory Law of the Muslims in India', *Islamic Culture*, 11 (1937), pp. 354–369, 444–454.

Ali, Mujtaba. *The Origins of the Khojahs and their Religious Life Today*. Bonn, 1936.

Amiji, Hatim M. 'The Asian Communities', in James Kritzeck and William H. Lewis, ed., *Islam in Africa*. New York, 1969, pp. 141–181.

___ 'Some Notes on Religious Dissent in Nineteenth-Century East Africa', *African Historical Studies*, 4 (1971), pp. 603–616.

Amin, Mahmud. *Ta'rikh Salamiyya fi khamsin qarn*. Damascus, 1983.

Amir-Moezzi, Mohammad Ali. *The Divine Guide in Early Shi'ism: The Sources of Esotericism in Islam*, tr. D. Streight. Albany, NY, 1994.

Anderson, James N. D. 'The Isma'ili Khojas of East Africa: A New Constitution and Personal Law for the Community', *Middle Eastern Studies*, 1 (1964), pp. 21–39.

___ *Islamic Law in Africa*. London, 1955; 2nd ed., London, 1970.

Appadurai, Arjun. *Modernity at Large: Cultural Dimensions of Globalization*. Minneapolis, MN, 1996.

Arkoun, Mohammed. *Rethinking Islam: Common Questions, Uncommon Answers*, tr. Robert D. Lee. Boulder, CO, 1994.

Arnould, Joseph. *Judgement of the Honourable Sir Joseph Arnould in the Khojah Case, otherwise known as the Aga Khan Case*. Bombay, 1867.

Asani, Ali S. 'The Khojki Script: A Legacy of Ismaili Islam in the Indo-Pakistan Subcontinent', *JAOS*, 107 (1987), pp. 439–449.

___ *The Bujh Niranjan: An Ismaili Mystical Poem*. Cambridge, MA, 1991.

___ *The Harvard Collection of Ismaili Literature in Indic Languages: A Descriptive Catalog and Finding Aid*. Boston, MA, 1992.

___ 'The Ismaili *ginans* as Devotional Literature', in R. S. McGregor, ed., *Devotional Literature in South Asia: Current Research, 1985–1988*. Cambridge, 1992, pp. 101–112.

___ 'Muslims in South Asia: Defining Community and the "Other"', *Bulletin of*

the *Royal Institute for Inter-faith Studies*, 2 (2000), pp. 103–113.
___ 'The Khojas of South Asia: Defining a Space of their Own', *Cultural Dynamics*, 13 (2001), pp. 155–168.
___ *Ecstasy and Enlightenment: The Ismaili Devotional Literature of South Asia*. London, 2002.
___ 'Isma'ili Muslim Americans', in *Encyclopedia of Muslim-American History*, ed. Edward E. Curtis IV. New York, 2010, vol. 1., pp. 303–305.
Al-Azmeh, Aziz. *Islams and Modernities*. London, 1993.
Bakari, Mohamed. 'Asian Muslims in Kenya', in Mohamed Bakari and Saad S. Yahaya, ed., *Islam in Kenya: Proceedings of the National Seminar on Contemporary Islam in Kenya*. Nairobi, 1995, pp. 58–63.
Barlas, Asma. *'Believing Women' in Islam: Unreading Patriarchal Interpretations of the Qur'an*. Austin, TX, 2002.
Barrès, Maurice. *Une enquête aux pays du Levant*. Paris, 1923.
Barrucand, Marianne, ed. *L'Égypte Fatimide, son art et son histoire*. Paris, 1999.
Basu, A. *The Growth of Education and Political Development in India, 1898–1920*. Delhi, 1974.
Batatu, Hana. *Syria's Peasantry, the Descendants of its Lesser Rural Notables and their Policies*. Princeton, 1999.
Bhabha, Homi. *The Location of Culture*. London, 1994.
Bianca, Stefano. *Urban Form in the Arab World: Past and Present*. London and New York, 2000.
___ , ed. *Karakoram: Hidden Treasures in the Northern Areas of Pakistan*. Geneva and Turin, 2005.
___ , ed. *Syria: Medieval Citadels between East and West*. Geneva and Turin, 2007.
Bianca, Stefano and Philip Jodidio, ed. *Cairo: Revitalising a Historic Metropolis*. Geneva and Turin, 2004.
Billimoria, N. M. *Bibliography of the Publications related to Sindh and Baluchistan*. 2nd ed., Lahore, 1977.
Blank, Jonah. *Mullahs on the Mainframe: Islam and Modernity among the Daudi Bohras*. Chicago, 2001.
Bliss, Frank. *Social and Economic Changes in the Pamirs*. London, 2006.
Bobrinskoy, Aleksey A. 'Secta Ismailiya v Ruskikh Bukharskikh Predelakh Sredniy Azii', *Etnograficheskoe Obozrenie*, 2 (1902), pp. 1–20.
Boivin, Michel. 'The Reform of Islam in Ismaili Shi'ism from 1885 to 1957', in Françoise 'Nalini' Delvoye, ed., *Confluence of Cultures: French Contributions to Indo-Persian Studies*. New Delhi, 1994, pp. 197–216.
___ 'New Problems Related to the History and to the Tradition of the Agakhani Khojahs in Karachi and Sindh', *Journal of the Pakistan Historical Society*, 46 (1998), pp. 5–33.
___ *La rénovation du Shi'isme Ismaélien en Inde et au Pakistan. D'après les écrits et les discours de Sultan Muhammad Shah Aga Khan (1902–1954)*. London, 2003.

___ 'Ginans and the Management of the Religious Heritage of the Ismaili Khojas in Sindh', in Tazim R. Kassam and F. Mallison, ed., *Ginans: Texts and Contexts, Essays on Ismaili Hymns from South Asia in Honour of Zawahir Moir*. New Delhi, 2007, pp. 25–53.

___ , ed. *Les Ismaéliens d'Asie du Sud*. Paris, 2007.

Bonnett, Alastair. *The Idea of the West: Culture, Politics and History*. New York, 2004.

Brennan, James. 'South Asian Nationalism in an East African Context: The Case of Tanganyika, 1914–1956', *Comparative Studies of South Asia, Africa and the Middle East*, 19 (1999), pp. 24–38.

Brett, Michael. *The Rise of the Fatimids: The World of the Mediterranean and the Middle East in the Fourth Century of the Hijra, Tenth Century CE*. Leiden, 2001.

Burckhardt, Titus. *Mirror of the Intellect: Essays on Traditional Science and Sacred Art*. Cambridge, 1987.

Burhanpuri, Qutb al-Din b. Sulaymanji. *Muntazaʿ al-akhbar*, vol. 2, partial ed. Samer F. Traboulsi. Beirut, 1999.

Burton, Richard F. *The Races that Inhabited the Valley of Indus*. Karachi. 1851; 2nd ed., Karachi, 1981.

___ *Zanzibar Island, City and Coast*. London, 1872.

Calder, Norman. 'Judicial Authority in Imami Shiʿi Jurisprudence', *Bulletin of the British Society for Middle Eastern Studies*, 6 (1979), pp. 104–108.

Capra, Fritjof. *The Web of Life*. London, 1996.

___ *The Hidden Connections*. London, 2003.

Chakrabarty, Dipesh. *Habitations of Modernity*. Chicago, 2002.

Chambon, Laurent. *Le Sel de la démocratie: l'accès des minorités au pouvoir politique en France et aux Pays-Bas*. Amsterdam, 2002.

Chevallier, Dominique, ed. *Les Arabes et l'histoire créatrice*. Paris, 1995.

Çinar, Alev. *Modernity, Islam, and Secularism in Turkey: Bodies, Places, and Time*. Minneapolis, MN, 2005.

Corbin, Henry. *En Islam Iranien. Aspects spirituels et philosophiques*. Paris, 1971–1972.

___ *Cyclical Time and Ismaili Gnosis*, tr. R. Mannheim and James W. Morris. London, 1983.

Cortese, Delia. *Ismaili and Other Arabic Manuscripts: A Descriptive Catalogue of Manuscripts in the Library of The Institute of Ismaili Studies*. London, 2000.

Cortese, Delia and Simonetta Calderini. *Women and the Fatimids in the World of Islam*. Edinburgh, 2006.

Daftary, Farhad. *The Ismaʿilis: Their History and Doctrines*. Cambridge, 1990; 2nd ed., Cambridge, 2007.

___ *The Assassin Legends: Myths of the Ismaʿilis*. London, 1994.

___ 'Hasan-i Sabbah and the Origins of the Nizari Ismaʿili Movement', in F. Daftary, ed., *Mediaeval Ismaʿili History and Thought*. Cambridge, 1996, pp. 181–204.

___ *A Short History of the Ismailis*. Edinburgh, 1998.
___ 'The Ismaili *Daʿwa* outside the Fatimid *Dawla*', in M. Barrucand, ed., *L'Égypte Fatimide, son art et son histoire*. Paris, 1999, pp. 29–43.
___ *Ismaili Literature: A Bibliography of Sources and Studies*. London, 2004.
___ *Ismailis in Medieval Muslim Societies*. London, 2005.
___ 'Religious Identity, Dissimulation and Assimilation: The Ismaili Experience', in Yasir Suleiman, ed., *Living Islamic History: Studies in Honour of Professor Carole Hillenbrand*. Edinburgh, 2010, pp. 47–61.
___ 'Shihab al-Din al-Husayni', *EI2*, vol. 9, p. 435.
___ 'Ṭayyibiyya', *EI2*, vol. 10, pp. 403–404.
___ 'Aga Khan', in *Encyclopedia of Muslim-American History*, ed. Edward E. Curtis IV. New York, 2010, vol. 1, pp. 25–26.
Daftary F. and Z. Hirji. *The Ismailis: An Illustrated History*. London, 2008.
Daftary, F., E. Fernea and A. Nanji, ed. *Living in Historic Cairo: Past and Present in an Islamic City*. London, 2010.
Dalton, Robert and Naznin Virji-Babul. 'Expressions of Cultural Identity in the Drawings of Two Ismaili Muslim Children', in T. Pelton, G. Reis and S. Stewart, ed., *Connections*. Victoria, BC, 2006, pp. 11–23.
van Dam, Nicolaos. *The Struggle for Power in Syria*. London, 1996.
de Smet, Daniel. 'Comment déterminer le début et la fin du jeûne de Ramadan? Un point de discorde entre Sunnites et Ismaéliens en Égypte Fatimide', in U. Vermeulen and D. de Smet, ed., *Egypt and Syria in the Fatimid, Ayyubid and Mamluk Eras*. Leuven, 1995, pp. 71–84.
Derrida, Jacques. *Writing and Difference*, tr. Alan Bass. London, 2004.
Dossa, Parin A. 'Women's Space and Time: An Anthropological Perspective on Ismaili Immigrant Women in Calgary and Vancouver', *Canadian Ethnic Studies*, 20 (1988), pp. 45–65.
___ 'Reconstruction of the Ethnographic Field Sites: Mediating Identities, Case Study of a Bohra Muslim Woman in Lamu (Kenya)', *Women's Studies International Forum*, 20 (1997), pp. 505–515.
Douwes, Dick. 'Tegenstellingen in noordwest Syrië in de periode 1840–1880 (Controversies in Northwestern Syria, 1840–1880)', *Sharqiyyat*, 2 (1989), pp. 47–64.
___ 'Knowledge and Oppression: The Nusayriyya in the Late Ottoman Period', in *La Shiʿa nell'impero ottomano*. Rome, 1993, pp. 149–169.
___ *The Ottomans in Syria: A History of Justice and Oppression*. London, 2000.
Douwes, Dick and Norman N. Lewis, 'The Trials of Syrian Ismaʿilis in the First Decade of the 20th Century', *International Journal of Middle East Studies*, 21 (1989), pp. 215–232.
Dumasia, Naoroji M. *A Brief History of the Aga Khan*. Bombay, 1903.
___ *The Aga Khan and his Ancestors*. Bombay, 1939.
Elias, T. O. 'The Evolution of Law and Government in Modern Africa', in H. Kuper and L. Kuper, ed., *African Law: Adaptation and Development*. Berkeley, 1965, pp. 184–195.

Emadi, Hafizullah. 'Breaking the Shackles: Political Participation of Hazara Women in Afghanistan,' *Asian Journal of Women's Studies*, 6 (2000), pp. 143–161.
___ 'Nahzat-e Nawin: Modernization of the Badakhshan Ismaili Communities of Afghanistan,' *Central Asian Survey*, 24 (2005), pp. 165–189.
Encyclopaedia Iranica, ed. E. Yarshater. London and New York, 1982–.
The Encyclopaedia of Islam, ed. H. A. R. Gibb et al. 2nd ed., Leiden, 1960–2004.
Engineer, Asghar Ali. *The Muslim Communities of Gujarat. An Exploratory Study of Bohras, Khojas and Memons*. Delhi, 1989.
___ *The Bohras*. New Delhi, 1980; rev. ed., New Delhi, 1993.
Enthoven, Reginald E. *The Tribes and Castes of Bombay*. Bombay, 1920–1922.
Esack, Farid. *On Being a Muslim: Finding a Religious Path in the World Today*. Oxford, 1999.
Esmail, Aziz. 'Islam and Modernity: Intellectual Horizons', in Azim Nanji, ed., *The Muslim Almanac*. Detroit, MI, 1996, pp. 483–487.
___ *The Poetics of Religious Experience: The Islamic Context*. London, 1998.
___ 'Introduction', in F. Daftary, ed., *Intellectual Traditions in Islam*. London, 2000, pp. 1–16.
___ *A Scent of Sandalwood: Indo-Ismaili Religious Lyrics (Ginans): Volume I*. Richmond, Surrey, 2002.
Euben, Roxanne L. *Enemy in the Mirror: Islamic Fundamentalism and the Limits of Modern Rationalism*. Princeton, 1999.
Fakhry, Majid. *A History of Islamic Philosophy*. 2nd ed., New York, 1983.
Forbes, Alexander. *Gujarat Ras-Mala: Hindoo Annals of the Province of Goozerat in Western India*, ed. H. G. Rawlinson. London, 1924.
Franke, Patrick. *Begegnung mit Khidr: Quellenstudien zum Imaginären im Traditionellen Islam*. Stuttgart, 2000.
Friedmann, Yohannan. *Prophecy Continuous: Aspects of Ahmadi Religious Thought and its Medieval Background*. Berkeley, 1989.
Frischauer, Willi. *The Aga Khans*. London, 1970.
Frye, Richard N. *The Heritage of Central Asia: From Antiquity to the Turkish Expansion*. Princeton, 1997.
Fulford, Robert. 'A Postmodern Dominion: The Changing Nature of Canadian Citizenship', in W. Kaplan, ed., *Belonging: The Meaning and Future of Canadian Citizenship*. Montreal, 1993, pp. 104–119.
Fyzee, Asaf A. A. 'A Chronological List of the Imams and Daʿis of the Mustaʿlian Ismailis', *Journal of the Bombay Branch of the Royal Asiatic Society*, New Series, 10 (1934), pp. 8–16.
___ *Outlines of Muhammadan Law*. 3rd ed., London, 1964.
___ *Cases in the Muhammadan Law of India and Pakistan*. Oxford, 1965.
___ 'The Study of the Literature of the Fatimid *Daʿwa*', in George Makdisi, ed., *Arabic and Islamic Studies in Honor of Hamilton A. R. Gibb*. Leiden, 1965, pp. 232–249.
___ *Compendium of Fatimid Law*. Simla, 1969.

Gardet, Louis. *La cité Musulmane*. Paris, 1954.

Gaudefroy-Demombynes, Maurice. *La Syrie à l'époque des Mamelouks, d'après les auteurs Arabes*. Paris, 1923.

Ghadially, Rehana. 'Daudi Bohra Muslim Women and Modern Education: A Beginning', *Indian Journal of Gender Studies*, 1 (1994), pp. 195-213.

___ 'Women Observances in the Calendrical Rites of the Daudi Bohra Ismaili Sect of South Asian Muslims', *Islamic Culture*, 77 (2003), pp. 1-21.

Ghalib, Mustafa. *Ta'rikh al-daʿwa al-Ismaʿiliyya*. Damascus, 1953; 2nd ed., Beirut, 1965.

___ *The Ismailis of Syria*. Beirut, 1970.

Gilroy, Paul. *The Black Atlantic: Modernity and Double Consciousness*. Cambridge, 1992.

Gitlin, Todd. 'Public Sphere or Public Sphericules?', in Tamar Liebes and James Curran, ed., *Media, Ritual, Identity*. London, 1998, pp. 168-175.

Gladney, Dru C. *Dislocating China: Reflections on Muslims, Minorities and Other Subaltern Subjects*. London, 2004.

Gray, John. *False Dawn: The Delusions of Global Capitalism*. London, 2002.

___ *Al Qaeda and What it Means to be Modern*. London, 2003.

Gregory, Robert G. *India and East Africa: A History of Race Relations within the British Empire 1890-1939*. Oxford, 1971.

Grunebaum, Gustave E. von, ed. *Unity and Variety in Muslim Civilization*. Chicago, 1955.

___ , ed. *Theology and Law in Islam*. Wiesbaden, 1971.

Gupta, Desh. 'South Asians in East Africa: Achievements and Discrimination', *South Asia*, 21 (1998), pp. 103-136.

Habermas, Jürgen. *The Structural Transformation of the Public Sphere: An Inquiry into a Category of Bourgeois Society*, tr. T. Burger. Cambridge, MA, 1991.

Halm, Heinz. *The Empire of the Mahdi: The Rise of the Fatimids*, tr. M. Bonner. Leiden, 1996.

___ 'The Ismaʿili Oath of Allegiance (ʿahd) and the "Sessions of Wisdom" (*majalis al-hikma*) in Fatimid Times', in F. Daftary, ed., *Mediaeval Ismaʿili History and Thought*. Cambridge, 1996, pp. 91-115.

___ *The Fatimids and their Traditions of Learning*. London, 1997.

___ *Die Kalifen von Kairo. Die Fatimiden in Ägypten 973-1074*. Munich, 2003.

Hardy, Peter. *Muslims of British India*. Cambridge, 1972.

Hart, W. E., ed. *Report of Cases Decided in the High Court of Bombay*. Rajkot, 1907.

Hobsbawm, Eric and Terence Ranger, ed. *The Invention of Tradition*. Cambridge, 1983.

Hodgson, Marshall G. S. 'The Ismaʿili State', in *The Cambridge History of Iran: Volume 5, The Saljuq and Mongol Periods*, ed. John A. Boyle. Cambridge, 1968, pp. 422-482.

Hollister, John N. *The Shiʿa of India*. London, 1953.

Holzwarth, Wolfgang. *Die Ismailiten in Nordpakistan*. Berlin, 1994.
Hourani, Albert. *Arabic Thought in the Liberal Age 1798–1939*. London, 1962.
Hughes, A. W. *Gazetteer of the Province of Sindh*. Karachi, 1876.
Hughes, Thomas B. *Memoirs on Sindh*. Karachi, 1855.
Hunsberger, Alice C. *Nasir Khusraw, The Ruby of Badakhshan: A Portrait of the Persian Poet, Traveller and Philosopher*. London, 2000.
Hunzai, Faquir M. 'A Living Branch of Islam: Ismailis of the Mountains of Hunza', *Oriente Moderno*, NS, 84 (2004), pp. 147–160.
Ibn al-Haytham, Abu 'Abd Allah Ja'far b. Ahmad. *Kitab al-munazarat*, ed. and tr. W. Madelung and Paul E. Walker as *The Advent of the Fatimids: A Contemporary Shi'i Witness*. London, 2000.
Idris 'Imad al-Din b. al-Hasan. *'Uyun al-akhbar wa-funun al-athar*; vol. 7, ed. Ayman Fu'ad Sayyid, with summary English trans. by Paul E. Walker and M. A. Pomerantz as *The Fatimids and their Successors in Yaman: The History of an Islamic Community*. London, 2002.
Inayatullah, Sohail and Gail Boxwell, ed. *Islam, Postmodernism and Other Futures: A Ziauddin Sardar Reader*. London, 2003.
Iskandarov, Bahadur I. *Vostochnaya Bukhara i Pamir v period presoedineniya Sredney Azii k Rosii*. Stalinabad, 1960.
Islam, Rafiqul. 'The Bengali Language Movement and the Emergence of Bangladesh', *Contributions to Asian Studies*, 11 (1978), pp. 142–152.
Ivanow, Wladimir. 'The Sect of Imam Shah in Gujarat', *Journal of the Bombay Branch of the Royal Asiatic Society*, New Series, 12 (1936), pp. 19–70.
___ *Brief Survey of the Evolution of Ismailism*. Leiden, 1952.
___ *Ismaili Literature: A Bibliographical Survey*. Tehran, 1963.
Jamal, Arif A. 'Principles in the Development of Ismaili Law', *Yearbook of Islamic and Middle Eastern Law*, 7 (2002), pp. 115–126.
Jani, Balvant. 'The Devotional Element in the Nasihats of the Bohra Writings in Gujarat', in A. W. Entwistle and F. Mallison, ed., *Studies in South Asian Devotional Literature*. Paris and New Delhi, 1988–1991, pp. 224–238.
Juwayni, 'Ala' al-Din 'Ata-Malik. *Ta'rikh-i jahan-gusha*, tr. John A. Boyle as *The History of the World-Conqueror*. Manchester and Cambridge, MA, 1958.
Kaiser, Paul J. *Culture, Transnationalism, and Civil Society: Aga Khan Social Service Initiatives in Tanzania*. Westport, CT, 1996.
Karamshoev, Dodikhudo. *Olimoni Soveti dar borayi Pomir*. Dushanbe, 1975.
Karim, Karim H. 'Relocating the Nexus of Citizenship, Heritage and Technology', *The Public: Journal of the European Institute for Communication and Culture*, 4 (1997), pp. 75–86.
___ 'Cyber-Utopia and the Myth of Paradise: Using Jacques Ellul's Work on Propaganda to Analyze Information Society Rhetoric', *Information, Communication and Society*, 4 (2001), pp. 1–22.
___ 'Public Sphere and Public Sphericules: Civic Discourse in Ethnic Media', in S. Ferguson and L. R. Shade, ed., *Civic Discourse and Cultural Politics in Canada*. Westport, CT, 2002, pp. 230–242.

___ 'Crescent Dawn in the Great White North: Muslim Participation in the Canadian Public Sphere', in Yvonne Haddad, ed., *Muslims in the West: From Sojourners to Citizens*. New York, 2002, pp. 262–277.
___ *Islamic Peril: Media and Global Violence*. Montreal, 2003.
___ 'Nation and Diaspora: Rethinking Multiculturalism in a Transnational Context', *International Journal of Media and Cultural Politics*, 2 (2006), pp. 267–282.
Kassam, Tazim R. *Songs of Wisdom and Circles of Dance: Hymns of the Satpanth Isma'ili Muslim Saint, Pir Shams*. Albany, NY, 1995.
___ 'The Aga Khan Development Network: An Ethic of Sustainable Development and Social Conscience', in Richard C. Foltz et al., ed., *Islam and Ecology: A Bestowed Trust*. Cambridge, MA, 2003, pp. 477–496.
___ 'Balancing Acts: Negotiating the Ethics of Scholarship and Identity', in José Ignacio Cabezón and Sheila G. Daveney, ed., *Identity and the Politics of Scholarship in the Study of Religion*. New York, 2004, pp. 133–161.
Keshavjee, Rafique H. *Mysticism and the Plurality of Meaning: The Case of the Ismailis of Rural Iran*. London, 1998.
Ketelbey, C. D. M. *A History of Modern Times*. 5th ed., New Delhi, 1973.
Khadur, Hisam. *Lamsat naqdiyya li-shu'ara' Salamiyya*. Salamiyya, 2000.
Khan, A. R. *The All-India Muslim Educational Conference: Its Contribution to the Cultural Development of Indian Muslims 1886–1947*. Oxford, 2001.
Khan, Dominique-Sila. *Conversions and Shifting Identities: Ramdev Pir and the Ismailis in Rajasthan*. New Delhi, 1997.
___ 'Diverting the Ganges: The Nizari Ismaili Model of Conversion in South Asia', in R. Robinson and S. Clarkes, ed., *Religious Conversions in India*. Delhi, 2003, pp. 29–53.
___ *Crossing the Threshold: Understanding Religious Identities in South Asia*. London and New York, 2004.
Khan, M. A. Muqtedar. *American Muslims: Bridging Faith and Freedom*. Beltsville, MD, 2002.
Kharyukov, Leonid N. *Anglo-Russkoe sopernichestvo v Tsentral'noy Azii i ismailizm*. Moscow, 1995.
___ *Istoriya Gorno-Badakhshanskoy Autonomnoy Oblasti*. Dushanbe, 2006.
King, Noel. 'Toward a History of the Isma'ilis in East Africa', in I. R. al-Faruqi, ed., *Essays in Islamic and Comparative Studies*. Washington DC, 1982, pp. 67–83.
al-Kirmani, Hamid al-Din Ahmad. *al-Masabih fi ithbat al-imama*, ed. and tr. Paul E. Walker as *Master of the Age: An Islamic Treatise on the Necessity of the Imamate*. London, 2007.
Klemm, Verena. *Memoirs of a Mission: The Ismaili Scholar, Statesman and Poet al-Mu'ayyad fi'l-Din al-Shirazi*. London, 2003.
Kohlberg, Etan. *Belief and Law in Imami Shi'ism*. Aldershot, 1991.
Kusno, Abidin. *Behind the Postcolonial: Architecture, Urban Space and Political Cultures in Indonesia*. London, 2000.

Lalu, Hashim. *Islam ain sanatan. Ilahu nur ya ishvari jot.* Hyerabad, 1926.

Lelyveld, D. *Aligarh's First Generation: Muslim Solidarity in British India.* Princeton, 1978.

Lerner, Daniel. *The Passing of Traditional Society: Modernizing the Middle East.* Glencoe, IL, 1958.

Lewis, Bernard. *The Assassins.* London, 1967.

Lewis, Norman N. 'The Isma'ilis of Syria Today', *Journal of the Royal Central Asian Society*, 39 (1952), pp. 69–77.

___ *Nomads and Settlers in Syria and Jordan, 1800–1980.* Cambridge, 1987.

Lokhandwalla, Sh. T. 'The Bohras, a Muslim Community of Gujarat', *Studia Islamica*, 3 (1955), pp. 117–135.

___ 'Islamic Law and Ismaili Communities (Khojas and Bohras)', in Sh. T. Lokhandwalla, ed., *India and Contemporary Islam: Proceedings of a Seminar.* Simla, 1971, pp. 379–397.

Lumbard, Joseph E. B, ed. *Islam, Fundamentalism, and the Betrayal of Tradition: Essays by Western Muslim Scholars.* Bloomington, IN, 2004.

Lyotard, Jean François. *The Postmodern Condition: A Report on Knowledge*, tr. G. Bennington and B. Massumi. Minneapolis, MN, 1984.

Madelung, Wilferd. 'Aspects of Isma'ili Theology: The Prophetic Chain and the God Beyond Being', in S. Hossein Nasr, ed., *Isma'ili Contributions to Islamic Culture.* Tehran, 1977, pp. 51–65; reprinted in W. Madelung, *Religious Schools and Sects in Medieval Islam.* London, 1985, article XVII.

___ 'Makramids', *EI2*, vol. 6, pp. 191–192.

al-Madju', Isma'il b. 'Abd al-Rasul. *Fahrasat al-kutub*, ed. 'Ali N. Munzavi. Tehran, 1966.

Malik, H. *Sir Sayyid Ahmad Khan and Muslim Modernization in India and Pakistan.* New York, 1980.

Mallison, Françoise. 'Hinduism as Seen by the Nizari Isma'ili Missionaries of Western India: The Evidence of the *Ginan*', in Günther D. Sontheimer and H. Kulke, ed., *Hinduism Reconsidered.* New Delhi, 1989, pp. 93–103.

___ 'Les chants *Garabi* de Pir Shams', in F. Mallison, ed., *Littératures médiévales de l'Inde du Nord.* Paris, 1991, pp. 115–138.

___ 'La secte Ismaélienne de Nizari ou Satpanthi en Inde. Hétérodoxie Hindoue ou Musulmane?', in Serge Bouez, ed., *Ascèse et renoncement en Inde ou la solitude bien-ordonnée.* Paris, 1992, pp. 105–113.

Mangat, J. S. *A History of the Asians in East Africa c.1886 to 1945.* Oxford, 1969.

Masov, R. M. et al., ed. *Ocherki po istorii Sovetskogo Badakhshana.* Dushanbe, 1985.

Masselos, James C. 'The Khojas of Bombay: The Defining of Formal Membership Criteria during the Nineteenth Century', in Imtiaz Ahmad, ed., *Caste and Social Stratification among Muslims in India.* New Delhi, 1973, pp. 1–20.

Mayo, Katherine. *Selections from Mother India*, ed. M. Sinha. New Delhi, 1998.

Menant, Dominique. 'Les Bohoras du Guzarate', *Revue du Monde Musulman*, 10 (1910), pp. 465–493.

___ 'Les Khodjas du Guzarate', *Revue du Monde Musulman*, 12 (1910), pp. 214-232, 406-424.
Mernissi, Fatima. *Women and Islam: An Historical and Theological Enquiry*. Oxford, 1991.
Metcalf, Barbara D. *Islamic Revival in British India: Deoband, 1860-1900*. Princeton, 1982.
___ 'India', in The *Oxford Encyclopedia of the Modern Islamic World*, ed. John L. Esposito. Oxford, 1995, vol. 2, pp. 188-195.
Millward, James A. *Eurasian Crossroads: A History of Xinjiang*. London, 2007.
Mirza, Nasseh A. *Syrian Ismailism*. Richmond, Surrey, 1997.
Misra, Satish C. *Muslim Communities of Gujarat*. Baroda, 1964.
Moir, Zawahir. 'Historical and Religious Debates amongst Indian Ismailis, 1840-1920', in Mariola Offredi, ed., *The Banyan Tree: Essays on Early Literature in New Indo-Aryan Languages*. New Delhi and Venice, 2000, vol. 1, pp. 131-153.
Moosa, Ebrahim. 'The Debts and Burdens of Critical Islam', in Omid Safi, ed., *Progressive Muslims: On Justice, Gender, and Pluralism*. Oxford, 2003, pp. 111-127.
al-Mu'ayyad fi'l-Din al-Shirazi, Abu Nasr Hibat Allah. *al-Majalis al-Mu'ayyadiyya*, vols. 1-3, ed. Hatim Hamid al-Din. Bombay and Oxford, 1975-2005; vols. 1 and 3, ed. M. Ghalib. Beirut, 1974-1984.
Muhammad 'Ali b. Mulla Jivabhai. *Mawsim-i bahar*. Lithograph, Bombay, 1301-1311/1884-1893.
Murison, William. *Zanzibar Protectorate Law Reports, Volume 1 (1868-1919)*. London, 1919.
al-Murtada, 'Abd Allah. *al-Falak al-dawwar fi sama' al-a'imma al-athar*. Aleppo, 1352/1933.
al-Nabulsi, 'Abd al-Ghani. *al-Haqiqa wa'l-majaz fi'l-rihla ila bilad al-Sham wa-Misr wa'l-Hijaz*, ed. Ahmad A. Huraydi. Cairo, 1987.
Nadwi, Abu Zafar. *'Iqd al-jawahir fi ahwal al-Bawahir*. Karachi, 1936.
Nafi, Basheer M. 'The Rise of Islamic Reformist Thought and its Challenge to Traditional Islam', in Suha Taji-Farouki and Basheer M. Nafi, ed., *Islamic Thought in the Twentieth Century*. London, 2004, pp. 28-60.
Nanji, Azim. 'Modernization and Change in the Nizari Ismaili Community in East Africa – A Perspective', *Journal of Religion in Africa*, 6 (1974), pp. 123-139.
___ *The Nizari Isma'ili Tradition in the Indo-Pakistan Subcontinent*. Delmar, NY, 1978.
___ 'Ritual and Symbolic Aspects of Islam in African Contexts', in Richard C. Martin, ed., *Islam in Local Contexts*. Leiden, 1982, pp. 102-109.
___ 'The Nizari Ismaili Muslim Community in North America: Background and Development', in Earle H. Waugh et al., ed., *The Muslim Community in North America*. Edmonton, AB, 1983, pp. 149-164.
___ '*Shari'at* and *Haqiqat*: Continuity and Synthesis in the Nizari Isma'ili

Muslim Tradition', in Katherine P. Ewing, ed., *Shariʿat and Ambiguity in South Asian Islam*. Berkeley, 1988, pp. 63–76.

___ 'Aga Khan', in *The Oxford Encyclopedia of the Islamic World*, ed. John L. Esposito. Oxford, 2009, vol. 1, pp. 63–65.

Nanji, Azim and Z. Hirji. 'Ismaʿilism. xvi. Modern Ismaʿili Communities', *EIR*, vol. 14, pp. 208–210.

Nanji, Azim and S. Niyozov. 'Silk Road: Crossroads and Encounters of Faiths', in *The Silk Road: Connecting Cultures, Creating Trust*. Washington DC, 2002, pp. 37–43.

Nasr, Seyyed Hossein. *Traditional Islam in the Modern World*. London, 1987.

___ *Ideals and Realities of Islam*. New rev. ed., Cambridge, 2001.

Needleman, Jacob, ed. *The Sword of Gnosis: Metaphysics, Cosmology, Tradition, Symbolism*. Baltimore, MD, 1974.

al-Nuʿman b. Muhammad, al-Qadi Abu Hanifa. *Daʿaʾim al-Islam*, ed. Asaf A. A. Fyzee. Cairo, 1951–1961. English trans., A. A. A. Fyzee, completely revised by Ismail K. Poonawala, as *The Pillars of Islam*. New Delhi, 2002–2004.

___ *Iftitah al-daʿwa*, ed. W. al-Qadi. Beirut, 1970; ed. F. Dachraoui. Tunis, 1975. English trans., *Founding the Fatimid State: The Rise of an Early Islamic Empire*, tr. H. Haji. London, 2006.

___ *Taʾwil al-daʿaʾim*, ed. M. Hasan al-Aʿzami. Cairo, 1967–1972.

Paz, Octavio. *Convergences*. New York, 1987.

Peletz, Michael G. *Islamic Modern: Religious Courts and Cultural Politics in Malaysia*. Princeton, 2002.

Penrad, Claude. 'La presénce Ismaʿilienne en Afrique de l'Est: note sur l'histoire commerciale et l'organisation communautaire', in D. Lombard and J. Aubin, ed., *Marchands et hommes d'affaires Asiatiques dans l'Océan Indien et la Mer de Chine 13e–20e siècles*. Paris, 1988, pp. 221–236.

Perry, Erskine. *Cases Illustrative of Oriental Life: The Application of English Law in India*. New Delhi, 1853; 2nd ed., New Delhi, 1988.

Pirumshoev, H. S. and A. H. Dani. 'The Pamirs, Badakhshan and the Trans-Pamir States', in *History of Civilizations of Central Asia: Volume V, Development in Contrast: From the Sixteenth to the Mid-nineteenth Century*, ed. Ch. Adle et al. Paris, 2003, pp. 225–246.

Poonawala, Ismail K. *Biobibliography of Ismaʿili Literature*. Malibu, CA, 1977.

___ 'Al-Qadi al-Nuʿman and Ismaʿili Jurisprudence', in F. Daftary, ed., *Mediaeval Ismaʿili History and Thought*. Cambridge, 1996, pp. 117–143.

___ 'Sulaymanis', *EI2*, vol. 9, p. 829.

Qorban, Shrin. *Zhongguo Tajikliri (Tajiks in China)*. Urumqi, 1994.

___ *Zhong guo Tajike shi liao hui bian (Historical Sources Concerning Tajiks of China)*. Xinjiang, 2003.

Qudrat Allah Beg. *Taʾrikh-i ʿahd ʿatiq-i riyasat-i Hunza*. Baltit, 1980.

Qutbuddin, Tahera. *Al-Muʾayyad al-Shirazi and Fatimid Daʿwa Poetry: A Case of Commitment in Classical Arabic Literature*. Leiden, 2005.

___ 'Arabic in India: A Survey and Classification of its Uses, Compared with

Persian', *JAOS*, 127, 3 (2007), pp. 315–338.

Rahman, Fazlur. *Islam and Modernity: Transformation of an Intellectual Tradition*. Chicago, 1982.

Rahman, Tariq. *Language and Politics in Pakistan*. Karachi, 1996.

Ramadan, Tariq. *Islam, the West and the Challenges of Modernity*, tr. S. Amghar. Leicester, 2001.

___ *Western Muslims and the Future of Islam*. Oxford, 2004.

Roberts, Richard and Kristin Mann. 'Law in Colonial Africa', in K. Mann and R. Roberts, ed., *Law in Colonial Africa*. London, 1991, pp. 1–48.

Ross-Sheriff, Fariyal and A. Nanji. 'Islamic Identity, Family and Community: The Case of the Nizari Ismaili Muslims', in Earle H. Waugh et al., ed., *Muslim Families in North America*. Edmonton, AB, 1991, pp. 101–117.

Roy, Olivier. *The New Central Asia: The Creation of Nations*. New York, 2000.

Roy, Shibani. *The Dawoodi Bohras: An Anthropological Perspective*. Delhi, 1984.

Ruthven, Malise. *Islam: A Very Short Introduction*. Oxford, 1997.

___ 'Aga Khan III and the Isma'ili Renaissance', in Peter B. Clarke, ed., *New Trends and Developments in the World of Islam*. London, 1998, pp. 371–395.

Safi, Omid, ed. *Progressive Muslims: On Justice, Gender, and Pluralism*. Oxford, 2003.

Salam, Hayat, ed. *Expressions of Islam in Buildings*. Geneva, 1991.

Salvadori, Cynthia. *Through Open Doors: A View of Asian Cultures in Kenya*. Nairobi, 1989.

Sanders, Paula. 'The Fatimid State, 969–1171', in M. W. Daly, ed., *The Cambridge History of Egypt:* Volume 1, *Islamic Egypt, 640–1517*, ed. Carl F. Petry. Cambridge, 1998, pp. 151–174, 560–561.

___ 'Bohra Architecture and the Restoration of Fatimid Culture', in M. Barrucand, ed., *L'Égypte Fatimide, son art et son histoire*. Paris, 1999, pp. 159–165.

Sayyid, Ayman Fu'ad. *al-Dawla al-Fatimiyya fi Misr*. 2nd ed., Cairo, 2000.

Scarcia Amoretti, Biancamaria. 'Controcorrente? Il caso della communità Khogia di Zanzibar', *Oriente Moderno*, NS, 14 (1995), pp. 153–170.

Schimmel, Annemarie. *Islam in the Indian Subcontinent*. Leiden, 1980.

___ *Islam: An Introduction*. Albany, NY, 1992.

Serjeant, Robert B. 'The Fatimi-Tayyibi (Ismaili) Da'wah: Ideologies and Community', in Dominique Chevallier, ed., *Les Arabes et l'histoire créatrice*. Paris, 1995, pp. 59–77.

Shackle, Christopher and Zawahir Moir. *Ismaili Hymns from South Asia: An Introduction to the Ginans*. London, 1992.

Sharabi, Hisham. 'Islam and Modernization in the Arab World', in J. H. Thompson and R. D. Reischauer, ed., *Modernization of the Arab World*. Princeton, 1966, pp. 26–36.

Sheriff, A. *Slaves, Spices and Ivory in Zanzibar*. 2nd ed., London, 1990.

Sheriff, A. and E. Ferguson, ed. *Zanzibar under Colonial Rule*. London, 1991.

Shihab al-Din Shah al-Husayni. *Khitabat-i 'aliya*, ed. H. Ujaqi. Tehran, 1963.

Shodan, Amrita. 'Legal Formulation of the Question of Community: Defining the Khoja Collective', *Indian Social Science Review*, 1 (1999), pp. 137–151.

___ *A Question of Community: Religious Groups and Colonial Law.* Calcutta, 2001.

___ 'The Entanglement of the Ginans in Khoja Governance', in Tazim R. Kassam and F. Mallison, ed., *Ginans: Texts and Contexts.* New Delhi, 2007, pp. 169–180.

Singh, R. P. *Education in an Imperial Colony.* New Delhi, 1979.

Smith, Wilfred C. *Islam in Modern History.* Princeton, 1957.

Stern, Samuel M. 'The Succession to the Fatimid Imam al-Amir, the Claims of the Later Fatimids to the Imamate, and the Rise of Tayyibi Ismailism', *Oriens*, 4 (1951), pp. 193–255; reprinted in S. M. Stern, *History and Culture in the Medieval Muslim World.* London, 1984, article XI.

Stowasser, Barbara F. *Women in the Qur'an: Traditions and Interpretation.* New York, 1994.

Tajddin Sadik Ali, Mumtaz Ali. *Ismailis through History.* Karachi, 1997.

___ *101 Ismaili Heroes.* Karachi, 2003.

Tamir, 'Arif. 'Furu' al-shajara al-Isma'iliyya al-Imamiyya', *al-Mashriq*, 51 (1957), pp. 581–612.

___ *Muraja'at Isma'iliyya.* Beirut, 1994.

al-Tawil, Muhammad. *Ta'rikh al-'Alawiyyin.* Latakiya, 1924.

Thorpe, C. L. *Education and the Development of Muslim Nationalism in Pre-partition India.* Karachi, 1965.

Toorawa, Shawkat. 'Tahir Sayf al-Din', *EI2*, vol. 10, pp. 103–104.

Turner, Bryan S. *Orientalism, Postmodernism and Globalism.* London, 1994.

al-Tusi, Nasir al-Din Muhammad b. Muhammad. *Rawda-yi taslim*, ed. and tr. S. J. Badakhchani as *Paradise of Submission: A Medieval Treatise on Ismaili Thought.* London, 2005.

Tyabjee, Husayn Badr al-Din. *Why Mussalmans Should Oppose Pakistan.* Bombay, 1946.

al-'Utaybi Abu 'Abd al-Malik Ahmad, *Dahaqinat al-Yaman: Tahqiqat wa mutala'at fi milaff al-Isma'iliyya.* Amman, 2002.

Utvik, Bjorn O. 'The Modernising Force of Islam', in John L. Esposito and Francois Burgat, ed., *Modernising Islam: Religion in the Public Sphere in the Middle East and Europe.* London, 2003, pp. 43–67.

van den Berg, Gabrielle R. *Minstrel Poetry from the Pamir Mountains: A Study on the Songs and Poems of the Isma'ilis of Tajik Badakhshan.* Wiesbaden, 2004.

Vassanji, M. G. *The In-Between World of Vikram Lall.* Scarborough, ON, 2003.

Viswanathan, Gauri. *Outside the Fold: Conversion, Modernity and Belief.* New York, 1998.

Wadud, Amina. *Qur'an and Women.* Kuala Lumpur, 1994.

Walker, Paul E. *Abu Ya'qub al-Sijistani: Intellectual Missionary.* London, 1996.

___ 'Fatimid Institutions of Learning', *Journal of the American Research Center in Egypt*, 34 (1997), pp. 179–200; reprinted in his *Fatimid History*, article I.

___ 'The Isma'ili Da'wa and the Fatimid Caliphate', in M. W. Daly, ed., *The Cambridge History of Egypt:* Volume 1, *Islamic Egypt, 640–1517*, ed. Carl F. Petry. Cambridge, 1998, pp. 120–150, 557–560.
___ *Exploring an Islamic Empire: Fatimid History and its Sources.* London, 2002.
___ *Fatimid History and Ismaili Doctrine.* Aldershot, 2008.
___ 'Institute of Ismaili Studies', *EIR*, vol. 13, pp. 164–166.
Wasfi, Zakariya. 'Salamiyya', *al-Insaniyya*, 3 (1933), pp. 601–610, and 4 (1934), pp. 17–27.
___ *Jawlat athariyya fi ba'd al-bilad al-Shamiyya.* Damascus, 1934.
Weber, Max. *The Theory of Social and Economic Organization*, tr. A. M. Henderson and Talcott Parsons. New York, 1947.
Weulersse, Jacque. *Le pays des Alaouites.* Tours, 1940.
Willey, Peter. *Eagle's Nest: Ismaili Castles in Iran and Syria.* London, 2005.
Winter, Stefan. 'The Nusayris before the Tanzimat in the Eyes of Ottoman Provincial Administrators, 1804–1834', in T. Philipp and C. Schumann, ed., *From the Syrian Land to the States of Syria and Lebanon.* Beirut, 2004, pp. 97–112.
Wright, Theodore P. 'Muslim Kinship and Modernization: The Tyabji Clan of Bombay', in Imtiaz Ahmad, ed., *Family, Kinship and Marriage among Muslims in India.* New Delhi, 1976, pp. 217–238.
Zamiri, Atikem and Shrin Qorban. *Tajik Adibiyati Tarihi (History of Tajik Literature).* Urumqi, 2005.

Index

Main entries are arranged alphabetically and the sub-headings are arranged thematically rather than alphabetically. The Arabic definite article 'al-' is ignored for the purposes of alphabetization. The abbreviation 'b.' for ibn ('son of') is alphabetized as written.

Abbasids 1, 2, 252, 253
'Abd al-Husayn Husam al-Din, Da'udi *da'i*, 301
'Abd al-Husayn Jeeva-ji, founder of Mahdibaghwalas 312, 314
'Abd Allah Badr al-Din, Da'udi *da'i* 301, 315–16, 319
'Abd al-Qadir Najm al-Din, Da'udi *da'i* 300–1, 311, 312–13, 324, 341
'Abd al-Rahman, King of Afghanistan 58
'Abd al-Tayyib Zaki al-Din, 'Alavi Bohra *da'i* 357
'Abd 'Ali Sayf al-Din, Da'udi *da'i* 297–8, 299–300, 309, 320, 321–2, 339–41
Abu 'Abd Allah al-Khadim, Ismaili *da'i* 47
Abu 'Ali al-Mansur al-Amir bi-Ahkam Allah *see* al-Amir, Fatimid caliph
Abu Tamim Ma'add al-Mu'izz li-Din Allah *see* al-Mu'izz, Fatimid caliph
Abu'l-Hasan Khan, Sardar, brother of Aga Khan I,
access 161–2
  education 178

adaptation
  Ismailis 69–70
  Ismailism 95
administration
  Bohras, Bohoras 306, 318–26, 345–8, 347
  centralization 321–3
  Nizaris 11
  Pamir 53–4
  reforms 304
  Salamiyya 30–1
Afghanistan
  Aga Khan Development Network (AKDN) 71
  Aga Khan Fund for Economic Development (AKFED), 211
  Aga Khan Trust for Culture (AKTC) 72
  Aga Khan I 7
  British invasion of,
  exchanges 121
  migration 69
  Nizari Ismailis 45, 57–61
  refugees from 265
  Roshan telecom Development Company 211
  Soviet occupation 61
Afghans 51
Africa 130, 189, 195, 208, 209, 213–14 *see also* East Africa
Aga Khan 6
Aga Khan Academies 197–8

381

Aga Khan Agency for Microfinance
  (AKAM) 203–4, 261
Aga Khan Award for Architecture 189,
  214, 222–4
Aga Khan Case of 1866 106, 107, 115, 134,
  135–6
Aga Khan Development Network
  (AKDN)
  activities 218
  Afghanistan 61, 71
  built environment 221
  Constitution of the Shia Imami Ismaili
    Muslims, The 122
  development 11, 70–2
  established 219
  exchanges 120–1
  Global Centre for Pluralism, Ottawa
    284, 286–7
  growth 189
  Islamabad 69
  modernization 284
  Pakistan 109
  School Improvement Programmes
    (Sips) 195
  Tajikistan, Central Asia 57
  transnationalization 266
  women 261
Aga Khan Education Services (AKES) 70,
  193, 248, 261
Aga Khan Foundation (AKF) 57, 71, 196,
  205, 261–2, 284
Aga Khan Fund for Economic
  Development (AKFED), 203, 207–13,
  209–10, 211–13, 214, 261
  Aga Khan Development Network
    (AKDN) 189
Aga Khan Health Services (AKHS) 70,
  193, 212, 248, 261
Aga Khan I, Hasan 'Ali Shah, Nizari
  Imam 6–7, 60, 105, 130, 132, 134, 139
Aga Khan II, Aqa 'Ali Shah, Nizari Imam
  81, 85–6
Aga Khan III, Sultan Muhammad Shah,
  Nizari Imam 9, 26–7, 38
  Bombay 26
  Bombay (Mumbai) 258–9
  communications 38
  court case 106
  Dual System of education 170

economic development 70
education 166, 174–5, 180–3, 260
female education 176, 256–7
Golden Jubilee 117
Great Game 50
India in Transition 167–8, 251–2
modernization 284, 287
Mombasa, Kenya 259
recognition as Imam 19, 31, 37
Recreation Club Institute 117
religious reforms 110
religious traditions 63–4, 95
schools 192
struggle 267
Supreme Council for Africa 146
Aga Khan IV, Prince Karim, Nizari Imam
  10, 208
  Aga Khan Development Network
    (AKDN) 189
  Canada 266
  Constitution of the Shia Imami Ismaili
    Muslims, The 39
  economic development 70
  exchanges 120–1
  Institute of Ismaili Studies, London
    199
  Living Imam 190–1
  media coverage 285
  modernization 284
  Nizaris xiii
  religious reforms 110, 130–1
  visits Pakistan 64
  visits Tajikistan 71
  vists Canada 281–2
  women 247, 260
  Xinjiang, China 81
Aga Khan IV, Shah Karim al-Husayni,
  Nizari Imam *see* Aga Khan IV
Aga Khan Case (1866) 106, 115, 134, 135,
  138, 141, 144
Aga Khan Museum, Toronto 190, 285
Aga Khan Music Initiative 71, 189–90
Aga Khan Programme for Islamic
  Architecture 222
Aga Khan Rural Support Programme
  (ARSP) 70, 201–7, 204–5, 206
Aga Khan schools 171
Aga Khan Trust for Culture (AKTC),
  Geneva

Aga Khan Development Network
  (AKDN) 190
 built environment 221, 222–4
 Canada 281
 Central Asia 71–2
 conservation 215–17
 cultural heritage 242–3
 al-Darb al-Ahmar project 231
 founded 12
 Stone Town, Zanzibar 210
 women 261
Aga Khan University (AKU), Karachi 11,
  71, 198–9, 212, 261
Aga Khan University Hospital 214
Aga Khans 119
Agha Khan I, Hasan 'Ali Shah, Nizari
  Imam *see* Aga Khan I
Agha Khan Mahallati *see* Aga Khan I
Ahmad al-Jundi 39
Ahmad al-Muhammad al-Hajj, Shaykh
  27
Ahmad, Aziz 103
Ahmad Khan, Sir Sayyid 163–4, 166–7
Ahmad Shah Mas'ud 59
Ahmed, Akbar 275
Ahmed, Imtiaz 104–5
Ahmed, Leila 254–5
alam 84
Alamut 4, 5, 12
'Alavi ('Alya), subgroup of Da'udi Bohras
  xiii, 355
'Alavi Bohras 4
Alawis 21, 23, 29–30, 32, 35
Alawis and Ismailis 25
Alawiyya 21
Aleppo, in northern Syria 217, 231
'Ali b. Abi Talib, Imam 1, 24, 333
'Ali b. Ibrahim, founder of the 'Alavi
  subgroup of Da'udi Bohras 355
'Ali 'Idu, Shaykh 39
Aligarh, University of
 converted to university status 167, 177,
  192
 educational reforms 163
 founded 164
 higher education 173
 Islam 179
 Tahir Sayf al-Din, Da'udi *da'i* 343
All-India Muhammadan Educational
  Conference (1902) 167, 252–3
All-India Muhammadan Educational
  Conference (1911) 176
All-India Muhammadan Educational
  Conference (1936) 181
allegiance 121, 334, 335–6
Aly Khan, Prince, son of Aga Khan III
  and father of Aga Khan IV 38
Aman Allah, King of Afghanistan 58, 60
America(s) 61, 69, 129 *see also* United
  States of America
'amil, Da'udi functionary 347
al-Amir, Fatimid caliph 297
Amir Isma'il 28–9
Amir Muhammad b. Haydar al-Baqir,
  Muhammad-Shahi Nizari Imam 29
Anglo-Indian case law 136–9, 140
Anjudan 6
Aqa 'Ali Shah *see* Aga Khan II
Aqa Qadamgoh (footprints of the Aga
  Khan) 85–6
Arabic (language) 121, 320, 338
architecture and development 217–18,
  223, 224–5, 238, 307
ArchNet 222
Area Development Projects 226
'Arif Tamir 26, 36
Ariya Samaj, group of Hindu reformists
  104
Arnould, Sir Joseph 135
Asani, Ali 280
Assassin Legends 5
Australia 265
authority
 'Abd 'Ali Sayf al-Din, Da'udi *da'i* 322
 Aga Khan I, Hasan 'Ali Shah, Nizari
  Imam 105–6
 decentralization 274
 Imam 333
 Ismaili rule books 152–3
 khalifa 55–6
 Khojas 97
 limitations 317
 pirs 54, 69
 Reformist Bohras 318
 Tahir Sayf al-Din, Da'udi *da'i* 316–17
 traditions 276
auto-poïesis 234–5
al-Azhar Park 216, 225–6, 229

al-Azhar University 307, 343
al-Azmeh, Aziz 276

Bachat Yojna 320
Badakhshan
  Afghanistan 57
  Autonomous Region 54
  Ismailis 53–7
  Nasir-i Khusraw 48
  Nizari Ismailis 47
  Nizaris of 45
  occupation 58
  political structure 49
  Roshan telecom Development
    Company 212
Baghlan 212
Bahrayn 1–2
Baltistan, Pakistan 61–4
Baltit Fort, Karimabad, northern Pakistan
  216, 225, 227
Bangladesh 265
Barlas, Asma 255
Baroda, (Vadodara), Gujarat 356, 357
Batinis, Batiniyya 96, 284
Bhabha, Homi 276
Bhakti tradition 100
Bharuch 206
Bhatia caste 98
Blank, Jonah 332
Blommaert, Jan 131
Bobrinskoy, Count Aleksey A. 49
Bohras, Bohoras
  affluence 308
  Bombay (Mumbai) 302–3
  British Raj 309–10
  Da'udi (Dawoodi) 297
  Da'udi-Sulaymani split 355
  diaspora 308
  ideology 311
  intermarriage 307
  internal dissent 311–12
  internal dynamics 318–26
  as minority community 308
  pan-Islamic associations 310
  partition 305
  public identity 305
  religious education 344–5
  secession 312
  Tayyibi Musta'lians xiii

Yemen 323–4
Boivin, Michel 114
Bombay High Court 134, 138, 139–40,
  315
Bombay Legislative Council *see* Imperial
  Legislative Council
Bombay (Mumbai)
  Aga Khan I, Hasan 'Ali Shah, Nizari
    Imam 7, 105
  Aga Khan III, Sultan Muhammad
    Shah, Nizari Imam 64, 258
  Aga Khans at 105
  elections 310
  Great Game 50
  Imams 26
  immigration to 319
  Khoja Law Commission 148
  library 343
  literature 332
  Prince Aly Khan Hospital 193
  Progressive Bohras 317
  riots 109
  Sayfi Hospital 320
  Tahir Sayf al-Din, Da'udi *da'i* 298, 302
Brethren of Purity *see* Ikhwan al-Safa'
British Raj
  Aga Khan I, Hasan 'Ali Shah, Nizari
    Imam 7, 105
  Bohras, Bohoras 297, 309
  East Africa 129–30
  education 162
  Ismailis 132–6
  Khojas 103, 107
  mass education 169
  nationalism 97
  policies 135
  religion 102
  Surat, Gujarat 319
  Tahir Sayf al-Din, Da'udi *da'i* 305
Buddhism 45
built environment 221, 222–4, 232–8, 243
Bujh Niranjan, South Asian Sufi work
  99–100
Bukhara, Uzbekistan 53
Burhanpur Dargah Case 302, 315–16
Burhanpur Hakimiyya School 316
Burhanpuri, Qutb al-Din b. Sulaymanji,
  Da'udi author 340–1
Burma 319

Burundi 129

Cairo 216, 225–6, 228, 305, 325, 333
Calgary, Canada 265, 279
Cameron, Sir Donald Charles 145
Canada
    Bohras, Bohoras 319
    ex-colony 277
    immigration to 265–6
    Ismaili communities 265, 270, 277–9
    multiculturalism 286, 287
    Nizari Ismailis 45
    postmodernism 267
Canadian Ismailis 279, 280, 285, 286, 287, 288
capacity development 208, 213, 242
castes and religions 147–8
Central Asia *see also* Badakhshan
    adaptation 69–70
    Aga Khan Development Network (AKDN) 70–2, 189
    Aga Khan Fund for Economic Development (AKFED), 209
    control 48
    fragmentation 50, 52
    Historic Cities Programme (HCP) 231
    history of Ismailis 46
    Ismaili *da'wa* 3
    isolation 50, 68–9
    mazars, shrines 85
    Nizari Ismailis 45
    oral traditions 65–6
    Panjtani (five bodies) 66
    School Improvement Programmes (Sips) 193, 194–5
    traditions 64–9
    visits by Imam 65
Central Asian Music Initiative 189–90
Ceylon 305, 318
Chandabhai Gulla Case 301, 315
Charagh-nama 67
Charogh Rawshan, rite for the dead in Badakhshan 56, 63, 65, 67–8, 88
China 45, 77, 81, 90–1, 319
Chitral, northern Pakistan 45, 61–4, 201, 205
Choryori (four friends) 66
Chunara, 'Ali Muhammad 117–18
    Ismaili, The 117

Çinar, Alev 275
civil society 71, 276, 285
civil war 57, 59, 69
coastal Syria 21–4
colonial policy 162–7
colonial powers 48–52
colonialism 102–8, 129, 238, 271
commerce 318
communal governance 146–53
communications 26, 37–8, 64, 80–1, 325
Communism 81
Congo 129
conscription 31, 58
conservation
    Aga Khan Award for Architecture 223
    Aga Khan Trust for Culture (AKTC) 215–17
    built environment 232, 234
    Historic Cities Programme (HCP) 225
    Hunza 227
    tourism 210–11
Constitution of the Shia Imami Ismaili Muslims, The 11, 39, 121–2, 247
Constitution, Rules & Regulations of His Highness the Agakhan Ismailia Councils of Africa, The 146
Constitution, Rules and Regulations of His Highness Aga Khan Shia Imami Ismailia Councils of Africa, The 146–7
constitutions 110–11
Contractor, Noman 317
control
    'Abd 'Ali Sayf al-Din, Da'udi *da'i* 322
    Central Asia 48
    development 240
    education 165, 168, 172, 178
    Ismaili Khojas 8
councils 11, 110
Court of Appeal for East Africa 140
Crusaders 5
cultivation 30
cultural development 223, 242
cultural heritage 215, 231, 232, 242–3, 287
cultural identity 221, 225, 238, 324
Cultural Revolution, China 82
Curzon, George N., Viceroy of India 165, 169, 173, 179, 184n9
customary law 134–5, 138, 141–2, 145

Daʿaʾim al-Islam, of al-Qadi al-Nuʿman 335
daʿi (summoner)
  Tayyibi 297, 305, 325
al-daʿi al-mutlaq
  Daʾudi Bohras 298, 334
  nass (designation) 302
  Sulaymani 355
  Tayyibi 298
Dar al-ʿIlm (House of Knowledge), Cairo 3
Dar es Salaam, Tanzania 145, 150, 171, 193
al-Darb al-Ahmar, district in Cairo 216, 228–31
darwiza 84
Das Avatara, ginan 99, 116
Daʾud b. Qutb Shah, first Daʾudi *daʿi* 331
Daʾudi (Dawoodi) 4, 297, xiii
Daʾudis, Daʾudiyya, branch of Tayyibis 298, 306, 331, 355 *see also* Bohras, Bohoras
daʿwa (Persian, *daʿwat*) 1, 2, 4, 304
  Chitral, Pakistan 63
  Daʾudi 304
  Fatimid 307
  Hunza 63
  Nizari 56
  poetry 67
  Sulaymani 355
  Tayyibi 306–8, 317
al-daʿwa al-hadiya (the rightly guiding mission), 1, 333
daʿwat see daʿwa
dawla 2
Delegation of the Ismaili Imamat 284
Delhi 231
democracy 252
Deoband, in India 163, 173
development
  Aga Khan Development Network (AKDN) 219
  Aga Khan Rural Support Programme 201, 204
  Aga Khan University (AKU), Karachi 198
  Badakhshan 71
  Bohras, Bohoras 318–26
  built environment 221, 225, 232

civil society 276
conservation 234
  Ismailis 69–70
  women 252
development agencies 189
devotional life 113–17
devotional literature 113–17, 119
al-Dhuʿayb b. Musa al-Wadiʿi al-Hamdani, first Tayyibi *daʿi mutlaq* 334
Diamond Jubilee 192
Diamond Jubilee Investment Trust Company (DJIT) 208
Diamond Trust Bank (DTB) 209
diaspora 137, 308
dispensaries 193
dissidents 313–14, 314–16
diversity 95, 199, 277, 286
diwan 339, 341
doctrine 99, 101, 111–12, 119, 270
Dossa, Parin 279
dress code 304–5, 306, 324, 335, 346–7, 356–7
duʿa, prayer 112–13, 120
Dual System of education 168–72, 172, 179

East Africa
  Anglo-Indian case law 136–9, 140
  Bohoras, Bohoras 318
  colonial law 139–46
  communal governance 146–53
  customary law 145
  Daʾudis (Bohras) of
  economic development 111
  education 260
  health care 193
  internal dissent 317
  Ismaili rule books 151
  Jubilee Insurance Company (JIC) 207
  Madrasa Early Childhood Programme 195–7
  migration to Canada 280
  modernization 284
  Nizaris (Khojas) of
  School Improvement Programmes (Sips) 193, 194–5
  Tahir Sayf al-Din, Daʾudi *daʿi* 305
East India Company 162, 297, 309
economic development 70, 110–11, 190,

207–13, 226
education
　access 161–2, 178
　Aga Khan Academies 197
　Aga Khan Development Network (AKDN) 70, 219
　Aga Khan III, Sultan Muhammad Shah, Nizari Imam 260
　Aga Khan University (AKU), Karachi 198–9
　architecture and development 217–18
　Badakhshan 71
　Bohras, Bohoras 306, 308, 320–1, 345; see also Da'udis
　British Raj 103
　Burhanpur Dargah Case 315–16
　China 82
　Da'udi Bohras 332
　free 176
　Historic Cities Programme (HCP) 225
　Khojas 8
　modernization 182
　multiculturalism 279
　Muslim revivalism 162–7
　Nizari Ismailis 9
　reforms 161, 304
　rural development programmes 36
　social access 172–8
　social development 191–200
　Soviet Union 54
　Sulaymani Bohras 356
　universal access 178
　women 248, 252–3, 257
educational curriculum 112, 120, 161, 178–82, 181, 195
Egypt 3, 36, 331
Engineer, Asghar Ali 317–18
England 140, 169 see also United Kingdom
English language 150, 192, 304
Esack, Farid 270
Esmail, Aziz 133, 268, 273–4
ethnicity 57, 79
Euben, Roxanne L. 272
Europe
　Aga Khan Development Network (AKDN) 284
　architecture and development 239
　Assassin Legends 5

　immigration to 69
　Nizari immigration to 61, 129
　Nizari Ismailis 45
European Commission 210
excommunication 315–16

faith 36, 110–13, 118, 320
*farman*s
　Aga Khan III 10
　Central Asia 65
　dissemination 112
　education 192
　guidance 116
　religious guidance 120
　religious reforms 110, 111
Fatima, daughter of the Prophet 1
Fatimi-Tayyibi (Ismaili) Da'wah: Ideologies and Community 332
Fatimid caliphate see also Fatimids
　Bohras, Bohoras 307
　demise 20
　historical sites 325
　Ismaili state 2
　pluralism 288–9
　Tayyibi literature 339
　texts 333
Fatimids 228
female education 176, 192, 196, 258–9, 321
female inheritance 138
festivals 68, 86–7, 88–9
First Microfinance Bank 203
France 33, 130, 169, 265
Fulford, Robert 278
fundamentalism 272
funeral ceremony 88
Fyzee, Asaf Ali Asghar 356

Gandhi, Mahatma 269, 310
Gazetteer of the Bombay presidency 98
*geet*s (songs) 281–2
gender 254
Geneva
　Aga Khan Development Network (AKDN) 190
　Aga Khan Trust for Culture (AKTC)
　　built environment 221, 222–4
　　Canada 281
　　Central Asia 71–2

conservation 215–17
cultural heritage 242–3
al-Darb al-Ahmar project 231
founded 12
Stone Town, Zanzibar 210
women 261
Getty Grant Programme 216
Ghalib, Mustafa 36
Gilgit, northern Pakistan 50, 61–4, 192
*ginan*s
authorized 114–17
Canadian Ismailis 280–1
devotional hymns 6
Khojas 98–9
Sadr al-Din, Pir 98
Satpanth 113
transformation 97
Global Centre for Pluralism, Ottawa 11, 284, 286
globalization 120, 239, 266, 274, 303
Golden Jubilee 305
Gorno-Badakhshan region, Tajikistan 52, 54
governance
British Raj 133
education 168–72
Ismaili rule books 152
Ismailis 131
Khojas 97
migrants 145–6
Zanzibar, East Africa 142–3
Gray, John 272
False Dawn 245n13
Great Britain *see* England; United Kingdom
Great Game 48–52
Gujarat 96, 109, 132, 206
Gujarati (language)
Bohras, Bohoras 346
*farman*s 111, 112
Ismaili history 117
Ismaili rule books 149–50
literature 332
ritual prayer (Khojas) 101
Guru Nanak 100
Gwadar 148

hadith 118, 252, 254, 270
Hafiz al-Asad 38

Hafizi 4, 331
Hahn, Kurt 197–8
Haji Bibi Case 106
al-Hajj Khidr 23, 25
hajj (pilgrimage to Mecca) 86
al-Hallaj, al-Husayn b. Mansur, Sufi master 24
Hamid al-Din al-Kirmani *see* al-Kirmani, Hamid al-Din
al-Hamidi, Hatim b. Ibrahim, Tayyibi *da'i mutlaq* 323
Hardy, Peter 103
Harvard University 10, 222
Hasan al-Mu'addil 24
Hasan-i Sabbah 3, 4, 5
Hastings, Warren 133
Hatim Amiji 137
Hazaras 45, 57–8, 59
Hazaristan, Afghanistan 57
healthcare
Aga Khan Development Network (AKDN) 219
Aga Khan University (AKU), Karachi 198–9
Bohras, Bohoras 320
education 192–3
Nizari Ismailis 9
rural development programmes 36
social development 191–200
women 248
Herat 231
heritage 270, 278
Hickling, Carissa 133–4
hidden imams (*al-a'imma al-masturin*) 284 *see satr*
hierarchy 68–9
High Court of Bombay *see* Bombay High Court
higher education 164, 165, 176, 177, 180, 306
Hilf al-Fada'il 313
Himadi al-'Umar 31–2
Himalayas 62
Hindu Kush, mountains, Central Asia 45, 49, 62
Hinduism 97, 102
Hindus 97, 103, 104, 108, 166
Hisham Sharabi 268
Historic Cities Programme (HCP) 71,

189, 215–16, 224–32, 242
history
   built environment 222
   Constitution of the Shia Imami Ismaili Muslims, The 122
   education 162
   Ismaili Khojas 110
   Ismailis 283–4
   Mawsim-i bahar 341
   Nizari Ismailis 12
   Tajik Ismailis 80–3
History of British India, The 249
Hong Kong 319
Hubib Ebrahim 103
*hujja*s 5, 47, 68, 83, 334
Hunza, northern Pakistan 62, 192, 227
Husam al-Din al-Hajj Ghulam Husayn, Sulaymani *da'i see* Ghulam Husayn
al-Husayn b. 'Ali al-Marwazi, Ismaili *da'i* 47
hybridity 274

Ibn Arabi, al-Shaykh al-Akbar 24
Ibn Hawshab, Mansur al-Yaman, Ismaili *da'i* and author 339
identity
   ambiguity 96
   Bohras, Bohoras 304
   built environment 221, 232–3, 235
   Canada 279
   dissimulation 6
   *ginan*s 280
   Ismailis 66, 283–4
   Khojas 97, 107, 110–19, 122
   law reports 141
   multiculturalism 275
   Nizari Ismailis 9, 12, 56
   pan-Ismaili 113, 119–20
   religion 103
   sectarianism 107
ideology 222, 239, 269, 311, 332, 333–8
Ifriqiya *see* Africa
Ikhwan al-Safa' (Brethren of Purity) 24
   see also Rasa'il Ikhwan al-Safa'
illiteracy 166, 174
Imam
   Alamut 5
   allegiance 121
   India 25

Khojas 99, 136
Mu'min-Shahis 26
religious dues 84
religious hierarchy 83
role 111
Imamate *see also* Imam
   authority 153, 333–4
   Da'udi Bohras 333
   Imami doctrine 1, 112
   modernization 284
   Persia 130
Imami doctrine 1, 112
Imami Shi'is 1
Imperial Legislative Council 167, 170, 175
India *see also* Indian subcontinent
   Aga Khan Rural Support Programme 205–7
   Bohras, Bohoras 298–9
   colleges of science and technology 180
   colonial law 139–46
   customary law 145
   Da'udi Bohras 332
   drip irrigation 207
   economic development 111
   education 195
   financial sector 209
   Imam 25
   independence 305
   Khojas 6
   literature 66
   migration from 265
   Muslims 109
   nationalism 97
   Nizari Imamate 7
   Nizari Ismailis 45
   partition 108
   primary schooling 173
   race division 173
   reforms 309
   religious identity 102
   School Improvement Programmes (Sips) 194–5
   Sulaymani Bohras 355
   Tayyibi *da'wat* 297, 308, 339
   women 249–50
India in Transition 167–8, 251–2
Industrial Promotion Services (IPS) 208
inqita' al-nass theory 302, 312–14, 315, 317, 321

Institute for Educational Development (IED) 71, 193
Institute of Ismaili Studies, London
   Aga Khan Development Network (AKDN) 284
   Central Asia 46
   education 199–200
   educational curriculum 72, 120
   founded 11
   scholarship 119
   teacher training 38–9
Integrated Cultural Development 226, 227
intermarriage 23, 51, 79, 256, 286, 307
internal dissent 311–12, 316–18
International Baccalaureate (IB) 197–8
investment 210, 211, 212–13
Iran 79, 99, 121, 265 *see also* Persia
'Iraq 101
irrigation schemes 201, 207
Islam
   built environment 221, 235–6
   China 77
   interpretation 111
   law 133–4
   pillars of Islam 335
   religious identity 102, 103–4
   revivalism 162–7
   Shi'i perspective
   state religion 108
   women 256
Islamabad 69, 203
Islamic education 179
Islamic finance 319–20
Islamic law 299
Islamic studies 181–2
Islamic traditions 111
Islamic values 271–2
Islamism 272
Isma'il al-Muhammad, Amir 31
Ismaili Association for Pakistan
   publications 119
Ismaili *da'wa*
   Yemen 3
Ismaili identity
   pan-Ismaili 121
Ismaili Khojas
   history 110
   post-colonialism 108–9

Ismaili law
   Fatimid period 2
Ismaili Muslim Youth Choir
   Canada 282
Ismaili Printing Press
   ginans 115
Ismaili rule books
   distribution 148–51
Ismaili Society, Bombay, Ismailia Associations *see* Ismaili Tariqah and Religious Education Boards (ITREB)
Ismaili state 2
Ismaili Tariqah and Religious Education Board (ITREB) 280–1
Ismaili Tariqah and Religious Education Boards (formerly Ismailia Associations), Ismailis, Isma'iliyya 11, 39, 72 *see also* Shi'is
Ismaili Tariqah and Religious Education Committees (ITREC) 72
Ismaili, The 117
Ismailis
   Aga Khan Rural Support Programme 205
   British Raj 132–6
   Canada 265, 279–87
   colonialism 147
   communal governance 146–53
   cult of the saints 23
   Diamond Jubilee Investment Trust Company (DJIT) 208
   diversity 95
   Dual System of education 170
   East Africa 130
   identity 122
   India 109
   media coverage 285
   modernism 266–7
   Ottoman Syria 19
   Pakistan 109
   privacy 288
   religious community 110
   social development 52
   status in Zanzibar 142
   Tajiks 78
   third space 276
   women 249, 256, 258, 263
Ismaily, Safar Ali 279
Ithna'ashariyya 57, 106, 135 *see*

also Twelvers, Twelver Shi'ism (Ithna'ashariyya)
Ivanow, W. (Vladimir Alekseevich Ivanov) 96, 101
Ivory Coast 212

Ja'far al-Sadiq 1, 24
Ja'far b. Sulayman, Sulaymani *da'i* 355
jama'atkhanas 82–3, 98, 279
Jamal, Shamshu 282
jama'at (jamat) 265–6, 286, 288, 348
Jameson, Frederic 276
Jami'a Sayfiyya *see* Dars-i Sayfi
Japan 319
Jubilee Insurance Company (JIC) 207
Junagadh 206

Kabul 57, 60, 211, 231
Kafat 30
Kahf, castle, Syria 20
kamadia (Nizari functionary) 64, 65
Kant, Immanuel 206
Karachi 109, 203, 212, 305
Karakorum Highway 64, 201
Karakorum, mountains, Central Asia 45, 62, 201
Karbala 101
Karim al-Husayni, Aga Khan IV *see* Aga Khan IV
Kassam, Sabrina 143
Kassam, Tazim 248
  Songs of Wisdom and Circles of Dance 281
Kayan valley, Afghanistan 59
Kayani *sayyids* 60
Kenya, East Africa
  Diamond Jubilee Investment Trust Company (DJIT) 208
  Diamond Trust Bank (DTB) 209
  Frigoken 212
  Ismailis 129, 130
  migration from 265
  Serena hotel Chain 210
khalifa
  Afghanistan 61
  Badakhshan 59
  da'wa 56
  education 82
  healing remedies 86

leadership 50
literature 66
religious authority 55–6
religious hierarchy 84
Khan, Dominique-Sila 104, 133
Khan, Muqtedar 276
Khawabi 33, 34, 38
Khayrbek Mosque 230
khidmat 321, 334–5
Khoja identity 107
Khoja Law Commission 148
Khoja Shia Imami Counsilna Kayadani Book: Prakaran Pelu tatha Biju 146
Khojas *see also* East Africa: India: Pakistan
  Aga Khan I 7
  Canada 280
  colonialism 102–8
  in court cases
  customary law 134
  dissimulation 7–8
  *ginan*s of
  governance 144
  histories of
  identity 110–19
  India 6
  Ismaili identity 106
  law reports 140–1
  migration 8–9
  *mukhi*s 8, 27
  multivalent identity 104, 110
  Muslims 105
  Nizari Ismailis 97
  Nizaris xiii
  Sunnis 101
  transnationalization 119–22, 121
  Zanzibar, East Africa 136–7
Khojki, script 98, 115
Khorog, capital Tajik Badakhshan 52, 53, 54
Khudonarazrov, Davlat 56, 74*n*23
khums (tribute payments) 28, 32
Khurasan 47
Khurshah, Nizari Imam *see* Rukn al-Din Khurshah
khwaja see Khojas
Kirman 7
al-Kirmani, Hamid al-Din 2, 339
Kitab al-najah fi ahkam al-nikah 341

Kivikes, E. K. 52
Kyrgyzstan, Central Asia 45

labour 32, 255
Lahore 231
Lalji Devraj 115–16
land reforms 35
language 37, 78, 116–17
Latakiya, Syria 20
legal battles 314–16
legitimacy 119, 302, 312–13
Lerner, Daniel
 Passing of Traditional Society: Modernizing the Middle East, The 268
Levant 5
Lewis, Bernard 95
liberal education 179, 181
libraries 5, 9–10, 38, 343, 357
Lisan al-Da'wat
 'Abd 'Ali Sayf al-Din, Da'udi *da'i* 340
 Bohras, Bohoras 345–6
 education 321
 Kitab al-taharat 341
 literature 332
 Mawsim-i bahar 341
 Tahir Sayf al-Din, Da'udi *da'i* 342
 Tayyibi literature 338
literacy 82, 165, 304
literary production 24
literary traditions xiv
literature *see also ginans*
 Da'udi Bohras 332, 338–44
 educational reforms 179
 Fatimid heritage 320
 Ismailis 66, xiv
 Khojas 117
 manuscript tradition 343–4
 Nizaris 5, 8
 religious reforms 111, 113–17
 Tayyibi
local government 31
Lohana caste 132, 198
Lucknow, India 163, 173
Lyotard, Jean François 274

Madagascar 129, 265
maddoh, devotional poetry 56, 66–7

Madrasa Early Childhood Programme 195–7
Madrasa resource centres 196
madrasas 321, 344–5
Mahdibaghwalas, Mahdibagh party, subgroup of Da'udis 312
majalis 336–7
Malaysia 275–6
Mali 231
Mamluks 20
mandate authority 33
Manichaeism 45
manuscript tradition 24, 343–4
Mara Mowal Canada Padharshe 282
marriage 87–8, 152, 256, 283, 335
martyrdom 325, 337
al-Masjid al-Mu'azzam 307
mass education 164, 168, 170, 175
Massachusetts Institute of Technology 222
Masyaf, Syria 20, 26, 27, 217
Mawsim-i bahar 341
Mayo, Katherine
 Mother India 250
mazars, shrines 85
Mecca 86, 335
meritocracy 174, 260
Mernissi, Fatima 252
microfinance 202–4, 207, 216
migration
 Aga Khan Rural Support Programme 206
 Bohras, Bohoras 318–19
 to Canada 265
 to East Africa 132
 encouraged 120
 Ismailis 23, 28–30, 69
 Khojas 119
 Salamiyya 32
military coup, Syria (1963) 36
Mill, James
 History of British India, The 249
mithaq 335–6
modernity 19, 238–43, 266, 269, 270–4, 279, 280
Moir, Zawahir 101, 118, 132–3
Mombasa, Kenya 145, 192, 193, 195, 259
Monaco Telecom International 211
Moosa, Ebrahim 272–3

mosques (*masjid*s) 77, 237, 279, 319
Mother India 250
Mozambique 129, 207, 210, 265
al-Mu'ayyad fi'l-Din al-Shirazi, Abu Nasr Hibat Allah, Ismaili *da'i* and author 2, 337, 339
Mughal empire 304
Muhammad al-Baqr, Shaykh 26
Muhammad al-Haydar, Shaykh 26
Muhammad al-Suwaydani 25
Muhammad Ali Jinnah 108
Muhammad 'Ali Rampuri 341
Muhammad Badr al-Din, Da'udi *da'i* 300, 309–10, 322–3
Muhammad Burhan al-Din, Da'udi *da'i* 301, 321, 322, 334, 343
Muhammad Burhan al-Din II, Da'udi *da'i* 306–8
Muhammad Hasan al-Husayni, Nizari Imam *see* Aga Khan I
Muhammad Ibrahim 34–5
Muhammad 'Izz al-Din, Da'udi *da'i* 300
  Tafsir 'Izzi 341
Muhammad, Prophet 1, 67–8, 114, 253–4, 333
Muhammad Zahir Shah, King of Afghanistan 60
Muhammadan Anglo-Oriental College *see* Aligarh, University of
al-Mu'izz, Fatimid caliph
  Da'a'im al-Islam, of al-Qadi al-Nu'man 335
*mukhi*s 8, 27, 64, 65, 83
multiculturalism 274–5, 277, 286, 287–8
Mumbai *see* Bombay (Mumbai)
Mu'min-Shahis 19, 26, 27–8
Mundra, India 171
murid 50, 51, 52–3, 83, 121
Murison, Sir William 144–5
murshid see also pir, qutb
al-Mustafa li-Din Allah 3
Musta'lawiyya *see* Musta'lians
Musta'lians 3, 4, 297, 331
Musta'lians, Musta'liyya (or Musta'lawiyya) *see also* Bohras, Da'udis; Hafizis; Sulaymanis; Tayyibis
al-Mustali bi'illah 3
Musta'liyya *see* Musta'lians
al-Mustansir, Fatimid caliph 3

mystical texts 24
mysticism 112

Naeem, Fuad S. 269
Nafi, Basheer M. 269–70, 272
  Rise of Islamic Reformist Thought, The 271
Nairobi, Kenya 193, 208
Najran, Saudi Arabia 355
Nandy, Ashis 269
Nanji, Azim 98, 267, 274
al-Nasafi, Muhammad b. Ahmad, Ismaili (Qarmati) *da'i* 47
Nasir al-Din al-Tusi 5 *see* al-Tusi, Nasir al-Din
Nasir-i Khusraw
  Charogh Rawshan, rite for the dead in Badakhshan 68
  Diwan 47–8
  oral traditions 65–6
  poetry 66–7
  religious traditions 80
  scholars 2
  Tajik Ismailis 81
  Xinjiang, China 61
Nasr al-Muhammad, Shaykh 32
nass (designation) 300–1, 302, 312–14
nation-building 175–6
Nation Group 213–14
National Council 39
National Endowment Steering Committees (NESCs) 196
national identity 275, 279
Nawruz 88–9
Nizar b. al-Mustansir, Nizari Imam 331
Nizar II, Nizari Imam 3
Nizari communities 5, 6
Nizari Imamate 7
Nizari Imams 6
Nizari Ismailis 96, 107, 162, 247
Nizari-Musta'li split 3
Nizaris, Nizariyya
  Afghanistan 57–61
  evolution 4–5
  historiography 117–19
  Ismailis xiii
  split from Musta'lians 3
normalization 30–2
North West Frontier Province 62

Pashtuns, Afghanistan 63
al-Nuʿman b. Muhammad, al-Qadi Abu Hanifa, Ismaili jurist and author 335, 24, 339, 341
Nur al-Din Muhammad II b. Hasan ʿala dhikrihi'l-salam see Hasan II, Nizari Imam
Nuram Mubin 117–19
Nusayris see also Alawis

Old Customs House 227
Old Dispensary 210, 225, 226–7
oral history 25
oral traditions 48, 65–6, 80, 339, xiv
orthopraxy 107–8, 345
Ottawa, Canada 265, 279
Ottawa Muslim Association 279
Ottoman-Safavid wars 21
Ottoman Syria 20
Ottoman troops 22
Oxus river 49

Pakistan see also Chitral; Gilgit; Hunza; Multan; Panjab; Sind
  Aga Khan Trust for Culture (AKTC) 216–17
  Aga Khan University (AKU), Karachi 198
  Aligarh, University of 177–8
  colleges of science and technology 181
  Daʾudi Bohras 332
  economic development 111
  education 195
  First Microfinance Bank 203
  higher education 180
  immigration to 61, 69
  Islamic state 108
  Islamization policies 112
  Ismailis 61–4
  migration from 265
  Nizari Ismailis 45
  Serena hotel Chain 210
Pamir 45, 46, 49, 51, 52
Panj river, Badakhshan 50, 53, 55, 70
Panjtani (five bodies) 66
partition 108, 209, 298–9, 305
Pashtuns, Afghanistan 63
Passing of Traditional Society: Modernizing the Middle East, The 268

Paz, Octavio
  Convergences 244n6
Perry, Justice Erskine 134
persecution
  abolition 52
  Alawis 21
  Bohras, Bohoras 297, 308, 323
  Ismailis 46, 47, 95–6, 284
  Pakistan 109
Persia (Iran) 3, 4, 79
Persian (language) 46, 78, 121, 338
Peterson, Alec 197–8
Piaget, Jean 194
Pilik 88–9
pillars of Islam 335
Pirbhoy, Adamji 302, 314, 315
pirs see also murshid, qutb
  Afghanistan 61
  alliances 51
  authority 54
  Badakhshan 59
  education 82
  *ginan*s 98–9, 113
  Great Game 50
  healing remedies 86
  importance 64–5
  Ismaili communities 63
  Nizari Ismailis 96
  politicians 60–1
  relationships 52–3
  Satpanth 97
  Xinjiang, China 81
Platinum Jubilee 193
pluralism 288–9
poetry 24, 39, 114, 339
politics
  Aga Khan Development Network (AKDN) 190
  Bohras, Bohoras 298–9
  pir 51
  religion 81
  stability 309
  Tahir Sayf al-Din, Daʾudi *daʿi* 311
  universal education 175
  women 251–2
polygamy 255, 256
Poona, India 148
Portugal 130, 197, 265
Position of Women Under Islam, The 256

post-colonialism 108–9
postmodernism 267
postmodernity 274–6
poverty 174–5, 203
Pragati Mandal 317
prayers 101, 112–13
pre-colonial Khojas 97–102
Prevention of Excommunication Act 316
primary schooling 173, 174
Prince Aly Khan Hospital 193
privacy 237, 286, 288
Privy Council 140, 316
Professional Development Centres (PDC) 71
professional interaction 258
Progressive Bohras 316–18
Punjab 96, 149, 203
purdah 253–4

al-Qadi al-Nu'man *see* al-Nu'man b. Muhammad
Qadmus, castle, Syria 20, 27, 32–3, 34
qa'im see also imam-qa'im; Mahdi; *qiyama*
qa'im al-qiyama
Qandahar 7
Qandil-nama see Charagh-nama
Qarmatis 1–2
qasidakhoni 67
Qasim-Shahis 19, 26–7, 36
Qasim-Shahis, Qasimiyya, branch of Nizaris *see also* Khojas; Nizaris
Qum, Iran 6
Qur'an 254–5, 257, 338

Rabani, Burhanuddin 59
Rajastan, India
  Ismaili ambiguity 96
Rajasthan High Court
  raza 317
Ramadan, Tariq 273
Rashid al-Din Sinan, Nizari leader in Syria 20, 5
Rashid, Ian Iqbal
  Touch of Pink, A 283
Rashid, Rai Mohamedali 143
Al Rashid Mosque 279
Rattansi, Diamond 256
Rawafid *see* Rafida

raza 317
Read, James S. 157n54
Recreation Club Institute 115, 117
Reformist Bohras 316–18
reforms
  Aga Khan III, Sultan Muhammad Shah, Nizari Imam 110
  Bohras administration 321–3
  education 161
  India 309
  modernization 271, 284
  Nizari Ismailis 9, 12–13, 27
  Tahir Sayf al-Din, Da'udi *da'i* 304
refugees 29, 34, 52, 57, 58, 248
regulation 165–6
religion
  Canadian Ismailis 288
  China 81
  higher education 180
  identity 102, 103
  Ismaili Tariqah and Religious Education Board (ITREB) 280–1
  modernity 269
  postmodernism 275
  reforms 110
  traditions 271–2
religious community 110, 168
religious dues 84, 105
religious education
  Bohras, Bohoras 320–1
  Ismaili Tariqah and Religious Education Boards (formerly Ismailia Associations), Ismailis, Isma'iliyya 72
  Ismailis 112
  Muslims 169–70
  policies 38
  reforms 164, 304
  Tayyibi *da'wat* 344–5
  Xinjiang Zongjiao Shiwu Guanli Tiaoli (Xinjian Religious Affairs Administration Regulation) 82
religious guidance 120
religious hierarchy 83–4
religious identity
  Bohras, Bohoras 307, 324–6
  China 78, 91
  ethnicity 79
  India 102

Khojas 8, 106
   reorientation 114
religious policy 9, 37–9, 55, 91
religious practices
   Central Asia 65
   doctrine 101
   Islam 235
   Khojas 119
   lack of political motivation 56
   reforms 130
   reorientation 110–13
   Tajik Ismailis 85–7
religious reforms 113–17
religious traditions 24–6, 55, 63–4, 82, 112, 241
Rise of Islamic Reformist Thought, The 271
Roshan telecom Development Company 211–12
Ross-Sheriff, Fariyal 267
Roy, Shibani 315
Rule Book of the Khoja Shia Imami Ismaili Council: Parts One and Two 146
rural development programmes 36, 201–7, 215, 223
Russia 45, 46, 48–52, 53 *see also* Soviet Central Asia
Russian Federation 69
Rwanda 210

al-Sadiq, Imam *see* Ja'far al-Sadiq
Sadr al-Din, Pir 98
Safavid dynasty, Persia
Safdarali Khan, *mir* of Hunza 62
Safi, Omid 273
Sahib, Sadiq Ali 341
Sahib, Sayfi
   Kitab al-najah fi ahkam al-nikah 341
Salamiyya, central Syria 27, 28, 30–2, 36–7, 38, 39
Salih al-'Ali, Shaykh 33–4
Saljuq dominions 4
Salman al-Farisi 24
sanitation schemes 214–15, 227
Sant tradition, South Asia 96, 100
Sardar, Ziauddin 275, 276
sarkuri 84
Sarv-i Jahan 6
Satpanth

   doctrine 99
   *ginan*s 98, 113
   Hindu practices 7
   Hinduization 104
   Khojas 6, 96–7, 133
   Nizari Ismailis 96
   sub-groups 97
satr (concealment) 297, 331, 333
Saudi Arabia 356
Sayfi Hospital 320
Sayfi Women's Organization 304
sayyid 83, 98–9, 113
Sayyid Farrukhsho 51–2
Sayyid Qutb 272
Sayyid Sa'id, Sultan 8–9
Sayyid Shah Sadeh 59–60
Sayyida Arwa, Sulayhid Queen 4
Sayyida Imam Begum 116
scholars
   *ginan*s 281
   Institute of Ismaili Studies, London 200
   Ismailis 2
   khalifa 84
   nass (designation) 312
   Tajik Ismailis 80
   taqiyya (precautionary dissimulation) 95
School Improvement Programmes (Sips) 193–5
schools
   Aga Khan Academies 197
   Aga Khan Education Services (AKES) 193
   Aga Khan III, Sultan Muhammad Shah, Nizari Imam 9–10, 171–2, 192
   Mombasa, Kenya 192
   religious education 112
secular education 316, 344–5
self-determination 179
Semenov, Aleksandr A. 49
Serena hotel Chain 209–10, 227
Serjeant, Robert 313, 332
sexual relations 257–8
Shackle, Christopher 101
Shah Karim al-Husayni *see* Aga Khan IV
Shah Khamush, Sayyid, Ismaili *da'i* 48
Shah Malang, Ismaili *da'i* 48
Shams al-Din al-Tayyibi 24

Shams al-Muluk, mother of Aga Khan III 9
shariʿa, sacred law of Islam 272, 322, 324, 335
Sheikh, Samira 148
Shiʿa *see* Shiʿis, Shiʿism
Shihab al-Din Shah 8
Shiʿi Islam 21
Shiʿis *see also* Imamate
  conception of religious authority 119
  Daʾudis, Daʾudiyya, branch of Tayyibis 331
  and dissident Nizari Khojas in Aga Khan Case 106
  doctrine of *taʿlim* 111
  historiography 117–19
  Ismaili rule books 153
  Khojas 135
  system of law 133
Shiʿism 108–9, 111, 117–19, 119, 133 *see also* Imamate
Shingun Duldul 86
Shodhan, Amrita 115, 132, 136, 147
Shohtemur, Shirinsho 54
shrine culture 23, 24, 37
Siddiqui, Haroon
  Toronto Star 285
al-Sijistani, Abu Yaʿqub, Ismaili *daʿi* 2
Silk Road Project 218
Sind 96, 105
Singapore 319
Sinha, Mrinalini 250
Smith, Wilfred Cantwell 107
social action 191, 202
social change 35–7, 110
social development 52, 54, 61, 190, 226, 304
social etiquette 89–90
social practices 332, 345–8
social reform 176, 183, 312
socio-economic conditions 90, 249
soft power 206
Songs of Wisdom and Circles of Dance 281
South Africa 129, 265
South America 265
South Asia 189, 193, 194–5, 208–9, 284, 332 *see also* India; Pakistan
Soviet Central Asia *see also* Central Asia
Soviet Union

Central Asia 46
  collapse 59, 265
  dissolution 69
  Pamir 53
  religious policy 55
  religious traditions 65, 67
  repression 55
spirituality 10, 25, 27, 233, 269, 313, 335
St. Petersburg 50
standard of living 39
state education 170, 171
Stewart, Tony 102
Stone Town, Zanzibar 210–11, 216, 226–7
suffrage 250–1, 255
Sufis 96, 99
Sulayman al-Hajj, Shaykh 27
Sulayman b. Hasan, Sulaymani *daʿi* 355
Sulayman b. Haydar, Shaykh, Nizari leader at Masyaf 26
Sultan Muhammad Shah, Aga Khan III *see* Aga Khan III
Sunni Islam 2, 21
Sunnis
  alliances 51
  Bohras, Bohoras 297, 308
  China 77
  conflict 33
  domination 34, 36, 38, 58–9
  hostility to Ismailis 47
  Islamic state 108
  Khawabi 23
  Khojas 101, 106, 135
  Madrasa Early Childhood Programme 195–6
  majority population 2–3
  as officiants 133
  as oppressors 50
  in Pakistan 108–9
Supreme Council for Africa 146, 147
Supreme Council of Antiquities, Egypt 229–30
Surat, Gujarat 297, 303, 307, 319, 332, 343
Syria *see also* Crusaders: and Nizaris
  Aga Khan Rural Support Programme 207
  Bohras, Bohoras 325
  exchanges 121
  Historic Cities Programme (HCP) 231
  Ismailis 19

Living Imam 26–8
local society 21–4
Nizaris 3, 5
Tahir Sayf al-Din, Da'udi *da'i* 305

Tafsir 'Izzi 341
Tagore, Rabindranath 269
Tahir Sayf al-Din, Da'udi *da'i*
    Bohras, Bohoras 301–4
    Golden Jubilee 305
    legitimacy 314–15
    Muslim denominations 310–11
    partition 305
    Tayyibi literature 339, 341–2
    Yemen 324
Tajik Ismailis 83–4, 86
Tajikistan, Central Asia
    Aga Khan Rural Support Programme 207
    civil war 56, 59
    exchanges 121
    Great Game 49–50
    independence 69
    migration from 265
    Nizari Ismailis 45
    Serena hotel Chain 210
Tajiks 78
Taliban 61
ta'lim 120
Tamir Mirza, Amir 31
Tang Dynasty Court History 79
Tanganyika, East Africa 145, 192 *see also* Tanzania
Tanzania, East Africa *see also* Tanganyika; Zanzibar
    Diamond Jubilee Investment Trust Company (DJIT) 208
    Diamond Trust Bank (DTB) 209
    hospitals 191–2
    internal dissent 317
    Ismailis 129, 130
    migration from 265
taqiyya (precautionary dissimulation)
    Badakhshan 58, 59
    dissimulation 6, 7–8
    Ismailis 284
    Khojas 106, 132–3, 135
    religious traditions 95
taqlid 270, 322

Tartus 20
Tashkurghan, Xinjiang, China 45, 80, 85, 90
tawhid 235, 333
taxes 51, 52, 58, 84, 209
al-Tayyib, son of the Fatimid caliph al-Amir, Tayyibi-Musta'li Imam 331, 333
Tayyib Zayn al-Din, Da'udi *da'i* 300, 320–1
Tayyibi *da'wat*
    Da'udi Bohras 348
    India 308
    literature 338–44, 339
    religious education 344–5
    revenues 313
    Surat, Gujarat 297–8
Tayyibi literature 343–4
Tayyibi Musta'lians 297
    Da'udi Bohras 331
Tayyibis, Tayyibiyya, branch of Musta'lians 4, 297, xiii *see also* Musta'lians; Da'udis; Sulaymanis; 'Alavis
    Da'udi-Sulaymani-'Alavi split of named areas *see* under India; Syria; Yemen
teacher training 38–9, 197–8, 217–18, 321
texts 24, 332, 333, 335, 335–6
Thanvi, Maulana Ashraf Ali 269
tithes 55, 192
Todd, Douglas 285
Toronto, Canada 265
Toronto Star 285
Touch of Pink, A 283
tourism 209–10, 229
trade 306, 318, 357
traders to East Africa 90
traditions
    architecture 217
    Bohras, Bohoras 303
    built environment 225, 233–4, 235–6
    Canada 278
    Canadian Ismailis 279, 286
    continuity 64–9
    education 181
    ginans 281
    heritage 278
    Ismailis 267, 268–70, xiv
    modernity 238–43, 267, 289

pluralism 287
religion 241, 271-2
transnationalization 119-22, 266, 274-5, 286-7, 288
Tripoli 20, 21
Tunisia *see also* Africa
Turkestan 49, 54
Turks *see* Ottoman Turks; Saljuqs; Turkomans
Twelvers, Twelver Shi'ism (Ithna'ashariyya) 205 *see also* Imamate; Imamis; Shi'is
Tyabji family, Bombay 356

Udaipur, India 316
Udaipuri, Ahmad 317
Uganda 129, 130, 208, 209, 210, 265
Umm al-Sultan Sha'aban Mosque 230
United Arab Republic 36
United Kingdom 46, 48-52, 130, 265, 319 *see also* England; India; British
United States of America 278, 319
universal education 172-8
University of Central Asia, Tajikistan 11, 71, 261
Utvik, Bjorn 272

Vadodara *see* Baroda
Vaishnaivate tradition, South Asia 96
Vancouver, Canada 265, 279
Vancouver Sun, The 285
Vassanji, Moyez
    In-Between World of Vikram Lall, The 283
village organizations (VOs) 201, 202-3, 204
virahini 100-1
volunteerism 120

Wadud, Amina 255
Walker, Paul E. 96
Weber, Max 280
welfare 8, 258, 306, 308, 319
well-being 9
Westernization 272, 319
Westropp, Chief Justice 138-9
women
    Aga Khan Development Network (AKDN) 261

Aga Khan Foundation (AKF) 196
Aga Khan Rural Support Programme 206
Aga Khan University (AKU), Karachi 198
Bohras, Bohoras 299, 306
Calgary, Canada 279
customary law 138-9
development 263
dress code 346-7
education 192, 257, 304, 345
equality 255
Islam 256
microfinance 202-3, 216
Nizari Ismailis 9, 247-8
Roshan telecom Development Company 211-12
Sayfi Women's Organization 304
social interaction 258
status 248-9, 251, 253
Sulaymani Bohras 356
teacher training 38-9
women's organizations (WOs) 201, 202-3, 304
Wood, Captain John 49
World Bank 216
World Monuments Fund 216
World War II 56, 270

Xinjiang, China 45, 61, 77-8, 81, 85, 86
Xinjiang Zongjiao Shiwu Guanli Tiaoli (Xinjian Religious Affairs Administration Regulation) 82

Yaqut Shah, Pir Sayyid, Ismaili *da'i* 63
Yemen
    Da'udi Bohras 323-4, 331
    Ismaili *da'wa* 3
    Sulayman b. Hasan, Sulaymani *da'i* 355
    Sulaymani Bohras 355-6
    supported Tayyibis 4
    Tayyibi *da'wat* 297
Yemenis (Yamanis), *satr* (concealment) 331-2
Youth Bohras 316-18

Zaidi, Syed
    Position of Women Under Islam, The 256

Zanzibar, East Africa
   Aga Khan schools 171
   Bombay High Court 139–40
   customary law 138
   Integrated Cultural Development 226–7
   Ismailis 136–7
   Khoja governance 142–4
   migration 8–9
   schools 192
   Serena hotel Chain 210
   status of Ismailis 142
   Zanzibar Protectorate Law Reports 144–5
Zarubin, Ivan I. 49
Zaydis, Zaydiyya 323
Zia ul-Haqq 108
Zoroastrianism 45